# EXECUTIVE ESSENTIALS

THE ONE GUIDE TO WHAT EVERY
RISING BUSINESSPERSON SHOULD KNOW

# EXECUTIVE ESSENTIALS

## MITCHELL J. POSNER

AVON
PUBLISHERS OF BARD, CAMELOT, DISCUS AND FLARE BOOKS

Because the English language lacks a generic singular pronoun that indicates both "he" and "she," it has been customary to use the masculine pronoun to refer to either sex. Although I've tried to use terms that encompass both sexes wherever possible, I have often resorted to the generic masculine pronouns for the sake of style, readability, and succinctness. With the obvious exception of things like "choosing a necktie," all the material in this book applies to both men and women.

Note: All prices, product information, addresses and telephone numbers are included to aid the reader, but are subject to change without prior notification. The author and publisher are not responsible for any loss, damages or other consequences resulting from such changes.

EXECUTIVE ESSENTIALS: THE ONE GUIDE TO WHAT EVERY RISING BUSINESSPERSON SHOULD KNOW is an original publication of Avon Books. This work has never before appeared in book form.

AVON BOOKS
A division of
The Hearst Corporation
1790 Broadway
New York, New York 10019

First Avon Printing, March, 1982

Library of Congress Cataloging in Publication Data:

Posner, Mitchell J.
   Executive Essentials.

   Includes index.
   1. Executive ability. 2. Executives — Time management.
3. Success. I. Title.
HF5500.2.P65      658.4'09      80-69883
ISBN 0-380-79079-3                AACR2

# CONTENTS

---

## PART III
## LIFE IN THE FAST LANE:
## EXECUTIVE HEALTH

---

---

---

# PART IV
# WINNING

---

---

your company to pay; attending the seminar and getting the most out of it; the big names in the seminar field; how to evalueate a seminar; the CEU (Continuing Education Unit): What's it worth?; selecting a school and a program: the MBA; the MS; the Phd: the EMBA; the glamour courses; teaching your way to the top; what you should know when you get out of school; who gets ahead; the influence of family background, education, cognitive skills, race, etc. on success

## PART V
## MOVING THROUGH
## THE JOB JUNGLE

ten questions interviewers love to ask, knowing what to listen and look for during the interview; passing the chemistry test: rapport with an interviewer; the corporate snoop: privacy and the job hunt

# PART VI
## GETTING YOUR SHARE:
### EXECUTIVE COMPENSATION

# PART VII
## THE OFFICE ARSENAL

automation: its advantages; what you should know about the
modern office

---

## PART VIII
## ON THE ROAD: WHAT THE
## TRAVEL GUIDES DON'T TELL YOU

---

The preparation of this book required the assistance of business executives and academic experts too numerous to mention. However, I would like to thank several people in particular for the valuable advice, assistance, patience and support: Frederic B. Poneman, International Trade Management, Inc.; Warren Berman, J&W Supply, Inc.; Harriet Berman; Beverly Poneman; Special thanks to Marlene Shama for her thorough research and keen insights; Marian Cohen for her major contribution to Parts V and VI; and to my wife Renee Z. Posner, whose help on this project transcends that which can be put into words.

# INTRODUCTION

On becoming an observer of the American business scene, I quickly reached a conclusion that is undoubtedly shared by a large segment of the business community: Success is not simply a matter of keeping one's nose to the grindstone, or a reward for years of unwavering loyalty and devotion to the firm. Proof that I am not alone in this view lies in the sizable and sustained audience for books on how to manipulate, dominate, intimidate, or otherwise aggravate one's way to the top. And books on how to look, dress, decorate, and impress for success.

*Executive Essentials* is not a book about one of these areas. It is an attempt to help you evaluate all of them—and then some. My goal is to identify and fill those "knowledge gaps" that, if left open, could create serious consequences in your career. These are the areas and issues that have a critical impact on the overall effectiveness and success of an executive, but are not generally taught (in some cases, are completely ignored) in colleges, business schools, and executive training programs. Like it or not, we are talking about knowledge that often makes the difference between success and stagnation.

I've tried to separate the wheat from the chaff, eliminating useless examples, anecdotes, redundancies, interviews with "Bill C.," and other kinds of fluff that authors use to stretch a single subject into a book. The result is a comprehensive source book that treats each topic in a straight-to-the-point manner.

*Executive Essentials* is organized into eight parts that correspond to the basic subjects on which we are least enlightened:

**Time management.** Time is surely the executive's most precious commodity. This section shows you how to recognize where you are wasting time and why, and what you can do to avoid squandering it.

**Information management.** Knowledge reaches us through the communications environment, and that environment is being flooded—and increasingly polluted. Trying to keep abreast can result in a loss of time, energy, and concentration. Yet no executive can afford to risk closing himself off. The modern businessperson has to learn to *select* what to read, listen to, and watch—and, at the same time, exploit one's mental potential to the fullest. This section shows you how to screen information and how to improve your cognitive abilities, so that you can take in more in less time and process it more effectively.

**Attitudes, insights, and key personal skills.** An American business cliché is that success is merely a matter of a winning attitude, with a dash of inspiration thrown in. You'll learn how you go about developing that winning attitude. Also, how to negotiate, delegate, take risks, speak in public, play the power game, and much more. In this part of the book there's advice on executive education and information about a few successful but relatively little-known approaches to more effective management, such as Japanese techniques and the Absolute Theory of Management.

**Health.** Success has as much to do with dependability, stamina, and vitality as it does with knowledge, ability, and skill. Poor health will slow one's career advancement; it happens more than most people realize. Beset by fatigue, stress, illness, depression, and other problems, many executives are perceived as health risks and, therefore, poor prospects for promotion. This section is not about how to pamper yourself—I'll assume that you are prepared to go flat out to get to the top. Rather, it's about how to take care of yourself now that you're traveling at a fast pace while carrying a heavy load.

**Career paths.** This is not a how-to-get-a-job guide for the unemployed or for the kid just out of college. The fact is that in today's business environment, the market for talent is open, freewheeling, and treacherous. It's also rife with opportunity. Even the executive who has a secure, enjoyable position with excellent potential must consider the ever-changing job picture and how it might affect him. This section is designed to provide you with the basic rules by which the job-changing game is played among accomplished executives. I hope that it'll entice you to remain always "available," and that it will also provide insurance against the unthinkable—the sack—which happens even to the best of us.

**Compensation.** Okay, so money isn't the only factor important to a job decision. But why accept less than what you are worth? You might think you have a good reason for doing so: Be advised that there are very few good reasons around. Remember, nobody is happy at a job if he feels he's being shortchanged or taken advantage of. And there's more to compensation than just a salary. What about "perks" and tax advantages? This section is designed to help you determine what you should be getting and what is available in the way of compensation, and to help you go about getting it without risking all.

**Home base: your office.** Mission Control for some, The Fortress of Solitude for others. Whatever the purpose your office serves, its design and operation is about to change. The office of 1992 will bear little resemblance to that of 1982. With the increased emphasis on office productivity, there's a good chance that you'll be seeing most of these changes long before the end of the decade. Many innovations are being introduced already, and more will be phased in over the next few years. You have two choices: Regard the automated office as sheer gimmickry, toys of eggheads that do no more than help secretaries type faster; or recognize and learn to capitalize on the vast potential of the modern office. And if you don't think you've got the time to work toward greater efficiency, effectiveness, and output, don't assume the competition thinks likewise. This section will tell you (1) what the office of the future is all about, (2) what are its assets and its drawbacks, (3) how to introduce office automation, and (4) how your job will be affected. Above all, you'll be well versed in the latest devices, their functions, and the accompanying lingo so that you won't be at the mercy of the equipment salesperson or, worse, some wiseacre from data processing.

**The field: doing business away from home.** Whether it's undertaken to buy, sell, make contacts, or generate goodwill, a trip requires preparation if it is to yield maximum results. The less affected you are by travel problems that upset schedules, health, and performance, the better. Some people learn to avoid nuisances through experience; others never quite manage to cope. Wouldn't you rather be briefed on how to "travel smart" than learn by making all the possible mistakes?

I've organized this book into sections with short chapters and subheadings, so a quick review of any of the topics covered is easy. You may even wish to clip out or photocopy a page or two for your desk or bulletin board. *Executive Essentials* was written to be used.

If I've done my job well, this book should help you identify and clarify the problems you face at work—and provide many of the solutions required to meet the challenges of business in the eighties.

# PART I

# PUTTING TIME ON YOUR SIDE

"The past is gone; the present
is full of confusion; and the
future scares hell out of me!"
David Lewis Stein

# 1

# A SHORT COURSE IN SAVING TIME

Don't underestimate the importance of effective time management. *The executive is judged by what he accomplishes, not by how many hours he puts in.* If you decide to work ten hours a day, it should be because you have a full ten hours of work to be done. More often than not, we fill ten hours with what should take us only eight. This pattern will not go unnoticed, and will undoubtedly be frowned upon.

Since there are an unlimited number of ways to waste time—Are you sure you should be reading this book now? Is there something more important to attend to?—there are countless ways to improve the situation. What you've got to do is figure out exactly where you are wasting time, and then start doing something about it. The ways in which people waste time seem obvious when you read them from a list, but because we are often unaware of them in our own lives and jobs, self-analysis is in order.

Some advice on this subject is pure common sense. There are also several creative, innovative, and even downright ingenious time-saving methods that are worth exploring.

Let's face it: It is very difficult to change behavior. So if you choose to follow the suggestions in this chapter, go easy on yourself. Don't attempt to turn your life upside down to save an hour. At least, not all at once.

## HOW TO SEIZE THE TIME

Every writer and consultant on time management presents a plan of some sort. No matter what the approach, each plan can be boiled down to five basic steps:

1. *Formulate a work plan.* How do you intend to spend your day?
2. *Complete a time log.* How did you actually spend your day?
3. *Do an analysis.* What went wrong? What went right? Major problems?

4. *Find solutions.* Formulate strategies to eliminate the problems, improve your work plan, and devise an efficient routine.
5. *Implement.* The hard part. Putting your plans and strategies into effect.

## FORMULATE A WORK PLAN

Plan your day. Make a list, and be specific. Note down activity and how much time you intend to allocate to it, either as a percentage of the work day or as actual time in minutes—or both.

Rank the activities in order of priority using a simple rating system such as the numerical one devised by noted time management consultant R. Alec Mackenzie:

1 = important and urgent
2 = important, not urgent
3 = urgent, not important
4 = routine

## COMPLETE A TIME LOG

There are several steps involved:

MAKE ONE   Devise your own, or try the simple five-column chart of Fig. 1.

FILL IN ABSOLUTELY EVERYTHING YOU DO   Professors Thomas Bonoma and Dennis Slevin* refer to the contents of a time log as *work incidents.* They define a work incident as "any change in what you are doing." This sensible approach leaves little room for fudging by not recording such things as reading a newspaper article. An interruption is defined by the professors as "any unprogrammed incident." Don't forget to record the nature and duration of every work incident and interruption while it is still fresh in your mind.

MAKE COMMENTS   Anything that comes to mind about the incident: complaints; frustrations; ways in which this incident or interruption could have been eliminated or expedited.

STICK WITH IT   Keep this log for a minimum of three days. A week or two is ideal. Obviously, it is unwise to pick a week you know will be atypical, because the results will not be as useful. However, don't use the excuse of "waiting for the typical week" to delay doing the log. If your work schedule changes after you complete the log, you can always start another time log.

---

*Thomas V. Bonoma and Dennis P. Slevin, *The Executive Survival Manual* (Belmont, CA: Wadsworth Publishing Co., 1978), p. 14.

---

| Time of Day | Activity | Duration | Priority Rating | Comments |
|---|---|---|---|---|
| | | | | |
| | | | | |
| | | | | |
| | | | | |
| | | | | |
| | | | | |
| | | | | |
| | | | | |
| | | | | |
| | | | | |
| | | | | |
| | | | | |
| | | | | |
| | | | | |

Fig. 1. Sample time log
If you like, leave a space at the top for goals and objectives.

## DO AN ANALYSIS

There are several methods, but the goal is the same for each—to locate the incidents that waste your time, and those you could deal with more effectively. Most important, you want to make certain that you are making progress toward achieving your objectives by allocating time to activities according to their priorities.

In order to do this, you've got to rate your daily activity. My favorite rating system is in the time log designed by William C. Giegold and included in his text *Strategic Planning and the MBO Process* (New York: McGraw-Hill, 1978).

Giegold employs a columnar rating system. One column is for *control*, a measure of how much time is spent on planned or unplanned activity; one is for *usage*, a measure of the priority of the activity; and one is for personal *satisfaction*. Each column is rated separately, and then they are combined for an overall "Effectiveness Rating," or ER. The three aspects of the rating system are weighed according to the individual's needs (*see* Fig. 2).

| Time period | Activity | Ratings | | | Comments and suggestions for improvement |
|---|---|---|---|---|---|
| | | A | B | C | |
| 8:00 | | | | | |
| 8:30 | | | | | |
| 9:00 | | | | | |
| 1:00 | | | | | |
| 1:30 | | | | | |
| 2:00 | | | | | |
| 2:30 | | | | | |

Rating codes (See Note 1)

Column A:   1 = planned   2 = unplanned
Column B:   3 = urgent   4 = important   5 = unimportant   6 = routine   7 = imposed
Column C:   8 = satisfied   9 = dissatisfied

Effectiveness Rating for the day (See Note 2)

A = percent of time rated "1" in Column A  _____
B = percent of time rated "4" in Column B  _____
C = percent of time rated "8" in Column C  _____

$\dfrac{A + B + C}{300}$ = Effectiveness rating  _____

## NOTES ON USE OF THE TIME LOG

*Note 1:*   Give every activity a rating in all three columns. Column A provides a measure of *control* of your time. Column B provides a *usage* measure. Column C is a subjective measure of your *satisfaction* with the way your time was spent.

Column B may contain more than one digit. For instance, you may rate this morning's 10:00 meeting with the boss as a 357—urgent, unimportant, and imposed. Likewise, an activity may be a 34, urgent and important, or a 35, urgent but unimportant.

*Note 2:*   The Effectiveness Rating (ER) is a combined score on control, usage, and satisfaction. Each rating, A, B, and C may vary from zero to one hundred. The formula for ER obviously weights these three factors equally. You may adjust these weights as you see fit, depending on the nature of your problem. For example, if your job is composed of unplanned activities or emergencies—typical of a fire fighter or trouble-shooter—there is little point in downgrading your ER just because "That's the job." In such a case, your formula for ER might be $\dfrac{B + C}{200}$.

Whatever formula you choose, *stay with it* so as to preserve a uniform basis for measuring changes in effectiveness.

Fig. 2. Daily time log and effectiveness rating

From *Strategic Planning and the MBO Process,* by William C. Giegold. Copyright © 1978 by McGraw-Hill, Inc. Used with permission of McGraw-Hill Book Company.

If you prefer, you can use the "1 to 4" rating system described earlier, the one used for formulating a work plan. If you choose to do so, add the number 5 to indicate "not urgent, not important"—an incident with so low a priority that it is virtually wasted time.

Compare the amount of time allocated to each activity with the actual time spent. Did the high-priority items receive the most attention? Were the activities carried out with maximum effectiveness?

If you look carefully at your analysis, you will see that the specific time management problems are of two basic types:

*tangibles.* The kind you are likely to record in the log: telephone interruptions, drop-in visitors, a disorganized desk.

*intangibles.* These problems stem from attitude and personality quirks, and they are difficult to pin down. The evidence of such problems will probably turn up in the "Comments" column of the log. Statements like "Just couldn't get started today" or "I'm such a nice person—it always gets me in trouble" are often an indication that something below the surface is affecting your ability to control your own time.

## FIND SOLUTIONS

Now that the problems are self-evident, what should you do about them? Once again, Bonoma and Slevin have reduced the problems to elegant simplicity. There are, they say, two basic ways to save time:

*Work faster.* This includes all solutions that involve increasing your speed and working ability.

*Do less.* This covers all methods of eliminating unnecessary tasks and streamlining the work load.

This section of the book is filled with all sorts of strategies and suggestions for saving and managing time. But they are all variations on one or the other—doing less or working faster.

| Time | Action | Priority | Comment, Disposition, or Results |
|------|--------|----------|----------------------------------|
| Goals: 1. _____  2. _____  3. _____  4. _____  5. _____  6. _____  Date: _____ |||| 
| | | 1 = Important and urgent<br>2 = Important, not urgent<br>3 = Urgent, not important<br>4 = Routine | Delegate to _____.<br>Train _____ to handle.<br>Next time ask his recommendation.<br>Consolidate, eliminate, or cut time.<br>Other. |
| 8:00 | | | |
| 8:30 | | | |
| 9:00 | | | |
| 9:30 | | | |
| 10:00 | | | |
| 10:30 | | | |
| 2:00 | | | |
| 2:30 | | | |
| 3:00 | | | |
| 3:30 | | | |
| 4:00 | | | |
| 4:30 | | | |
| 5:00 | | | |
| 5:30 | | | |
| Evening | | | |

Fig. 3. Daily time analysis
*(above and opposite)*
Reprinted, by permission of the publisher, from *The Time Trap*,
by R. Alec Mackenzie, © 1972 by AMACOM, a division of the
American Management Associations (pp. 26-27). All rights reserved.

1. Enter the date and list the goals for the day in terms of results, not activities. (Include the agenda in the time allocated for a sales meeting, *not* just the meeting itself.)
2. Record all significant activities in terms of results during each 15-minute period. Do not wait until noon or the end of the day. The major benefit is lost.
3. Answer the following questions immediately after the completion of the daily time log.

## QUESTIONS

1. Did setting daily goals and times for completion improve my effectiveness? If so, why? If not, why not?
2. What was the longest period of time without interruption?
3. In order of importance, which interruptions were most costly?
4. What can be done to eliminate or control them?
   a. Which telephone calls were unnecessary?
   b. Which telephone calls could have been shorter or more effective?
   c. Which visits were unnecessary?
   d. Which visits could have been shorter or more effective?
5. How much time was spent in meetings?
   a. How much was necessary?
   b. How could more have been accomplished in less time?
6. Did I tend to record "activities" or "results"?
7. How many of my daily goals contributed directly to my long-range objectives?
8. Did a "self-correcting" tendency appear as I recorded my actions?
9. What two or three steps could I now take to improve my effectiveness?

# 2
# TACKLING THE
# TIME-WASTERS

When executives fill out time logs or talk about time management, a number of common time-wasters usually emerge. These problems are encountered by almost every manager at one time or another. What follows are a few suggestions on how to solve them.

## MEETINGS

The business community has a love-hate relationship with its meetings. They can be great fun; they can be excruciatingly boring. They can be very productive—or they can be the biggest time-wasters of all. Despite the following insights and advice, I must point out that I have yet to find an executive who claims to be in complete control of meetings or his meeting time.

### REDUCING THE NUMBER
### AND DURATION OF MEETINGS

LOG YOUR MEETINGS   See which ones can be eliminated, and which can be cut down. Of course, it isn't always up to you.

AVOID COMMITTEES UNLESS YOU THINK THEY HAVE AN IMPORTANT PURPOSE   Committees = meetings; therefore, fewer committees = fewer meetings. Dissolve committees when they have accomplished their purpose.

NEVER CALL A MEETING UNLESS THERE IS NO ALTERNATIVE   If there is another way to deal with a situation, pursue it. Almost anything is more efficient, whether it be letter, conference call, or doing the job yourself. Meetings are required only when group action is necessary.

DON'T GO UNLESS YOU HAVE TO   If it's unimportant, skip it altogether. If it's important, ask yourself if *you* have to be there. Is there someone else you can send? You'll find ways to duck the real sleepers, saying, "I wasn't informed," or "There is a conflict in my schedule, and it's an appointment I can't change." Tell someone to tape the meeting so you can be sure to be brought up to date. Chances are, if it's not worth going to, it's not worth listening to, either. But jump around on the tape to get the gist of it, or ask a trusted colleague where the meat of the meeting lies, and listen to that.

## PREPARING FOR A MEETING

BRING THE MEETING INTO FOCUS IN ADVANCE   Know what you hope to accomplish. Set priorities.

SET TIME LIMITS   When will it start? When will it end? Sometimes you won't finish, and will have to schedule another meeting. Nobody wants that, so they will all push to finish on time. But if you leave it open-ended, the meeting will tend to fill as much time as it has been allotted. By the way, start on time. Don't wait for anyone—well, almost anyone. If a VIP is late, use your charm, and tactfully tell him that it sets a bad example and to please be prompt in the future.

USE CHECKLISTS   Prepare a checklist for yourself. Perhaps make a version that you can give out to participants.

CHOOSE THE TIME AND PLACE WITH CARE

DEAL WITH POTENTIAL INTERRUPTIONS IN ADVANCE

## IMPROVING MEETINGS

MAKE SURE THERE IS AN AGENDA, AND STICK TO IT   Try to get someone else to keep saying, "Let's move on," or "Let's stick to the agenda," unless you have real command of groups. Otherwise, you come off sounding like a nurd who wants to go by the book when one of the senior execs is telling everyone "the one about the one-legged sailor." Nevertheless, the agenda is not for nurds only. It really makes a difference in reducing wasted time and increasing efficiency.

IF YOU HAVE NOTHING TO CONTRIBUTE AND NOTHING IMPORTANT TO LEARN, STAY AWAY   And if you have done your part and feel that you are no longer needed, split. If it's your meeting, excuse anyone who is no longer needed. This way *you won't waste the time of others*, and they will respond better when you *do* need them.

EVERYONE AT THE MEETING SHOULD BE THERE FOR A PURPOSE   If this is the case, and it should be, make sure you involve everyone. This will help curtail boredom and make sure no one holds back a valuable contribution.

ENCOURAGE PEOPLE TO LISTEN

BE FIRM BUT TACTFUL IN DEALING WITH PROBLEM PERSON-
ALITIES:

    The Negative Element
    The Over-aggressor
    The Introvert
    The Attention Seeker
    The Non Sequitur Specialist
    The Lobbyist
    Mr. Cool
    Mr. Showbiz
    The "Dirty Laundry" Man
    The Bleeding Heart
    The Devil's Advocate

ENCOURAGE THOSE WHO HELP THE MEETING PROGRESS:

    Mr. Initiative
    The Good Humor Man
    The Opinion Leader
    The Clarifier
    The Elaborator
    The Acid Tester
    The Scrutinizer
    The Compromiser

---

# TELEPHONES

---

How ironic that a device that has saved the business community so much time and money, eliminating unimportant correspondence and business trips, has turned out to be the biggest time-waster of all.

As with the automobile, TV, and most other technological advances, the danger lies in overuse.

### THE DISEASE: TELEPHONE ABUSE

WE TALK TOO MUCH   At work, the phone is primarily a business tool. It should be treated as such. Our calls last much longer than they should.

WE CALL TOO OFTEN   Picking up the phone at the slightest whim is a serious offense against your valuable time. It breaks your train of thought and your work flow, and exposes that much more of your time to situations you do not completely control. The party at the other end may put you on hold, put you off, confuse you, abuse you, and mislead you.

---

**WE ARE UNABLE TO REGULATE THE INCOMING CALL PATTERN**
If you are like most executives, you have at least two bosses—your immediate superior and the phone. When the phone summons, you answer. Ridiculous!

**WE LACK THE SAVVY TO CUT A PHONE CALL SHORT AND BE NICE AT THE SAME TIME**

## THE CURE: CUTTING TELEPHONE TIME

By now you've probably figured out how to solve a few of these problems. Time management experts agree on how best to cut down on phone interruptions.

CALL LOG   Record incoming/outgoing; party/nature of call; length; time of day. Do this for a solid week, or for several days a week over a two- or three-week period. You'll be shocked at how much time you spend talking to your buddies about getting together over the weekend, and at how long it takes you to complete a call that was intended to get a simple yes or no answer to something.

CALL CLUSTERS   Placing and receiving calls is an activity unto itself. Block out a period of time each day for placing calls and, if possible, for receiving them. Some prefer early morning. Others late afternoon before quitting time. Or you can have two periods, early A.M. and late P.M. Calls that fill this period of clustered activity are not interruptions.

CALL SCREENING AND CALL-BACK   This requires a secretary. When you do not wish to be interrupted, tell your secretary to have the party call back, or take the number so that you may return the call when it is more convenient. Of course, make a priority list of individuals whose calls you will take under any circumstances. If this list is very long, then you are not being selective enough. If you trust your secretary's cordiality in requesting that an important person allow you to return his or her call, so much the better. A priority list should reflect urgency, not just rank. Only a very privileged few should have carte blanche access to your time.

Often, your secretary can provide the caller with the information required, thus eliminating the need for a call-back. If she says, "Perhaps I can help you," in many cases the caller will turn elsewhere to seek the information he's looking for and will therefore tell your secretary, "Never mind, I'll call so-and-so instead"; or "Never mind, I'll go look it up."

*If you answer your own phones:* Lots of executives prefer to answer their own phones. It allows them to maintain contact with what's going on at all levels of their business and gives their business associates a feeling of accessibility to the top. If you feel this way, by all means follow through, but remember that it will cost you in time. One compromise is a daily period for incoming calls: Have a secretary say that you take calls personally between nine and ten each morning. You'll get your share of inane calls, but at least they won't interrupt anything else.

SET THE TONE OF THE CONVERSATION AT THE START   Cut the bull and get down to it. If you start with pleasantries, you are opening Pandora's box. After the how-are-you's, say, "The reason I'm calling is ..." In some cases a simple "How are you?" is too much, because he'll actually tell you, in detail. There are those social critics who say our culture is in a sorry state when people ask how you are and don't really want to know. They may be right. My solution is don't ask if you don't want to know. If you say, "This'll only take a minute," then only take a minute. Don't be afraid to say, "Listen, Bill, I have only about five minutes to talk. If you need more time, let's talk later." Then, if the guy starts running off at the mouth, you have an out. "As I said, Bill—I'm in quite a rush, so let's continue this another time." One rule: Be nice! (But also be firm.)

Again, there are exceptions. Salesmen and politicians often claim that "talking it up" is part of their approach. They feel uncomfortable saying, "Hi. The reason I'm calling is to sell you a seventy-five-thousand-dollar computer." Okay. If you must chat, do so. But be aware of the problem and don't overdo it. Incidentally, I know several salesmen who use the straight-ahead "I'm out to sell you" approach quite effectively.

LEARN HOW TO CLOSE THE CALL   End it when you've accomplished the purpose. Don't be afraid to cut it off. Unless you are a shrink or a priest, you are not a confessor. A great trick (this will blow my cover) is to press the receiver button or cradle down while you are talking a blue streak. The other party won't be upset at you, because he'll think he's been cut off. He probably won't call back if it's just to make idle chatter. But safeguard against it by alerting your secretary to pick up the phone and tell him you've stepped away from your desk. Don't tell this to all your friends or it'll never work again.

DON'T DIAL YOUR OWN CALLS   Impersonal? Stuffy? Yes, but it's also a great time-saver, because frequently the person isn't in, or you've reached the wrong party and you must be transferred, or you're put on hold. To some, the words "Mr. Doe? Please hold. Mr. Smith calling" sound very impressive. Some others will be annoyed. But since you know who you want to reach, you are in control.

GET IT TOGETHER FIRST   Take a few minutes and outline, mentally or on paper, what you want to say or find out. Get the main points in so that you don't forget and have to call back.

**PAY ATTENTION** Listen. Take notes if necessary. Get it right the first time. You'll sound more alert and attentive. You'll be more productive. And you won't have to call again to "double check." The "double-check" is, 80 percent of the time, simply a cover phrase for inattention or feeblemindedness.

**DON'T KEEP PEOPLE WAITING** Their time is valuable, too. If you do it to them, they'll do it to you. It's a bad pattern to start. If you are victimized, hang up. If your party doesn't call back, try again later. It's less humiliating than wearing your neck out by cradling a phone in it, and it frees you to go back to your work.

**CONSIDER THE NEW DEVICES** Don't go gadget crazy, but there is a wide range of telephone accessories—answering devices; automatic dialers; speaker phones; call timers; wireless phones—and many of them can be helpful. This will be discussed in a later chapter.

## THE BEST WAY TO ELIMINATE INTERRUPTIONS: THE HIDEOUT

If you've got some money to spend:

**RENT A SMALL APARTMENT NEAR YOUR HOME OR OFFICE** Don't give out the address or phone, except to those who may need to reach you in an emergency. Or don't install a phone. If you carry a beeper, then you can call in when needed. Perhaps your company can cover the rent.

**RENT A HOTEL OR MOTEL ROOM** This has certain advantages over an apartment. You can rent it only when you need it; besides, you get the use of room service, pool, sauna, and other conveniences, especially relaxing when you are holed up for several days.

**RENT AN OFFICE FROM ANOTHER COMPANY** Just a small 9 x 12 where no one knows you and no one cares.

If you don't have money to spend:

**WORK AT HOME A DAY OR TWO A WEEK** But don't tell many people, or you'll get those calls at home.

**WORK IN YOUR CAR** Drive it to a secluded spot, take a clipboard and a pocket dictation unit, and you're all set.

**USE THE LIBRARY** Great place. Everyone minds his own business and you are unlikely to get into distracting conversations.

**IF YOU ARE REALLY HARD UP, TRY THE REST ROOM** Several

executives I know consider this the place for mind-busting reading and thinking. A bathroom stall has an inner-sanctum feeling.

RELIGIOUS RETREAT HOUSES   For a very reasonable fee you can stay at a rectory or some such place. Your room will be stark, but the setting is usually idyllic country beauty and the atmosphere is very calming.

SUGGEST THAT YOUR COMPANY DESIGNATE AN EMPTY OFFICE AS A QUIET ROOM   Unfortunately, it may not be vacant when you need it the most.

## THE PERMISSIBLE INTERRUPTION: THE BREAK

Stopping work because of a drop-in visitor, phone call, or other distraction is clearly unproductive. But regular, self-imposed breaks can be extremely valuable. Research has shown that short interruptions leading to higher recall of material. Five- to ten-minute breaks are best.

## THE TYRANNY OF THE URGENT

"We live in constant tension between the urgent and the important," wrote Charles Hummel. "The problem is that the important tasks rarely must be done today, or even this week. The urgent task calls for instant action—endless demands pressure every hour and day."*

You have your day planned, and it's beautiful. Everything's rolling along on schedule; everything's going to get done. Then it hits: the urgent; the unexpected. The crisis. Suddenly the day is no longer beautiful. The meetings get canceled. Paperwork is put aside. Those important calls never get made. Your excuse? "There was an emergency and I had to deal with it."

*The lure of the crisis is almost irresistible, because it demands your immediate attention. But in retrospect, it is the high-priority items that count.* The real danger in such a situation is that the urgent matters tend to assert priority over the important, instead of the other way around.

There's not much you can do about this except exercise good judgment: *Think before you throw things aside to attend to a "crisis."* Can you let the crisis work itself out? Is there someone else who can handle

---

*Charles Hummel, *Tyranny of the Urgent* (Chicago: Intervarsity Press, 1967) quoted in R. Alec Mackenzie's *Time Management* (Greenwich, NY: Alec Mackenzie and Associates, 1976), p.58

it? What will be the repercussions if you let a crisis persist versus the repercussions if you interrupt your priorities?

PLAN AHEAD  It's amazing how many problems can be avoided when you have considered in advance how to deal with them. Keep careful records and thorough notes to avoid forgetting anything that is routine now, but could turn into a crisis if neglected until the last minute. More often than not, the roots of crisis lie in routine tasks.

DON'T PANIC  Under pressure, the natural thing to do is to act to eliminate whatever is exerting the pressure. But remember—the thing causing the pressure isn't necessarily the most important thing you could be attending to at the time. Once you realize that urgency is not necessarily synonymous with priority, you will feel less pressure.

FORMULATE CONTINGENCY PLANS  Whenever you are involved in something the outcome of which is uncertain (that covers just about everything), consider what you will do if it doesn't work out as you plan. Developing contingencies involves time and effort, but the consequences can be grave if you don't have them to fall back on. And as a result of your efforts to come up with a contingency, you might discover a new and better way of doing things.

---

# PROCRASTINATION

---

I put off writing this section for quite a while. No kidding. But if any area requires biting the bullet, procrastination is it. Management experts have few pearls of wisdom to offer here, and the reason is apparent to any amateur analyst: *Procrastination is primarily a psychological problem*, symptomatic of some glitch in our personalities. In some people the result is a general problem, while in others, just a tendency to postpone certain tasks or responsibilities.

Depressed people procrastinate a lot. Those who hate to say no will often put off that nay-saying phone call.

If procrastination is a truly debilitating problem that has been affecting your performance, you must do something about it before it's too late.

You might consider one of the many methods of self-improvement, from TM to psychotherapy. You choose.

### FOR RELIEF OF MILD PROCRASTINATION SYMPTOMS

In many cases procrastination is far less serious than a personality disorder. It is merely the bad habit of putting off something unpleasant, or what grandma would call "just plain laziness." Here, time management experts such as Alan Lakein and Edwin Bliss have been

---

helpful with a few clever little strategies for psyching yourself up (or out?) and plowing into action. Here are the best:*

DIVIDE AND CONQUER  If you have taken to procrastinating because of the sheer awesomeness of the task before you, break it up into smaller, less unwieldy jobs that don't leave you weak in the knees. Once you start accumulating small victories and accomplishments, you'll be on your way. Momentum is the buzzword for this feeling.

This method is referred to by Bliss as the "Salami Technique" (because you slice up the task like a salami) and by Lakein as the "Swiss Cheese Method" (because you bore small holes in the big job). Cute.

THE BALANCE-SHEET METHOD   This method, so named by Bliss, is essentially an exercise in self-humilation. This may be just what the doctor ordered. Get a sheet of paper and make a balance sheet. One side of the sheet is for all the wonderful things that will result if you do this job now. The other side is for listing all the reasons why you're putting it off. If there are solid, concrete reasons for postponing the job, they will show up clearly. But if you are simply procrastinating, the reasons for putting if off will look pretty silly when compared with the benefits of completing it. If the balance sheet fails to reveal good reasons for doing the job now, you should question whether the job is worth doing at all. Nothing saves time like eliminating work.

The chief advantage of this method is in seeing all the lily-livered, lame excuses you have for procrastinating. The effects are often very dramatic. Executives have been known to go to their windows and shout, "Man the battle stations," "I've not yet begun to fight," or, my favorite, "Whatever could be done tomorrow should be done today."

BITE THE BULLET  Unfortunately, as time management expert Michael LeBoeuf points out, the "divide and conquer" technique won't help you when you are putting off a one-shot task like firing your secretary; I don't recommend firing someone over a week's time, five minutes a day. And when you've got to report disappointing sales figures to your boss, there doesn't appear to be much sense in bothering with the "balance sheet" method. You have to do it, and you needn't waste time convincing yourself.

Biting the bullet is for the time when you must be bold. It's not so bad. Everyone jumps into a cold swimming pool once in a while.

PRIORITIZE  Do the important things first. Learn to assign priorities and organize your work so that you give the greatest and most immediate attention to the most important jobs. If you've got to take the heat because something isn't done, at least make sure it's minor. You want to be known as someone who always comes through on the big

*Reprinted, with permission, from *How to Get Control of Your Time and Your Life*, by Alan Lakein, Copyright © 1973 by Alan Lakein. Published by David McKay.

ones. That's where you make your reputation—not by accomplishing lots of little things that don't matter much.

AVOID THE PERFECTIONISM TRAP   That's when you never finish anything because you are never satisfied. If you are obsessive about a project, it could be that you are trying to delay moving on to the next—more difficult or unpleasant—task. Or trying to put off the discomfort associated with being judged on your work.

The way to avoid this is to set standards of performance, both at the company level and the individual level. "In our company, we don't want memos that are great works of literature," says one chief executive. "We discourage even the excessive correction of typos in interoffice communication. On the other hand, I get terribly annoyed at the sight of a misspelled word or outdated statistics on an important report. If it happens often, I'll call the perpetrator on the carpet."

*Know how good the job must be, and when you reach that level, move on.* The points you might gain for that little bit extra might very well be offset by a reputation for being slow and unable to let go of something.

DO IT RIGHT THE FIRST TIME   So many things must be done a second or third time simply because there is a lack of understanding between you and your superiors about what the project is all about. Make sure you get it straight. And keep the lines of communication open throughout the project.

If you find that you are doing things over because you have overlooked items the first time around, you might consider using checklists and taking better notes. If you plan to rely on your memory, make sure it's reliable.

SET DEADLINES   It is difficult to conceptualize a task without placing it in some sort of time frame. You can set a deadline for practically anything. Use every means, including the above techniques, to get things in on time.

---

# LATENESS

---

Lateness has become an epidemic in a country where punctuality is considered a virtue. In some cultures lateness is not only accepted, but encouraged. But in the United States, it has always been an indication of poor character. "Punctuality" appears on every school child's report card.

So why are there so many Johnny- and Janey-come-latelys in the U.S.? Perhaps, like other puritan ethics, punctuality is considered old-fashioned. If adultery is on the rise, what chance does being on time have?

There could be other reasons. The deterioration of essential services in some of our larger cities makes it difficult to get something or somebody to another place. And the proliferation of the computer—intelligence that never sleeps—means that traditional time limits, such as those set for banking and regular mail deliveries, have less meaning.

Do not be fooled into thinking that being late will have no consequences. Nobody likes to be kept waiting. And during the time a person spends waiting for you, he is likely to be thinking about all your negative traits. He will not be in a good frame of mind when you arrive.

Remember the days when the person would worry about your well-being when you were late, because it was "not like you"?

Being prompt has class. It shows respect for others and is just plain good business. When you arrive is as much a part of your initial impression as what you are wearing.

## HOW TO BE ON TIME

ASSUME AND PREPARE FOR THE WORST   This is Murphy's Law applied to lateness. If it takes ten minutes to get somewhere, allow more time than that. You just never know when they will start construction on Washington Street, or when a truck will turn over on the freeway. Sure, if things go smoothly, you might arrive early. But if you think that this will make you look overeager, you can always stop into a nearby coffee shop and read or do some light work. (Always carry some reading and/or light work with you—not only for the times when you arrive early, but also for the times *you* are kept waiting.)

DEFINE YOUR TERMS   If you mean "around three," make it clear that you mean "approximately three," "between 2:30 and three," etc., not "exactly three." Giving an approximate time of arrival is usually acceptable when the other party is at home or in his office and there is always something to do until you arrive. It is not okay if the person has a tight schedule—for example, another appointment at 3:30.

IF YOU ARE GOING TO BE LATE, CALL

IF YOU HAVE TROUBLE GAUGING TIME, USE A TIMING DEVICE THAT SIGNALS WHEN YOU MUST GO   And follow it religiously. Many of the newer electronic watches come with alarm functions. So do many pocket calculators.

LEARN HOW TO END A PREVIOUS ENGAGEMENT IN SUFFICIENT TIME   This is not as simple as it sounds. It involves setting priorities, because you may wish to keep a less important party waiting while you finish up with a more important one. Don't do this often. Most VIPs will respect your desire to be prompt in meeting with your next visitor. If you are late, the person cooling his heels will feel that you don't consider his time as valuable, and he will reflect that perception in his dealings.

AVOID, AT ALL COSTS, MEETING SOMEONE IN FRONT OF SOMEPLACE   If one of you is late, the other will be obliged to stand there waiting. It is difficult, if not impossible, to make use of that time.

IN ADVANCE, FIGURE OUT HOW MUCH TIME AN APPOINTMENT WILL TAKE   Then, allow at least 30 percent more. This applies even to getting out of the house in the morning. One industrial psychologist told me that I would be amazed at how many people are late because they spent ten minutes wrestling with a cowlick, trying to hide a blemish, or picking out a tie. Naturally, people don't confess to such things, so they are forced to lie, making some incredible remark about the traffic.

IF YOU SEE THAT YOUR SCHEDULE IS TOO TIGHT, CHANGE IT IN ADVANCE   Give yourself some room.

START LEAVING A MEETING BEFORE IT'S TIME TO LEAVE   You need a few extra minutes to work your way out the door. If you wait to the last minute to say, "I must be going," you may find yourself sitting back down to hear the last few points the party was saving for the end.

LEARN YOUR ENVIRONMENT   How long does it take to get there? By bus? Rail? Cab? Get the lowdown on making time from the natives. For example, New Yorkers know that you've got to allow time to hail a cab, as well as time to reach your destination. In the rush hour, or in the rain, getting a cab can take almost as long as the ride itself.

DON'T MAKE PROMISES THAT YOU CAN'T KEEP   Be realistic. And if you see that you have overcommitted yourself, let the parties involved in on the situation.

AVOID REPEAT PERFORMANCES   If you are late for a meeting once, don't let it happen again with the same party. Such behavior tends to form patterns. The sooner you break it, the better. What's more, the other party will form a pattern of his own, and begin to classify you as "always late." Once he does, that reputation will be very hard to break.

### IF YOU ARE ABSOLUTELY HOPELESS

CARRY A BEEPER   And have your secretary beep you before each appointment.

ASK THE OTHER PARTY IF HE WOULD MIND CALLING TO RECONFIRM ON THE DAY OF THE APPOINTMENT

PSYCH YOURSELF OUT   You'll need the help of your secretary: Have her set appointments for you. Sometimes you will be given the actual time of the appointment. Sometimes you will be given a time that is anywhere from five to fifteen minutes early. This unpredictable schedule will keep you on your toes. You will never know whether you are arriving early or on time. So it will be tough to cheat.

IDENTIFY THE UNDERLYING PSYCHOLOGICAL REASONS FOR CHRONIC LATENESS:

- fear of being early and having nothing to do
- poor judgment of time
- disorganization
- lack of respect for the other party
- little value placed on promptness
- "subconscious" reasons, such as lateness as a form of aggressive behavior

How far inside yourself you need to go in order to solve this problem is something only you can determine. Base your decision not only on the severity of the problem, but on the potential damage to your career. In some situations lateness does not matter as much as in others. A film star who is constantly late on the set will eventually cost the studio many thousands of dollars in resulting production schedule overruns. Very few can afford to do this repeatedly and expect to work. But in some professions, only deadlines are important—not punctuality.

---

# INEFFECTIVE DELEGATION

---

The ability to delegate is an essential ingredient of effective time management. Many of us feel that we got where we are on our own merits and are therefore reluctant to place even a tiny sliver of our fates in someone else's hands. Then there are those who are arrogant enough to believe that nobody else can do the job. Often, this is just a way of masking an insecurity—the fear of being shown up. When this problem is taken to extremes, we can wind up victims of *reverse delegation*, in which we take on the work of subordinates.

All of these attitudes are distinct liabilities. There is virtually unanimous agreement that without some form of delegation, proper use of time is impossible. Equally important is the *skill* of delegating. It's one thing to decide to delegate tasks and responsibilities. It's quite another to make it work.

### HOW TO DELEGATE

FIND THE RIGHT PERSON FOR THE JOB  The right person isn't always the most obvious, the most available, or even the most qualified. There may be someone highly motivated, with lots of drive, who will get excited about the task. Often, such a person will outperform a more

---

experienced person who might be passive or even resentful about the task.

ONCE YOU'VE CHOSEN THE PERSON, MAKE SURE HE IS PROPERLY OUTFITTED   Supply aids to doing the job well—resources, contacts, advice, a budget.

MAKE SURE YOU ARE ON THE SAME WAVELENGTH   What exactly is it you want done? What is your subordinate's accountability? What are the limits and breadth of his responsibility? Make it all clear at the beginning. It will save you a lot of heartache.

STROKE   Give credit where and when it is merited. It's simple human nature: People like to receive recognition for a job well done. But you should mean it. Insincere praise backfires, because the subordinate will think you are being obsequious, or substituting praise for a raise or bonus.

TRUST   Give your delegatee a vote of confidence. Understand that he may disagree with you, or even go wrong. That's the chance you take. Outwardly demand perfection; but remind yourself nobody's perfect, and don't be unreasonable.

BEWARE OF REVERSE DELEGATION   This occurs when the person you are delegating the job is able to get *you* to do the job. Sometimes it's that one adorable, sweet, lovable person you just can't say no to. Sometimes it's the one who says he needs advice, who flatters you into helping him by making you feel needed. If you're not careful, you'll wind up doing his work as well as your own—and praising him for its quality. Know where to draw the line.

ACCEPT RESPONSIBILITY   That is one thing you cannot delegate. It's your decision to assign the task, and you have got to take the heat. Funny how these things work. If you are called in to get praise heaped upon you, it always looks gracious to say, "Well, I had some terrific help," or "My staff deserves most of the credit," or "It was a team effort." But if you get called on the carpet and say, "Well, it was Spofford's fault, he's so sloppy," or "I'm having trouble getting a competent staff together," you are digging yourself a big hole in which you may get buried. Better off getting your head bloodied. The cowboys in the boardrooms love the spirit of the rugged individualist, the leader. Don't overdo it by taking the rap for everything, though.

BE A NICE PERSON   Remember Captain Bligh? Well, this ain't the navy, and you're not at war. When you want something done, ask; don't bark orders. Be courteous to those who treat you with respect. Just because you are a higher-up in your company doesn't mean that you are worth more as a human being. The only time you should pull rank is when being nice doesn't work. You'll know when that happens, and it won't be often.

**LAY YOUR CARDS ON THE TABLE**   Don't hold back. Make sure your subordinate knows what is expected, and how to go about it. If there are certain caveats connected with the task, such as keeping something confidential or avoiding a confrontation with Mr. X, say so. If possible, say why you want this job done, how it fits into your overall scheme, and what the consequences will be. The more your appointee knows, the less often he'll have to say to others, "I'll have to get back to you on that one." It also allows him to think on his feet.

Occasionally I receive calls from business associates to discuss the price of a service and the person delegated to speak with me is empowered only to make *the offer*, not to negotiate; in fact, quite often he doesn't know what kind of compromise his boss would accept. Not only does that annoy me, but it makes him look like a lackey, and I quickly demand to speak to the boss. You can bet that this gentleman resents his boss more than he resents me.

**FOLLOW UP**   Make sure that the job gets done—on time, correctly. Don't leave your subordinate hanging. It's a good idea to set a time to discuss the job with him. I've been in situations in which I tried to discuss a particular job with a superior and was told, "Handle it." So I would. Six months later, the guy would barge into my office, his blood pressure so high I could hear the blood coursing through his veins, to tell me that I hadn't done that job right, and what was the matter with me. *He* was to blame.

**LEAVE THE GUY ALONE**   You gave him the job, now let him do it. If you trust him—and if you don't, what's he doing on your staff?—give him the chance to prove himself.

**GO SLOW**   It takes years to acquire the judgment to delegate effectively. For your sake and his, go slow with every subordinate. Don't start dumping stuff on him out of the clear blue. Let him know that you want to start delegating, ask him how he feels about it, and control the flow. Give him a chance to get in the groove.

**BE SELECTIVE IN WHAT YOU DELEGATE**   Ask yourself if the task at hand is an appropriate one for delegation. Delegation can be overdone, possibly creating the impression that you don't want to get your hands dirty.

**DELEGATE IN ADVANCE**   Let the subordinate know what kinds of things you'll be wanting him to handle, rather than waiting for the job to come along and prompt the thought, "Aha, this is just what I want to give to Arnold. Send him in." Arnold will be more prepared if he knows what kind of work has his name on it.

**DON'T JUST DELEGATE THE DULL OR THE DIRTY**   Some guys think that subordinates exist primarily to do their busy-work. They save all the plums for themselves. This is such a rotten way to do things, nothing more need be said. If you delegate some of the more stimulating and challenging jobs, it will be easier to get top-drawer performances from your staff.

# POOR PLANNING

This problem is self-evident, and symptomatic of the entire time management problem. Objectives? Formulate them carefully and clearly. Priorities? Set them. Planning? Always plan. This is primarily an analytical function—learning to deal with certain variables, assigning values to them, putting them in order, and identifying the essence of the task. You learned this in school if you took philosophy, mathematics, logic, or any science. It's just that nobody told you it had anything to do with everyday business. If you learned anything in college, you learned to be critical of fallacious arguments; of unethical policies; of ineffective strategies. So, use your mind.

# TAKING ON TOO MUCH

This problem is almost always self-generated, and it is intimately bound up with attitudes toward work. Often, we have a desire to "make up for lost time," or feel that by taking on that much work, we will get ahead that much faster. Whether it is driving ambition, a healthy success orientation, or an insecurity or need for approval, the effect is often the same—taking on too much at once. Realize that *the amount of things that one is handling at any given time often bears no fruitful relationship to overall productivity.* Don't overburden yourself; you'll end up doing lots of things in a mediocre manner, but nothing well.

## SYMPTOMS

Overeagerness to assume new tasks translates into some behavioral quirks at the job:

POOR ESTIMATION OF TIME   We want to take on this job so badly that we underestimate how much time it will take, or how much time we'll need for the other tasks we have. Research has shown that, on the whole, jobs take longer than most executives estimate they will take. So allow more time—*give yourself a cushion,* even if you have to pass on something in order to create that cushion.

HYPERRESPONSIVITY   That's when you respond to all and everything that comes your way. It's nice to champ at the bit, but don't overdo it. And if you do take on something, *give what is needed or what is asked for.* Don't overwork the assignment. *Volume is often a negative rather than a positive, because the superior has to cope with unnecessary detail and increased paperwork.*

POOR PRIORITIZING  You can't decide what's most important, so you approach everything with equal weight.

---

# JUST CAN'T SAY NO

---

Like procrastination, this is largely a personality problem, and a serious one. The inability to say no is obviously a major root cause of another time-waster, "attempting too many things at once."

## MAJOR CAUSES

LACK OF CONFIDENCE AND ASSERTIVENESS  You may wish to engage in assertiveness training, TA, est, or whatever you feel will help you become more confident and self-assertive.

BEING TOO NICE  One of the more positive aspects of our Judeo-Christian culture is the overall emphasis on being "nice," being generous, and helping thy neighbor. But this may be taken too far, leading to a distorted view of what it means to be a nice person and continual effort to go to great lengths to avoid offending people.

If you are a nice, cooperative, helpful person, there is no reason to feel that you betray that self-image every time you say no.

THE NEED TO FEEL USEFUL  Many executives encourage others to ask for help solely because of the ego boost it gives. This signifies insecurity.

THE DESIRE TO AVOID CONFRONTATION AND/OR UNPLEAS-ANTNESS  Saying yes is so much easier. And less risky.

## MAJOR SOLUTIONS

In this book we can't examine these personality problems in depth, but we can attack this particular hangup in a few practical ways:

IF YOU ARE THINKING "NO," DON'T HESITATE  Say it right away, before your ambivalence betrays you and gives someone a chance to apply pressure. A quick "no" will often convey that it's useless to argue or brown-nose.

EXPECT TO SAY NO SEVERAL TIMES A DAY—THIS IS YOUR SOLEMN RIGHT  When it happens, you won't be surprised and tinged with guilt, because you've already come to terms with it.

BE CIVIL, POLITE, AND UNDERSTANDING  Find alternative ways

---

of helping others with their problems, such as referrals or suggestions on how they might handle the problems themselves.

DON'T GET DEFENSIVE AND MAKE EXCUSES   Easier said than done, but try. Being defensive is so common in business circles that even when you aren't being defensive, people will accuse you of it. Be nice, but be firm. And never waver.

IF YOU WANT TO SAY NO AND CAN'T THINK OF A VALID REASON, EITHER DON'T OFFER ONE OR REMAIN SILENT UNTIL YOU CAN THINK OF ONE   Saying "yes" to fill a void is the real sucker's way out.

### THE UNIVERSAL ANTIDOTE: YOUR SENSE OF HUMOR

A funny is great when you are in a tough spot. If you are trying to get someone to leave your office, it's always better to send him out laughing. If you can't say a flat-out "no" to a person, why not disarm him with a witticism?

But what if you aren't funny, or have a tendency to put your foot in your mouth? What if you overdo it—too much sarcasm? The results can be fatal. So if you can't do the humor thing well, don't do it at all. Practice at home.

---

# SCHEDULING: THE TO DO LIST

---

The need to sketch out a plan for the day's activities is so obvious it hardly needs mentioning. As schoolkids we wrote down our homework assignments at the end of each day as a reminder. And most executives write reminders in their diaries, calendars, and planners.

### REMINDING IS DIFFERENT FROM PLANNING

So from now on, when you scribble in your list of things to do, keep these points in mind:

SET PRIORITIES   Take several minutes to consider what must be done tomorrow and what is most important in the long run. You'll need this information to schedule your day sensibly.

SCHEDULE   Have a deliberate order for your tasks. Try to tackle the most important things first.

BEWARE OF THE "SMALL THINGS" SYNDROME   Don't fill up precious time with a collection of small things to get out of the way before taking on the major jobs. It's the easiest way to eat up your day without accomplishing anything significant. Contrary to the opinions

---

of most management experts, though, I think it's okay to warm up with a little thing—something that will sharpen your mind, get you in focus, and give you a sense of accomplishment without taking up much time—in short, an aid to psyching yourself up. Example: a short, clever "complaint" letter. A goodwill note to a client. Or compute your sales record, when you know all along it's going to be sensational.

LOOK FOR THINGS TO DELEGATE   Just because an item appears on your To Do list doesn't mean that *you* have to do it. It simply means that you must see that it *gets done*. If at all possible, find somebody else.

---

## YOUR MIND, YOUR BODY, AND YOUR SCHEDULE

---

"Each person with a little introspection can begin to sense his own inner timing—hunger contractions, the chill of dropping temperature, the quality of fresh vigor, emotional ebullience or anxiety and irritation. An hour-by-hour evaluation of mood, alertness, and sensations will begin to give each person the shape of his daily changes."[*]

Nobody in the business community is likely to argue with you if you were to point out that every individual has a different personality, intellectual approach, and perception of the environment in which one works. To a large degree, this diversity is what makes a successful company tick. However, most of us do not realize that there are significant differences in physiological functioning from individual to individual. Not everyone is "sharp" at the same time; not everyone is able to sustain complete concentration for hours. Some can go fifteen minutes at a stretch, but do it several times a day. Some are intellectually useless after two P.M.  And some don't have any real energy or drive until mid-morning.

These physiological differences are due to a wide variety of variables—hormonal, genetic, nutritional, metabolic, biochemical, sleep related, and environmental. *The important thing is that you should become aware of your own patterns.* Careful scrutiny of the time log should help. When making entries, note your mood (grouchy/feeling great; confident/dull; mind wanders/sharp/focused) and your physical feelings (sluggish; tired; bloated from lunch; energized, relaxed, calm). Patterns will emerge that reflect your energy levels, mental and physical peaks, and the kinds of activities that have positive or negative effects.

---

[*]From *Body Time: Physiological Rhythms and Social Stress* by Gay Gaer Luce, Copyright © 1971 by Gay Gaer Luce. Reprinted by permission of Pantheon Books, a division of Random House, Inc.

---

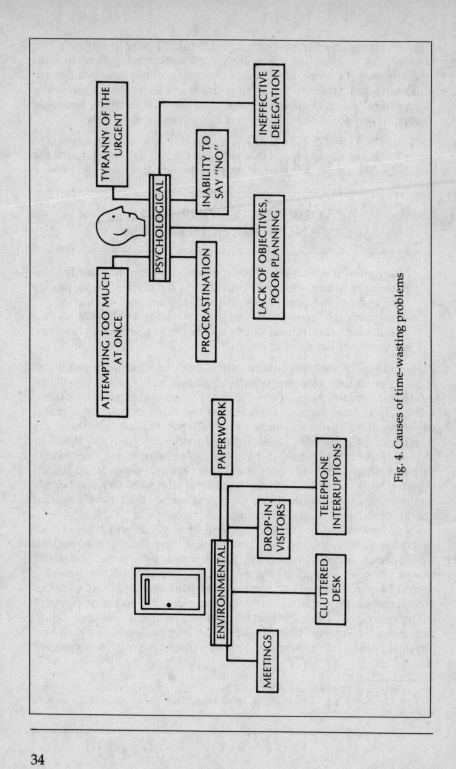

Fig. 4. Causes of time-wasting problems

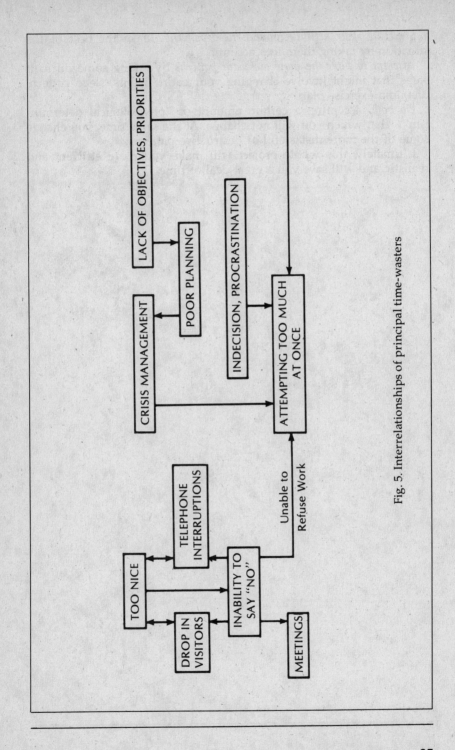

Fig. 5. Interrelationships of principal time-wasters

*Structure your activity around these patterns.* Make the best of the situation by taking them into account.

*Attempt to alter the more awkward patterns* by taking some difficult steps that might involve changing your eating habits, sleep pattern, diet, and exercise plan.

*Do both,* accepting a certain amount of "physiological determinism"—that which you will not change. At the same time, you change some of the more distasteful or destructive patterns.

Ultimately, this whole project will make you more efficient and realistic and will save you a great deal of time.

# 3

# THE PAPERWORK PROBLEM

Everyone agrees that there is simply too much paper floating around the American business community. If the pile on your desk or in the mail won't tell you, take a long look at the way things are done in your office.

## SYMPTOMS

**Copier consciousness.** One "coffee boy" told me that by parking his coffee-and-donuts wagon by the copier of a large office, he did a larger business than he did during coffee breaks. Take a look at your bills for paper, toner, and repair if you need confirmation of this tale.

**Formulosis.** I'm not sure who invented the standard form, but I'll bet his or her intention was to *reduce paperwork*. And in fact, if forms are used properly, they will save time and paper. Unfortunately, the federal government has managed to turn a bright idea into a blight—and many companies have followed suit. Are there standard forms in your firm that leave you at a loss to explain their value?

**Typing backlog.** Does the wait to get something typed remind you of the wait for gasoline in the summer of '79? If so, it could be that your typists are slow, inefficient, or overloaded with work, but it could well be because they are processing too much unnecessary wordage. The belief is that typing equals official and businesslike. But remember there are times when a handwritten note has more class and warmth. Use the phone more often. With the cost of a page of typing over $12, a phone call, unless it's to Peking, is almost certainly going to be cheaper and faster.

**Reading yourself to sleep in your own office.** Do you find that the most useless, irrelevant information crosses your desk, requiring your initials? You probably assume it's coming from the higher-ups. Maybe. But maybe it's some exec trying to make points by showing how on-top-of-things he is. If you'd rather he keep his statistics on paper clip usage and his Vince Lombardi-type "win" pep talk quotes to himself, say so.

**You can't always get what you want.** You ask for an important file. But you get a file that is worthless. Or a file so thick that it takes fifteen minutes to find what you're looking for—and you with only three minutes to read it. Files shouldn't be like gold mines, where you have to move tons of useless earth to find a precious little bit of ore. Files should be like bank vaults, holding only the stuff that counts.

**Clerical glut.** Is everyone's nephew or niece working at your place during the summers and after school? How many clerks do you need, anyway? They may be busy filing and all, but what if they are spending all day processing unproductive paper? Better check.

**Document fever.** Documents, reports, and memos about everything. Are they really necessary? Especially if they're thick, reports impress people; they show that the author did lots of work. But reports should have an objective—one achieved as efficiently as possible. *That's* what should be impressive.

**Too many files.** We run out of space, we buy more files. Right? A waste of space, a waste of money. If you have a business that necessitates a steady increase of its volume of filed material, consider the many space-saving alternatives, such as micrographics and microforms (see Chapter 34), or frequently purge the files of obsolete or other unnecessary paper.

---

## THE PAPER TEST:
## SHOULD THIS PAPER BE CREATED?

---

1. *What is its purpose?*
2. *How will it be used, and where is it going?* Perhaps a call or a short memo would work better.
3. *Do I plan to put the right amount of information in the document?* Too much is waste of time and paper. Too little means that you may have to do it all over again, but more thoroughly.
4. *Is it redundant?* Can the information be found elsewhere with little time and effort?
5. *Is this the best time?* Or will you have to summarize the situation again later?

---

6. *Can this task be accomplished in a paperless manner?*
7. *What happens to the paper after it is read?* If you have ideas, include them: "File under . . . " or "You may discard," for example.
8. *Can we do without this?* The bottom line.

---

# THE CULPRITS

---

**The Creator.** * In principle, there's nothing wrong with someone creating paperwork. But if the person is on a power trip, thinks he's the literary light of the office, or, even worse, is insecure enough to think that his work will be evaluated by the volume of paper he produces, he's a serious problem.

Trevor Bentley has isolated three types of dementia that, personified, result in uncontrolled paper.

> *Memo Man.* Inarticulate, so uses memos to cover it up.
> *Bookworm.* Likes words and numbers. Compulsive about writing everything down. This is the guy who used to copy every word the teacher said in class, but usually didn't do so hot.
> *The Copier Freak.* To some, copiers are like motorcycles, fast cars, or even drugs. They love using them, and they'll use any excuse. They love the bright yellow-green light, the moaning noise, the smell of the chemicals.

**The Reader.** He's got to read absolutely everything that crosses his desk. He's afraid he'll miss something. As a result he is not selective in his reading and wastes lots of time. He subscribes to mailbags full of magazines, newsletters, and brochures, making for lots of clutter.

**The Checker.** Has to check and double-check everything before it goes out. Finding errors isn't always cost effective. Sometimes it takes more time than it's worth. How important is a typo in an interoffice memo? Years ago someone invented spot checking and sampling. It works quite well to keep people on their toes—and their work accurate.

**The Converter.** He takes statistics broken down by month and breaks them down by year. If he doesn't like metric, he'll convert to pounds, inches and quarts. He's a specialist in the kind of work known as NVA—No Value Added.

**The Filer.** This is usually a team effort. First there's *the one who creates*

---

*This "paperworker" and the others that follow were so named by Trevor J. Bentley in *Information, Communication, and the Paperwork Explosion* (Maidenhead, England: McGraw-Hill, 1976), pp. 15–30.

---

*the file in the first place.* Then there's *the person who actually does the filing.* The file maker often uses a system that only he can understand, or that follows rules of logic so obscure that the clerical staff would have to be trained at Scotland Yard to follow the clues. The file "stasher" takes the blame for lost files when it is often not his fault. Or, on the other hand, he may file an item under a heading that an executive might never think of checking. It is estimated that 20 percent of all clerical activity is spent in filing, 15 percent in retrieving.

**The Destroyer.** This is the one who goes too far. The joy of clearing a paper-filled desk, of moving through documents and consigning most of them to the wastebasket, gives him or her the exhilarating feeling of a job well done. Often, however, items that are important to others get pitched, because *the destroyer, in his zeal, forgets to check with others.* If there is something in dispute that requires referral to written documentation, keep the document away from a destroyer.

**The Fountain of Knowledge.** This one can be very dangerous—the person who feels personally slighted if he doesn't know absolutely everything going on in the office. "Why wasn't I told?" is his favorite expression. Often, he will go to improper lengths to find out what's going on, reading communications of a confidential nature, for instance, or glancing over memos on someone's desk when that person is at lunch or a meeting.

---

# THE CLUTTERED DESK

---

Before I suggest to you what should be on your desk, or even what a desk is for, let's dwell on what to remove from your desk. For this exercise you will need:

- *at least one large trash can.* If you are into recycling paper, get a smaller can as well for nonpaper items.
- *a table or other large surface.* You will need this to sift through the mountains of junk that you probably have in and on your desk.
- *file folders*
- *file cabinet*, if your desk drawer doesn't have one built in
- *a few storage boxes*

**Scan for known garbage.** This is junk mail, candy wrappers, last week's papers and last month's magazines, and anything else that is sitting on your desk which you have already sentenced to become part of a landfill. Just remind yourself that it feels so good to throw things away! Savor the experience; enjoy it to the fullest.

---

Now you should feel euphoric and ready to move on to the next step.

**Dump everything from the top of your desk onto the table or other surface, and add the contents of your desk drawers.** Obviously, be careful with vases, full ashtrays, etc. Disgusting, isn't it, all that junk?

**Eliminate.** When in doubt, throw it out. Believe me, you don't need most of what is there unless you've been extremely vigilant already. And if that is the case, your desk isn't cluttered, so you don't need to do this exercise. Sorry.

**Sort.** Now you've thrown out what's not needed, *make piles according to category.* There are several ways to do this sorting procedure: by subject, by category, or by recent/dated. You will be filing from these piles. Some of the material may belong in your desk drawer file for ready access; other material is to be kept for records only and will probably not be needed, except in the case of such events as an IRS audit or an insurance claim.

**File.** Yes. But as you hit each file folder, make sure that nothing in it can be pitched. Over 90 percent of filed material over a year old is never referred to. If it's legal and/or financial, you might want to hold on to it. If not, throw it out.

---

## ORGANIZING YOUR DESK

---

A desk is a work space, or, more accurately, a work tool. It should be styled that way and not as a storage depot for papers, food, books, what-have-you. Your desk should contain only those things specifically related to your day's work, and items you will use to enhance overall performance.

**Do not put things on your desk because you feel that you will be reminded to attend to them.** This doesn't work. Soon a pile of things not to be forgotten develops and the pile must be sifted to find that item—that is, if you remember to look for it. Another hitch: If the memory-jogging effect does succeed, it is likely to distract you or break your train of thought, because every time you look up, there's that paper beckoning to you.

**Purge your desk of various useless items.** It's not a museum, a window display, a souvenir shop, a trophy case, a photography exhibit, a retrospective of the past ten years of your life, or your equivalent of King Tut's tomb. Therefore, remove various awards, gift paperweights, pen-and-pencil sets that you don't use, too many pictures, etc.

---

| LEGEND FOR AUTHORITY TO DISPOSE | LEGEND FOR RETENTION PERIOD |
|---|---|
| AD—Administrative Decision | AC—Dispose After Completion of Job or Contract |
| ASPR—Armed Services Procurement Regulation | AE—Dispose After Expiration |
| CFR—Code of Federal Regulations | AF—After End of Fiscal Year |
| | AM—After Moving |
| FLSA—Fair Labor Standards Act | AS—After Settlement |
| ICC—Interstate Commerce Commission | AT—Dispose After Termination |
| | ATR—After Trip |
| INS—Insurance Company Regulation | OBS—Dispose When Obsolete |
| | P—Permanent |
| ISM—Industrial Security Manual, Attachment to DD Form 441 | SUP—Dispose When Superseded |

*After Disposed    **Normally         †Govt. R&D Contracts

| TYPE OF RECORD | RETENTION PERIOD YEARS | AUTHORITY |
|---|---|---|
| **ACCOUNTING & FISCAL** | | |
| Accounts Payable Invoices | 3 | ASPR-STATE, FLSA |
| Accounts Payable Ledger | P | AD |
| Accounts Receivable Ledgers | 5 | AD |
| Authorizations for Accounting | SUP | AD |
| Balance Sheets | P | AD |
| Bank Deposits | 3 | AD |
| Bank Statements | 3 | AD |
| Bonds | P | AD |
| Budgets | 3 | AD |
| Capital Asset Record | 3* | AD |
| Cash Receipt Records | 7 | AD |
| Check Register | P | AD |
| Checks, Dividend | 6 | |
| Checks, Payroll | 2 | FLSA, STATE |
| Checks, Voucher | 3 | FLSA, STATE |
| Cost Accounting Records | 5 | AD |
| Earnings Register | 3 | FLSA, STATE |
| Entertainment Gifts & Gratuities | 3 | AD |
| Estimates, Projections | 7 | AD |
| Expense Reports | 3 | AD |
| Financial Statements, Certified | P | AD |

Fig. 6. Records retention timetable
This table can be used as a guide to how long to save records.
(*through page 46*)

From "Records Retention Timetable" (New York: Electric Wastebasket Corp., 1977). Reprinted courtesy of Electric Wastebasket Corp., New York, NY 10036.

| TYPE OF RECORD | RETENTION PERIOD YEARS | AUTHORITY |
|---|---|---|
| Financial Statements, Periodic | 2 | AD |
| General Ledger Records | P | CFR |
| Labor Cost Records | 3 | ASPR, CFR |
| Magnetic Tape and Tab Cards | 1** | |
| Note Register | P | AD |
| Payroll Registers | 3 | FLSA, STATE |
| Petty Cash Records | 3 | AD |
| P & L Statements | P | AD |
| Salesman Commission Reports | 3 | AD |
| Travel Expense Reports | 3 | AD |
| Work Papers, Rough | 2 | AD |

## ADMINISTRATIVE RECORDS

| | | |
|---|---|---|
| Audit Reports | 10 | AD |
| Audit Work Papers | 3 | AD |
| Classified Documents: Inventories, Reports, Receipts | 10 | AD |
| Correspondence, Executive | P | AD |
| Correspondence, General | 5 | AD |
| Directives From Officers | P | AD |
| Forms Used, File Copies | P | AD |
| Systems and Procedures Records | P | AD |
| Work Papers, Management Projects | P | AD |

## COMMUNICATIONS

| | | |
|---|---|---|
| Bulletins Explaining Communications | P | AD |
| Messenger Records | 1 | AD |
| Phone Directories | SUP | AD |
| Phone Installation Records | 1 | AD |
| Postage Reports, Stamp Requisitions | 1 AF | AD |
| Postal Records, Registered Mail & Insured Mail Logs & Meter Records | 1 AF | AD, CFR |
| Telecommunications Copies | 1 | AD |

## CONTRACT ADMINISTRATION

| | | |
|---|---|---|
| Contracts, Negotiated. Bailments, Changes, Specifications, Procedures, Correspondence | P | CFR |
| Customer Reports | P | AD |
| Materials Relating to Distribution Revisions, Forms, and Format of Reports | P | AD |
| Work Papers | OBS | AD |

## CORPORATE

| | | |
|---|---|---|
| Annual Reports | P | AD |
| Authority to Issue Securities | P | AD |
| Bonds, Surety | 3 AE | AD |
| Capital Stock Ledger | P | AD |
| Charters, Constitutions, Bylaws | P | AD |

| TYPE OF RECORD | RETENTION PERIOD YEARS | AUTHORITY |
|---|---|---|
| Contracts | 20 AT | AD |
| Corporate Election Records | P | AD |
| Incorporation Records | P | AD |
| Licenses - Federal, State, Local | AT | AD |
| Stock Transfer & Stockholder | P | AD |

### LEGAL

| | | |
|---|---|---|
| Claims and Litigation Concerning Torts and Breach of Contracts | P | AD |
| Law Records - Federal, State, Local | SUP | AD |
| Patents and Related Material | P | AD |
| Trademark & Copyrights | P | AD |

### LIBRARY, COMPANY

| | | |
|---|---|---|
| Accession Lists | P | AD |
| Copies of Requests for Materials | 6 mos. | AD |
| Meeting Calendars | P | AD |
| Research Papers, Abstracts, Bibliographies | SUP, 6 mos. AC | AD |

### MANUFACTURING

| | | |
|---|---|---|
| Bills of Material | 2 | AD, ASPR |
| Drafting Records | P | AD† |
| Drawings | 2 | AD, ASPR |
| Inspection Records | 2 | AD |
| Lab Test Reports | P | AD |
| Memos, Production | AC | AD |
| Product, Tooling, Design, Engineering Research, Experiment & Specs Records | 20 | STATUTE LIMITATIONS |
| Production Reports | 3 | AD |
| Quality Reports | 1 AC | AD |
| Reliability Records | P | AD |
| Stock Issuing Records | 3 AT | AD, ASPR |
| Tool Control | 3 AT | AD, ASPR |
| Work Orders | 3 | AD |
| Work Status Reports | AC | AD |

### OFFICE SUPPLIES & SERVICES

| | | |
|---|---|---|
| Inventories | 1 AF | AD |
| Office Equipment Records | 6 AF | AD |
| Requests for: Services | 1 AF | AD |
| Requisitions for Supplies | 1 AF | AD |

### PERSONNEL

| | | |
|---|---|---|
| Accident Reports, Injury Claims, Settlements | 30 AS | CFR, INS, STATE |
| Applications, Changes & Terminations | 5 | AD, ASPR, CFR |
| Attendance Records | 7 | AD |
| Employee Activity Files | 2 or SUP | AD |
| Employee Contracts | 6 AT | AD |

| TYPE OF RECORD | RETENTION PERIOD YEARS | AUTHORITY |
|---|---|---|
| Fidelity Bonds | 3 AT | AD |
| Garnishments | 5 | AD |
| Health & Safety Bulletins | P | AD |
| Injury Frequency Charts | P | CFR |
| Insurance Records, Employees | 11 AT | INS |
| Job Descriptions | 2 or SUP | CFR |
| Rating Cards | 2 or SUP | CFR |
| Time Cards | 3 | AD |
| Training Manuals | P | AD |
| Union Agreements | 3 | WALSH-HEALEY ACT |

## PLANT & PROPERTY RECORDS

| | | |
|---|---|---|
| Depreciation Schedules | P | AD |
| Inventory Records | P | AD |
| Maintenance & Repair, Building | 10 | AD |
| Maintenance & Repair, Machinery | 5 | AD |
| Plant Account Cards, Equipment | P | CFR, AD |
| Property Deeds | P | AD |
| Purchase or Lease Records of Plant Facility | P | AD |
| Space Allocation Records | 1 AT | AD |

## PRINTING & DUPLICATING

| | | |
|---|---|---|
| Copies Produced, Tech. Pubs., Charts | 1 or OBS | AD |
| Film Reports | 5 | AD |
| Negatives | 5 | AD |
| Photographs | 1 | AD |
| Production Records | 1 AC | AD |

## PROCUREMENT, PURCHASING

| | | |
|---|---|---|
| Acknowledgements | AC | AD |
| Bids, Awards | 3 AT | CFR |
| Contracts | 3 AT | AD |
| Exception Notices (GAO) | 6 | AD |
| Price Lists | OBS | AD |
| Purchase Orders, Requisitions | 3 AT | CFR |
| Quotations | 1 | AD |

## PRODUCTS, SERVICES, MARKETING

| | | |
|---|---|---|
| Correspondence | 3 | AD |
| Credit Ratings & Classifications | 7 | AD |
| Development Studies | P | AD |
| Presentations & Proposals | P | AD |
| Price Lists, Catalogs | OBS | AD |
| Prospect Lines | OBS | AD |
| Register of Sales Order | NO VALUE | AD |
| Surveys | P | AD |
| Work Papers, Pertaining to Projects | NO VALUE | AD |

| TYPE OF RECORD | RETENTION PERIOD YEARS | AUTHORITY |
|---|---|---|
| **PUBLIC RELATIONS & ADVERTISING** | | |
| Advertising Activity Reports | 5 | AD |
| Community Affairs Records | P | AD |
| Contracts for Advertising | 3 AT | AD |
| Employee Activities & Presentations | P | AD |
| Exhibits, Releases, Handouts | 2 - 4 | AD |
| Internal Publications | P (1 copy) | AD |
| Layouts | 1 | AD |
| Manuscripts | 1 | AD |
| Photos | 1 | AD |
| Public Information Activity | 7 | AD |
| Research Presentations | P | AD |
| Tear-Sheets | 2 | AD |
| **SECURITY** | | |
| Classified Material Violations | P | AD |
| Courier Authorizations | 1 mo. ATR | AD |
| Employee Clearance Lists | SUP | ISM |
| Employee Case Files | 5 | ISM |
| Fire Prevention Program | P | AD |
| Protection - Guards, Badge Lists, Protective Devices | 5 | AD |
| Subcontractor Clearances | 2 AT | AD |
| Visitor Clearance | 2 | ISM |
| **TAXATION** | | |
| Annuity or Deferred Payment Plan | P | CFR |
| Depreciation Schedules | P | CFR |
| Dividend Register | P | CFR |
| Employee Withholding | 4 | CFR |
| Excise Exemption Certificates | 4 | CFR |
| Excise Reports (Manufacturing) | 4 | CFR |
| Excise Reports (Retail) | 4 | CFR |
| Inventory Reports | P | CFR |
| Tax Bills and Statements | P | AD |
| Tax Returns | P | AD |
| **TRAFFIC & TRANSPORTATION** | | |
| Aircraft Operating & Maintenance | P | CFR |
| Bills of Lading, Waybills | 2 | ICC, FLSA |
| Employee Travel | 1 AF | AD |
| Freight Bills | 3 | ICC |
| Freight Claims | 2 | ICC |
| Household Moves | 3 AM | AD |
| Motor Operating & Maintenance | 2 | AD |
| Rates and Tariffs | SUP | AD |
| Receiving Documents | 2 - 10 | AD, CFR |
| Shipping & Related Documents | 2 - 10 | AD, CFR |

**Place upon your desk only the item you're working on at the moment.** Everything else should be filed or otherwise kept out of sight. When you've finished with it, get rid of it by sending it to the appropriate place. If you will need the item later, file it and make a note under the appropriate space in your planner where you have filed it.

**Do not allow periodicals and correspondence to be placed on your desk by others.** The in and out boxes are a must, but don't keep them on your desk. Go to the in box only at a specified time each day, so that you aren't tempted to sift through it during working hours. But never neglect it, or the in pile will become a meaningless stack of papers.

---

## THE PERSONAL PAPERFLOW SYSTEM

---

Now that your desk is uncluttered and organized, the challenge lies in keeping it that way. Remember, just as appearance and apparel make a personal statement, so does the look of your desk. Unless you are a chief exec, your desk should not be too empty: People will think that you are not very busy, which is bad, or that you are obsessively neat, which is worse. You should have work—mail, memos, statistics, orders, etc.—on your desk, but well placed and organized. It is better not to wait until the desk looks like the mailroom, then go on a neatness spree only to watch the piles mount up so that next week you start all over. Stay in control of your paper.

**Screen unnecessary paper.** Cancel subscriptions to unwanted newsletters, magazines, and catalogs. Get the office manager to bypass you on irrelevant interoffice memos. Have your secretary handle paper that does not require your personal attention.

**Try to handle each piece of paper only once.** Most time management experts treat this as an absolute. That is of course ridiculous. Some papers will get handled dozens of times with good reason. But don't shuffle paper that can be acted on and disposed of, or passed on to someone else. It is truly amazing how many times a letter can get read before one gets around to writing a simple reply.

**Classify paperwork as it comes in.** Some recommend three piles: *Immediate Action, Pending,* and *Informational.* And of course, there's the throwaway pile. Vary this according to your own needs—almost everyone has a *To Be Filed* stack. And some add an *Urgent* pile, used only for the projects that must be acted on instantly. This pile should come into being only on occasion.

---

**Spot junk mail before it lures you into reading it.** Junk mail has its own language. I offer the following observations as a former author of some high-quality junk mail. Most of you are experts already, so you bear me out:

| *When they say:* | *What they are really saying is:* |
|---|---|
| • "Free!" | If we give you something that doesn't cost us much, will you buy something on which we will make much more? |
| • "You may have already won" | But we won't tell you until you give us a chance to sell you, and then mail in this coupon. Of course, you need not buy anything to win a prize, but if you think it'll help, so much the better. And if you are considering buying, but are not motivated to mail the card, the lure of a prize might push you over the line. |
| • "An important message" | It's important to us that you read this and respond. |

Also watch for the visual cues: odd-shaped envelopes; offbeat printed matter—stamps, wheels, brochures, etc.; return addresses that don't identify the sender.

*Shop junk mail quickly—go to the offer card first.* This is either a postcard or a card to be stuffed into a provided envelope. This is the bottom line. You will find out in 30 seconds (a) who the offer is from, (b) what is offered, (c) for how much, (d) for how long, (e) length of guarantee, (f) delivery time, (g) payments accepted. If you are interested, then go back and read the stuff. If not, to the basket with it.

**When something is no longer "active," but must be kept as a record, file it immediately!** Your desk top is not a file cabinet.

# CUTTING DOWN ON PAPERWORK

The best way to cut down on paperwork is to locate the people responsible and take them to task. The next best way is to dig in and fight from your own desk.

*Put only what is absolutely necessary in writing.*
*Screen out unnecessary paper.* Junk mail. Junk memos.
*Cut down on copier use.*
*Use the telephone.* It's faster and cheaper than letters.
*Use the dictating machine.* Avoid writing out rough drafts of letters or instructions to your secretary. You can speak at 200 wpm with ease, but can write only about 20 wpm. Using a dictating machine saves your secretary's time, too.
*Use cassettes.* A cassette memo can be recorded even while you are driving or waiting for a plane. Pop it into the mail and the recipient will be able to reuse it afterward.
*Throw away even more paper.*

# 4

# TOOLS TO SAVE TIME AND ELIMINATE PAPER WITH

Although effective time management is primarily a matter of will power, there are a number of products that can be of great help:

## PLANNERS, DIARIES, APPOINTMENT CALENDARS

I know a doctor who relies on the first "freebie" appointment book he receives each year (the drug firms send them) and gets along quite well with it. Then there's the multimillionaire investment manager who has been using the girlie calendar supplied to him by his garage at Christmastime. And the key executive at a major corporation who makes up his own daily forms, has his secretary run off and date 365 of them, and then has them bound.

You should have a planner of some type, but there is little agreement on what is the ideal type for the executive. It's a very personal matter.

Will a specific type contribute to your effectiveness? That depends more on how you schedule and manage your time than on how you record it. Nevertheless, most managers do view the choice of a planner as a considered purchase. Planners appear by the thousands in late fall, and even sooner in the mail-order and ad specialty markets. It seems that any guy with a printing press and a calendar figures he has a chance in this business.

### WHAT EXECUTIVES LOOK FOR IN A PLANNER

The following data is based on a survey conducted by *Business Week*'s new-product development department.

EXECUTIVES PREFER A "PLANNER" FORMAT OVER A SIMPLE DIARY They view their appointment book as a planning tool, not simply as something in which to record their daily activity. The simple diary format is a carry-over from the original English design.

AESTHETIC APPEAL   A planner is a highly personal tool. It says something about the user; so, naturally, you'll want yours to look good. You have to consult it several times a day, often in front of others.

TIME MANAGEMENT SECTION   Time is the eternal equalizer—everyone has the same number of hours in a day, no matter what one's lot in life. It's how you use it that makes the difference. Apparently, many believe that the proper planner can help them manage time.

PERSONAL DATA PAGE   Here you list credit card numbers, bank account and insurance policy numbers, etc. While the demand for this feature is strong, it is greater in the upper echelons. The reason appears to be that upper level executives tend to involve their secretaries, who then need handy access to basic information, in personal financial matters. Lower level executives often don't use this feature, because they don't want such data lying around.

A BINDING THAT LIES FLAT   The book should lie open on a desk, without the help of hands.

A DOUBLE-RIBBON BOOKMARK   To keep place in two pages at the same time.

"800" NUMBER DIRECTORY   Such numbers can be hard to find, and directories are real time-savers. Many of the toll-free "800" numbers are in service 24 hours a day.

SPACE FOR MOST FREQUENTLY USED NUMBERS

OPTIMAL PAGE LAYOUT:

- *quarter-hour subdivisions*
- *extra space for luncheon engagements,* so one can note all details
- *simple layout;* easy on the eyes, uncluttered
- *proportionally less space for weekends and nights.* The lower on the totem pole, the greater the need for "overtime" space

A PLANNING FEATURE   Space for weekly, quarterly, and yearly planning—and, ideally, a planning calendar for five years ahead, plus last year's calendar for reference.

## WHAT EXECUTIVES DO NOT WANT IN A PLANNER

Many diaries are filled with such things as air distance charts, postage rates, census and business statistics, and other extraneous reference materials. All these features do is make the book thicker and more expensive. The fact is, executives don't want this stuff in their planners.

*BW* found that most of them don't use it. If an executive wants to know the weather in Hong Kong, he'll contact his travel agent or some other appropriate party. The survey respondents claimed that this kind of data simply served to distract.

*When choosing a planner, pick one that will provide quick access to information that is vital to your everyday work.*

Since about 85 percent of all your calls are placed to a pool of 30-40 numbers, sufficient space for recording those key numbers is perhaps the most important extra.

## TIME LOGS

For several reasons, planners don't contain time logs. First, time logs are highly personal and should be structured by the individual. Second, they are used only for a few weeks at a time. Third, the planner is not a workbook. It is not meant to train people in time management or to function as a means of conducting research. You'll get the most out of your planner if you take the trouble to do a time log first.

## POCKET PLANNERS

Executives like flexible covers; space for expenses, notes, and phone numbers; and, as an extra, "800" numbers. Keep the size down, as "thin is in." If you carry it in your jacket pocket, its outline shouldn't bulge through.

## SEVERAL GOOD PLANNERS

BUSINESS WEEK EXECUTIVE PLANNER   Taking into account the results of their survey, the *BW* staff has come up with one of the best planners around. Layout, binding, and graphics are all excellent. And it contains just the right amount of supplemental information. It is also competitively priced.

The pocket version (they come as a set) is not as superb as the desk size. But BW assures me it's working on the "ultimate."

DAYTIMERS   The GM of the planner industry. The largest users of Daytimers are lawyers, accountants, and salespeople, and one look at the format tells you why. The Daytimer is for people who literally must time their day—a godsend for those who bill by the hour, or whose profits are dictated by how many sales calls they can cram into a single day.

The time record section is split into twelve-minute segments. The appointment section is a series of open lines. There is also a "To Be Done Today" planning section.

The ink is eye-ease green, but the paper wasn't meant for anything but a ballpoint. A fountain pen or marker will probably bleed through in the pocket version.

| **Thursday** **21** | **Friday** **22** | **January 1982** |
|---|---|---|

January 1982

| S | M | T | W | T | F | S |
|---|---|---|---|---|---|---|
|  |  |  |  |  | 1 | 2 |
| 3 | 4 | 5 | 6 | 7 | 8 | 9 |
| 10 | 11 | 12 | 13 | 14 | 15 | 16 |
| 17 | 18 | 19 | 20 | 21 | 22 | 23 |
| 24 | 25 | 26 | 27 | 28 | 29 | 30 |
| 31 |  |  |  |  |  |  |

February 1982

| S | M | T | W | T | F | S |
|---|---|---|---|---|---|---|
|  | 1 | 2 | 3 | 4 | 5 | 6 |
| 7 | 8 | 9 | 10 | 11 | 12 | 13 |
| 14 | 15 | 16 | 17 | 18 | 19 | 20 |
| 21 | 22 | 23 | 24 | 25 | 26 | 27 |
| 28 |  |  |  |  |  |  |

| Thursday 21 | Friday 22 | |
|---|---|---|
| 8 | 8 | |
| 9 | 9 | **Saturday** **23** |
| 10 | 10 | |
| 11 | 11 | |
| 12 | 12 | |
| Lunch | Lunch | |
| 1 | 1 | |
| 2 | 2 | **Sunday** **24** |
| 3 | 3 | |
| 4 | 4 | |
| 5 | 5 | |
| Eve | Eve | |

Fig. 7. Page format of Business Week Executive Planner

From *Business Week Executive Planner* (New York: Business Week 1980). Reprinted by permission of publisher.

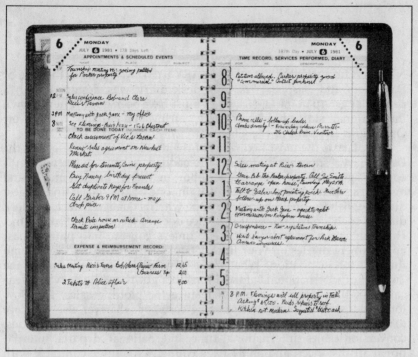

Fig. 8. Illustration of Pocket Day-Timer
Courtesy of Day-Timers, Allentown, PA 18001.

When you buy a Daytimer, you are buying into a system of planning paraphernalia. Pages can be added and/or deleted, and there is a wide range of formats. You can, in effect, customize your planner.

At the end of the R. Alec Mackenzie Time Management Seminar I attended, Mackenzie handed out a little gift: several months' worth of Pocket Daytimers (little monthly spiral-bound books), with a low-grade vinyl wallet sturdy enough to get you through the sample months and a pen that clips to the wallet (very tacky). Also included was a Daytimer Six Year Planner (very handy if, like the Soviets, you are into five-year plans), and a small address book that allots only two lines per entry.

This sampling is a great hook, because Daytimers are very good; to use them is to love them. And most people have never used a good planner before. If you have a *BW* or other good planner, you might resist the temptation to send for a Daytimer set. But if you've been using scraps of paper and stuff, the Daytimer will change your life. And if you fill out a form with the names of three of your friends who need one, they'll get a sample kit and you'll get three more cheapo pens. My guess is that this is the backbone of Daytimers' sales campaign.

Contact:
Daytimers
Allentown, Pa. 18001

NEWSWEEK INTERNATIONAL DIARY SYSTEM    If, as in the case of Daytimers and *BusinessWeek*, this desk diary was designed with a particular group in mind, *Newsweek* must have been going after its own international staff, heads of state, airline pilots and the Covert Operations Division of the CIA.

This diary is the most luxurious of the three. As the flyer says of the Desk Diary, "superbly bound in soft-padded, grained cover with gilt-edged pages and two silky black ribbon markers." Printed and bound by Charles Letts & Co. in Great Britain, one of the oldest and largest diary publishers, one cannot take issue with its quality. In fact, the desk diary is such a nice book that the price doesn't seem too far out of line. However, it's good only for a year, unless you are into putting past appointment diaries on your library bookshelf for your kids to thumb through for inspiration. What makes this diary very unusual is the "wealth of international information." It's got the obligatory six-year calendar, time graphs—a useful feature for plotting sales, the Dow Jones Industrials, company operating costs, or whatever else you care to track on a week-by-week basis over the year—weights and measures, conversion tables, international time, international airports, international air distances, and an 84-page country/city guide complete with maps. There's ample space for personal information, addresses and phone numbers, a "Forward Planner" for next year and a 32-page full-color world atlas in the back, including a map of air and sea routes. Why an atlas? When you need to know the capital of Mongolia, you can just as easily pull an atlas off the shelf as have it in your diary. This feature, according to *Newsweek*, is a time-saver. If you travel a great deal, maybe so. But judging from the weight and construction of the desk planner, it was meant to stay home.

With all that material, it's pretty hard to part with your diary at the end of the year. If the folks at *Newsweek* thought that this stuff was so important, why didn't they put it all into a companion volume? After all, they are happy to sell you the entire "diary system" which includes the Wallet Pocket Diary, the Pocket Diary Alone, the Desk Address Book, and the Pocket Address Book (with 28-page international hotel, restaurant, and airline guide).

They could have added a "Newsweek International Quick Reference Book" or something like that. Custom imprinting and quantity orders available. Contact:
Newsweek International Diaries
Newsweek Building
P. O. Box 425
Livingston, New Jersey 07039

One Dallas-based time management consultant commented that diaries should avoid built-in clutter. On a desk, the amount of clutter equals the amount of distraction. When you reach for the book to record an appointment or find a phone number, you shouldn't find yourself reading about the Swiss restaurant in Kuala Lumpur.

EXEC'MINDER This is the brainchild of Lawrence Resnick, a successful CPA and business school instructor. A time management buff, he could find nothing on the market that was good enough for him. So he created his own system, called it Exec'minder, and made a lot of people happy in the process.

In many respects Exec'minder is similar to the pocket Daytimer. But the differences are by no means trivial. Exec'minder, for example, uses a brighter, better quality paper that will not allow even marking-pen ink to soak through. Each day has a memos/calls received section in addition to the "Things To Do" section it provides in common with Daytimer. Resnick used his experience as a CPA to design a more practical and sensible expense record section. The preplanner for next year is in the front of the book instead of the back, and there is a 7 A.M. hour, which is very helpful if you are on the West Coast and doing business with the East. The high-quality wallet includes an extra flap that will hold a memo pad, but swings open to expose the credit-card pockets.

The principal difference in the two planners is how you get them. Exec'minder is sold through finer department stores in one-year sets. (Each month, the sets in the stores are updated.) Admittedly, it is a classier and higher-quality product, but it also costs much more—$55, including the wallet. The filler books alone are $21.

Daytimers are sold through the mail. A set comparable to Exec'minder, with a top-of-the-line wallet, is around $35; the refills cost just $12.95.

Daytimers wants your name on its mailing list so it can remind you to order your Daytimer each year. And the company sells other office supplies. Thus Daytimers will send you several months of fillers free of charge—an excellent way to get familiar with this kind of format. If you like it, you can either order the Daytimer or walk into a department store and buy Larry Resnick's Exec'minder.

THE ENGLISH IMPORTS: LETTS OF LONDON AND LEATHERSMITH OF LONDON The English are diary fanatics, which is not surprising when you consider how long diaries have been available there. In 1816 Charles Letts produced the first Letts Diary or Bills Due Book and Almanack. T. J. & J. Smith Ltd. started competing with Letts in 1839 and now sells its products under the name Leathersmith.

Both firms produce well-made diaries and planners with exquisite bindings and high-quality paper. Most have leather covers, gilt-edged paper, and ribbon bookmarks. In the pocket editions the emphasis is clearly on producing a very slim coat or shirt-pocket diary that is rich looking and does not cause a "bulge." Clearly, the weight is on elegance over utility, since neither company has done much with the page design: a page consists of simple boxes bearing the date or, in some cases, boxes that include lines with time of day. To keep it thin there are between three and seven days to the page, depending on the model.

The leather desk versions are beautiful and have much more space. Matching address books are available at additional cost. Letts has a "Timeplan" system that includes a desk planner with a useful time management section. It is very nearly identical to the *Newsweek* planner. The desk versions start at $20. Pocket versions start at $4.

For name of nearest dealer, contact:

Letts of London, Ltd.
400 Oser Avenue
Hauppauge, New York 11787

Leathersmith of London Ltd.
3 East 48th Street
New York, New York 10017

---

# CHECKLISTS

---

Getting it right the first time is an important time-saver, and that often means not leaving anything out the first time. Any aid in doing a thorough job will save you time. One such aid is the checklist. Checklists serve several purposes:

*They let you get a view of the entire job* before you. All steps written out, one after the other.

*At a glance, you can see how far you've gone and what remains.*

*Checklists serve as memory joggers, reminding you* to complete tasks that might have slipped your mind.

*A completed checklist, with dates and figures filled in, is an excellent record.*

*Checklists facilitate communication with superiors.* Once approved, they signify that there is agreement on what it is you are supposed to be doing.

*Checklists can make you look good at meetings.* You'll be prepared and can help keep the group on track. If someone overlooks something, you'll be able to remind him about it.

## HOW TO MAKE A CHECKLIST

WRITE DOWN, IN LIST FORM, ALL THE THINGS THAT YOU MUST DO    Show the list to your boss, secretary, and other interested parties

---

## ADVERTISING AND SALES PROMOTION FUNCTIONS

The purpose of this questionnaire is to enable you and your management to determine whether your advertising and sales promotion functions are being performed economically and effectively. It should also assist you in determining when to obtain the services of an advertising agency.

### Advertising

1. Does your firm provide quality workmanship and efficient service, which are bases for your advertising?  ☐ Yes ☐ No
2. Has your firm established an advertising program?  ☐ Yes ☐ No
3. Have you considered these determinants of advertising:
   a. The nature of your business?  ☐ Yes ☐ No
   b. Company objectives (strategy)?  ☐ Yes ☐ No
   c. Industry practice?  ☐ Yes ☐ No
   d. The media used?  ☐ Yes ☐ No
4. Is your advertising program primarily of a continuous nature?  ☐ Yes ☐ No
5. Do you use noncontinuous advertising to:
   a. Prepare your customers to accept a new product? ☐ Yes ☐ No
   b. Suggest new uses for established products to your customers?  ☐ Yes ☐ No
   c. Bring special sales to your customers' attention? ☐ Yes ☐ No
6. Do you use your advertising to pave the way for your sales representatives by making your company and product well known?  ☐ Yes ☐ No
7. Have you developed an advertising budget showing the outlay of funds for advertising?  ☐ Yes ☐ No
8. Do you use standard advertising ratios for your line of business or type of industry as guides?  ☐ Yes ☐ No
9. Is your company's advertising set as a percentage of projected sales?  ☐ Yes ☐ No
10. Have you decided to spend the major portion of your company's total advertising outlay on one of your products and to give only incidental advertising to others?  ☐ Yes ☐ No
11. Do you vary your advertising expenditures seasonally?  ☐ Yes ☐ No
12. Is your company's advertising truthful and in good taste?  ☐ Yes ☐ No
13. Has your firm obtained assistance from suppliers and trade associations concerning your advertising program?  ☐ Yes ☐ No

Fig. 9. Sample checklist
*(above and next page)*

From *The Dow Jones-Irwin Business Papers,* by Tate, Megginson, Scott, and Trueblood, Copyright © 1977 by Dow Jones-Irwin. Reprinted by permission of Dow Jones-Irwin.

14. Are you attempting to measure the results of your advertising?
    □ Yes □ No

15. Before an advertisement is composed, do you consider what you expect the advertising to do for your firm?     □ Yes □ No

16. In planning your ads, do you use these pointers:
    a. Identify your store completely and clearly?     □ Yes □ No
    b. Select similar illustrations?     □ Yes □ No
    c. Select a printing typeface and stick to it?     □ Yes □ No
    d. Develop easily read copy?     □ Yes □ No
    e. Use coupons for direct mail advertising response? □ Yes □ No
    f. Get the audience's attention in the first five seconds of a television or radio commercial?     □ Yes □ No

17. Check which of these tests you use for immediate-response ads:
    □ Coupons to be returned to your store?
    □ Letters or phone requests referring to the ads?
    □ Split runs by newspapers?
    □ Sales made of the particular item?
    □ Checks on store traffic?

18. Do you attempt to evaluate the relative effectiveness of each of your advertising media?     □ Yes □ No

**Sales Promotion**
19. Check which of these sales promotion techniques you use:
    □ Special displays
    □ Premiums
    □ Contests
    □ Free samples
    □ Free introductory services
    □ Demonstration products

20. If you are a retailer, are your window and counter displays changed frequently?     □ Yes □ No

21. If you are a manufacturer, are you using trade shows? □ Yes □ No

22. Are your sales representatives furnished with:
    a. Good sales kits?     □ Yes □ No
    b. Up-to-date promotional materials?     □ Yes □ No
    c. Catalogs?     □ Yes □ No

23. If you are selling two or more products, are you promoting them:
    a. Jointly?     □ Yes □ No
    b. Separately?     □ Yes □ No

**Using an advertising agency**
24. Are you aware that most newspaper advertising is developed by creative skills possessed by the newspaper staff?     □ Yes □ No

for additions and other suggestions. You may wish to have someone else do the first draft. A checklist is a blueprint of your thinking, and if yours does not meet with approval by the boss, you may be open to some criticism. If you can, ask the boss to draft a checklist.

DO A STRAW POLL OF EVERYONE INVOLVED You'll come up with a long list of items to be included.

# TIMING DEVICES

Solid state technology has made it possible to incorporate timing devices into many personal items, such as watche',calculator'c console clocks, even desk diary sets. Reminders such as these are valuable, especially if you have a lateness problem or tend to loose track of time when involved in your work. But avoid using them so often that you become dependent on them, never checking your watch unless it "goes off." Having one sound off in an important meeting or when you are with a client is a no-no.

# BEEPERS

Beepers are wireless, portable paging systems. They can alert you to a crisis or urgent message or serve as a means of reminding you of an appointment or something you must do.

**Tone-Only Models.** These signal you with a beep or tone. You can choose one that has a memory feature, which means that you can switch the thing off and if a signal comes in during that time, the unit will "remember" to signal you as soon as you turn it back on. Very useful at times when you don't want it going off and embarrassing you, or disturbing a train of thought—or a nap.

Another feature is two-signal capability, which allows you to be paged from two separate points. The identity of the paging party is distinguished by the kind of signal you get. For example, one signal might be a beep-beep, the other a long tone.

The signal is sent over phone lines to a computer that identifies the sequence of numbers dialed on the phone and selects the proper frequency for transmission by radio wave. This takes from ten seconds to three minutes, depending on the broadcast traffic. This type of system is generally effective within a 100-mile radius.

Tone-only comes in two basic types—the squat model that can clip onto a belt and the long, slim model. Both types weigh around six ounces.

**Tone-And-Voice.** This unit will transmit a voice, but it has serious limitations. It works only within about a 40-mile radius. The caller has 10-20 seconds to speak, and there is no memory feature. If your unit is not on, or if the room is noisy and you can't hear, that's tough.

**Costs.** Tone-onlys cost around $175 per unit at the time of this writing, and you'll pay a monthly charge of around $15. You can rent a unit, and it'll cost around $30 per month with everything included.

Tone-and-voice units cost between $250 and $450 plus around a $25 monthly charge. If you prefer to rent, it'll cost around $50 per month, all included. Most major cities have several firms that specialize in this service. Check the Yellow Pages under "Paging and Signaling Services."

---

# A DAY WITH R. ALEC MACKENZIE

---

At the start of his one-day time management seminar, Mr. Mackenzie guarantees that if you apply the principles he articulates, you will save two hours per day. He follows that statement with an offer to work with you personally if you fail to achieve that objective. No doubt R. Alec knows that most executives would simply be too embarrassed to admit failure—especially because everyone who attends this seminar should be able to see how it is possible to save those two hours. In a fast-paced audience participation seminar, Mackenzie takes you through the major time-wasters, their causes and solutions, and voices the major management principles that, when violated, give rise to these problems.

Mackenzie is a dynamic speaker who works hard at his specialty. He employs role playing and other histrionics to illustrate some of the common problems that arise. The participants are given a short introduction to the topic and are shown the excellent film "Time to Think." Then they get into analyzing their own situations, searching for the "top ten time-wasters." They are aided in this search by a useful and comprehensive workbook that appears to be a summary of Mackenzie's cumulative knowledge resulting from ten years of research in this field. Then all the teams make their reports, and the result is a thorough examination of the major problems and their solutions.

Occasionally a participant will take him to task over a specific suggestion, such as whether to place your own calls or have your secretary do it. A point quickly emerges: His word is far from gospel. For example, Mackenzie advises that you do the number-one priority first, reasoning that energy level declines steadily as the day wears on; this, of course, isn't true for everyone. And Mackenzie opened the seminar I attended with a spiel about starting on time, but he failed to

---

make suggestions on how to prevent tardiness. Regarding those "creative" tasks that are often at the mercy of inspiration, he admitted that there was difficulty in planning and scheduling creativity. I found some of the problems and solutions redundant.

Perhaps the biggest problem with a seminar such as this is that it deals only with *awareness* of the time-wasting problems. The solutions often involve behavior or personality changes, which cannot be learned in a seminar. For example, Mackenzie advises us not to "overreact" in crisis situations. That's fine, but will writing ourselves a reminder, "don't overreact" do the trick? And while learning to delegate tasks is a good suggestion for the manager, some of us have great difficulty doing so.

The seminar is a great awareness-builder, but it's only a start. Execution of new approaches and systems is up to you. Mackenzie admits that many participants fall back into their old habits.

Learning to manage time efficiently is not a one-day affair. It is not easy, but it is extremely profitable for both you and your company. And such a seminar is an excellent way of "turning over a new leaf," getting started on a more efficient use of time.

Most of the participants I spoke to found the course valuable in that it made them more aware of time. Some were quite enthusiastic, enrolling their secretaries in a special Mackenzie seminar for secretaries conducted the following day.

For information on Alec Mackenzie seminars, contact:

Alec Mackenzie and Associates
P. O. Box 232
Greenwich, New York 12834

## The Top Ten Time-wasters according to MacKenzie*

    telephone interruptions
    drop-in visitors
    ineffective delegation
    meetings
    lack of objectives, priorities, planning
    crisis management
    attempting too much at once
    cluttered desk/personal disorganization
    indecision/procrastination
    inability to say no

---

*From R. Alec Mackenzie, *Time Management Notebook*, (Greenwich, NY: R. Alec Mackenzie, 1976), p. 23. Reprinted by permission from Time Management Notebook.

# SUGGESTED READING

Time management books are incredibly redundant; the biggest waste of time would be to read more than one of them cover to cover. If you must look at several, read one and skim the others. Otherwise, you'll wind up reading over and over about time logs and telephone interruptions.

Here are some of the best books on saving time:

*How to Get Control of Your Time and Your Life,* by Alan Lakein (New York: Peter H. Wyden Inc., 1973)

The one and only. This book talks about time and your entire life. It is only partly a tips book. It is also motivational, and very helpful if you are in the "it's-time-to-make-a-new-start" mood. Lakein is recognized as the leading authority on time management.

*Getting Things Done,* by Edwin Bliss (New York: Charles Scribner's Sons, 1976)

Ed Bliss is also a well-known expert on time management. His book is very practical and to the point. It consists of short, pithy sections on each of the principal time management issues.

*The Time Trap,* by R. Alec Mackenzie (New York: AMACOM, 1972)

A perennial business best-seller, this book teaches the subject from a manager's point of view. It is well researched through both personal and academic investigation and provides some valuable insights into effective time management in the corporate structure.

*Working Smart,* by Michael LeBoeuf (New York: McGraw-Hill, 1979)

This book reads like an amalgam of the better parts of all the foregoing books. It is eminently practical, offering the most in-depth analysis of problems and possible solutions. LeBoeuf covers personal as well as business life. He has obviously lifted time management tips from other popular works on the subject, but he does come up with some creative approaches of his own. While not quite as "inspiring" as Lakein's book, it is the best written.

*The Dow Jones-Irwin Business Papers,* by Curtis E. Tate, Jr., Leon C. Megginson, Charles R. Scott, Jr., and Lyle R. Trueblood (Homewood, IL: Dow Jones-Irwin, 1977)

A different type of time management book, this is just a bunch of checklists and forms—but they are helpful. Some of the checklists in the book can be applied to your business just as they are. Others will have to be modified. In any event, you'll see what a checklist is and how it functions, and the ones in the book will serve as a good foundation upon which to build your own. In addition, the questionnaires included in this book serve as an excellent way to learn some valuable management techniques by identifying the variables that you must confront in many different situations.

*Information, Communication, and the Paperwork Explosion,* by Trevor J. Bentley (Maidenhead, England: McGraw-Hill [U.K.], 1976)

This book is one of the most substantive and practical guides to setting up and improving paperwork and information flow. Of course, techniques for designing forms and making and filing flow charts hardly make for scintillatingreadinxcbut there are so many illustrations and nifty little symbols jazzing up the text that one doesn't mind such a dry topic. Most of the execs I gave it to got through it quickly and considered it worthwhile.

Bentley has obviously put a great deal of effort into this book, because it outlines methodology rather than offering simple "common sense" tips. A real find.

# PART II

# COPING WITH THE INFORMATION EXPLOSION

"Try to know everything of something,
and something of everything."
Henry Peter, Lord Brougham

# 5
# THE DATA DELUGE

In *Future Shock,* author Alvin Toffler\* points out that ideas have been estimated to enter and leave our awareness at a rate twenty to one hundred times faster than they did a hundred years ago. Scientists suggest that although a large portion of our brain is, theoretically, underutilized, especially in the area of perceptual and reasoning ability, the typical individual is approaching the upper limits in his ability to assimilate and process information. In short, our circuits are overloaded.

A breakthrough in microcircuitry, computer science, or semiconductors can revolutionize an entire industry. Firms spring up overnight and go bankrupt or get gobbled up just as quickly. As a businessperson, you have the special problem of trying to maintain the efficiency of a system, of a routine, while at the same time being on the lookout for ways to update and, if necessary, jettison the status quo.

A look at any of the major business magazines reveals that editorial coverage has been expanded in recent years in the areas of global affairs, science and technology, social and environmental issues, and even religion. Everything affects business, and business affects everything. Because the American economy is the world's most powerful, with the most advanced communication systems, business here affects the whole world, and international business in turn affects the American economy.

You cannot just watch the stock markets, the trade publications, and the markets that you work in. But *while information is expanding rapidly, and the need for its consumption increasing, the amount of time available for such activity is not increasing to keep up with it.* Already, most successful executives spend their leisure time trying to catch up on important reading and viewing.

\*From Alvin Toffler, *Future Shock,* Copyright © 1970 by Alvin Toffler. Reprinted by permission of Random House, Inc.

# HOW WE REACT NEGATIVELY
## TO "INFORMATION OVERLOAD"

Toffler has characterized various responses. They are nothing more than simple stress symptoms applied to the information problem, but that stress is what makes the responses so marked.

**The Denier.** Overwhelmed by the information explosion, the denier refuses to accept any more. He blocks out certain realities and often clings to the philosophy that the old way is still the best way, the tried-and-true way. In the current business environment, this attitude will lead to disaster. Unless you are a demigod at your corporation, the very embodiment of success, this static approach will make you a sitting duck for anyone with any foresight.

**The Specialist.** Unable to absorb and master the material being shot at him, or uninterested in doing so, this person picks a narrow field and learns all he can to keep pace: know a lot about a special thing instead of a little about a lot of things. While the specialist's approach to survival may not be the best prescription for a full, diverse life, it is not a bad strategy for executive survival in a society that has great use for specialists in highly complex fields—provided, of course, that your particular field of expertise remains in demand. A single innovation may wipe out your turf in one stroke. And then where are you? So the specialist, as he prospers, must cast a wider net and absorb information to keep his options open. Since the degree of interrelatedness of all fields of business is increasing, everything affects your specialty. So you must keep track, if only superficially, of events outside your area.

**The Reversionist.** The Denier, when confronted with rapid change, clings to the status quo. The Reversionist turns tail and tries to dredge up the past in some sort of absurd defense against the future through use of nostalgia. If this is you, see a shrink; take a rest from your job. One doesn't often encounter this type in business, because, unless he is an officer through family clout or ownership, he just can't last.

**The Supersimplifier.** Just as the name implies, he is the reductionist, simplifying complex information, turning grey areas into black and white, moral ambiguities into simple rights and wrongs. It takes great intellectual ability to see the essence of a chunk of information and simplify it, boiling it down to a few essential facts. But the supersimplifier attempts to do this with his defense mechanisms, not his intellect. He is drowning in a sea of facts, and he must simplify in order to comprehend and to survive. This person can be dangerous, because when you've used all your powers of analysis and concentration to come to grips with difficult issues, he will stand up in the meeting and brush it all aside with some rinky-dink platitude. The real trouble is that many of your colleagues would rather swallow his bromides than dig into the meat of the issues.

To Toffler's list I add one of my own:

**The Information Junkie.** This one realizes the extent of what is taking place in terms of the information explosion and makes an energetic, if utterly unrealistic, attempt to keep up with it all. He buys every newspaper, magazine, book, and newsletter he can get his hands on, and saves each one because he can't bear to throw it out unread, fearing that he might be missing something. Often, such a person doesn't enjoy the process of learning new things, because he is so frantic about it. While reading one thing, he thinks about what's next. This behavior can apply to television, movies—any and all media. I know someone who listens to an all-news station for hours at a time, even though the entire news report repeats itself every half hour. Why? "Because," he says, "something might happen after I've heard the news the first time." Now, regular listening makes sense, but continual monitoring? You may know him as the person who holds up everyone's plans for Sunday because he has got to get through the entire Sunday paper before leaving the house.

Not only does he continually acquire the same information several times in different forms; he will also become very boring, because he is not taking in another very valuable kind of information—the kind that comes from being around people. As Voltaire said, "The multitude of books is making us ignorant." That was in the eighteenth century, before shopping centers and bookstore chains.

In coping with the information explosion, it's quality, not quantity, that counts. Digest a smaller amount of material that is richer in information, not a gluttonous amount filled with starchy nonsense.

Enjoy what you read. And by no means must everything you absorb have a specific purpose. You can learn a lot about how to survive in the corporate world from reading *War and Peace*. But read it because it's a good book, not because of some work-related benefit.

---

## COPING

---

**Become an "information ecologist."** Keep your environment free of unhealthy elements: Screen out unreliable information, word pollution, redundancy, irrelevance.

---

- Identify material worthy of your attention.
- Develop the discipline to discard the unworthy.
- Learn to seek out and home in on the pertinent facts and figures.
- Discard all else.

**Make greater use of your mental potential.** Do just what the IBM boys do when their computers are no longer up to the job—increase capacity, speed, power, and storage capability. You can upgrade the same functions of your own brain by learning to:

- read more efficiently
- increase your brain's retentiveness
- reduce stress that might be negatively affecting your performance
- improve your work environment for improved performance
- sharpen your listening skills and note-taking ability.

**Learn new information-gathering techniques.** Most of us are still gathering information in the same manner we learned in school. Many alternatives exist, some of them the result of recent innovations. Here is a list of principal information sources:

- data bases
- business libraries
- microfilm/microfiche
- video/audio cassettes
- magazines
- books
- radio
- television
- reference services

---

# HOW EXECUTIVES GET THE NEWS

---

## CURRENT EVENTS AND HARD NEWS

NEWSPAPERS AND MAGAZINES   Most executives rely exclusively or in part on:

- *The New York Times*
- *The Washington Post*
- *The Wall Street Journal*
- Local dailies
- *Time*
- *Newsweek*
- *U.S. News and World Report*

---

TELEVISION   A survey reported in *Industry Week* found that only 40 percent of managers and professionals watch TV news, mostly because of "not being home for it."

ALL-NEWS RADIO   In this format there is no programming other than hard-news reports, wire services, and features. It is very popular among executives, expecially during "drive time," a radio-biz term for 7-9 A.M. and 4-6 P.M., when people are on their way to work or home and have their car radios turned on. This time slot is the radio equivalent of TV's prime time.

## BUSINESS NEWS

In order of preference, according to *Industry Week*'s survey:

- *The Wall Street Journal*
- *BusinessWeek*
- *Forbes*
- *Fortune*
- *The Economist*

*Note:* This is a ranking of the publications based not on their excellence, but on their use as a primary source of news. Since *Business-Week* is the only domestic weekly, it seems logical that it would be at the top of the list of business magazines.

## OTHER NEWS SOURCES

CONSUMER MAGAZINES   Executives do not appear to allot much time to the reading of consumer magazines, although it is apparent from other readership surveys that many subscribe to them.

NEWSLETTERS   These are popular, especially among upper level executives. Financial newsletters, especially those dealing with investments and tax planning, are popular, as are association and industry newsletters.

CATALOGS   Many executives scan the catalogs they receive in the mail; they are helpful in gauging marketing trends and consumer preferences, as well as pricing structures.

On the average, executives spend one-third of their day reading. But studies recently conducted here and in Britain suggest that most executives do not read enough to keep pace, that they are not well informed, and that they understand the spoken word far better than the written.

Part of the problem is an overreliance on several passive information-gathering methods:

NEWS GATHERED BY STAFF   This includes news summaries prepared by staff members, and information gleaned from subordinates who point out important news as it happens. Unfortunately, news and information relayed by others eliminates the intuitive and creative insights of the executive himself. Chances are, given the same article, a topflight executive will pick up on a few things that others will miss. In addition, the brain has a tendency for us to "file" seemingly unimportant things that are called forth later on. If one never scans the relevant material, one misses the opportunity to make associations and connections.

CLIPPING SERVICES   An efficient way of monitoring press coverage on a particular subject, individual, or company. For a fee, a clipping service scans newspapers (in some cases, magazines as well) for mention of any name or subject you wish. The articles are then clipped, appropriately underlined to call relevant data to your attention, and sent to you. One drawback is that many of the ideas you get each day are sparked by bits of information that have overtly little or nothing to do with a particular name or subject. So by relying on a clipping service, your focus could become too narrow.

There are clipping services in most major cities. Look under "Clipping Bureaus" or "Clipping Services" in the Yellow Pages.

CONFERENCES AND SEMINARS   Pleasant (if you're lucky), great for making contacts, but often insufficient in scope and depth. Large meetings attract many publicity hounds who are more interested in self-aggrandizement or in riding a hobbyhorse than in providing valuable information.

Good judgment is a most important requirement for a successful executive; yet most fail to exercise that judgment in gathering information.

# 6

# INFORMATION ECOLOGY: GETTING THE MOST IN THE LEAST TIME

By estimate, the number of books and scientific papers is doubling every eight years. We can't possibly read everything we wish to read. *The act of selecting worthwhile reading material is as big a time-saver as reading very fast*, if not bigger.

## SCREENING PRINTED MATTER

Let's begin with a typical situation. A book or magazine arrives at your desk. What do you do?

### THE FIRST GLANCE

TITLE    This should tell you something. But it doesn't always.

AUTHOR    When reading a book or article, do note the author's name. If you like how and/or what he writes, next time you spot the name, you'll have good reason to invest time in reading the material; and chances are you'll know something about it even before you read it.

*Use the trash can.* If you don't want to read something, throw it away—now. Or give it away. But get rid of it. Otherwise, you might, in a moment of weakness, decide to read it. It's like wasting an hour or two watching something on TV that you know is trash, and feeling crumby afterward because you wasted the time. Reading material can also be a "vast wasteland." The printed word, contrary to what your grade-school teachers and school librarians may have told you, is not sacred.

### IF IT'S A BOOK

CONTENTS    This is a good place to begin your survey. Lately publishers and writers have begun using the contents page as a means of selling a book, so it may promise more than the book delivers; rarely does it promise less. If you don't see what you want, it's probably not in there.

DUST JACKET   Sometimes the jacket blurbs give you a good idea about what's inside. A quote from a critic or authority you know and respect may help you decide. If not, ignore the quotes. Comments and introductions are a big part of the book business ; often, someone will write an introduction or comment about someone else's book merely to keep in the public eye. While most do not lie about their opinions, neither are they likely to be unprejudiced. Dust jackets often include an upbeat capsule description of the book's subject matter and summarize the author's credentials. Unfortunately, the intention is usually to advertise the book rather than describe it, so the jacket often oversells.

INDEX   Scan it quickly. You'll get a more thorough idea of the subjects covered and the author's point of view, as well as a good idea of what other authors or experts are invoked. When you pick up several books on management and see in the index that huge passages are devoted to "Drucker, Peter, on management," you have to at least ask yourself whether you should be reading Drucker's books instead. A quick scan of the book in question will tell you whether you'd rather get the subject matter in another author's style, or from another's perspective.

PREFACE OR INTRODUCTION   This is usually written *after* the book and often provides a good idea about what is coming in terms of the author's goals and point of view, and/or it summarizes the contents. Do not read the acknowledgments during the screening period. Besides, most first authors dedicate most of that space to thanking wives, parents, children, lovers.

### IF IT'S A MAGAZINE

In magazines for general audiences, articles assume the reader has little or no prior knowledge, so there must be some introductory material on the subject. If an article in such a magazine is just a few pages long, it rarely goes beyond the basics. So if you are well versed in the subject, you won't learn anything new. If the article is long, skim to see if there is some new material or in-depth analysis that might be of some value.

For example, in a period no longer than several weeks, *The Wall Street Journal, Business Week, Forbes, Fortune,* and *U.S. News and World Report* all ran articles on recent trends in the movie business, based on a conference and a reporting of studio earnings. *The Wall Street Journal* broke it first (unsurprisingly, because they are a daily), and the others followed suit with one- or two-page items covering essentially the same information. (The exception was *Forbes*, which did an in-depth study of motion picture financing and marketing techniques and how Hollywood is changing, in an article that included pictures and graphs.) One of the news versions of this item would have been sufficient to get the gist, and a look at the *Forbes* article would have been worthwhile.

## IF IT'S A NEWSLETTER OR TRADE JOURNAL

Prior knowledge is assumed, so authors waste little time on preliminaries. Article length is not a reliable screening method here. *Give special attention to pictures, graphs, and diagrams.* These are used to illustrate or make a point. If there are many of them, you can get a good idea of what the article is about, and the information contained therein. The inclusion of just one illustration could be misleading, because authors wanting to add eye appeal often throw in a visual that has little to do with the text.

## SKIMMING

The key to skimming is to (a) move your eyes in broad sweeps, very rapidly, one line at a time, and (b) look for key words, words that are outstanding or significant that convey the general ideas of the text. The uses of skimming:

A QUICK LOOK AT SOMETHING IMPORTANT   If you are really under the gun, but you can't possibly attend that meeting without some familiarity with the report, skim it. But remember that at best, skimming will provide half as much comprehension. So it's a sort of gamble if you really must "own" that material.

WEEDING OUT THE BULL   Skimming will help you decide which parts of a book, magazine, article, or report you will go back and read. You will be able to pick out the digressions, the "fluff" paragraphs, the meaningless quotes, and the spoon-feeding.

CHECKING FOR REDUNDANCY   In my opinion, redundancy is one of the biggest problems in coping with the information explosion. Frankly, some parts of this book contain information you may have seen elsewhere. Don't bother reading them! Key words can be an excellent clue.

Example: In 1979, the AFL-CIO had a convention during which (1) George Meany made his resignation speech, (2) President Carter spoke, and (3) the labor policies for the troubled times ahead were discussed. Fine; you read all about it in a newspaper or magazine.

Then you picked up another magazine, and it contained an article on labor. You saw the words "AFL-CIO Convention" and knew that much of what followed chronicled what was done and said there. The item was straight news, so you skipped it; you already knew what was done and said. Then you came upon an editorial and skimmed it to find the editorial meat. You skipped the tedium of reading who said what all over again.

The act of skimming is subjective. Not everyone will pick out the same key words or form exactly the same opinions about the material.

## PREVIEWING

Like skimming, previewing is a screening and time-saving method; but it is a bit more methodical. It serves two main purposes: (1) preparing you for a second, more conventional reading, familiarizing you with the material; (2) searching out the essential elements of the material. When you must familiarize yourself with a report before the big meeting, previewing is far better than skimming, although doing both is ideal. Previewing is recommended by experts for material that is critical, technical, and lengthy; skimming works better for general, light reading.

- *Read the beginning of the material.* At least the first two paragraphs.
- *Read all the section, subsection, chapter, and subchapter headings.* Nonfiction books are filled with more and more subheadings and divisions, because it's been found that people like their information in smaller packages. Maybe it's because people can read an entire section whenever they've got a free moment. Whatever the reason, the numerous section headings are flags to the content of the material.
- *Read the first sentences of subheadings and paragraphs that catch your eye.*
- *Read anything marked "summary."*
- *Read eye-catchers like underlined, italicized, bold-type, or capitalized portions.* One exception: In previewing, stay away from footnotes. Often quite fascinating, they are not critical, or they would be part of the text.

## QUALITY

There is a lot of reading material being passed off as new, significant, or controversial when in reality it is old, banal, and tiresome. When reading, be on the alert for empty words, sift them out and do not read the sentences that surround them. A few danger signs of poor workmanship:

IRRELEVANT HISTORICAL PASSAGES   When you're reading about the advantages of electronic typewriters, do you really want to know who invented the manual in 1817?

MEANINGLESS QUOTATIONS FROM IMPORTANT PEOPLE   We have all seen politicians in action. Do you think that they are the only VIPs that speak and say little? Very often an author will interview an expert for some insight. If the interviewee has nothing to say, it looks bad for him and makes the interviewer uncomfortable. So he often obliges with some articulate but essentially no-value-added drivel.

OUT-OF-DATE MATERIAL   Who wants yesterday's papers?

FLUFF   Articles and even books often have to meet length requirements. Thin books tend not to sell as well as thick ones. Magazines must fill the space they have blocked out for articles. Sometimes an author gets carried away with his ability and just keeps on writing. The result tends to be fluff. I could be a wise guy and fluff up this section to three times the size, but then I would be having fun at your expense. (See? I already added another three lines!)

EXAMPLEMANIA   Teach by examples. Illustrate by examples. All our teachers did it, and taught us to do it. But unless examples are worthwhile, they just waste space. Many authors overdo it.

FAULTY ANALOGIES   Some analogies just don't work.

FALSE ARGUMENTS   Circular reasoning, faulty generalizations, etc.

OVERUSE OF STATISTICS   Sometimes they help build an argument. That's good. Sometimes they are signals from the author: "Look at me, I'm thorough. I'm accurate. I'm scientific. I back up what I say!" That attitude breeds lots of numbers mixed in with words. Too many statistics = ZZZZZ.

*Save only what you can use.* If there is an article you want to read after skimming the magazine, save the article by tearing it out. Throw away the magazine; eliminate temptations.

---

# SCREENING NONPRINT MEDIA

---

## TELEVISION

Our ability to screen television programs is perhaps the best developed of all screening techniques (no pun intended). This is because we can't accumulate every television program. We must make choices. How do we do this?

- *Familiarity.* Programmers like to build audience loyalty. They do this by giving you just what you've come to expect. The only time they depart from their norm is when the ratings slip. So the more successful a show, the more consistent it will be. This allows you to make a guess as to which shows will be "message," which exposé.
- *Program guides.* Recent years have seen an increase of specials at the expense of series. Program guides do a reasonable job of summarizing a show.

---

- *Reviews.* Increasingly, television programs are being reviewed in the press and on radio—and on television itself. Fortunately, these reviewers seem to have no loyalties to the stations or networks for which they work.
- *TV skimming and previewing.* Flipping the dial. Watching the first ten minutes, etc. We all know how to do it.

The most important aspect of TV screening: When you've concluded that something isn't worth watching, DON'T WATCH!! Remember that TV news is redundant. The same items are repeated on news broadcasts throughout the day. A film report from Iran may start out on "Today" or "Good Morning America," with portions of it appearing on local news and the whole thing shown again on the network evening news. If the first few seconds of the film and voice-over are exactly the same, you know you've got a rerun.

VCR   VCRs, or videotape recorders, make selecting a TV program a bit easier, since you can tape a show and watch it later, or tape it while watching another show at the same time. All the more reason to be on your guard against garbage. The newer VCRs offer some help with a "preview" mode. This is a fast-forward mode that allows you to jump ahead and view segments in fast action. The drawback here is that you don't get any intelligible audio, so it's often difficult to determine what is going on. But help is on the way: Several companies have announced devices that speed up picture *and* audio in a manner that allows you to see *and* hear clearly.

## RADIO

*Listen to the radio for news. If nothing new has developed since the last time you watched the TV news, you can afford to skip TV*—unless you are happily addicted to the little color stories and features.

## AUDIO CASSETTES

These can be skimmed, although not as easily as print. If your tape machine has a "cue" feature:

1. Listen at regular intervals.
2. Be sensitive to "silent spots" that occur when the speaker pauses excessively, or stops to listen to a question from the audience. Using the "cue" device, you can chop off as much as 30 percent of the listening time in silent spots.
3. Preview the tape. Listen to the first five minutes to determine:
   a. the nature of the tape. Who is the main speaker?
   b. Is it a conference? A prepared speech? A professionally produced tape?
      - Conferences recorded "off the cuff" are hard to skim

because they are largely unstructured and poorly organized.

- Prepared speeches usually have a structure to them. See if you can lock into the structure. If you can, you'll know where the speaker is going and be able to skip his examples, asides, sick jokes, etc.
- Professional tapes are easiest to skim. They have introductions and summaries and are often divided into small listening sections. You can easily jump ahead and/or play over parts of the tape, according to your need.

## ON USING YOUR INTUITION

Screening is, to a large degree, intuition. The decision to buy a book and read it is not as easy to pin down. Many times you will decide to read or listen to something that on the surface seems silly, simplistic, or boring—but you have a feeling that it will turn out to be "special" in some way.

On the other side of the coin, anxiety over missing something may cause you to buy something wasteful. I have a lawyer friend who decided to "get into" real estate. He can't resist buying a real estate book, even though he invariably reports that the book contains "nothing new." He has hundreds of real estate books cluttering his bookshelves.

If in doubt, wait. Put it off for an hour. Or several days. And look again.

### I.O.A.

The information explosion clearly has lots of people at wit's end. As a relief from what the prominent organizational psychologist Warren Bennis calls "Information Overload Anxiety" (I.O.A.), he has proposed "the Fat-Free Daily Reading Diet." To my way of thinking his diet is a bit lean, but I think the leanness is a deliberate attempt on Bennis's part to shock us into perceiving how little we need in order to get by.

# THE FAT-FREE DAILY READING DIET

| *according to Bennis** | *according to me* |
|---|---|
| • **Newspapers** *The Wall Street Journal.* | Add one local paper. |
| • **News magazines** Limit one. Prefers *Newsweek.* | Read one selectively, skim one or two others. No preferences. |
| • **General Culture and Ideas** *Vogue, The Listener,* the Sunday *New York Times.* Beware of the Sunday *Times.* It can cause "terminal I.O.A." if the entire contents is attempted. | Agreed. |
| • **Reference** Random House Dictionary, National Directory of Addresses and Phone Numbers. | There are several first-rate unabridged dictionaries. And why put a limit on reference works? The limit should be on the amount of time spent reading them. See the "personal reference library" section of Chapter 8 for recommended works. |
| • **Management and Business** *BusinessWeek,* for its timeliness and concise coverage. | Agreed. But skim *Forbes* and *Fortune* for important and relevant features. Mags like *Inc., Venture,* and *Free Enterprise* tend to be a bit fluffy. |
| • **Science and Technology** *Scientific American* "gives the specialist too little and the nonspecialist too much." Bennis prefers *New Scientist,* from England. | Problematic; depends on your background and special interest. *New Scientist* is good. So is *New Products and Processes,* published by *Newsweek.* It is unlikely that you will read any publication in this category cover to cover. Skim *Science 81, Psychology Today.* If you are involved with computers, be careful not to overdo it with technical and trade mags. |

---

*From Warren G. Bennis, "A Prescription for Information Overload Anxiety" (*Technology Review,* June/July 1979), pp. 12-13, 88. Reprinted by permission.

---

- **Other Items** Monthly Economic Report, free from Morgan Guaranty Trust Co.; Statistical Bulletin, free from Metropolitan Life Insurance Company; *Manas* (philosophy/ideas); *Brain/Mind* (psychology/behavior). Stock, bond, and commodity market analyses, free from major brokerage houses like Merrill Lynch and Smith Barney. Limit: one or two magazines and one or two newsletters of your choice. If you find *Manas* or *Brain/Mind* too heady, why not choose a mag or two for recreational reading? *Smithsonian, Natural History, Harper's, Quest, Sports Illustrated, Esquire,* or the irrepressible *New Yorker* are a few suggestions. And by all means, make time to read through an occasional book—but choose carefully.

---

## DEVELOPING YOUR OWN MEDIA MIX

Managing the format and flow of information is really an offshoot of management. So you should begin by logging your "information time." Using the list below, log just how much time is spent daily in gathering information from each of these categories. Be specific. At the end of the day, evaluate your activities and set priorities. Are you spending too much time on *Sports Illustrated*? Not enough on *The Bank Credit Analyst*? Perhaps you aren't reading enough. Whatever the case, use the log results to construct a media-mix plan in which you allot time to specific information activities. Always take into account the flow of material. If it's a weekly magazine, when does it arrive? If it's a TV program, it has a specific viewing time. (If you have a video recorder and you tape the show, when will you watch it?) If it's a tape, book, or magazine, is it borrowed? When must it be returned? After a short time, patterns will form naturally. And you will better understand and control your own methods of coping with the information explosion.

## MEDIA LOG

| Date | Time | Type of Media | Title | Priority | Comments (Value; sections read, etc.) |
|------|------|---------------|-------|----------|----------------------------------------|
| 9/3 | 8:15 – 9:00 | magazine | Business Week | important | Valuable article on German consumer mkt in Int'l Business. Spent too much time on article about skiing and book reviews. |
| 9/3 | 3:10 – 3:30 | magazine | People | unimportant | Read while waiting to see doctor. Next time, bring important reading to doctor's office! |

Fig. 10. Sample media log
Use this format, or design one of your own.

**Magazines**

business
news
consumer
special interest

**Television**

business related
educational
general entertainment
social issues oriented entertainment
public affairs
religious
news

**Radio**

news
public affairs
self-improvement features
religious

**Books**

business
technical
general nonfiction
fiction
history
case studies

**Audio cassette/Videocassette**

business conferences
business courses
self-improvement
business book condensations
fiction and nonfiction
    book condensations
magazines on tape

**Data bases**

statistics

Fig. 11. Media checklist
This list can be used in planning your own media mix.

# 7

# USING YOUR HEAD

All the craziness caused by information overload serves to underscore a fascinating paradox: We have trouble coping with the tremendous amount of information bombarding us from our environment, but in reality our brains are far from overloaded.

In fact *our brains have virtually unlimited potential.* If you feel intimidated by the office computer, just remember that next to your brain, that computer is like comparing the rubbing together of two sticks to the operating of a nuclear reactor. The human brain far outclasses even the largest computer in versatility and complexity.

Peter Russell, in his stimulating and useful *The Brain Book,** gives a few examples of the brain's capacities and capabilities. A brief summary:

- *Storage.* The brain can store 1,000 bits of new information per second from the moment of birth to old age with room to spare. Recent research indicates that we may remember everything that happens to us.
- *Recognition.* The brain can recognize a face in less than a second. No computer can do that.
- *Miniaturization.* Are you amazed by those pictures of powerful computer chips no bigger than a fingertip? Well, even with such miniaturization, a computer that could do all the brain could do would weigh more than ten tons and would be too large to fit in Carnegie Hall.

*The brain is still the best thinking machine we know.*

*So, why the problem?* Scientists estimate that we use only a small percentage of our brains. These estimates range from one to ten percent, and Russell puts the figure at an even smaller .1 percent or less. Some believe that geniuses of Einsteinian magnitude are capable of using perhaps a little more of their brain's capacity. Imagine what they could do with 50 percent.

---

*From Peter Russell, *The Brain Book.* Copyright © 1979 by Peter Russell. Reprinted by permission of the publisher, Hawthorn Books, a Division of Elsevier-Dutton Publishing Co., Inc.

---

We have never been properly taught how to use the brain. We don't know how it works, how to get the most out of it, or the kind and form of information that it responds to best. There is still a great deal that we don't know about the brain, but we have learned a lot since today's adults were in grade school. What follows are some tips on how to improve your brain's ability to absorb, process, and retain information.

---

## READING BETTER

---

Many books have little to offer in the way of new information and are poorly written to boot. It is therefore understandable that one would not want to spend the same amount of time reading a business or technical book, newsletter or office paperwork as one would spend reading Shakespeare, John Cheever, Thoreau, or even Peter Drucker.

One way in which executives cope is to learn what must be read and what can be skimmed. The difference is like that between food and vitamins. Food is to be savored and enjoyed; vitamins are gulped down, as quickly and painlessly as possible.

Another popular solution to the reading problem, besides skimming, is rapid reading. Before we see just how this can help you and how you can learn the technique, consider what we have learned about reading in recent years:

| MYTH | TRUTH |
|---|---|
| • *Words are read one at a time.* | We read from meaning, so we fixate on phrases—groups of words that convey meaning. |
| • *500-plus wpm is impossible.* | Still some controversy, but it does appear likely that we can read faster than 500 wmp. |
| • *A fast reader can't really appreciate what he reads.* | This is a matter of degree. A good reader knows that he shouldn't read everything as fast as possible, but as fast as comfortable. If you read at a rapid rate, appreciation of the material can actually be improved: There is less boredom, more rhythm to the reading process, and less muscular fatigue. |

---

- *High speeds mean lower compre-hension.*

Wrong. Faster speeds mean less starting and stopping, and therefore greater concentration. Seeing a greater amount of words in less time enables one to get a more comprehensive overview and better perspective on the material. Thus there is a better chance of perceiving order and association—further aids to comprehension and memory.

- *Average reading speeds are best.*

Nonsense. Average does not mean natural. Everyone, from health food freaks to auto buffs, knows that statistics on national averages don't always denote something positive. An average is just a mathematical term; it doesn't tell us much about individual capacities. And when it comes to reading, average speeds reflect abnormally slow speeds resulting from inadequate teaching methods—the Jugheads in the sample who pull the average down.

## PROBLEMS ASSOCIATED WITH READING

Rapid reading involves unlearning inadequate techniques as much as it does learning useful new ones. Here are some of the problems that may be slowing you down, and what can be done about them.

BACK-SKIPPING OR REGRESSION Going back over words and phrases. This is unnecessary and useless. It is primarily the result of apprehension and in no way aids comprehension. The experts try to cut this out completely.

SLOW FIXATION Your eyes stay with a word grouping longer than they should. This problem is tackled by training you to increase your speed, spending about one quarter-second on each fixation, and also learning to take in more words per fixation.

VISUAL WANDERING Eyes wander off during reading. This is eliminated by vastly increasing speed, much in the way that a trainer builds intensity and concentration in athletes by moving them through a workout at a faster pace. It's also like watching a comedian: If he tells his jokes fast enough, he can keep your interest even if only half his jokes are good, because if you hate one, there's usually a good one not far behind. We tend to wander off our reading when we hit slow or boring spots, but if we're moving fast enough, we tend to wander off course less. There is almost always better material not far ahead.

CONSCIOUS REGRESSION   Reading something over again on purpose, because you didn't think you got it the first time. Once you learn to read properly, your comprehension will improve and you won't be doing this. But you might occasionally pause at some point to think about an unusually difficult concept. Reading something over doesn't provide anything new.

ALTERED BREATHING AND SUBVOCALIZING   While reading, many of us breathe as if we are speaking out what we read; or we may actually vocalize the words as they are read, usually (but not always) at an inaudible level. If you move your lips when your read, or feel activity in your larynx, you've got one of these problems. Your reading speed then tends to be limited by how fast you can speak.

## RAPID READING

The average reading speed of the American executive is 200-250 words per minute. This is slower than college level. In today's business climate it is unacceptable, since you will have difficulty reading as much as you should. A slow reading rate can hold you back considerably. Here are the pros and cons of rapid reading:

| CON | PRO |
|---|---|
| • *The rapid-reading firms make exaggerated claims.* Evelyn Wood, the Coca-Cola of the industry, claims to have taught more than ten million people to read three to ten times faster with improved comprehension. Most experts on reading believe our maximum reading speed is between 800-1200 wpm. (After that, they say, you're skimming, with great loss in comprehension.) | Many academics are short-sighted, claiming that the maximum reading speed is 600 wpm—until shown otherwise. |
| • *They teach skimming, not reading.* | They teach both. And skimming is a very useful skill. |

| • Rapid reading takes the joy out of reading. | Some rapid-reading experts deny this outright. Others say that you needn't speed-read everything. If you would rather read poetry or the Bible more slowly, do so. |
| • Rapid reading emphasizes speed over comprehension and retention. | Speed is essential for good comprehension and retention. The reader gets a better view of the whole because he sees more in less time; thus he can place things in context and see patterns that will enable him to remember. |

Both sides have their points, which makes it that much more difficult to decide whether or not to take a rapid-reading course, or, if you have already done so, to continue reading in this manner. Most courses emphasize two principal benefits: increased speed and comprehension.

SPEED   This is highly subjective. Some people have the ability to read faster than others. One thing is clear—almost everyone can improve reading speed. Is it actually beneficial to do so? Again, that depends on you—and on what you read. Several reading teachers I have spoken to point out that what many people really need is remedial reading, not speed reading, because they lack the basic reading skills. Speed reading will be of little benefit to these people.

COMPREHENSION   Recognition of words and sentences is not the same as understanding the ideas they are communicating. And understanding is different from remembering. Therefore, what counts is how fast you can grasp what you are reading, not how fast your eyes can move down the page. And you must be able to retain what you've understood so it doesn't leave you two pages later. There is a good indication that in this regard the words-per-minute come-on is bunk. If your ability to read outstrips your ability to comprehend, you are not accomplishing anything. And if your ability to comprehend something does not include some means of fixing the ideas in your memory, you will not be able to make much use of what you've read. *Speed must vary with material, because the material will determine how long it will take you to grasp its contents.*

Some time ago a Columbia University reading teacher prepared a one-page test for a roomful of speedreading graduates. He was amazed to discover they read at speeds of almost 6,000 words a minute. To be sure they understood what they read, he asked them to do it again—in fact, two more times. Their average quickly parachuted to about 1700 wpm, still extremely impressive. Then the teacher told them the sad fact: What they read had absolutely no meaning. The teacher had stitched together a page of pure mumbo-jumbo, taking two lines from one magazine article and then two lines from another—all the way down the page.

—"Faster, Faster," by Randall Poe, in
*Across the Board*, February, 1978

## THE BASIC PRINCIPLES OF RAPID READING

INCREASE THE NUMBER OF WORDS PER FIXATION    In order for the eyes to see a moving object in focus, they must move. If the object is still, the eyes must be still. And since words are still, the eyes must stop, at least micromomentarily, to allow them to focus on the words.

So the eyes don't move smoothly across the printed page, like an express train, but rather in a series of jumps and stops, like a local train rushing to get back on schedule. The jumps take very little time, but the stops take more. Using our train analogy, it's as if the ride between stations was very short, because the stations are so close together, but the time spent at each stop is long. In speed-reading lingo, these stops made by the eyes on words or groups of words are called *fixations*. These fixations take place between one-quarter and one-half second.

A main principle of speed reading is *to train the eye to see more words per stop*—a whole phrase perhaps, instead of one or two words—and that will result in faster reading.

USE PERIPHERAL VISION IN READING    We do see out of the corners of our eyes, and although whole words and phrases gathered in by our peripheral vision may not be in focus enough so that they may be read conventionally, they do cue us to what is coming next. Reading specialists believe that they can train people to be able to absorb the words that are captured by their peripheral vision, and also to increase the scope of peripheral vision to take in more words—from above and below as well as from the sides.

INCREASE THE NUMBER OF FIXATIONS PER SECOND    Studies indicate that the eye can register five words per one-hundredth of a second. Specialists have been successful in reducing fixation time at least to the faster end of the acceptable range, one quarter-second. Obviously, this increases speed.

SPOT REDUNDANCY IN PRINTED ENGLISH    Our brain can recognize letters and even words by seeing just parts of them—shapes, curves, and only a few key letters instead of all. In addition, many words and phrases can be omitted from written material without loss of meaning.

The principles that form the basis of all speed-reading techniques are without a doubt valuable and, if practiced, will increase your speed and comprehension.

*Applying the principles*
1. *To some degree, the manner in which you read is a habit.* And habits are hard to break. You must retrain yourself to read. This is tough, and it's the best reason for going to a speed-reading course; it will force you to break old habits. If you are doing it on your own, practice for a few minutes before reading.
2. *Once you learn the principles, use them.* People have a tendency to slip backward to old patterns developed as a child.
3. *Satisfy yourself.* Forget words-per-minute. If you feel comfortable with your reading and comprehension, and have sufficient time to finish all the material, that's just fine.

Using the basic principles, rapid-reading experts make lots of money teaching people to read faster.

## WHAT THEY DO

- Eliminate regression and back-slipping.
- Increase number of fixations per second.
- Expand area of fixation.
- Increase motivation.
- Teach previewing, skimming, and other aids that help you cut down on the sheer volume of reading material.
- Make greater use of peripheral vision and the redundancy factor in reading.

## HOW THEY DO IT

- *High-speed training.* If you drive at 90 mph for a few hours, when you come back down to 70, it'll feel like it's pretty slow, even if 70 was fast by comparison to your usual 55. The reading teachers go for broke, pushing you to break boundaries even to the point of telling you to move your hand, eyes, across the page as fast as physically possible and turning the pages as fast as you can. This encourages the reader to take in more with his eyes, to break the habit of reading at a set pace, and to use the right side of the brain in the reading process (when we read left to right, the material seen in the right visual field goes to the left side of the brain). When you read fast, both sides of the brain are brought into play more readily. High-speed training also improves the ability to pick out key words—often the only things you ever see when you do this exercise. High-speed training helps break the subvocalizing habit because you are forced to read much faster than you can subvocalize.
- *Visual guides.* Some kind of pointer—your finger or a book

mark, etc. By learning to follow the pointer, back-skipping can be eliminated. The visual guide can also increase speed, because as we increase the movement of the pointer, the eyes will tend to go along with it. By altering the pattern of the pointer's movement on the page, we can expand the focus of the fixation and thereby increase speed and comprehension.

- *Breathing exercises.* Regular, even breathing is best for reading, and the experts use exercises in which awareness of breathing takes precedence over speed and comprehension.
- *Metronome training.* This can establish a smooth rhythm. It also helps build speed.
- *Motivational training.* What you get when you cross an Evelyn Wood with a Vince Lombardi. People at these courses get geared up for speed. Sample lessons do more than just hook the person into taking the course. The small accomplishment of experiencing an increase in reading speed in just one night makes us hungry: Students return with a burning desire to read faster. Of course, instructors must keep students aware of the basic fact that it is the responsibility of the individual student to put the technique into practice. Many claim that the motivational aspect of these courses is far more productive than are the actual techniques. Certainly, the charged atmosphere and constant "take it to the limit" evaluations are what make these courses more effective than study-at-home cassette and workbook courses offering the same techniques.

## LISTENING BETTER

Listening is unquestionably the weakest link in the communications chain. Poor listening ability can hurt your career more than just about anything else.

Very little that is heard is actually remembered. Even less is understood. As with reading, the problem is not with our cognitive capacities. We are capable of absorbing and reacting to hundreds, even thousands of auditory bits each second. And good listening is not a matter of hanging on every word. We hear on many levels—phrases, sentences, sounds, tones and intonations—complemented by nonverbal cues such as gestures and facial expressions.

The failure, says noted communications expert Tony Schwartz, is not in the listening, but in the failure to *attend* to what we hear. Again, this is analogous to reading, where the problem is not in reading the words, but in how we process what we read.

The business world is filled with poor listeners. It's tough enough to communicate with peers, but this problem pales by comparison to the difficulty of communicating downward. There is evidence that as much as 80 percent of an original item of information is lost in three sequential downward transmissions.

There is little that can compare to the exhilaration of beginning a response to a speaker by reeling off a lucid summary of what he has just said. It is a great way to shower respect and laudation on the speaker—or a great way to begin to cut his argument to pieces. The choice is yours. Either way, good, careful listening is so rare you are bound to be remembered.

## HOW TO BE A BETTER LISTENER

PREPARE   Familiarize yourself with the subject to be discussed. Be fresh, well rested, and comfortable. This will minimize distractions and help you to pay close attention.

PUT THE SPEAKER AT EASE   Make sure that the speaker is comfortable, and look and act interested. If the speaker is comfortable and feels that the listener is receptive, he'll do a better job.

LISTEN WITH COMMITMENT   Listening to someone is not just a matter of placing yourself within earshot. It is an act of will, and you may have to work at it. In the business world it is said that the higher up you go, the harder you must work to listen to others.

MAINTAIN A GOOD MENTAL ATTITUDE   Be open-minded, interested, and empathetic. Try to see the subject from the listener's point of view. If you are unable or unwilling to do this, you are probably wasting your time.

KNOW YOUR BIASES AND PREJUDICES   While self-examination alone doesn't often change a person, it is important to be aware of one's own biases and prejudices. You will be more alert, and therefore better able to keep those biases under control and prevent them from interfering with your listening ability. Let's be frank. If you are one of those who think that, say, women are not as smart as men, you should be listening extra carefully and attentively when a woman speaks to you. You must try to compensate for your tendency to devalue—on account of her sex—anything she says.

Value judgments apply to occupations, life-styles, and geographical areas as well as to sex, race, and religion. For example, many people are suspicious of so-called experts, or specialists in a given field. Others prefer to hear the word from an expert than from a dynamic professional speaker. There are those who care little about the speaker's credentials or communications skills as long as he seems trustworthy. Where do you stand? Ask yourself how receptive you will be to the speaker because of such prejudgments.

CONCENTRATE   Most people start out paying close attention. After a while, that attention drops off, and then increases again toward the end of the listening period. Try to hear more than just the beginning and the end of what someone is saying by staying with him during the bulk of the talk.

DON'T LET YOURSELF GET DISTRACTED   Once you get used to the sound of the speaker's voice and to the accompanying gestures, and get a rough idea of what he is saying, there is a tendency to seek out some other object of attention. It could be anything from the newspaper on your desk, to a hangnail, to admiring someone's looks. This will obviously interfere with your reception ability. Another key source of distraction is your own thoughts. Whether reflections on what has just been said or just simple daydreaming, your thoughts can interfere with the listening process. Try to focus on what is being said, keeping your inner thoughts at bay.

It is not easy to cut out distractions, especially if the speaker is dull. If this is the case, try to cut him off, get him to cut it short, or make a conscious decision not to listen. Don't let the situation get away from you, because giving in to distractions is a bad habit, and you may find yourself doing it to an important speaker or someone with something very worthwhile to say.

LISTEN CRITICALLY   Look for specious arguments, poor logic, improper assumptions, half-truths, and inaccurate statistics. This will keep you sharp and involved in the listening process. And if by chance you find yourself on an opposing side, you'll have accumulated enough ammunition to torpedo the speaker.

TRY TO ISOLATE THE MAIN POINTS   Many people have difficulty getting to the point. They give all sorts of examples, faulty analogies, and anecdotes that are off the topic. Zero in on the main points. That the speaker's mind is cluttered or muddled doesn't mean yours must follow suit. Good listening means separating the grain from the chaff.

WATCH FOR NONVERBAL CUES   Social scientists tell us that much of what is communicated is expressed in a nonverbal manner—by tone of voice, facial expressions, and gestures. While there are several good books purporting to teach you how to interpret body language, you already know a great deal. For example, when you see a speaker clenching and unclenching his fists, what does that tell you? All you really have to do is be observant.

TAKE AN ACTIVE ROLE   Give feedback whenever possible. Let the speaker know that you understand, that you are following him. Or that you don't and aren't. Ask for more information when needed.

SEEK OUT A GOOD LISTENING POST   You should be comfortable too. Find a seat or location where all the information is available to you without strain. In a lecture situation, that might mean you should be in the center of the room, or up front, or just away from the window and the noise from the street.

DELAY FORMULATING YOUR ARGUMENTS  The most common listening problem is that the would-be listener is preparing his reply while the speaker is talking. This is the chief reason why so little actual listening takes place. If you can't repeat what the speaker has just said to his satisfaction, you haven't been listening, and your reply, whatever it is, will carry less credibility.

DON'T INTERRUPT  Rude. Boorish. Breaks the speaker's train of thought. And makes it tougher to follow his thread.

HOLD YOUR TEMPER  Something that was said got you angry? That doesn't automatically entitle you to take the floor. Besides, few people can think or speak clearly when they are fighting mad. Sit on it until your turn comes.

DON'T TALK TOO MUCH  Many of us love to hear ourselves. But that is not the purpose of a discussion. You already know what you think. Express yourself only when appropriate. When you've made your point, give the other person a chance to respond.

GO EASY  When you are criticizing or arguing, be careful. Unless you are going for a knockout, you don't want to put the other person on the defensive to the extent that he tightens up or gets angry. Communication then breaks down. You may win the battle, but lose the war.

## HOW TO AVOID COMMON LISTENING TRAPS

Listening is *the* basic skill for negotiation, arguing a point, and carrying out orders. Here are a few suggestions that will safeguard against costly mistakes:

WHEN YOU HAVE JUST LISTENED TO SOMETHING OF VITAL IMPORTANCE, REPHRASE IT ACCORDING TO YOUR UNDERSTANDING  Repeat it to the source to check whether you have it right. Say, "So what you're saying is . . ." or "Let me see if I understand you correctly. . . ."

WHEN YOU MUST ACCEPT AND CARRY OUT AN ORDER THAT YOU DISAGREE WITH, MAKE SURE YOU HAVE IT RIGHT  First, you often become so involved with your counter-argument that you may miss the details of the order. And second, if you carry out an order improperly because you didn't hear it right, it could be taken for a rebellious act, since you are already on record as a dissenter. *In many cases an inverse relationship exists between the degree of excitement generated by something you've just been told, and the level of comprehension of that information.* When you get particularly worked up about something, make sure you have the facts right and any instructions clear.

**WHEN YOU FIND SOMETHING BORING, DON'T STOP PAYING ATTENTION** It may be boring because you are lost, not because the information is dull or irrelevant. Besides, a boring speaker can at any moment become lucid and start spitting out important information.

# NOTE TAKING

Most business people take crumby notes. Either they attempt to capture every word on paper, missing the sense of the whole they would get from relaxing, listening to, and watching the speaker; or they take haphazard, poorly organized, sketchy notes, which are of little or no value when they are needed. Many executives eschew taking notes, undoubtedly because they think it's bad for their image.

Just like school, isn't it? In high school or college, poor notes mean poor study and mediocre grades. But this is the real world, where a B— can cost thousands of dollars. At a crucial meeting, a tête-à-tête with your boss, lawyer, or accountant, you've got to nail it right.

## WHY CONVENTIONAL NOTE TAKING IS INEFFICIENT

**WE WASTE TIME WRITING WORDS THAT WON'T HELP US RECALL THE CONTENT** And then waste time rereading those unnecessary words. Learning-methods specialist Tony Buzan estimates that these words account for over 90 percent of note taking.

**WE SPEND TOO MUCH TIME SEARCHING FOR THE KEY WORDS THAT CONVEY MEANING AND IMPORTANT CONCEPTS** This is difficult and time consuming, because key words are mixed in with all those irrelevant words and phrases. With these words few and far between, it is hard to form the associations and connections between the key words and their concepts. Psychologists believe such associates are necessary for learning and memory.

**WHILE WE ARE BUSY TAKING NOTES, WE RISK MISSING MUCH OF WHAT THE SPEAKER IS SAYING** Since nine out of ten words are useless, we should be able to take good notes in one-tenth the time of verbatim note taking.

In spite of all this, note taking is worthwhile. Whether or not you consult your notes afterward, items that are written down are six times as likely to be remembered as those that are not. Good note taking is a method of encoding information and organizing it in the way most useful for you. If you do it right, you should have time to jot down interpretations and inferences. When you return to your notes, they should immediately draw your attention to what is important.

Some recent innovations based on learning research can make the task a great deal easier.

# THE MIND MAP

A mind map is simply a means of taking notes that is more in accord with the modes of association and memory utilized by the brain.

*The brain responds to organization.* It thrives on it, searches for it. And if the material is not organized, the brain seeks to impose its own order. Mind maps allow material to be more easily, rapidly, and clearly organized.

*The higher the percentage of key words in the notes, the higher the recall.* Mind maps involve the recording of only key words and ideas. This reduces bulk wordage and insures that the words written are rich in meaning. Maps also aid comprehension of the material by forcing one to listen actively in order to extract the key words and concepts.

*The brain is aided in its associative ability if the words and ideas are clustered together visually.* A mind map allows you to write key words near related ideas. With conventional linear notes, ideas often appear in the chronological order of their presentation. If the speaker is disorganized or skips around, so do the notes.

*The brain will more easily retain that which is visually interesting or outstanding.* The mind-map method completely rejects the grade-school concept of neat, orderly notes. With conventional notes, every page looks the same. Not so with mind maps, since the note taker is encouraged to vary sizes, shapes, colors, and images used. When pictures work better than words, they are used.

We respond more readily to that in which we become more involved. Mind maps are the antithesis of mindless copying. They are engaging, original, and fun. You are actively involved in creating a highly personal set of notes. And since the process is less time consuming, it's easier to pay attention to what's being said.


## HOW TO MAKE MIND-MAP NOTES

*Put central ideas at the center of the page.* Mind maps should be organized in an organic manner, like cells. The nucleus—the main idea—is at the center, and as we move away from it, we encounter more specialized organs.

*Use key words.* Print the words rather than using script. Use lower case except where added emphasis is desired.

*Use lines and arrows to link related or associated concepts.* The best way is to write the key words on separate lines, and then connect those lines with other lines. If you run words together in a given line, you'll quickly close up the map and run out of room to add more key words to their proper places. The idea is to leave the map open-ended at all times, so that you can put a key word in its proper place even if a central concept comes at the end of the talk.

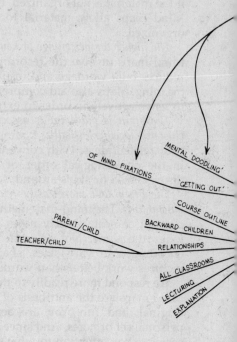

MENTAL 'DOODLING'

OF MIND FIXATIONS

'GETTING OUT'

COURSE OUTLINE

PARENT/CHILD

BACKWARD CHILDREN

TEACHER/CHILD

RELATIONSHIPS

ALL CLASSROOMS

LECTURING

EXPLANATION

Fig. 12. Sample mind map
This map outlines the many uses of mind maps,
as detailed in Tony Buzan's book.

From *Use Both Sides of Your Brain*, by Tony Buzan, p. 103.
Copyright © 1974 by Tony Buzan. Reprinted by permission
of the publisher, E. P. Dutton.

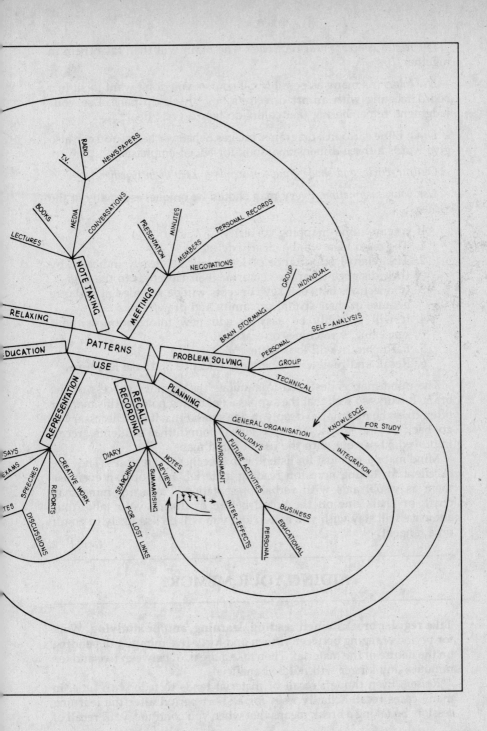

*Put related concepts near each other.* The brain will then take them in together.

*Use colors.* As many as possible. Of course, you don't want to sit in a board meeting with an art director's box of felt-tip pens. Use your judgment, remembering that colors do help a great deal.

*Draw.* Little cartoons, diagrams, images, whatever helps. You can also give words a three-dimensional look for added emphasis.

*Outline, circle, and shade groups of words to keep them together.*

*Use your imagination.* Every map should be unique, especially at the center.

If you are mind-mapping correctly:
1. The main idea will be clearly defined.
2. The relative importance of ideas will be clearly indicated by their distance from the center or their closeness to the edge.
3. Connections between key concepts will be revealed at a glance because of their spatial proximity and drawn links.
4. It will probably be easy to add new information without squeezing, scratching, or erasing.
5. Each pattern will look different.
6. Recall and review will be more effective and take less time.

The mind map is designed to simulate the memory process of the brain. It works so well that the simple act of taking notes in this manner often fixes the material so deeply in one's mind that it isn't necessary to go back to the maps. Michael Howe found that students' recall improved 50 percent with the use of mind maps.

Mind maps aren't just for listening to speeches and lectures. They are excellent for taking notes on reading material, and you can even use them as visual aids with verbal presentation. Prepare a mind-map chart, or chalk one on the board before or during your talk. Your audience will stay with you better, and you will be less likely to go off on a tangent.

## AIDING YOUR MEMORY

**Take regular breaks when reading, learning, and/or studying.** Work for periods ranging between fifteen and forty-five minutes, depending on the nature of the material. Then take a break of between five and ten minutes; any longer will not be beneficial.

*Reason:* Even though recall of material tends to fade with time, in many cases recall actually rises for a short period after the learning session. So taking a break means that when you continue, your recall of the material you just worked with will be better than if you had just gone right on. It may save you lots of time in looking back over what you just read.

*Another reason:* In any learning situation, the beginning and the end of a session is remembered better than the rest. So if you break up the sessions into smaller ones, you have more sessions and thus more beginnings and ends.

**Before beginning, plan the time and work schedule in advance—and stick to it.** Remember what the break is for. Breaking too often or too long means too little time spent on the material to make any real sense of it or to allow you to get an overview. Very long work sessions, on the other hand, will defeat your purpose.

*Reason:* At certain times you'll feel that you are really rolling along, and that there is no need for a break. Actually, it has been found that interrupting people at times like this, when they are very much involved in their work, leads to even greater recall. If you go by the clock and not by your subjective mood, you won't fall into the habit of skipping breaks.

*Another reason:* When you get absorbed in your work, you may have a sense of profound understanding and insight into what you are reading. You may not think a break is necessary. But what we are talking about here is *remembering.* And as both Buzan and Russell are quick to point out, *understanding something and remembering it are two different things; they don't necessarily go hand in hand.*

**During the breaks, rest, relax, get some air; take a total rest from the type of material you've been working on.** If you merely switch to something similar, you will not get the full benefit of the rest.

*Reason:* During the rest period the mind will organize and condense what it has learned. Let it do that unimpeded by still more material.

**When returning to work, spend a minute or two going over the previous material.** This may seem ridiculous, since you stopped only five or ten minutes ago, but it has been found that such a review acts as a warm-up. It brings the material into focus, and gets you set to begin anew.

But isn't the habit of taking breaks considered a time-waster? Yes, it is, in the negative form discussed in my section on time management; but those breaks are the result of distractions or procrastination. Here we are talking about breaks that serve a very specific purpose, and that must be performed with discipline according to a planned routine. Do not decide to take a break just because a phone call has come in. Rather, use your ten-minute break to make phone calls; have your secretary tell the caller that you will get back to him later (when you take your break).

**Apply these same memory-aiding principles to oral communications.** You've probably heard the adage "First tell them what you are gong to say, then say it, and finally, tell them what you've said." This makes sense in light of what we know about our memory patterns.

1. Give the most important information during periods of high recall for the auditor—ideally, at the beginning and at the end of your talk.
2. Use high-recall periods to summarize, preview the next portion of your talk, or drive home the key concept.
3. If your talk is much longer than fifteen minutes, take a short break (tell your listeners how long). Or simply stop to pour some coffee, etc. Try this even in a conference or meeting when you have the floor.

**Make your ideas stand out.** Exaggerate an idea or otherwise embellish it. In reacting, you can underline, make colorful notes and doodles, and think about how the idea is unique.

*Reason:* Research has shown that we tend to remember elements that stand out from things around them.

**Associate.** Association is a basic memory tool utilized by the brain, which makes all sorts of connections between things that are remembered. Research has shown that the context and the environment in which the information is learned or experienced play a very important role.

Take stock of your surroundings and situation and associate these with the material you are learning.

Try to form clear associations between ideas.

**Organize.**

LOOK FOR A PATTERN, RULE, OR PRINCIPLE THAT MAY GOVERN OR APPLY TO OR UNITE THE MATERIAL YOU ARE TRYING TO REMEMBER   There is evidence that the mind attempts this involuntarily, because it is a basic strategy for memory. Help it along voluntarily. The better the organization, the easier the memory.

BREAK UP LARGE AMOUNTS OF MATERIAL INTO SMALLER CHUNKS   Find some classification or means of organizing them that will break them down. A common example is to break down major markets into smaller chunks by geographic regions.

**Visualize.** *Visualize what you want to remember, whether it be a graph, a face, or a warehouse shelf.*

*Reason:* We take in through our eyes most of what we learn. And although many scientists believe that we have some capacity for a "photographic" memory, the ability remains latent. We are so unaccustomed to forming mental pictures of things, places, and people that we have failed to develop that ability, or allowed it to atrophy.

*Be more aware of your surroundings and try to picture them with eyes closed.* Do the same for other senses. Imagine smells, noises, touches that you've recently experienced. Awaken these lost abilities. Note how often children do it. Research has shown that children are better than adults at remembering what they have seen. Children rely more on what they see of the physical world than on symbols like words and numbers.

If you feel that your memory could use substantial improvement, you might consider a book, cassette course, or classroom course in mnemonics (memory techniques). Suggested reading: Robert L. Montgomery's *Memory Made Easy* (New York: AMACOM, 1979), and *The Memory Book*, by Harry Lorayne and Jerry Lucas (Briarcliff Manor, New York: Stein & Day, 1974).

# 8

# INFORMATION GATHERING

"Knowledge is of two kinds," wrote Samuel Johnson. "We know a subject ourselves, or we know where we can find information upon it."

Knowing a subject is the direct outgrowth of experience. And for experience there is no substitute. But the next best thing is knowing where to look for the best information gathered through the experience of others.

## CHOOSING A BUSINESS MAGAZINE

### GENERAL BUSINESS PUBLICATIONS

LOOK AT A FEW COPIES FIRST  Borrow them from friends or pick them up around the office or in waiting rooms. I would suggest buying an issue or two off the newsstand, but that doesn't make much sense pricewise: Often, a trial subscription is just a few dollars more than the price of several issues. If you can't find a few issues to look at, but you have a feeling that this magazine is for you, take a trial subscription that can be canceled for a full refund. Then look at the first issue; if you're not satisfied, write "cancel" on the invoice and mail it back. Do not pay the bill out of laziness. You don't want useless magazines cluttering your house or office. They will seduce your attention and take valuable reading time away from better information sources.

GET A FIX ON THE EDITORIAL POLICY  Something should emerge from reading the magazine. Is it very newsy? Or does it concentrate on case studies, dealing with contemporary business issues by giving examples of how successful companies deal with them? Does the content seem weighted in terms of marketing information, or is it geared more toward finance? How about approach: Does it assume too much knowledge or experience on your part, or, perhaps, too little?

If you are still confused, just drop a note to the publisher asking for a summary of readership statistics. This will tell you who reads the magazine, where he works, how much he makes, what his interests are, etc. You can get an idea of the target audience, and then determine whether you stand to benefit from a magazine geared toward such a group. I know many male executives who read *Redbook* and the *Ladies Home Journal* because it puts them in touch with a market that is primary for their products, and there are women who read *Playboy, Esquire,* and *Sports Illustrated* for similar reasons. Thus, even consumer magazines can function as business magazines.

IS IT FUN TO READ?  Style is important, because some people prefer the bare facts and others like anecdotes, or articles with a sense of humor. Some magazines give the pros and cons of an issue; others take one side or the other. Since even business-related reading should be enjoyable, pick magazines you like to read. But keep their strengths and weaknesses in mind and try to compensate for the latter in other ways.

FREQUENCY  Monthly or weekly or daily? You'll have to plan your reading schedule accordingly.

## TECHNICAL AND TRADE PUBLICATIONS

Follow procedures for general publications, and take a good look at who writes the articles and who publishes.

Are the writers and contributors industry experts or those working in industry? Or are they staff writers?

Although staff writers are more objective, they are often novices in the industry and are unable to dig out the truly useful or "inside" information.

Many periodicals are published solely as a vehicle for advertisements; the features don't say much about anything. Some executives rely on advertisements as a source of information and as a way of keeping in touch with the competition. If this is your bag, then such a publication is worthwhile. A general rule: If the mag is free or very cheap, it is advertiser supported and thus laden with ads.

Sometimes a trade journal is not published by an independent company, but is the publishing arm of a national organization or a lobby of some sort. Thus it may carry a strong editorial bias; keep this in mind.

## CHOOSING A NEWSLETTER

Newsletters are a multimillion-dollar industry. They are usually very expensive to subscribers, but very inexpensive to produce. This translates into big profits. Why do people pay $100 and more for a four-page, single-color report with no fancy paper or pictures? The primary reason is advice—and newsletters can be a valuable and convenient way to get information. The newsletter concept is predicated on the principle that the advice found in it is the sole property of those who subscribe to the letter; in a sense, it is an extension of the consultant idea. Some newsletter writers go to great lengths to support this notion, setting up "hotline" phone numbers to provide daily updates of the advice provided in the newsletter, and holding seminars around the country from time to time to which newsletter subscribers are invited free or at a reduced rate.

The concept gained momentum on Wall Street. Various analysts supply their stock market tips and picks each week to eager but confused traders, speculators, and investors. Some of the analysts—such as Jim Dines, author of the *Dines Letter*, and Joseph Granville—have been so successful with this activity that is has become primary rather than secondary. The current Cinderella of the field is entrepreneur Howard Ruff, a former actor, whose *Ruff Times* newsletter, combined with books and a syndicated TV show, grosses several million dollars. Ruff is not a stock expert; he counsels people on prudent investment strategies in these troubled times.

Newsletters exist covering all kinds of things—diamonds, gold, art, tax shelters, inflation, etc. Since the circulation is small and the information highly specialized, supposedly worth a great deal of money in potential profits or savings, the newsletters seem worth the price even at a hundred or two hundred bucks. But simple arithmetic will tell you that any one of these that catches fire will net the author a pretty sum. So the lure to publish is often irresistible, and many newsletters in the field simply do not provide truly expert advice, privileged information, or hot tips. Some don't even provide sound advice, and when their subscribers go broke after a few months of following the letter's suggestions, they eventually disappear from the scene. The author? Well, he's made a couple of hundred thousand, so he's okay.

Newsletters can be a valuable and convenient way of getting information. Or they can be a rip-off. The key is learning to choose wisely.

**Choose a newsletter on the basis of a strong recommendation from a savvy investor.** Preferably, one who is rich. Ask how long he has been a subscriber, whether he has followed the advice in the letter, and how it has all turned out. Even if he hasn't chosen to follow the advice, can he tell you how accurate the author's predictions were?

**Ask for a sample copy and look it over carefully.** If the author declines to send you one, forget it. Any reputable newsletter writer worth his salt will be glad to do so.

**Take advantage of the trial subscription approach.** A newsletter that costs $225 per year is hardly an impulse purchase for most people. So the newsletter publisher will often offer a trial rate of, let's say, eight weeks for $35. Of course, the publisher isn't losing any money on this deal, but you can get a reasonable chance to assess the worth of the letter for a lot less expense than that of a full year's subscription.

**Evaluate the basic investment philosophy of the writer and the soundness of his analytical techniques.** Most newsletter writers will provide some background concerning their approach and outlook. If you think it sounds suspect, don't waste your money. You'll have trouble working up the resolve to act on the advice.

**Consider the credentials of the author—and don't be misled by good PR.** Getting one's name in a magazine or newspaper doesn't make anyone a leading expert, no matter what the PR and advertising boys write. Judge the author by his performance in his field, not on his shrewdness in hiring a PR person and the size of his budget committed to advertising and PR.

Remember that past performance is in the past. Many newsletter ads point out that if you invested just $1,000 in 1975 according to Charles H. Nurd's advice, you'd be worth $59,963 today. Impressive? Yes. So you buy the man's newsletter, follow his advice, and lose all your dough in the next three months. Charles will be quick to note that he can't be right all the time, but that those who invested with his system in '75 are still ahead. The SEC requires that a caveat be printed at the bottom of such ads. It's there for a reason.

**Watch out for hard sell.** A newsletter publisher doesn't waste time following subscription leads outside the special field that the letter deals with. But he will pound away at the potential audience, trying to turn the prospect into a subscriber. If you are in his target audience, he will try to make you feel that you will be left behind and left out, and will lose time and lose money if you don't subscribe. Most of the time you'll be offered a money-back guarantee. If you subscribe, but are not satisfied, avail yourself of the guarantee.

## MONITORING ALL-NEWS RADIO

This is an excellent news source. Major news, weather, and sports are repeated about every 20 minutes. With the exception of a late-breaking story, the items don't vary much with each 20-minute report. So a quick listen several times a day is good, but sticking with the station for another go-round of the same items is a waste of time and will drive you crazy. Many stations set particular times for reports, such as business news, featuring stock market quotes and gold settings, etc. Some of the time is filled with quickie movie reviews and consumer tips and inflation fighter information, with things like how to get the most for your money when buying chocolate syrup. All things considered, this is a good way to get concise and up-to-the-minute news; and, best of all, you can assimilate it while you are doing something else. In general, *radio is the most accessible of all information sources.* A survey revealed that during the major blackout in the Northeast in 1977, 77 percent of those surveyed listened to radio, and 95 percent of the respondents rated radio's performance good to excellent.

Another survey shows that 49 percent of all business executives rely on radio as the first source of news in the morning, ahead of newspapers (42 percent) and TV (8 percent). It is also the primary source of news during the day.

See the All-news Radio Guide in the Appendix to Part II. It gives the stations in the U.S. that carry this format. Check a newspaper or your hotel desk for the location of the station on the dial. Note: The guide gives format only; quality and tone of the news may vary widely from station to station.

## RESEARCHING: SKILLS AND RESOURCES

Research skills are among the most underrated skills of executives. Anyone who has ever watched a Senate hearing knows the value of having done one's homework. Research helps you:

- defend your position
- attack the positions of others
- formulate sound strategies
- uncover potential pitfalls and opportunities
- sound much more knowledgeable than you are

There are two basic reasons why some executives don't research well: They are intimidated by the apparent complexity of the information-seeking process; and research takes time.

This is also why superiors may turn the job over to you. If you can research things more quickly and thoroughly than your peers, you will have more time available for more creative and innovative tasks and will also gain a reputation as a person who has his act together.

Know your research sources:

- libraries
- data bases
- private research organizations

- public or nonprofit research organizations
- reference book publishers
- nonbook research sources

Libraries are still the primary and least expensive source of information. The hang-ups: You have to leave your office and go there; material is on a first-come, first-served basis, so it might not be there when you want it; you can't take reference books outside the library; in large part, libraries operate on limited budgets, and their reference sources aren't always up to date.

Data bases are an excellent investment if your company can afford a service and you use it enough to justify the cost. There's a full discussion of data bases later in this chapter.

Many other public and private research sources are enormously useful. It's just a matter of knowing which research organization to contact for what kind of information.

The best way to begin solving this research problem and many others is to compile your own research library. Remember, books are tax deductible. And if it's a simple fact or statistic you need, a call to the publisher of the appropriate reference book will often suffice.

## THE PERSONAL REFERENCE LIBRARY

Not every little need for data or a statistic should send you or your secretary scurrying to the library. It is a very good idea to have some basic business information at your fingertips. You expect other professionals, like your doctors, lawyers, and accountants, to depend on reference works. Why not you, the manager?

The best reference books for business and industry (a) are expensive and (b) become outdated quickly. But many companies willingly pick up that tax-deductible tab.

Here is my suggestion for a basic business reference library. To this list add reference works specific to your industry or profession.

*Where To Find Business Information*, by David M. Brownstone and Gorton Carruth (New York: John Wiley & Sons, 1979)
   A super book, worth every penny it costs. It is clearly organized and easy to use. International in scope, it provides information on English language publications, including the name and address of the publisher of each book or periodical listed, the complete title, price, frequency of publication, and range of subjects covered. The Source Finder subject index appears to have been written with the executive in mind: It is one of the few with subject headings that make sense to people in business. This book won't give you any specific data on a subject, but it will save you a great deal of time in finding what you are looking for. And it can help you make your research much more complete.

*The Dow Jones-Irwin Business Almanac,* edited by Sumner N. Levine (Homewood, Illinois: Dow Jones-Irwin) Annually.

A useful compendium of hard statistics, business facts, names and addresses, and other useful bits of information that appear to have been pulled from various sources.

*Business Services and Information, the Guide to the Federal Government,* by Management Information Exchange, Inc. (New York: John Wiley & Sons)

This book attempts to organize by topic the tremendous volume of business information available from the federal government. It is very worthwhile and will undoubtedly be used often once you acquire it. There are a few problems: Any book like this is outdated the instant it goes to press, and there is little the book can do to reduce the headaches that come from dealing with the federal bureaucracy. Often, in your quest for data, you will be directed to an office in a division of a federal agency, only to be told that it no longer makes the data available.

*A Deskbook of Business Management Terms,* by Leon A. Wortman (New York: AMACOM, 1979)

A dictionary of management terms. Great for finding impressive terms to spice up reports and speeches, or for deciphering those used by others. The listings are very brief; they do little more than define the word or phrase.

Publications of the Baker Library, Harvard Business School:

Baker Library, one of the nation's finest business libraries, makes a number of its publications available to the public. Among them is a short book called *Business Reference Sources: An Annotated Guide for Harvard Business School Students.* It is a good, concise bibliography that includes the call numbers by which the books are shelved in the Baker Library. Other bibliographical books include *Business Intelligence and Strategic Planning* and *Executive Compensation;* and each of a series of twenty "mini-lists," 2-6 pages long, suggests where to look first for information on a particular business topic.

For a complete listing and order form, contact:
Publications Office
Baker Library
Harvard Business School
Soldiers Field
Boston, Massachusetts 02163

*A Researcher's Guide to Washington,* by Washington Researchers

This book is not simply a list of what is available; it is intended to help you through the Washington maze. Included: a complete

GSA phone directory, a directory of over 1,500 key statistical personnel, a list of every government document room and what is in each, and some valuable tips on how congressional committees function and how to get information from their researchers. Contact:

Washington Researchers
910 Seventh Street, NW
Washington, D.C. 20006

*Guide to American Directories* (Coral Springs, Florida: B. Klein Publications)

This guide lists over 6,000 directories. Use it to locate the directory you need. You can then contact the publisher if your need is just a matter of one or two listings. Or you can get the directory from the library. The book is also an excellent "shopping guide" for your company, because the staff can go through it and decide which directories are worth ordering. Contact:

B. Klein Publications
P. O. Box 8503
Coral Springs, Florida 33065

*The Encyclopedia of Associations* (Detroit: Gale Research Company)

Lists and briefly describes over 13,000 organizations in the United States. Besides data on membership and a statement of the objectives of each listed organization, this encyclopedia defines specific research interests and projects and lists personnel who can be of assistance. Such organizations are an excellent reference source, because one of their principal functions is to compile and disseminate information for and about their constituencies. Contact:

Gale Research Company
Book Tower
Detroit, Michigan 48226

*Ulrich's International Periodicals Directory* (New York: R. R. Bowker)

Trade journals and magazines are an excellent source of information. More than 60,000 of them are listed here by subject, and they are cross-referenced by title. Most libraries carry this one. Contact:

R. R. Bowker Company
1180 Avenue of the Americas
New York, New York 10036

*National Information Center for Educational Media:*

NICEM puts out several indexes, one each for educational films, educational video tapes, and educational audio tapes. Nonbook media can be the superior source of information in many cases, and the index offers the most complete list. The *16mm Educational Films Index* comes in four volumes. Contact:

National Center for Educational Media
University of Southern California
University Park
Los Angeles, California 90007

*Dictionary of Business and Economics,* by Christine and Dean S. Ammer (New York: Free Press)

My favorite of the business and economics dictionaries on the market, because it is the most up to date and the best written. Such books are usually written by eggheads, and I have trouble understanding them. Dean S. is the academician. Christine is a professional lexicographer with a great deal of experience in writing encyclopedias, dictionaries, and other reference works; it shows. This book is clear, well-organized, and intelligently cross-referenced. It is also a good buy. Free Press is a division of Macmillan, so the book should be widely available.

*Research Centers Directory* (Detroit: Gale Research Company)

In any business it is worthwhile to get the jump on the competition. When it comes to research, there is often a big lag between the completion of a study and the publication of the data in a place meant for consumption by the executive. An aggressive businessperson goes right to the source. This directory lists those sources—a few thousand university and nonprofit research organizations. Use this book to find the research groups that might be working in your field of interest, select one person in each group to contact (this is important; don't just write the lab), and you just might see such a connection result in a relationship of mutual benefit. You can also use this directory to select organizations to do research specifically for you or your firm. Since they are nonprofit and often rely on highly trained but low-paid students, they can usually do the job for much less than a private research facility that serves the business community.

*Industrial Research Laboratories in the United States* (New York: Jacques Cattell Press)

This book lists labs serving business and industry, the recent publications by each lab, and their relevant personnel. These labs see every firm as a potential client and will often bend over backward to help you. Contact:

Jacques Cattell Press
R. R. Bowker Company

1180 Avenue of the Americas
New York, New York 10036

*International Directory of Published Market Research* (New York: Undine Corporation)
Over 4,000 listings. Studies are categorized according to the British Industrial Classification System. This book is a must for any company thinking of striking out in a new direction, whether it be new-product development, expansion of an existing line, a new-service business, or import-export. Contact:
Undine Corporation
575 Madison Avenue
New York, New York 10022

*Exhibits Schedule, Annual Directory of Trade and Industrial Shows* (New York: Successful Meetings Magazine)
The most complete list available. Includes trade shows here and abroad, classified by industry, geographic area, and date. The only hitch—the book is an annual and becomes worthless after that year. Contact:
Exhibits Schedule
Successful Meetings Magazine
633 Third Avenue
New York, New York 10017

*The National Directory of Addresses and Telephone Numbers,* edited by Stanley Greenfield (New York: Bantam Books)
Has over 50,000 useful phone numbers nationwide. These include local and federal agencies, freight lines, communications services, etc.

*Survey of Buying Power* (New York: Sales and Marketing Management Magazine)
This survey includes data on American cities with populations of over 40,000, and on foreign countries. It concentrates on consumer income, buying patterns, and purchasing power. Contact:
Sales and Marketing Magazine
633 Third Avenue
New York, New York 10017

# THE DATA BASE

A data base is simply a set of information that a computer can draw upon to perform operations and draw conclusions. For our purposes we can think of it as a source of information, a place where data is stored as if in a bank, and, like a bank, a place from which we can withdraw in one of several forms what is put in.

The data base is a concrete reality and is here to stay. It is likely to become the primary source of all information regarding your business and your personal life. Rather than being concerned with what it is likely to mean in the future, let's take a look at what it means now.

HOW IT WORKS You go to a terminal, which is equipped with a keyboard so that you can address the data base. You ask for something, using a series of steps and classifications by subjects, dates, titles, etc. You get that information, on a cathode ray tube (CRT) or by hard copy (paper printout), or even spoken out to you through a robot larynx.

In order to keep the data base up to date, people are hard at work—eliminating obsolete material and adding new or current information. At the New York Times Information Bank, a popular data base, this process goes on around the clock.

Sometimes the information is in the form of abstracts, rather than the entire article you request. Sometimes the data base will have only several articles or other limited bits of information that the people who program the base felt were important. And sometimes a data base may offer only a bibliography or an index that will tell you where to look further.

## ADVANTAGES

*Speed.* Computers are fast, much faster than a librarian with a card catalog.

*Accuracy.* The computer never forgets where it puts things, and that "Mc" comes before "M" in alphabetizing.

*Currentness.* Directories, annuals, indexes are published only periodically. But a good data base will be up to date as of a few days ago.

*Less redundancy.* It will be easier to avoid reading the same data several times, since the computer will give you a side-by-side listing of related materials.

## DISADVANTAGES

*Terminals.* You can take a book or magazine on the bus...but a terminal? Well, you can at least make a hard copy to take with you.

*Limited availability of intact items.* If you need the entire article exactly as it originally appeared, you won't always find it in the data base. This will present a problem in preparing a letter to the editor or replying to allegations in the article you're seeking.

*The point of view of a third party.* Data base managers take great pains to insure a complete and sensible abstracting procedure. But it always comes down to an individual or a small group deciding what is worth going into the data base and what is not. What looks minor to an abstracter, may be a touchstone for a brilliant idea when read by you.

*Cost.* There are equipment costs, hookup costs, time costs, and telephone line fees.

*Language barrier.* Programmers are making tremendous strides in developing languages that make it possible for the layman to communicate directly with the computer. But when it comes to data bases, there are still some problems. Sooner or later you will find yourself mired in a "Who's on first" conversation with the electronic brain, and you'll call for help (which, incidentally, is usually graciously provided).

*Concept barrier.* How are items classified? Would you look for the Ayatollah under Iran? Islam? OPEC? all three? A data base comes with a thesaurus, or a kind of index to help you cross-reference. Also, the computer will scan its banks for related items—even, for example, items in which the word *Ayatollah* appears in the title.

Nevertheless, I had tremendous difficulty finding "jet lag" in one of the largest data bases. It wasn't under "aviation, " or "medicine," or "travel," or "airlines," or any other category I could think of. I gave up, although I'm sure it's in there somewhere.

## USES OF THE DATA BASE

*Planning.* The data base is useful when preparing forecasts and projections, designing new-product-entry programs, and doing industry analyses, because the base provides a large number of statistical and editorial items on the industry and consumer markets.

*Marketing.* The base assists in developing strategies by providing information on market forces, competitors, and buying trends.

*Public relations.* You can order up information for a speech, or a letter to the editor, or to your congressperson. And you can monitor the press coverage of your company and industry.

*Administrative.* Keep track of all issues affecting the successful administration of your company, from labor statistics, and reports of union activities to business and economic indicators and national affairs.

*International affairs.* Keep abreast of business, social, political, and economic developments in current and potential import or export markets.

*Finance.* Economic trends, stock market figures, banking information, money-market statistics, industry performance figures, all at your fingertips.

*Government.* Keep track of tax incentive programs, key legislation affecting your business, and other government activities.

*General information.* Who, what, where, when, why, how . . .

*Sports.* Settle arguments, win bets.

## DATA BASE SERVICES

*The New York Times Information Bank.* This service claims that over 300 of the Fortune 500 are regular subscribers. That is not a surprising figure when you consider that the largest corporations are obliged to monitor their public image and important government activities as well as new developments here and around the world. The Information Bank stores over 1.7 million abstracts from over 60 publications. It is a good, well-thought-out, user-oriented service.

You can order the service two ways:

*On demand.* Just as you call the deli for lunch, you can call your local Information Bank office. A research professional will help you assess your needs and will tell you whether the Info Bank can help. (Which it, almost always, can in some way. Whether it's worth the dough is, of course, your decision.) The Information Bank office will retrieve the data the same day and will mail or messenger-deliver a printout or even a microfiche.

*On-Line.* This is direct access to the data base via a terminal of your own that is hooked up to the computer by telephone lines. Using an access code, you can tap the Bank at any time, paying only for the time you use. There is no minimum usage charge.

Contact:
The Information Bank
Corporate Headquarters
Mt. Pleasant Office Park
1719-A Route 10
Parsippany, New Jersey 07054
(201) 539-5850

*DIALOG Information Retrieval Service.* One of the world's leading on-line data base systems, DIALOG is actually a collection of data bases—over 70 to choose from, for a total of around 20 million records. What is Lockheed doing in a business like this? Well, originally this system contained data bases on mostly scientific and technical subjects, and Lockheed was quick to see the value of being able to check patents and research papers, technical specifications, and test results by computer rather than manually. (Most scientists and engineers are now more comfortable with computers than books, anyway.) In recent years DIALOG has added data bases of interest to academicians, consumers and businesspersons. There are data bases in the arts, public affairs, humanities, mass media, and business and management, to name a few specific bases.

DIALOG is priced on a pay as-you-go system: no minimums, no monthly charges. Of course, you'll have to buy or lease a terminal if you don't already have one. And optional training on the use of DIALOG is extra, as are a wide variety of other services that you will probably use from time to time. The user's manual costs $10. The usage charges vary depending on the data base you run, running about 50 cents per minute to $1.50 per minute.

Although the DIALOG system can be very useful for the businessperson, many of the data bases are things like "BHRA Fluid Engineering," ("world-wide information on all aspects of fluid engineering,") and "Surface Coatings Abstracts," ("research literature on all aspects of paints and surface coatings including pigments, dyestuffs, resins . . ."). But there are also about 20 business/economics data bases, such as "Management Contents and Economic Abstracts International," along with an excellent series of general-reference data bases.

My favorite, for those pensive moods when you have time to reflect: "The Philosopher's Index." How about a little Kant when you can't take it anymore?

Contact:
DIALOG
Information Retrieval Service
3460 Hillview Avenue
Palo Alto, California 94304
All other locations: (415) 493-4411, Ext. 45412

# SCHEDULE 1-A DATA BASE RATES

*[Numbers in Parentheses Refer to Supplier Terms and Conditions listed on Order Forms]*

Connect time rates **include** all royalties paid to Database Suppliers.

*\*Database copyrighted by indicated supplier.*

*†Not available through the DIALOG Classroom Instruction Program.*

*‡Forthcoming database.*

*☆ 50¢ per full record typed online or printed offline for nonsubscribers after 3 months.*

| | Online Connect Time Rate Per Hour | | Online Type Rate | Offline Print Rate |
|---|---|---|---|---|
| Database (Supplier) | Mini-mum | Maxi-mum | Per Full Record | Per Full Record |
| * ABI/INFORM (Data Courier, Inc.) | $58 | $73 | | 30¢ |
| AGRICOLA 1970 - 1978 (U.S.D.A. Technical Info. Systems) | 10 | 25 | | 5 |
| AGRICOLA 1979 - Present (U.S.D.A. Technical Info. Systems) | 10 | 25 | | 5 |
| AIM/ARM (The Center for Vocational Education, Ohio State University) | 10 | 25 | | 10 |
| * AMERICA: HISTORY AND LIFE (ABC-Clio, Inc.) | 50 | 65 | | 15 |
| APTIC (U.S. Environmental Protection Agency) | 20 | 35 | | 10 |
| AQUACULTURE (NOAA/EDIS/ESIC/LISD) | 20 | 35 | 10¢ | 15 |
| AQUALINE (Water Research Centre) | 20 | 35 | 25 | 25 |
| † AQUATIC SCIENCES & FISHERIES ABSTRACTS (FAO, Rome & Intergovernmental Oceanographic Comm. of UNESCO) (17) | 32 | 47 | | 20 |
| * ARTBIBLIOGRAPHIES MODERN (ABC-Clio, Inc.) | 45 | 60 | | 15 |
| *‡ ASI (Congressional Information Service, Inc.) | 75 | 90 | | 15 |
| BHRA FLUID ENGINEERING (British Hydromechanics Research Association) | 50 | 65 | | 15 |
| *‡ BIOGRAPHY MASTER INDEX (Gale Research Company) | 40 | 55 | | 15 |
| * BIOSIS PREVIEWS 1969 - 1973 (BioSciences Info. Service) | 34 | 49 | | 10 |
| * BIOSIS PREVIEWS 1974 - Present (BioSciences Info. Service) | 34 | 49 | | 15 |
| ‡ BOOK REVIEW INDEX (Gale Research Company) | 40 | 55 | | 15 |
| *† CA SEARCH 1967-1971 (Chemical Abstracts Service) (1) | 55 | 70 | | 20 |
| *† CA SEARCH 1972 - 1976 (Chemical Abstracts Service) (1) | 55 | 70 | | 20 |
| *† CA SEARCH 1977 - Present (Chemical Abstracts Service) (1) | 55 | 70 | | 20 |
| CAB ABSTRACTS (Commonwealth Agricultural Bureaux) (10) | 20 | 35 | 25 | 25 |

Fig. 13. An excerpt from current data base listing
(*through page 125*)

From DIALOG Information Retrieval Service,
Palo Alto, CA. Reprinted by permission.

| Database (Supplier) | Online Connect Time Rate Per Hour | | Online Type Rate Per Full Record | Offline Print Rate Per Full Record |
| --- | --- | --- | --- | --- |
| | Minimum | Maximum | | |
| *† CHEMICAL INDUSTRY NOTES (Chemical Abstracts Service) (1) | $45 | $60 | | 20¢ |
| *† CHEMNAME™ (Lockheed Information Systems and Chemical Abstracts Service) (1) | 55 | 70 | | 20 |
| *† CHEMSEARCH™ (Lockheed Information Systems and Chemical Abstracts Service) (1) | 40 | 55 | | 16 |
| *† CHEMSIS™ 1972 - 1976 (Lockheed Information Systems and Chemical Abstracts Service) (1) | 55 | 70 | | 20 |
| *† CHEMSIS™ 1977 - Present (Lockheed Information Systems and Chemical Abstracts Service) (1) | 55 | 70 | | 20 |
| CHILD ABUSE AND NEGLECT (National Center for Child Abuse and Neglect) | 20 | 35 | | 10 |
| * CIS (Congressional Information Service, Inc.) | 75 | 90 | | 15 |
| † CLAIMS™/CHEM (IFI/Plenum Data Company) | 80 | 95 | | 15 |
| † CLAIMS™/CHEM UNITERM 78 - Present (IFI/Plenum Data Co.) | 285 | 300 | | 15 |
| CLAIMS™/CLASS (IFI/Plenum Data Co.) | 80 | 95 | | 10 |
| † CLAIMS™/CHEM/UNITERM 50 - 70 (IFI/Plenum Data Co.) | 285 | 300 | | 15 |
| † CLAIMS™/CHEM/UNITERM 71 - 77 (IFI/Plenum Data Co.) | 285 | 300 | | 15 |
| † CLAIMS™/U.S. PATENTS (IFI/Plenum Data Co.) | 80 | 95 | | 15 |
| † CLAIMS™/U.S. PATENT ABSTRACTS (IFI/Plenum Data Co.) | 80 | 95 | 25 | 50 |
| † CLAIMS™/U.S. PAT. ABS. WEEKLY (IFI/Plenum Data Co.) | 80 | 95 | 25 | 50 |
| * COMPENDEX (Engineering Index, Inc.) | 53 | 68 | 10 | 20 |
| * COMPREHENSIVE DISSERTATION INDEX (University Microfilms International) (2) | 40 | 55 | | 12 |
| * CONFERENCE PAPERS INDEX (Data Courier, Inc.) | 58 | 73 | | 20 |
| ‡ CONGRESSIONAL RECORD (Capital Services, Inc.) | 60 | 75 | | 15 |
| CRIS/USDA (Current Research Information System, U.S. Department of Agriculture) | 25 | 40 | | 10 |
| DIALINDEX (Lockheed Information Systems) | 20 | 35 | | N/A |
| DIALOG PUBLICATIONS (Lockheed Information Systems) | N/A | 15 | | N/A |
| * DISCLOSURE (Disclosure, Inc.) | 45 | 60 | 3.00 | 5.00 |
| † ECONOMICS ABSTRACTS INTERNATIONAL (Learned Information, Ltd.) (15) | 50 | 65 | | 20 |
| * EIS INDUSTRIAL PLANTS (Economic Info. Systems, Inc.) (8) | 75 | 90 | 50 | 50 |
| * EIS NONMANUFACTURING ESTABLISHMENTS (Economic Information Systems, Inc.) (8) | 75 | 90 | 50 | 50 |
| ENCYCLOPEDIA OF ASSOCIATIONS (Gale Research Co.) | 40 | 55 | | 15 |
| * ENERGYLINE® (Environment Information Center, Inc.) (9) | 75 | 90 | | 20 |

| Database (Supplier) | Online Connect Time Rate Per Hour | | Online Type Rate Per Full Record | Offline Print Rate Per Full Record |
|---|---|---|---|---|
| | Minimum | Maximum | | |
| * ENVIROLINE® (Environment Information Center, Inc.) (9) | $75 | $90 | | 20¢ |
| * ENVIRONMENTAL BIBLIOGRAPHY (Environmental Studies Institute) | 45 | 60 | | 15 |
| ERIC (National Institute of Education, Educational Resources Information Center) | 10 | 25 | | 10 |
| EXCEPTIONAL CHILD EDUCATION RESOURCES (Council for Exceptional Children) | 10 | 25 | | 10 |
| * EXCERPTA MEDICA 1974 - 1979 (Excerpta Medica) (11) | 50 | 65 | | 20 |
| * EXCERPTA MEDICA 1980 - PRESENT (Excerpta Medica) (11) | 50 | 65 | | 20 |
| * EXCERPTA MEDICA (In process) (Excerpta Medica) (11) | 50 | 65 | | 20 |
| ‡ FEDERAL REGISTER (Capitol Services, Inc.) | 60 | 75 | | 20 |
| * FOOD SCIENCE AND TECHNOLOGY ABSTRACTS (International Food Information Service) | 50 | 65 | | 15 |
| FOODS ADLIBRA (K&M Publications, Inc.) | 40 | 55 | | 10 |
| † FOREIGN TRADERS INDEX (U.S. Dept. of Commerce) (18) | 30 | 45 | 25 | 25 |
| * FOUNDATION DIRECTORY (The Foundation Center) (6) | 45 | 60 | | 30 |
| * FOUNDATION GRANTS INDEX (The Foundation Center) (6) | 45 | 60 | | 30 |
| FROST & SULLIVAN DM$^2$ (Frost & Sullivan, Inc.) | 75 | 90 | | 25 |
| * GEOARCHIVE (Geosystems) | 55 | 70 | | 20 |
| ‡ GEOREF (American Geological Institute) | 50 | 65 | | 20 |
| GPO MONTHLY CATALOG (U.S. Government Printing Office) | 20 | 35 | | 10 |
| ‡ GRANTS (Oryx Press) | 45 | 60 | | 30 |
| * HISTORICAL ABSTRACTS (ABC-Clio, Inc.) | 50 | 65 | | 15 |
| † INPADOC (International Patent Documentation Center) (19) | 80 | 95 | | 20 |
| * INSPEC 1969 - 1977 (The Institution of Electrical Engineers) (4) | 55 | 70 | | 20 |
| * INSPEC 1978 - Present (The Institution of Electrical Eng.) (4) | 55 | 70 | | 20 |
| * INTERNATIONAL PHARMACEUTICAL ABSTRACTS (American Society of Hospital Pharmacists) | 35 | 50 | | 15 |
| * IRL LIFE SCIENCES COLLECTION (Information Retrieval, Ltd.) | 30 | 45 | | 15 |
| * ISMEC (Data Courier, Inc.) | 58 | 73 | | 20 |
| * LANGUAGE AND LANGUAGE BEHAVIOR ABSTRACTS (Sociological Abstracts, Inc.) | 40 | 55 | | 15 |
| * LEGAL RESOURCE INDEX (Information Access Corporation) | 75 | 90 | | 20 |
| *† LISA (Learned Information, Ltd.) | 35 | 50 | | 10 |
| * MAGAZINE INDEX (Information Access Corporation) | 60 | 75 | | 20 |

| Database (Supplier) | Online Connect Time Rate Per Hour Mini-mum | Maxi-mum | Online Type Rate Per Full Record | Offline Print Rate Per Full Record |
|---|---|---|---|---|
| * MANAGEMENT CONTENTS® (Management Contents, Inc.) | $55 | $70 | | 15¢ |
| MENTAL HEALTH ABSTRACTS (National Clearinghouse for Mental Health Information) | 15 | 30 | | 10 |
| * METADEX (American Society for Metals) | 65 | 80 | | 12 |
| METEOROLOGICAL AND GEOASTROPHYSICAL ABSTRACTS (American Meteorological Society, NOAA) | 80 | 95 | | 15 |
| * MLA BIBLIOGRAPHY (Modern Language Association) | 40 | 55 | | 15 |
| *† NATIONAL FOUNDATIONS (The Foundation Center) (6) | 45 | 60 | | 30 |
| * NATIONAL NEWSPAPER INDEX (Information Access Corp.) | 60 | 75 | | 20 |
| ‡ NCJRS (National Criminal Justice Reference Service) | 20 | 35 | 10¢ | 15 |
| *† NEWSEARCH (Information Access Corporation) | 80 | 95 | | 20 |
| *† NICEM (National Information Center for Educational Media) | 55 | 70 | | 20 |
| † NICSEM/NIMIS (National Information Center for Special Education Materials) | 20 | 35 | | 10 |
| NONFERROUS METALS ABSTRACTS (British Nonferrous Metals Technology Center) | 30 | 45 | 10 | 20 |
| * NTIS (Nat'l Technical Info. Service, U.S. Dept. of Commerce) | 25 | 40 | | 10 |
| * OCEANIC ABSTRACTS (Data Courier, Inc.) | 58 | 73 | | 20 |
| * ONTAP CA SEARCH (Chemical Abstracts Service) (1) | N/A | 15 | | N/A |
| * ONTAP CHEMNAME™ (Lockheed Information Systems and Chemical Abstracts Service) (1) | N/A | 15 | | N/A |
| * ONTAP ERIC (ERIC and Lockheed Information Systems) | N/A | 15 | | N/A |
| * PAIS INTERNATIONAL (Public Affairs Info. Service, Inc.) (16) | 45 | 60 | | 15 |
| * PHARMACEUTICAL NEWS INDEX (Data Courier, Inc.) | 75 | 90 | | 20 |
| PHILOSOPHER'S INDEX (Philosophy Documentation Center) | 40 | 55 | | 15 |
| * PIRA (Research Association for the Paper and Board, Printing and Packaging Industries) | 40 | 55 | | 15 |
| * POLLUTION ABSTRACTS (Data Courier, Inc.) | 58 | 73 | | 20 |
| POPULATION BIBLIOGRAPHY (University of North Carolina, Carolina Population Center) | 40 | 55 | | 10 |
| * PSYCH INFO. (American Psychological Association) (5) | 50 | 65 | | 10 |
| *☆ PTS F&S INDEXES 1972-1975 (Predicasts, Inc.) (7) | 75 | 90 | | 20 |
| *☆ PTS F&S INDEXES 1976 - Present (Predicasts, Inc.)(7) | 75 | 90 | | 20 |
| PTS FEDERAL INDEX (Predicasts, Inc.) | 75 | 90 | | 20 |
| *☆ PTS INTERNATIONAL FORECASTS (Predicasts, Inc.)(7) | 75 | 90 | | 20 |

| Database (Supplier) | Online Connect Time Rate Per Hour | | Online Type Rate | Offline Print Rate |
| --- | --- | --- | --- | --- |
| | Minimum | Maximum | Per Full Record | Per Full Record |
| *☆ PTS INTERNATIONAL TIME SERIES (Predicasts, Inc.) (7) | $75 | $ 90 | | 20 ¢ |
| *☆ PTS PREDALERT (Predicasts, Inc.) (7) | 75 | 90 | | 20 |
| *☆ PTS PROMT (Predicasts, Inc.) (7) | 75 | 90 | | 20 |
| *☆ PTS U.S. FORECASTS (Predicasts, Inc.) (7) | 75 | 90 | | 20 |
| *☆ PTS U.S. TIME SERIES (Predicasts, Inc.) (7) | 75 | 90 | | 20 |
| † RAPRA ABSTRACTS (Rubber and Plastics Research Association of Great Britain) | 50 | 65 | | 15 |
| * RILM ABSTRACTS (City University of New York, International RILM Center) | 50 | 65 | | 15 |
| * SCISEARCH® 1974 - 77 (Institute for Scientific Information) (Subscribers to print) (3) | 25 | 40 | | 10 |
| * SCISEARCH® 1974 - 1977 (Institute for Scientific Information) (Non-subscribers) (3) | 115 | 130 | | 20 |
| * SCISEARCH® 1978 - Present (Institute for Scientific Information) (Subscribers to print) (3) | 15 | 30 | | 10 |
| * SCISEARCH® 1978 - Present (Institute for Scientific Information) (Non-subscribers) (3) | 105 | 120 | | 25 |
| * SOCIAL SCISEARCH® (Institute for Scientific Info.) (3) | 55 | 70 | | 10 |
| * SOCIOLOGICAL ABSTRACTS (Sociological Abstracts, Inc.) | 40 | 55 | | 15 |
| † SPECIAL EDUCATION MATERIALS (National Information Center for Special Education Materials) | 50 | 65 | | 15 |
| SPIN (American Institute of Physics) (12) | 20 | 35 | | 10 |
| * SSIE CURRENT RESEARCH (Smithsonian Sci. Info. Exchange) | 63 | 78 | | 20 |
| † STANDARD & POORS NEWS (Standard & Poors Corporation) (20) | 70 | 85 | | 15 |
| * SURFACE COATINGS ABSTRACTS (Paint Research Association of Great Britain) | 50 | 65 | | 15 |
| † TRADE OPPORTUNITIES (U.S. Dept. of Commerce) (18) | 30 | 45 | 25 | 25 |
| † TRADE OPPORTUNITIES WEEKLY (U.S. Department of Commerce) (18) | 30 | 45 | 50 | 50 |
| † TRIS (U.S. Department of Transportation) (13) | 25 | 40 | | 10 |
| TSCA INITIAL INVENTORY (Lockheed Information Systems and Environmental Protection Agency) | 30 | 45 | | 15 |
| † U.S. EXPORTS (U.S. Department of Commerce) | 30 | 45 | 25 | 25 |
| U.S. POLITICAL SCIENCE DOCUMENTS (University of Pittsburgh, University Center for International Studies) | 50 | 65 | | 15 |
| U.S. PUBLIC SCHOOL DIRECTORY (National Center for Educational Statistics) | 20 | 35 | | 10 |
| WELDASEARCH (The Welding Institute) | 50 | 65 | | 15 |
| WORLD ALUMINUM ABSTRACTS (Amer. Society for Metals) | 35 | 50 | | 10 |
| WORLD TEXTILES (Shirley Institute) (14) | 40 | 55 | | 10 |

*SDC Search Service of System Development Corporation.* SDC is a comprehensive on-line retrieval service featuring data bases under the name ORBIT. The data bases in the ORBIT bank come from other suppliers, and there are over 50 to choose from. It is a well-thought-out collection, with a good number of data bases of particular interest to both general and specialized management personnel (see Fig. 14). Users pay as they go: no subscription fee or minimum use. In fact the SDC people will give new subscribers two free hours of computer connect-time. Hourly rates range from $35 to $120, depending on the data base involved. You are billed for time used, rounded off to the nearest one hundredth of an hour.

SDC also provides an "Electronic Maildrop" system, which allows you to order full-text hard copies of any documents in several of the data bases in the ORBIT banks. The request is delivered by computer to the document supplier. The only charges are the time used to place the order (seconds) and, of course, the charge by the document supplier.

Contact:
SDC Search Service Headquarters
2500 Colorado Avenue
Santa Monica, California 90406
Toll-free telephone numbers:
(800) 352-6689 (CA only)
(800) 421-7229 (U.S. except CA)
Telex: 65 2358
Twx: 910 343-6443


*THE SOURCE.* A service of Telecomputing Corporation of America, this is one of the first computer time-sharing information services to spring up for home-computer and small-business users. While not a data base in the sense of the others mentioned, it is an extremely useful information service. You can get up-to-date news via UPI, business and financial information, weather, home entertainment; you can take language courses, send and receive electronic mail, and access several data bases, including a special offshoot of The *New York Times* Information Bank. The charges are quite reasonable, with a $5-per-month minimum and about $15 per hour for prime-time use, $2.75 for nonprime. The hookup and registration will set you back a hundred bucks, assuming you have your own keyboard, printer, and/or CRT. TCA will sell you what you need in packages ranging from $600 to $1,000. You can also store data on a disc at TCA's central computer for a modest charge.

Contact:
Source Telecomputing Corporation
1616 Anderson Road
McLean, Virginia 22102
(703) 821-6660

## CHEMDEX/CHEMDEX2

These two chemical dictionary files are companion files to the Chemical Abstracts databases. All compounds cited in the literature from 1972 to date are contained in these files. Each record contains a Registry Number, the molecular formula, Chemical Abstract's rigorous nomenclature for a specific compound, and many common synonyms ⹁recognized by Chemical Abstracts Service. The Registry Numbers retrieved are then used as search terms in the CAS77, CAS7276, and CAS6771 files. Search CHEMDEX or CHEMDEX2 by chemical name or fragment, molecular formula, molecular formula fragment, or group or row within a periodic chart.

Prepared by: Chemical Abstracts Service of the American Chemical Society

Printed Publication: *CA Substance Index, CA Registry Handbook, CA Index Guide,* and *CA Formula Index*

File Size: Approximately 2.6 million citations

Coverage: 1972 to present

Updating: Quarterly

Cost: $70/computer-connect hour
$.20/citation for offline printing

## Chemical Abstracts
see CAS77/CAS7276/CAS6771

## Chemical Abstracts Source Index
see CASSI

## Chemical Industry Notes
see CIN

## Chemical Reactions Documentation Service
see CRDS

## CHEMSDI*

Covers information cited in the last six weeks of *Chemical Abstracts*. This file will contain detailed information about chemical compounds cited as well as the indexing parameters available in CAS77, CAS7276, and CAS6771. CHEMSDI can be used as a current awareness file for both new compounds and new developments in chemical and related fields.

Prepared by: Chemical Abstracts Service of the American Chemical Society

Coverage: Last six weeks

Updating: Every 2 weeks

Cost: $70/computer-connect hour
$.20/citation for offline printing

*Available 1981

## Christian Science Monitor
see MONITOR

## CIN

Chemical Industry Notes contains citations to business literature in the chemical industry, including pharmaceutical, petroleum, paper and pulp, agriculture, and food industries. Subject coverage includes production, pricing, sales, facilities, products and processes, corporate activities, government activities, and people. Covers over 80 U.S. and non-U.S. publications.

Automatic SDI service is available on this file.

Prepared by: Chemical Abstracts Service of the American Chemical Society

Printed Publication: Chemical Industry Notes

File Size: Approximately 52,000 citations per year

Coverage: 1974 to present

Updating: Weekly

Cost: $75/computer-connect hour
$.20/citation for offline printing

## CIS

Covers publications emanating from the work of committees and subcommittees of the U.S. Congress: hearings; committee prints; House and Senate

Fig. 14. A sampling of data bases from SDC Search Services
Reprinted by permission.

# Master Index to the SOURCE

This Master Index of over 600 subjects introduces you helpfully and reliably to the world of the SOURCE. There are many, many more programs that are indexed further within the major Library Data Bases listed here.

After each listed subject, command notations are clearly given. Simply type in the command exactly as it is printed in this Master Index. Multiple commands for a particular subject are separated by semicolons and should be entered as separate commands.

## A

Abort—to stop any program employ break; type QUIT or STOP
Abortion—NYTCDB(P0001)
Absurdity—POST READ SAYINGS; PLAY POETRY; PLAY SONNET; WISDOM; R MADLIBS
Ace—(trick) DATA ACES; (Bridge) UPI F 1209
Acupuncture—NYTCDB(P0003)
Addition—R ADDMANY; DATA CHILD
Adjectives, German—INFO GADJEC
Adjustments (Customer Service)—MAIL TCA088
Adolescence—UPI F 1217; NYTCDB (P0114)
Adoption—NYTCDB(P0004)
Advanced Applications/Programs—DATA ADAPPR
Adventure—INFO (or PLAY) ADVENTURE
Advertisements—DATA CLASSI
Advice—DATA ASTRO-LIB, DATA ESP, DATA LORE
Age (elderly)—UPI F 1469, 1225
Aid for Ailing House—UPI F 1205
Aid, financial for college—AID
Aircraft—POST READ AIRCRAFT
Airline Schedules—AIRSCHED
Airline Toll-Free Numbers—TOLL-FREE (INDEX)
Alabama News or Sports—UPI S AL N or S
Alaska News or Sports—UPI S AK N or S
Alcoholism—NYTCDB(P0005)
Alert—(astrology) DATA ASTALT; (travel) DATA ALERT; (personal) DATA PERSON
Alphabet—R BETWEEN
American Stock Exchange:
  Daily Listing—UNISTOX (141, 144, 149)
  Daily Prices—UNISTOX (141, 144, 149)
  Most Active—UNISTOX (117)
  Wknd Comp. Prices—UNISTOX (161)
  Wknd Bond Prices—UNISTOX (164)

Amortization of Loan—R LAMORT
Amortization of Loan, Unk Term—INFO YRMORT
Amperage—INFO OHM
Amusement—DATA GAMES; DATA MAGIC; WISDOM; UPI F 1277
Anderson, Jack—UPI F 1123, 1127; NYTIMES (P0006)
Angle, quadrant ref—INFO TRIG
Anniversary Memo—DATA PERSON
Announcements—DATA ANNOUN
Annuities Analysis—R ANNUIT
Annuity Debt Payment—R LDEBTS
Antiques—UPI F 1285; NYTCDB(P0007)
Amphorisms—WISDOM
Apartments (rent)—POST READ APARTMENTS—RENT
Apple Info—POST READ APPLE
Aquarius—DATA ASTTRA-2
Aries—DATA ASTTRA-1
Arizona News or Sports—UPI S AZ N or S
Arkansas News or Sports—UPI S AR N or S
Armed Services (tollfree nos.)—TOLL-FREE (P081)
Arms Control—NYTCDB(P0008)
Art Objects—NYTCDB(P0009) ; POST READ ART
Arts—UPI F 1425
"Ask Kleiner" (entertainment)—UPI F 1449
Assets—DATA TAXTIP
Astrology—DATA ASTRO-LIB; UPI F 1221
Automobiles—NYTCDB (P0010, 11, 12); POST READ AUTOMOBILE-DOMESTIC OR AUTOMOBILE-FOREIGN
Aware Financial Service—DATA AFS
Aylward, Jim—UPI F 1159

## B

Backgammon—PLAY BACKGAMMON; PLAY BACKGAMN
Balancing Checkbook—R CKBAL
Bargains—DATA BUCKS; (travel) DATA ALERT
Base Conversions—R FROMTEN

Baseball—UPI N S
Basic (computer language)—SYSINFO;POST READ BASIC
Basketball—UPI N S
Battered Wives—NYTCDB(P0013)
Beauty—UPI F 1477, 1229
Behavior—UPI F 1393; DATA ASTRO-LIB
Bessel function (stat.)—INFO BESSEL
Binomial Coefficients (stat.)—INFO BINOM
Binomial Probabilities (stat.)—INFO BINOPO
Biorhythm (analysis)—BIOQUEST; PLAY BIORHYTHM
Birth Control—NYTCDB(P0014)
Birthday—DATA ASTTRA-1; DATA ASTTRA-2; UPI F 1221
Blackjack—INFO BLACKJACK
Black Studies—NYTCDB(P0016)
Bonds:
  AMEX Daily Listing—UNISTOX (141, 144, 149)
  Fed. Land Bank, Dly—UNISTOX (061)
  NYSE Daily Listing—UNISTOX (151, 155, 028)
  Treasury OTC, Dly—UNISTOX (024, 058)
  World Bank, Dly—UNISTOX (060)
  Volumes, Dly Sumy—UPI N B
  BC—BNDSLS
  Weekend Summary—UPI N B
  BC—BONDS
  Treasury, Wknd—UNISTOX 170
Bond Yield—INFO BNDYLD
Bond Price, accrued interest—INFO BNDPRC
Bordeaux—WINE (P017)
Boston & Northeast OTC Exchange—see "Over-the-Counter"
Boxscores (sports)—UPI N S
Brandies—WINE (P042)
"Break" Key—interrupts program flow
Bridge—UPI F 1209, 1349; INFO AUTOBRID;DATA AUTOB9; DATA BRCL;DATA BRGL;DATA BRIDGE
Bulletin-Board—POST READ BULLETIN-BOARD
Burgundy—WINE (P018, 19)
Businesses—try POST READ BUSINESSES
Business News—UPI N B
Business in Politics—NYTCDB (P0016)
Buying Wines—WINE (P010, 34)

## C

Cabernet Sauvignon—WINE (P050)
Cable Television—NYTCDB(P0017)
Calculation of Income Stmt—INFO BALSHT
Calendar (for any year 1582 onward)—PLAY YEARS
California News or Sports—UPI S CA N or S
California North & South OTC Exchange—see "Over-the-Counter"
California Wines—WINE (P012, 13, 14)

Fig. 15. Sample listings of the SOURCE data bases

READING TV: DATA BASES ON THE HOME SCREEN   Just around the corner is the opportunity to read your television, instead of merely watching it. This heralds an era in which the viewer will interact with the TV. The technology is here, and systems are in the testing stages at this moment. The Europeans have the jump on us this time, primarily because most of the airwaves on the other side of the Atlantic are government owned and controlled, and the British and French governments have pushed for this innovation.

Three basic approaches are being tried. Two involve the TV screen; the third involves hitching a video display to the phone.

*Teletext.* Developed by the British, this system capitalizes on the fact that the TV picture does not utilize all of the 525 lines available. A minimum of 21 lines is reserved for technical purposes, and the Teletext system uses these lines to transmit printed messages. In this system an entire library of several hundred information pages is transmitted every two minutes. The set is equipped with a "decoder," and using an index to select the appropriate page number, the user communicates the number to the system, which grabs the correct signal and flashes the page onto the screen. Teletext is designed to be supported in part by sponsored pages, in which ad messages will be conveyed as well as the data. Stations in Salt Lake City and St. Louis are currently testing the system.

*Viewdata.* Sometimes called videotex, Viewdata utilizes a phone-line hookup to link the viewer to an information bank. This would operate in much the same way as the data bases currently in operation and would allow for two-way communication between the information bank and the user, with the user able to access a wide variety of information and services via a keyboard. The British Post Office is testing such a system; a test is scheduled for Miami in the near future.

*Costs.* Teletext is much cheaper than Viewdata. All you need do is equip your set with a decoder, about $150. New sets will come with decoders built in for an additional charge of about $50. Advertising pays for the rest. Viewdata, on the other hand, means about $2,000 for a suitably equipped TV.

*Telematique.* The French term denotes a system that is essentially a telephone unit equipped with its own video display that allows users access to data bases and to perform a variety of electronic transactions. Success hinges on the production of cheap video terminals of under $100, which experts believe is unrealistic at this time. Nevertheless, many phone company officials feel that the money saved through eliminating phone directories (you can consult listings through the video display) will more than justify the cost of supplying a free video display. And many users will want an optional facsimile system to make hard copies. AT&T is testing a similar system in Albany soon.

The French have also developed a TV-based system, called Antiope, which can be adapted to both Teletext and Viewdata formats.

---

# INFORMATION AND THE FUTURE

---

As in the case of the office, where electronic storage is largely supplanting paper, information gathering and access is trending toward the nonbook forms. This is occurring in two ways:

- increased use of tried-and-true nonbook approaches such as video, slides, audio cassettes
- the development of new modes based on electronic data transmission and the availability of new technologies such as fiber optics and satellite transmissions

## LIBRARIES

Libraries will rely on a network of data bases, linking information stored in libraries all over the country and the world. Access will be by phone or by terminal. In some cases, access will be direct from the home or office. In others, it will be on-site. Books and articles will be produced as hard copies by the library, or by the user if his terminal is equipped with a printer. However, it is very likely that libraries will continue to shelve books and magazines, at least popular current and classic titles, for a long time to come. Somehow, the thought of reading a computer printout of *Romeo and Juliet*...*

## CUSTOM-TAILORED PERIODICALS

Before he moved to California, my father bought the *New York Post* every day. He hated the paper but loved its sports section, and he rarely read anything else in that paper. I have friends who get home delivery of *The Wall Street Journal*, yet read only the stock market page. In the future we will be able to order exclusively what we wish to read. The capability of receiving a daily "information sheet" consisting of the stock market page of *The Wall Street Journal*, the sports section of the *New York Post*, and the front page of *Women's Wear Daily* will be available to all. This is sometimes called an *information menu*.

Another strategy made available by the new technologies will be an increase in the number of "special editions" published by newspapers

---

*One expert points out that there is no reason why *Romeo and Juliet* could not be reproduced to look much like a classic English edition: Laser copiers can produce an exact image of an original, rather than render the same words in a "billing statement" typeface.

---

and magazines, tailored for special audiences. For example, New York lawyers might have a special edition of *Time* magazine all their own.

## PROBLEMS

Special editions and information menus will allow people to narrow the range of information that they absorb to a highly specialized mix—at the expense of the general. Specialized news will breed more specialists and a specialized mode of thinking. Studies on creativity have shown that many of the solutions to problems are found in fields lying outside the discipline in which the problems reside.

## HOW TO COPE

When you gain access to data bases, computerized libraries, and the like, consider that the best way to use such technology is to eliminate the redundant and the superficial. The information networks of the future should help you eliminate clutter, just as some home video systems let you edit out commercials. Do not use the systems to feed yourself a steady diet of shop talk. A properly used information and research system should allow you to cast a wider net than ever before and to learn about and absorb more information than ever.

## THE KNOWLEDGE/EXPERIENCE PARADOX

*Premise:* The amount of innovation is so rapid that the "half-life" of worker knowledge is shortening. What you learned in school is often of little value, if not obsolete, after just a few years on the job. So:

- New workers, fresh from formal education, will have a greater command of the most up-to-date technologies and concepts;
- but older workers will have extensive experience.

A report by the Diebold Group suggests that unless something is done to solve this paradox, we may see a shift in the compensation patterns, with more money being given in earlier years, when knowledge is most current and therefore most valuable, and less when you are past your knowledge prime. In this sense the corporation man may become more like a pro athlete. With the population getting steadily older, at least through the end of the century, this potential problem could become fearful reality for many and bring about sweeping changes in the economy.

WHAT YOU CAN DO   Turn the tables and make the paradox work for you. *Experience* is an asset that the new workers cannot provide, no matter what they do. But their asset, *up-to-date knowledge*, is readily accessible to you. The experienced executive who conscientiously fights the obsolescence of his own knowledge will command both advantages.

# 9

---

# APPENDIX TO
# PART II

MAJOR ENGLISH-LANGUAGE
BUSINESS PERIODICALS

ALL-NEWS RADIO STATIONS
IN THE UNITED STATES

# MAJOR ENGLISH-LANGUAGE
# BUSINESS PERIODICALS

**ABA Banking Journal.** $15. m ABA Banking Journal. Subscription Department. P.O. Box 530, Bristol, Conn. 06010

**AFL-CIO American Federationist.** See American Federationist

**Academy of Management. Journal.** $20. 4 times a yr Dr. Dennis F. Ray. P.O. Drawer KZ, Mississippi State University, Mississippi State, Miss. 39762

**Academy of Management Review.** $24. q Academy of Management Review, Walter B. Newsom, Business Manager, P.O. Box KZ, Mississippi State, Miss. 39762

**Accountancy.** £16.80. m Accountancy. The Institute of Chartered Accountants in England and Wales, 56-66 Goswell Rd, London EC1M 7AB, England

**The Accountant.** £27. w Accountant, Gee & Co (Publishers) Ltd., 151 Strand, London. WC2R 1JJ, England

**Accounting and Business Research.** $12. q Institute of Chartered Accountants in England and Wales, 56-66 Goswell Rd, London EC1M 7AB, England

**The Accounting Review.** $25. q Mr. Paul L. Gerhardt, American Accounting Association, 5717 Bessie Dr, Sarasota, Fla. 33583.

**Across the Board.** $30. m The Conference Board, Inc. 845 Third Avenue, New York, N.Y. 10010

**Administrative Management.** $16. m Geyer-McAllister Publications, Inc, 51 Madison Ave, New York, N.Y. 10010

**Administrative Science Quarterly.** $32. q Administrative Science Quarterly, Malott Hall, Cornell University, Ithaca, N.Y. 14853.

**Advertising Age.** $40. w Advertising Age. Circulation Department, 740 Rush St, Chicago, Ill. 60611

**Air Conditioning, Heating & Refrigeration News.** $34. w Air Conditioning, Heating & Refrigeration News, P.O. Box 2600, Troy, Mich. 48084.

**Air Transport World.** $24. m Air Transport World. Gloria S. Adams, Circulation Department, P.O. Box 95759 Cleveland, Ohio 44101.

**American Business Law Journal.** $8. 3 times a yr American Business Law Association, c/o Indiana University School of Business, Bloomington, Ind. 47401

**American Druggist.** $12. m The Hearst Corporation. 250 W 55 Street, New York, N.Y. 10019

**American Economic Review.** $43. 5 times a yr (Mr, My, Je, S, D) American Economic Association, C. Elton Hinshaw Secretary, 1313 21st Ave. South, Suite 809, Nashville, Tenn. 37212

**American Federationist.** $2. m American Federation of Labor and Congress of Industrial Organizations, 815 16th St, N.W. Washington, D.C. 20006

**American Import/Export Bulletin.** $15. m North American Publishing Company. 401 N Broad St, Philadelphia, Pa. 19108

**American Journal of Agricultural Economics.** $35. 5 times a yr American Agricultural Economics Association, c/o John C. Redman, Department of Agricultural Economics, University of Kentucky, Lexington, Ky. 40506

**American Printer and Lithographer.** $20. m American Printer and Lithographer. Circulation Department, 300 W Adams St, Chicago, Ill. 60606

**American Real Estate & Urban Economic Association. Journal.** $20. q American Real Estate & Urban Economic Association, J. Rabianski, Department of Real Estate and Urban Affairs, Georgia State University, Atlanta, Ga. 30303

**American Statistical Association, Journal.** $40. 5 times a yr American Statistical Association, 806 15th St, N.W. Washington, D.C. 20005

**Antitrust Law and Economics Review.** $67.50 q Antitrust Law and Economics Review, Inc, P.O. Box 3532, Vero Beach, Fla. 32960

**Applied Economics.** £45. q Applied Economics, Subscription Department, A.B.P. North Way, Andover, Hampshire, U.K.

**Appraisal Journal.** $25. q American Institute of Real Estate Appraisers of the National Association of Real Estate Realtors, 430 N Michigan Ave, Chicago, Ill. 60611

**Arbitration Journal.** $20. q American Arbitration Association, Inc, 140 W 51st St, New York, N.Y. 10020

**Automotive Industries.** $20. m Chilton Co, Chilton Way, Radnor, Pa. 19089

**Automotive News.** $35. w (semi-w 4th w Ap, 2d w Je) Automotive News, Circulation Department, 740 Rush St, Chicago, Ill. 60611

**Aviation Week & Space Technology.** $47.

w Aviation Week & Space Technology, Fulfillment Manager, P.O. Box 430, Hightstown, N.J. 08520

**The Banker.** £29. m Minister House, Author Street, London, EC4R 9AX, England

**The Bankers Magazine.** $48. bi-m Warren Gorham & Lamont, Inc, 210 South St, Boston, Mass. 02111

**Bankers Monthly.** $15. m Bankers Monthly, Inc, 601 Skokie Blvd, Northbrook, Ill. 60062

**Barron's.** $49. w Dow Jones & Co, Inc. 200 Burnett Rd, Chicopee, Mass. 01021

**Best's Review Life/Health Insurance Edition.** $14. m A.M. Best Co, Inc, Oldwick, N.J. 08858

**Best's Review Property/Casualty Insurance Edition.** $14. m A.M. Best Co, Inc, Oldwick, N.J. 08858

**Beverage Industry** $15. bi-w Beverage Industry, 747 Third Avenue, New York, N.Y. 10017

**Beverage World.** $15. m Keller International, 150 Great Neck Rd, Great Neck, N.Y. 10021

**Black Enterprise.** $10 m Earl G. Graves Publishing Co, Inc. 295 Madison Ave, New York, N.Y. 10017

**Broadcasting.** $50. w (last w D bi-w) Broadcasting Publications, Inc, 1735 DeSales St, N.W. Washington, D.C. 20036

**Buildings; the Construction and Building Management Journal.** $25. m Stamats Publishing Co, 427 Sixth Avenue, S.E. Cedar Rapids, Iowa 52406

**Business America; The Journal of International Trade.** $41. bi-w Superintendent of Documents, U.S. Government Printing Office, Washington, D.C. 20402

**Business and Society Review.** $38. q Business and Society Review, 870 Seventh Ave, New York, N.Y. 10019

**Business Economics.** $15. 4 times a yr David L. Williams, Executive Secretary-Treasurer, National Association of Business Economics, 28349 Chagrin Blvd, Suite 201, Cleveland, Ohio 44122

**Business History Review.** $15. q Business History Review, 215 Baker Library, Soldiers Field, Boston, Mass. 02163

**Business Horizons.** $15. bi-m Business Horizons School of Business, Indiana University, Bloomington, Ind. 47405

**Business Insurance.** $30. w Business Insurance, 740 Rush Street, Chicago, Ill. 60611

**Business Quarterly.** $16. q University of Ontario, School of Business Administration, London, Ontario, Canada N6A, 3K7

**Business Week.** $34.95. w (except for one issue in Ja) Business Week, P.O. Box 430, Hightstown, N.J. 08520

**CA Magazine.** $20: m Canadian Institute of Chartered Accountants, 250 Bloor St, E. Toronto, Canada M4W 1G5

**CLU Journal.** $9. q CLU Journal, The American Society of Chartered Life Underwriters, 270 Bryn Mawr Ave, P.O. Box 59, Bryn Mawr, Pa. 19010

**The CPA Journal.** $24. m New York State Society of Certified Public Accountants, 600 Third Ave, New York, N.Y. 10016

**California Management Review.** $15. q California Management Review, Graduate School of Business Administration, 350 Barrows Hall, University of California, Berkeley, Calif. 94720

**The Canadian Banker and ICB Review.** $12. 6 times a yr The Canadian Banker & ICB Review, Editor, Box 282 Toronto-Dominion Centre, Toronto, Ontario M5K 1K2 Canada

**Canadian Business.** $21. m Canadian Business, Suite 214, 56 The Esplanade, Toronto, Ontario M5E 1R5 Canada

**The Canadian Business Review.** $15. q The Canadian Business Review. Suite 100. 25 McArthur Road, Ottawa, Ontario, Canada

**Chain Store Age Executive with Shopping Center Age.** $20. m (semi-m Ja) Executive Offices. Chain Store Age Executive, 425 Park Ave. New York, N.Y. 10022

**Challenge; the Magazine of Economic Affairs.** $30. bi-m Challenge, 80 Business Park Dr, Armonk, N.Y. 10504

**Chemical and Engineering News.** $24. w Director of Financial Operations, ACS, 1155 16th St, N.W. Washington, D.C. 20036

**Chemical Business.** $38. (included with subscription to Chemical Marketing Reporter) M. Schnell Publishing Company, Inc. 100 Church St, New York, N.Y. 10007

**Chemical Marketing Reporter.** $45. w Schnell Publishing Company, Inc. 100 Church St, New York, N.Y. 10007

**Chemical Week.** $26. w Chemical Week. Fulfillment Manager, P.O. Box 430, Hightstown, N.J. 08520

**Citibank Monthly Economic Letter.** m. Citibank, Economics Department, 399 Park Ave. New York, N.Y. 10043

**Columbia Journal of World Business.** $16. q Columbia Journal of World Business, Graduate School of Business, Columbia University. 408 Uris Hall, New York, N.Y. 10027

**The Commercial and Financial Chronicle: Statistical section.** $118. w Subscription Service Department, 4 Water Street, Arlington, Mass. 02174

**Commodities; the Magazine of Futures Trading.** $34. m Commodities Magazine, Inc. 219 Parkade, Cedar Falls, Iowa 50613

**Communications News.** $15. m Communications News, 124 South First St, Geneva, Ill. 60134

**Compensation Review** $21.75. q American Management Associations, Subscription Services, Box 319, Saranac Lake, N.Y. 12983

**Computer Decisions.** $26. m Hayden Publishing Company, Inc, P.O. Box 13803, Philadelphia, Pa. 19101

**Computers and People.** $14.50 bi-m Berkeley Enterprises Inc., 815 Washington St., Newtonville, Mass. 02160

**Computing Surveys.** $30. q Association for Computing Machinery, 1133 Ave of the Americas, New York, N.Y. 10036

**Construction Review.** $19. m Superintendent of Documents, U.S. Government Printing Office, Washington, D.C. 20402

**The Cornell Hotel and Restaurant Administration Quarterly.** $15. q Cornell University, School of Hotel Administration. Ithaca, N.Y. 14853

**Credit & Financial Management.** $15. m (bi-m Je-Jl) National Association of Credit Management, 475 Park Ave. S. New York, N.Y. 10016

**Data Management.** $16. m Data Management, Circulation Department, 505 Busse Highway, Park Ridge, Ill. 60068

**Datamation.** $36. m Technical Publishing Co. 666 Fifth Ave. New York, N.Y. 10019

**The Director; Journal of the Institute of Directors.** £24. m The Director Publications Limited for the Institute of Directors, 116 Pall Mall, London, SW1Y 5ED, England

**Distribution.** $20. m Distribution, P.O. Box 2105, Radnor, Pa. 19089

**Drug & Cosmetic Industry.** $15. m Drug & Cosmetic Industry. Circulation Offices, 1 E. First St. Duluth, Minn. 55802

**Drug Topics.** $26. semi-m Litton Publication, Inc. Business & Editorial, Box 334, Oradell, N.J. 07649

**Dun's Review.** $22. m Dun's Review, Circulation Department, 666 Fifth Ave. New York, N.Y. 10019

**EDP Analyzer.** $48. m EDP Analyzer Subscription Office, 925 Anza Ave, Vista, Calif. 92083

**EFTA Bulletin.** m European Free Trade Association, Press and Information Service, 9-11 rue de Varembe, CH-1211 Geneva 20, Switzerland

**Economic Development and Cultural Change.** $22. q Economic Development and Cultural Change, The University of Chicago Press, 5801 Ellis Ave. Chicago, Ill. 60637

**Economic Record.** $A27. 3 times a yr Stechert-Macmillan, Inc. 7250 Westfield Ave. Pennsauken, N.J. 08110

**The Economist.** $85. w The Economist Newspaper Ltd. P.O. Box 190, 23a St. James's St. London, SW1A 1HF, England

**Editor & Publisher.** $25. w Editor & Publisher Co, Inc. 575 Lexington Ave, New York, N.Y. 10022

**Electrical Word.** $36. m McGraw-Hill Inc, P. O. Box 430, Hightstown, N.J. 08520

**Electronic News.** $22. w Fairchild Publications, Inc. 7 E 12 St. New York, N.Y. 10003

**Energy International.** Continued as Modern Power Systems with the January 1981 issue

**The Engineering Economist.** $11. q Engineering Economist AITE. 25 Technology Park/Atlanta, Norcross, Ga. 30092

**Engineering News-Record.** $26. w Engineering News-Record, Fulfillment Manager, P. O. Box 430, Hightstown, N.J. 08520

**Euromoney.** $89. Euromoney Publications Ltd. Nestor House, Playhouse Yard, London EC4V 5EX England

**European Chemical News.** £45. (including Chemscope) w IPC Industrial Press, Ltd. Quadrant House, The Quadrant, Sutton, Surrey, SM2 5AS United Kingdom

**The Federal Home Loan Bank Board Journal.** $29. m The Federal Home Loan Bank Board Journal, Superintendent of Documents, U.S. Government Printing Office, Washington, D.C. 20402

**Federal Reserve Bank of New York, Quarterly Review.** q Federal Reserve Bank of New York, 33 Liberty St. New York, N.Y. 10045

**Federal Reserve Bulletin.** $20. m Board of Governors of the Federal Reserve Systems, Division of Administrative Services, Washington, D.C. 20551

**Finance and Development.** q Finance and Development. International Monetary Fund Bldg, Washington, D.C. 20431

**Finance: the Magazine of Money and Business.** $35. bi-m Finance Publishing Corporation. 8 W 40th St, New York, N.Y. 10018

**Financial Analysts Journal.** $36. bi-m Financial Analysts Journal, 1633 Broadway, New York, N.Y. 10019

**Financial Executive.** $18. m Financial Executive Institute, Circulation Manager, 633 Third Ave, New York, N.Y. 10017

**Financial Management.** $30. q Financial Management Association. c/o Prof. Donald L. Tuttle, Graduate School of Business, Indiana University, Bloomington, Ind. 47401

**Financial World.** $36. semi-m Financial World Macro Communications, Inc, 150 East 58th St, New York, N.Y. 10155

**Fleet Owner.** $25. m Fleet Owner, Fulfillment Manager, P.O. Box 430, Hightstown, N.J. 08520

**Food Processing.** $24. m (semi-m Jl) Putman Publishing Co, 430 N. Michigan Ave, Chicago, Ill. 60611

**Food Product Development.** $18. m Food Product Development, Circulation Department, 747 Third Ave. New York, N.Y. 10017

**Food Service Marketing.** $24. m Food Service Marketing EIP, Inc. 2132 Fordem Ave, Box 7158, Madison, Wis. 53704

**Forbes.** $30. bi-w Forbes, Inc, 60 Fifth Ave, New York, N.Y. 10011

**Forest Industries.** $30. m (semi-m My) Forest Industries, Circulation Department, 500 Howard St, San Francisco, Calif. 94105

**Fortune.** $30. bi-m Fortune, 541 North Fairbanks Court, Chicago, Ill. 60611

**Fueloil & Oil Heat and Solar Systems.** $11. m Fueloil & Oil Heat, Circulation Department, 200 Commerce Rd, Cedar Grove, N.J. 07009

**Governmental Finance.** $12. q Governmental Finance, 180 N Michigan Ave, Chicago, Ill. 60601

**Graphic Arts Monthly and the Printing Industry.** $30. m Graphic Arts Publishing Co, 666 Fifth Ave, New York, N.Y. 10019

**Handling & Shipping Management.** $24. m(2 issues S) Handling & Shipping, P.O. Box 95759, Cleveland, Ohio 44101

**Hardware Age: the Hardlines Merchandising Magazine.** $5. m Chilton Co, Chilton Way, Radnor, Pa. 19089

**Harvard Business Review.** $24. bi-m Harvard Business Review, Subscription Service Department. P.O. Box 9730, Greenwich, Conn. 06835

**Hospital Financial Management.** $30. m Hospital Financial Management Association, 1900 Spring Road, Suite 500, Oak Brook, Ill. 60521

**Hotel & Motel Management.** $8. m Harcourt Brace Jovanovich Publications, 757 Third Ave. New York, N.Y. 10017

**Housing.** $33. m Housing, Fulfillment Manager, P.O. Box 430, Hightstown, N.J. 08520

**Human Resource Management.** $8. q University of Michigan Business Review, Graduate School of Business Administration, University of Michigan, Ann Arbor, Mich. 48109

**Industrial and Labor Relations Review.** $12. q Industrial and Labor Relations Review, Circulation Manager, Cornell University, Ithaca, N.Y. 14853

**Industrial Development.** $39. (including Site Selection Handbook) bi-m Conway Publications, Inc. Peachtree Air Terminal, 1954 Airport Rd, Atlanta, Ga. 30341

**Industrial Distribution.** $20. m Industrial Distribution, Circulation Manager, 2 Park Ave, New York, N.Y. 10016

**Industrial Management.** £17.50 m Industrial Management, Building 59, GEC Estate, East Lane, Wembley, Middlesex, HA9 7PG, England

**Industrial Marketing.** $20. m Industrial Marketing, Circulation Department, 740 Rush St, Chicago, Ill. 60611

**Industrial Marketing Management.** $62. q Elsevier North-Holland, Inc. 52 Vanderbilt Ave, New York, N.Y. 10017

**Industrial Relations; a Journal of Economy and Society.** $10. 3 times a yr Institute of Industrial Relations, University of California, Berkeley, Calif. 94720

**Industrial Research & Development.** $36. 13 times a yr Industrial Research, Circulation Department, 666 Fifth Ave. New York, N.Y. 10019

**Industry Week.** $36. bi-w Penton Publishing Company, Penton Plaza, 1111 Chester Ave, Cleveland, Ohio 44114

**Infosystems.** $40. m Infosystems, Hitchcock Publishing Company, Hitchcock Bldg, Wheaton, Ill. 60187

**The Insiders' Chronicle.** $145. w Insiders' Chronicle, 1111 East Putnam Ave, Riverside, Conn. 06878

**Institutional Investor.** $90. m Institutional Investor, Circulation Department, 488 Madison Ave, New York, N.Y. 10022

**Institutions.** Continued as Restaurants and Institutions with the January 1, 1981 issue

**Interavia.** $40. m Interavia S.A. 86 Avenue Louis-Casai. P.O. Box 162, 1216 Cointrin. Geneva, Switzerland

**Interfaces.** $18. q Institute of Management Sciences, 146 Westminster St, Providence, R.I. 02903

**The Internal Auditor.** $16. bi-m Internal Auditor, 249 Maitland Ave. Altamonte Springs, Fla. 32701

**International Labour Review.** $20. bi-m ILO Publications, International Labor Office, CH-1211, Geneva 22, Switzerland

**International Management.** £19. m International Management, Circulation Director, Mc-Graw-Hill House, Maidenhead, Berkshire, SL6 2QL, England

**International Monetary Fund. Staff Papers.** $7. 3 times a yr International Monetary Fund, Washington, D.C. 20431

**International Trade Forum.** $10. q International Trade Forum, International Trade Center UNCTAD/GATT, P.O. Box 30, CH-1211, Geneva 21, Switzerland

**Iron Age.** $50. 36 times a yr Chilton Co. Chilton Way, Radnor, Pa. 19089

**The Journal of Accountancy.** $20. m American Institute of Certified Public Accountants, Inc. 1211 Avenue of the Americas. New York, N.Y. 10036

**Journal of Accounting Research.** $25. semi-ann Journal of Accounting Research, Graduate School of Business, University of Chicago, Chicago, Ill. 60637

**Journal of Advertising.** $16. q J. Patrick Kelly, Subscription Mgr, 391 JBK, Brigham Young University, Provo, Utah 84602

**Journal of Advertising Research.** $45. bi-m Journal of Advertising Research. P.O. Box 1292, Long Island City, N.Y. 11101

**Journal of Bank Research.** $20. q Bank Administration Institute, 303 South Northwest Highway, Park Ridge, Ill. 60068

**The Journal of Business (Graduate School of Business of the University of Chicago)** $20. q The Journal of Business, University of Chicago Press, 5801 Ellis Ave, Chicago, Ill. 60637

**Journal of Commercial Bank Lending.** $13.50. m Robert Morris Associates, 1616 Philadelphia National Bank Bldg, Philadelphia, Pa. 19107

**Journal of Common Market Studies.** $49.50. q Basil Blackwell, 108 Cowley Rd. Oxford OX4, 1JF, England

**Journal of Consumer Affairs.** $20. semi-ann American Council on Consumer Interests, 162 Stanley Hall, University of Missouri, Columbia, Mo. 65201

**Journal of Consumer Research.** $36. q Journal Consumer Research, 222 South Riverside Plaza, Chicago, Ill. 60606

**The Journal of Developing Areas.** $16. q Journal of Developing Areas. Western Illinois University, 900 W Adams St, Macomb, Ill. 61455

**Journal of Economic Issues (JEI)** $20. q Association for Evolutionary Economics, 509 Business Administrative Bldg, Pennsylvania State University, University Park, Pa. 16802

**Journal of Economics and Business.** $13. triannual Robert H. Deans, Ed, Journal of Economics and Business, School of Business Administration, Temple University, Philadephia, Pa. 19122

**The Journal of Finance.** $35. 5 times a yr R. G. Hawkins Executive sec-treas. Graduate School of Business, New York University, 100 Trinity Pl. New York, N.Y. 10006

**The Journal of Human Resources.** $13. 4 times a yr Journal of Human Resources, University of Wisconsin Press, Journals Department, P.O. Box 1379, Madison, Wis. 53701

**Journal of Industrial Economics.** $30. q Basil Blackwell & Mott Ltd. 108 Cowley Rd. Oxford OX4 1LR, England

**Journal of Management Studies.** $42.50. 3 times a yr Manchester Business School, Booth St. West, Manchester, M15 6PB, England

**Journal of Marketing.** $40. q American Marketing Association, 222 South Riverside Plaza, Chicago, Ill. 60606

**Journal of Marketing Research.** $30. q American Marketing Association, 222 South Riverside Plaza, Chicago, Ill. 60606

**Journal of Occupational Medicine.** $25. m American Occupational Medical Association, 150 N Wacker Dr. Chicago, Ill. 60606

**Journal of Occupational Psychology.** $55. q The British Psychological Society, The Distribution Centre, Blackhorse Road, Letchworth, Herts SG6 1HN, United Kingdom

**Journal of Property Management.** $15. bi-m National Association of Realtors. 430 N. Michigan Ave, Chicago, Ill. 60611

**Journal of Purchasing and Materials Management.** $10. q Journal of Purchasing and Materials Management, National Association of Purchasing Management, Inc. 49 Sheridan Ave. Albany, N.Y. 12210

**Journal of Retailing.** $15. q Eleanor M. Rak, Journal of Retailing, New York University, 202 Tisch Hall, Washington Sq, New York, N.Y. 10003

**Journal of Risk and Insurance.** $25. 4 times a yr R. E. Johnson, Executive Director College of Business, University of Georgia, Athens, Georgia 30602

**Journal of Small Business Management.** $10. 4 times a yr General Secretary, NCSBMD, UW-Extension. 929 N Sixth St. Milwaukee, Wis. 53203

**Journal of Systems Management.** $17.50. m Association for Systems Management, 24587 Bagley Rd, Cleveland, Ohio 44138

**The Journal of Taxation.** $60. m Journal of Taxation, Inc. Warren, Gorham & Lamont, 210 South Street, Boston, Mass. 02111

**Journal of the Operational Research Society.** $150. m Subscription Fulfillment Manager. Pergamon Press, Ltd. Headington Hill Hall, Oxford OX3 0BW England

**Journal of Urban Economics.** $106. bi-m. Academic Press, Inc. 111 Fifth Ave. New York, N.Y. 10003

**Labor Law Journal.** $45. m Commerce Clearing House, Inc. 4025 W Peterson Ave, Chicago, Ill. 60646

**Land Economics.** $28. q Journals Departments, The University of Wisconsin Press, 114 North Murray St. Madison, Wis. 53715

**Long Range Planning.** $120. bi-m Pergamon Press Ltd. Subscriptions Manager, Headington Hill Hall, Oxford OX3 OBW, England

**MSU Business Topics.** $6. q Graduate School of Business Administration, Berkey Hall, Michigan State University, East Lansing, Mich. 48824

**Management Accounting.** members $20. m National Association of Accountants. 919 Third Ave. New York, N.Y. 10022

**Management International Review.** $45. q Betriebswirtschaftlicher Verlag. Dr Th. Gabler KG, 54 TaunustraBe, D 62 Wiesbaden, Federal Republic of Germany

**Management Review.** $24. m Management Review, American Management Association, Inc. Trudean Rd. Saranac Lake, N.Y. 12983

**Management Science: Journal of the Institute of Management Sciences.** $50. m Institute of Management Sciences, Circulation Dept. 345 Whitney Ave. New Haven, Conn. 06511

**Management Today.** £20. m Management Today. Haymarket Publishing Ltd. 53-55 Frith St, London W1A 2HG England

**Management World.** $18. bi-m Management World. Julia Bradley, Circulation Mgr. AMS Bldg, Maryland Rd, Willow Grove, Pa. 19090

**Managerial Planning.** $18. bi-m Planning Executive Institute. P.O. Box 70. Oxford, Ohio 45056

**Marine Fisheries Review.** $13. m U.S. National Marine Fisheries Service, Scientific Publications. U.S. Department of Commerce, Room 450, 1107 N.E. 45th St, Seattle, Wash. 98105

**Marketing & Media Decisions.** $36. m Decisions Publications Inc. 342 Madison Ave, New York, N.Y. 10017

**Merchandising.** $30. m Merchandising Week, Fulfillment Manager, P.O. Box 2157, Radnor, Pa. 19089

**Mergers & Acquisitions; the Journal of Corporate Venture.** $48. 4 times a yr Mergers & Acquisitions, Circulation Department, Box 36, McLean, Va. 22101

**Metropolitan Life Insurance Company Statistical Bulletin.** q Metropolitan Life Insurance Company, 1 Madison Ave, New York, N.Y. 10010

**Milbank Memorial Fund Quarterly/ Health and Society.** $25. q Milbank Memorial Fund Quarterly, 156 Fifth Ave. Room 502, New York, N.Y. 10010

**Mini-Micro Systems.** $30. m Mini-Micro Systems, 221 Columbus Ave, Boston, Mass. 02116

**Modern Plastics.** $22.50. m Modern Plastics, Fulfillment Manager, P.O. Box 430, Hightstown. N.J. 08520

**Modern Power Systems.** $30. m Modern Power Systems, Circulation Department, 500 Howard St. San Francisco, Calif. 94105

**Money.** $19.95. m Time Inc. 541 N Fairbanks Court, Chicago, Ill. 60611

**Monthly Labor Review.** $18. m Superintendent of Documents, Government Printing Office, Washington, D.C. 20402

**Mortgage Banker.** $20. m Mortgage Bankers Association of America, 1125 Fifteenth St, N.W. Washington, D.C. 20005

**National Institute Economic Review.** $36. q National Institute Economic Review, 2 Dean Trench St, Smith Sq. London, SW1P 3HE, England

**National Petroleum News.** $34.50. m (semi-m Je) National Petroleum News, 53 W Jackson Blvd, Chicago, Ill. 60604

**National Real Estate Investor.** $38. m (bi-m Je) National Real Estate Investor, 6285 Barfield Rd, Atlanta, Ga. 30328

**National Tax Journal.** $18. q NTA-TIA, S. J. Bowers, Exec. dir, 21 E State St, Columbus, Ohio 43215

**The National Underwriter Life & Health Insurance Edition.** $22. w (extra issues Jl, S, O) National Underwriter Co, 420 E 4th St, Cincinnati, Ohio 45202

**The National Underwriter Property & Casualty Insurance Edition.** $22. w (extra issue third w N) National Underwriter Co, 420 E 4th St, Cincinnati, Ohio 45202

**Nation's Business.** $45. (2 yrs) m Chamber of Commerce of the U.S. 1615 H St, N.W. Washington, D.C. 20062

**Nursing Homes.** $12. bi-m Nursing Homes, 4000 Albemarle St, N.W. Washington, D.C. 20016

**OECD Observer.** $9. bi-m OECD Publications Center, Suite 1207, 1750 Pennsylvania Ave. N.W. Washington, D.C. 20006

**Ocean Industry.** $15. m Ocean Industry Magazine, Circulation Mgr, Box 2608, Houston, Tex 77001

**The Office.** $20. m Office Publications,

Inc. 1200 Summer St, Stamford, Conn. 06904

**Oil & Gas Journal.** $78. w Oil & Gas Journal Subscriber Service Manager. P.O. Box 1260. Tulsa, Okla. 74101

**Omega; International Journal of Management Science.** $160. bi-m Subscription Fulfillment Manager, Pergamon Press Ltd. Headington Hill Hall, Oxford OX3 0BW, England

**Operations Research.** $50. 6 times a yr Operations Research Society of America, 428 E Preston St. Baltimore, Md. 21202

**Organizational Behavior and Human Performance.** $124. bi-m Academic Press, Inc. 111 Fifth Ave, New York, N.Y. 10003

**Organizational Dynamics.** $24.50. q American Management Associations, AMACOM, 135 W. 50th St, New York, N.Y. 10003

**Paper Trade Journal.** $15. semi-m Paper Trade Journal, Circulation Department, 300 W Adams St, Chicago, Ill. 60606

**Paperboard Packaging.** $11. m Paperboard Packaging, 747 Third Ave, New York, N.Y. 10017

**Pension World.** $34. m Pension World, 6285 Barfield Rd. Atlanta, Ga. 30328

**Personnel.** $24. bi-m Personnel Magazine, American Management Associations, Subscription Service, Box 319, Saranac Lake, N.Y. 12983

**Personnel Administrator.** $26. m American Society for Personnel Administration, 30 Park Dr, Berea, Ohio 44017

**Personnel Journal.** $28. m Personnel Journal, Inc. 866 W 18th Street, Costa Mesa, Calif. 92627

**Personnel Management.** £20. m Business Publications, Ltd. 75/77 Ashgrove Rd. Ashley Dorun, Bristol BS7 9LW, England

**Personnel Psychology.** $32. q Personnel Psychology, Inc. P.O. Box 6965 College Station, Durham, N.C. 27708

**Petroleum Economist.** $92. m Petroleum Economist, 5 Pemberton Row, Fleet St, London, England EC4A 3DP

**Pipeline & Gas Journal.** $25. m(semi-m Ap, Jl) Pipeline & Gas Journal, P.O. Box 1589, Dallas, Tex. 75221

**Plastics World.** $30. 13 times a yr Plastics World Circulation Manager, Box 5391, Denver, Colo. 80217

**The Practical Accountant.** $36. 12 times a yr Practical Accountant, 964 Third Ave, New York, N.Y. 10155

**Product Marketing.** $20. m Charleson Publishing Co. 124 E. 40th St. New York, N.Y. 10016

**Professional Builder/Apartment Business.** $30. m (2 issues Je) Professional Builder, 270 St Paul St, Denver, Colo. 80206

**Progressive Grocer.** $30. m Progressive Grocer, 708 Third Ave, New York, N.Y. 10017

**Public Personnel Management.** $20. q Public Personnel Management, Suite 870, 1850 K St, N.W. Washington, D.C. 20006

**Public Relations Journal.** $20 m (semi-m Jl) Public Relations Society of America, Inc. 845 Third Ave, New York, N.Y. 10022

**Public Relations Quarterly.** $12. q Public Relations Quarterly. 44 W Market St, Rhinebeck, N.Y. 12572

**Public Utilities Fortnightly.** $64. bi-w Public Utilities Reports, Inc, Suite 2100, Rosslyn Center Bldg. 1700 N Moore St, Arlington, Va. 22209

**Publishers Weekly.** $45. w (Last 2w D bi-w) R. R. Bowker Co. P.O. Box 13746, Philadelphia, Pa. 19101

**Pulp & Paper.** $30. m(2 issues in Je, N) Circulation Department, Pulp & Paper, 500 Howard St, San Francisco, Calif. 94105

**Purchasing.** $30. semi-m Circulation Department, Purchasing Magazine, 270 St Paul St, Denver, Colo. 80206

**Quarterly Review of Economics & Business.** $17. q The Quarterly Review of Economics & Business, 408 David Kinley Hall, Urbana, Ill. 61801

**Quick Frozen Foods.** $15. m Quick Frozen Foods, 1 E First St, Duluth, Minn. 55802

**Railway Age.** $20. semi-m Railway Age. Subscription Department, P.O. Box 530, Bristol, Conn. 06010

**The Real Estate Appraiser and Analyst.** $25. bi-m The Society of Real Estate Appraisers, 645 N Michigan Ave, Chicago, Ill. 60611

**Real Estate Review.** $38. q Real Estate Review, Warren, Gorham & Lamont, Inc. 210 South St, Boston, Mass. 02111

**Real Estate Today.** $19.50. m(bi-m My/Je, N/D) Realtors National Marketing Institute, 430 N Michigan Ave, Chicago, Ill. 60611

**Research Management.** $32. bi-m Research Management, 265 Post Road West, Westport, Conn. 06880

**Restaurant Business.** $40. m Restaurant Business Inc, 633 Third Ave, New York, N.Y. 10017

**Restaurants & Institutions.** $30. Semi-m Restaurants & Institutions, 270 St Paul St, Denver, Colo. 80206

**Review of Black Political Economy.** $15. 4 times a yr Transaction Periodicals Consortium. Rutgers University, New Brunswick, N.J. 08903

**The Review of Business and Economic**

**Research.** $7. 3 times a yr Division of Business and Economic Research, College of Business Administration, University of New Orleans, Lake Front, New Orleans, La. 70122

**The Review of Economics and Statistics.** $56. q North-Holland Publishing Co, P.O. Box 211, Amsterdam, the Netherlands

**Risk Management.** $21. m Risk and Insurance Management Society, Inc. 205 E 42nd St. New York, N.Y. 10017

**SAM Advanced Management Journal.** $13. q American Management Associations, Trudeau Road, Saranac Lake, N.Y. 12983

**Sales & Marketing Management.** $35. m (bi-w F, Ap, Jl, O) Sales Management, Inc, 633 Third Ave, New York, N.Y. 10017

**Savings & Loan News.** $14. m United States League of Savings Associations, 111 E Wacker Dr, Chicago, Ill. 60601

**Security Management.** $27. m American Society for Industrial Security, 2000 K St, N.W. Suite 651, Washington, D.C. 20006

**Site Selection Handbook.** $45. (or $39 with subscription to Industrial Development) 4v Conway Publications, Inc, 1954 Airport Rd, Atlanta, Ga. 30341

**Sloan Management Review.** $24. 3 issues a yr Sloan Management Review, Alfred P. Sloan School of Management, Massachusetts Institute of Technology, Cambridge, Mass. 02139

**Social Security Bulletin.** $16. m Superintendent of Documents, U.S. Government Printing Office, Washington, D.C. 20402

**Special Libraries.** $26. m(Jl-Ap) bi-m (My-Je) Special Libraries Association, Circulation Department, 235 Park Ave. S, New York, N.Y. 10003

**Stores.** $20. m National Retail Merchants Association, Inc, 100 W 31st St, New York, N.Y. 10001

**Supermarket Business.** $26. m Gralla Publications, 1515 Broadway, New York, N.Y. 10036

**Supervision.** $20. m Supervision, Subscription Department, 424 N Third St, Burlington, Iowa 52601

**Supervisory Management.** $16. m Supervisory Management. American Management Associations, Subscription Services, Box 319, Saranac Lake, N.Y. 12983

**Survey of Current Business.** $22. m Superintendent of Documents, U.S. Government Printing Office, Washington, D.C. 20402

**Taxes.** $45. m Commerce Clearing House, Inc. 4025 W Peterson Ave, Chicago, Ill. 60646

**Telecommunications.** $36. m(semi-m S) Telecommunications, 610 Washington St, Dedham, Mass. 02026

**Telephony.** $27. w Telephony Publishing Corporation, 55 E Jackson Blvd. Chicago, Ill. 60604

**Textile Industries.** $35. m W. R. C. Smith Publishing Co, 1760 Peachtree St, N.W. Atlanta, Ga. 30357

**Textile World.** $30. m Textile World, Circulation Manager, 1175 Peachtree St, N.E. Atlanta, Ga. 30361

**Training and Development Journal.** $30. m American Society for Training & Development, Subscription Department, Box 5307, Madison, Wis. 53705

**Transportation Journal.** $20. q American Society of Traffic and Transportation, Inc, 547 W Jackson Blvd, Chicago, Ill. 60606

**Trusts & Estates.** $42. m Trusts & Estates, Subscription Department, 6285 Barfield Rd. Atlanta, Ga. 30328

**World Mining.** $35. m (semi-m Jl, O) World Mining, Circulation Department, 500 Howard St, San Francisco, Calif. 94105

**World Oil.** $12. m(semi-m F, Ag) Robert C. Slick, Circulation Manager, P.O. Box 2608, Houston, Tex. 77001

# ALL-NEWS RADIO STATIONS
# IN THE UNITED STATES

From *Broadcasting Yearbook*. Reprinted by permission of *Broadcasting Magazine*.

| | | | |
|---|---|---|---|
| WHLO | Akron, OH | KAXZ | Forth Worth, TX |
| WABY | Albany, NY | WFRL | Freeport, L.I., NY |
| KZIA | Albuquerque, NM | | |
| WOUB | Athens, OH | WMAX | Grand Rapids, MI |
| WAVA | Arlington, VA | WKEU | Griffin, GA |
| WGST | Atlanta, GA | | |
| KLBJ | Austin, TX | WMPL | Hancock, MI |
| | | WMPL-FM | Hancock, MI |
| KMOU | Berlin, NH | WPOP | Hartford, CT |
| WXLO-FM | Berlin, NH | KHVH | Honolulu, HI |
| WMLO | Beverly, MA | KEYH | Houston, TX |
| KSPO | Boise, ID | | |
| WEEL | Boston, MA | WSIU | Iowa City, IA |
| CHIC | Brampton, Ont. | WUPM-FM | Ironwood, MI |
| WEBR | Buffalo, NY | | |
| | | KJSN-FM | Klamath Falls, OR |
| WBYS | Canton, IL | KRLS-FM | Knoxville, IA |
| WSOC | Charlotte, NC | | |
| WBBM | Chicago, IL | KNOU | Las Vegas, NV |
| WALE | Chicopee, MA | KFWB | Los Angeles, CA |
| KLYX-FM | Clear Lake City, TX | KNX | Los Angeles, CA |
| WERE | Cleveland, OH | WAMZ-FM | Louisville, KY |
| KSJR-FM | Collegeville, MN | | |
| | | WMOA | Manetta, OH |
| WRR | Dallas, TX | WMVI | Mechanicville, NY |
| WAVI | Dayton, OH | KINZ | Miami Beach, FL |
| KLCD-FM | Decorah, IA | KRMC | Midwest City, OK |
| KDEN | Denver, CO | WRIT | Milwaukee, WI |
| WWJ | Detroit, MI | KDAN | Minneapolis, MN |
| WKEN | Dover, DE | WWTC | Minneapolis, MN |
| KDAC | Duluth, MN | KMGA | Moultrie, GA |
| WDCL | Dunedun, FL | WSIG | Mount Jackson, VA |
| KURV | Edinburg, TX | | |
| KGDN | Edmonds, WA | WCBS | New York, NY |
| KISM | El Paso, TX | WINS | New York, NY |
| KASH | Eugene, OR | WRNG | North Atlanta, GA |
| KCNW | Fairway, KS | | |
| KARM | Fresno, CA | KYNN | Omaha, NE |
| WAVS | Fort Lauderdale, FL | KYXI | Oregon City, OR |
| KFPW | Fort Smith, AR | CKO-FM-1 | Ottawa, Ont. |

| | | | |
|---|---|---|---|
| WPBR | Palm Springs, FL | KJOE | Shreveport, LA |
| WCAU | Philadelphia, PA | WCOW-FM | Sparta, WI |
| KIAR | Phoenix, AZ | KMOX | St. Louis, MO |
| KQV | Pittsburgh, PA | KSJN-FM | St. Paul, MN |
| WIBU | Poynette, WI | | |
| WFAN | Providence, RI | WAMP-FM | Toledo, OH |
| | | CKO-FM-2 | Toronto, Ont. |
| WPOM | Riviera Beach, FL | WBVD | Trenton, NJ |
| KPRO | Riverside, CA | KCOK | Tulare, CA |
| KARV | Russellville, AR | KTUC | Tucson, AZ |
| | | | |
| KCRA | Sacramento, CA | WRC | Washington, DC |
| KFBK | Sacramento, CA | WTOP | Washington, DC |
| WVAI | San Antonio, TX | KWSO | Wasco, CA |
| KWMS | Salt Lake City, UT | WSCQ-FM | West Columbia, SC |
| KGB | San Diego, CA | WBRI | Westerly, RI |
| KGB-FM | San Diego, CA | WBRI-FM | Westerly, RI |
| KSDO | San Diego, CA | WNUS | West Springfield, MA |
| KGO | San Francisco, CA | WBRE | Wilkes-Barre, PA |
| KNAI-FM | San Francisco, CA | WILM | Wilmington, CO |
| KXRX | San Jose, CA | WKBX | Winston-Salem, NC |
| KAAP | Santa Paula, CA | | |
| WQSA | Sarasota, FL | WBBW | Youngstown, OH |

# PART III

# LIFE IN THE FAST LANE: EXECUTIVE HEALTH

*"The tragedy of life is what dies
inside a man while he lives."*
Albert Schweitzer

# 10

# YOUR HEALTH AND YOUR JOB

Personal health is not just a personal matter. Corporations lose millions of dollars each year as result of employee illness. It's not just sick pay: A key executive's illness can hold up deals, and result in missed opportunities, confusion, and chaos. More and more, top management is paying close attention to the medical history of its personnel. Your career may suffer if you accumulate a history of health problems, or if you wear your problem—obesity or chain smoking, for example. Such conditions signal not only a health risk, but a lack of discipline. Very bad for your reputation.

Most of us are intellectually aware of the tremendous toll a job can take on our health. But it appears that few see the direct connection between physical condition and job performance. "Most executives don't believe that an hour spent on physical fitness is more valuable to the business than one spent at a meeting," says Stan deLisser, president of Executive Health Examiners Group.

What motivates executives to exercise? To some extent, an intelligent desire to reduce the risk of an early death. And executives who wish to remain athletic know the value of regular exercise. But above the demands of work, the pleasures of play, and concern for longevity, vanity is the principal motivating factor.

It's difficult to relate to longevity as a goal—and even tougher to associate the striking of a good business deal with an exercise program. But an exercise program or diet will make a real difference in how you look. Inversely, a potbelly is taken as an indication that fitness is not important to you.

If your life-style includes activities that offer more enjoyment when you are healthy, you have a built-in incentive to shape up, or to stay in shape. But if you are sedentary, you will probably need additional motivation. That's why a sport is so helpful. It provides both a health-related activity and a goal.

All vanities aside, fitness *is* an important component of job success. Just feeling good about yourself will help you, on the job and everywhere else.

What follows in the next five chapters is a frank appraisal of factors that influence executive health, job performance, and longevity—and a basic guide to getting and staying in condition for the big game of life and the daily scrimmages of the business world.

Most job-related health problems are emotional in origin and can be traced to anxiety and stress. Therefore, a large portion of Part III of this book is devoted to the origins of stress, its symptoms, and the methods of controlling it.

## HEALTH AND THE EXECUTIVE WOMAN

Women in the executive suite have no pronounced health problems due to their sex. In fact they are generally healthier. Very few of the chronic "executive diseases" affect women as much as they affect men.

There is some indication that this situation might be changing. More women have entered the work force in recent years, and doctors have begun to see more women afflicted with executive diseases. But many experts do not expect women to achieve the morbid equality of a male-level disease rate.

Speaking of equality, sex discrimination does add an extra measure of stress for the woman executive. So does the problem of sexual advances on the job.

Another stress producer is the conflict that many women feel between career and motherhood. Menstruation is generally not a problem, although it can result in a few extra sick-days.

Strange as it may sound, the most common problems among executive women are dermatological. And women are worse offenders of the rules of good nutrition than men are.

The greatest concern is that women are picking up the bad health habits common in the business: alcohol, smoking, sedentary life-style.

## OVERVIEW OF TYPES OF EXAMINATIONS

*The Standard Examination*—The components of this examination, all of which are *tests present in the Comprehensive and Senior Examinations,* are basic procedures to detect the more common chronic diseases such as glaucoma, hypertension, diabetes, heart disease, emphysema and cancer of the colon/rectum plus glandular abnormalities and kidney/liver malfunction. It evaluates major body systems and functions and provides base line data to build an individualized preventive health program. Recommended for age 35 and over.

*The Comprehensive Examination*—The Comprehensive has additional procedures designed to detect esophagus, stomach, and gallbladder problems more common to people in executive capacities and/or 40 years of age or older. The added procedures, employing contrast media (barium/iodine pills), detect abnormalities such as tumors, cancer and gallstones.

*The Senior Examination*—This examination focuses on cardiac evaluation and the organs of the abdomen area. We perform a lateral chest x-ray to determine the size and shape of the heart muscle; abdomen x-ray to define the size and position of the liver, spleen, intestines, bladder and kidneys and exercise tolerance EKG. Tolerance testing consists of stressing the heart by exercising on a bicycle ergometer (pedaling against preset resistance) for four or five minutes, then three EKG readings are taken over a five-minute period. Recommended for age 40 and over.

*The Periodic Examination*—This evaluation omits tonometry screening for glaucoma and the proctoscopic inspection of the Standard Examination but contains all of the other procedures to detect common chronic diseases. Recommended for those under age 35.

---

*Cardiac Stress*—The treadmill test is a sophisticated diagnostic tool to help uncover underlying heart disease. It is a predictive indicator of the risk of heart attack. This procedure evaluates the condition of the cardiovascular system and appraises the functional capacity of an individual to perform under stress. Cardiac Stress testing is a succession of uninterrupted and increasing work stages with continuous oscilloscope monitoring of the heart rate. Our physician and a registered nurse are present throughout the testing. Recommended annually for senior executives and those in stressful positions.

Fig. 16. Physical examinations offered by Executive
Health Examiners Group

Reprinted by permission of Executive Health Examiners Group.

STANDARD EXECUTIVE EXAMINATION

*Required Time: Approximately 2 Hours*

Complete personal and family history
Physical examination of all body systems
X-ray of the heart and lungs (14" x 17")
12-Lead resting electrocardiogram with interpretation
Audiometric Screening
Visual Screening
Tonometry for Glaucoma
Spirometer test of vital capacity
Proctosigmoidoscopy (inspection of the rectum and lower colon)
Stool for occult blood
Hematology:

| | |
|---|---|
| Red blood count | Hemoglobin |
| White blood count | Hematocrit |
| Differential Screening | |

SMA-12 Blood Chemistry Analysis plus Triglycerides

| | |
|---|---|
| BUN (Urea Nitrogen) | SGOT (Oxalecetic Transaminase) |
| Glucose (Sugar) | LDH (Lactic Dehydrogenase) |
| Cholesterol | Phosphorous |
| Calcium | Albumin |
| Uric Acid | Total Protein |
| Bilirubin (Total) | Triglycerides |
| Alkaline Phosphatase | |

Urinalysis:

| | |
|---|---|
| Sugar | Specific Gravity |
| Albumin | Microscopic |

Pap Smear (Women, extra)

Test evaluation, written report and consultation by the examining physician.

Fig. 17. Standard Executive Examination, Executive
Health Examiners Group
Reprinted by permission.

PERIODIC B EXAMINATION

*Required Time: Approximately 2 Hours*

Complete personal and family history
Physical examination of all body systems
X-ray of the heart and lungs (14" x 17")
12-Lead resting electrocardiogram with interpretation
Audiometric Screening
Vision Screening (near/distant)
Spirometer test of vital capacity
Stool for occult blood
Hematology:

| | |
|---|---|
| Red blood count | Hemoglobin |
| White blood count | Hematocrit |
| Differential Screening | |

SMA-12 Blood Chemistry Analysis Plus Triglycerides

| | |
|---|---|
| BUN (Urea Nitrogen) | SGOT (Oxalacetic Transaminase) |
| Glucose (Sugar) | LDH (Lactic Dehydrogenase) |
| Cholesterol | Phosphorous |
| Calcium | Albumin |
| Uric Acid | Total Protein |
| Bilirubin (Total) | Triglycerides |
| Alkaline Phosphatase | |

Urinalysis:

| | |
|---|---|
| Sugar | Specific Gravity |
| Albumin | Microscopic |

Pap Smear (Women, extra)

Test evaluation and written report by the examining physician.

Fig. 18. Executive Health Examiners Group
Periodic B Examination, for those under 35
Reprinted by permission.

# 11

# STRESS: A USER'S GUIDE TO BODILY WEAR AND TEAR

One sure sign that a thing is popular is that everybody has heard of it but almost nobody is quite sure what "it" is. These days, stress is "it." This product of pressure is commonly equated with nervous tension, probably because we are a pretty wound-up culture. We ingest over five billion doses of tranquilizers to calm ourselves, five billion doses of barbiturates to help us unwind and sleep, and then three billion doses of amphetamines to make us feel perky.

Stress is a term that was once strictly medical and is now so mangled that the definition seems dictated more by the cure than the cause. One thing is certain: The scope of stress extends far beyond simple anxiety. And the sources, signs, and symptoms are far more numerous than most executives imagine them to be.

## WHAT IS STRESS?

Basically, stress is the nonspecific response that the body elicits to any demand. This definition by Dr. Hans Selye, one of the leading stress researchers, is obviously very broad. It can be taken to mean simply the wear and tear on the body that comes with living life.

So what's so bad about that? Nothing. In fact, the body is built to handle stress and even, in many instances, thrive on it; many of us function better when demands are made on us. Only when the demands are excessive and/or prolonged or too frequent does stress become dangerous. Stress can also take a great toll when it focuses on a particular organ. Such conditions have become commonplace, especially in the business world.

To distinguish between the natural, constructive form of stress that comes from a competitive environment and excessive stress that overburdens people and does bad things to them, Selye uses two terms: "eustress" for the good, "distress" for the bad. Since this chapter is devoted to counting the ways in which stress can impair your performance and shorten your life—and to finding ways of dissipating that stress—assume I'm speaking of distress unless otherwise noted.

*Misconceptions*
- Stress is simple anxiety.
- Stress results only from negative occurrences.
- Stress is always bad.

# WHAT CAUSES STRESS?

Virtually anything can be a source of stress. Because we differ from one another in our psychological and physical makeup, we differ in our reactions to external events and demands. One man's joy is another man's distress. So, by necessity, any discussion of the causes of stress centers on the *most common* sources—those that elicit stressful responses in many executives. Most experts have by now accepted the future shock theory, which states that the accelerating rate of change, innovation, mobility, and depersonalization of our technologically advanced culture makes each new day a bout with potentially damaging stress. In short, our culture, with its technology, is changing at a rate that outstrips our ability to adapt. Organizational psychologist Jere E. Yates, has produced a chart that effectively summarizes the sources and symptoms of stress that commonly affects the manager.

## JOB-RELATED STRESSORS

The chart clearly demonstrates that most causes of stress are psychological. Noise, crowding, air pollution, and such can take their toll, but the body shows a remarkable ability to adapt to such physical stressors.

Job-related stresses are a bit peculiar. While they are clearly a factor in health problems, they also appear to contribute to job satisfaction. A recent survey by Ruder and Finn found that most executives wouldn't change jobs because of pressure. More often, greater opportunity for fulfillment or challenge is the reason to walk. The bottom line is that many of the things that we like about our jobs are the very same things that make us sick.

Let's look at these inverse stressors.

SUCCESS   Success, and what comes with it, is one of the best methods of reducing stress. Many of us like to think that everything is not rosy at the top, that success has its drawbacks: Powerful and wealthy people must, underneath it all, be unhappy. Well, it just ain't so. Most successful people experience less frustration on the job, have high self-

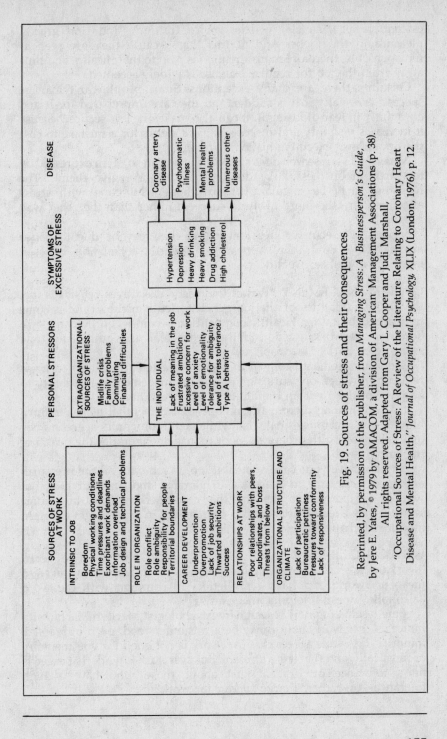

Fig. 19. Sources of stress and their consequences

Reprinted, by permission of the publisher, from *Managing Stress: A Businessperson's Guide*, by Jere E. Yates, © 1979 by AMACOM, a division of American Management Associations (p. 38). All rights reserved. Adapted from Gary L. Cooper and Judi Marshall, "Occupational Sources of Stress: A Review of the Literature Relating to Coronary Heart Disease and Mental Health," *Journal of Occupational Psychology,* XLIX (London, 1976), p. 12.

esteem, fewer financial worries, more freedom, and find greater pleasure in their jobs. Add to this that because they are seen as indispensable, therefore more attention is paid to their health, and time away from the job for regular exercise is widely accepted.

Certainly there are many exceptions. Some people can't manage success, especially if it is sudden and they are unprepared for it and constantly in fear of losing it. It can also make one less secure, because it increases visibility and responsibility. It's easy for a mistake to cost the upper level executive his job.

Nevertheless, research does support the notion so often expressed by top men in business: "We don't get ulcers. We give them!" The reasoning may be circular. Perhaps those who cope with stress effectively are the more likely to succeed, rather than the other way around.

Successful executives live longer, but that may be due to better medical care. And there appears to be little correlation between longevity and sheer wealth.

GOOD MANAGEMENT   Part of the reason executives get sick is that the positive qualities of the job get distorted somehow, and become ugly and debilitating. Healthy competition becomes conflict; ambition becomes overwork. Responsibility breeds fear and guilt. And time seems to be part of a conspiracy.

Good management is one of the most neglected approaches to stress reduction. In fact, one sure sign of good management is the ability to keep a workload within the limits of manageability.

In a well-managed company, no one should feel that he has to burn himself out. It is unfortunate that while many companies spend money on gyms and health programs, poor management erodes the health of the employees.

Why not have your cake and eat it too? A job with all the pressures and risks necessary to keep you exhilarated and on your toes, but without the pernicious elements that could send you to the cardiac ward. It may even be necessary to change jobs in order to get the right mixture of challenge and moderation.

WORKAHOLISM: THANK GOD IT'S MONDAY   The term "workaholic" has a negative connotation to most people. It is taken to mean *over*work; and having six letters in common with the word "alcoholic" doesn't help its image any.

Some fascinating new research by psychologist Marilyn Machlowitz indicates that workaholics may be a misunderstood, even oppressed, minority. Everyone agrees that overwork is not good for you mentally or physically, and that it is a stressor. But overwork is work that exceeds one's tolerance or limits. What about those who have a high tolerance—or, rather, a large *appetite* for work?

156

Such people don't complain about overwork, because they don't mind or don't notice. Many love their work and thrive on it, almost to the exclusion of all else. Thus, if you complain about being a workaholic, you probably aren't one. You are just overworked.

Workaholics are the victims of discrimination for much the same reasons that other minorities are: They threaten the majority. Workaholics like their jobs and appear to live satisfied lives. And they don't work solely to please others. Primarily, they work to please themselves.

Some workaholics do have serious problems—feelings of inadequacy, inability to relax—that lie at the root of this behavior. But, according to Machlowitz, just as many workaholics weave together work and play almost as a continuum—or two sides of the same coin—rather than as two separate aspects of life. In such cases, it appears that the rigorous work load doesn't produce excessive stress. More often, it is a source of enjoyment.

The real problems lie in one's relationship with family and friends. If you are always working, neglect is inevitable. Children can suffer from lack of attention. Workaholism is a primary factor in many broken marriages.

Machlowitz, in her book *Workaholics*,* offers a diagnostic quiz that will help you determine if you are a workaholic:

YES     NO

1. Do you get up early, no matter how late you go to bed?
2. If you are eating lunch alone, do you read or work while you eat?
3. Do you make daily lists of things to do?
4. Do you find it difficult to "do nothing"?
5. Are you energetic and competitive?
6. Do you work on weekends and holidays?
7. Do you find vacations "hard to take"?
9. Do you dread retirement?
10. Do you really enjoy your work?

If you answered "yes" to eight or more questions, you, too, may be a workaholic.

---

## PERSONAL STRESSORS

Such stresses can be extremely serious, especially if they are centered around home life. While the office is often perceived as a jungle, the home is considered a source of stability. A stressor that rocks the domestic boat can hurt a great deal. Divorce is an obvious possible source of stress. So is adultery. It appears that many of our moral judgments are attempts to minimize stress-producing events. Respondents to a recent survey considered adultery more immoral than homosexuality, perhaps because adultery is seen as more destabilizing and therefore more stressful.

## ANXIETY AND DEPRESSION

Anxiety and depression are frequently mentioned as symptoms of stress. They can also be a source. Many people simply cannot tolerate high levels of anxiety or deep depression, or they respond to it with negativism. Often, the symptoms can be more of the same, resulting in a physical and mental vicious cycle—and a downward spiral for the victim. This may help explain why relaxation techniques are often so effective against stress. Not only do they attack the *symptoms* by helping the individual to feel relaxed and uplifted, but at the same time they alleviate a major *cause* of stress.

# WHAT MAKES SOMETHING A "DISTRESSOR"?

What makes one event or outside influence a stressor, and another simply a run-of-the-mill occurrence, has a lot to do with how you perceive the situation and how you react to it. *In reality, there's no such thing as a stressful situation—only a stressful response.* Here's why some situations cause stressful responses:

## INDIVIDUAL DIFFERENCES

Everyone's physiology is different. Say you are in shape. You run five miles a day. For you, a five-mile run is a constructive situation, stressing the heart in such a way as to improve its condition. Your colleague, on the other hand, hasn't done any exercise in years. And he's got angina and hypertension to boot. For him, a five-mile run might mean a stroke. Obviously, a recommendation to run five miles a day can't be applied across the board. You've got to take the individual's condition into account.

It's a good idea to know where you stand. *Learn as much as possible about yourself and how you function.* Otherwise, you can get caught unaware. Everyone is talking about taking more time off because it's good for their health. But suppose you love your job, and it's idleness that sends your blood pressure up and sets your nerves on edge? For you, a long vacation may not be what the doctor ordered. Regular medical examinations to keep you aware of your physical condition are a good idea. In some cases, personality testing may be warranted to help you identify your basic personality traits.

## UNPREDICTABILITY

People can put up with even the most annoying and rotten things if they know they are coming. But the very same things can produce stress if they appear unexpectedly.

The flip side of unpredictability is overanticipation. Stress can be caused by anticipation of something unpleasant—having to fire someone or preparing to ask for a raise, for example.

On balance, a regular routine and a well-planned work day can be beneficial, precisely because adherence to a routine cuts down the unexpected. And a sober, sensible analysis of the unpleasantries ahead won't hurt you.

## LACK OF CONTROL

It is amazing how much people can endure when they feel in control of a situation. In a now classic study, two groups of workers were subjected to identical irritating noise. The only difference was that the members of one group had buttons with which they could silence the noise at will. Most members of that group chose not to touch the buttons, and so voluntarily worked under the same conditions as the helpless group. But the work output of the group with the *option* to cut the noise was far superior to the group that had no choice.

This doesn't mean that we have to be power-hungry in order to avoid stress. It means that we do better when we feel that we are calling the shots in our lives. Stress can result from the feeling of being at the mercy of the clock, of the bill collector, of the boss. But as the study serves to point out, what is important is not the time, the bills, or the boss, but our perception of the situation.

## SOCIAL CONTEXT

Have you ever noticed how you can shrug off your own mistake when it's witnessed by a casual friend, but the very same gaffe will make you want to crawl under the desk if it happens in front of certain other people? It appears that one's environment and social context are factors in stress.

Culture also plays a role in determining stress. A Brazilian businessperson might do a slow burn if you are a few minutes late for an appointment. To him, you're a stressor. An Arab businessman will most likely spend the time calmly drinking coffee, not feeling slighted in the least. The two react differently due to the differences in cultural conditioning.

Whenever one is in an unknown or openly hostile social or cultural environment, the potential for stress rises markedly. That is why there is such a great need for diplomatic protocol, meetings on "neutral soil," and the like.

---

## WHAT STRESS CAN DO TO YOU

---

Stress can make you unhealthy and unhappy; it can even kill you. If that isn't bad enough to consider, ponder further: Much of what we do in attempting to alleviate the psychological effects of stress, such as smoke, drink, overeat, and take medication, can also do us in. Fortunately, as we learn more about stress, we become better at identifying the danger signs and symptoms commonly caused by high levels of stress. Unfortunately, by the time many of us take notice of the symptoms and decide to take action, they have already developed into full-fledged diseases.

This section is not intended to turn you into a hypochondriac or a stressphobic (a stress-fearing creampuff). Rather, it is intended to alert you to signs that you may be under excessive stress. This awareness will enable you to monitor the situation closely—and to do something about it should it get out of hand.

Regular physical exams are a must; and you will help your doctor and yourself by calling attention to possible stress-related symptoms.

---

## WARNING SIGNS

---

### THE FIGHT-OR-FLIGHT RESPONSE

This is a common response by the body to a perceived external threat. The body prepares itself to confront the threat or to run from it. The changes that take place in our physiology at this time are quite noticeable:

- increases breath rate rapidly
- blood pressure increases
- muscle tension increases
- heart rate increases
- pupils dilate
- digestion slows or stops
- blood sugar rises

---

- bowel and bladder control loosens
- perspiration and saliva increase
- adrenaline flow increases
- the senses sharpen

The fight-or-flight response allows us to act more quickly, powerfully, and efficiently to a situation in which having "something extra" might make the difference between our survival and our demise. But two basic situations can turn this key response into a problem:

- The fight-or-flight response is triggered inappropriately. There are times when we believe we are being threatened, but in reality we are not.
- A threat is correctly perceived, but the physical response called for by the fight-or-flight mechanism is inappropriate. Suppose a business associate says something that you take as a threat. Your fight-or-flight mechanism is now switched on. Punching him would be a bad move. Running away is utterly insane. So you basically do nothing but steam. You break a few pencils, perhaps; you call your mate and curse the guy out. But that's it.

Clearly, in our competitive world, the fight-or-flight mechanisms may be triggered too often. And because the physical reactions that the response calls for are socially unacceptable, we are deprived of the most natural outlets for that response. Every fight-or-flight reaction puts a great deal of stress on the body. And being forced to internalize it just makes it worse.

If you find yourself frequently experiencing the reactions associated with the fight-or-flight response, you had better look at what is causing your engine to race.

## LIFE CHANGES

Any abrupt change in the status of an individual's life can produce stress. So goes the theory advanced by Drs. Thomas Holmes and Richard Rahe of the University of Washington School of Medicine. Basically, they are saying that health is directly affected by the rate and severity of change in one's life. And there is some evidence that this is true.

Life-change events are potentially harmful because of the *stress* of change, not because the event itself is negative; many life-change events are, in themselves, neutral or downright positive. If it causes a great change, it can cause stress.

Holmes and Rahe have put together a Social Readjustment Rating Scale, which is all the rage in books and magazine articles about stress. It is a list of 43 life events, each of which is assigned a value in terms of Life Change Units. All you do is go through the list looking for events that have taken place in your life over the past year. Tally up the total

# THE SOCIAL READJUSTMENT RATING SCALE

| LIFE EVENT | MEAN VALUE |
|---|---|
| 1. Death of spouse | 100 |
| 2. Divorce | 73 |
| 3. Marital separation from mate | 65 |
| 4. Detention in jail or other institution | 63 |
| 5. Death of a close family member | 63 |
| 6. Major personal injury or illness | 53 |
| 7. Marriage | 50 |
| 8. Being fired at work | 47 |
| 9. Marital reconciliation with mate | 45 |
| 10. Retirement from work | 45 |
| 11. Major change in the health or behavior of a family member | 44 |
| 12. Pregnancy | 40 |
| 13. Sexual difficulties | 39 |
| 14. Gaining a new family member (e.g., through birth, adoption, oldster moving in, etc.) | 39 |
| 15. Major business readjustment (e.g., merger, reorganization, bankruptcy, etc.) | 39 |
| 16. Major change in financial state (e.g., a lot worse off or a lot better off than usual) | 38 |
| 17. Death of a close friend | 37 |
| 18. Changing to a different line of work | 36 |
| 19. Major change in the number of arguments with spouse (e.g., either a lot more or a lot less than usual regarding child-rearing, personal habits, etc.) | 35 |
| 20. Taking on a mortgage greater than $10,000 (e.g., purchasing a home, business, etc.) | 31 |
| 21. Foreclosure on a mortgage or loan | 30 |
| 22. Major change in responsibilities at work (e.g., promotion, demotion, lateral transfer) | 29 |
| 23. Son or daughter leaving home (e.g., marriage, attending college, etc.) | 29 |
| 24. In-law troubles | 29 |
| 25. Outstanding personal achievement | 28 |
| 26. Wife beginning or ceasing work outside the home | 26 |
| 27. Beginning or ceasing formal schooling | 26 |
| 28. Major change in living conditions (e.g., building a new home, remodeling, deterioration of home or neighborhood) | 25 |
| 29. Revision of personal habits (dress, manners, associations, etc.) | 24 |
| 30. Troubles with the boss | 23 |
| 31. Major change in working hours or conditions | 20 |

Fig. 20. Social Readjustment Rating Scale
A method of cataloging stress and estimating the probability
of stress-related illness within the next two years.
*(above and opposite)*

Reprinted with permission from T. H. Holmes
and R. H. Rahe, "The Social Readjustment Rating Scale,"
*Journal of Psychosomatic Research* 11 (1967): 213-18.
Copyright © 1967 Pergamon Press, Ltd.

| 32. | Change in residence | 20 |
| 33. | Changing to a new school | 20 |
| 34. | Major change in usual type and/or amount of recreation | 19 |
| 35. | Major change in church activities (e.g., a lot more or a lot less than usual) | 19 |
| 36. | Major change in social activities (e.g., clubs, dancing, movies, visiting, etc.) | 18 |
| 37. | Taking on a mortgage or loan less than $10,000 (e.g., purchasing a car, TV, freezer, etc.) | 17 |
| 38. | Major change in sleeping habits (a lot more or a lot less sleep, or change in part of day when asleep) | 16 |
| 39. | Major change in number of family get-togethers (e.g., a lot more or a lot less than usual) | 15 |
| 40. | Major change in eating habits (a lot more or a lot less food intake, or very different meal hours or surroundings) | 15 |
| 41. | Vacation | 13 |
| 42. | Christmas | 12 |
| 43. | Minor violations of the law (e.g., traffic tickets, jaywalking, disturbing the peace, etc.) | 11 |

There seems to be a well-documented and clear relationship between life change and physical disease. It is impossible to make accurate predictions on an individual basis, since most of these findings are statistical. In our subjective judgment, we would estimate that you might be able to interpret your life change scores as follows:

| LIFE CHANGE SCORE FOR PREVIOUS YEAR | PROBABILITY OF ILLNESS WITHIN NEXT 2 YEARS |
| --- | --- |
| Less than 150 (low stress) | Low |
| 150-199 (mild stress) | 30% |
| 200-299 (moderate stress) | 50% |
| 300 or more (major stress) | 80% |

number of Life Change Units accumulated and you can estimate the probability of illness over the next two years. Simple? Yes. That's why health writers love it. Accurate? Not really.

There are so many factors and variables involved. No distinction is made between eustress and distress: Some of the events on the list may be good for you. And as I pointed out earlier, the major factor in stress formation is not the event itself, but the individual's ability to cope with that event. The Holmes-Rahe list fails to take this into account.

On the positive side, the Social Readjustment Rating Scale can be a valuable tool for increasing your awareness of possible danger points. If you feel you have been having a pretty hard time of late, one look at the rating scale might tell you why. And if you are anticipating having to "work a few things out" in your life, you can prepare to compensate for the possible toll the ordeal could take on your health.

# ATYPICAL BEHAVIOR ON THE JOB

When people are under stress, they often do things out of character. It's easy to excuse such behavior by saying "I'm not myself today." We expect that people will understand. And that is why we tend to bend over backward with a subordinate we know to be competent. But whether it be our subordinates or ourselves, the best approach isn't always to look the other way. There are some common behavior patterns that are, in effect, warning lights that something is amiss. It may indeed appear that the individual is "slipping." If recognized early, the problems causing the stress can be confronted and overcome—and you can probably avoid having to fire somebody, or getting canned yourself.

EXCESSIVE ABSENTEEISM  Often an indication of problems at home, low morale or self-esteem, and a general wish to avoid problems, absenteeism is also coupled with depression; we feel like staying in bed and shutting out the world.

PROCRASTINATION  When a worker who is normally "a real go-getter" starts pushing pencils around the desk, it's probably not because he's getting lazy. Something has taken the fight out of him, and he is simply running out the clock—stalling for time, avoiding the challenges he used to eat for breakfast.

POOR TIME MANAGEMENT  People under stress often feel tyrannized or oppressed by time. When you feel that way, often you wind up losing control of your own schedule and work routine.

DEFENSIVENESS  This is perhaps the most common sign of all. But since defensive behavior is so widespread in the business world, its significance as a sign of something more serious is often overlooked. If an individual starts displaying defense mechanisms that are out of the ordinary, take notice. Be especially on guard for:

*Avoidance of reality,* either by denying that problems exist ("Relax, there's no problem") or by creating an illusion ("Things are great; everything's going really well").

*Excessive suspicion, or xenophobia* (fear of that which is foreign). The individual thinks that so-andq'o is out to get him, can't be trusted, or is to blame.

NOT CUTTING THE MUSTARD  The quality of work is substandard, or below the individual's normal performance levels. Putting on the pressure may be the worse thing you can do in this situation. If it's a subordinate, try to find out what is going on. If it's you, take stock of the situation and try to weed out the cause of your slide, rather than trying to ride it out unexamined.

Keep in mind that even events that are neutral or positive can induce such behavior. So even when things are going smoothly and well, an executive can be under stress.

## PHYSICAL AND MENTAL DISTRESS SIGNALS

Dr. Selye has prepared a list of 31 common danger signs. The list is long because it runs the gamut of signs that appear among a great range of individuals. If even a few are turning up regularly in your life, they could mean trouble.

## PRIMARY SYMPTOMS

**Depression.** Depression is best defined as a feeling of dejection about life. It can vary in intensity and is often accompanied by inactivity, feelings of sadness, worthlessness, and futility, and a lack of energy and goals. It is not unusual for people to experience a depression of limited duration as a direct reaction to a marked life change or crisis, such as the illness or death of a loved one or the loss of one's job. But the more debilitating form of depression is a chronic, unrelenting brand that often appears to have no immediate justification. This is the kind of stress that psychiatrist David Viscott describes as "a sadness which has lost its relationship to the logical progression of events."*

Depression is often associated with (or is even a direct cause of) several other stress symptoms, such as changes in appetite and sleep patterns. Many depressed people feel better after raiding the refrigerator; or they eat without pleasure, just to take their minds off their problems. Others lose their appetites completely. Then there are those who can't sleep or who wake up in the middle of the night—and those who are too depressed to face the world, so they stay under the sheets all day long. The sudden appearance of pains, soreness, and aches is also associated with depression.

One estimate puts the number of people with serious depression at 15 percent of the U.S. population.

**Anxiety.** This feeling of tension, apprehension, and worry certainly needs no description. But anxiety should be distinguished from such feelings as fear and frustration. Fear is a response to a pending or immediate danger; it may save your life someday. Anxiety, on the other

*Reprinted from *Executive Health,* by Philip Goldberg, Copyright © 1978, by McGraw-Hill, Inc., New York, NY 10020. All rights reserved.

1. General irritability, hyperexcitation, or depression
2. Pounding of the heart, an indicator of high blood pressure
3. Dryness of the throat and mouth
4. Impulsive behavior, emotional instability
5. The overpowering urge to cry or to run and hide
6. Inability to concentrate, flight of thoughts, and general disorientation
7. Feelings of unreality, weakness, or dizziness
8. Predilection to become fatigued, and loss of the "joie de vivre"
9. "Floating anxiety"—that is to say, we are afraid, although we do not know exactly what we are afraid of
10. Emotional tension and alertness, feeling of being "keyed up"
11. Trembling, nervous tics
12. Tendency to be easily startled by small sounds
13. High-pitched, nervous laughter
14. Stuttering and other speech difficulties
15. Bruxism, or grinding of the teeth
16. Insomnia
17. Hypermotility
18. Sweating
19. The frequent need to urinate
20. Diarrhea, indigestion, queasiness in the stomach, and sometimes even vomiting
21. Migraine headaches
22. Premenstrual tension or missed menstrual cycles
23. Pain in the neck or lower back
24. Loss of appetite or compulsive eating
25. Increased smoking
26. Increased use of legally prescribed drugs, such as tranquilizers or amphetamines.
27. Alcohol and drug addiction
28. Nightmares
29. Neurotic behavior
30. Psychoses
31. Proneness to accidents

Fig. 21. Danger signs and symptoms of stress

Reprinted, by permission of the publisher, from *Managing Stress: A Businessperson's Guide*, by Jere E. Yates, © 1979 by AMACOM, a division of the American Management Associations (pp. 82-83).

hand, is a reaction to *anticipated* danger, and usually this reaction is far out of proportion to the actual threat. Frustration results from your apprehension of an obstacle that prevents, or threatens to prevent, attainment of a goal.

Like depression, chronic or intense anxiety may be associated with changes in appetite and sleep.

# SECONDARY SYMPTOMS

**Insomnia.** This symptom usually goes hand in hand with anxiety or depression, but can occur by itself. Chronic insomnia can be quite a problem on its own. There are many approaches to relief, among them sleep clinics, nutritional and folk remedies, relaxation techniques, and, as a last—and, ideally, temporary—resort, drugs. (Many researchers believe that drugs inhibit some therapeutic qualities of sleep.)

**Neck or back pain.** Many people tend to tense their muscles repeatedly when under stress. The back and neck are often the first areas to tighten up. Some people feel the muscle tension in other areas, such as the jaw and head. Maybe the word "uptight" is worth using after all, on account of its physiological accuracy. Mom and dad used "pain in the neck," didn't they?

# POOR SOLUTIONS
# TO STRESS-RELATED PROBLEMS

Sometimes a symptom is nothing more than a poor attempt at a solution. In the case of stress, many of the solutions that we adopt to improve the situation do very little to ameliorate it. In fact they often make it worse.

**Eating.** Some people stuff themselves just to get some relief. Others hope to accomplish the same thing by starving. Neither approach works. You just get fat or undernourished, or you wind up a junk-food junkie.

**Drinking.** Excessive drinking is very popular among stress addicts. It can aggravate the symptoms of stress. But usually it works too well and the victim becomes the victim of chronic tranquilization. Thus, the root causes of the stress reaction are never confronted—and the liver and stomach pay the price.

**Smoking.** Smoking more now to escape the stress? But nicotine acts as a stimulant. Besides, imagine how stressful it must be to know you're increasing your chances of becoming a statistic.

**Drinking caffeine.** It is not unusual for coffee, tea, and cola drinkers to increase their consumption of these caffeine-bearing beverages during periods of stress in order to get a "lift." But excessive amounts produce symptoms similar to anxiety. And caffeine has been linked to nervousness, insomnia, ulcers, even heart disease.

One rule of thumb: If the solution can become a stressor, it's probably not a very good solution.

---

## STRESS-RELATED DISEASE
## AND DISORDERS

---

Excessive stress, if unchecked, is certainly a contributing factor in the onset of many diseases. In some cases it may be the most important factor; in others it may simply accelerate the appearance of a disease. Hans Selye believes that although many factors (such as heredity, diet, and environment) may indeed make an individual a candidate for a particular disease, it is excessive stress that causes a potential problem to blossom into a full-fledged disease. By this way of thinking, there are millions of potential heart attack victims who can avoid having one by controlling stress. Many doctors disagree. But it is worth noting which diseases appear closely linked to excessive stress.

**Heart disease.** Heart attack, stroke, hypertension, and angina have all been linked to excessive stress. In that linkage, stress joins a long list of other factors, including smoking, obesity, and heredity. We do not know to what extent stress plays a role in cardiovascular disease, but there is little doubt that excessive stress can trigger a heart attack in a "high risk" individual. Selye has been able to trigger heart attacks in rats by inducing stress in them.

Stress itself often induces the "fight-or-flight" response that results in an elevation of the blood pressure. If this happens repeatedly, the result can be that the pressure eventually ceases to return to normal. The result is hypertension, or high blood pressure, greatly increasing the risk of stroke.

Angina pectoris, a tightening or pain in the chest area, is caused by temporary blood deprivation in some part of the heart muscle. It is known to occur during periods of physical and emotional stress.

---

### Physical Signs

1. Excess weight for your age and height
2. High blood pressure
3. Lack of appetite
4. A desire to eat as soon as a problem arises
5. Frequent heartburn
6. Chronic diarrhea or constipation
7. An inability to sleep
8. A feeling of constant fatigue
9. Frequent headaches
10. A need for aspirin or some other medication daily
11. Muscle spasms
12. A feeling of fullness although you've not eaten
13. Shortness of breath
14. A liability to fainting or nausea
15. An inability to cry or a tendency to burst into tears easily
16. Persistent sexual problems (frigidity, impotence, fear)
17. Excessive nervous energy which prevents sitting still and relaxing.

### Mental Signs

1. A constant feeling of uneasiness
2. Constant irritability with family and work associates
3. Boredom with life
4. A recurring feeling of being unable to cope with life
5. Anxiety about money
6. Morbid fear of disease, especially cancer and heart disease
7. Fear of death—your own and others'
8. A sense of suppressed anger
9. An inability to have a good laugh
10. A feeling of being rejected by your family
11. A sense of despair at being an unsuccessful parent
12. Dread as the weekend approaches
13. Reluctance to take a vacation
14. A feeling you can't discuss your problems with anyone
15. An inability to concentrate for any length of time or to finish one job before beginning another one
16. A terror of heights, enclosed spaces, thunderstorms, or earthquakes

Fig. 22. Physical and mental signs of stress

Jack Tresidder (ed.), *Feel Younger, Live Longer* (Chicago: Rand McNally, 1977). Reprinted, by permission of the publisher, from *Managing Stress: A Businessperson's Guide*, by Jere E. Yates, © 1979 by AMACOM, a division of American Management Associations (pp. 89-90). All rights reserved.

**Headache.** Excessive stress is a principal cause of both tension headaches and migraines, but for different reasons. Tension headaches are the result of muscular tension in the scalp and neck. Muscle contraction is a common response to stress. The condition tends to be self-aggravating because the muscles may respond to the pain by tightening further.

Migraines are caused by a dilation of blood vessels in the head and neck. The pain can be excruciating and incapacitating. Curiously, migraines tend to come not during, but after the stress has subsided. Dr. Harold Wolff has observed that migraines are common on Sundays, when the contrast between the high stress of the week and the relaxation of the day of rest is greater.

**Backache.** Many of us have weak back muscles as a direct result of the sedentary life-style that comes with a desk job. Add to that the tightening of these muscles as a result of stress and you've got a backache. While stress is a common factor here, chronic back pain should not be subject to a spot diagnosis. There may be some structural damage. Get thee to a physician.

**Ulcers.** The relationship between stress and ulcers is part of American folklore. The expression "It's giving me an ulcer" is tantamount to saying that something is causing aggravation.

There is wisdom in this assertion. Constant stress prevents the gastrointestinal system from returning to a dormant stage and thereby increases the acidity in the stomach and intestines. A single, ultra-high-stress event occasionally results in bleeding in a matter of hours.

According to Dr. I. Mendeloff, "It's what's eating you rather than what you're eating"* that causes ulcers.

**Diabetes.** It appears that diabetes is to a large extent genetically determined. But many people with the genetic predetermination never develop the disease. Apparently, environmental considerations and the way the body reacts to stress determine whether the disease remains latent or surface. There is no question that high levels of stress can make a diabetic's condition worse.

**Cancer.** Yes, even cancer appears to have some connection with stress—at least in theory. The reasoning is that stress lowers our resistance to disease by weakening our immune system. Perhaps, say some researchers, the stress-weakened immune system is unable to neutralize malignant cells before they establish themselves in the body.

---

*From Kenneth Lamott, *Escape from Stress* (New York: Berkeley Medallion, 1975).

## Selye's tips on stress reduction

Because we have such a highly developed nervous system, we are quite vulnerable to psychological insults from others. From a lifetime of research and practical experience, Selye offers several tips (paraphrased here) for dealing with these insults:

1. Don't waste your time trying to befriend those who don't want to be recipients of your love and friendship.
2. Don't be a perfectionist; strive to do something that is within your capabilities.
3. Don't underestimate the genuine pleasure that can come from the simple things of life.
4. Carefully assess each situation to see whether a syntoxic or catatoxic response will serve you best. Only fight for that which is really worth it.
5. Concentrate on the pleasant side of life and on the activities which can improve your lot. As the old German proverb says, "Imitate the sundial's ways; count only the pleasant days."
6. When you do experience a setback or defeat, reestablish your self-confidence by remembering all your past accomplishments.
7. Don't procrastinate in tackling the unpleasant yet necessary tasks you have to do. Get them over with quickly.
8. Realize that people are unequal in many ways at birth. All people should have access to equal opportunities, and their progress should be evaluated on the basis of their performance. Leaders are leaders only as long as they have the respect and loyalty of their followers.
9. Live in such a way as to earn your neighbor's love, and your life will be a happy one. Selye believes that this adapted version of the Golden Rule (love your neighbor as yourself) is more in line with the way humans really are, i.e., egotistical. He's not against the Golden Rule; he just believes that almost no one can love his neighbor as much as he loves himself. So for him the important thing is to work on perfecting yourself so that you will have some usefulness in society.

Fig. 23. Dr. Hans Selye's advice on how to reduce stress

Reprinted, by permission of the publisher, from *Managing Stress: A Businessperson's Guide*, by Jere E. Yates, © 1979 by AMACOM, a division of American Management Associations (p. 113).

**Other diseases.** Many specialists believe that intense stress can bring on allergy attacks in those who suffer from them and can aggravate existing symptoms. Stress has also been linked with arthritis and sexual dysfunction.

---

# STRESS REDUCTION
# AND RELAXATION TECHNIQUES

---

Wherever there is a problem, there are people ready to make money by offering solutions. In the stress-control business, the techniques offered as solutions usually involve some form of physical or mental relaxation. What follows is a cataloging of the most popular and successful approaches to relaxation. However, before we begin I'd like to point out that you already know some of the most effective methods of stress reduction: exercise, good nutrition, good living habits, effective management of time and work load.

## THE TRANSCENDENTAL
## MEDITATION PROGRAM™

The TM Program™ reduces stress by triggering a state of very deep rest during which the body seeks to normalize, or to correct any negative effects of stress. Practitioners report feeling relaxed, yet alert after a typical session. Scores of studies of TM technique done at many independent research facilities have monitored physiological changes and verified the unique state of rest that the Transcendental Meditation Program engenders. Other studies confirm the generally positive effects that regular practice of the TM Program has on the body, mind, and behavior.

Although it is difficult to determine exactly what benefits you will derive from the regular practice of the TM Program, it does appear safe to say that the technique is good for you. And, despite the claims of detractors, there appears to be no conclusive evidence that there is any other mental technique quite like TM, in terms of either the physical and mental state it elicits, or the benefits that result.

In addition to the physiological studies, which indicate a reduction in oxygen consumption, cardiac output, and other signs of deep rest, several studies have been done on the TM Program in the business environment. Organizational psychologist Dr. David Frew studied the effects of the TM Program on 500 male and female workers. His findings:

- Job satisfaction increased.
- Performance improved.

---

- There was an improvement in relationships with co-workers and supervisors.
- There was less of a desire to leave the company.

A pilot study done at a General Motors plant in Fremont, California, was even more dramatic:*

Those practicing the TM Program filled out questionnaires after completing the program. They claimed that they:

- required less sleep: 37%
- fell asleep faster: 50%
- drank less hard liquor: 37%
- drank less beer and wine: 23%
- eliminated or reduced the use of tobacco: 55% of the smokers in the study
- used less aspirin: 20%
- drank less coffee: 20%
- felt more confident: 53%
- felt improved emotional stability: 60%
- noticed improvement in organizing ability: 53%

Many enthusiastic executives have gone a step further and made TM instruction available to interested employees. In some cases the courses are conducted on company premises. Overwhelmingly, the results have been positive.

It should be noted, however, that the TM Program is a holistic method of self-development, affecting all aspects of life. Reduction of stress is only a small part of the potential benefits.

Although several unauthorized "how-to" books have appeared in an attempt to capitalize on the popularity of the TM program, there is really only one way to learn—from a trained instructor. There are TM Program centers in every major city where you can take the course.

For more information on the Transcendental Meditation Program, check your local phone directory under "International Meditation Society" or "TM," or contact:

International Meditation Society
World Plan Executive Council
17310 Sunset Boulevard
Pacific Palisades, California 90272

SUGGESTED READING

*TM and Business* by J. B. Marcus (New York: McGraw-Hill, 1978)
*Management of Stress: Using TM at Work* by David R. Frew (Chicago: Nelson-Hall, 1977)

---

*From *TM and Business* by Jay B. Marcus, pp. 164-166, Copyright © 1978 by Jay B. Marcus. Used with permission of McGraw-Hill Book Company.

*The TM Program: The Way to Fulfillment,* by Philip Goldberg (New York: Holt, Rinehart & Winston, 1976)

*TM: Discovering Inner Energy and Overcoming Stress,* by Harold Bloomfield, Michael Cain, Dennis Jaffe, with Robert Kory (New York: Delacorte Press, 1975)

## BIOFEEDBACK

In recent years investigators have demonstrated that we can exert some control over so-called involuntary body functions through the use of an electronic "feedback system." The feedback system allows us to monitor and manipulate body mechanisms once thought to be beyond our voluntary control. One function commonly manipulated is circulation: People have been enabled through conscious effort to lower blood pressure and increase the blood flow to different parts of the body. That's why biofeedback has been effective in relieving certain types of headache pain. In terms of its usefulness as a stress-control method, the results have been mixed.

Essentially, patients are trained to relax by manipulating certain physiological functions. The biofeedback device doesn't do anything but monitor a bodily change, keeping you aware of your progress. If all goes as planned, you eventually are able to associate specific subjective feelings with bodily changes. Eventually you develop the ability to elicit certain responses at will.

Most biofeedback training involves hooking up to a machine that monitors a bodily change associated with relaxation. The most common approaches involve monitoring GSR (skin's resistance to electric current, an indication of perspiration), skin temperature, EEG (brain waves), or EMG (muscle tension). All of these are good indications of the degree of relaxation or tension in the body. And it appears that, to a degree, increase in GSR, increase in skin temperature in extremities, reduction in muscle tension, and the presence of alpha brain waves are all associated with relaxation.* The machine signals you when you have achieved a given objective. Some experts claim that after a while, the feedback machine is no longer necessary.

Does it work? Sometimes, for some people. Feedback involves learning, and where there is learning, variances in native ability will be reflected in results. In order for biofeedback to work, conditions must be optimal: You must thoroughly understand what you are trying to accomplish, and you must be certain that the malady you are trying to alleviate bears some relationship to the function you wish to control. For example, a machine that monitors muscle tension will do little for

---

*However, other approaches, most notably the technique used in TM, bring about such changes in concert and without focused effort.

---

you if you are suffering from migraines or a cerebrovascular condition, neither of which causally involves the muscles.

You must be on guard against artifacts—false signals generated by "noise" in the feedback system. For example, gritting the teeth or assuming certain facial expressions will often produce "desirable" brain wave patterns. If care is not taken, you could wind up training yourself to grit your teeth.

The best way to get into biofeedback is through a reputable clinic where you will be under the care of trained specialists who use reliable equipment. Always begin with a visit to your doctor. And do not rush out and buy a commercial biofeedback machine without making sure that it is reliable and the proper machine for you.

## BENSON'S RELAXATION RESPONSE

Herbert Benson, M.D., of Harvard Medical School, was one of the original researchers on the physiological effects of the TM technique. He became convinced that TM was only one of many methods of eliciting a deep state of rest he calls "the relaxation response." He never learned the TM technique himself, but developed his own technique, derived from what he believes that TM'ers do when they meditate. What really counts is the effectiveness of Benson's technique. But although his research does indicate that some restfulness results, there is little to back up Benson's claim that it works as well as TM: The studies on the the TM technique were more rigorous than those conducted on the relaxation response. And Benson appears to be reasoning as follows:

1. The TM Program does good things.
2. Basically, the Benson technique functions according to the mechanism by which The TM Program functions.
3. Therefore, the Benson technique does all the good things The TM Program does.

Trouble is, nobody has yet proven statements 2 and 3.

All the basic information on the Benson technique is contained in Herbert Benson's book *The Relaxation Response* (New York: William Morrow, 1975 and Avon Books, 1976).

The TM technique is a conservative, time-tested method that stems from a tradition thousands of years old. Benson's technique is the invention of one man and has been practiced for less than ten years.

## SELF-HYPNOSIS AND AUTOSUGGESTION

Hypnosis is a trancelike state that results from focusing the attention on a set of suggestions and being receptive to them. We've all seen the more theatrical versions in nightclubs or on television. But a quieter, simpler form can be self-administered. Usually this involves being trained by an expert.

The hypnotic state can produce a feeling of calm. But the rest the body receives is no deeper than that of sitting quietly in a chair. In some cases, breathing becomes shallower. Many people find self-hypnosis relaxing and refreshing. But not everyone can learn it.

A variation, in which we "suggest" to ourselves certain attitudes or behavior changes, is called *autosuggestion*. This technique is often used to facilitate the breaking of habits, such as overeating and smoking. But conventional hypnosis, administered by a hypnotist, is more effective than autosuggestion in controlling habits.

## PROGRESSIVE RELAXATION

In some respects, Progressive Relaxation is the granddaddy of biofeedback. In 1929 Edmund Jacobson published this technique, which is based on a very simple theory: Emotional and inner tension manifests itself in muscular tension; by becoming aware of the nature and location of that tension and then relaxing the tensed muscles, we can produce a state of overall relaxation and thus a reduction of tension in the mind as well as the body. Progressive relaxation is a set of sequential physical and awareness exercises to achieve this state.

Since its introduction, many other specialists have modified the basic technique or developed their own versions. But Jacobson's basic approach is still around—and it does work to undo at least some of the effects of stress. You need a good half hour in a quiet place where you can lie down. And while the feeling of relaxation is subjectively quite satisfying, I have found no strongly persuasive evidence that Jacobson's technique is effective in fighting chronic deep-rooted stress.

A good summary of the Progressive Relaxation method appears on pages 204-206 of *Executive Health*, by Philip Goldberg (New York: McGraw-Hill, 1978).

## AUTOGENIC TRAINING

This sequence of exercises designed to induce deep relaxation was developed by German psychiatrist Johannes H. Schultz. This technique draws from self-hypnosis, autosuggestion, Jacobson's Progressive Relaxation, and yogic breathing exercises. In many cases it does produce some relaxation. But, as with the Jacobson technique, the scope of its effectiveness is problematic.

It's best to learn Autogenic Training from a knowledgeable psychiatrist or psychologist. But Jere Yates's book *Managing Stress* (New York: AMACOM, 1979) offers a reasonably good do-it-yourself summary.

## BREATHING DEEPLY

Most of us breathe in a shallow manner, taking short breaths and never actually filling the lungs with fresh air or emptying them entirely of old air. Breathing deeply from the diaphragm, filling the lungs, will reduce tension and fatigue.

## MASSAGE

Massages can be very relaxing and beneficial. If you are seeking a professional massage, make sure the masseur or masseuse is licensed. One who is not properly trained can cause injury.

Rubdowns are generally less effective than Swedish or Shiatsu massage. You can do a lot of good through self-massage. And if you are careful and follow instructions, a massage by a spouse or a friend can be quite effective.

## STRETCHING

An important part of any exercise program, stretching also greatly encourages relaxation. The most comprehensive and clearly illustrated book on stretching techniques is *Stretching*, by Bob Anderson (Bolinas, CA: Shelter Publications, 1980).

## YOGA

This term means, literally, union, and it applies to many systems of mental, physical, and spiritual development. Hatha yoga, the form of yoga most commonly practiced in the West, employs, among other techniques, a series of asanas (poses, or postures) and breathing exercises to achieve a state of physical and mental well-being and an expansion of awareness.

Hatha yoga practiced health-spa style is simply a set of stretching exercises used out of context. They may help you loosen up, but this approach misses the ultimate aim of hatha yoga—enlightenment. And in order for hatha yoga to have any real affect on stress, it must be practiced diligently, with a proper sequencing. Such discipline is time-consuming and requires the attention of a good teacher; such teachers are few and far between.

# 12

# USE IT OR LOSE IT: EXERCISE FOR EXECUTIVES

Being in shape is, of course, a question of life-style. It involves stress control, proper nutrition, and sufficient rest, as well as exercise. But, increasingly, researchers are finding that exercise may be the most important aspect of health maintenance. The effects of regular exercise seem to spill over into other phases of life: Exercise has a profound impact on both weight control and stress control; and it builds self-confidence, an important component of good health.

## WHAT IS "IN-SHAPE"?

There are many different opinions and parameters. Apart from purely medical concerns, getting in shape is a highly personal matter, dependent on individual goals and needs. If your hobby is mountain climbing, you'll have to train harder than your friend the golfer. But, in general, there are certain minimum standards that must be applied if your exercise program is going to help keep you healthy.

In this sense, the executive—or, indeed, anyone who wants to use exercise effectively—has some things in common with the athlete. The exercise programs that prepare one for sports competition are often those that also lead to health, happiness, longevity, and better job performance; and the basic rules of training and diet apply equally to the executive and the athlete. Further, the primary goals of a soundly structured exercise program are the same for athlete and nonathlete. Each one of these goal should be served in your workouts:

**Flexibility.** Often neglected, this goal is a must. Even if you are fit in other ways, tightness in the muscles, ligaments, and joints will restrict your movement and make you more susceptible to strains and sprains.

Gaining flexibility is simple. Do stretching exercises before and after strenuous activity and on a regular basis (daily if possible) as part of your fitness routine. Books for runners, tennis addicts, and even roller skaters usually include some recommended stretches, but most people I know skip over those parts. That's a mistake.

The goal of stretching is not the sort of flexibility required for contortionist tricks. Rather, we stretch to tone our muscles and connective tissue, and to relax our body and increase fluidity of movement. Nor is stretching meant to be painful. A stretching sensation is not the same thing as pain.

A do-it-yourself test of flexibility: Sit on the floor with your legs straight out in front of you. Touch your toes, holding the position for sixty seconds. Next, sit with your legs spread. Bend forward, placing your elbows on the floor between your legs, fists together. Bring your forehead to your fists; hold for sixty seconds. These two positions test the bare minimum in flexibility. If you have difficulty, you should be especially conscientious in your stretching.

**Strength.** Strength alone is not an important requirement for fitness. But a healthy body is usually a strong one: The muscles are firm and in good tone. In addition, it is important that opposing muscles be well-balanced. If one muscle is very well developed and an opposing muscle is very weak, it could produce instability in the body. Many executives have sufficient strength in their arms and chests, but weak lower-back and abdominal muscles.

One popular method of increasing strength is isotonic exercise. The muscles are pitted against a moving, steady resistance. This brings about a gradual increase in strength. Weights and exercise machines are often used.

**Muscle mass.** This is perhaps the least important aspect of fitness. Unless, of course, you are vain and want to hold your own at muscle beach or the company picnic. Don't underestimate the power of vanity. According to the director of one of the nation's largest executive health consulting firms, the principal motivation of businessmen to get in shape is vanity. "They aren't as afraid of a coronary as they are of looking bad as they grow older."

You build muscle mass through maximum effort—isometric exercise, in which the muscle works against an unmoving resistance. Weights and machines can be used to build mass.

Enlarged muscles are not necessarily strong. But they are heavy—heavier than fat. So if building muscle is your bag, don't be surprised to see your weight increase rather than decrease.

**Endurance.** The main event. Endurance depends upon the ability of the muscles to store and burn energy and the ability of the cardiovascular system to deliver large amounts of oxygen. In short, it comes down to how long you can last at a particular activity or sequence of activities.

180

In a larger sense, endurance is concerned with how long you can last at the activity we call life. Endurance training increases the body's ability to meet the physical and mental demands made on it each day. That is why endurance training is far and away the most important phase of any fitness program.

Endurance is primarily a function of the cardiovascular system (abbreviated CV from now on). CV fitness programs involve pushing the body well beyond its "normal" operating capacity, but still within the limits of health. The idea is to throw the body into high gear for a short time, which is something the typical American rarely does in day-to-day activity.

There are various viewpoints concerning just how hard you should push. They range from 80 percent of maximum attainable heart rate for 12 minutes every day, to 60 percent of maximum for 30 minutes three times a week. One plan calls for reaching a pulse rate of 130 beats per minute and keeping it there for five minutes every other day.

Exercise that brings about this effect is called *aerobic,* because it is designed to increase the maximum amount of oxygen that the body can process in a given time. Aerobic exercise does this by increasing the lungs' ability to suck in large amounts of air, expanding the heart's capacity to deliver large amounts of blood, and improving the vascular system's capability to deliver the increased blood volume to all parts of the body.

Increasing your aerobic capacity delivers an important by-product that can greatly reduce the risk of coronary accident. Regular aerobics actually results in the enlargement of coronary arteries, which reduces the likelihood of blockage. There is evidence that in some cases, the body grows new vessels to supply the heart; these new vessels could provide an alternate in case of blockage. But such findings are far from conclusive.

Since one uses a great deal of energy during strenuous exercise, the fat concentration in the blood is lowered. So is blood pressure, in many cases, because of the enlargement of the vessels.

No one can say for certain how much protection aeorbics provides against heart disease. But judging from studies done on athletes, there is little doubt that it strengthens the heart. The heart of a well-trained athlete is more muscular and therefore pumps the same amount of blood with 50 beats as the average Joe pumps in 75. That's a saving of 13 million beats a year! So the jock heart works less and rests more. All other things being equal (they never are, though), a heart that maintains this efficiency should last longer than the average.

WHAT DOES AEROBIC EXERCISE CONSISTS OF?  Anything that gets it up—your heart rate, that is. The most accessible aerobic exercise is running, but any vigorous exercise that moves your entire body will probably do the job. Some popular methods are biking, swimming, rowing, cross-country skiing, and machines that simulate these activities. Any exercise shown to be aerobic (and safe) will do. The key is to pick something you like; otherwise, you'll have difficulty staying with it. And, because of a phenomenon known in sports-medicine circles as reversibility, if you don't do the exercise regularly, you won't accrue its benefits.

*Reversibility.* This is backsliding. The body is constantly adapting, and just as it adapts positively to the increase in physical demands made upon it, it will adapt negatively to inactivity. This negative adaptation takes place a lot faster than positive adaptation—which is why you get out of shape a lot faster than you get in shape. A layoff of just a few days produces noticeable backsliding. A few weeks will be serious.

Every desk jockey who exercises irregularly experiences this reversal. The muscles slacken, permitting us to slouch easily. The rear end fattens to make sitting more comfortable. And with neither an increased demand for oxygen nor the aid of active muscles, the heart beats in a quick and shallow fashion.

*What about weekend workouts?* Great fun, but they don't work. Whatever endurance gains you make over the weekend, you give back if you are inactive during the week. Your skill at a particular activity may very well improve, but not your overall fitness.

Another important point: *Light exercise provides no real endurance benefit.* In most cases, it won't even cause you to lose any weight, unless you spend hours at it.

---

## EXERCISE AND WEIGHT CONTROL

---

Most experts agree that exercise and weight control are the main ingredients of health maintenance. No matter what the diet program involves, the only way to lose weight is to burn more calories than you take in. And this is where exercise comes in.

**Exercise burns calories.** The amount of fuel you burn is a question of how much weight you move, and the distance you move it. How the weight is moved—what type of exercise you do—doesn't matter. For example, if you move your body 18 inches off the floor with each pushup, you burn the same number of calories as you do when you take an 18-inch stride during running. If it seems tougher to do a pushup than to take a running stride, that's because the pushup (using your arms to lift your body off the ground) is a tougher way to move weight than is running (using your legs—which are longer and more powerful).

If you are interested primarily in burning calories, choose the way that's fastest and/or most congenial for you. If you want endurance benefits too, you may have to modify your plan.

---

**Exercise helps control appetite.** Research indicates that the appetite control mechanisms of the body work better in active people. After adopting an exercise regimen, some people eat more than they did before; some eat less. But usually, the result of regular exercise is movement toward a healthier body weight and better eating habits. When active people eat more, it is usually a justifiable increase rather than a case of gluttony.

Exercise helps stabilize the blood-sugar levels. Fat is utilized, so there is less often a need to take sugar out of the bloodstream. Since a drop in blood sugar triggers hunger, it isn't surprising that active people are less hungry than inactive people.

Many people eat out of nervousness or anxiety. The relaxing effects of a swim or a jog can help them cut down on compulsive eating.

**Exercise helps you lose the right kind of weight.** When you diet, you lose muscle as well as fat. If you don't exercise, about 25 percent of the weight lost will be muscle. If you are active during dieting, you will tend to lose a lower percentage of muscle, because your body needs that tissue. Rather, the loss will come more from the stores of fat in your body. Many executives who convert rapidly from inactives to exercise freaks find that they lose not pounds, but inches. That is, they replace the lost fat with muscle, so there is minimal weight loss. But because what is left is solid, the appearance is trim and healthy.

If you choose not to exercise while dieting, you should do so when you go off the diet. When you start eating normally, you will gain back some weight, and unless you exercise, all of that weight will be fat. So the net result of the diet will be that you lost some fat and some muscle—and replaced it with 100 percent fat. You may weigh a few pounds less, but the percentage of body fat will have increased. Women must be especially careful, because their bodies normally contain a higher percentage of fat than men's bodies do, and that percentage increases with age.

## EXERCISE AND MOOD

Undoubtedly, you've heard runners speak of the "natural high" they get. Well, there does appear to be a correlation between exercise and a more positive mood. There are various theories, none proven.

**A matter of balance.** The upshot of all this is that there is no easy or quick way to stay in shape; you just can't get by on a few minutes a week. However, exercising can be enjoyable. Pick a program you like and a structure that you can live with. A well-balanced workout should include some stretching, some endurance, and, if possible, some strength exercises.

Be sensible. Don't train too hard or too much. Such effort can actually reduce your training time by causing you to slack off early in the workout, or by making too many demands on your schedule, causing you to skip workouts. On the other hand, expect that once in a while a skipped workout and a rich meal will be unavoidable. If you can keep them to a minimum, there's no need to feel guilty.

## WHERE TO WORK OUT: CHOOSING AND USING A HEALTH FACILITY

Health spas, health clubs, gyms, and fitness centers all purport get you in shape, help you lose weight, and mold a movie-star figure out of your once-flabby or once-skin-and-bones self, as the case may be. The simple fact is, all of these places are only facilities—that is, rooms with machines, pools, saunas, and whatever the latest wonder-gizmo happens to be. If any molding and shaping is done, it is done by the individual. It's his time. And his sweat. Which brings us to the first rule:

**Before joining a health facility, be prepared to go there three to five times a week.** If you are not, don't waste your money. A spa can't do a thing for you if you don't put in the time.

**Examine the facilities first.** A wide range of facilities call themselves health clubs or spas. Some have pools, tennis courts, saunas, and exercise rooms. Others are strictly for exercise. You've got to see for yourself, because the advertising can be misleading. A place may have one tennis court that is poorly kept and always in use, but the ad would have you believe that tennis is a principal feature. Ask yourself if the facility is the kind you want. Does it emphasize training and conditioning, or sports? Does it seem more like an "urban country club" than a serious fitness center? If it isn't what you want, look elsewhere.

**Is the staff qualified?** Many spas claim to have fitness experts, nutritionists, even physiotherapists who will custom-tailor a program to meet your needs. Experienced, well-trained professionals in these areas cost money to hire. You should be able to get an idea of how qualified such supposed experts really are by talking to them and watching them work. If the facility offers you a trial membership, make sure that you put the staff (as well as the machinery) through its paces.

**Beware of high-pressure sales tactics and false claims.** The FTC has found evidence of misleading sales and advertising tactics, unsubstan-

184

tiated claims, unqualified medical claims, false benefits of the spa, and even confusing fine-print contracts that don't say what the salesperson says they say. In some cases, spa owners put most of their money into ads and sales; once you sign up, they actually try to discourage you from coming often, so they can keep signing members without overcrowding.

**Make sure you receive proper instruction in using the exercise machines.** Progressive-resistance machines like Nautilus and Universal are the rage. But most experts point out that they can cause injury if not used properly. Once you've had a bad experience with a machine, you will tend to avoid it, missing out on its benefits.

**A unique approach.** When people are left to themselves, they rarely train properly. There is a tendency to work the parts of the body that are already in good condition. One avoids pain and looks vigorous in the gym, but the benefits are minimal.

As for machines, they are only as good as the people who operate them. And if you've got to wait in line to use a particular one, there might be a tendency to skip it.

With this in mind, professional athletic trainer Michael O'Shea opened the Sports Training Institute in Manhattan. His approach is to give each member his own trainer, who takes him through the entire workout. The choice of which machines to use (as well as when to use them, with how many repetitions) and the structure of the aerobics workout are all left to the trainer. With a trainer on your back, it's tough to slack off or cut corners, and the machines get used properly.

Originally, STI was a gym geared primarily toward the needs of pro athletes who had to get or stay in shape, or who required special programs because of an injury. But the word got out, and soon, many top executives were asking O'Shea if they could join. Now the membership includes executives, athletes, actors, models—anyone who is serious about fitness, willing to work hard at least three times a week and able to afford the $2,000 that membership can cost for a year.

I hope the concept will catch on in other cities. It really works.

# 13

# A LEAN COURSE IN NUTRITION

According to a 1978 survey conducted by ABC News and Louis Harris, eating is the number-one leisure activity of American men and women. We do so much of it, it is amazing that we aren't better at it. And since we're among the best-fed people in the world, good nutrition should be . . . er, a piece of cake.

If you don't maintain a well-balanced diet and good eating habits, sooner or later you will do yourself a lot of damage. Here's what you need to know.

## CARBOHYDRATES

These are sugars, starches, and cellulose. Carbohydrates are the chief source of energy, providing the body with fast, cheap fuel. They also help us utilize fat and protein. Snacks high in carbohydrates are good before exercise or other demanding activity, because they are quick energy. The trouble is, many of us tend to include too much carbohydrate in our diet, thus crowding out other important foods. Diets high in carbohydrates tend to be low in vitamins and minerals mostly because they include large amounts of refined foods such as white flour and white sugar.

## PROTEINS

Protein has become an "in" food, primarily because experts have found few bad things to say about it. However, its importance is overrated. By that I mean that since the average American eats twice the protein required, there is little reason to worry about not getting enough. Next to water, protein is the most plentiful substance in the body.

Protein is the major building material of muscles, skin, hair, and internal organs. The body requires about twenty-two amino acids to synthesize protein, and it can make fourteen all by itself. The remaining eight, which must come from the diet, are called "essential amino acids" (looks great on food labels). Foods that contain all eight are called "complete proteins."

Most meat and dairy products are complete proteins. Vegetables and fruit are incomplete.

To clear up a few common misconceptions: Protein needs don't increase with activity—even an athlete needs no more when competing than he does at rest. As an energy food, protein is rather inefficient. Its energy yield is lower than that of both fats and carbohydrates, and it costs more.

Protein-rich animal products also contain lots of fat, so it is wise not to derive all your protein from them. Eat fresh fruits and vegetables, grains, and beans.

---

# FATS

---

Ounce for ounce, fats furnish more energy than any other major class of food provides. They also serve to carry the fat-soluble vitamins, help maintain body temperature, cushion internal organs, and round out the body contours.

Fats are made up of fatty acids, of which there are two types—saturated and unsaturated. Saturated fats are solid at room temperature and come from animal sources. Unsaturated fats are usually liquid at room temperature and are derived from grains, vegetables, nuts, and seeds. Sometimes they are hardened by a process known as hydrogenation.

Unsaturated fat has become popular in the forms of margarine and cooking oils, because it is cholesterol-free or low in cholesterol. (More about cholesterol later.)

Because of the high caloric content of fats, eating excessive amounts of them will lead to obesity. They can cause poor digestion by slowing it abnormally.

---

# VITAMINS

---

Vitamins have no energy value, and they are not used in the composition of bodily structures. But without them, the body couldn't convert food into energy or make tissue. Vitamins are vital constituents of enzymes, which regulate almost all bodily biochemical reactions. Vitamins are derived from animal products, fruits, and vegetables; and the human body can synthesize only a few.

---

The importance of vitamins is one of the most hotly contested topics in nutritional science. What is at issue is not whether we need them or not, but the dosages required. Recommended Dietary Allowances (RDAs) have been established by the National Research Council, and these standards are undoubtedly safe levels, designed to meet the vitamin needs of the "typical American." The trouble is that the "typical American" exists only in statistics. Climatic conditions, amounts of physical activity, eating habits, and the types of food eaten all have an effect on nutritional requirements. And, recently, research has demonstrated that stress can increase vitamin needs.

The fact is, very little is known about vitamins and the proper amounts needed. Most doctors know very little about the subject. In medical school, only minimal time is devoted to nutrition.

Use the RDA figures as a guide, but be sensitive to signals from your body that your diet might be lacking in some way. Excessive fatigue, anxiety, depression, or chronic aches and pains are common signs of vitamin insufficiency. If you can't identify the nature of the problem yourself (see Fig. 24, at the end of this chapter), then it might be wise to consult a nutritionist. Certain chemical analyses performed on blood, urine, and hair have proved helpful in nutritional analysis.

Unfortunately, taking vitamin supplements can be as dangerous as suffering a deficiency, because excessive amounts can be harmful. Some vitamins are actually toxic at high levels, while an excess of others is simply excreted in the urine, rather than stored. And there is no conclusive evidence that vitamin supplements improve performance, strength, or endurance, increase energy, or prevent colds or injury.

Another important point: It's not what you eat that matters most, but what you *assimilate*. Even a vitamin-rich diet can turn out to be deficient if you're a heavy smoker or a heavy user of laxatives or aspirin—substances known to interfere with vitamin absorption.

There are a great many athletes and executives that swear that vitamin supplements have done remarkable things for them. If you feel they are helpful to you, then go right ahead in spite of the smirks of your doctor. Just make certain that you are aware of the maximum safe dosages, the potential side effects, the best time to take the vitamins, and the adjustments you must make in your diet. And try to establish beyond a reasonable doubt that it is the vitamin program that deserves the credit for your improved health, not another positive step, such as an exercise or a diet regimen, that you may have taken around the same time.

## THE "IN" VITAMINS

There are at least twenty known vitamins, but, lately, people have become the most concerned and excited about:

VITAMIN C   Ascorbic acid is a water-soluble vitamin most commonly found in citrus fruit and fresh vegetables. We've known for years of its importance in maintaining the health of connective tissue and its role in promoting healing.

Any amount of Vitamin C that you can't use immediately passes out of the body within a few hours after you've swallowed it; the excess is eliminated in the urine and perspiration. The controversy over vitamin C concerns the minimum dosage, with estimates ranging from the 45 milligrams RDA, to the 2,300-9,000-milligram range recommended by Linus Pauling.

Another aspect of the controversy focuses on the benefits. Recently, claims have been made that megadosages of C can prevent or cure the common cold, treat drug addiction, fight common viral diseases, or even cure cancer. Once again, there is no conclusive evidence supporting any one of these claims, but no shortage of people willing to step forward and testify to their validity as a result of personal experience.

The most common side effect of vitamin C overdose is diarrhea. But since we pointed out the proposed-but-not-fully-substantiated benefits of the vitamin, we'll do the same for possible negative side effects. Massive doses of C have been linked to kidney stones, decreased fertility, liver damage, miscarriage, bone fractures, destruction of vitamin $B_{12}$, and iron poisoning. And some studies have revealed the possibility of a vitamin C "drug dependence": There is a tendency for those who get lots of vitamin C to get scurvy more quickly, when deprived of the vitamin, than those who normally got a lot less C.

VITAMIN E   This fat-soluble vitamin appears to have several important functions. Very little is known about vitamin E and the proper dosages of it. Most of the claims made concerning vitamin E therapy are still unsubstantiated.

Vitamin E burst into the American consciousness because of its reputed role in sexual potency. Can vitamin E do anything for your sex life? Probably not. But a serious deficiency of E could possibly result in problems in the reproductive organs. Such deficiencies are rare.

Vitamin E supplements could be toxic. Almost as bad, they could be a waste of money.

VITAMIN $B_{12}$   Deficiency of this vitamin can be quite serious, both physically and mentally. The earliest and most common symptoms are fatigue and weakness.

Vitamin $B_{12}$ deficiency is rare. But since the substance is found almost exclusively in animal protein, pure vegetarians are susceptible to deficiency; those who shy away from animal products may require a supplement. If you eat dairy products, meat, fish, or eggs, you are probably getting all you need.

There is virtually no scientific evidence that large amounts of $B_{12}$ will have any value to someone who is getting enough. But there are a great many people who are hooked on $B_{12}$ injections and make all sorts of claims as to their benefits, especially as an energizer. Since no cases of $B_{12}$ toxicity have been reported, I suppose there's nothing wrong with the shots if you feel that they help you. But I have observed that most people who use them are people who don't eat properly, or don't get enough rest and exercise. They could be suffering from a deficiency that a glass of milk could solve just as easily. But then again, there are a few pro athletes who sing the praises of $B_{12}$.

# MINERALS

The body uses about seventeen minerals in making tissues and regulating biological reactions. Even though the body requires only trace amounts, they are vitally important, and often overlooked. The minerals are interrelated in their action, and a shortage of one can seriously inhibit the effectiveness of the others.

The most important minerals are calcium, potassium, sodium, and magnesium. These minerals interact in the body, and often a deficiency in one will occur in tandem with a deficiency in another.

**Calcium** is the most abundant mineral in the body. A great deal of it is stored in the bones, and the average diet is rich in calcium. So our supplementary requirements are minimal, with the exception of growing children and pregnant or lactating women.

There is some belief that we lose calcium when we exercise. This is untrue.

The treatment of certain diseases with calcium has been attempted, without conclusive results. However, calcium does appear to function well in some people as a natural tranquilizer or sleep-inducer. Excessive amounts of calcium or vitamin D can lead to hypercalcemia, which is the calcification of bones and tissue. Milk, cheese, and other dairy products are the primary sources of calcium. Dark green vegetables, dried legumes, and sardines also contain calcium.

**Potassium** serves many important functions in the body, including the regulation of activity in the circulatory and nervous system. Potassium helps keep muscles from overheating during exercise. In the process, it is released in the blood and excreted in the urine. As a result, exercise can deplete potassium supplies. So can high intake of alcohol, coffee, and sugar.

Potassium is found in virtually all fruits and vegetables, in fish, eggs, seeds, and nuts.

**Magnesium** is intimately connected with calcium. Increasing the calcium levels in the body calls for an increase in magnesium, both to counterbalance the effects of potassium and to aid in its absorption. Magnesium has other important roles to play in metabolic activity. Low levels can result in muscle cramps and/or fatigue.

Nuts and green vegetables are excellent sources.

**Sodium** is a very important mineral, found primarily in the body fluids. It is contained in virtually all foods, especially salt. We get so much of it that the concern is over too much, never over too little. More on that in the section on salt.

The only people who use sodium supplements, in the form of salt tablets, are athletes who sweat a great deal. But this remedy has been shown to be unnecessary, as serious salt depletion rarely occurs outside of deserts.

# WATER

Water is by far the most important food substance. It is the primary constituent of tissue, and it helps transport nutrients and waste products and helps control body temperature. You must make sure that you drink plenty of it. Fruits and vegetables are excellent sources of pure water.

With the recent popularity of bottled mineral water, debate has been raised over its value. Some drink it because of the good things (presumably minerals) it contains. Others drink it because of the bad things in tap water (chemicals, carcinogenic agents, bacteria). The jury is still out.

# THE BAD BOYS OF NUTRITION

These are the foods that recently have been insulted, maligned, and, in many cases, shunned. It's no fault of theirs, really. Each of these substances is a healthy, wholesome, nutritious food. The problem lies, as usual, in our abuse of these foods and our ignorance concerning their proper use.

### SUGAR

Well, it definitely promotes tooth decay. But it has taken the rap for more. The sugar we refer to is white sugar, a refined form that is pure carbohydrate and contains no vitamins or minerals. Some claim that it has no nutritional value. That is not quite fair. It is an excellent source of quick energy, and anyone who has experienced a "sugar rush" knows that in the right circumstances, the lift is welcomed.

We eat a lot of sugar, about a hundred pounds a year. You think you are cutting down by staying away from table sugar? Nice try, but most sugar enters our body through many other foods that we eat. White sugar is probably the most common food additive, next to salt. Besides the obvious, like cake, ice cream, cookies, and candy, white sugar is added to foods like ketchup, canned fruits, and soups. And foods such as spaghetti, white bread, and pancake mixes contain refined starches that quickly turn to sugar once digested.

A large intake of sugar appears to be a negative factor in health. Some nutritionists feel that sugar depletes the body of vitamins, minerals, and other nutrients by upsetting the delicate nutritional balances: Bombarding the body with about two pounds of sugar a week is sort of a nutritional bull-in-the-china-shop.

Many medical experts are skeptical about the extent of the damage caused by high-sugar diets. They maintain that we get so much more than we need in the way of nutrients, that even if sugar does have this depletion effect (and they don't all agree that it does), it causes little if any harm.

Others are not so sure. While they eschew the prohibition-era rhetoric of the anti-sugar movement, they have found certain links between sugar intake and several degenerative diseases. The most alarming are a connection with heart disease and the possibility that sugar elevates serum cholesterol levels. Sugar, of course, is bad for people suffering from diabetes and a disease called reactive hypoglycemia (low blood sugar brought on as a reaction to sugar intake), but there is little evidence to suggest that excessive sugar intake causes these diseases.

From what I've been able to discover, it certainly can't hurt to cut down on sugar. If you are average in your sugar intake and then cut your consumption in half, you will still be swallowing fifty pounds per year. That is not what I call depriving yourself of sweets. You should cut out table sugar, or at least cut down. Read food labels, and if sugar is one of the first ingredients mentioned (ingredients are listed in order of amount), try to avoid that food. Rely on foods containing more complex carbohydrates, such as bananas, beans, vegetables, and whole grains. This is especially important, because many people begin to crave sugar when they cut down on it. Satisfy your craving with a carbohydrate source other than refined sugar or starches.

Sugar provides energy. Period. Chances are, you eat plenty of energy foods in the forms of fats and complex carbohydrates; you just don't need that much sugar. It's just that you have developed a fondness for its sweet taste. Cut down. You'll probably feel better, and you just might save some money on dental bills.

## SALT

Since we sprinkle salt on food, we tend to overlook it as a major constituent of our diet. Foods like nuts, canned soups, and cold meats, and snack foods like chips and popcorn are loaded with the stuff. Fact: We don't need nearly as much salt as we consume. The average American consumes sixty times the minimum daily requirement.

There is a lot of evidence that high-sodium diets (a major ingredient of salt) do harm. Too much salt can contribute to the onset of hypertension, raise the body's potassium levels, cause blood clotting, and even interfere with the body's ability to *retain* salt.

Most people would do well to cut down on salt. Some dishes might taste a bit bland at first, but the taste buds will adjust rapidly and you will begin to notice subtle flavors in foods that heretofore had been obscured by the presence of lots of salt.

## CHOLESTEROL

Some years ago, heart specialists teamed up with certain food manufacturers to blacken the word *cholesterol* until it became synonymous with certain death. Cholesterol is a fat substance that the body uses to make hormones, nerve fiber, bile, and other substances and tissues. It is also a source of very high energy. It is important enough that our bodies are equipped to manufacture it. However, the more we eat, the less we make.

Cholesterol has been linked with heart disease. It travels through the bloodstream as part of substances called lipoproteins. Cholesterol is a major factor in the formation of plaque on the inside walls of blood vessels, which may lead to atherosclerosis, or hardening of the arteries, and eventually to heart attack or stroke.

In this regard, cholesterol has been considered the primary dietary culprit in the onset of cardiovascular disease. It has been treated unfairly for several reasons. First, it is only one of many elements that make up the glop that contributes to the clogging of vessels. There are also triglycerides, minerals, and collagen, to name a few. And there are other factors involved, such as heredity, fitness, and stress. For example, during the fight-or-flight response, the increase in blood pressure slams the fatty substances against the arterial walls. Most important, there is a great deal of disagreement on the relationship between serum cholesterol (cholesterol in the blood) and cholesterol in the diet.

Those who feel that there is a relationship between ingested cholesterol and cholesterol in the blood obviously advocate cutting down on the stuff—some drastically, like Nathan Pritikin, who puts his patients on a diet of 5-10 percent fat, with only five milligrams of cholesterol, down from about 600. Pritikin has had very good results, but other experts are quick to point out that his diet includes other significant changes for the better, and that his patients are put on exercise programs, which encourage weight loss and fitness. Many of his patients are treated at his Longevity Center in California, in an environment that encourages rest and relaxation—other signifcant factors.

Some manufacturers have tried to capitalize on the cholesterol scare by offering low-cholesterol and cholesterol-free food products. Some safflower oils and the like are quite healthy and natural. Others, like some margarines and egg substitutes, are largely chemical concoctions that many experts feel aren't so hot themselves. The best thing to do is cut down on fat by learning to eat less of it, rather than by hunting for substitutes.

Although there is little doubt that, as a general health practice, cutting down on fat is a good idea, many fail to accept the pernicious effects of cholesterol. And there is a lot of evidence to back up this stance. For example, men and women consume the same amount of cholesterol, but men have more heart attacks. Americans, Swedes, and Britons consume the same percentage of fat, but the death rate from heart disease in Americans is three times that of the Swedes and twice that of the Britons. Other comparative studies, between the Finns and the Dutch and between native Irishmen and their American immigrant brothers, also support the notion that fat consumption alone is not a major factor in cardiovascular disease. And then there is the well-known study done on the Masai tribe of Kenya. Their diet is almost exclusively meat and milk—high-cholesterol heaven—but the Masai are virtually free of coronary heart disease and hypertension.

The bottom line: Cut down on saturated fats, but don't single out cholesterol as the ultimate dietary evil.

## diet analysis

| Food Item | | Measure | Weight g | Calories | Protein g | Fats g | Carbohy-drates g | Water g | Calcium mg | Iodine mg | Iron mg | Magne-sium mg | Phos-phorus mg | Potas-sium mg |
|---|---|---|---|---|---|---|---|---|---|---|---|---|---|---|
| **Breakfast** | egg, fried. | 1 med. | 50 | 108 | 6.2 | 8.6 | 0.4 | 34.0 | 30.0 | — | 1.20 | 5.0 | 111.0 | 70 |
| | whole wheat toast | 1 slice | 19 | 55 | 2.4 | 0.6 | 11.0 | 5.6 | 22.0 | — | 0.50 | 18.0 | 52.0 | 62 |
| | honey | 1 tbsp. | 21 | 64 | 0.1 | — | 16.0 | 3.6 | 1.0 | — | 0.11 | 0.6 | 1.3 | 11 |
| | skim milk | 1 cup | 246 | 89 | 8.9 | 0.2 | 13.0 | 223.0 | 298.0 | — | — | 35.0 | 234.0 | 357 |
| | orange juice | 1 med. | 180 | 88 | 1.8 | 0.4 | 20.0 | 154.0 | 74.0 | — | 0.72 | 19.8 | 36.0 | 360 |
| | | | | | | | | | | | | | | |
| | | | | | | | | | | | | | | |
| | **Sub total** | | 516 | 404 | 19.4 | 9.8 | 60.4 | 420.2 | 425.0 | — | 2.53 | 78.4 | 434.3 | 860.0 |
| **Lunch** | | | | | | | | | | | | | | |
| | **Sub total** | | | | | | | | | | | | | |
| **Dinner** | | | | | | | | | | | | | | |
| | **Sub total** | | | | | | | | | | | | | |
| **Snacks** | | | | | | | | | | | | | | |
| | **Sub total** | | | | | | | | | | | | | |
| | **Total** | | | | | | | | | | | | | |
| **RDA** | | | | | | | | | | | | | | |
| **+ or −** | | | | | | | | | | | | | | |

*sample*

Fig. 24. Diet analysis chart
Enter the foods eaten at each meal, and use a nutrition table
to fill in the basic nutrition information for each food.
Then you can easily compute your total intake of the basic
dietary components and see where you are lacking.

196

| Sodium mg | Copper mg | Vitamin A IU | (Thiamine) B₁ mg | (Riboflavin) B₂ mg | Vitamin B₆ mg | Vitamin B₁₂ mcg | Biotin mcg | Choline mg | Folic Acid mg | Inositol g | Niacin mg | Pantothenic Acid mg | Vitamin C mg | Vitamin D IU | Vitamin E mg | Vitamin K mg |
|---|---|---|---|---|---|---|---|---|---|---|---|---|---|---|---|---|
| 169.0 | 0.03 | 71.0 | 0.05 | 0.15 | — | — | — | — | — | — | 0.10 | — | 0 | 27.0 | — | — |
| 119.0 | — | — | 0.04 | 0.02 | — | — | — | — | 0.010 | 0.01 | 0.60 | — | — | — | — | — |
| 1.1 | 0.04 | 0 | — | 0.01 | 0.004 | 0 | — | — | 0.001 | — | 0.06 | 0.04 | 0.21 | — | — | — |
| 118.0 | 0.01 | 998 | 0.10 | 0.44 | 0.100 | 1 | — | — | — | — | .25 | 0.90 | 2.50 | 100.0 | — | — |
| 1.8 | 0.14 | 360 | 0.18 | 0.05 | 0.108 | 0 | — | — | 0.010 | 0.38 | 0.72 | 0.45 | 90.0 | — | 0.43 | 0.002 |
| | | | | | | | | | | | | | | | | |
| 408.9 | 0.22 | 2,068 | 0.37 | 0.67 | 0.212 | 1 | — | — | 0.021 | 0.39 | 1.73 | 1.39 | 92.71 | 127.0 | 0.43 | 0.002 |

*Sample*

From *Nutrition Almanac,* by Nutrition Search Inc.,
John D. Kirschmann, Director, © 1979 by John D. Kirschmann.
Used with permission of McGraw-Hill Book Company.

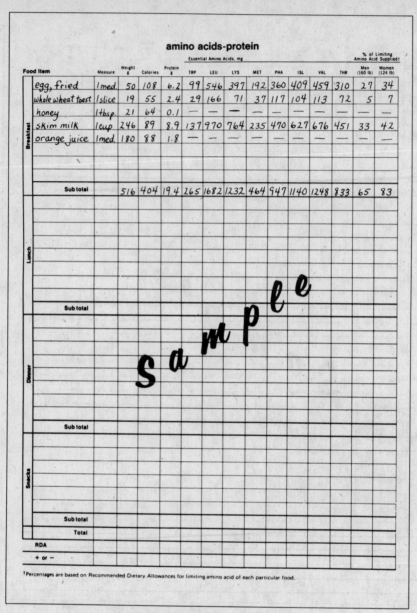

# amino acids-protein

| Food Item | Measure | Weight g | Calories | Protein g | TRP | LEU | LYS | MET | PHA | ISL | VAL | THR | Men (160 lb) | Women (124 lb) |
|---|---|---|---|---|---|---|---|---|---|---|---|---|---|---|
| **Breakfast** | | | | | | | | | | | | | | |
| egg, fried | 1 med. | 50 | 108 | 6.2 | 99 | 546 | 397 | 192 | 360 | 409 | 459 | 310 | 27 | 34 |
| whole wheat toast | 1 slice | 19 | 55 | 2.4 | 29 | 166 | 71 | 37 | 117 | 104 | 113 | 72 | 5 | 7 |
| honey | 1 tbsp. | 21 | 64 | 0.1 | — | — | — | — | — | — | — | — | — | — |
| skim milk | 1 cup | 246 | 89 | 8.9 | 137 | 970 | 764 | 235 | 470 | 627 | 676 | 451 | 33 | 42 |
| orange juice | 1 med. | 180 | 88 | 1.8 | — | — | — | — | — | — | — | — | — | — |
| Sub total | | | 516 | 404 | 19.4 | 265 | 1682 | 1232 | 464 | 947 | 1140 | 1248 | 833 | 65 | 83 |

*Essential Amino Acids, mg*

*% of Limiting Amino Acid Supplied†*

†Percentages are based on Recommended Dietary Allowances for limiting amino acid of each particular food.

Fig. 25. Protein analysis chart

Use this chart as you would the diet analysis chart. In this case, you are tracking your intake of essential amino acids.

From *Nutrition Almanac*, by Nutrition Search Inc., John D. Kirschmann, Director, © 1979 by John D. Kirschmann. Used with permission of McGraw-Hill Book Company.

# 14
# THE PHYSIOLOGY OF JOB PERFORMANCE

In a sense, your job is no different from that of an astronaut or a professional athlete. Even if you are in excellent health, your performance will be affected by several external and internal factors that act directly on your nervous system and, consequently, affect your ability to think and act.

## LIGHT

Sunlight is a nutrient; it is used by our bodies. Several experts have proposed that we aren't getting enough of it and our health is suffering as a result.

Artificial light is not a poor substitute; it is *no* substitute. "Cool white" fluorescent light is utterly unlike sunlight. Incandescent light, although it offers some benefits, cannot compare to sunlight.

Of the three, only sunlight contains the full light spectrum. There is some evidence that full-spectrum light influences endocrine activity in the body and stimulates the production of vitamin D (in a form superior to any form you can buy as a supplement, and therefore irreplaceable). The lack of sunlight may also retard our immune system, affecting our ability to fight off disease, including cancer.

What can you do? Well, if this makes sense to you and you want to get more sunlight, you can do so without burning yourself to a crisp on some beach. What you really want is natural daylight—you don't need bright sunlight. A fifteen-minute walk each day will help. And you can install a special "full-spectrum" fluorescent bulb in your work areas. Several companies make them. Full-spectrum light affects your brain most directly through your eyes. But the glass in most eyeglass lenses, including contact lenses, distorts the solar spectrum. You can get full-spectrum lenses through your optometrist.

LIGHT ON THE JOB   Natural daylight is the most useful form of light for the workplace, but it is getting scarce. Artificial light produces more strain and fatigue. If you haven't a choice, make sure that the artificial light is diffused, rather than shining directly onto the page. Bounce it off walls and ceilings, or use good-quality reflectors. The result will be a more even light, with less glare. Avoid spotlights as a source of work light. They force the eyes to readjust constantly as they move from objects illuminated by the spot's beam to those outside it. However, spots are okay if used as part of a general illumination system or as attention-getters.

## SEATING COMFORT

Offices do not do nice things for the human body. In fact years of office work eventually take their toll, probably hastening the onset of circulatory diseases and contributing to chronic lower-back problems.

Since you spend a great deal of time sitting, you should spend some time selecting the proper *chair:*

The seat should be high enough so that your lower legs rest comfortably at a right angle to the floor and your feet rest "flat flooted." The thighs should then be horizontal, or approximately parallel to the floor.

The seat should not be so high that it puts pressure on your legs and thighs by "lifting" your legs off the ground and placing your thighs on an incline.

The seat should not be so low that your thighs are inclined and body weight is centered on your upper thighs. This is extremely tiring and bad for circulation.

You should sit upright with your back inclined *slightly* forward.

*Your desk or table* should not be so low as to cause slouching or so high that your arms seem jammed into your shoulders.

## HEAT

According to Peter Russell, your brain works best at 65°F (18°C). A temperature of 68-70° is simply too warm for optimal brain functioning. Wear a sweater and heavier socks if you feel chilled.

## CIGARETTE SMOKE

Even if you don't use tobacco, you may be one of millions of "second-hand smokers" due to the environment in which you live or work. In a smoke-filled room the nonsmoker is exposed to about 75.5 milliliters of carbon monoxide gas for each cigarette consumed. If you are sensitive to smoke, you could be running the risk of a health hazard. But even if you fail to notice any immediately adverse reactions, your performance could be affected.

Dr. Steven Thacker has noticed a decrease in attention span and an impairment of psychomotor abilities in people exposed to cigarette smoke. And since many find the smoke annoying, it can be a distraction and cause tension in the office.

Although it is not my intention to get into the controversy of smokers' rights versus nonsmokers' rights, it is worth noting that a resolution of the problem is a positive and significant step in terms of overall office performance. It should not be allowed to fester.

If you are a smoker, don't forget that some people have very strong feelings about cigarettes, and their perception of you will be affected if you light up. If a superior is annoyed by a smoke-filled room and you are sitting there with a lit cigarette, he will consider you the source of his annoyance. Some executives see smoking as a sign of weakness. For the sake of your career as well as your health, it pays to quit. But don't preach or boast or berate others. Being free of a bad habit is a plus; being obnoxious about it is not.

THE AMERICAN CANCER SOCIETY sponsors clinics, usually run by ex-smokers. The methods used involve an awareness of the behavioral aspects of smoking—what leads us to light up. Gradual withdrawal is aided by a buddy system and by a regimen of such substitutions as chewing on coffee stirrers or gum and keeping the hands busy with rubber bands. The sessions are free.

SMOKENDERS is a private program involving weekly two-hour seminars for two months. The general idea is to motivate you to *want* to stop, and then to help you withdraw. The first five weeks are spent learning about your smoking habits. By the end of that time you have quit, and the remaining weeks are spent in coping with the pangs of withdrawal. SmokEnders claims a 92 percent success rate by the end of the course. A year later, 22 percent of the initially successful group will have gone back to smoking. About 12 percent of beginners never finish the course. Taking backsliders and dropouts into account, about 45 percent of those who begin the program end up ex-smokers.

Contact:
SmokEnders World
Phillipsburg, New Jersey 08865

HYPNOSIS This involves making unpleasant suggestions regarding smoking while the subject is under hypnosis.

BEHAVIOR MODIFICATION The act of smoking is punished by such methods as electric shock.

AVERSION THERAPY Ever smoke three cigarettes at once? Most people get very sick, and the traumatic experience is one you don't forget easily. Not for people who have weak hearts or who are in generally poor health.

ACUPUNCTURE Smoking is treated by acupuncture in many different ways. Some are intended to reduce tension and relieve stress, helping the smoker who lights up out of anxiety. Other methods involve inserting needles in certain areas to alleviate the effects of nicotine withdrawal or to suppress the desire to smoke.

*Do all these methods work?* Yes. But none of them work for everyone. Some people claim that one or two sessions of hypnotherapy or acupuncture did the job; others required two years. It is important that you investigate the clinic and/or therapist before placing yourself in their hands.

## DRUGS

Drugs are a very serious problem among executives. The use of both marijuana and cocaine has increased markedly in recent years. But the real scare comes from the prescribed drugs. And of course, alcohol.

Alcohol is a drug. It also brings out the worst in other drugs. Since it impairs judgment and motor coordination, it lowers efficiency. Drinking at lunch puts you at a disadvantage. Even though a drink or two may relax you, it's better to find another way.

Taking more than two drinks a day can have a negative effect on health. (In this context, a drink equals two ounces of 80 proof liquor, six ounces of wine, or 16 ounces of beer.)

The Drug Abuse Warning Network (DAWN) has compiled a list of the ten most dangerous drugs. Some of them may surprise you:

- Valium
- alcohol in combination with other drugs
- heroin and other morphine derivatives
- aspirin
- flurazepam (tranquilizer)
- Darvon
- Librium
- Elavil
- phenobarbital
- secobarbital

## NOISE

Excessive noise levels can be downright harmful; and insistent, irregular sounds can cause distraction and annoyance. You can learn to live with the hum of an air conditioner, but the sequence of buzzers, beeps, hums, and clicks generated by a copier can be annoying if it's very near your desk.

## DESK FATIGUE

Doing desk work for prolonged periods can result in a syndrome that consists of mental fatigue, tired eyes, and tense muscles. Take frequent breaks to stretch, rest your eyes, and allow your mind to retreat, if only for five minutes at a time, from the task on which you were working.

## "FAR-OUT" FACTORS: DO THEY AFFECT YOUR PERFORMANCE?

### BIORHYTHMS

Scientists have known for years that many of our bodily functions operate in a cyclical, or at least rhythmic, fashion. But they have been unable to get data reliable enough to allow us to predict or regulate our performance or bodily functions.

Recently, however, several self-styled experts have advanced the theory of "biorhythms." It is loosely based on the work of Wilhelm Fliess, who formulated a half-baked theory of biological rhythms in 1887. The concept was okay, but the formulas were simplistic and awkward. Fliess probably would have faded into obscurity faster than the Dave Clark Five had he not hung around with Dr. S. Freud. Fliess was a skilled surgeon who operated on Freud's nose and was among the first to use cocaine as an anesthetic. (I wonder what *that* does to biorhythms.)

The theory states that among our many cycles are three biorhythms—physical, emotional, and intellectual. These cycles follow rigid patterns from low to peak: The physical cycle lasts 23 days, the emotional, 28 days, and the intellectual, 33 days. Supposedly, they are triggered at birth. The critical days of each cycle are at the start, the middle, and the end. If all three cycles are at a low point on the same day, stay home and watch soap operas; you are in for a bad time. But if they all reach their peak on the same day, you are in top form; now is the hour to mount your takeover attempt of General Motors. Thus you predict your probable performance.

This theory of biorhythms has attracted a surprising number of adherents, considering there is no conclusive evidence that they function as charted. Lately, however, few seem to care that much about objective studies, or about whether evidence is conclusive or not. If there's a chance, say athletes, airline pilots, and even executives, it's worth a try.

Nevertheless, I call your attention to an article in the April, 1978, issue of *Psychology Today*, in which Arthur M. Louis zapped the biorhythm theory but good. He pointed out that the biorhythms of one Reggie Jackson indicated that he would be a "bum," as we say in New York, during the 1977 World Series. Indeed, noted biorhythm expert

Bernard Gittleson had gone on record saying that Reggie would find it "very tough to get a hit."

Close. Jackson, you will recall, batted .450 and set a Series record by hitting five home runs. Louis, however, anticipated the rebuttal that one isolated case does not a counter-theory make. So he analyzed 100 no-hit baseball games between 1934 and 1975 and 100 heavyweight title fights between 1899 and 1976. There was no significant correlation between the presumed biorhythms and individual performance.

More studies are being done—on injury patterns of railroad workers and drivers of automobiles, for example. I confess that while I wait for the results, I'll continue to regard biorhythms as bunk.

## WEATHER

There is some evidence that the weather may affect your performance. And I don't mean that you might miss a day's work on account of snow.

ARE YOU "WEATHER SENSITIVE"? Many people have adverse reactions to excessive heat, precipitation, winds, high or low pressure fronts. Physicians and psychiatrists have observed a relationship between weather and:

- sleepless nights
- back pain
- upset stomach
- migraine
- depression
- loss of appetite
- irritability
- lack of judgment

Some estimates put the rate of weather sensitivity in its various forms at 33 percent of the population. There is not much you can do about it, except to be aware of the problem—and even that is difficult. There are so many other causes of the above-listed symptoms that it is almost impossible to tie them to the weather. The exception is when you change climates. If you live in Chicago and feel terrible in Miami on a winter trip, it could be that you are sensitive to heat and/or humidity. See how you feel when you return to Chicago—and note whether history repeats itself during any subsequent Miami trip.

If you are fairly certain you have a weather sensitivity, keep it in mind when you must select a location for a business meeting.

Most people are uncomfortable when the THI (temperature-humidity index) is over 73.

STORMY MONDAY  In 1960 *Reader's Digest* published an article on the possible effects of negatively charged oxygen ions in the air. Shortly afterward, GE and Emerson Electric started making ionizers for their air conditioners. The interest died down (GE and Emerson ceased production long ago), but the speculation did not.

*The theory:* Desert and mountain winds, thunder and lightning (electrical storms), and cigarette smoke are several of the conditions that give air a positive charge. Positive ions are said to be bad for you because they stimulate the thyroid to overproduce adrenaline and cause serotonin to be released in the brain. Serotonin, the theory states, is the real villain, because it causes the usual nonspecific stress symptoms: irritability, uneasiness, headache.

Ever notice how good you feel *after* a thunderstorm? Or in a mountain valley or by the seashore or a waterfall? The reason, believers say, is that these environments have an abundance of negative ions, which suppress the secretion of serotonin and clear viruses and bacteria from the air.

The cities are hotbeds of positively charged air, what with all the smoke, central heating (a big producer of positively charged air), pollution, and winds generated by "skyscraper canyons."

If you believe that there is something to this, get yourself an *ion counter* and/or a *negative ion generator.* Since the above claims have not been officially substantiated, negative-ion generators can be sold only as air cleaners. Indeed, they do take suspended particles out of the air (unfortunately, those particles can wind up on your walls).

Several mail order houses specializing in consumer electronics offer compact, efficient, inexpensive units.

You might want to spend some time in a negative-ion environment—they tend to be attractive places—and observe whether you feel better.

ALTITUDE  There is no doubt that altitude affects our performance. Some acclimate more quickly than others. Be careful not to exert yourself until you get used to the altitude.

POLLEN  Rain and ocean breezes tend to rid the environment of pollen. Forests are not good, because they trap the stuff.

SMOG  Not much you can do about it short of joining the Sierra Club. Listen to the radio for air-quality announcements. On "fair" or "poor" days, don't overexert yourself. When the conditions are more serious, stay indoors, limit activity, or get out of town!

## THE ATMOSPHERE AND YOUR BODY

Extreme heat, cold, altitude, or any sudden change in the weather can affect your bones and joints, and your heart.

# BURNING THE CANDLE AT BOTH ENDS

Not a good idea—but sometimes unavoidable. And if you have some discipline and a clear understanding of your own physiology, you can on occasion put out 500 percent without getting caffeine fits, hallucinations from sleep deprivation, malnutrition, or atrophied muscles.

Amid all the recommendations, estimates, and approximations made in this chapter, one fact emerges as irrefutable: Every individual is different from the "average," and requirements for effective health maintenance vary accordingly. We differ from one another in our tolerance of drugs and in our nutritional requirements. The stress symptoms that we display vary from one person to the next. No wonder everyone has an opinion on what is good for you and what is not.

Saying that everyone requires eight hours' sleep is absurd. That everyone requires 2,000 milligrams of vitamin C daily is equally absurd. But the more you can find out about your own needs, the better able you will be to gauge your own limits and live freely within them.

## SKIPPING SLEEP

There is no "normal" amount of sleep. Many people quite naturally sleep less than others. Even those who require less than four hours a night are not wildly unusual. It should come as no surprise that lower-than-average sleep requirements are quite common among the very famous or successful. Recent studies of confirmed "workaholics" also show less need for sleep.

Personally, I envy people who need less sleep than I do. It gives them that much more time to work and play. Until recently, I believed that you couldn't push it. But this is not quite true.

First of all, there may be a great deal of difference between what your body actually *needs* and what it is *conditioned* to getting. Years and years of sleeping about the same number of hours each night has its effect: If, now and then, we don't get that amount, the body reacts negatively. It's sort of like a bad habit, such as overeating. When you diet, you feel hungry at first, even though you are getting enough nutrition. If you are disciplined, you will eventually get used to eating less.

According to several researchers, the same thing appears to be true of sleep. You can retrain the body to sleep less, perhaps as much as an hour or so, without harmful effects. You just cut down gradually, about a half hour every two weeks. If you've been getting more sleep than you need, the fatigue and irritability should recede.

You won't lose much in the way of deep sleep. Rather, you will spend less time in a lighter stage of sleep, called REM (for "rapid eye movement"), during which you do most of your dreaming. The loss of some of this REM, or dream time, doesn't appear to be serious. Unfortunately, we don't know that much about the function of dreams: There may in fact be some side effects of dream deprivation yet to be discovered.

If you decide to attempt a sleep-reduction program, remember to keep a daily log and to sleep regular hours. Otherwise, you'll have trouble. Be psychologically prepared for some discomfort, and don't forget that you may require more sleep during times of great stress. (Don't begin this program during such a period.) Most important, don't overdo it. That means that you shouldn't cut down any faster than one-half hour every two weeks: Everyone needs sleep, and it is unlikely that you can get by on less than five hours. If you try to live on less than that and don't adjust after about two weeks, you've passed your limit; sleep a little more. Some scientists believe that sleep requirements may be in part hereditary—and you can't fight your genes.

A few other tips. Make sure that:

- the room is not hot
- your bed is comfortable
- you are not too hungry or too full
- the room isn't noisy
- the room is reasonably dark
- you exercise regularly during the day

FOR ONE OR TWO NIGHTS    Practically anyone can get by for one or two nights on less sleep than usual. Sometimes, just knowing that you'll be okay helps you get through the day without incident. But don't press it. Get a good night's sleep at the first opportunity. Naps can be helpful. Of course, there is a difference between needing less sleep and depriving yourself of what you need. Even a confirmed workaholic couldn't sustain a pace that required him to consistently come up short in the sleep department.

Have little doubt that being well rested is an important ingredient of success. The degree of rest and the degree of alertness are intimately connected. Robbing yourself of sleep will eventually rob you of good health as well. In order to maximize performance, and be able to skip a few hours of sleep when necessary, you must be able to sleep regularly and well. If you are troubled by persistent insomnia, see your doctor.

### FORGETTING FOOD

Skipping one meal, or even several, does not present a problem for a healthy person. It can even be a good thing. In our well-fed society, even several days without food won't result in any serious nutritional problems.

You should keep in mind that intense hunger can be quite distracting. And those with weak stomachs or poor digestion should avoid going for long periods with an empty stomach. It is usually wise to pull yourself from your work long enough to have a quick meal—one that is served quickly, not eaten quickly. Wolfing your food down to save ten minutes is unhealthy and absurd.

## ELIMINATING EXERCISE

You don't get out of shape overight, so it's okay to skip a workout here and there. But it's not a good idea to go too long without some form of exercise. If you are putting in ten-hour days at the desk, get up and go for short walks, even if it's only around the room. A little stretching is also a good idea.

## STAYING ALERT: AIDS TO CANDLE-BURNING

A cup of strong coffee is still the fastest and most reliable way to stay sharp under siege. As a general rule, avoid drinking too much coffee or tea. However, if you are usually moderate in your consumption, a few heavy-caffeine days won't hurt you, unless you are the type that has an adverse reaction to large doses of the stuff. It can cause irritability, tremors, nervous tension, and insomnia.

Stay away from drugs, including amphetamines. Some of them do stimulate the central nervous system and increase activity levels, but there is little evidence that they improve cognitive ability. And the depression and fatigue that follow, aptly called "crashing," can be disastrous. One other drawback: They can be habit forming.

Partaking of alcohol and cigarettes other than very sparingly will cause your performance to deteriorate rapidly. So will ingesting a very large meal, which tends to make one feel sluggish and dull.

I'm going to share a secret known only to the most successful workaholics. A great invigorator is ... fresh air. Open the window, breathe deeply. Or get outside. In general, air quality is important. Many people find central heating or air-conditioning very tiring. Negative-ion generators, humidifiers, and air filters all have their proponents.

# 15
# HEALTHY HARDWARE

A very large industry manufactures hundreds of devices, each claiming to be the "scientific" or "most effective" or "easiest" or "newest" way to good health. If you want to avoid throwing money away on useless—and sometimes dangerous—equipment, you had better educate yourself before purchasing. Many of the marketing tactics used in the industry are a mixture of hype, myth, pseudoscience and, in some cases, outright exploitation of our insecurities and vanity. Fortunately, the scientific facts are accessible, and the firms that make products with verifiable tangible benefits will always be eager to back up their claims with hard data from a third party.

## EXERCISE MACHINES

Most of this equipment is worthless, for at least one of several reasons. First, many involve unfamiliar or uncomfortable movements. Second, many lose their effectiveness with repeated use. Third, many are unsafe. Fourth, we easily become bored with them and stop following the routine.

If you are serious about acquiring exercise equipment for your home, you've got to have the available space—and be prepared to spend some bucks. These are the best investments. Choose from among:

**Aerobic machines.**
- exercise bicycles
- rowing machines
- cross-country ski machines
- treadmills
- jump ropes

Machines cost $300 and up for a model that will take the punishment of daily usage.

Of course, jump ropes are an exception. However, you should spring for more than a clothesline. Get a jump rope that is the proper length (it should reach your armpits while you are standing on it with *one* foot) and that has ball-bearing handles. Some have "jump counters" in the handle to keep track of the number of jumps.

**Strength machines.** Free weights are still the best, and they are even better if you get the benches, belts, and other accessories. But you can easily hurt yourself, so get expert instruction before beginning a lifting program.

Reviews of isometric exercisers like the Bullworker are mixed.

## ELECTRONIC MONITORING DEVICES

**Pulse rate monitors.** There are several types. Some involve inserting your fingers into the device. Some are placed directly on the pulse point. A unique bar-shaped device called Insta-pulse need only be gripped and an LED (light-emitting diode) readout registers your pulse.

Most of the devices I've tried are reasonably accurate. You'll want one that is portable enough to run with or use in the gym—and that responds quickly to changes in your pulse, so that you can monitor your heart's ability to return to its resting rate.

**Home blood pressure units.** These almost always involve the use of the inflatable cuff—similar to the one professionals use—called a sphygmomanometer. But many home models do not require that you listen for diastolic and systolic sounds with a stethoscope; this is done electronically.

The stethoscope method is more accurate, if and when you learn the proper sound. But any blood pressure device is a good idea for people with hypertension. And since most hypertension remains undetected, don't hesitate to take your own blood pressure if you get near one of these gizmos.

## EYEGUARDS

The most common injuries in racket sports involve the eyes. The damage can be extremely serious, and even a minor blow can cause complications. If you get hit, resist the macho urge to shrug it off: Go see an eye doctor.

The growing interest in squash and racquetball has led to the development of impact-resistant eyeguards. Your basic eyeguard is about $7, but eyeguards can run upward of $30 for the flashy, padded, goggle type. If you wear glasses, it's best to have prescription sports glasses made by an optometrist.

Adequate eye protection is also important in skiing, scuba and skin diving, and hunting. You can get prescription ski goggles, scuba masks, and swim goggles. Seeing well is important during these activities.

## BRACES

Most of the over-the-counter knee, arm, ankle, and back braces are helpful only in the case of a mild strain. Very often, especially in the case of the knee, a $3 brace provides a false sense of security. A good doctor will not only diagnose your injury, but will also prescribe the best brace for your problem. The high-priced professional athletes have subsidized great advances in the design of braces and supports. For example, I wear a knee brace originally designed for Julius Erving! You won't find it in any drugstore.

## SUGGESTED READING

A good health maintenance program might well begin with the hefting of a good book. If you want to delve further into topics discussed in Part III of *Executive Essentials,* check out these titles:

*Executive Health,* by Philip Goldberg (New York: McGraw-Hill, 1978)

*Managing Stress,* by Jere E. Yates (New York: AMACOM, 1979)

*Sportsmedicine,* by Gabe Mirkin, M.D., and Marshall Hoffman (Boston: Little, Brown and Co., 1978)

*Nutrition Almanac,* by Nutrition Search, Inc. (New York: McGraw-Hill, 1979)

*Stretching,* by Bob Anderson (Bolinas, California: Shelter Publications, 1980)

*Sleep Less, Live More,* by Everett Mattlin (New York: J. P. Lippincott, 1979)

*Running Away from Home,* by David Colker (New York: Jove Publications, 1979)

*The New Aerobics,* by Kenneth Cooper (New York: Evans and Co., 1970)

*Royal Canadian Air Force Plans for Physical Fitness* (New York: Pocket Books, 1972)

# PART IV

# WINNING

"Success is simply a matter of luck.
Ask any failure."

Earl Wilson

# 16

# THE SUCCESS SCRIPTURES AND WHAT YOU CAN LEARN FROM THEM

There is considerable overlap in the subject matter of business success books, but that is not surprising when you consider that power, money, happiness, and even sex are intimately interconnected in the minds of the public. It's tough to write about power without writing about money too. And a book about succeeding in company politics can't ignore the concepts of power and negotiation skills.

The primary differences among these books lie not in subject matter, but in perspective: The author perceives the obstacles to success in a certain context. The key is finding a book that reflects a point of view you can identify with.

Therein lies the reason that many bad self-help books become best-sellers. So many readers identify with the *problems and obstacles* set forth by the author that they willingly snap up the book even though solutions may be sorely lacking. For example, if you feel that politics and infighting are holding you back, you'll be drawn to a book on company politics. If you think you've got to become a better leader, you'll find yourself reading much the same information in a book on leadership or power. Sloppy or forgetful? How about a memory book? Disorganized? There are time management books.

Another consideration is the author's personal philosophy. Some people would not welcome advice that they lie in order to accelerate success; others wouldn't think twice before adopting this tactic.

The number of success formulas is unlimited. No seminar speaker, author, or business leader has a lock on "the best method." So if a friend of yours thinks that Robert Ringer is America's greatest living genius, but you feel unreceptive to his message, don't feel obliged to absorb his teachings.

There are several hundred self-help titles on the bookstore shelves. And there will be many more by the time this book appears. What follows is not an extensive review of success books, but, rather, a guide to the major criteria for choosing a success guru.

By the way—there is one principle of financial gain that most (but not all) authors omit: "There will always be people out there looking for a shortcut to success." If the number of success books in print is any indication, there must be plenty of such people around.

# WHO'S WRITING THIS STUFF?

Success formulas are based primarily on the author's observation, experience, and point of view. The successful entrepreneur might be quick to point out that you should rely only on yourself, but a corporate man who has built a successful career as part of a team might see it another way. So before you accept any of these books as gospel, consider where the authors are coming from. I've divided the exploding population of success gurus into several types:

## SELF-MADE MILLIONAIRES

In the publishing world, being a self-made millionaire appears to be a kind of qualification for writing a success book, as having a PhD in American lit would be for writing a Hemingway study. Why does a millionaire write a book on success? (1) He is not really a millionaire. (2) He is a millionaire, but doesn't feel he's quite rich enough. (3) Making money turns him on, even when he doesn't need it. (4) Pure vanity, plain and simple: He's rich, now he wants to be famous. (5) He really believes that he has something of value to share with the world. (6) His book is an attempt at self-discovery.

The most interesting kinds of "millionaire success books" are those written by those who do so for reasons (5) and (6). Many of this ilk feel somehow "plugged in" to the cosmic order of things. They wish to give expression to those principles, and they believe—in earnest—that they will work for everyone if applied.

Sounds weird? You should take a look at some of these books. Judging by some of the "rules" and "laws" laid down, we can conclude that in America, you needn't be a rational thinker to succeed—just a passionate one.

Personally, I do believe that there are some basic laws of nature that are so primal in form that they escape the awareness and perception of our complex and culturalized minds. And I do believe that some successful people have become so because of the sheer simplicity and basic truthfulness of their approach. Since such people often operate from intuition, their methods are often considered mystical, or just so much armchair motivational psychology.

If you pick up a book by Napoleon Hill, Clement Stone, or Og Mandino, take a second look before dismissing it as nonsense.

## INSIDERS

These writers succeed for many of the same reasons that made Hedda Hopper and Walter Winchell so successful. They orbit amid the inner circles of business, where they are surrounded by, if not steeped in, success (stories). This proximity arms them with a store of great anecdotes and rags-to-riches sagas. The problem comes when they attempt to extract useful "tips" and principles of success from their observations and conversations. This is a formidable job for even the most disciplined sociologist, who will at least strive to make his sources varied and well balanced, and will attempt to be objective. But the methods of popular authors appear to be strictly catch-as-catch-can.

Everyone learns by example. And the stories of the rich, famous, and powerful make fun reading. But even the winner himself may not be able to adequately explain why and how he got where he is. Therefore, it may be unwise to model your approach after an author's description of how several of his acquaintances or interviewees "made it."

Glean what you can from the success stories, even if it's only inspiration and a small tip about how to answer a phone. But be aware that many authors shoot from the hip—it saves time and trouble. Sometimes they hit. Sometimes their stories and principles strike a responsive chord, but following their advice on that basis alone can be disastrous.

## SCHOOLBOYS

The academics. Academics are hooked on scientific methodology. This means hypotheses, research, and theories. If they are successful, they come up with findings that encourage them to run grey areas into black-and-white. Often, they do so even if they are unsuccessful. I mean, who would spend three years studying "cross-cultural relations within the business community," only to announce that he has emerged with no theories? And, of course, there is the pressure to publish.

On balance, academic studies of the business community are quite useful. Just keep in mind that they often deal in norms, averages, probabilities, and statistical significance. So what they say may—or may not—apply to you, your co-workers, or your company. Studies of success in business can be valuable because they give you a sense of the values and methods of the environment in which you earn your living. They can give you a better view of the total picture.

Since academic studies often make no value judgments, but, rather, emphasize what is, and why it is, you get a "cleaner" feeling about success. An academic may subconsciously try hard to vindicate his theories, but it is less likely that he will be espousing a personal moral (or immoral) ethical philosophy—the stuff of so many how-to books on success.

Many studies are not published in books, but in journals; or they may be available only as limited editions through sponsoring research institutions or foundations or universities. You must peruse business abstracts or some type of business index if you wish to stay informed. Browsing through a bookstore, or even through *Business Week*, will not keep you abreast of the latest intelligence.

## TECHNICIANS

These are the authors whose bag is technique. Industrial psychologists. Engineers. Organizational psychologists. Management consultants. Logistics specialists. They will talk to you of procedures, principles, and methods. Organization. Reorganization. Flowcharts. Follow-through. Education. Communication. Evaluation. Backup. Feedback.

These authors can be very redundant, because many of the methods they evolve in seemingly endless variations are reducible to a few tried-and-true approaches to problem solving. But if you don't spend a lot of time reading such books, you won't notice the repetition. Besides, some of them are very inventive.

The basic tenet of the technicians' books is that success is the direct result of a job well done. Improve the workings of the company and your own lot will improve automatically.

One of the reasons, I suspect, that the managerial techniques books don't teach back stabbing, throat cutting, or even the tamer power games is that most of them are written from the point of view that the corporation is paramount; the needs of the individual come second. While this may be a good attitude to cultivate among American executives, a few facts belie it: Most of the people who *started* the companies were rugged individualists, with loyalties rarely extending beyond family and a few trusted friends.

Although many executives live happy, fulfilled lives as company men and women and are rewarded with nice benefits when they retire, most experts believe that the way to the top is not straight, but a zigzag through many companies. The reason: Competence is more important than loyalty, and other firms are less likely to be eager for your skills when you've all but blended into the woodwork as a loyal member of the "team." America is not Japan: U.S. corporations (with few exceptions) simply cannot be counted on to "take care of you." More important is the good old American tradition of striving for a bigger piece of the pie.

## GUNSLINGERS

These are the authors who are interested in telling you how to survive. To them, the executive's road to success is a matter of guerilla warfare, or kill-or-be-killed. In the unhappy event that you are working in a dog-eat-dog environment, you may need such books. But first you should ask yourself if this is really the kind of job you want to have.

Most gunslingers are erstwhile victims of business treachery who decided to fight fire with fire. It worked for them, they feel, and now they stand at the top of the hill, bloodied but unbowed. Fortunately, they are going to share with you their knowledge of the tactics of corporate combat, so you too can come out a winner. Unfortunately, these guys won't be around to help if you stumble and wind up like General Custer rather than Alexander the Great. Worse, you will probably have trouble getting them on the phone when you need a friend to talk to and you've already lost all the friends you had in your pregunslinger days.

There's nothing wrong with picking up a few secret weapons to protect yourself from the business world's seedier elements; these authors can help. Just remember that a weapon is only a weapon if you know how to use it properly. See such books for what they are—not blueprints for success, but tools of last resort—the lowest road to success.

---

# WHAT THEY PROMISE

---

## POWER

Books on power vary according to the definition of the term. A "power book" could be about getting the things you want, being able to influence, control, or manipulate people, gaining control over your own life, or any combination of the above.

The best-known book on the subject is *Power! How to Get It, How to Use It,* by Michael Korda (New York: Random House, 1975). This book is often interesting, but very uneven. Some of Korda's insights are worthwhile, but in my opinion much of the book is shoddy, offering advice based on questionable values and ethics.

I recommend to you *Power in Management,* by John P. Kotter (New York: AMACOM, 1979) as tops among the "power" books. It is based on a study of over 200 executives in 26 organizations. Kotter, an associate professor of organizational behavior at Harvard Business School, has a great deal to say on power-oriented behavior, the positive functions it serves, and how it operates. The findings ring true. The book is well written and well organized and gives you far more significant

---

information on power than Korda's book, in less than half as many pages.

## SUCCESS

Books about success arrive at a definition (or help you define it for yourself) and then give you tips on how to achieve it. Be careful, though: Many of these books attempt to prey on our weaknesses. For example, some books de-emphasize the role of skill and hard work in success. The authors will tell you that appearances and visibility count most; you are as great as anybody around, but you haven't been letting the world know. This explains the emphasis on the trappings of success. Don't be lulled into thinking that the only difference between you and the other guy is a matter of PR. Promoting yourself is fine, but not at the expense of performance.

In the world of publishing, one successful book begets another. Michael Korda followed *Power!* with another popular work, *Success!* (New York: Random House, 1977). Here's a notable quote that's bound to get you in trouble if you swallow it whole: "Ability and talent won't take you very far. You can even succeed through failure if you are calculating enough."

For all its "hard-nosed" observations and unrepresentative examples, *Success!* is not a bad book. Appearances *are* important, and Korda's book will help you maintain them. Just don't be fooled—there is more to success than what lies within its pages.

If ever there were a challenger to Michael Korda for the title of head success guru, it would have to be Robert Ringer. He is at least as good as Korda in devising gut-level book titles, just as fast in following up his first best-seller with another (*Winning through Intimidation* succeeded by *Looking Out for Number 1*), and far better at obscuring questionable ethics.

Ringer believes that successful people are not nice. His message, as I read it, is that there is some conspiracy to deceive people into being good while all the "winners" are out there putting the screws to everyone.

As in the case of Korda, Ringer does provide some specific advice that can be of value to the would-be king of the hill. But in doing so, he mangles and degrades human nature, and preys on the very weaknesses of others that he claims to abhor in himself. I suspect he does it for the shock value.

Where does money fit into all of this? As Korda says, "It's *always* better to be rich."

# WEALTH

You would think that if you have success and power, you would probably make money as well. Not necessarily. Some money books are *economic battle plans*. Others take the attitude that all the world is a Las Vegas casino, and you can beat the house. Just because a strategy for making money succeeds for some, it doesn't necessarily follow that it will succeed for you.

There are also "psych" books on money. You know, "the power of the subconscious mind": Dream about a Cadillac (or Mercedes, if you prefer) and you'll soon own one.

The most famous is *Think and Grow Rich*, by Napoleon Hill, originally published in 1937. This is a pretty good book. Hill is a true original. He is practical and thoughtful, and he has done his homework. While his principles may not always get you a million, they will usually help. It takes a special kind of person to lock into Hill's formula and follow his principles to the letter; they leave some people cold. But many have told me that upon reading Hill's book, they realized that they were doing what he suggests all along. His book validated their approach, thus firing them up. For those who can't get into this type of reading (I empathize), try the cassette version of *Think and Grow Rich*, published by the Success Motivation Institute and narrated by Earl Nightinggale, with a special guest pep talk by Napoleon Hill (yes, he's still alive). This tape is great while shaving or driving to work. Some like it before bed in place of the "Tonight Show" or "Starsky and Hutch." It'll give you the gist of what Hill is saying. If you like what you hear, go out and read the books, which are more detailed.

For a discussion of money books see Investment section.

# INSPIRATION

Inspiration comes in all packages:

EGO-MASSAGE   "I'm okay, you're okay, so why can't we both make it?" Learn to be your own best friend and pull your own strings.

RELIGIOUS   Do God's work and you'll get a commission.

MOTIVATIONAL   Success is within your grasp if you have the energy, willpower, and determination to go out and get it.

Inspiration and optimism are vital ingredients in everyone's life. Get them any way you can. Sometimes you can inspire yourself with the help of an insight or creative idea. One comment comes to mind, said by a well-known actor: "Talent is commonplace. What is rare is the ability to develop and exploit that talent." Chances are you've got what it takes. Go forth and figure out how to make it work for you. Don't take all this self-help stuff too seriously, but when you do pick up an insight, use it. And if you're uptight about being accused of being part of the "Me Generation," keep your how-to books to yourself.

A few popular inspirational books are *Self Love,* by Robert Schuller (Old Tappan, New Jersey: Fleming H. Revell, 1975), *Psycho-cybernetics,* by Maxwell Maltz, M.D. (Englewood Cliffs, New Jersey: Prentice-Hall, 1960), and *The Power of Positive Thinking,* by Norman Vincent Peale (Englewood Cliffs, New Jersey: Prentice-Hall, 1954).

Motivation expert Zig Ziglar, author of *See You at the Top,* offers a typical example of inspirational fare with a four-step formula:

- *Reverse the way you get out of bed.* Don't attack the alarm clock, Ziglar advises. Get up, clap your hands, and say, "Oh, boy, it's a good day to get up and go get 'em!"
- *Establish some symbols.* Change your vocabulary. Transform "stoplights into golights," "weekends into strongends," and so forth.
- *Set your gyroscope for success.* "If you want to be optimistic . . . you have to act it." Answer the phone with "Hello, it's a great day."
- *Feed your mind.* Listen to motivational tapes. Read inspirational books.

### RELIEF FROM FRUSTRATION

Many people are just plain unhappy with their lot. They are frustrated and bitter. Some books take their side, telling their readers that they are justified in feeling that the world stinks. Then the books turn to telling how to dish it out, giving tips on infighting, maneuvering, manipulation, and naked deceit.

Some people claim to have turned their lives around as a result of such a book. But they are the exceptions.

Other books provide relief in a more soothing, constructive manner. The most popular book for relieving pain is the Bible. Other pep talks designed to make you aware of what's wrong and how to set it right include Wayne W. Dyer's *Your Erroneous Zones* (New York: Funk & Wagnalls/T. Y. Crowell, 1976) and *I'm O.K., You're O.K.* by Thomas A. Harris (New York: Harper & Row, 1969).

### SPECIFIC SKILLS

These are the original self-help books. There is a wide selection of books on all sorts of business, management, and noncognitive skills. For example, the popular *Memory Book,* by Harry Lorayne and Jerry Lucas (Briarcliff Manor, New York: Stein & Day, 1974). Or *Memory Made Easy,* by Robert L. Montgomery (New York: AMACOM, 1979).

Will these books help? Depends. Some skills can be learned out of a book; some require personal instruction.

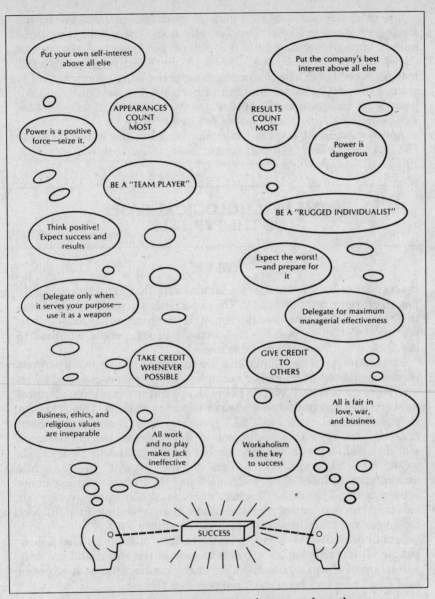

Fig. 26. Different perspectives on the success formula
Often, apparently contradictory viewpoints can be reconciled.
Success, to a large extent, depends on the ability to live with
ambivalent feelings, resolve dichotomies, and selectively
accept and reject values. The bubbles above represent
common points of view on success. As you can see,
many conflicts arise.

The most popular books on general management skills are by the manager's manager, Peter Drucker. His books have sold over three million copies (over one million copies of *The Practice of Management* [New York: Harper & Row, 1954]). To be effective, says Drucker, managers need both a basic competence and the will to perform. Profits are not the goal of a company, but rather a need. A vast distillation of his ideas and opinions appears in *Management: Tasks, Practices, Responsibilities* (New York: Harper & Row, 1974).

Another excellent work is *Leadership: What Effective Managers Really Do . . . And How They Do It*, by Leonard Sayles (New York: McGraw-Hill, 1979).

---

# THE PSYCHOLOGICAL BASIS
# OF THE PEP TALK

---

## SET

Psychologists have been able to demonstrate that expectation clearly has an effect on our perception. The expectations are called "set." Set is the basis for the common criticism, "He sees only what he wants to see." It is also quite possible that, because of set, people will tend to overlook what they are not expecting.

Further research has shown that we may help people live up to our own expectations of them. For example, a group that is expected by its teacher to do very well will do better than a group of children identical in every way except that they are not expected to excel. This is known in psychological circles as the Pygmalion effect,* and it has been observed not only in schools, but in the business and professional world as well. It may be that the teacher or other authority figure tends to notice and encourage success in the "smart" group, while overlooking failures. The teacher's "set" is toward above-average achievement. The same teacher may be set toward average or substandard performance in the other group, tending to point out lackluster work and pass over displays of ability.

Set not only affects our perceptions; it affects our beliefs. That is why people with strong beliefs are able to look at the world and see only validation of them, while others see many contradictions. It has been said that "religious people see religion everywhere."

This may be a news flash for you, but it comes as no surprise to the success gurus who preach "positive thinking" and other variations on the same theme: By creating a positive set—expectation—of success for ourselves and a positive self-image, we increase the likelihood of

---

*From Peter Russell, *The Brain Book* (New York: Hawthorn, 1979), p. 213.

---

fulfillment of our goals. Set programs our minds to lock into elements or events in our environment that support our activities.

Call it what you will—"psyching yourself up," "mind over matter," "positive thinking"—it does work, to varying degrees, in everybody. A problem may arise when you pick up a "pep talk" book that aims at creating a positive mental set: To begin with, you need to have the kind of set that leads you to expect that the book will work. And so it goes. That's why a book that comes highly recommended by a friend or relative you admire and respect is more likely to work for you. You are more favorably disposed toward it, and therefore it is more likely that the author's words will elicit a positive response in you.

There is an inspirational, pep-talk book for every "set" and every taste. Don't sell them short. Find one that you like. Better yet, don't sell yourself short. Many people don't need to be told how to create a positive set about themselves. And besides the books, there are other ways—like religious faith, warm family relationships, a pat on the back.

## IMAGINATION

It has also been shown that imagining or visualizing a situation helps to create a mental set in which the fulfillment of that "vision" is more likely.

Several psychotherapists have been able to help patients who don't interview well by showing them how to imagine themselves doing well at the interview, visualizing each step.

This may be related to hypnosis or autosuggestion. Napoleon Hill often speaks of visualizing the specific amount of money you wish to have. Just wanting to be rich is not enough, because it is too abstract. The greater the detail, the greater the ease and effectiveness of imagining and visualizing.

A good time to imagine or visualize is at bedtime, as you are drifting off, or when you awake in the morning. Any "quiet time" is suitable. But please, not at a staff meeting.

## WOMEN'S SUCCESS MATERIALS

Books and seminars on success in business directed at women are very much in vogue. Everyone is out to make a buck here, and because job discrimination has held women back, there is a shortage of genuine experts.

There are no real "rules" of success. And very little can be learned in a one-day seminar. Books for women contain essentially the same material included in those written for either sex, except that they usually give some attention to problems like sexual harassment, affirmative action, and the home/career conflict. But if you want only the basic facts about investments, skills, or general management, pick what you like without regard for the sex of the author or for whether the word *women* is in the title.

---

## COMMON ERRORS OF SUCCESS BOOKS

---

- Generalizing from the specific
- Assuming that survival-oriented behavior is premeditated
- Assuming that, for most people, power, money, and success are their own rewards
- Assuming that getting people to do what you want them to do requires deceit or coercion
- Appealing to, rather than debunking, the myth that acquiring power, influence, and success is for the hard-boiled who do nothing out of sheer altruism
- Assuming that the contents of their books can change the readers' behavior
- Believing that *admitting* that you are doing something purely for money or power places you above reproach
- Assuming that a quotation or two from a highly respected, definitive work constitutes a validation or approval of the author's point, just because the author being quoted may appear to be saying a similar thing

# 17

# WHAT EVERY BUSINESS PERSON OUGHT TO KNOW SOMETHING ABOUT

This chapter looks at important skills and concepts as though they were independent entities, for the sake of convenience and because we vary in our needs, strengths, and knowledge. But, in the final analysis, it's how you put them all together that counts.

## WHAT IT TAKES: A THUMBNAIL SKETCH OF THE SUCCESSFUL EXECUTIVE PERSONALITY

Psychologist Roger Birkman has compiled a list of major personality traits that set successful executives apart from their peers:[*]

**A need for power.** The successful executive appears to need power to accomplish his goals. For him, though, power is a *tool*, not an end in itself. Power must not become an addiction, and it shouldn't be exercised needlessly.

**A need for challenge.** All executives thrive on challenges; it's just that the more successful ones are better at selecting and managing them. When faced with a challenge, they are better at calculating risks. They don't create or accept challenges they can't meet.

The successful executive appears to have a need to put himself to the test, and a great deal of his satisfaction is derived from overcoming challenges.

---

[*]Adapted from Roger Birkman, "What Sets an Executive Apart from His Peers?", *S.A.M., Advanced Management Journal*, Summer 1978 (New York: S.A.M., a division of American Management Associations, 1978), pp. 59-63.

**Ability to delegate.** Effective delegation is very difficult to master. It involves a fair amount of risk. Often poor delegation is really not delegation at all. Rather, it is an attempt to impose one's methods or to pass the buck. The less successful executive may attempt to derive satisfaction by applying his own skills and getting things done his way. The more successful executive derives satisfaction from motivating, inspiring, influencing, and guiding others into turning in a superior performance. An executive who can effectively lead several subordinates is obviously worth more than an executive whose contribution is limited to his own output.

There should, however, be no misunderstanding: The executive himself must make the hard decisions and take responsibility for results.

**Ability to balance empathy and objectivity.** A successful manager can understand and empathize with the predicaments of subordinates, but at the same time view the situation in an objective light. This gift of balance is important, because the best interests of a worker and the firm are often at odds. And the worker's own view of what's best often differs from the manager's.

Less successful executives are often insensitive to the needs and feelings of others—or blinded by them to the extent that they lack objectivity.

It is emotionally easier to take a simple stand—either a confirmed disinterest in co-worker feelings and problems or a confirmed feeling of empathy. But the successful executive is the one who steps up and confronts the ambivalence, often making a decision that proves agonizingly difficult, precisely because he can see both sides.

Some years ago, psychologist Abraham Maslow noted that one sign of a healthy personality was the ability to accept and integrate ambivalent or ambiguous feelings and values.

**A need for competition.** This is common to most executives. But the more successful ones appear to have an expanded view of the process of competition and the joy of winning. They want to win, but in a manner consistent with their own methods and ethics. They are interested in long-range results—the war, not the battle. Effectively, they superimpose a code of honor upon the concept of "survival of the fittest."

In order to be successful, one has to stay on top. Those that do stay there know that honor and consistency—playing by the rules—makes one less susceptible to treachery.

**Independence.** Successful executives tend to avoid group-dependence. That is to say, they *do not require* group approval, reinforcement, or risk sharing. On the other hand, such executives *don't object* to working in groups when appropriate—and when they get results. Because their source of self-esteem and confidence comes from within, they see groups as vehicles for problem solving, idea and information sharing, and (as a sometime bonus) enjoyment of camaraderie.

**A need for change.** Birkman's analysis reveals that successful executives are more restless than the average. They prefer to achieve a broad perspective or overview and then move on, rather than to spend a great deal of time intensely probing a single subject.

Of course, this may be because, as successful executives, this is the nature of their jobs: They have larger responsibilities and cannot afford to dwell on one subject when they have subordinates on staff to do follow-up work. However, it is possible that it takes a special type—one who likes to "shift gears" often—to be successful in top management. Such a person must be able to quickly grasp the essence of a situation or problem and integrate the parts into a whole. Such minds are not content to stay with one thing for very long.

The successful executive is far from being a stereotype composed of the traits summarized above.

Birkman points out that although most top executives will have many of these traits, very few have them all.

Besides personality differences, other factors influence success. There are genetic factors, specific skills learned on the job and in our social environment, and several other factors, identified by Birkman:

**Opportunity.** The sociopolitical-economic structure of our society makes opportunity more elusive for some, more readily available for others. Race, sex, educational background, parental income, and where you spent your childhood all play a role in determining the opportunities available to you.

For more information on these factors, see my own discussion and the book *Who Gets Ahead?*, by Christopher Jencks (New York: Basic Books, 1979), which is discussed further in Chapter 19.

**Motivation.** This takes the form of a desire to achieve goals, accomplish objectives, and get to the top.

**Insight.** Defined for our purposes as the ability to size up a situation and acutely perceive the actions, motives, and feelings of others, insight also involves *self-awareness*—the ability to see yourself as you really are, accurately assessing your own needs, strong and weak points, and other special traits.

**A drive to action.** This is where you put it all together, translating motivation and insight into concrete, realistic, effective action, taking advantage of the opportunities afforded and transcending the obstacles. All successful individuals are doers.

If you wish to read more on Birkman's findings, get a copy of the Summer, 1978, issue of the *S.A.M. Management Journal,* and read the article "What Sets an Executive Apart from His Peers?" by Roger Birkman (S.A.M. stands for Society for Advancement of Management, a division of American Management Associations). Any good business library will have it.

---

# DELEGATING

---

Good management is terribly difficult without effective delegation. Delegation enables you to control your workload; to communicate with and evaluate your subordinates, to bring them along; and, in general, to make life easier.

## HOW NOT TO DELEGATE

- planning poorly
- issuing too many orders and directives
- overcontrolling
- undercontrolling
- overworking subordinates
- applying pressure
- criticizing too much
- imposing too many rules
- imposing too few rules
- being indecisive
- lacking objectives and priorities
- passing the buck
- exemplifying disorganization

## HOW TO DELEGATE

THE ONE THING YOU NEVER DELEGATE IS ACCOUNTABILITY You are still on the line. If you have delegated well and effectively, you'll come out well. But if the situation doesn't pan out, *do not blame the delegate involved.* You'll lose the respect of your superiors and the loyalty of your subordinates. Never delegate blame.

THE OTHER THING YOU DON'T DELEGATE IS A JOB THAT HAS YOUR NAME ON IT You are where you are because you do something well—even if it's only delegating.

---

CHOOSE CAREFULLY   Don't delegate a task to someone because he's there, but because he's right for the job. If there is no such person available on your staff, try to find someone in another part of the organization. Or do it yourself.

MAKE SURE YOUR DELEGATES UNDERSTAND THE OBJECTIVES   *You* set the objectives, perhaps with the input of others. *They* must carry them out. So first you must have well-defined goals; then you'd better make sure they are understood.

STATE THE LIMITATIONS UP FRONT   Budget? Authority? Deadlines? Let your helpers know the rules of the game.

DELEGATE RESPONSIBILITY, NOT JUST JOBS   You've got to keep accountability. But you can—and should—give a degree of free rein. If you can't do that, at least engender a sense of responsibility in your delegates.

DELEGATE AUTHORITY, NOT JUST RESPONSIBILITY   Authority is part of what your subordinates need to get the job done. But define the limits of that authority; and make sure that they check with you at even the slightest question of overstepping it.

YOU MAKE THE BIG DECISIONS. THEY ADVISE, RECOMMEND, AND ANALYZE

ANALYZE THE RISKS   Delegation is a form of risk taking.

LET THEM DO IT THEIR WAY   You are interested in the "what." How your delegates do it should be left to them as long as they understand the limits. You can offer help, but don't push your methods on them.

KEEP YOUR EAR TO THE GROUND   Establish checks and balances, building your delegates into the process. Request progress reports concerned with spending, time periods, or fulfillment of certain tasks or needs—or a combination of these considerations—any method that allows you to monitor the situation.

ESTABLISH STANDARDS OF PERFORMANCE   Whatever your subordinates do reflects on you. Make sure their work is up to snuff. The best way is to set the standards in advance.

ENCOURAGE INDEPENDENCE   If delegates must check with you before every move, you might as well do it yourself—but then how will you ever develop a competent support staff that you can rely on?

BE SUPPORTIVE   As a superior, you should be more like a coach to your team than a dictator. Be firm, stern, and tough. But you will all benefit if your team has a high morale. You've got to be supportive.

GIVE CREDIT WHERE IT IS DUE   If a job has been done well, say so.

And not just to them. Allow at least some of the praise to filter upstairs. If a subordinate feels that you have his best interests at heart and want him to succeed, you've won his dedication. (There are exceptions.)

IF THINGS GO AMISS, MOVE! Don't sit by while the job gets plagued by crisis after crisis. Step in and set it back on track. Or use a subtle guiding hand. This is not meddling. You step in if it's a critical situation, not something minor.

BUILD TRUST You may have to take a few chances. But mutual trust is a very potent weapon in the business world, precisely because there is so little of it in circulation.

DELEGATE THE GOOD AND BAD Don't just pass along what's distasteful. We all know how that feels.

DON'T RUSH THE JOB It takes time to build an atmosphere of trust, respect, cooperation, and proper communication.

DELEGATE IN STAGES First delegate small tasks. Don't dump the whole work load on subordinates. Many managers are quick to do that when they get their first assistant, or a new one. Even if it means that you must do more than your share of the work at the beginning, remember that training is a gradual, steady process. Don't burn out your staff.

IF POSSIBLE, DELEGATE IN ADVANCE Results tend to be better when a staff member knows in advance that a problem or task is his "department."

MAKE THE DELEGATED TASK "COMPLETE" Give your delegates the whole story—background and desired results. Too often, they just get the tip of the iceberg and never fully understand what they are doing, or why. If possible, give them a whole job, not just a part—and *specific results to achieve.*

DON'T DELEGATE JOBS THAT ARE "OVER THE HEADS" OF THE DELEGATES It's okay to give them a challenge, or tax their limits. But if the goal is way out of their range, the results could be disastrous—a botched job, mistrust, poor morale, and a bad career move for you.

BE CONSISTENT If your subordinates don't know what to expect from you, they will be either too timid (fearing your wrath) or too bold (expecting no response)—or both.

### WHEN YOU ARE THE DELEGATE

SEIZE THE OPPORTUNITY! Someone is giving you a chance to show your stuff. If it's a crummy job, you can still profit by building a relationship.

DON'T ACCEPT BLINDLY   If you feel the job is not right for you, say so. If it could be done simpler elsewhere, say so.

IS THE WORK BEING DELEGATED CONSISTENT WITH YOUR GOALS?   If you see the delegated tasks and responsibilities moving you into an area where you don't want to go you might want to decline the job. Don't be afraid to say as much.

GET YOUR SUPERIORS TO TELL YOU WHAT YOU NEED TO KNOW

MAKE SURE THAT THEIR FEEDBACK IS VALUABLE   "Good" or "Could be better" doesn't tell you much. You want to learn how your superiors think and what their standards are. Draw it out of them. Will they think you a pest? That's a risk you take.

### INSIDERS' TRICKS

The delegation game can be played dirty. For the most part, you don't need me to tell you how. But here—in case of need—are a couple of delegation strategies that management experts don't like to talk about.

NEGATIVE DELEGATION   If you've got a subordinate who is after your job or threatens you in some other way, freeze him out by delegating only the most mundane tasks. Never ask for his opinion, and never comment on his good work. He'll ask for a transfer; or he'll be "broken" and continue, in harness, with considerably less initiative. But there's one other thing he might do—turn the subtle power battle into an all-out war.

VOLUNTEER FOR EVERYTHING   This takes the pressure off the boss when he's got things that nobody wants to handle. This kind of eagerness is so rare that you will become famous. But, you ask, how do I avoid becoming overcommitted? Simple. Make sure that you know how to delegate effectively, so that you do the volunteering and somebody else does the work. Devilish.

## MODIFYING BEHAVIOR: B. F. SKINNER
## AND THE BUSINESS WORLD

Thomas Bonoma and Dennis Slevin have applied the basic principles of behavior modification to the manager's job. These principles are based on research that was first conducted at Harvard by B. F. Skinner using pigeons. Now behavior modification is used to help people stop smoking and cure phobias—and to get them to do what you want.

## THE BASIC CONCEPTS

1. *If you reward a certain behavior, it is more likely to be repeated than is unrewarded behavior.* Reward for behavior is called reinforcement.
2. *Reward behavior intermittently rather than continuously.* This is called partial reinforcement. The idea is to keep 'em guessing. Sometimes you give the reward; sometimes not. Studies have shown that this uncertainty is a more effective inducement to effort than is certainty of reward.
3. *Complex behavior patterns are made up of simple behavior patterns linked together.* To reinforce complex behavior, you merely reinforce the simple behaviors and link them together.

There you have it: an approach for improving compliance by systematically reinforcing certain behaviors. For any given behavior, you can provide either a reward or a punishment—or you can simply ignore it.

## HOW TO MAKE BEHAVIOR MODIFICATION WORK

(A) Look for and isolate the behavior you want to change. (B) Decide on the desired behavior pattern. (C) Set up a feedback system so you can keep track of the degree of change from the undesirable to the desirable behavior. (D) Determine the rewards, or consequences, if the behavior is, or is not, changed. (E) Reinforce the desired behavior by doling out the reward or punishment at a time when the relationship between the reinforcement and behavior will be clear.

Sounds a bit scary, doesn't it? This kind of conscious manipulation reeks of *1984*. But most of us do it to some degree without ever seeing it in these terms. And although you may not wish to establish a specific behavior-and-reward pattern for every task in the office, awareness of these principles can help you avoid some of the more destructive patterns.

AVOID CRITICISM OF A GENERAL NATURE  It is destructive, because it tends to attack the more general attributes of a person, rather than a specific behavior. In essence, you are telling someone that he is no good, rather than that you did not like the way he did this or that.

IF YOU ARE GOING TO REWARD SOMEONE, DON'T WAIT TOO LONG  Annual bonuses work because they are perceived as a kind of profit sharing for a good job or a profitable year. But they are not linked to specific behaviors. If you want to reward somebody for something, do it soon after the accomplishment so that the relationship is established.

WHEN SIZING UP SOMEONE'S WORK, TRY TO DO IT FREQUENT-LY, SPECIFICALLY, AND IN SMALL DOSES  The longer you wait, the more nonspecific the appraisal becomes and the smaller the opportunity to reward or punish an isolated, specific behavior. This is why *coaching*, a frequent appraisal and pep talk (the this-is-right/this-is-not approach) works better than a formalized, judgmental performance appraisal.

## IS BEHAVIOR MOD BEING USED ON YOU?

What incentives does your boss create for you? How does he try to influence your behavior? A common managerial mistake is choosing the wrong kind of punishment or reward. If you detect that your superiors are attempting to encourage a certain kind of behavior, you have several options:

If you feel comfortable "doing it their way," do so. But make sure that you get a meaningful reward. Suppose they want to give you money, but you want power. Let them know.

IF YOU CONSIDER THE BEHAVIOR YOUR BOSS IS TRYING TO ELICIT IN YOU TO BE UNACCEPTABLE, TURN THE TABLES  It is possible for subordinates to reward management by getting desired results, assuming responsibility, and providing desired information. Establish a link between "doing it your way" and the reward. Chances are the bosses will chuckle about how you've got a mind of your own, but as long as you do your job, it's okay. Such behavior turns to defiance only when you fail to provide suitable rewards to your superiors.

WHEN USING BEHAVIOR MOD TO MANAGE YOUR BOSS, MAKE SURE THAT YOU DON'T FORGET PARTIAL REINFORCEMENT  It's great to be loyal and trustworthy. But it's very easy to be taken for granted. Don't salivate every time the bell is rung. Throw a few curves. Let superiors know that a simple pat on the back doesn't always work, nor does increased responsibility or a bonus. Contrary to popular belief, the rewards will not cease. Rather, your unpredictability will keep them on their toes. On the flip side, don't reward them every time they behave to your liking.

More than an attempt at manipulation, partial reinforcement is a defense against being regarded simplistically. You've heard people say the equivalent of "Oh, Jones'll do anything if he thinks there's a few extra bucks in it. Let's call him." Jones may get a bit richer, but probably never very powerful.

# METHODS OF LEADERSHIP

Nobody leads in quite the same way. Some leadership roles call for vastly different approaches from others. And the specific needs and requirements of the individual play a role in determining how one approaches a leadership position.

Professors Thomas Bonoma and Dennis Slevin, of the University of Pittsburgh, have identified four basic types of leadership in their book *Executive Survival Manual* (Belmont, California: Wadsworth Publishing, 1978):

- *Autocrat.* The autocrat makes decisions alone, requesting little or no information from subordinates.
- *Consultative autocrat.* This leader gets as much data as possible from his staff, but then makes the key decisions alone.
- *Consensus manager.* This manager encourages not only group input, but also group decision making.
- *Shareholder manager.* The manager does not encourage input or information exchange, but allows the group to make the decision.

Essentially, the differences in these approaches are purely in terms of (a) where the information comes from and (b) who makes the decisions:

- *Autocrat.* Relies on self for information—maintains authority.
- *Consultative autocrat.* Subordinates get increased access to information and increase input, but the boss still calls the shots.
- *Consensus manager.* The group gets more involved in exchanging information and in making the actual decisions.

These three approaches are all valid, given the conditions propitious to them. Bonoma and Slevin deride the "shareholder" approach as bad management—an unjustified delegation of authority without foundation.

It is worthwhile to determine which leadership style you and your boss each display:

- *Where do you get your information?* Peers? Superiors? Subordinates? The conventional information sources (libraries, books, computers)? Anywhere you can?
- *Who decides?* You alone? Your staff? Who above you?

Now ask yourself if this is your preferred modus operandi. If not, what can you do to change it? Every style of leadership has its own unique set of problems and advantages. And not all styles suit every situation. Manage as an autocrat and run the risk of making a decision without benefit of crucial information and other points of view.

Manage by consensus and run the risk of the problems that come from group pressures and conflict. Take a look at the kinds of decisions you have to make, the kinds of people you work for, the kinds that work for you, and your company in general. Then take into account the kind of person you are and decide on an approach to leadership.

Your approach need not fit neatly into one of the three categories. It could be your own hybrid of two or more approaches. Sometimes different responsibilities call for different methods.

---

# RISK TAKING

---

Explaining the obstacles to innovation, many Westerners cite peculiarities of the Soviet economic system. At its most basic, there is a disinclination to take chances. "There is a constant fear among bureaucrats," says a U.S. metals executive, "that if an unproven technology doesn't work, they will end up in Siberia." But to a U.S. manager, one Western economist comments, "risk is an opportunity, because that's where the pay-offs are."

—"Russian Know-How,"
*The Wall Street Journal*,
March 21, 1980, page 1.

Having "potential" won't get you much further than getting hired for your first job. You've got to bring that potential out. In the competitive business environment, you can rise to the challenge and display your talent openly. Or you can freeze up, "choke," or just turn in an average, lackluster performance.

Often, what determines how well you put out, and whether you get noticed, is the way you take chances. To get ahead, you must put yourself on the line. That's how individuals succeed, and that's how companies succeed. With the increasing rate of change, "the status quo" is almost nonexistent—you are constantly at risk.

## WHAT DOES RISK TAKING MEAN?

In the final analysis, risk taking comes down to either betting on yourself (and influencing the outcome) or betting on chance (the probability that things will go in your favor). Even when you bet on others, you are betting, to an extent, on yourself—on *your judgment* of the ability of others.

Risk taking means going from a situation of some security to another, less secure, situation. Every executive must place himself at risk in order to advance.

---

HOW FAR ARE YOU WILLING TO GO? This is the critical issue. And it differs according to the individual. Some people are willing to take greater risks than others. They perceive situations differently. They differ in personality and intellect. It may even be a matter of genes. Each person sizes up the situation—gauges odds, risks, and rewards in a different way. *A great many people are unwilling to take risks that directly involve themselves*. Often, this is the critical difference between the executive who goes places and the one who marks time.

WIN OR LOSE, YOU'VE GOT TO PLAY THE GAME IF YOU WANT TO GET GOOD AT IT If you play it safe for an extended period, you may begin to lose your touch. Keep trying, even in the face of failure. You will learn how to assess risks and rewards more accurately and can then formulate a set of rules that work for you.

THERE ARE TWO BASIC TYPES OF RISKS IN BUSINESS: ECONOMIC AND INTERPERSONAL You take economic risks to make money. For your company and for yourself.

In the interpersonal area, you take a risk every time you decide to hold on to or let go of power. In this sense, you are taking a risk when you delegate, but also if you do the job yourself. Another kind of personal risk involves the decision to open up to someone—let someone know what you *really* think or feel. The flip side is to play your cards close to your chest. If your boss asks you how you feel about his pet project, you might want to assess the risks of telling him the truth—it stinks—possibly saving the company megabucks—versus the risks of stroking him while he goes ahead to disaster.

RISKS CAN BE ACTIVE OR PASSIVE Some risks involve inaction—an attempt to avoid risks (to avoid losses). But an active, dynamic risk is one in which one "goes for it"—an attempt to make gains.

CREATIVITY AND RISK TAKING ARE INTIMATELY CONNECTED There are lots of creative ideas, but few creative achievers. Creative ideas are often unusual; unconventional. Fighting for them almost invariably involves risks.

YOU CAN HEDGE AGAINST RISK BY MAKING IT A GROUP DECISION But, you say, the group will want to play it safe, talk you out of it. Not so. Research has shown that groups usually influence individual decision making toward higher risks. If it's your idea and the group decides to go ahead, you'll probably get the credit for proposing it. But you've spread the risk around, as a safeguard against failure.

# HOW TO TAKE RISKS

**NEVER RISK MORE THAN YOU CAN AFFORD TO LOSE** An old gambling rule. The tough part is determining how much you can afford to lose and the degree of risk to that money or thing.

*Make sure that the risks are justified.* Don't risk a lot for a little. It's very tough to follow this rule. But it may help to remember and heed it when you are about to expose yourself to considerable risk just for a little satisfaction, face-saving, or a "matter of principle" that is less than fundamental. And remember, revenge may be sweet, but not in the corporation.

**DON'T DISCOUNT INTUITION** The risk should "feel" right.

**CONFRONT THE FEARS THAT MAY BE HOLDING YOU BACK** Fear of failure, fear of uncertainty, fear of disapproval, to name a few.

**KNOW YOUR LIMITATIONS** It is to your credit that you are willing to step up and bet on yourself. But don't let that satisfaction lull you into making a bad bet. There will be times when you will be outclassed, outranked, or outfoxed. Don't be foolhardy. A long shot is one thing. An impossible or no-win situation is quite another.

**ALWAYS HAVE A CLEAR IDEA OF HOW MUCH AUTHORITY YOU HAVE AND HOW MUCH POWER YOU YIELD** Authority is officially sanctioned control. Power can and often does go beyond this sanction. If you have a "power base" among your peers and key superiors, you can take the risk of exceeding your authority, but you must appraise the situation *before* acting.

**KNOW THE RULES** There are virtually no rules—everything is subject to change; but the idea is to be an observer of human and organizational behavior. See if you can isolate the favored modus operandi of your peers, supervisors, and subordinates. You can then venture a guess as to how they will react to any move you make. And that will help you assess the risks.

**HAVE A CONTINGENCY PLAN** Suppose your risk doesn't pay off. Are you ready to cut your losses? Perhaps you can save face, or even make a small gain. Seasoned risk takers prepare with a variety of alternatives or contingencies. They are better equipped to compromise, cooperate, and negotiate. One executive told me, "I like to go in feeling 'heads I win, tails I win.' " Of course, if that were really the case, where would be the risk? But it's an ideal worth striving for.

**PAY ATTENTION TO TIME AND PLACE** Be tactful. Don't use social situations for tactical moves. Don't make your move at a time or place in which someone will be unnecessarily degraded or embarrassed.

Most people understand that risk taking is part of the game. But your insensitivity and your victim's humiliation won't be forgotten. Behave that way often and you'll have lots of people gunning for you.

Rather, try to orchestrate any risk-taking move involving others so that it's kept "in the family."

GAUGE IN ADVANCE JUST HOW FAR YOU CAN GO   Never (well, almost never) exceed these limits. There are times when the spoils go to the risk taker who goes where wise men never tread. But you should know when you are stepping over the line.

GO FOR MAXIMUM IMPACT   Lawyers know that it isn't just the strength of the argument, but how it is argued that counts. When you take a risk, be dramatic. Do it orally, with style. A memo or other "paper risk" cools it off and leaves you vulnerable to behind-the-scenes moves and varying interpretations. Avoid any risk-taking methods that blunt your momentum.

GIVE 'EM SOME SPACE   Don't push too hard. When you take a risk, it's okay to apply pressure to help things along. But if you push too hard, you may bust your hand.

KNOW WHEN TO QUIT   Ever notice how one risk leads to another? And another? At the time you take the first risk, you should already know how far to go. When you reach that point and you're not ahead, cash in your chips. Maybe.

JUDGE YOUR WINNINGS AND LOSSES OVER THE LONG TERM   Unless it's a winner-take-all situation (which should be avoided, if possible), you shouldn't be discouraged if you lose. The important thing is where you stand over the long haul.

## FOUR MAJOR RISKS

According to Richard Byrd, author of *A Guide to Personal Risk Taking* (New York: AMACOM, 1974), these are the rough ones:

THREATENING TO QUIT   This is an all-out risk unless you've got a better job already lined up. Do so only when your most basic rights and principles are being violated.

SEEKING A CONFRONTATION   Leveling with someone about your opposition to his apparent interests or his position on an issue is a risk to you, because you are threatening him, thereby prompting retaliation. However, the risk is even greater to the other side, because he must frame a response: mount an offense or a defense, or neutralize by agreeing with you. Confrontation can be a healthy risk if those in your work environment can deal with emotionalism.

GOING OVER OR AROUND THE BOSS   This is akin to threatening

to quit, because it is also a high-stakes risk, and you may lose your job if it backfires. Even if it doesn't, you'll lose your boss's trust. Do the rewards justify it? Well, if you stand to gain enough, you might not need his trust. Maybe you'll even wind up *his* boss.

STICKING TO YOUR GUNS If you firmly believe you are right, holding out against all odds may be the only thing to do. Just make sure you do it with class, without acrimony and bitterness. And make sure that the issue is important enough to be obstinate about.

# NEGOTIATING

Negotiation is called for in any situation involving incompatible goals between parties.

## IS THIS NEGOTIABLE?

ARE YOU IN A POSITION TO DEAL? First, consider whether there is an insurmountable power gulf. If you carry much more weight than the opposition, you won't need to negotiate. If the other party carries much more power than you, he will take what he wants. So the time to negotiate is when there are no gross power differences.

HAS HE GOT SOMETHING YOU WANT? Or: Have you got something he wants?

ARE THERE ANY PHYSICAL, TEMPORAL, OR LEGAL OBSTACLES?

## HAVE A PLAN

WHAT ARE YOU LOOKING FOR? What is your best deal? You must have a clear notion of your best deal if you hope to move the other party in that direction.

WHAT WILL YOU ACCEPT? Besides knowing what the best deal is, you must know what the worst deal consists of. The bottom line represents the minimum acceptable offer, beyond which you will not go.

WHAT IS YOUR OPPONENT AFTER? The idea is to find out what the other party's bottom line is while keeping him from finding out yours. Then you want to move his bottom line in a direction more favorable to you: Get him to give ground without relinquishing much of your own.

DECIDE WHO WILL DO THE NEGOTIATING You are not in this for ego massage; you are in it to win. Sometimes that means delegating the negotiation to someone else. Or bringing in a team. Team negotiation has the advantage of sheer numbers, and your case may be buttressed by several different points of view and areas of expertise. Just make sure everyone understands the strategy and agrees on tactics and the chain of command.

Going it alone has advantages, too. You call the shots and don't have to worry about someone else screwing things up.

DECIDE ON YOUR APPROACH    Tackle the tough issues first? Or last? Take up points one at a time or in blocks? Negotiate each point as separate, or use Kissinger-type "linkage"? What are your basic assumptions? Does your opponent share them, or does he have a set of his own? How will you get him to see it your way?

DECIDE HOW TOUGH YOU WILL BE    Will you compromise, and to what extent? Are you prepared to come away empty-handed, or must you strike some kind of deal? What can you afford to give away?

TIME AND PLACE    This is more important than it might seem. Always go for the home-court advantage. If not, seek a "neutral" site.

Keep time on your side. The best time to negotiate is when your adversary is feeling the pressure of time and you are not. If he is in from out of town, try to find out how long he is planning to stay. If you are from out of town, you might want to conceal that information.

REHEARSE    Not only might this prepare you for the unexpected, but it will also provide some valuable insights. Do some role playing.

BRAINSTORM    Throw out ideas, tactics, strategies. The key rule in brainstorming is that "no idea is too stupid to be mentioned." One never knows.

CONTINGENCIES    You should now be equipped to develop a few contingencies in case the opponent has a few curves of his own (which he undoubtedly will).

## AT THE BARGAINING TABLE

Use all the tactics, as needed, against your opponent:

- *Wait him out;* show patience.
- *Surprise him.*
- *Back off* for no apparent reason.
- *Table an issue.* Bring it up later when conditions are optimal for you.
- *About-face.* He is following your reasoning and direction; then you go the opposite way.
- *Fake-out.* Make it seem like you are going one way. All the while, you are setting up your opposite number, surreptitiously moving in another direction.

- *Use endorsements.* Break out statements of support by experts or prominent people. Better yet, get them there in person.
- *Bracket.* Try to flush out the truth by shooting left, right, center, high, low, middle—and watching what happens.
- *Use questions for several approaches.* They can get attention, be provocative, and give direction: "Have you given any thought to doing it *this* way?" "What would you say if I told you . . . ?"

Questions can bring things to an end—get to the bottom line: "So, do we have the job?" "Where do we go from here?"

Then there are the more conventional uses of questions—to gain information, or to give it: "What is . . . ?" "Did you know that . . . ?" "Why is . . . ?"

**DON'T MERELY LISTEN; WATCH!** Everyone displays a wide variety of nonverbal cues. Is your adversary clenching his fists? Scratching his head? Leaning forward across the table? Are his arms folded? These things tell you a great deal about how he is feeling at the time—tense; puzzled; aggressive; defensive.

Be aware of your own nonverbal cues. A nimble negotiator may actually use them to create a false impression; he may, for example, look nervous or fidgety to give the impression he's on the ropes. The adversary, smelling blood, moves in for the kill, only to be met by an effective counter-punch.

**IT'S NOT JUST WHAT HE SAYS, BUT HOW HE SAYS IT** Listen to the tone of voice. Watch for gestures. And be aware of exactly how the point is made. "Off the top of my head" is meant to imply a spontaneous remark, an estimate, a ball-park figure. Is it really? Or does he merely want you to think so? How about this one: "By the way . . . " implies that what follows is an aside, a minor or secondary point. In fact, it may be *the* point he's been working on all meeting long. Or this one: "This is strictly confidential" tells you that you are privileged to be let in on a secret, and that he wants you to share it with him alone. Well, who else has been told this "confidential" information? And does he really expect you to keep it to yourself? Or does he hope you'll spread it around? Similar expressions: "Between you and me . . . " and "Off the record . . . "

**PUT THE OTHER PARTY AT EASE** Pay attention to his needs, physical and psychological. It is understood that you are bargaining in your best self-interest, but negotiation sessions shouldn't be attempts to beat each other's brains in. If everyone is relaxed and functioning well, you will do business. When someone feels that he's lost control, he often freezes and refuses to budge. So you get nothing done and must have another meeting. (Of course, if he's under the pressure of a deadline, you can really put the screws to him by forcing him to deal under duress. But he'll remember that for a long time.)

Putting someone at ease can mean accommodating the nonsmoker. And it can mean displaying some empathy—letting your opponent know that you see his side of it.

## IF YOU REACH AN AGREEMENT

Often, unfortunately, the game is not over now that it's contract time. It's amazing how many deals break down or get delayed at this stage. Usually, the disagreement involves one or more of three basic issues:

- the amount of legal protection afforded the principal parties
- the duration of the agreement
- how much of the specifics gets written into the contract—and how much remains a gentlemen's agreement, subject to interpretation

The first question you should consider is whether you need a formal contract. Often, a person's word or good faith means more. People with their integrity and honor on the line will comply with the spirit of an agreement, especially if they've committed themselves in front of others.

Legal contracts are, of course, easier to enforce, but many clauses will prove subject to interpretation. Besides, they are far from black-and-white. People tend to look to the paper, rather than to themselves, for guidance on how to comply.

If you go with a formal contract, you then have to decide how specific to get. If it is a deal to distribute a product, will it specify a set sales volume that must be reached, or will it be "best efforts"? Many deals have been killed because lawyers crowded them with clauses and subclauses. Sometimes, a compromise can be reached in which the conditions are neither set nor open-ended; rather, they are tied to changing conditions in the company, marketplace, etc. This way, neither party is locked into a static agreement, and each can share in the profits or losses in a manner that reflects the environment and performance.

## IF YOU FAIL TO REACH AN AGREEMENT

Besides the obvious approaches like backing off or going elsewhere to get what you want, there's always mediation and arbitration. You can use a nonaligned consultant, industry expert, or attorney to help fashion an agreement. Many trade and professional organizations will arbitrate. Arbitration is a binding judgment, so both parties must first agree to accept the decision.

# A FEW FINAL WORDS ON NEGOTIATION

**WALKING AWAY SATISFIED DOESN'T ALWAYS MEAN THAT YOU'VE DONE WELL** When they finally reach an agreement, people tend to feel reduced tension and, therefore, are usually happy. Research shows that, in most cases, both sides are satisfied when they come to terms. But this has little to do with the terms of the deal. What did you gain? What did you give up? These are the questions that your superiors and colleagues will be interested in, not the smile on your face.

**DON'T PROJECT** Most people, in trying to analyze the opponent's point of view, project their own attitudes, perceptions, and assumptions. There is an excellent chance that your adversary does not see the issues, the goals, and the world the way you see them.

**AIM HIGH—BUT NOT TOO HIGH** Always shoot for the maximum deal you can reasonably expect. Chances are, you'll have to come down. But it's better to come down from a top offer than from a mediocre one. However, remember that if you are too high, you can bring about a deadlock, because people will react negatively to your goal and think that you don't really want to negotiate.

**HONESTY REALLY WORKS SOMETIMES** I've heard many executives say, "He knows what I'll accept, and I know what it's really worth, so why can't we cut the bull and quit wasting time?" In reply, many salesmen say that just one slip—that one time in a dozen that he gets the better of you—makes all those extra hours worthwhile.

However, when you are dealing with a principled executive who is *well prepared* and each of you knows exactly where the other stands, being up front can be exhilarating. You won't be able to do it with everyone, because your honesty will often be met with deception. But there will be a few who you can deal with without guile. These people usually turn out to be lifelong friends.

---

# PUBLIC SPEAKING

---

Any talk should:

- get audience attention and keep it
- be interesting
- be delivered in clear, simple language
- summarize key points
- motivate people

---

# HOW TO PREPARE

**WRITE A SHORT "PLAN OF ATTACK"**  State your purpose and how you propose to go about fulfilling it.

**NOTE THE KEY POINTS ON INDEX CARDS AND SPREAD THEM OUT IN FRONT OF YOU**  You may also wish to use the "mind map method" (*see* Chapter 7).

**STRUCTURE THE TALK**  First, you want to arouse your listeners' interest. Get them interested in you, the subject, a problem you are addressing, or a specific, provocative issue. *The opening* will depend on the overall structure. Some common approaches are: (1) stating the problem, the solution, and the rewards; (2) itemizing the causes of something, and pointing out the effects; (3) bringing out your theme in a historical perspective by offering details in chronological order.
*Always end with a summary.*

**PREPARE VISUALS**  Photos, diagrams, charts, important words or numbers are all helpful, where appropriate. If a visual doesn't add anything or aid in comprehension, don't use it.

**KNOW YOUR AUDIENCE**

- How much do they know about your subject? Does everyone know about the same amount, or is there a large gulf in knowledge?
- How much background and introductory material is needed?
- Will they be interested? Why?
- What are their attitudes? Opinions and other background?
- What do they know about you? Your authority and expertise?
- In terms of status or power, are you speaking "up" or "down"? (Is this the board of directors of your company? Or a group of prospective job applicants?)
- Learn what you can about past speeches given to this group: speeches and topics its members liked and disliked; the kind of delivery they prefer.
- Anything objectionable? Is an off-color joke okay? Any subject touchy?
- Now, taking all this into account, formulate the style, content, and delivery of the speech. And try to anticipate the reception the audience will give you—hostile? friendly? questioning? skeptical?

**REHEARSE**  Get familiar with the material, both the words to be spoken and the visuals to be shown. Time your run-through and make sure it fits the allotted period, leaving ample time for questions. If poor transitions or poor logic become apparent in rehearsal, eliminate them and then rehearse again. Several rehearsals will help you to look and feel more comfortable.

IF IT'S A NEW SPEAKING ENVIRONMENT, ARRIVE EARLY   Get the feel of the surroundings. Perhaps you can place the chair, blackboard, or other props in a way that's more to your liking. If there are cables, wires, or other obstacles, you can get rid of them or at least be forewarned. It's also good for your attitude—a feeling of familiarity helps delivery.

MAKE SURE THAT YOUR EQUIPMENT IS SET UP AND OPERA-TIONAL   Is the film or slide projector set up and plugged in? Film threaded? Are slides loaded? Projectors prefocused? Tapes cued? Can everyone see?

## GIVING THE TALK

BE WELL GROOMED AND MAINTAIN GOOD POSTURE   Look smart; sound smart.

BE CLEAR   Use short sentences and short words. Simplify complex ideas.

BE LOGICAL   Good, crisp, graceful transitions.

KEEP THE INTENDED PACE   The talk should not be markedly longer—or shorter—than planned.

BE AWARE OF AUDIENCE RESPONSE   Are they bored? If they are yawning, dozing, doodling, reading, giggling, or cleaning fingernails, it's time to try to recapture their attention.

TAKE BREAKS   One or a few, depending on how long you speak and on the format of your speech. Presentations that have variety—films, etc.—require fewer breaks than "all-talk" speeches.

SPEAK AT A NATURAL VOLUME AND IN A NATURAL TONE   Do not read; it will create a monotone. You may raise your voice to gain attention.

SPEAK CLEARLY   Don't slur or mumble. Think before and as you speak. *Listen* to yourself. How do you sound?

BREATHE NATURALLY

CHOOSE YOUR PHRASES CAREFULLY   Try to avoid "um," "uh," and "you know."

DON'T BE NERVOUS ABOUT BEING NERVOUS   Most audiences expect some unease in all speakers but the professional. They tend not to notice excessive nervousness; just ignore it.

WATCH WHAT YOU DO WITH YOUR HANDS   When standing,

never let your hands drop below your waist. You can hold something: index cards, pencil, pen, eyeglasses, papers, a pointer. You may also gesture with your hands or fold them. When you sit, it's okay to rest one hand in your lap.

LET YOUR ENTHUSIASM SHINE THROUGH  If you are not enthusiastic, you haven't prepared well enough. You should be able to get "up" for even the most uncongenial subject.

MAKE EYE CONTACT WITH PEOPLE IN THE AUDIENCE  Shift your attention about the room to different people, but always look at the audience.

USE FACIAL EXPRESSIONS AND GESTURES  They help you communicate. You use them in everyday conversation. Why not now?

WHEN A QUESTION IS ASKED, MAKE SURE YOU ANSWER IT  It's usually a mistake to use a question as a lead-in to another point. But if you should do that, make sure you answer the question along the way; or say, "I'll answer your question, but with your permission, I'd like to first . . . " Don't go off on tangents.

### AFTERWARD

- Ask yourself how it went. Did the audience enjoy it? Did they respond? Were they persuaded? Motivated?
- Ask others who were there what they thought.
- Is there any way to measure the outcome?

### IF YOU ANTICIPATE SPENDING MUCH TIME BEFORE THE BROADCAST MEDIA, GET PROFESSIONAL ADVICE

Perhaps you are called upon to be a company spokesperson. You've got to defend the firm against the charges of a consumer advocate on a local talk show, or testify at a Senate or EPA hearing on environmental impact.

There are several firms that will, in several days, put you through the paces—a simulated TV studio setup, complete with interviewer and antagonistic questions. You'll analyze the videotapes and learn how to look and act on TV, and how to handle yourself better in the hot seat.

Among the best-known media training companies are:

JACK HILTON, INC.  Hilton runs the two-day TeleCounsel program limited to eight participants. It consists of interview situations and videotape replays of them, with constructive criticism from "faculty" members. Hilton believes in as much realism as possible in order to get participants away from the "it's not for real" psychology, so he uses a fully equipped TV studio and professional interviewers. Past courses have featured such luminaries as Edwin Newman, Sander Vanocur, and George Reedy. The cost is over $10,000.

    Contact:
        Jack Hilton, Inc.
        60 East 42nd Street
        New York, New York 10017

SPEECH DYNAMICS is the brainchild of former actress and talk-show personality Dorothy Sarnoff. Ms. Sarnoff has written several books and numerous articles on speech and personality training. It is a wholly owned subsidiary of the Ogilvy and Mather ad agency. The Speech Dynamics program is flexible: Depending on the needs of the clients, it can consist of a two-day seminar, private studio sessions, even large group meetings. The program includes media training, but also concentrates on speeches and presentations.

    Contact:
        Speech Dynamics and Communications Service, Inc.
        111 West 57th Street
        New York, New York 10020

---

# HOW TO ARGUE*

---

Ever since we were kids, we've been told not to argue. We argue all the time. And there is nothing inherently wrong with arguing. It's a legitimate method of resolving a disagreement and ends in your (a) convincing the other party that you are right, (b) becoming convinced that your opponent is right, (c) arriving at a compromise, or (d) arriving at an impasse. It needn't degenerate into a brawl, although it frequently does.

Verbal brawling, like the physical kind, demonstrates a lack of control and an inability to persuade peacefully. And it often brings out the darker side of your personality—the part that's best left below the surface, or expressed, if need be, at more appropriate times.

Since an argument is something you want to win—and it is usually in your best interests to do so—keep the basic tactical pointers in mind:

TRY TO SIZE UP THE ARGUMENT AS IT TAKES SHAPE, BUT BEFORE IT GETS GOING   Are you going to be on the defensive, or on the offensive? Is the subject or position really worth arguing about? By the way, exactly what *will* you be arguing about?

AVOID ARGUING WITH FANATICS

---

*Some material adapted from *How to Win an Argument*, by Michael A. Gilbert, Copyright © 1979 by McGraw-Hill. Used by permission of McGraw-Hill Book Company.

---

## BE NICE

UNTIL SHOWN OTHERWISE, ASSUME THAT THE OTHER PARTY
HAS SOME REASONABLY GOOD REASONS FOR THE POSITION
HE IS TAKING  Most people are rational. If they aren't, you won't be
able to convince them anyway.

LISTEN CAREFULLY AT ALL TIMES  Speed of reply counts for very
little in an argument. Therefore, it is not necessary to formulate a reply
while the other person is talking. Listen to what he has to say, retaining
just a vague idea of your reply. Acute listening allows you to spit back
precisely what the opposer has said. This makes any attack on him
more credible. Besides, how are you going to compose an effective
reply if you don't know what has been said?

IF THE OTHER PERSON IS NOT LISTENING TO YOU, DON'T LOSE
YOUR COOL

PATIENTLY REPEAT

CONCENTRATE  Not only will you make a better argument, but you
will generate more intensity: Brain power can be "felt."

RELAX  Thanks to Clint Eastwood spaghetti westerns, we have all
learned that we can be quite deadly when we are relaxed. We also
demonstrate that we can't be intimidated—and this can be quite
unnerving to an opponent who tries to win by getting under your skin.

WHENEVER YOU ARE UNSURE OF WHAT YOU ARE ARGUING
ABOUT, SEEK A CLARIFICATION  You may have already reached
agreement on the important issues and are now just debating a minor
or procedural question. Having a point explained to you also serves as
a break in case you need time to think. If the opponent has "pulled a
switch," compel him to come back.

DON'T ATTACK THE CONCLUSIONS OF YOUR OPPONENT;
ATTACK THE REASONING THAT GOT HIM THERE  Disagreeing
with a conclusion does not produce any movement: He thinks one way,
and you another—impasse. To get him to move, you've got to erode the
foundations upon which his conclusions are built.

IF YOUR OPPONENT USES ANALOGIES OR EXAMPLES, TRY TO
BREAK THEM DOWN BY SHOWING THAT THEY ARE NOT REALLY
ANALOGOUS OR SIMILAR TO THE SITUATION IN QUESTION
 Most people love to fall back on examples or shoddy analogies. Don't
let them get away with it. On the other hand, if you think you can drive
a point home with an analogy or example and (a) feel you can get away
with it, or (b) can defend it, by all means use it.

ESTABLISH THE BASIC PRINCIPLES THAT UNDERLIE YOUR
ARGUMENT AND THAT OF YOUR OPPONENT  The idea is to

defend yours and attack his. The main principles are the lifeline of your argument. Or they can be its Achilles' heel.

DEFEND YOUR PRINCIPLES, EVEN IF IT MEANS CONCEDING A NEGATIVE OR UNCOMFORTABLE CONSEQUENCE  If you are willing to desert your basic position just to avoid the heat generated by an unpleasant situation, you are on shaky ground.

WATCH OUT FOR CIRCULAR REASONING  This is the name of the game when an argument assumes something it's supposed to be proving—as, for example, in saying that if you want to win an argument, you should follow these rules, because without them, you will certainly lose. Unless you are dealing with a dummy, never use circular reasoning. Even if you get away with it, onlookers will think that you are a sloppy thinker. When you see circular reasoning in others, attack! Point it out, but not derisively. Make sure that others are aware of the fallacious argument.

DON'T ARGUE OVER LABELS  There are umpteen definitions of a communist, a good Christian, a capitalist, etc. It's too subjective. Find out what is meant and argue at that level.

DEMAND THAT THE OPPONENT JUSTIFY ONE-WORD, GLIB CONCLUSIONS  "Nonsense!" "Absurd!" "Ridiculous!" do not constitute part of an argument; they are conclusions. Demand to know precisely why your opponent feels this way.

THE WILL OF THE MAJORITY HAS LITTLE TO DO WITH RIGHT OR WRONG  Just because "most people use this" or "think that," it doesn't automatically follow that such behavior or opinions are valid. And if your opponent says that "everyone knows this" or "does that," and you or someone you know does not, then he is wrong.

BE CAREFUL WHEN INVOKING THE EXPERTS  An expert is only an expert if he is one on the subject you are discussing. Dr. Spock had strong opinions on the Vietnam War, but his expertise is in child care, not international affairs. Therefore his Vietnam stand didn't carry much weight as expert opinion. *A posture becomes flawed if it relies on the opinions of an expert inappropriate to the subject.*

WHEN AN EXPERT IS INVOKED, BE SURE TO DISTINGUISH BETWEEN HIS PROFFERED FACTS AND HIS EXPERT OPINION  Opinions, even from experts, can always be challenged. But when an expert is able to supply crucial facts, he strengthens one side or another of the argument.

Examine the character of the expert. Is he given to making rash statements? Outlandish predictions? For example, relying on the views of Nobel laureate William Shockley could get you in trouble, because he has been associated with the view that certain races are genetically inferior. This view is so unpopular, that even the most erudite and innocuous statements of the man are often suspect.

IF THE EXPERT HAS GONE OVER YOUR HEAD, DON'T TRY TO FAKE IT    Never agree with him if you don't know what he is saying. Make him explain—and back up—his statements.

ATTACKS ON A PERSON'S CHARACTER ARE USUALLY OUT OF BOUNDS    Name-calling and character assassination are common. Deal with them by demanding that your opponent justify any slur or allegation and explain why he feels it is relevant to the argument.

KEEP TRACK OF ASSUMPTIONS    You may want to attack a basic assumption of your opponent. Or retract one of yours.

THAT SOMETHING SEEMS LOGICAL, PROBABLY TRUE, OR APPARENTLY ELEMENTAL IN A CAUSE-AND-EFFECT RELATION-SHIP DOES NOT MEAN THAT IT IS TRUE    Be skeptical. Question everything. Believe nothing. If you point out that there is even one other explanation for the cause of a problem or situation, you have cast doubt on the validity of the opponent's claim that his explanation is *the* explanation.

JUST ONE EXCEPTION IS SUFFICIENT TO FALSIFY GENERALIZA-TION    It is unwise to shoot for eternal truths or universal conclusions; you are very vulnerable to even a minor exception. Don't generalize any more than you have to. Generalizations are a common trap, because they often sound learned and authoritative.

WHEN YOU ARE OFFERED AN EITHER-OR CHOICE, BE ON YOUR GUARD    Some opponents make a conscious attempt to limit your choices artificially. Philosopher Michael A. Gilbert cites the example "America—Love It or Leave It."

An excellent book on the art of arguing is the one from which much of this material was drawn: *How to Win an Argument,* by Michael A. Gilbert (New York: McGraw-Hill, 1979).

## MBO

If ever there was a term that was self-explanatory, MBO—Management by Objectives—has got to be it. There is more to it than just three letters, but not so much that you have to go to business school to understand what it's all about. The basic structure of the MBO process is exceedingly simple. It's the application of the process to your management functions that is difficult.

**A Definition:** "A management process whereby the supervisor and the subordinate, operating under a clear definition of the common goals and priorities of the organization established by top management, jointly identify the individual's major areas of responsibility in terms of the results expected of him or her, and use these measures as guides for operating the unit and assessing the contributions of each of its members."*

## THE MBO PROCESS

SETTING OBJECTIVES  This is the strategic planning phase. Objectives should be clear, specific, well-defined, and mutually understood. There are several types:

*Organizational Objectives* are set for the entire company.

*Unit Objectives* are those of a specific division.

*Individual Objectives* are usually formulated as a complement to the larger-scale objectives. This is important because the individual is the key work unit and, therefore, must know exactly what his part in this process is all about.

*Personal Objectives* are those that an individual sets on his own—his objectives for accomplishment, achievement, promotion, etc.
Objectives can be set for virtually any kind of job, from the routine through the most innovative, problem-solving variety.

IMPLEMENTATION  Objectives are one thing; deciding how to attain them is quite another. The action plan should be detailed and thorough, but also flexible. It should include contingencies.
Going back over the plan is one way of insuring that it is valid. Flaws often show up. Better to catch them here than after you've embarked on your course.

REVIEW OF PERFORMANCE  At this stage, review the situation to see where you stand. Appraise the results and if necessary, modify your objectives or add new ones. You, as an individual, should do this frequently—on a daily or weekly basis. More formally, on a quarterly basis, meet with your boss for a review. This should not be a traditional appraisal by a superior of a subordinate: Because you both have objectives to work with, the review should be a cooperative venture intended to *improve* performance, not place blame. Of course, how and when you review the situation depends on the objectives involved and the timetable you are laboring under.

---

*From George S. Odiorne, *Management by Objectives.* Copyright © 1965. Reprinted by permission of Pitman Learning, Inc., Belmont, CA, pp. 55-56.

---

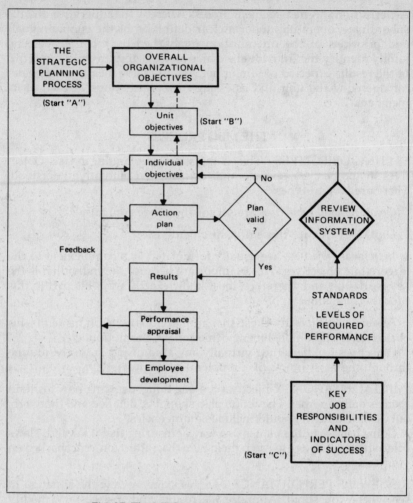

Fig. 27. The MBO process in flow chart form

Reprinted from *Strategic Planning and the MBO Process,*
by William C. Giegold. Copyright © 1978 by McGraw-Hill.
Used with permission of McGraw-Hill Book Company.

REPORT AND FEEDBACK  It's a good idea to prepare periodic reports that cover points of progress vis-à-vis the action plan, discuss performance, and reevaluate the objectives.

Then use the report to readjust objectives and actions. Formulate any additional actions needed to remove obstacles. One of the biggest advantages of MBO is that it treats management as a continual *process:* ongoing, always in a state of flux. If conditions change, objectives change, and it's likely the kind of action will change. Maybe even the personnel. MBO encourages input to facilitate this ability to "feed back" into the system so that it can readjust. Encourage input from everyone involved.

## REQUIREMENTS FOR EFFECTIVE MBO

AWARENESS OF EMPLOYEE NEEDS  MBO should result in an increase in the competence of employees and the development of important skills. You've got to create a supportive atmosphere in which they view the frequent assessments, evaluation, and measurement of their performance and accomplishments as a constructive thing.

CLEAR DELINEATION OF INDIVIDUAL RESPONSIBILITIES AND PRIORITIES  The staff must have no doubts concerning what they must do and when it must be done.

ESTABLISHED STANDARDS  Expected levels of performance should be crystal clear. "A job well done" means different things to different people. Arriving at standards not only provides an understanding of what is expected, but also serves as a baseline for measuring any dropoff or improvement in performance.

A GOOD INFORMATION NETWORK  Information should flow upward as well as downward, easily and rapidly. And the staff should be able to tell the difference between important data and clutter; otherwise, the network will rapidly become clogged with irrelevant memos, printouts, etc. If something is important, it should be put in writing. Records should be kept. MBO should not be too informal.

A MANAGEMENT TEAM WILLING AT ALL LEVELS TO PUT IN THE TIME TO MAKE MBO WORK  It is often upper management that scoffs at having "performance meetings" or writing things down. But MBO requires commitment.

OBJECTIVES AND ACTIVITIES COMPLEMENTARY TO THOSE IN OTHER PARTS OF THE ORGANIZATION  What good are sales objectives if they bear no relationship to production objectives? MBO requires interlocking objectives and priorities. Sometimes, personnel will play a key role in the implementation of MBO in several different phases of corporate activity.

OBJECTIVES FRAMED IN A MANNER THAT ALLOWS THEM TO BE MEASURED   It may not be possible to measure quality or quantity in a strictly numerical way. But some systematic method can always be worked out.

DEADLINES   Most of us need the discipline of a time limit.

REALISTIC OBJECTIVES AND A PLAN OF ATTACK ACCEPTABLE AND CHALLENGING TO ALL   Involve subordinates in the setting of the objectives and creation of the action plan. *All parties involved must be given the authority needed to get their jobs done.* If this means delegating, so be it.

*Are the objectives within the capabilities of the individuals involved? Are they technically feasible?* The very asking of these questions explains why the process of arriving at an objective is so important. Goals that are out of reach just result in frustration.

MBO is not just another gimmick. Nor is it a panacea. You've got to go into it carefully, because employees can easily mistake it for a punitive approach meant to keep tabs on them—a sign of suspicion and distrust. It is also important to follow through once you've started on MBO. Many executives simply get tired of it.

If implemented with conviction, MBO will produce many benefits, including greater efficiency and communication, better planning, a more informed, committed work force, greater trust, fairer evaluation, and even personal growth.

## WHERE TO LEARN MORE ABOUT MBO

Most of the principal business schools and university adult education programs offer courses in MBO. You might also try one of these good books:

- *Management: Tasks, Responsibilities, Practices,* by Peter F. Drucker (New York: Harper & Row, 1973)
- *Management by Objectives,* by William C. Giegold (New York: McGraw-Hill, 1978)

# "IF THE CUCKOO WON'T SING, LET'S WAIT UNTIL IT DOES": THE JAPANESE WAY*

The advice about the cuckoo is translated from a traditional Japanese short poem, or *haiku*. According to management expert Mitz Noda, this haiku characterizes the modern Japanese management system.

No manager can afford to be ignorant of Japanese methods. He may choose not to incorporate any of the practices, but he's got to know how his competition operates.

**The Japanese prefer to encourage achievement by setting goals, stimulating motivation, and attempting to make work pleasant.** They avoid intimidation and threats.

At one level, the approach is similar to the positive-reinforcement aspect of behavior modification. But there are differences, too. First, the Japanese methods are institutionalized; they are, in effect, modern applications of ancient tradition. Second, Japanese managers begin with certain basic assumptions about their workers: They enjoy being productive; working is a natural part of life for them; they take pride in their work and will conduct themselves with honor and self-control.

**The Japanese are expert delegators.** In many companies, lower level management makes major decisions.

**In Japan, the company's interest in the worker extends beyond the workday.** Management provides recreational facilities and sponsors social gatherings in addition to granting such benefits as company-built residences and retreats, job retraining, and the financing of weddings.

**They put great emphasis on face-to-face communications.** The Japanese manager tries to avoid communication via memo. He will seek out his superiors or subordinates, and be welcomed.

**Top management personnel move around.** They are shifted to different markets and divisions so that they can get a feel for different marketing and distribution approaches and the forces at play in different world markets.

**The Japanese rely on the "ringi" system of decision making.** Put

*Adapted in part from "Business Management in Japan," by Mitz Noda, *Technology Review*, June/July 1979, pp. 20-29. Used with permission from *Technology Review*, Copyright © 1979 by the Alumni Association of the Massachusetts Institute of Technology.

simply, it's the middle management that makes decisions and choices. Top management reviews the decisions, discussing them with middle management and making certain that everyone is satisfied.

**The government is presumed to operate in the best interests of business.** In the United States, government often acts as an antagonist of the corporation—protecting businesses from each other; protecting workers. While the relationship between Japanese government and business has justifiably come under fire, it should be noted that most people do not fear that companies will exploit them; therefore, relatively few of them feel a need for the government to function as an advocate of workers' rights.

**Sushin koyo.** Perhaps the most famous aspect of the Japanese system, because it differs so markedly from ours, sushin koyo is employment for life.

*How it works.* Management tends to hire fresh out of school. This makes for a generally younger work force. Executives come up through the ranks—never from the outside.

Mandatory retirement is strictly enforced at 55—60 for most males, but at older ages for top level management. Senior directors often remain active into their seventies, but mostly in an advisory capacity.

Retirement always brings financial reward. Employees who put in 35 years of service get, in addition to pension, a lump sum that equals a multiple of their average annual pay. The bonus is tax-free. If an employee resigns, he is considered "retired" and receives retirement pay based on length of service.

*Does it work?* "The employees I raised are never dismissed," says Saizo Idemitsu, founder of Idemitsu Kosan Co. "We are one big family and have no need for such things as time sheets and labor unions."

The facts appears to bear Mr. Idemitsu out: Unemployment in Japan runs about 1 or 2 percent; per capita personal savings are more than double American levels; Japan loses only one-eighth as many days to strikes as the U.S.; and, currently, capital investment in new equipment is double the American figure.

Sushin koyo may also explain the remarkable Japanese gift of innovation: Job security means that employees are not afraid to take risks—or even make suggestions that could eliminate their jobs. They know that the company will find a place for them.

**Japanese promotion and pay practices.** Except at the highest levels, promotion is based on age and length of service. Therefore, employees are confident that if they work hard, promotion to a managerial position is inevitable. And they needn't fear being bypassed for a position in favor of an outsider.

As time passes, the worker's age and length of service naturally increase. So does his salary. Education is also taken into account in establishing pay levels. But efficiency and performance just don't play a very large role. There are allowances made for hardship, exemplary attendance records, and job rank.

In top management ranks, promotion and pay are more directly a function of performance and position.

**What all this means to American managers.** To some extent, absolutely nothing. We are a nation of diverse cultures, rugged individualists, highly suspect of authority. We are excellent team players, but we'll work on that basis only as long as it suits us.

In Japan, employees often must wait 16 years, or until they are about 37, before they are eligible for a management position. We are a nation of impatient people, and expect quick rewards for performance.

This is not to say that the United States does not have the kind of employees who are willing to trade loyalty and dedication for security and fair and consistent increases in pay and position. But few of its citizens dould welcome such a situation as the only established method of getting ahead.

Nevertheless, as a lesson for Westerners the Japanese ideal of the company in a "parental" role is valuable, if not for what it provides, then for the feeling generated—a sense of community, cooperation, and trust.

Matsushita, one of the world's leading electronics firms, has set these principles for all employees to follow:

- Seek progress through hard work.
- Make contributions to world harmony.
- Display the true form of a human being in national society.
- Be fair about responsibilities to owners and employees.
- Be successful in business by achieving these goals.
- Understand that profits are merely the reward of good service.

There are a few signs that the traditional Japanese approach is coming apart. It is essentially t method that was built on a feudal system, in which the business replaced the fiefdom. But now, many individuals have increased influence and independence. Some experts predict that ringi, sushin koyo, and other pillars of the Japanese system will have to be modified.

### SUGGESTED READING

*Theory Z: How American Business Can Meet the Japanese Challenge*, by William Ouchi (Reading, Massachusetts: Addison-Wesley Publishing Company, 1981; reprint paperback ed., New York: Avon Books, 1982).

*The Art of Japanese Management: Applications for American Executives,*
by Richard Tanner Pascale and Anthony G. Athos (New York:
Simon and Schuster, 1981).

---

# COMPETITION IS FOR THE COMPETENT: THE ABSOLUTE THEORY OF MANAGEMENT (ATOM)

---

This expanded vision of management is that of Maharishi Mahesh
Yogi, who gave us the Transcendental Meditation program.

The Absolute Theory of Management looks at management in terms
of natural law, drawing on principles from physics, mathematics,
chemistry, biology, and philosophy, among other disciplines. The result
is really quite practical.

The ATOM is systematically presented in a series of videotapes
moderated and with commentary by Maharishi. One of the central
themes of the course is that nature itself knows best how to organize
and manage. By undertaking a systematic, interdisciplinary study of
natural laws, we can uncover the basic principles of management. A
few examples:

## FROM PHYSICS

1. Thermodynamics explains that nonliving systems increase in
entropy, or disorder, over time. That's why a file cabinet eventually
becomes disorganized, and why a paper clip winds up in the container
that holds rubber bands. Inherently, this condition is irreversible: The
odds are overwhelmingly against order spontaneously reasserting
itself over disorder.

2. Thermodynamics also tells us that by creating a state of least
excitation—by quieting things down—we can increase orderliness.

3. This doesn't mean that, in the name of increased orderliness, we
cease all business activity. It does suggest that we should *periodically*
reduce the activity or excitation in the workplace and in the nervous
systems of the people in it. By doing so, we reduce the entropy, counter
its buildup, and therefore reduce mistakes. Physicists have observed
that in super-fluid states, when the entropy is virtually at zero, the
molecules of substances are elegantly organized. An overall reduction
in activity could very well introduce that basic organizational
intelligence into the human management system.

Maharishi teaches that a technique that produces a state of least
excitation in the human nervous system—a state of profound
rest—should be incorporated into the management system. Such a
technique is the Transcendental Meditation Program.™ Some of the

results of regular daily practice of the TM technique in the workplace have already been measured, largely through the work of Dr. David Frew.* (See Chapter 10)

## FROM BIOLOGY

Life is elegantly organized. The simple cell is "managed" by its nucleus, and the DNA within the nucleus possesses all the vital information to be tapped as needed. Other portions of the cell pursue their specialized functions, as directed by the "manager."

This principle operates on more gross levels as well:

The reticular formation in the brain "manages" the human nervous system, directing "data" to its various parts.

Study the function of the enzyme: It behaves as a catalyst, reducing the barriers, the time and energy necessary for a reaction to take place, but remaining unchanged. Many occasions call for this kind of behavior on the part of the manager—not actually taking part in the performance of a task, but helping it along.

For more information on the Absolute Theory of Management and the Transcendental Meditation program, contact:

World Plan Executive Council
17310 Sunset Boulevard
Pacific Palisades, California 90272

Department of Business Administration
Maharishi International University
Fairfield, Iowa 52556

---

# STATISTICS

---

"There are two realities simultaneously playing themselves out before our eyes: the way we feel and the way we are told the data show we feel. It is a very insecure society that won't credit its own experience." So said Meg Greenfield in the September 10, 1979, issue of *Newsweek*.

No modern executive can avoid playing the numbers game.

Will the product sell? The numbers say, Probably not. But your gut feeling is, Yes, in a big way.

The conflict exists between numerical data and our own feeling about the reliability of our intuition.

Often you will use research and data, not as a primary method of making decisions, but as a means of backing up decisions you've

---

*See David R. Frew, *Using TM at Work* (Chicago: Nelson-Hall, 1977).

---

already arrived at. You do this to put everyone at ease. Then, if the project doesn't fly, they can always say, "The numbers looked good."

So it's no surprise that a perennial best-seller among researchers is the book *How to Lie with Statistics* by Darrell Huff and Irving Geis (New York: Norton, 1954).

The executive who is interested in results must be equally wary of statistics, on the one hand, and his own logic, judgment, and intuitive feelings, on the other.

# 18

# POWER: OUT OF
# THE CLOSET

Power, put simply, is the ability to get people to do what you want them to—and the ability to resist being forced to do what you don't want to do.

You cannot get ahead without acquiring some power and learning to use it. Not only is power both a prerequisite and an attribute of one's success as an individual; it is necessary for good, effective management.

Colleges, universities, even business schools don't teach you about power. Perhaps it's because they are unable to do so. More likely it's because of some moral trepidation. Power and sex used to be treated in a similar manner: Everybody needs it, but won't talk about it, and society regards it as slightly immoral. The difference is that sex is out of the closet—now considered a healthy, natural part of life—while power, on the other hand, is still a dirty word.

Power is healthy. It is the *misuse* of power that is not. And there is entirely too much worry over its abuses. Everyone has power to some degree—as a parent, supervisor, organization member, buyer, or seller. Most people handle it well. But it's the abuses that make headlines. As George Bernard Shaw once said, "Power does not corrupt men; but fools, if they get into a position of power, corrupt power."

## POWER AND JOB-RELATED
## DEPENDENCE ON OTHERS

Professor John P. Kotter of Harvard Business School has made a study of power in business organizations. According to his findings, an important component of managerial work is the manager's dependence on the activities of other people. This dependence leaves one very vulnerable and, indeed, is quite contrary to the dynamics of power, because it restricts the control you have over your own job and limits your ability to assert control over others. Unfortunately, as one rises in

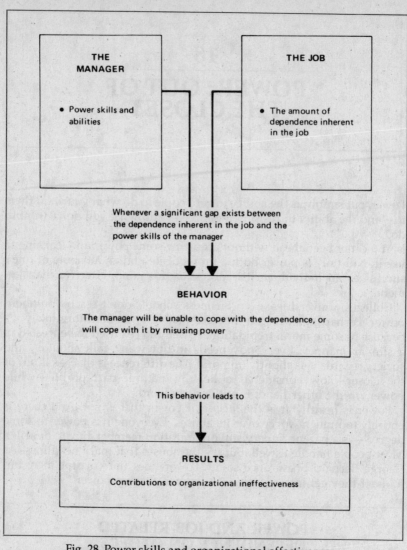

Fig. 28. Power skills and organizational effectiveness
This chart summarizes what happens when there is a gap
between the abilities of the manager and the amount of
dependence on others required by his job. He wants to break
out and grab for power, but the job structure holds him back.
The result is misuse of power and organizational
ineffectiveness.

Reprinted, by permission of the publisher, from
*Power in Management: How to Understand, Acquire,
and Use It,* by John P. Kotter, © 1979 by AMACOM,
a division of American Management Associations (p. 78).

the corporate hierarchy, the problem gets worse, not better. You have a wider range of responsibility, and although you may exert authority over more people, you are also more dependent on them. Add to that dependency the increasing complexity of dealing with greater numbers of subordinates.

**Power derived from authority is inadequate.** You are dependent upon the performance of some people over whom you have no authority. Besides, very few subordinates "blindly obey" anymore just because you are in charge. They often have recourse, and they know it. And they can follow your orders in a variety of different ways, depending on how they regard themselves, and you.

Professor Kotter's central theme is that power dynamics are not the result of a lust for power, or even of a burning desire to succeed. Rather, they are *the result of a disequilibrium in which the degree of on-the-job dependence on others far exceeds the power or control given the individual.* In other words, you have only a limited control over your own destiny, and there are a great many people who might act to reduce that measure of control.

Everyone needs some power. And every manager will attempt to gain enough power so that he feels comfortable.

**The greater the job-related dependence, the greater the time and energy spent playing power games.** The manager copes with job dependence by trying to expand and increase his control in the work environment.

As this job-related dependence increases, the manager gets more desperate, and his tendency toward the more risky, negative, and disruptive power tactics increases.

Job dependence is related to four internal factors:

- *responsibilities.* The greater your responsibilities, the more you need to rely on the help and cooperation of others.
- *span of control.* The more people under you, the more difficult it is to keep tabs on them, on how they do their jobs, and on whether to replace them.
- *degree of interdependence.* If a job involves interacting with other departments and personnel, it is more dependent than a job that involves self-contained tasks you handle alone.
- *bosses.* The greater the number of bosses, the more answerable you are.

With the exception of the number of bosses, all these factors increase as you move up the corporate ladder. That is why you have to be a better player near the top. Most can't handle it and make a desperate, clumsy attempt to consolidate power because they can't cope with their increased dependence on others. That's tough on the "rugged individualist." No wonder they're a dying breed.

Other factors related to job dependence can come from the outside. For example, you can be dependent on suppliers if you are in production, or on technology if you are in product design, or on a few people at an ad agency if you are in marketing.

---

# THE TACTICS OF POWER

---

This section will tell you, in the most basic terms, *what* people do to acquire and perpetuate power. What it will *not* tell you is *how* you go about doing these things. Every situation is different.

**Build relationships.** Let's look at some of the methods of forming binding relationships.

*Get other people to feel obligated to you in some way.* Good managers make this happen automatically. They don't do a favor or make a gesture just to "hook" someone; they do such things because they make sense, and because they enjoy doing them. Usually the result is the company benefits, the people directly involved benefit, and gratitude is a natural outgrowth.

*If you can't create a situation in which people are dependent on you, make them feel that they are.* This is an area where you can be perfectly justified in creating an "illusion." First convince the people in question that they need someone or something. Then convince them that you can deliver.

People don't have time to probe deeply into the true nature of things—or of people. Often, the first impression is the only impression they ever have time to form. They keep dredging it up every time they see the person. "Bill Hawkins...gold Rolex watch." "Steve Fischer...corner office with that beautiful ship in a bottle; very rich, I think." And so on.

Creating the illusion of power goes beyond how you look, dress, and decorate your office. The company you keep is also an indication. So if one of your high-school buddies is now famous, exploit it. This, by the way, is one of the themes of *Smart People,* by John Spooner (Boston: Little, Brown and Co., 1979).

**Establish credibility.** Back up your work and your word. That's how you build trust and, eventually, dependence.

**Develop a reputation.** Establish yourself as an expert and people tend to rely on you and defer to your judgment. The best way to earn a good

---

reputation is to perform. But you've also got to make sure your performance is noticed.

**Control as much information as possible.** Data control is a power weapon, because people rely on access to data to do their jobs. The intelligent use of data is also the best defense against attack. Privileged information is, of course, an even greater power tool.

The easiest method of controlling data is controlling its flow—the information channels. This is not merely a question of power for your own selfish ends. In large part, the modern corporation lives or dies by the way it handles information. (Look at the different ways automakers responded to the news that gas was going up in price.) The more information you have, the greater your ability to analyze and solve problems. With that kind of advantage, you probably won't need to manipulate the flow of information.

**Control resources.** This is the oldest of the power-grabbing methods; I can picture two roving bands of Neanderthals fighting for control of their mutual water supply. Money; equipment; employees; space; transportation—these are just a few of the resources worth winning.

**Become a Willie Stargell.** If you speak and act in a manner that expresses the "spirit" and sentiments of others, they tend to identify with you and elevate you. They will almost always bestow a greater amount of power on you than you deserve.

Civilization is full of examples. What did Che Guevara mean to Latin American radicals? The '69 Amazin' Mets to a faltering NYC? The 1980 U.S. Olympic Hockey Team to a frustrated nation?

This is no easy quality to culture; you are asking people to develop an idealized view of you. But it can be done. You must win respect; be visible; keep your ear to the ground so you know how people feel about important issues.

Most important, be sincere. Phonies do not last in this land of power play. You've got to develop understanding, a deep insight into the people around you. It's a matter of feelings as well as intellect.

Sometimes a particularly skilled politician will come on like the JFK of the corporation, and pull it off. But if he's not the genuine article, don't bet on his lasting long.

People need to look up to someone. Why not you?

**Locate the sources of power in your organization.** Don't rely solely on organization charts.

**Take risks with the power you have in order to build more.** In order to make a grab for something greater, sometimes you'll have to "use up" some of the power you've built.

---

**Stay away from activities and projects that could result in decreasing your power.** (Here is where risk analysis bears most directly on the attainment of power.)

**Don't overstep the acceptable limits of fair play.** Even the less-than-lily-white game of power has its code of behavior. Outfox and outmaneuver. But don't lie, cheat, or break your word. Not if you can help it.

**Count the ways you can influence people.** Go at 'em face to face and/or use more indirect methods, such as controlling schedules, meetings, agendas, memos, etc.

**Remember that playing the power game may begin in the genes.** Or at least in early childhood experiences. There is undoubtedly some intuitive ability involved in all this. Either you have a lot of intuition or you have a little. Make the best of it.

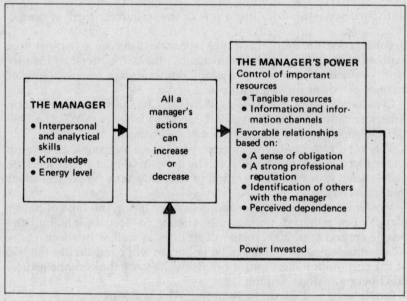

Fig. 29. Managerial behavior and the acquisition of power
How the manager acquires power by using his personal
skills, knowledge, and energy to attain control
of resources and form strong relationships.

Reprinted, by permission of the publisher, from
*Power in Management: How to Understand, Acquire,
and Use It,* by John P. Kotter, © 1979 by AMACOM,
a division of American Management Associations (p. 37).

Make sure that the energy and time you put in trying to get people to do something your way is justified by the importance of the situation. The more important it is, the more intolerant and inflexible you'll want to be. Don't play power games over unimportant matters.

---

## ABUSES OF POWER

---

**Lack of integrity.** If we learned anything from Watergate, it was that driving ambition that ignores the greater good is potentially self-destructive. Effective managers are able to balance their individual goals with those of their colleagues and the company. Ideally, better service to the institution fosters personal power, which in turn leads to increased service, which leads to greater consolidation of personal power, and so on. Often it doesn't work that way, but that's not a reason to abandon goals outside the personal sphere. Besides, the psychologists tell us that we are a species with strong altruistic tendencies, for whom doing good things for others is a primary source of satisfaction.

**The power-dependence mismatch.** Professor Kotter found that power is often abused by those who feel there is too much dependence in their jobs, and not enough power.

**Bad examples.** Misuse of power in upper levels not only sets a bad example; often it also forces the abuses downward, thus institutionalizing them.

---

## GETTING READY TO PLAY THE POWER GAME

---

**How well equipped are you to play?** Do you possess the abilities necessary to use the strategies and tactics needed to acquire power? What are your strengths? Weaknesses?

**Always be aware of how your actions are seen by others.** This is one way to avoid committing costly errors, making crude attempts to attain power, and misusing the power you have.

**Analyze your own power/dependence situation.** Whom are you dependent on? How are you dealing with these dependencies? What have you been doing to accumulate power to offset them?

---

Are you in a job in which there is too much dependence and not enough power? You are in trouble if the answer is yes. Redefine your job (power and dependence), or get a new one.

---

## LETTING 'EM KNOW YOU'RE THERE: COMPANY POLITICS

---

**Assume that every company has some politics.** No matter *what* they tell you. It's in every company.

**Locate the political factors (political climate):**

- what gets people promoted
- who's got the *real* power
- who's in the "in" crowd
- who's on the "outs"

**Give the "power people" what they want.** Aim to please.

**Run with the "in" crowd.**

**Know your job, know your company, know the business.**

**Work your butt off.** Some books say that hard work alone will get you nowhere. That may well be true. But politics or power games will also get you nowhere if you can't justify your claim to power. People who can't perform or deliver have to resort to treachery—pass the buck, or look good by making others look bad. Sooner or later it catches up to them. And until it does, they're always looking over their shoulders.

**Seek out and go after opportunities.** Be aggressive.

**On the other hand, don't take risks that aren't justified.**

**Learn how the game is played.** Cliques; alliances; double-crosses; tactics—and who uses them against whom.

**Always know what you want before you act.**

**Size up the competition.** Age? Experience? Background? Ability? Attitudes? Do they have what it takes? More important, do they possess the qualities that people in power will like?

---

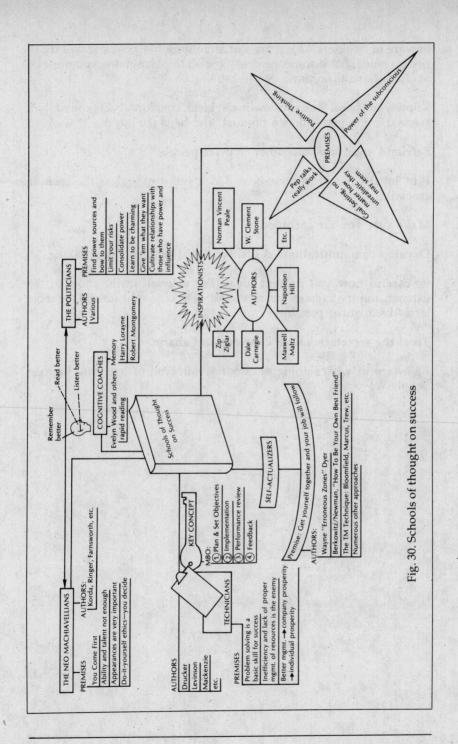

Fig. 30. Schools of thought on success

**Beware of "comers."** Most are just ambitious, like you, and will try to rise on merit. But if someone doesn't wish to play square, you must be ready to neutralize him.

**Know your boss.** Study his methods, ideas, opinions, background. You are marketing yourself as a product, and he is the buyer.

**Befriend your boss and other "power people."**

**Win loyalty.** Back up your boss: Do it his way (unless the issue is crucial).

**Make sure you are included.**

**Develop communications skills.** Writing, listening, and speaking.

**Be careful how you present ideas.** Put yourself in the shoes of the listener, and try to gauge his receptivity. Package your idea in the most attractive manner possible.

**Treat the secretaries with courtesy and charm.**

**Be aware** of what's going on around you. And of how you impress people.

# 19

# LEARN AND EARN: EXECUTIVE EDUCATION

The flow of technical knowledge is so rapid that your education may be obsolete before you graduate. Some experts predict that in the future, employees will earn top dollar fresh out of school, when they have the latest skills and technical know-how. Later on in their careers, when their knowledge is less current, they become less valuable and are therefore worth less. Knowledge appears to be taking on more importance than experience.

Frankly, you can't afford to stay out of school. You must protect yourself against lagging behind by taking advantage of the many educational options available to you. You do not have to quit your job. You probably won't even have to pay for your continuing education. Most companies will subsidize job-related education, if not completely cover its cost.

There are many alternatives, from one-day seminars to degree programs lasting several years.

## SEMINARS

### WHO GIVES THEM?

Almost anyone with enough cash to hire a meeting room and mailing list can hold a seminar. And practically everyone is doing it. The reason, of course, is that it is big business. The old-timers in the field include the American Management Associations, university adult education divisions of institutions such as Wharton (University of Pennsylvania) and New York University. But anybody who thinks he can pass himself off as an expert, speaks somewhat dynamically, and can write good direct-mail copy has jumped on board.

The independents tend to carve out a niche for themselves by concentrating on the soft areas that are less academic and more motivational, marrying business and self-help psychology. Examples include time management, negotiating skills, salesmanship, positive thinking, getting rich in real estate.

Seminars and conferences are a major source of education, training, and development for the U.S. business community. Anthony Whyte of AMR International, a leading seminar firm, estimates that American firms spend about $1.2 billion annually on employee seminars—57 percent (about $700 million) on in-house training and 43 percent (about $500 million) on external programs. There are over 1,000 organizations, trade associations, and educational institutions offering these courses. There are also countless one- and two-man operations.

## WHY ARE THEY POPULAR?

Although some seminars last a day or two, they can be a very efficient use of time, because the eight or so hours involved are often less time than it takes to read a tedious book on the same subject; and seminars can be fun. You tend to retain more, you can ask questions, and you are usually provided a workbook or manual that you can review as needed. And you can make worthwhile contacts. I'd rather hear about the arts of negotiation or tax shelters than read about them, any day. True, books are cheaper, and you can read them on your own time. But they are less up to date.

## SELECTING A SEMINAR

"It is becoming extremely difficult for individuals to delineate [sic] between the programs which are not going to be any good, many of them very trendy, versus programs that really cover some meaty topics and give them three or five or ten ideas which can be implemented when they get back to work," says Heidi Kaplan of the New York Management Center. Here are a few suggestions from Kaplan and others:

PICK A COURSE OR SEMINAR BASED ON YOUR ACTUAL NEEDS  Don't go to a seminar because it's in New Orleans and that's where your brother lives. Or even because it sounds interesting. The important question to consider is, Will this seminar prove useful in my current position or future career plans? Many training experts have discovered that negative experiences with seminars are often attributable to casual selection. Don't wait for a brochure to cross your desk and then fill out the coupon. Actively seek out the most valuable seminars.

SCRUTINIZE  The seminar field is so crowded with so many types of firms that no one is quite sure just how large the industry is. There are universities, publishing firms, consulting firms, individuals—anybody who thinks he can say something meaningful—all giving seminars. It's becoming more and more difficult to make a decision. Here are a few basic considerations:

- What are the credentials of the person leading the seminar? Does he have adequate experience?
- Is this his first seminar? (Can he teach?)
- Who is sponsoring it?
- Does the brochure provide a detailed analysis of what will be covered?
- Is it accredited by an educational institution?
- Is it tax deductible?
- What is the quality of the advertising? Is this a shoestring deal? Beware if the instructor solicits you directly.
- Has there been coverage of the seminar or its central figure by the news media?
- Has the person conducting the seminar published anything on the subject? Look at his book or his magazine articles.
- How does he demand payment?
- Is there really enough material on the subject to merit a seminar?
- Guarantees?
- Endorsements?
- Can the sponsor provide you with data on the students in past seminars? If reputable, the sponsor should have records of who has been attending the seminar and, possibly, would refer you to people in your industry.
- Is this a "promotional" seminar, meant to push a product or service?

## OBTAINING COMPANY APPROVAL

Seminar choices are usually left to the individual, but most companies will foot the bill. It is therefore important to keep your superiors abreast of the reasoning behind your use of their dollars spent on courses. In addition, without feedback afterward, firms have no way of evaluating the quality, content, and effectiveness of a course or seminar. Consulting with the people in your firm who oversee educational programs is a sure sign that you take the subject seriously. Educational expenditures are investments made by the company in its executives and, consequently, in its future. They should be respected as such.

HAVE A GOOD IDEA OF WHAT YOU WANT TO LEARN   Do your goals and ideas about your development and future responsibilities agree with those of your superiors? Don't assume that certain skills will be helpful later on. Explain the reasoning behind your decision to attend a seminar.

BE SURE A SEMINAR IS THE BEST APPROACH   Some of us hate school and see seminars as an easy way to get knowledge. They are short, little is expected of us, and the work isn't graded. But, often, seminars are simply insufficient. In other cases, a firm's training staff can provide a program in-house. And then there's the learn-on-the-job approach, which can work quite well. If, after you've examined the alternatives, the seminar still seems like the way to go, you should have little trouble getting approval.

COME PREPARED   Presumably, you've done some research on the seminar in question. You should have the course outline, brochures, and other pertinent information with you to support your case.

MAKE A "NO-FRILLS" REQUEST   An increasing number of seminars are being given in vacation spots so that attendees can come for a seminar and get a deductible vacation; your boss probably won't be interested in sending you to one of these. Since many of the seminars are "road shows" given in various cities, find the location nearest you. The exception: You have business to attend to in a distant city and the seminar can be combined with the business trip.

## ATTENDING THE SEMINAR

PREPARE   If you receive seminar materials in advance, read through them, or at least skim them.

Remember that the time before the seminar is critical. If you do not delegate effectively and clear your schedule, you are headed for trouble. You could well be spending seminar time on the phone, or on ducking out for appointments. Be ready to give the seminar your full attention.

GET INVOLVED   Question; list; outline. If there's something you want to know and it isn't covered in the seminar, catch the instructor during lunch or coffee break.

## WHEN YOU GET BACK

USE IT OR LOSE IT   If the seminar is worthwhile, you will come away full of new ideas and procedures. You should take some time to put into practice what you've learned. If you don't do it soon after returning, you probably never will.

FEEDBACK TO OTHERS   If your organization has a training department, provide its personnel with a detailed evaluation. If not, write up a memo about the seminar and send it to someone in the personnel department who would be interested; keep a copy for your files. If the program is so valuable that you think the entire staff should attend, you can arrange to have the seminar given on company premises. It's cheaper that way, and will probably be more effective.

HAVE REALISTIC EXPECTATIONS   More training is not always the sole answer. Personality or environmental problems may make it difficult for you to utilize what you've learned. And if you are an underpaid or underutilized employee, you will probably gain little from a "motivational" seminar; it doesn't address what is, for you, the real problem.

## SOURCES OF SEMINAR AND COURSE INFORMATION

TRADE ASSOCIATIONS  Many associations sponsor seminars and keep members up to date (usually by newsletter) on relevant seminars held by various firms. Organizations such as the National Association of Accountants have made a major commitment to providing continuing education to their membership.

TRADE MAGAZINES  Such magazines usually have calendar sections that include information on seminars. Sometimes they even sponsor a few of their own. Also watch for advertisements by seminar givers.

COMPANY TRAINING OFFICES  Training-office staff will be familiar with many of the seminars and their sponsors. They will also have the brochures on file, and perhaps some evaluations from others. There is also a good chance that they can get the lowdown on an unfamiliar seminar by calling their counterparts in other companies.

UNIVERSITIES  Most major universities and many smaller colleges offer some form of continuing education programs. They are very eager to tell you about their offerings.

DIRECT MAIL  Seminar givers rely on direct mail to reach you. They often get their lists from business magazines, so you're probably receiving at least a few brochures. If you aren't, call several of the larger seminar sponsors; they'll be glad to put you on their mailing lists.

MANTREAD, INC.  Mantread is a nonprofit clearinghouse for information on education and training programs. It maintains an unbiased National Training Registry, which summarizes experiences and evaluations of subscribers. It will also provide brochures and other printed material supplied by the seminar sponsor. Your organization must become a subscriber before you can avail yourself of Mantread's services. The fees are nominal, and will be still less if your firm has an experienced personnel or training director who is willing to help Mantread by submitting evaluations of programs taken by employees.

Many Fortune 500 companies belong. If the service prevents even a few of your company's employees from attending the wrong seminar, the subscription fee will be recovered.

Contact:
Mantread, Inc.
46 East 4th Street
Saint Paul, Minnesota 55101

## EVALUATION FORM

You recently attended a program on the subject of _____
_____ which was put on by
_____

Will you please take about ten minutes to complete this form. This will help us in our continuing analysis of the effectiveness of the management training, education and development programs that we use. Please be open and candid in answering all the applicable questions in PART I. If you wish, use PART II for any additional information that you feel would be helpful to us. Please return to me by _____ if possible.
                     (date)

If our identification of the program title and sponsor stated above is incorrect or incomplete, will you please show it correctly on the attached.


_____
                          Coordinator of Evaluation Program




Copyright 1972 by Mantread, Inc.

A non profit corporation for evaluation of MANagement TRaining, Education And Development  MANtread Inc.

Fig. 31. Evaluation form for seminars,
prepared by Mantread Inc.
(*through page 281*)
Reprinted by permission.

## PART I – BASIC EVALUATION

Name of Program:

Approx. Dates of Participation:

Month:            Year:

Sponsoring Agency or Resource Used:

Where Attended:

Place an "X" on the line which denotes your evaluation of each of the following questions which are applicable:

|  | POOR | FAIR | GOOD | EXCELLENT | For Office Use ONLY |
|---|---|---|---|---|---|
| 1. How were the physical facilities? | — | — | — | — |  |
| 2. How well was program run, as for example in scheduling, administration and creating a learning atmosphere, etc.? | — | — | — | — |  |
| 3. How well did the subject matter fulfill the stated objectives of the program? | — | — | — | — |  |
| 4. How effective did you think the leaders and other resources were considering purpose of the program? | — | — | — | — |  |
| 5. List the names of the leaders and key staff people and then evaluate their effectiveness. | | | | | |
| _____ | — | — | — | — | |
| _____ | — | — | — | — | |
| _____ | — | — | — | — | |
| _____ | — | — | — | — | |
| 6. Was there group participation? YES_____ NO_____ If yes, how useful and constructive was it? | — | — | — | — | |
| 7. What is your overall evaluation of this program? | — | — | — | — | |
| 8. Indicate how well each of the following contributed to the program. Cross out items that don't apply. | | | | | |
| – Reading materials | — | — | — | — | |
| – Bull sessions outside meeting | — | — | — | — | |
| – Ideas explored and studied | — | — | — | — | |
| – Visual aids | — | — | — | — | |
| – Contacts with others in program | — | — | — | — | |
| – Others (describe please) | | | | | |
| _____ | — | — | — | — | |
| _____ | — | — | — | — | |

9. Would you recommend this program for others in your organization?   YES _____ NO _____
   If yes, what type of person (or job title) would you recommend?

10. Please give an example as briefly as possible of something you gained from this program which may
    help you on your job. (If more space is needed, continue into PART II, pp 4).

11. Please state as briefly as possible what caused you to attend this program.

12. (Personal information so that your reactions can be most effectively used in our summary.) PLEASE
    CHECK APPROPRIATE BOXES.

|  | Less than 1 | 1-3 | 4-10 | Over 10 |
|---|---|---|---|---|
| • Years with present employer? | ☐ | ☐ | ☐ | ☐ |
| • Years in present position? | ☐ | ☐ | ☐ | ☐ |

|  | 20-29 | 30-39 | 40-49 | Over 49 |
|---|---|---|---|---|
| • Age? | ☐ | ☐ | ☐ | ☐ |

|  | HS Grad or Less | Some College | College Grad | Graduate Degree |
|---|---|---|---|---|
| • Years of Formal Education: | ☐ | ☐ | ☐ | ☐ |

|  | None | 1-2 | 3-4 | Over 5 |
|---|---|---|---|---|
| • How many other off-the-job programs taken in last 3 years? | ☐ | ☐ | ☐ | ☐ |

Please place check mark in front of the key words which come closest to generally describing your position:

Level of Position:   _____ Top & Upper Management   _____ Middle Management   _____ Supervisory Management   _____ Non-Supervisory

Primary Duties:

_____ Executive (Manages enterprise, department, or subdivision)
_____ Administrative (Assists executives or higher level administrators on policy interpretation or works in a specialized staff area)
_____ Professional (Position requires advanced knowledge in a field of science or learning)
_____ Outside Sales (Makes sales at customer's place of business)

NOTE: If you think additional information is needed to generally describe your position, place check here _____ and add information at end of PART II

## PART II – ADDITIONAL INFORMATION (OPTIONAL)

To conserve your time, questions in PART I were purposely very brief. However, if you can take the time, your completion of as many of the following items as possible would give us a more in-depth understanding of the program.

A. About how many people were enrolled in the group? _____

B. About what percentages of them fell into each category:

    Foreman, first line supervisors, staff assistants    _____ %

    Middle management and mid-level staff    _____ %

    Upper management – division heads, officers, etc.    _____ %

C. About what percentage of the program was:

    Theoretical? _____ %     Practical? _____ %

D. About what percentage of the material presented was:

    New? _____ %     Refresher? _____ %

E. Were there handout materials to take home? YES _____ NO _____ If yes, how likely that you will find use for them?

    Likely _____     Unlikely _____     Don't Know _____

F. Were there handout assignments to do before the program? YES _____ NO _____ If yes, how much did they add to the value of the program?

    Much _____     Little _____     Doubtful _____

G. What was the length of the program in days? _____

    Was the length of the program:

    Too long? _____     Too short? _____     About right? _____

H. Please use this space to add any additional feelings or opinions you have that may not have been adequately covered above or in PART I:

═══════════════ FOR EVALUATION COORDINATOR USE ONLY ═══════════════

# THE BIG NAMES IN BUSINESS SEMINARS

THE AMERICAN MANAGEMENT ASSOCIATIONS (AMA) is the largesf seminar giver in the nation. AMA is a nonprofit organization that boasts 70,000 members, and giving seminars is consistent with its goal of encouraging dialogue among its members, keeping them informed and facilitating contact with leading management thinkers.

The AMA's Center for Management Development offers over 2,000 courses a year, from 12 divisions:

- Finance
- General Management
- Marketing
- Research and Development
- Packaging
- Purchasing
- Insurance and Employee Benefits
- Manufacturing
- Management Systems
- Human Resources
- International Management
- General and Administrative Services

The Center maintains a full-time staff of coordinators and program directors who monitor course quality, recruit instructors, and develop new courses. They draw from a "faculty" of over 800 guest speakers.

In addition, there are 13 major "councils"—committees of top executives who examine seminar quality, content, and delivery and assess postseminar evaluations by attendees.

There are indications that AMA has been working very hard to maintain and upgrade the quality of its courses. In 1977, postseminar surveys revealed that 66 percent thought the seminars "excellent"—up 37 percent from 1973; 30 percent rated them "good," and only 4 percent thought them "fair," an 8 percent decrease from '73.

AMA officials claim that they have been able to get 100 percent of the managers to take part in postseminar evaluation. As for the 1/2—1 percent that consistently rates the seminars "poor," AMA officials are reluctant to take the blame. They say the response may be the result of a negative attitude on the part of employees pressured or even ordered to take the course; or the attendee made a poor choice in attending a seminar that was ill suited to his needs.

Contact:
American Management Associations
Center for Management Development
135 West 50th Street
New York, New York 10020

AMR INTERNATIONAL is a New York-based, profit-making educational firm that offers about 700 seminars a year on approximately 60 topics.

AMR, clearly at a disadvantage because of AMA's nonprofit status, goes in for more topical, freewheeling courses. The company doesn't have the same kind of accountability as AMA, so perhaps it can be a little more controversial and innovative: There are no advisory councils to please.

AMR has no in-house instructional staff. It draws instructors from the business community, and many approach AMR, rather than the other way around.

With over 250,000 past customers, AMR strives for repeat business. It claims a renewal rate of almost 100 percent from its clients—about 20,000 private and governmental organizations.

Contact:
AMR International, Inc.
1370 Avenue of the Americas
New York, New York 10019

THE CONFERENCE BOARD, INC. is a prestigious nonprofit organization that conducts a great deal of business and economic research.

The Conference Board's approach to seminars is markedly different from that of either AMA or AMR. It holds three basic types of meetings that tend not to overlap or compete with others in the industry:

*Large "theme" conferences.* Attendance ranges from about 300 to 1,500. These conferences are open to both members and nonmembers and usually deal with basic issues: antitrust, exporting, new-product development, etc.

*Private, invitational meetings.* These are very prestigious and are aimed at the members that really make the Conference Board work—the chief executive officers. There are usually about 50 in attendance.

Usually held in a retreat or conference center over a weekend, these meetings are exchanges among an elite from top corporations worldwide. The speakers usually come from their own ranks—and they are always heavyweights. On occasion they'll bring in an outsider to discuss a new idea, if none of the conferees has gained the necessary expertise in the field in question. In such cases they always go with a well-known name. And they try to avoid people with strong biases.

*One-day seminars.* These are open to all. Since the Conference Board deals in research, it sends resident experts and authorities on tour to give seminars on important topics. This is as close as the board comes to conventional seminars, but they are treated as methods of disseminating research findings and other information resulting from the board's other activities. In that sense, they are not really "products" for the training marketplace; i.e., not developed to meet specific training needs.

The Conference Board can operate this way because it gets plenty of cash from its prestigious membership—enough so that it could make ends meet without seminars.

In 1979 the Board conducted about 20 open conferences, 15 CEO invitational meetings, and 32 briefing seminars.

Contact:
The Conference Board, Inc.
845 Third Avenue
New York, New York 10016

## OTHERS IN THE FIELD

PROFESSIONAL ASSOCIATIONS AND FIRMS  In fields such as accounting, many states require Continuing Education Units for the professional who wishes to retain his license. Nonprofit associations such as the National Association of Accountants and profit companies such as the prestigious accounting firm of Peat, Marwick, Mitchell & Co. fulfill this need by giving seminars.

MAGAZINE PUBLISHERS  In the case of industries that are poorly organized, trade magazines often act as de facto professional organizations, organizing forums, and seminars. Recently, business magazines with a more general readership have jumped in. Among them: *BusinessWeek, Forbes,* and *Dun's Review.*

PACKAGERS  These are companies that administer and market seminars conducted by institutions with little experience in running the business end of the seminars themselves, or little inclined to do so. One of the largest and best known is the New York Management Center, Inc.

*New York Management Center, Inc.* NYMC coordinates programs primarily for prestige universities like Wharton School of Business (University of Pennsylvania), New York University, and the University of Chicago.

Generally, NYMC leaves the planning and content of the seminars to its clients and concentrates on the marketing and finance end. An important part of their effort is the direct-mail campaign; but billing, evaluation, facilities management, and the printing of course materials are also included.

NYMC has helped a great many schools compete successfully in the seminar marketplace. And since the schools are in it for prestige and donations as well as tuition profits, they are generally sticklers for quality. They want to to create a positive image in the public and private sector. You'd probably think twice before sending your son or daughter to a school that offered bush-league seminars. And there are alumni, individual and corporate supporters to please.

Contact NYMC for information about the seminars being offered by their client schools:

New York Management Center, Inc.
360 Lexington Avenue
New York, New York 10017

---

# THE CEU: WHAT'S IT WORTH?

---

The CEU, or Continuing Education Unit, is a halfhearted attempt to give legitimacy to noncredit courses. In some professions the units are required for relicensing or recertification, but they are little more than records of attendance. CEUs are also popular because they make the courses more attractive—the promise of credentials, no matter how ludicrous, lures people to the courses.

Serious-minded students interested in education for personal enrichment couldn't care less about CEUs. And those who feel the need for a substantial increase in education or the acquirement of additional skills would be wise to go for a degree or, at least, credit courses. When credit is offered, the instructor evaluates your performance and proficiency as well as your attendance. But there will always be those who spend their time, and the company's money, attending noncredit courses. They lack the need, motivation, time, or interest in additional formal schooling. The CEUs stand as the business world's equivalent to the Good Housekeeping Seal of Approval—CEUs mean the course actually did exist, one actually attended it, and the records are there to prove it. The value? Perhaps the course can go on your résumé without embarrassment, and it may have a certain promotional value—such as in a curriculum vitae or a company brochure.

Wisely, organizations such as the American Management Associations grant CEUs for all their courses.

---

# HOW TO SELECT A SCHOOL AND PROGRAM

---

If you've been to college, you already have some idea about what is involved: You pick the school and the program, the teachers, and the classes.

---

# THE SCHOOL

If you intend to keep your job, you obviously must choose a local school. Get all the catalogs and bulletins and read them. Look for evidence that the school is keeping pace with the changes in the business environment and is abreast of the latest techniques. The best way to tell is by the courses the school offers. Any school that claims to be in touch should have courses on computer applications in business, international business, systems analysis, information systems, and macro- and micro-economics. Few schools will have them all; if the school you're considering has none, or even very few, it is suspect.

Once you've established that the school has what you want in the way of courses and degree programs, you should find out something about its reputation. Ask around; people in personnel or training and development departments should know. Check with friends who faced a similar choice. And, by all means, ask school officials for placement records, starting salary levels of graduates, and any form of independent rankings. Ask about the intellectual caliber, academic achievement, and business experience of the students; you want to construct a profile of the typical student. If you do not fit the profile, you might find that the school would not meet your needs.

Ask the American Assembly of Collegiate Schools of Business for information on the school's accreditation status. Or consult *The AACSB Membership Directory.*

Contact:

American Assembly of Collegiate Schools of Business
11500 Olive Street Road
Suite 142
St. Louis, Missouri 63141

# THE TEACHERS

The best way to find out about a teacher is by asking current and former students. If you have an idea that you may be taking a particular instructor's course next semester, try sitting in on a class or two this semester. Don't be shy about arranging a meeting with the instructor. Talk about your needs and how his course may fit into your educational and professional plans. And size him up in terms of sincerity, ability to articulate, clarity of thinking, knowledge, and experience. Credentials can be deceptive. Not every instructor with an illustrious background in academia is a good teacher, nor is every highly successful businessperson.

# PLANNING YOUR COURSES

What exactly do you wish to learn? More important, how, if at all, do you expect this education to help you? If you attend classes because you enjoy learning, fine. But if you are interested in career advancement, your courses must have a focus. You can't afford to be a dilettante. Pick a goal—a degree, a certificate, or a level of proficiency in an important specialty. Companies are sometimes more willing to pick up the tab if you work at developing a skill in which the company is sorely lacking.

You might want to start your planning by consulting *Graduate Study in Management,* a complete guide to business degree programs. You'll find it in college and major bookstores. Or contact:

Admission Council for Graduate Study (ACGS)
Box 966
Princeton, New Jersey 08540

## YOUR DEGREE OPTIONS

THE MBA   Generally, the MBA requires 60 semester hours over two full-time years, or three to four years part-time (two or three hours, two nights a week). People who make job and promotion decisions are familiar with MBAs; they know what you have to learn to get one. The vast majority of graduate business degrees are MBAs. In 1980 approximately 52,000 MBAs were awarded—up from 21,000 in 1970. This glut, combined with economic uncertainties, means that the degree is no longer a ticket to a job.

MBAs typically come with a higher price tag, and they are generally hired into training positions where they don't at first contribute much to the company. In periods of recession or slow growth, companies simply hire fewer. Don't be surprised to see MBA programs scrapped at some schools.

If you have prior business experience along with your MBA, you are in a much better position. Most top companies prefer at least two years of work experience.

Now let's assume that you have a job, but not an MBA. You may feel that, in a poor business climate, the extra degree won't make a difference in terms of promotions or pay raises. But consider a part-time MBA. You don't give up your job. And when things rebound, you might find yourself sitting pretty. Another option: If you've got the smarts to get yourself accepted to one of the top B-schools—like Harvard, Stanford, M.I.T., Yale, Wharton—and you think that you'll do reasonably well, you needn't worry about getting a job. There are always openings for the cream of the crop.

*The part-time MBA.* This can mean the slow and steady route of three or four years of night school one day a week, or an occasional semester-long "educational leave of absence." It depends on your desire, on your work load, and, of course, on your company. Recently many schools have begun "early bird" and lunchtime classes.

The MBA is still the degree most in demand, but you do have other options: You can get an MS in business with less effort, in less time; or a PhD in business with more effort and a lot more time.

THE MS IN BUSINESS   requires only about 30 semester hours. You can get it in as little as one year, part-time. This program is a maverick, invented by Columbia University. The MS program cuts down on class time by de-emphasizing general business training and concentrating on a specialized area—accounting; personnel; computers. It has caught on at other schools, primarily because of its lower costs, fewer hours, and emphasis on a specialty. New York University, the University of Massachusetts, Florida State, Northwestern, San Diego State, Ohio State, Georgia Tech, and University of Southern California are among the schools that offer it.

THE PhD   Doctoral programs in business shouldn't be undertaken without considerable forethought; they do not give you much more general business training than you get with the MBA. The PhD in business is a prestige degree that will help you establish credentials as an authority, spokesperson, teacher, journal editor, or consultant. But in terms of its value to a manager, it hardly justifies the time and effort—unless, of course, you enjoy the quest for knowledge.

Doctorates are offered in economics, computer science, finance, and marketing. Part-time, it will take between five and eight years and will set you or your company back as much as $12,000.

THE EMBA   or executive MBA, was devised to appeal to older executives in middle to upper management. The emphasis is on top-level management skills, with less time spent on specialties. Only 45 semester hours are required. One of the main attractions of an EMBA program is the scheduling. It usually consists of one full day per week (Friday or Saturday), or two days every other week.

EMBA students like learning with their peers, rather than being mixed in with younger students in the MBA program. For this reason, it is generally unwise to enroll in an EMBA program if you are relatively young or hold a lower-level management position.

GLAMOUR COURSES   These are the blue chips—the prestige non-degree management programs intended for key executives. If your company sends you to one of these courses, it's a pretty good indication that you are being groomed for a promotion. If that doesn't pan out, you'll be in a better position by virtue of the contacts made at the course.

It's difficult to measure what one gets out of such courses; there are no grades. And the fact that most graduates succeed begs the question, since the very fact that you are chosen by your firm to attend is a sure sign you're on your way up. In most cases, such courses will broaden your perspective on problem solving and give you an opportunity to learn about areas outside your own field.

*Stanford* offers an eight-week program intended for those who have more than ten years of managerial experience or who hold a senior management post.

There are seven courses of instruction: Financial Management and Control; Management of Marketing Strategy; Management of Human Resources; Economics, Public Policy and Business; Management Science and Computers; Management of the Total Enterprise; The International Economy.

In 1978 the class had a median age of 43.

Contact:
Stanford Executive Program
Graduate School of Business
Stanford University
Stanford, California 94305

*Harvard's* Advanced Management Program is perhaps the best known and most respected. It lasts thirteen weeks. You live on campus. The program is very structured, with six hours of lectures and seminars each day. But you can't just sit in the back of the room and coast through it: The Harvard B-School "casebook" method is used. You must prepare for class and be ready to participate. The curriculum includes Operations Strategy and Structure, Business Policy, Business and the World Society, Management Control, Human Behavior in Organizations, Financial Management, Marketing Management, Management Control, and a few electives.

If you get an opportunity to attend this course, do not turn it down. It is a sure sign that you are headed for bigger things.

Contact:
Advanced Management Program
George Pierce Baker Hall
Harvard Business School
Boston, Massachusetts 02163

*Columbia's* executive program takes a different approach. For one thing, it is conducted not on Columbia's New York City campus, but 50 miles upstate, at Arden House. The program is less structured, and there is more emphasis on the exchange of ideas than on classroom learning. Topics taken up include the relationship between the planning and implementation functions, and the impact of the environment on business. The session lasts six weeks.

Contact:
Executive Program in Business Administration
Columbia Graduate School of Business
Columbia University
New York, New York 10027

*MIT* The Massachusetts Institute of Technology likes numbers. True to form, the cost of its Senior Executive Program is exceptionally high but includes a field trip to Washington, D.C. The approach is quantitative, with courses covering finance and accounting, electronic data processing, computer technology, control techniques, information systems, and quantitative analysis.

Contact:

MIT Program for Senior Executives
Room E-52-456
Sloan School of Management
Massachusetts Institute of Technology
Cambridge, Massachusetts 02139

*Other good glamour programs* are offered by Wharton (University of Pennsylvania), University of Chicago, University of Virginia, University of North Carolina, Carnegie-Mellon, Berkeley, and Northwestern.

Harvard has an additional course—the Program for Management Development (PMD)—designed for middle management—that lasts 14 weeks.

## WHERE TO GET INFORMATION
## ABOUT MANAGEMENT PROGRAMS

The best sources are:

- *Bricker's Directory of Management Enhancement Programs*
- *American Management Associations Directory of Management Education Programs,* an excellent source, contains over 1,100 primary program entries in all major management fields. It includes a comprehensive listing of the important data on each course.

Both of these directories are available in most public and university libraries.

---

# TEACHING YOUR WAY TO THE TOP

---

Power is built on influence. And influence is, in part, built on knowledge, reputation, and visibility. More and more, career-minded executives are viewing teaching as a success strategy, rather than a refuge for those who can't cut it in the business world.

The surge in demand for MBAs has created a need for good teachers with practical business experience. And long gone is the antagonism that existed between academia and the business world in the sixties.

More professional teachers have accepted off-campus work as consultants, and this trend has made it easier for executives to accept part-time teaching posts. The interchange between business and universities is out in the open.

---

Teaching is not easy. You don't stand in front of a class and tell them tales of your exploits. You've got to prepare, stick to a curriculum, and maintain strict academic standards. You'll be spending a fair amount of out-of-class time preparing for class and reading students' work.

For a good teacher, the rewards are numerous. As your course becomes more refined, you may develop an approach and a body of knowledge worthy of being published. Teaching and publishing form a symbiotic relationship: One helps the other.

When you teach, you come in contact with dozens of students who will be entering the working world (if they are not already working). They'll know who you are, and you will get to know many of them. So you will be forming the nucleus of a reputation, at least on a local level.

A good teacher usually learns a great deal from the teaching process. Your own understanding of the subject will deepen and your communications skills will improve. This will undoubtedly help you on your job in the business world.

Last, but not least, is the joy of teaching—sharing knowledge and helping others succeed.

If you are unsure about making a commitment, you might start by giving or participating in a seminar. Then move on to night school. Contact the school or sponsoring agency and offer your services and credentials. The need for knowledgeable teaching executives is greater than you might imagine.

---

## WHAT YOU SHOULD KNOW:
## OPINIONS FROM BUSINESS AND ACADEMIA

---

The American Assembly of Collegiate Schools of Business (AACSB), in an effort to upgrade and standardize the curricula of accredited business schools, has undertaken a major study. The first phase involved scanning business-school catalogs and consulting with faculty and administrators to come up with a list of "major knowledge areas." The result was a list of thirteen major knowledge areas, or "modules" (see Fig. 32).

This list was used as a basis for surveying over a thousand business people, students, alumni, and the general public in order to determine just how much time should be spent on each of these areas while in B-school.

Since this work will eventually form the basis of a standardized B-school curriculum and, maybe, an accreditation exam, the list is a useful indicator of what B-school students will be learning—and the kinds of things you should know within the knowledge areas most closely associated with your job.

---

## ACCOUNTING

Module No. 1—Managerial & Financial Accounting
 Nature & uses of accounting; accounting as measurements of managerial performance; structure & analysis of financial statements.
Module No. 2—Financial Accounting (Mod. No. 1—prerequisite)
 Capital structure; long-term debt; stockholders equity; capital budgeting and cost of capital.
Module No. 3—Accntng. Systems & Internal Control (Mods. 1 & 2—prerequisites)
 Flexible budgeting; standard costs; break-even analysis & pricing for profit planning; accounting systems & planning.

## ECONOMICS

Module No. 1—Microeconomics I
 Theory of demand & individual utility functions; measures & determinants of demand elasticity; cost & production theory.
Module No. 2—Microeconomics II (Mod. No. 1—prerequisite)
 Theories of firm; price & output decisions under varying market structures & environments; role of prices & profits in a decentralized economic system; impact of government policy on firm behavior.
Module No. 3—Macroeconomics
 Theory of national income determination; economic fluctuations, growth, inflation; monetary & fiscal policies & the role of government; economic forecasting.

## FINANCE

Module No. 1—Financial Structure (Econ. & Accntg. are prerequisites)
 Financial institutions; sources of financing; role of financial management & financial analysis.
Module No. 2—Financial Management (Mod. No. 1—prerequisite)
 Financial forecasting & budgeting; management of working capital; management of current assets.

## HUMAN BEHAVIOR & ORGANIZATION THEORY

Module No. 1—Individual Behavior
 Personality & individual differences; perception & cognition; theories of motivation; learning & development; styles of problem solving & decision making.

Fig. 32. Major business knowledge areas
These categories emerged from a study conducted by the
American Assembly of Collegiate Schools of Business (AACSB)
and involving B-school professors and business executives.
(*through page 294*)

From AACSB Accreditation Research Committee.
Reprinted by permission.

Module No. 2—Small group dynamics (Mod. No. 1—prerequisite)
Group process & dynamics; group effectiveness; leadership & influence; interpersonal conflict; inter- and intra-group conflict.
Module No. 3—Organizational Theory
Alternative organization models; approaches to organization design; organization development & change; organization effectiveness.

## INFORMATION SYSTEMS

Module No. 1—Management and MIS
Systems approach; systems design concepts in management; data base management systems.
Module No. 2—Mgmt. Information Systems (Mod. No. 1—prerequisite)
Design & implementation; general knowledge of computer; use of computer in management.

## INTERNATIONAL BUSINESS

Module No. 1—International Economics
Foreign exchange market; balance of payments & adjustment process; national & international monetary policy; international trade; national & international trade policy.
Module No. 2—Foreign Investment
Methods of pursuing international business; characteristics of direct foreign investment; impact of host state, parent state, & international policies on business strategies.

## LEGAL AND SOCIAL ENVIRONMENT

Module No. 1—The Systems Nature of the Bus. Environment
Linkages between bus. & society; social system, process, and structure; political system, process, and structure; government system, process, & structure; relationship with business.
Module No. 2—Legal & Regulatory Subsystems (Mod. No. 1—prerequisite)
Characteristics of these subsystems; political nature of these subsystems; impact on business; points of influence.
Module No. 3—Law & Business (Mods. 1 & 2—prerequisites)
Antitrust; uniform commercial code; law as an expression of social values.

## MANAGEMENT OF HUMAN RESOURCES

Module No. 1—Management of Human Resources
Human resource policy in organizational context; manpower planning for the organization; recruitment & selection including affirmative action factors; training & development; performance appraisal, compensation, & reward systems.
Module No. 2—Labor Relations
Historical evolution of union-management relations; legal framework; collective bargaining; mediation & arbitration; grievance systems.

## MANAGEMENT POLICY & STRATEGY

**Module No. 1—Development of a Strategic Plan**
Relationship to general management; analysis for strategic decisions; corporate structure, development & strategy; acquisition analysis; developing a strategic plan.

**Module No. 2—Implementation of Strategy (Mod. No. 1—prerequisite)**
Corporate structure; environmental context for strategy; personal values & strategy; managing the implementation process; integration of functional strategies.

**Module No. 3—Planning & Control (Mods. 1 & 2—prerequisites)**
Development of goals for planning & control; budgeting as a control mechanism; sources, costs, & uses of information for planning & control; computer-based planning systems; PPBS.

## MARKETING

**Module No. 1—Principles of Marketing**
Marketing concept; competition & demand models; product, price, promotion, & place issues & strategies; contemporary social, ethical, & governmental issues in marketing.

**Module No. 2—Marketing Management (Mod. No. 1—prerequisite)**
Consumer behavior models; industrial marketing; marketing research strategies.

## QUANTITATIVE ANALYSIS

**Module No. 1—Probability & Sampling**
Probability theory; sampling distributions & theory; measures of central tendency & dispersion.

**Module No. 2—Estimation & Hypothesis Testing (Mod. No. 1—prerequisite)**
Analysis of variance; multiple regression; covariance analysis.

**Module No. 3—Decision Theory & Analysis**
Decision & Utility theory; Bayes' Theorem; prior & posterior analysis.

## OPERATIONS RESEARCH

**Module No. 1—Use of Ops. Res. (Quantitative Analysis courses are prerequisites)**
Operations research & problem solving; model design; linear programming; dynamic programming.

**Module No. 2—Ops. Res. Techniques (Mod. No. 1—prerequisite)**
Inventory models; queuing theory; game theory; simulations.

## PRODUCTION (OPERATIONS) MANAGEMENT

**Module No. 1—Production**
Design of production function & physical system; job design; measurement of output.

**Module No. 2—Quantitative Techniques & Production (Mod. No. 1—prerequisite)**
Inventory systems & problems; quality control systems & problems; production scheduling (PERT, etc.); simulation models.

# NONCOGNITIVE SKILLS

There is some question whether noncognitive skills can be taught: Unlike cognitive or empirical skills, they do not involve set bodies of knowledge. They are primarily a matter of innate aptitude and abilities, personal attributes, character traits, and attitudes. But since everyone agrees that such skills are critical to business success, the AACSB decided to go ahead in an attempt to identify and define various noncognitive skills, or traits.

Using an extensive search of literature and lists compiled by academic and corporate experts, the AACSB research team arrived at a list of 89 traits (*see* Fig. 33).

The list was reduced to six basic "noncognitive characteristics groups" (*see* Fig. 34).

There is no question that you should become familiar with the noncognitive characteristics noted here; they are vitally important for success. The sooner you assess your strength and weaknesses, the better.

Although the list is a good one, it is interesting that it makes little mention of the kind of skills that may be necessary to insure personal career advancement and survival, such as power tactics, politics, and delegation skills. The skills mentioned in the AACSB are certainly those that make for a good and effective manager—but not necessarily a successful one.

For more information on this research project, contact:

American Assembly of Collegiate Schools of Business
11500 Olive Street Road
Suite 142
St. Louis, Missouri 63141

Your request for information should refer to the AACSB Accreditation Research Project.

SKILLS AND ABILITIES

1. Quantitative Ability
2. Analytical/Problem Definition & Analysis
3. Resources Management
4. Interpersonal Relations
5. Communications
   a. Oral
   b. Written
6. Listening
7. Reading
8. Decisiveness
9. Learning Ability
10. Imagination/Innovation
11. Risk Tolerance
12. Judgment
13. Ability to Generalize
14. Leadership
15. Application of Knowledge
16. Ability to Identify Alternatives
17. Questioning Skills
18. Creativity
19. Implementation Skills
20. Objectivity
21. Organizational Skills (Administrative)
22. Persuasiveness
23. Memory
24. Reasoning Ability
25. Problem Solving Ability
26. Ability to Synthesize
27. Assessment of Reasonableness
28. Ability to Set Priorities
29. Mental Ability
    a. Organization of Thinking
    b. Discriminatory Thinking
    c. Decision Making Skills
    d. Concentration
30. Negotiation Skills
31. Ability to Exercise Authority
32. Ability to Deal with Government Regulations

ATTITUDES AND VALUES

33. Respect for Authority
34. Motivation
    a. Desire to Work
    b. Willingness to Work

Fig. 33. Results of AACSB survey of noncognitive traits
Findings were grouped by skills, attitudes, and personal
characteristics of B-school graduates.
*(above and opposite)*

From AACSB Accreditation Research Committee.
Reprinted by permission.

35. Realism
36. Entrepreneurial vs. Organizational Ambitions
37. Level of Expectation
38. Functional vs. General Management Orientation
39. Balance of Rights and Responsibilities
40. Appreciation for
    a. Economic Values
    b. Private Enterprise
41. Global Perspective
42. Meritocracy Awareness
43. Risk/Benefit Sensitivity
44. Goal Orientation
45. Citizenship
    a. Social Responsibilities
    b. Loyalty/Commitment
46. Belief in Human Worth
47. Appreciation for Legislative Process
48. Optimism/Positivism
49. Sense of Tradition
50. Contribution vs. Exploitation Ethic
51. Desire to Expand Personal Influence/Power
52. Need Achievement
53. Compatibility of Personal & Corporate Ethics
54. Career Orientation
55. Competitiveness
56. Positive Understanding of Corporate Goals and Responsibilities
57. Tolerance
58. Commitment to Results
59. Long Range Viewpoint
60. Personal/Career Values (Balance)
61. Profit Motive/Value
62. Sense of Responsibility


## PERSONAL CHARACTERISTICS

63. Honesty
64. Maturity
65. Grooming
66. Mental Alertness
67. Inquisitiveness
68. Manners
69. Emotional Stability
70. Sincerity
71. Social Skills
72. Objectivity (Integrity)
73. Sense of Humor
74. Perceptiveness
75. Self-Discipline
76. Sensitivity

77. Humility
78. Self-Respect
79. Self-Starter
80. Empathy
81. Toughness
82. Flexibility/Adaptation to Change
83. Intelligence
84. Common Sense
85. Competitiveness
86. Energy
87. Self-Confidence/Esteem/Ego
88. Perseverance
89. Resiliency

1.  Administrative Skills
    a.  Organizing and Planning
    b.  Decision Making
    c.  Creativity
2.  Interpersonal Skills
    a.  Behavior Flexibility
    b.  Personal Impact
    c.  Social Objectivity
    d.  Perception of Threshold Social Cues
    e.  Oral Communication Skills
    f.  Leadership
3.  Intellectual Ability
    a.  Range of Interests
    b.  General Mental Ability
    c.  Written Communication Skills
4.  Stability of Performance
    a.  Tolerance of Uncertainty
    b.  Resistance to Stress
5.  Work Motivation
    a.  Primacy of Work
    b.  Inner Work Standards
    c.  Energy
    d.  Self-Objectivity
6.  Values of Business

Fig. 34. Important noncognitive skills

From AACSB Accreditation Research Committee.
Reprinted by permission.

# WHO GETS AHEAD?

In *Who Gets Ahead? The Determinants of Economic Success in America* (New York: Basic Books, Inc., 1979), Christopher Jencks, a Harvard sociology professor, along with a team of researchers, analyzes the question. In a study of American males between the ages of 25 and 64, based on the statistical analysis of 11 different surveys conducted over the course of a decade, Jencks et al examine the relationship between a worker's personal characteristics (measured in terms of family background, cognitive skills, personality traits, and education) and his economic success (measured in terms of occupational status and level of earnings).

If you have Horatio Alger—like illusions about who makes it in America, you may be surprised to read some of the study results.[*]

## FAMILY BACKGROUND: HAVE PEDIGREE, WILL TRAVEL

### EFFECT ON OCCUPATIONAL STATUS

- *The Silver Spoon Syndrome:* Being born into the "right" family pays. For instance, a doctor owes 48 percent of his occupational advantage directly to his family background and 52 percent to factors that differentiate him from his own brother.
- *Like Father, Like Son:* Father's occupational status is the single most significant effect on his son's status. Even after Jencks controlled for variables such as educational attainment, this factor yielded a "modest" influence. The implication of this finding is "that we are not necessarily dealing with general effects of privileged upbringing, but with something specific to occupations." Jencks suggests that the explanation may lie in the "direct transmission of specific jobs."
- Race, ethnicity, religion, and farm background exert a consistently strong effect on occupational status, independent of educational attainment.

### EFFECT ON EARNINGS

- Again, having the "right" family pays—a lot. As the study concluded, if a family's sole concern "were to increase their sons' earnings, the most 'successful' fifth of all families could expect their sons to earn" 45 to 80 percent "more than the average man."
- Race substantially affects level of earnings.

---

[*]Adapted from Christopher Jencks, *Who Gets Ahead?* (New York: Basic Books, Inc., 1979).

---

- Father's occupational status affects sons' earnings only insofar as it affects occupational status.
- Religion: Catholics and Jews have greater incomes than Protestants with similar demographic backgrounds and schooling.

## COGNITIVE SKILLS:
## AMERICAN "MERITOCRACY"—A MYTH?

If test performance is a measure of ability (a dubious assumption, Jencks notes), then the findings of this study would indicate that America is *not* a "meritocratic" society: Ability, per se, is not a determinant of success.

### EFFECT ON OCCUPATIONAL STATUS

- An adolescent's cognitive skills seem to have only an indirect effect on occupational status. Such skills affect educational attainment, which in turn affects entry into initial occupation and may later influence career mobility.

### EFFECT ON EARNINGS

- A "modest" association. To achieve a high level of earnings, "high scores are neither necessary nor sufficient. They are merely helpful."

## PERSONALITY TRAITS:
## MOST LIKELY TO SUCCEED?

### EFFECT ON BOTH OCCUPATIONAL STATUS AND EARNINGS

- The traits associated with occupational status are quite different from those identified with level of earnings. Industriousness seems associated indirectly with occupational status, in that that quality influences educational attainment, which in turn affects occupational status. Measures of leadership are to some degree particularly associated with earnings. However:
- "No single, well-defined trait emerged as a decisive determinant," but the combined impact of various traits was comparatively strong.

## SCHOOLING

Educational attainment was measured in terms of the last year of formal schooling completed. Jencks and his team offer no definitive explanation for the positive correlation established between completed schooling and subsequent economic success. They do conclude, however, that evidence suggests "only part of the association between schooling and success can be due to what students actually learn from year to year in school."*

## EFFECT ON OCCUPATIONAL STATUS

- Of all measurements taken, the single most significant indicator of adult occupational status is the highest school or college grade completed upon entry into the labor market.
- The completion of last year of high school, first year of college, or last year of college has a particularly strong impact—more so than any of the intervening years.
- "Differences in college quality [ranked according to selectivity] had no impact on occupational status" in subjects of equivalent educational attainment.

## EFFECT ON EARNINGS

- Of all measurements taken, the single most significant indicator of level of earnings is the highest school or college grade completed upon entry into the labor market.
- Each successive year of schooling completed raises level of earnings to some extent. Certification, per se, does not carry extra weight.
- Attendance at any selective college (not necessarily the most selective) increased earnings by 28 percent over men with similar backgrounds who attended unselective schools.
- Good grades are linked to high earnings only because they are associated with completion of school rather than with dropping out.
- Higher education increases earnings by helping people enter high-status occupations, which may have licensing and other devices that exclude those with less education. In that sense, it is not what college teaches the student, but rather the doors that it opens in the high-status job market that render it valuable.

*Christopher Jencks, *Who Gets Ahead?* (New York: Basic Books, 1979), p. 266.

# PART V

# MOVING THROUGH THE JOB JUNGLE

**"Without work
all life goes rotten."**
Albert Camus

# 20

# DO YOU SINCERELY WANT TO BE A CORPORATE EXECUTIVE?

*Wanting* to be an executive, say the experts in career counseling, is a matter of desire. There is no room at the top for the fainthearted or the wishy-washy. Commitment is crucial.

To get *there* from *here*, first find your bearings: That is, make an intelligent, clear-sighted evaluation of where you are now; then set the goal. Without a sense of direction, you are bound, at best, to proceed hesitantly; at worst, to travel aimlessly.

What *is* a corporate career? Before you sign your life away, you'd better find out.

Management consultant David J. McLaughlin writes, in *The Executive Money Map* (New York: McGraw-Hill, 1975), "When one's current position is a way station to greater things, we speak of having a career instead of a job." In the corporate world, those "greater things" to which one aspires are the executive positions—preferably the upper echelon of executive positions. But if you're not already privy to the inner sanctum of the executive suite, you still may be in the dark as to what executives do there day to day.

## 191 WAYS AN EXECUTIVE FILLS HIS DAYS

In 1959, the Educational Testing Service of Princeton, New Jersey, asked 93 executives at five major corporations just what it is they do. For the purposes of the study, an executive position was defined as one that "entails responsibility for supervising someone who is also a supervisor." That is, a management position above the "second line." The study, conducted by John K. Hemphill, identified ten major types of work performed by executives:

- providing a staff service in nonoperational areas
- supervision of work

- business control
- technical-product and markets
- human, commodity, and social affairs
- long-range planning
- exercise of broad power and authority
- business reputation
- personal demands
- preservation of assets

The study concluded that:

- Executive positions are complex (any *one* position encompassing three to five different types of work without apparent pattern).
- Work type is not informed by job title.
- What work an executive performs is only in small part dependent upon his place in the organizational hierarchy, his area of function, or the company characteristics.*

In other words, it's not easy to pin down the nature of the executive animal. For that very reason, the ETS researchers compiled a questionnaire. Based on the original responses of the participating executives, "The Executive Position Description" contains 191 statements of position elements. By rating each element on a 7-to-0 scale in terms of the part it plays (ranging from "most significant" through "substantial" and "minor" to "none at all") in the executive's position, the executive can arrive at a practical description of the job.

So take a look at the questionnaire (*see* Chapter 26) and learn the 191 ways an executive fills his day. It is a useful standard against which to measure your own skills, interests, and experience, and it will provide a handy reference when you are ready to put together a *personal* executive description, your résumé (Chapter 25).

---

## CHARTING A COURSE

---

Okay. You're committed. You have a *sense* of direction. To insure your arrival at the top, however, some career planning is essential. Though good luck may play a part in its achievement, success is rarely gained through serendipity alone. Particularly in these times of increased career mobility, an advancement strategy is required. Chart a course. You will want to consult your plan, perhaps revise it, at critical points along the way. Current thinking on the subject of career planning, as popularized by such people as Richard Bolles, in his widely acclaimed

---

*From John K. Hemphill, "Dimensions of Executive Positions" (Princeton, NJ: Educational Testing Service, 1959). Reprinted by permission of the author.

---

book *What Color is Your Parachute?* (Berkeley: Ten Speed Press, 1979), emphasizes the first important step: taking a self-inventory. The theory is that what you have in the future is in large measure determined by what you have now. If you have begun to "find your bearings" as suggested, you have already begun this crucial process of taking stock of your personal (not financial) assets and liabilities.

## SELF-ANALYSIS

**What are your aptitudes?** Also known as a cognitive skill, an aptitude is a natural or acquired ability, a capacity as well as an inclination to do a given thing. Commonly called intelligence, aptitude reflects *potential*, or readiness, in learning and understanding. If you aren't aware of what your aptitudes are, do some psychological testing.

**What are your talents?** A talent is defined as a skill for which you have demonstrated an aptitude. Typically, a talent is an activity you perform well and joyfully.

**What are your interests? hobbies?** What places, people, activities, ideas, or things arouse your curiosity? What fascinates you? What absorbs your attention? What do you *love* to do? What might you *like* to do? Also, what do you *hate* to do?

**What experience do you have?** This question requires specific answers: "I do bookkeeping, accounts payable and receivable," or "I supervised an office staff of seven people." Experience does not have to be on-the-job. ("I directed the fund-raising campaign for my church.") Of your actual experience, what have you enjoyed the most? the least?

**What are your personal priorities?** This is probably the most critical and most difficult question you will have to answer—and ask again and again—in the course of your career. To assess your priorities, consider the principles by which you guide your life. It is an emotional process as well as an intellectual one: What are the *feelings* that inform your actions? What do you value above all else? *In order to answer some practical questions, you must often first ask philosophical ones.* What are you willing to do to get ahead? What and how much are you willing to sacrifice? Your leisure time? Time with your family? Is that time for sale? What is the price tag?

For many people, work does have its own rewards. Through working, people gain a sense of self-respect, a sense of usefulness, a sense of purpose, a sense of accomplishment. For some people, a job offers a genuine challenge, an opportunity to demonstrate abilities, an opportunity to grow and develop. The corporate arena provides ample opportunities for those seeking power or status. But, for most people, the bottom line is this: When you work, you effect a trade-off; you exchange a degree of personal autonomy for a degree of financial security with the hope that financial security brings its own brand of freedom.

So be prepared to make some choices—practical ones. Would you exchange your present life-style—say, a house in the country, fresh air and open spaces for your kids—for a better position in a big city, or even in a different country?

Some of your choices will be simpler, a question of personal style: Do you prefer big corporations to smaller ones? The nonmanufacturing industries over manufacturing ones? Or a service-oriented company over both? Are you more interested in working with people or figures, personnel or finance? The point is, in establishing your career strategy, you must begin to narrow the vast field of opportunity around you.

# 21
# NARROWING THE FIELD

The first step to planning a career is to look inward. The second step is to look up and around. When you embark on your career, you enter what is known as the labor force. The labor force competes in what is known as the job market. What chance you have in succeeding in your career depends in some part upon the kind and number in the labor force as compared to the kind and number of jobs on the market. To translate that into personal terms, to maximize your career opportunities, locate your place in the labor force by identifying your particular skills and experience, then locate that sector of the job market that has a high demand for people with your abilities. If you can't locate a market that calls for your brand of expertise, then go back to square one and develop some new expertise. It's a simple principle, not unlike the one upon which certain intelligence tests are based: Only the mentally deficient try to fit large square pegs into small round holes.

## FITTING IN: THE JOB OUTLOOK
## OF THE EIGHTIES

The factors that affect the availability of jobs are economic, social, and political.

### GNP

The economic growth of this country is traditionally measured in terms of the Gross National Product (GNP), or the total goods and services produced per year. Judging by that index alone, the American economy has been generally thriving, with an average annual increase in the GNP of 4 percent per year since World War II, according to Thomas C. Hayes, in a recent article in *The New York Times*. However, Hayes reported a projected deceleration of the GNP to an average of less than 3 percent per year in the coming decade. This represents a reduction in overall productivity of the nation, which usually means increased job cutbacks and unemployment. Not an encouraging sign.

While productivity is declining, costs are rising and cutting into company profits. Consequently, corporations will seek to cut costs while maintaining productivity and increasing the volume of sales. According to Russell Reynolds Associates, this means industry will put its focus on those areas that most directly affect productivity and profitability: data processing and information systems, research and development, marketing and sales. Less attention will be paid to such areas as public relations, personnel, and legal functions.

## GOVERNMENT CUTBACKS

Government may be making some budget cuts as well. Depending on which services are cut and which government projects are suspended, certain industries will feel the blow directly.

## TIGHTER REGULATIONS

In addition to possible cutbacks in government projects, experts foresee more government regulation, particularly with regard to retirement, job safety, environmental protection, and equal employment opportunity. Such regulation would have some direct impact on the distribution of jobs within the labor force.

## EXPANDING LABOR FORCE

While government and industry may be tightening their belts, the labor force is suffering middle-age bulge: The baby-boom generation has come of age. During this decade workers between the ages of 25 and 44 will expand the work force by 21 million; they will fill 70 percent of the jobs. And although the Labor Department predicts that new jobs will continue to be created, their growth will be at a reduced rate. Only 23 million newly created positions are expected to open up between 1980 and 1990. In other words, there will be more workers vying for (possibly) fewer jobs, and those who will have it toughest are those who are already counted within the present ranks of the work force, not those who will be entering into it.*

## CONSUMER TRENDS

Unlike the sun, however, which is said to shine on all things equally, the factors that affect business conditions do not cast light, or even shadows, in quite so democratic a fashion. Even while some industries will suffer in the coming decade, others will thrive. Certain kinds of businesses are more susceptible than others to economic swings. For instance, those businesses, such as travel and advertising, that do not

---

*From supplement of *The New York Times;* articles by David E. Rosenbaum and Thomas C. Hayes.

produce essential goods or services are likely to feel a pinch in the current downswing. If the dollar weakens against major foreign currencies, on the other hand, tourism *in* the U.S. could boom.

Also, the factor known as "consumer tastes" is likely to exercise its fickle finger upon the future of certain businesses. Again, according to David Rosenbaum's recent article in *The New York Times*, consumer tastes these days apparently are running more towards gourmand than gourmet, and it's projected that a fast-food franchise will prove a better business bet in the eighties than a fine, full-service restaurant.

---

# PROSPECTS FOR THE EXECUTIVE

---

Different experts manage to draw differing conclusions from the same data. There are, of course, always those who, given a donut, will contemplate the hole. Those who prefer to regard the sweeter side of things predict that although the job outlook for the eighties is less than rosy, at least it promises to be better overall than the dismal picture that developed in the seventies. For the executive, in particular, the future holds some promise. The key to maintaining steady employment and a chance for growth is to come up with the right mixture of skills and experience, industry, and location.

More than half the new job openings in the eighties will be filled by white-collar workers, who also happen to constitute half the present-day labor force. What is particularly promising about that statistic is that white-collar jobs are expected to continue growing at an accelerated rate compared to blue-collar jobs. Thirty years ago, professionals and managers filled one in every 12 jobs. Today, they occupy 25 percent of all positions.

## EXPERTISE

The toughest executive positions to fill in the coming years, according to a survey conducted by the search firm of Haskell & Stern Associates, New York, will be "general management" openings. Apparently, the lack of qualified generalists is due to the fact that lower management these days tends to produce specialists. The same survey observed, however, that after general managers, qualified technical specialists, computer specialists, and engineers will be hardest to find. Although Haskell & Stern cited the financial function as one that will be easy to fill, an article in *Esquire* magazine named management accounting as an area that *needs* qualified candidates and is an open field especially for women.* To a lesser degree, a need is identified for personnel

---

*Myra Friedman, "Is This Any Way to Make a Living?" (*Esquire*, July, 1977), p. 66.

---

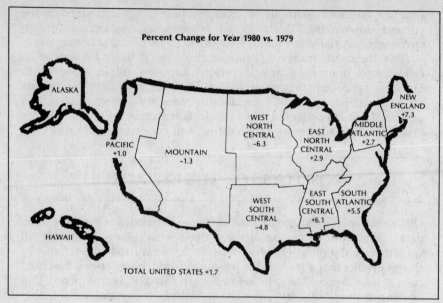

Fig. 35. New business incorporations

Source: Business Economics Division,
Dun & Bradstreet, Inc., 1981

managers, particularly in industrial relations, and for purchasing managers whose job will be to cut down company costs.

## INDUSTRY

The consensus seems to be that *service industries* will offer the most job opportunities in the eighties, particularly:

- *business services,* including insurance and banking. Barring major economic disaster, banking remains one of the most stable professions and, as it continues to expand its services, is currently thriving. Although banks tend to offer good benefits, they are also very paternalistic and *very* selective. They can afford to be. Beyond the ground floor, however, it is not easy to get a foot in the door.
- *information gathering and data processing,* considered *the* business technology of the future
- *computers and related industries, including electronics.* For those with the special or technical backgrounds, these fields continue to yield a bumper crop of opportunities, particularly in the fertile "sunbelt" region.
- *communications,* including radio and TV broadcasting, especially cable TV

- *entertainment and leisure industries*
- *medical services,* including health care and hospitals
- *transportation services*

Other growth industries:

- *energy,* petroleum and petrochemicals
- *synthetic fibers*
- *copper-ore mining*
- *retailing,* particularly department stores and restaurants. The retail sector, according to a 1979 report in *The New York Times,* is the nation's largest employer and is expected to generate the greatest number of new jobs in the coming decade. In the past ten years, the major chains, such as Sears, Roebuck, K Mart Corporation, Saks Fifth Avenue, and Neiman Marcus, experienced an average growth of 10 percent per year. A need is predicted in retailing for middle and upper management personnel, particularly in merchandising, real estate (investments in store property), and marketing and promotion.

## LOCATION

For many executives, finding the right job may be a matter of picking up and relocating to a new community. While a field of work may be glutted in New York City, for example, many able, unemployed executives could find work within their functional area if they were willing to relocate. For the most part, cities with the fastest rate of population growth tend to offer the highest numbers of employment opportunities. Older, established industrial centers, such as New York, long ago reached their demographic peaks. The word is: Young man, young woman, go west—to the West South Central, that is; or south, perhaps—to Florida. According to a study by Chase Econometrics,* the following cities are currently enjoying the fastest growth; note that many of them fall along the sunbelt. In descending order of annual growth rate, 1979-1990, for total non-agricultural employment:

Houston, Texas 4.6%
Ft. Lauderdale, Florida 4.4
Tucson, Arizona 4.3
Las Vegas, Nevada 4.3
Dallas/Ft. Worth, Texas 4.0
Austin, Texas 3.8
Phoenix, Arizona 3.7
El Paso, Texas 3.6
Tulsa, Oklahoma 3.6
San Diego, California 3.6

*Chase Econometrics, October, 1981.

# THE MAIN PROBLEM

In many fields, competition for the top executive jobs will be very stiff. People are concerned not so much about the loss of their careers, according to Barry A. Stein, co-author, with Rosabeth M. Kanter, of *Life in Organizations: Workplaces as People Experience Them* (New York: Basic Books, 1979), as they are about the loss of *opportunity to grow.* A survey of the chief executive officers of about 1,300 major, and primarily industrial, firms revealed a slackening in the number of available openings at the senior management level in coming years. Only 20 percent of the chief executive officers (CEOs) had plans to *increase* hiring in 1980, compared to 30 percent in 1979; and 30 percent of the CEOs expected to do *less* hiring in 1980, compared to only 17 percent polled in 1979. In still another survey, this one covering 1,050 companies, most CEOs predicted that of all the positions they expected to fill in 1980, only 10 percent or less would be newly created positions; all other openings would become available through promotion, termination, or retirement.

# 22

# A LOOK AT YOUR
# ENTIRE CAREER

A useful aid in charting your own executive career is studying the careers of those who already have made it to the top. However, each person's career is unique, just as each person is unique. Apparently, the path to the top is not necessarily the most predictable or the most logical.

In the course of a thirty-year, perhaps forty-year, career, your direction may take many turns, and the particulars cannot be predetermined. Nevertheless, management consultant David McLaughlin has described four basic phases through which most executives might well pass while traversing the corporate countryside, and he has sighted specific guideposts and milestones that mark the way. Below is an "atlas" compiled primarily on the basis of McLaughlin's overview. Insofar as it helps to delineate the choices, it is a handy travel guide for anyone planning to embark upon a corporate career.

# THE CORPORATE CAREER ATLAS

## KEY:

The fully achieved corporate career is divided into four periods: the preparatory; the formative; the critical stage, or watershed; negotiating the heights. Each period is described according to the following classifications:

TIME FRAMEWORK:   approximate duration of phase and/or approximate age of "traveler"

COMPENSATION:   expected salary range and projected net worth

CHARACTERISTICS:   includes noteworthy sights and things to do

OPTIONS:   major crossroads commonly encountered at that particular stage of career

ALERT:   a guide to possible pitfalls and high-risk options

TIPS:   helpful hints on how to insure a first-class route to your destination (practical principles to guide your career choices)

MILESTONES:   your objective for that phase of journey, the achievement of which marks passage into the next

## PREPARATORY STAGE

TIME FRAMEWORK:   the school years: undergraduate as well as graduate training; usually ages 18–25

COMPENSATION:   usually no substantial income

CHARACTERISTICS:
• Acquire a broad-based formal education. Focus on preparing for career by taking at least supplemental business courses.

(continued)

316

- Teachers, parents, friends offer career guidance. Begin to investigate career options and job market.
- Develop good work habits, character, and personality.

OPTIONS:
- Get broad liberal arts background as an undergraduate. Worry about particulars later, or take heavy course load in mathematics, economics, or business. Go right into job market with undergraduate degree.
- Specialize in a highly technical field. Go for advanced academic degree.
- Go on to MBA program.
- Work/study. Through an internship or part-time work, begin to get some field experience while attending school.

ALERT:
- Most campus job recruiters will not even talk to general liberal arts students unless thay have exceptional grades or class rank. Generalists are useful at the top of the corporate ladder, but lower ranks require some useful focus.
- Specializing in a very narrow field too early could limit future options.
- Companies are sometimes wary of corporate "converts"—people with advanced academic degrees who are trying to break into industry. Beware of appearing over-qualified.
- Higher education, including the MBA degree, may buy you a first-class ticket to only the first stop on your career itinerary. Statistics show that amount of schooling does not influence level of earnings much beyond the initial entry into the job market.

TIPS:
- A degree has little intrinsic value to a prospective employer. Perceived potential is what the employer is willing to pay for.
- Therefore, the value of "good" academic credentials is judged in terms of those skills and personal qualities that one hopes are developed in the course of earning a degree: character, personality, creativity, energy, focus, motivation.

MILESTONE:
- Aim to be in a position at the end of your schooling that maximizes the number and quality of potential job offers.

(continued)

# FORMATIVE STAGE

TIME FRAMEWORK: first 10—15-year postpreparatory period; ages 25—35

COMPENSATION: $20,000—$35,000 annual salary (no perquisites)

CHARACTERISTICS:
- Greatest number of options in this period and, therefore, greatest mobility and fastest growth.
- Promotions and compensation will be rewarded increasingly on the basis of on-the-job experience and demonstrated abilities vis-à-vis educational background and perceived potential.

OPTIONS:
- Options are almost unlimited: Almost every size and type of industry and company has entry-level positions in the $20,000—$35,000 range.
- The formative years are usually spent within one of three specific functional areas—personnel, marketing, and accounting. Therefore, your choice of functional area is, at this stage, more crucial than choice of industry or size of company.
- Join a "career" corporation within the first five postgraduate years. The bastions of the corporate world, such as General Motors, generally recruit for entry-level positions *only*. Barring unusual circumstances, this early phase in your career is the only chance you will have to join these ranks.
- Typically a period of much movement, through promotions within a company or through a new job in a new company.
- Make a lateral shift from one area of responsibility to another.

ALERT:
- The advantage of opting for a "career" organization is that you gain excellent experience. On the other hand, these granddaddies of the business world tend to offer a conservative pay scale to newcomers that doesn't make any great jumps for as long as 15 years; they tend to give little autonomy; and, unless it is a big company that has managed

(continued)

to stay young and keep small by developing new products and by diversifying, it may tend to be entrenched in its ways—a stifling environment for an eager young executive.

- Beware of too-early industry specialization. Five to eight years of one-industry experience is a salable commodity, but could lock you in. Beyond a point, breaking into a new industry is difficult.
- Beware the lure of fast-track promotions or job-hopping that increase the value of your paycheck only. Look for meaningful growth in experience: A lateral shift is justified only if the move increases your level of responsibility, results in a new kind of responsibility, or seems to broaden the possible channels for growth.

TIPS:
- Make frequent and *meaningful* job changes, once every two or three years at first; then, every three or four years.
- Look for the companies that offer the greatest growth potential.
- At this stage of the game, it is acceptable to sacrifice substantial financial gain to opt for new and greater responsibility. However, a truly better job usually means better pay.

MILESTONES:
- Acquire in-depth experience while increasing visibility through job performance. This should land you in the most advantageous position with maximized future options.
- Your goal in the organizational hierarchy should be, generally, an upper-middle management position.
- Your salary objective: approximately $1,000–$1,500 per year of your age; i.e., 35 years old/$35,000–$52,000 a year.

## CRITICAL STAGE OR WATERSHED

TIME FRAMEWORK: second 10-year postpreparatory period; ages 35–45

COMPENSATION: salary range $50,000–$70,000, plus some stock options. Net worth is beginning to accumulate, but probably remains below the $100,000 level.

(continued)

CHARACTERISTICS:
- Pivotal mid-life period. Time to take new self-inventory and make major reassessment of priorities and goals as measured against actual accomplishments and unactualized potential.
- Typically a period of increased financial growth, but also of increased financial responsibilities: home, family, children's education.
- Time to make major career commitment or change of course.
- Size of compensation package becomes increasingly dependent on job performance.

OPTIONS:
- Change course and try something completely new: Become an entrepreneur or take over a small, but growing establishment.
- Scale down. Take a position of less responsibility in a less high-powered organization.
- Commit your career to your present corporation or to a new one that offers equal or better opportunities for growth.

ALERT:
- To become an entrepreneur is to fulfill a great American dream. It is probably the only means still available to amass a truly great fortune—if you possess the right combination of talent, know-how, and luck. Nevertheless, the early years of any new business are likely to be characterized by hard work, long hours, and short cash. A new business is a risky business. Success in the long term makes all the risk seem worthwhile. But are you willing and able in the short term to make the necessary sacrifices? Moreover, do you possess the qualities of self-confidence, courage, ingenuity, and business acuity that make a successful entrepreneur?
- You always have the option to step backward or *out*, if that is in tune with your personal desires. But if you do make such a career decision, it's always wise to maximize future options and not to burn bridges behind you unnecessarily.
- Keep an eye on the changing scene and avoid a commitment to a career position that is bound for obsolescence.

(continued)

TIPS:
- Weigh the demands of your professional life against the requirements of your private life and determine what personal needs you are willing to sacrifice to your career ambitions. Make the necessary adjustments.
- When you do settle upon a career commitment, look for a situation within a company that suits your tastes in terms of overall style and function and that is willing and able to meet your financial requirements. Compensation packages vary from industry to industry; find a company that offers the kind of package you want. Also, fittingly, statistics show a correlation between a company's performance and executive pay potential. Look for a strong company with sound prospects.

MILESTONES:
- Have a practical program to meet your financial needs as well as your net-worth goals.
- Take a reading of the real progress made in your career. Measure realized potential against unrealized aims. Reconcile the difference and adjust your course accordingly.

## NEGOTIATING THE HEIGHTS

TIME FRAMEWORK: the final lap of the journey; age 45+

COMPENSATION: big bucks

CHARACTERISTICS:
- More expanded responsibility and more challenging opportunity.
- Increased opportunity for higher earnings through negotiation of incentive plans, stock options, etc.
- Very substantial growth in personal net worth.
- Achievement of full professional potential.

OPTIONS:
- Move up as high as you can go within your present

(continued)

corporation. Then hope for a corporate merger or acquisition, or the departure of a key executive, or some other act of fate to make room at the top available to you.

- If waiting your turn doesn't suit you, take over a young company looking for new leadership, become the professional manager of a family-held business needing new blood and your expertise, or take the helm of an established enterprise in troubled waters and turn it around.
- If you don't have what it takes to make it to the peak, keep out of trouble, keep busy, and hope the corporation doesn't outgrow its need for your talents.

ALERT:
- This is high stakes. Protect your share with an employment contract, if you can negotiate one.
- When you walk fresh from the outside into the top spot in an established business, you risk the cold-shoulder treatment due an outsider. This can make your job unpleasant, at best; impossible, at worst.

MILESTONES:
- Top Dog.
- Top Dollar.
- A bundle put aside for your old age.

# CHANGING TIMES

If you recall singing that refrain along with Bob Dylan in the sixties, you may be pleased to note that even in the corporate sector, some windows have been shaken and walls rattled. The old guard still thrives in the likes of IBM, 3M, and AT&T, of course, and, thank goodness, the demise of the capitalistic system is in no way imminent. (After all, you do have a vested interest now.) Nevertheless, the changing social trends of the past few decades are reflected today by changing corporate trends as characterized by executives' career patterns. The one-corporation career man, though not quite an endangered species, is, however, a declining phenomenon. His territory is being usurped by a new breed of executive called the "mobile managers," so named by Dr. Eugene Jennings of Michigan State University, who first observed their unique habits in the mid-sixties.

## YESTERDAY

Traditionally, the prudent aspiring executive valued job security and stability: He found himself a "good" company, applied himself to his work, and maintained his faith in the paternalistic corporate system, which, if he did his job well and with enthusiasm, would reward him regularly with promotions and increased pay. If you were loyal to the company and excelled in your work, you could hope one day, with time (maybe 30 or 40 years) and some luck, to be president, CEO, or even chairman of the board. It was sort of like believing in America: Anyone could "grow up" to be president.

## TODAY

A recent survey of 1,700 executives showed that if you began your career in marketing, finance, or a professional or technical field, there is a 66-75 percent chance (in personnel, a 48 percent chance; and in manufacturing, a 30 percent chance) you will continue your career within that *industry* . However, other studies show that although many stick to one industry, an estimated 17-20 million Americans change *jobs* each year. The average American changes jobs once every five years. In 1977, 11.5 percent, or more than one-tenth of the *entire* employed work force, made a job switch.

Particularly in the corporate world, there is no progress without change. A recent report by the National Personnel Association on mid-level managers (incomes of $14-75,000) stated that at any given time, approximately 29 percent of all managers have their résumés in circulation, and other experts estimate that another 40 percent are *considering* sending theirs out. Of people holding managerial positions, according to one survey, 75 percent who make the move *choose* to leave secure positions to take new ones. The high value once attached to "company loyalty" is to a great extent inappropriate to today's corporate executive. Mobility characterizes the current trend in building a corporate career.

## THE TREND: MOVING ON, MOVING UP

What is the official attitude toward all this change? Judging by the proliferation of mobile managers, corporations today take a favorable view toward job mobility—that is, of course, when the change is made with obvious forethought and purpose. Although only 19 percent of people moving into new jobs actually accept the same or reduced salaries, studies indicate that most people do not choose to make a change primarily for financial reasons, but for reasons related to their work. In fact, of the 9 percent of would-be switchers who end up staying in their old jobs because the employer made a good counter-offer, most switch jobs within a year anyway. Experts cite the following motivations behind an employee's decision to seek a new position:

- He feels a lack of autonomy or responsibility in his present job.
- He is impatient because he feels his progress is hampered by a slow-moving superior, or by the lack of corporate growth or creativity.
- He feels there is a conflict of philosophy or personality between himself and his superiors and/or the company.
- He feels a lack of attention from, support by, or access to top management.
- He feels stuck in a dead-end job, unfairly passed over for promotion, or "lost" in a too large organization.

In other words, the quest for personal fulfillment, rather than for financial gain, has become the major force behind the current trend favoring career mobility.

## A NEW ETHIC

This shift in emphasis from the material rewards of work to the nonmaterial is rooted in some fundamental changes in both the economic fabric and the social fabric of society. We are an affluent society to a degree unprecedented in history. For most American executives, this means we already possess those essentials—and quite a few extras—that money can buy. We have secured for ourselves a relatively high degree of material comfort and as a result, the traditional work ethic is called into question: We have worked hard and earned our daily bread, and stomachs comfortably full, have sat back in our chairs and begun to realize that indeed man does not live by bread alone. Less concerned with the size of their paychecks, many people have become more concerned with the quality of their lives, and this shift in concern has begun to alter long-held attitudes about work.

## WOMEN IN THE WORK FORCE

Causing another wave of social economic change, women are entering the labor force in increasing numbers. Two-paycheck households decrease the financial demands made on the traditional breadwinner in two ways: First, such households tend to have fewer children; second, the burden of bringing home the bacon is redistributed between two

# EXECUTIVE DEMAND INDEX

## NATIONAL SUMMARY

The total demand for business executives during the year ended March 1981 increased 4%, compared with the year ended March 1980.

Other comparisons showed that increases in executive demand were realized in the International region, up 85%; the Southwest, up 29%; the Southeast, up 16%; and the Northeast, up 8%. Demand declined in the Midwest, down 6%, as well as in the West, down 4%.

Administration executives realized the greatest increase in demand during the year ended March 1981, up 87% over the year ended March 1980. Other gains were experienced by marketing and sales executives, up 34%; general management executives, up 15%; and operations executives, up 1%. Three functional categories showed decreases in executive demand: finance, down 18%; engineering and science, down 15%; and personnel, down 11%.

All three industry groupings registered increased executive demand during the year ended March 1981. The highest gain—11%—occurred among financial services companies.

In the first quarter of 1981, compared with the same quarter of 1980, demand increased 11% in the International region; 6% in the Southwest; and 3% in the Southeast. Declines in demand were noted in the Midwest, down 10%; the West, down 8%; and the Northeast, down 2%.

Demand for administration executives increased 26% during the first quarter of 1981, compared with the same quarter of 1980. The largest decrease—28%—was experienced by finance executives.

An analysis of changes in demand among industry groupings during the first quarter of 1981, compared with the same quarter of 1980, showed an increase in demand among financial services companies, up 23%. Non-manufacturing and manufacturing companies registered decreases in executive demand—down 12% and 8%, respectively.

## TERMS AND EXPLANATIONS

This report analyzes the results of the AY/ERC Executive Demand index for the current quarter. The index is compiled by sampling advertisements in major U.S. business publications, and the statistical methodology used is designed to reflect the demand for top and middle management positions in profit oriented businesses. The demand has been analyzed by geographic region, executive function, and industry grouping.

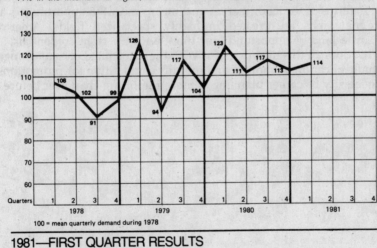

100 = mean quarterly demand during 1978

**1981—FIRST QUARTER RESULTS**

Fig. 36. Executive demand as measured and indexed by Arthur Young & Co.

Courtesy of Arthur Young & Co./Executive Resource Consultants.

earners, and, therefore, neither is so strictly bound to make career choices on the basis of financial motivation.

## COMPACT CAREERS

Not only are more workers making more and more changes during the course of their careers, they are making them in less and less time. This is particularly true in the corporate world. First of all, executives tend to take on more responsibility at an earlier stage in their careers. In 1950, 57 was the average age of a corporate president; twenty years later the average age had dropped to 49.

Also, the average length of time executives hold a given office has markedly decreased. In the ten years between 1962 and 1972, the number of company presidents (in a study including 500 major industrial companies) in office over five years dropped from 45 percent to 25 percent.

Finally, with the lowering of the mandatory retirement age and the increase in the number of attractive retirement packages, more executives are simply calling it quits sooner than they used to. The overall result: a compressed career span.*

## THE AGE OF SPECIALIZATION

Concurrent with the rise of affluence has been the accelerated growth of technology, and the two forces together have reshaped the course of many careers. Advanced technology has created an age of specialization: In terms of the labor market, that means more job opportunities as more new jobs are created in highly specialized fields. America remains a land of opportunity for those with the right credentials.

What does all this mean for *you?* With the accelerated pace of change, the multiplication of choices, and the stiff competition for promotions, the necessity of career planning is more important than ever before.

---

*From David J. McLaughlin, *The Executive Money Map* (New York: McGraw-Hill, 1975), pp. 14-15.

# 23

## ROADBLOCKS

The necessity of career planning is clear, but, as the poet said, even the best-laid schemes go oft astray. You follow the rules. You plan your career step by step. You get a good job. You make all the right moves. Then all of a sudden you are out on the street again, unemployed and looking for a job. *That* was not in the plan.

An unexpected roadblock, a detour, can set you off your path temporarily. Once it happens, stay steady and clear and you will find your way back.

---

### GETTING FIRED

---

#### THE FACTS

Twenty thousand middle and upper level managers changed jobs in 1979. Of those, 8,500, or almost 43 percent, were given their walking papers. The turnover rate of executives doubled in the period from 1960 to 1970, and experts warn that the number of executives fired each year will continue to grow.

In most fields, the higher you go, the greater are the chances for dismissal. And if you are forty years old or over, there is only one chance in five you won't be forced to take a step backward and/or accept a lower salary in your next job.

Furthermore, a currently unemployed person faces unusually stiff competition in the job market.

Seventy-two percent of all job applicants are already employed in secure positions, and they get 81 percent of the available jobs. They also receive, on the average, a compensation package 18 percent higher than an equally qualified but unemployed candidate. Being fired can be a depressing experience, and, unfortunately, the foregoing hard facts don't help to make things brighter.

## WHO GETS FIRED?

- *The Problem Personality:* Personality conflicts between employee and supervisor, often over operating style, account for 33 percent of all terminations. That means *most people are not fired for personal reasons.*
- *The Fifth Wheel:* Company mergers and acquisitions, the numbers of which are on the rise, often create overstaffing problems.
- *The Lame Duck:* Office politics: The new boss decides to bring in his "own team."
- *The Obsolete Veep:* The company reorganizes or takes a new direction and no longer needs your particular skills.
- *The Cut Corner:* In these inflationary times, financial cutbacks are, unfortunately, a growing phenomenon.

## THE NOT-SO-SURPRISED PARTY

You know how difficult it is to give a surprise party at which the guest of honor is actually caught by surprise. When people are conspiring around you, for whatever purpose, their behavior is usually quite transparent—at least to the alert eye.

Why should you be the last to know you are getting fired? Don't be caught by surprise. Keep a lookout for telltale signs:

- Old friends in the office seem to be unusually *un*friendly.
- Old enemies in the office seem to be unusually friendly.
- Conversations stop cold when you enter a room unexpectedly.
- You are given a new office. It has no window or carpet. Your old one had both.
- You are asked if you wouldn't mind sharing your secretary with the new exec in the next office.
- The new exec in the next office seems to know a lot about your work.
- Everyone in the office gets new name plaques. Yours, however, is "not ready yet."

## THE TERMINATION INTERVIEW, OR
## WHAT TO DO WHEN THE GUILLOTINE FALLS

You have been asked into the boss's office for what seemed like a friendly chat. Somewhere into the conversation you hear your boss tell you that you are being dismissed, terminated, laid off, let go, severed, asked to leave, or told to leave. No matter what euphemism your boss has used to blunt his instrument, at some point you will register the impact of the blow, and it will hit hard: *You are fired. You have lost your job.* What do you do?

FIRST OF ALL, DON'T PANIC At least not in front of your executioner. This is easier to do when you realize that, unless he has a reputation for sending heads rolling, what he is doing is probably as hard on him as it is on you. Remember, the odds are 2 to 1 that your "termination" is really nothing personal. The person delivering the message just pulled the short straw in the "who's-gonna-be-the-one-to-tell-him" office lottery. Most people are decent enough and truly hope they will never have to conduct a termination interview; therefore, they have not made a career of learning *how.* Your interviewer may seem overly harsh or overly solicitous. In either case, he is probably just trying his best to get through an unpleasant and awkward task.

PULL YOURSELF TOGETHER Again, this is not easy to do when you have just been axed. It's not a nice feeling under any circumstances to lose a job, but you have nothing to gain by indulging your emotions. Self-pity will not pay the rent or get you another job. The interview is the time to begin to take action.

NEGOTIATE FOR SEVERANCE COMPENSATION Severance compensation is not a game-show booby prize and should not be doled out in that fashion. Most terminated employees have played a fair game, and when circumstances "disqualify" a worker from continuing on his job, the company has a real responsibility to see he doesn't suffer unduly. If you are terminated, recognize three things:

1. You have a right to be fairly compensated and to negotiate for the best severance arrangement to suit your needs.
2. Your terminating interviewer may not be fully aware of the company's severance policies.
3. Your interviewer, at the moment he drops the ax, may appear:
   - remote and stingy, in which case he is probably just uncomfortable, and you should politely decline his current offer and suggest you discuss the severance package at a later date (when you've both had time to think it over), or with a personnel person, or both; or
   - sweet and generous, in which case he probably feels uncomfortable and guilty, and you should hit him hard for all you can get.

### THE TYPICAL SEVERANCE COMPENSATION PACKAGE

As executive turnover becomes more commonplace due to an increasing number of mergers, company cutbacks, and reorganizations, corporations generally are developing more responsible and liberal attitudes toward severance compensation. The principal parts of a typical severance package are:

THE FINANCIAL PACKAGE   Severance pay is usually a percentage of your yearly salary—anywhere from 50 percent to 100 percent, depending on your status in the hierarchy. You should be sure to get the maximum due you, because this may be your only rent money for as long as six months to a year. Insurance and medical benefits are fairly standard parts of the pay package. Depending on what other forms of compensation you received or had coming to you (stock options, deferred compensation, etc.), find out what your rights are to such monies.

OFFICE SUPPORT SYSTEM   You should negotiate for use of office space, including a desk, a telephone, and secretarial assistance. A reasonable employer will usually agree to have the switchboard take calls and messages for you. When you are unemployed and hunting for work, this support is a practical necessity.

COUNSELING OR OUTPLACEMENT   This is a recent, but growing development in severance compensation. Outplacement counseling, the domain of a rising number of specialized consulting firms, has a double-edged function. Under contract to a particular corporation, the outplacement counselors provide their clients with advice and strategies for use in terminating both individuals and groups of employees. Then, in turn, the counselors are commissioned to provide employment counseling as well as moral support to dismissed personnel for the duration of their job search. The purpose of outplacement is to re-place the terminated employee.

*Mixed reviews for outplacement:* Reviews are mixed as to the effectiveness of these outplacement professionals. They claim excellent results—in some instances, 80 percent of their cases employed within four to six months, 60 percent of those in better jobs. Many newly placed executives happily confirm this track record. However, outplacement counseling, although it represents a relatively minor cost to the corporation—maybe $3,000 to $5,000 per terminated employee who receives counseling—is a hefty portion of the entire severance package. Some severed employees have noted ruefully that they might have spent that better had they received it direct from the employer.

Some major outplacement firms: Fuchs, Cuthrell and Company, New York; Drake-Beam and Associates, New York; the TH Inc. Consulting Group, New York; Challenger, Gray, and Christmas, Chicago; and Eaton-Swain Associates, New York.

## A FINAL WORD ON THE FINAL WORD

The reality of termination is simply this: A job hunt is a job hunt no matter what the cause behind it. Granted, being fired and unemployed makes it tough on the ego, but that is all the more reason to attack the job market with a vengeance. Develop your search plan and follow through!

# BEWARE THE CORPORATE MERGER

Rumors of an imminent corporate merger are a sure sign of future organizational shuffling. Depending upon the nature of the merger (that is, the intent of the acquiring company in merging with your own) and also upon your own status and experience within your company, you are as likely to be singled out for termination as you are to be targeted for promotion.

Mergers are taking place in the business world with greater frequency, and they are one of those wrinkles in your career path for which you cannot plan. Take it as it comes. There is no guarantee that you won't be one of the terminal cases when the merger epidemic reaches your quarters, but you can be alert and take measures to protect your career interests.

# THE TRANSFER NOTICE

## WHO GETS IT?

Experts have estimated that corporations transfer 250,000 to 500,000 employees a year, and the number seems to be swelling. There are three different circumstances under which an executive may receive a transfer notice:

- as a prerequisite condition of being offered a job in a new corporation
- as a prerequisite condition of being offered a promotion within the present corporation
- as a result of a corporate relocation in which the plant or headquarters are moved and the employees are asked to move along with it.

According to an Atlas Van Lines "Survey of Corporate Moving Practices," cited in a 1979 issue of *D&B Reports*, "The typical employee being relocated by the companies [surveyed] is male between the ages of 31 and 40 years old [62.4 percent]... with 53.2 percent in the sales/marketing field. The salary range with the greatest frequency of employee transfers is in the $21,000-30,000 range [64 percent]." In another survey, conducted by Merrill Lynch Relocation Management, Inc., an estimated 62 percent of the transferred employees owned homes that they would be required to give up as a result of relocation.

# What to do when a takeover comes

| Situation | Your response |
|---|---|
| A merger is probable but not definite | Keep cool, don't take sides on the merger, and stay out of the office rumor mill. If you are in line for a job contract or have one that is expiring, try for three years' coverage. |
| A merger is definite, and you are nervous | Research the aggressor company's history in past takeovers. Learn all you can about your boss —and your counterpart—in the new company. Make no overt job-hunting moves, but use business friends discreetly for a line on new jobs. Stay close to the scene, avoiding extended travel if you can. |
| The merger date is close, and you fear being frozen out | Use a low-key campaign to find a new job. Contact friends and several executive recruiters known to be reliable. If your salary is less than $40,000, see top-rate employment agencies as well. Don't discuss the merger, but concentrate on selling your own experience and strong points. |
| The merger date is close, and you want to stay on | Make your feelings known to your old boss, and— if possible—to your expected new boss. Talk candidly about what you want. Then concentrate on work. |
| The merger is set, and you own stock in your old company acquired via a stock option | Don't make a hasty sale. Sit tight and be guided by the advice of the board of directors. Selling out will make you look bad to both sides. |
| You hold an unexercised stock option | Don't buy the shares hastily. Seek advice from your boss and your company's top financial officer. Remember that your option—and any premium growing out of the merger—will probably carry over to the merged operation. |
| The merger has happened, and you feel your job is in danger | Work hard, but make a strong new-job effort. Be candid about the merger in job interviews, but avoid any impression that you are fleeing a tough situation. If fired, fight for the best severance settlement you can get—such as 50% to 100% of a year's pay, which is common. Pay $150 for a consultation with a good lawyer who, if necessary, will represent you in severance negotiations. |
| Same as above, but you're over 50 | The same advice holds, but also review all fringe and retirement benefits. If eligible, figure out your income under early retirement. A lump-sum payout under a qualified pension or profit-sharing plan can be put into an Individual Retirement Account (IRA), with taxes not due until a later date. This is true even if you retire from your company and take a new job. |
| You have survived six months since the merger | Do your best work. If no added rewards come within a year, consider starting a discreet job search. |

Fig. 37. Merger advice from *Business Week*

# WHAT DO YOU DO WITH IT?

You can take it or leave it, of course. But if you refuse to accept a transfer, your refusal could cost you your job: The Merrill Lynch study noted that "45% of companies don't hold it against employees when they refuse to be transferred. About 20% said they didn't mind refusals as long as the reason is 'valid.' But 8% definitely said refusal was looked upon unfavorably and could harm an employee's career." So consider the following questions and determine for yourself if you stand to gain more than you lose by making the move:

WHAT WOULD THE MOVE COST YOU OUT-OF-POCKET? Moving your home and family, particularly if you are a home owner, can be a costly affair. Consider the following types of expenses, named in *D&B Reports*, you might incur in the process:

- travel expenses
- house-hunting expenses
- interim living expenses (for executive and dependents)
- moving costs (including insurance, storage, automobile)
- lease cancellation or mortgage-rate differentials
- income-tax consequences
- real estate expenses (costs of selling old home and buying new home)

WHAT IS THE RELOCATION POLICY OF THE COMPANY? More and more corporations are formalizing policy on relocation as well as expanding the coverage offered to transferred employees. According to one estimate, a transferring employee spends an average of four months (not full time) organizing a move. *The Wall Street Journal* reported that the number of relocated employees reporting difficulty selling homes rose from 16 percent to 28 percent as a result of "tight money markets and a dearth of buyers."* The costs of making a transfer should be covered by the company. Be sure you won't be left holding a hefty bill.

IS THIS TRANSFER REALLY A PROMOTION? Or just a fast track to nowhere? Are you being offered more responsibility or just a bit more money? Is the money alone worth the disruption in your life? Beware of some companies who put their young executives on a fast-track transfer circuit that is long on cash but short on real job growth.

IS YOUR SPOUSE CURRENTLY EMPLOYED? The Merrill Lynch study revealed that of the 686 corporations surveyed, only 30 percent offered to help employed spouses of transferred workers in finding new positions, although this figure is almost doubled over the previous year's. Of those employees who declined to accept a transfer, 17 percent

---

*"Relocation Blues," *The Wall Street Journal*, September 25, 1979, p. 1.

### 1. REAL ESTATE

a. Purchase old home . . . . . . . . . . . . . . . . . . . .  _____
b. Pay expenses incidental to sale . . . . . . . . .  _____
c. Pay loss on sale of real estate. . . . . . . . . . .  _____
d. Pay lease breaking expenses. . . . . . . . . . . .  _____
e. Loan for purchase of new home . . . . . . . .  _____
f.  Mortgage interest differential . . . . . . . . . . .  _____
g. Other real estate assistance . . . . . . . . . . . .  _____

### 2. PERSONAL EXPENSE

Pre-move visit by spouse: . . . . . . . . . . . . . . . .  _____
a. One trip . . . . . . . . . . . . . . . . . . . . . . . . . . .  _____
b. More than one trip . . . . . . . . . . . . . . . . . . .  _____
c. No trips. . . . . . . . . . . . . . . . . . . . . . . . . . . .  _____
d. Children or baby-sitting included. . . . . . . .  _____

Family travel at time of transfer. . . . . . . . . . .  _____
a. Actual expenses (including meals, motels,
    etc.). . . . . . . . . . . . . . . . . . . . . . . . . . . . . . .  _____
b. Daily allowance . . . . . . . . . . . . . . . . . . . . . .  _____
c. Limited expenses . . . . . . . . . . . . . . . . . . . . .  _____

Temporary living expenses. . . . . . . . . . . . . . . .  _____
a. Temporary quarters . . . . . . . . . . . . . . . . . . .  _____
b. Meals and incidental expenses. . . . . . . . . .  _____

### 3. SELECTION OF CARRIER

a. Traffic Manager selection . . . . . . . . . . . . . .  _____
b. Traffic Manager-employee preference . . . .  _____
c. Employee make selection . . . . . . . . . . . . . .  _____

### 4. PACKING

a. Full pack authorized. . . . . . . . . . . . . . . . . . .  _____
b. Pack breakables only . . . . . . . . . . . . . . . . . .  _____
c. Maximum limitation. . . . . . . . . . . . . . . . . . .  _____
d. Mobile homes . . . . . . . . . . . . . . . . . . . . . . .  _____

### 5. TRANSPORTATION

Normal household goods: . . . . . . . . . . . . . . . .  _____
a. Unlimited weight . . . . . . . . . . . . . . . . . . . . .  _____
b. Limited weight . . . . . . . . . . . . . . . . . . . . . . .  _____
c. Limited weight, new employees only . . . .  _____

Fig. 38. Moving Policy Check List
*(above and opposite)*

From "Corporate Moving Policy Manual," (Evansville, IN:
Atlas Van Lines, 1979), pp. 33-34. Reprinted by permission
of Atlas Van Lines.

    d. Automobiles......................... _____

    e. Second Automobiles.................. _____

   Unusual items:......................... _____

    a. Limitation on items such as boats, trailers,
       statuary, etc.......................... _____

    b. Air express frozen foods............... _____

    c. Air express pets..................... _____

## 6. APPLIANCE SERVICE
    a. All appliance service.................. _____

    b. Origin service only................... _____

    c. No appliance service................. _____

## 7. SPECIAL SERVICES
    a. Housecleaning or maid service.......... _____

    b. Carpet removal....................... _____

    c. Disassembly of unusual items such as
       playhouses, swimming pools, regulation
       pool tables, etc...................... _____

    d. Altering rugs and drapes............... _____

## 8. VALUATION
    a. Release of 60 cents per pound per article _____

    b. Release at $1.25 per pound............ _____

    c. Lump sum value in excess of $1.25 per
       pound............................... _____

    d. Additional insurance for items of unusual
       value................................ _____

    e. Claims handling assistance............. _____

## 9. STORAGE
    a. Unlimited storage-in-transit............ _____

    b. Limited (time) storage-in-transit......... _____

    c. Limited (dollars) storage-in-transit....... _____

    d. No storage-in-transit.................. _____

    e. Extra pickups and deliveries............ _____

    f. Permanent storage.................... _____

## 10. PERFORMANCE REPORT
    a. Required on all moves................. _____

of them so chose in order to protect a spouse's career. Of all transferred employees in the U.S. in 1978, only 3 percent were female executives.

WHAT WOULD THE TRANSFER COST YOU—AND YOUR FAMILY—EMOTIONALLY, PSYCHOLOGICALLY, AND PHYSICALLY?   The psychic costs of moving can be devastating to a family. Children must leave their schools and their friends; everyone in the family gives up the security and comfort of a familiar community for the problems confronted as a stranger in a new one. Of course, many families adjust to change well or go through the difficulty of the move to find themselves enjoying their new life. Relocation can be a stressful operation and carries no guarantee that it will result in a change for the better.

DO YOU WANT TO MOVE YOUR FAMILY FROM BIG SUR TO THE BIG APPLE?   From Los Angeles, California, to Columbus, Indiana? From Houston, Texas, to Fairbanks, Alaska? From Boston, Massachusetts, to Montgomery, Alabama? A change of location can mean a drastic change of life-style as well as a change in the quality of your life. Are you giving up the good life for a better one?

---

# WHERE THE GRASS IS GREENER

---

You may recall a social studies lesson back in your school days in which your teacher instructed that America had (and the term would be chalked on the blackboard) the *highest per capita income* of any nation. This meant, the teacher explained, the average American earned more money than the average person in any other country. The teacher concluded, remarking, no doubt, with pride: "Americans enjoy the highest standard of living of any people in the world." Hearing this news then, do you remember sighing just a little, feeling somehow relieved and reassured to know that life in America was so *good?*

Thus many Americans grew up with the belief that life in America *is* good and will remain so as long as all *capita* earn an average income. In the final analysis, however, the pursuit of a good wage does not seem to insure the enjoyment of a "good" life. Despite their high *standard* of living, some Americans have become concerned about the lack of *quality* in their lives.

### A STUDY ON THE QUALITY OF LIFE

In 1970 the Midwest Research Institute, questioning the moral of that long-ago lesson, conducted a study to measure and compare the "quality of life" (QOL) in the 50 United States. (Later the study was revised to assess the U.S. metropolitan areas particularly.) The

---

researchers believed that standard measures such as per capita income and GNP are not accurate indicators of the quality of life. If "quality" were strictly a function of "quantity," or material wealth, then why were so many substantially well-to-do people feeling discontent with their lot?

THE COMPONENTS OF QUALITY   In the introduction to the study, the Institute suggests that such by-products of economic growth as changes in institutional structures and the allocation of resources are sometimes so costly to the quality of life as to more than offset the gains made by raising our standard of living. The researchers therefore developed five separate components by which to measure *overall* national well-being:

- economic
- political
- environmental
- health and education
- social

Altogether, the five indicators comprised 120 variables, including, for example, quantitative measures of income inequality; level of informed citizenry; levels of air, visual, and noise pollution; available means to promote maximum development of individual capabilities; and the availability of sports and cultural events in each Standard Metropolitan Statistical Area (SMSA). The SMSAs were divided into three groups according to size of population:

- large (500,000 or more)
- medium (200,000 to 500,000)
- small (200,000 or less)

and the SMSAs in each population group were separately rated:

A: outstanding
B: excellent
C: good
D: adequate
E: substandard

for each of the 120 components. The ratings were based on the QOL index values relative only to the respective group means. Therefore, comparisons between SMSAs can only be made within the same-size population group.

THE BEST LIFE   On the basis of collected data, the study concluded:

- "QOL is not necessarily a direct function of income and material wealth, at least beyond a certain level of subsistence." In other words, "an outstanding rating in the economic component did not simultaneously have outstanding ratings in social, political, environmental, health, and education components."

- The *major* disparities in QOL among SMSAs are *not* economic and political, but have to do with social, health, educational, and, to a lesser degree, environmental considerations.
- Data suggested that those geographical regions with the greatest relative number of SMSAs of outstanding and excellent ratings are:

  the West Coast
  East North Central states
  Mountain states
  New England

The conclusions of the research in the long term will have far-reaching implications for our policymakers who continue to measure the quality of our lives solely in terms of output and income.

In the short term, the study yields immediately useful information to an executive considering relocation or transfer. The study provides practical bases for determining the real worth to you of a proffered career opportunity that necessitates relocation of your home to a new community. Is the quality of your life a negotiable item in the bargain?

For a copy of the Midwest Research Institute report on *Quality of Life Indicators in the U.S. Metropolitan Areas, 1970,* write to Midwest Research Institute, 425 Volker Boulevard, Kansas City, Missouri 64110. Copies are $5 each.

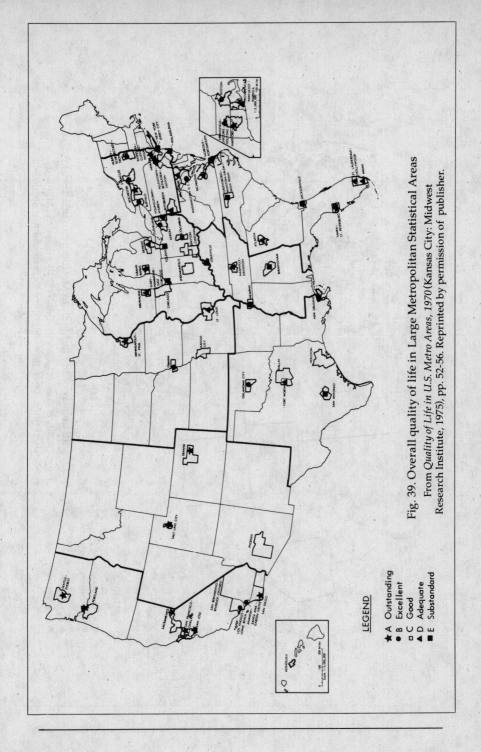

Fig. 39. Overall quality of life in Large Metropolitan Statistical Areas

From *Quality of Life in U.S. Metro Areas, 1970* (Kansas City: Midwest Research Institute, 1975), pp. 52-56. Reprinted by permission of publisher.

LEGEND

★ A Outstanding
● B Excellent
□ C Good
▲ D Adequate
■ E Substandard

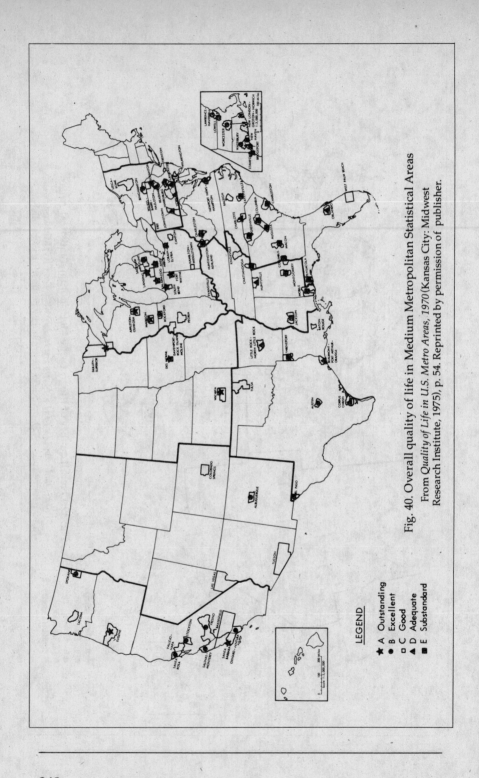

Fig. 40. Overall quality of life in Medium Metropolitan Statistical Areas

From *Quality of Life in U.S. Metro Areas, 1970* (Kansas City: Midwest Research Institute, 1975), p. 54. Reprinted by permission of publisher.

LEGEND

★ A  Outstanding
● B  Excellent
□ C  Good
▲ D  Adequate
■ E  Substandard

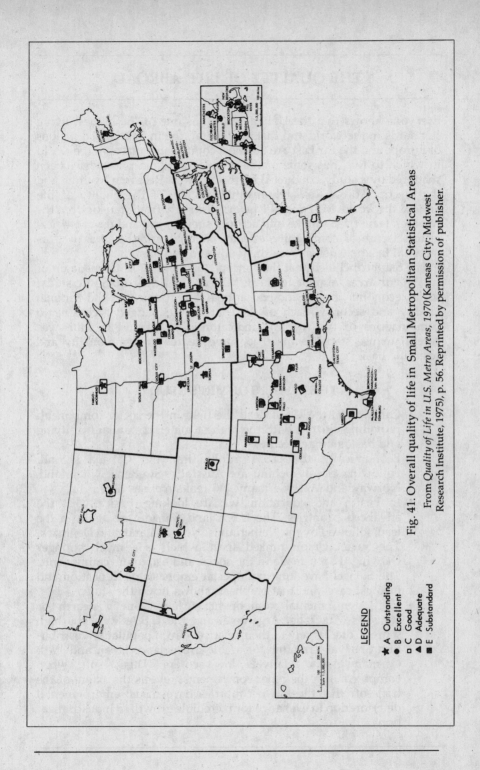

Fig. 41. Overall quality of life in Small Metropolitan Statistical Areas

From *Quality of Life in U.S. Metro Areas, 1970* (Kansas City: Midwest Research Institute, 1975), p. 56. Reprinted by permission of publisher.

LEGEND

★ A Outstanding
● B Excellent
□ C Good
▲ D Adequate
■ E Substandard

# THE QUALITY OF LIFE ABROAD

Everyone knows that the United States has one of the highest living standards in the world and that, in general, the industrialized nations of Europe and the Far East are the most comfortable places in the world in which to live. But some of the popular misconceptions have been shattered by a study, conducted by the Midwest Research Institute and the Electric Power Research Institute (EPRI), of the quality of life around the world. MRI and EPRI worked strictly from statistics, but the research team tried to take into account sociological and psychological factors (sense of community, esteem, national pride, etc.) as well as material factors (such as wealth, goods and services).

The team concluded that the concept "quality of life" is made up of five major areas, similar to those MRI used in their domestic study: social, economic, health and educational, environmental, and national vitality and security. Each of these areas was judged according to combinations of twelve basic indicators. The MRI/EPRI team was careful to use statistics that had some degree of commonality and scientific basis.

## THE RESULTS OF MRI'S STUDY

- Canada and the U.S.A. lead the field in the social component, providing citizens with the highest material standard of living and basic human needs.
- Economically, the U.S.A. ranks first and Canada second. Following closely behind are Australia, Sweden, Switzerland, Norway, and West Germany. No real surprises here.
- In health and education, we are looking, basically, at the advanced countries. The U.S.A. and Canada are again in the lead, followed by the Netherlands, New Zealand, and Denmark. The Soviet Union ranked .sixth, which is a much stronger showing than it made in the social and economic components. The Soviets have long put special emphasis on education and medical care, and that emphasis shows up in the study.
- The environmental component suffers from a dearth of statistics. Australia, Argentina, and the U.S.A. were the high scorers, due largely to their relatively even population distribution and vast amounts of arable green land. Japan and West Germany were relatively low scorers. This result, when compared with the other components, reveals the extent of the trade-off that these two countries have made: environmental deterioration in exchange for incredible growth in industrialization.

- National security? No punches pulled here. Israel and the U.S.S.R. top the list. Not surprising when you consider that both countries have undergone a massive military buildup. Next come Taiwan, the U.S.A., Australia, Czechoslovakia, Bulgaria, and Poland. This component also measures the national vitality—the overall stability of a nation and its relative economic self-sufficiency. In this regard, many of the advanced nations are much more vulnerable than those with totalitarian regimes and limited foreign trade.

When the figures were compiled to produce an overall QOL (quality of life) ranking, the list that resulted could set the State Department back twenty years:

- Oil-rich nations like Saudi Arabia, Kuwait, Libya, and Venezuela did very poorly. It takes more than money.
- The Soviet Union held its own. And several "iron curtain" countries outscored western nations such as France and Italy.
- In general, Latin American nations, along with the Africans, brought up the rear (South Africa being no exception).

This study was based on 1975 figures and, therefore, doesn't reflect the incredible political, social, and economic changes that have taken place since then. Scientists at both MRI and EPRI refuse to speculate on how the rankings may have changed since then. But a close look at the data used in this ranking suggests that the Arab countries won't improve much, because economic gains will probably be offset by increasing unrest and dependence on foreign trade. Runaway inflation might serve to drop some countries, such as Israel, while giving a boost to other countries, such as Switzerland, that have kept inflation under control. With so many variables, one can see why MRI is unwilling to venture a guess.

If you would like a detailed summary of the MRI/EPRI study, you can write to the Electric Power Research Institute, requesting a copy of "Income, Energy Requirements, and the Quality of Life Indicators: An International Comparison, 1975." There is no charge.

Contact:
Electric Power Research Institute
3412 Hillview Avenue
Palo Alto, California 94304

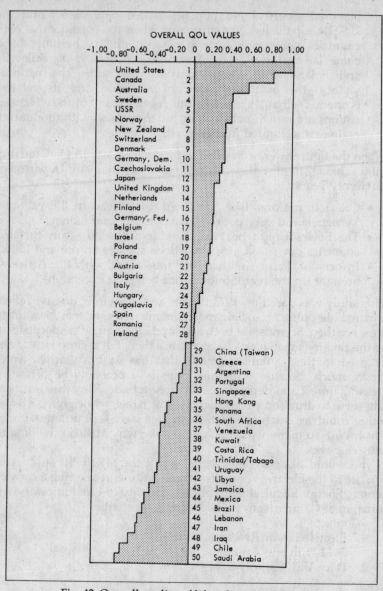

Fig. 42. Overall quality of life values, per Midwest
Research Institute Study. The values are based on an
index with the United States equal to 1.

From *Income, Energy Requirements and Quality of Life Indicators:* An
International Comparison by Ben-chien Liu, PhD, Claude F.
Anderson, PhD (Kansas City: Midwest Research Institute, 1979),
p.12. Reprinted by permission of sponsor, Electric Power Research
Institute, Palo Alto, California.

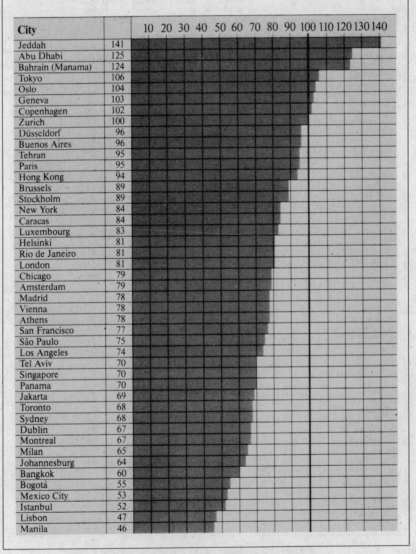

## Price Level

Zurich = 100

| City | | 10 | 20 | 30 | 40 | 50 | 60 | 70 | 80 | 90 | 100 | 110 | 120 | 130 | 140 |
|------|---|----|----|----|----|----|----|----|----|----|-----|-----|-----|-----|-----|
| Jeddah | 141 | | | | | | | | | | | | | | |
| Abu Dhabi | 125 | | | | | | | | | | | | | | |
| Bahrain (Manama) | 124 | | | | | | | | | | | | | | |
| Tokyo | 106 | | | | | | | | | | | | | | |
| Oslo | 104 | | | | | | | | | | | | | | |
| Geneva | 103 | | | | | | | | | | | | | | |
| Copenhagen | 102 | | | | | | | | | | | | | | |
| Zurich | 100 | | | | | | | | | | | | | | |
| Düsseldorf | 96 | | | | | | | | | | | | | | |
| Buenos Aires | 96 | | | | | | | | | | | | | | |
| Tehran | 95 | | | | | | | | | | | | | | |
| Paris | 95 | | | | | | | | | | | | | | |
| Hong Kong | 94 | | | | | | | | | | | | | | |
| Brussels | 89 | | | | | | | | | | | | | | |
| Stockholm | 89 | | | | | | | | | | | | | | |
| New York | 84 | | | | | | | | | | | | | | |
| Caracas | 84 | | | | | | | | | | | | | | |
| Luxembourg | 83 | | | | | | | | | | | | | | |
| Helsinki | 81 | | | | | | | | | | | | | | |
| Rio de Janeiro | 81 | | | | | | | | | | | | | | |
| London | 81 | | | | | | | | | | | | | | |
| Chicago | 79 | | | | | | | | | | | | | | |
| Amsterdam | 79 | | | | | | | | | | | | | | |
| Madrid | 78 | | | | | | | | | | | | | | |
| Vienna | 78 | | | | | | | | | | | | | | |
| Athens | 78 | | | | | | | | | | | | | | |
| San Francisco | 77 | | | | | | | | | | | | | | |
| São Paulo | 75 | | | | | | | | | | | | | | |
| Los Angeles | 74 | | | | | | | | | | | | | | |
| Tel Aviv | 70 | | | | | | | | | | | | | | |
| Singapore | 70 | | | | | | | | | | | | | | |
| Panama | 70 | | | | | | | | | | | | | | |
| Jakarta | 69 | | | | | | | | | | | | | | |
| Toronto | 68 | | | | | | | | | | | | | | |
| Sydney | 68 | | | | | | | | | | | | | | |
| Dublin | 67 | | | | | | | | | | | | | | |
| Montreal | 67 | | | | | | | | | | | | | | |
| Milan | 65 | | | | | | | | | | | | | | |
| Johannesburg | 64 | | | | | | | | | | | | | | |
| Bangkok | 60 | | | | | | | | | | | | | | |
| Bogotá | 55 | | | | | | | | | | | | | | |
| Mexico City | 53 | | | | | | | | | | | | | | |
| Istanbul | 52 | | | | | | | | | | | | | | |
| Lisbon | 47 | | | | | | | | | | | | | | |
| Manila | 46 | | | | | | | | | | | | | | |

Fig. 43. Price levels of major international cities,
indexed to Zurich

From "Prices and Earnings Around the Globe," by M. Gutmann and
Dr. A. Kruck (Zurich: Union Bank of Switzerland Economic
Research Department, 1979), p. 7. Reprinted by permission.

The table shows the percentage by which price, salary (wage) and purchasing power levels in the various cities are above or below those of Zurich. For all indices, Zurich = 100

| City | Price Level[1] | Salary (Wage) Level gross[2] | Salary (Wage) Level net[3] | Purchasing Power Level[4] gross | Purchasing Power Level[4] net |
|---|---|---|---|---|---|
| Abu Dhabi | 125 | 36 | 46 | 28 | 37 |
| Amsterdam | 79 | 81 | 68 | 102 | 86 |
| Athens | 78 | 31 | 34 | 40 | 43 |
| Bahrain (Manama) | 124 | 38 | 49 | 31 | 39 |
| Bangkok | 60 | 11 | 12 | 18 | 20 |
| Bogota | 55 | 13 | 13 | 24 | 24 |
| Brussels | 89 | 74 | 67 | 83 | 74 |
| Buenos Aires | 96 | 29 | 30 | 30 | 32 |
| Caracas | 84 | 49 | 59 | 58 | 70 |
| Chicago | 79 | 89 | 87 | 112 | 110 |
| Copenhagen | 102 | 95 | 71 | 93 | 70 |
| Dublin | 67 | 42 | 42 | 62 | 62 |
| Dusseldorf | 96 | 83 | 76 | 86 | 78 |
| Geneva | 103 | 95 | 92 | 91 | 88 |
| Helsinki | 81 | 54 | 45 | 66 | 55 |
| Hong Kong | 94 | 22 | 27 | 23 | 29 |
| Istanbul | 52 | 18 | 12 | 35 | 23 |
| Jakarta | 69 | 10 | 10 | 14 | 14 |
| Jeddah | 141 | 52 | 63 | 36 | 45 |
| Johannesburg | 64 | 38 | 39 | 59 | 61 |
| Lisbon | 47 | — | — | — | — |
| London | 81 | 46 | 44 | 56 | 55 |
| Los Angeles | 74 | 78 | 79 | 105 | 106 |
| Luxembourg | 83 | 78 | 78 | 94 | 94 |
| Madrid | 78 | 42 | 47 | 54 | 60 |
| Manila | 46 | 7 | 8 | 15 | 17 |
| Mexico City | 53 | 24 | 27 | 45 | 50 |
| Milan | 65 | 40 | 36 | 60 | 55 |
| Montreal | 67 | 66 | 64 | 98 | 94 |
| New York | 84 | 84 | 76 | 99 | 90 |
| Oslo | 104 | 76 | 63 | 72 | 60 |
| Panama | 70 | 21 | 24 | 30 | 34 |
| Paris | 95 | 58 | 61 | 61 | 64 |
| Rio de Janeiro | 81 | 30 | 34 | 37 | 41 |
| San Francisco | 77 | 86 | 80 | 111 | 103 |
| Sao Paulo | 75 | 33 | 36 | 43 | 48 |
| Singapore | 70 | 17 | 16 | 23 | 22 |
| Stockholm | 89 | 77 | 64 | 87 | 71 |
| Sydney | 68 | 66 | 66 | 96 | 97 |
| Tehran | 95 | 39 | 44 | 41 | 46 |
| Tel Aviv | 70 | 27 | 27 | 38 | 38 |
| Tokyo | 106 | 66 | 73 | 62 | 69 |
| Toronto | 68 | 66 | 68 | 96 | 98 |
| Vienna | 78 | 63 | 59 | 81 | 75 |
| Zurich | 100 | 100 | 100 | 100 | 100 |

[1] A basket of more than 100 different goods and services weighted by consumer habits

[2] Calculated on the basis of the gross average hourly earnings in 12 different occupations

[3] Calculated on the basis of the net average hourly earnings after deducting taxes and social insurance contributions in 12 different occupations

[4] Ratio of labor expended (measured in terms of the number of working hours) to the costs of the basket with goods and services. The higher the purchasing power, the fewer the number of working hours needed to purchase the goods and services in the basket

Fig. 44. Price, salary and purchasing power
in 45 international cities

From "Prices and Earnings Around the Globe," by M. Gutmann and
Dr. A. Kruck (Zurich: Union Bank of Switzerland, Economic
Research Department, 1979), p. 6. Reprinted by permission.

# 24

# THE HUNT

A career strategy is concerned with long-range, broad objectives. The job hunt is conducted within the context of an overall career plan for the purpose of accomplishing a specific and immediate goal: getting employed.

## A PHILOSOPHY OF JOB HUNTING: DON'T BE RULED BY PROJECTIONS AND STATISTICS

In the previous few chapters I've offered lots of projections, replete with statistics, about the job market for the eighties. Now, let's throw a wrench into the works: *Forget the projections.* The fact is, the economy is an unwieldy creature whose ways are to a large extent unfathomable. These days, many observers of the economy are frankly bewildered as to how best to domesticate the beast. The statisticians, the analysts—they all run behind, grabbing at its tail or any handle they can get on the wild animal.

The prophets of boom and bust do not have access to crystal balls. They make informed predictions, well-educated guesses; but they don't have a hotline to the future. Don't discount the economic projections altogether; but don't let them scare you into passivity, either. Appraise them. Digest them. Then move on. The point is, have a "take charge" attitude toward your job hunt. Go after the job you *want,* not the one that's most likely to be available five years from now. If you truly enjoy the work you do, you will excel. If you excel, there will always be jobs to choose from. As long as one job is available, believe that you can have it. *That* is the key to a successful career.

# WHO ARE THE HEADHUNTERS AND WHY ARE THEY AFTER YOU?

Not every unexpected detour in your career path will be unwelcome. In 1977, according to *Fortune* magazine, 16,000 executives were snared by professional "headhunters" and lured into new corporate habitats. In fact, of all executives in the $30,000-$50,000 income bracket, 60 percent of those who exchange their present positions for new and often better ones are "searched out," as are 75-80 percent of executives in the $50,000-plus bracket.

Headhunters, who are not terribly fond of that appellation and prefer to be known as management consultants, are specialized recruiters who are employed by businesses to "search out" top executive talent for hire in new jobs. Executive search firms (to use another preferred term) generally work strictly for the corporation (vis-à-vis the individual executive), and the corporation pays the search firm a very substantial fee—as much as 30 percent of the new recruit's annual salary—for its services. The headhunter offers the corporation know-how, access to the crème de la crème of executive talent, objectivity, and anonymity in the recruitment process. Before the recruiter begins his search, he conducts a comprehensive interview with the client company in order to determine the job specifications and the kind of talent the corporation wants for the job. Armed with this information, the headhunter sets to work.

## WHO IS FAIR GAME FOR THE HEADHUNTER?

Any resident of the executive suite. Headhunters stalk their prey in current business directories, through data banks, by word of mouth, by keeping files of press clippings and dossiers on any newsworthy executive, and by keeping close tabs on all other industry sources that might turn up the name of a likely candidate. The one most "likely" is almost invariably an already employed executive. The *best* candidate is an executive who is not only employed, but happily employed and not even looking to leave.

## WHAT LURES THE HAPPY EXECUTIVE AWAY?

Usually it's the opportunity to gain additional "psychic" income such as expanded territory of influence, greater power and status, and, of course, extra cash benefits and noncash rewards.

# HOW TO TALK TO A HEADHUNTER

KNOW THE NOMENCLATURE If the voice on the telephone identifies its owner as a "recruiter," the company pays the fee and this is a voice worth listening to. On the other hand, if the voice says "job counselor," cut it off; otherwise, the call may cost *you* money in the long run.

BE OPEN AND DIRECT WITH THE RECRUITER He makes a living on that phone and has already heard every cute remark in the book. That recruiter is in a position to turn you on to possibly the best career opportunity in your life. Don't turn *him* off. Save your biting wit for another occasion.

ON THE INITIAL CONTACT, THE RECRUITER WILL WANT SPECIFIC INFORMATION:

- Your present salary. On this point you don't have to be too specific. A ball-park figure will do: high thirties, low fifties, etc. However, don't try to fool the recruiter. He has his ways of finding out the truth without your help.
- Your willingness to relocate. The recruiter will want to put a price tag on this: How much would it take to convince you to move? Again, be nonspecific. Leave the point open for negotiation.

ASK QUESTIONS OF YOUR OWN At this time it's fair game for you to find out:

- a basic job description
- what the position pays
- why the position is available and how long it's been available
- how long your predecessor held the position and why he vacated it

On the other hand:

- DO NOT push for the name of the company.
- DO NOT pursue an interview if you are not really interested in the job opportunity. It wastes the recruiter's time—and yours—and it won't endear you to him. Maybe this position isn't for you, but a more attractive offer might come in the future.

If you do choose to pursue the current opportunity, be sure you feel confident the recruiter has your best interests at heart as well as those of the client corporation. Once the matchmaking begins, a good recruiter has the concerns of both parties in mind and, in pursuit of a happy union, should be willing to educate you about the prospective employer.

---

# WHAT TO DO WHEN THE
# HEADHUNTER DOESN'T CALL

Courtships are lovely, and everyone likes to feel pursued. But it's possible you'll have a long and unproductive wait if you spend your professional life sitting by a telephone waiting for Mr. Right to call.

Taking it as it comes is a useful attitude in coping with the unexpected obstacle and even the unexpected opportunity. If you want to advance your career, however, you are usually going to have to take a more active approach to your future than waiting in fear of a pink slip or in hope of a telephone call. So take charge. Go out and get the job you want.

A headhunter conducts a particular search with a pretty clear idea in mind of the credentials of the ideal candidate. If he has a large square vacant hole, he wants a large square peg to fit it. Generally, he has no use for carrying a lot of extra large round pegs in his back pocket. He works almost exclusively for corporate clients and isn't equipped to serve the individual executive looking to make a career change.

One day, however, the headhunter may be looking around for a peg just about your size. In that case, *you want to make yourself as visible as possible.* When trying to attract the attention of a headhunter, the trick is, *don't* be coy. If you expect to lure him with your extraordinary qualities, first he has to notice you.

- *Publish* in professional journals or even in popular periodicals.
- *Make speeches* at your trade or professional associations.
- *Be newsworthy.* Be active in social and civil affairs. Make a good name for yourself.
- *Cultivate professional contacts.* Headhunters are plugged into the corporate grapevine.


# THE LAST RESORT:
# APPROACH A HEADHUNTER DIRECTLY

Still no phone call? It's possible, of course, that you may never turn the head of a hunter and the only way to get his attention is, finally, to introduce yourself to him. Collectively, recruiters represent thousands of job opportunities a year, and they usually have exclusive knowledge of the positions they fill; so you don't want to give up on them too easily.

To approach a headhunter directly is a delicate affair, and experts suggest the following etiquette be applied in making your contact:

- Never walk in cold to a recruiter's office expecting an interview.
- Send a résumé. Wait one week and call for an interview.
- If you don't get an interview, wait a month and resubmit your résumé.

- If you do get an interview, keep it very brief: 30 minutes or less, unless the recruiter keeps it going.
- Follow up the interview with a thank-you note and a *short* reiteration of your present situation. *Do not* follow up with a phone call.
- Keep in mind that recruiters work for client corporations and not for you. They generally do not have the office systems to keep efficiently maintained files of inactive résumés, and they generally do not give any interviews unless they have a job in mind for you. Don't let that stop you, however; you could be lucky, time it right, and get an instant response.

## WHERE TO FIND A HEADHUNTER

*Consultant News* publishes a national directory of executive search firms. You can write direct to the publisher to obtain a copy. The address is Templeton Road, Fitzwilliam, New Hampshire 03447. Copies are $10 each, $15 for the international edition.

Some management consulting firms also do executive searches. Many of the large accounting firms have executive search departments as well. Fig. 45 is a list of names (with home offices) of major recruiters. Most of them have branch offices in other cities.

**Bacci, Bennett, Gould & McCoy, Inc.**
375 Park Avenue
New York, NY 10022
(212) 688-8671

600 Montgomery Street
San Francisco, CA 94111
(415) 989-8212

**Bartholdi & Company, Inc.**
65 William Street
Wellesley Hills, MA 02181
(617) 237-3710

1415 West 22nd Street
Oak Brook, IL 60521
(312) 325-8474

610 Fifth Avenue
New York, NY 10020
(212) 489-7280

**Battalia, Lotz & Associates, Inc.**
342 Madison Avenue
New York, NY 10017
(212) 986-4380

**J. W. Bauder Associates, Inc.**
5580 LBJ Freeway/Suite 550
Dallas, TX 75240
(214) 386-0481

**Billington, Fox & Ellis, Inc.**
20 North Wacker Drive
Chicago, IL 60606
(312) 236-5000

Atlanta Center/Suite 1420
250 Piedmont Avenue, N. E.
Atlanta, GA 30308
(404) 659-8300

1100 Superior Avenue, N. E.
Cleveland, OH 44114
(216) 781-1000

One Main Place/Suite 920
Dallas, TX 75250
(214) 744-4900

3701 Wilshire Boulevard
Los Angeles, CA 90010
(213) 661-2500

529 Fifth Avenue
New York, NY 10017
(212) 661-2500

**Billington, Fox & Ellis International**
529 Fifth Avenue
New York, NY 10017
(212) 661-2500

*Australia, Belgium, Brazil, Canada, England, France, Germany, Italy, Japan, Netherlands, New Zealand, South Africa, Sweden

**Booz Allen & Hamilton Inc.**
245 Park Avenue
New York, NY 10017
(212) 697-1900

229 Peachtree St., N.E.
Atlanta, GA 30303
(404) 659-3600

135 South La Salle Street
Chicago, IL 60603
(312) 346-1900

1100 Chester Avenue
Cleveland, OH 44115
(216) 696-1900

Suite 550
523 West Sixth Street
Los Angeles, CA 90014
(213) 620-1900

2210 Republic Bank Tower
325 North St. Paul Street
Dallas, TX 75201
(214) 741-5011

*Belgium, Brazil, England, France, Germany, Iran, Japan, Venezuela

**Boyden Associates, Inc.**
Suite 2000
260 Madison Avenue
New York, NY 10016
(212) 949-7600

Suite 1738
Lenox Towers
3390 Peachtree Road, N.E.
Atlanta, GA 30326
(404) 261-6532

Suite 1650
10 South Riverside Plaza
Chicago, IL 60606
(312) 782-1581

*Denotes Foreign Offices or Affiliates

Fig. 45. Association of Executive Recruiting
Consultants, Inc., Member Firms (New York).
(*through page 357*)
Used by permission.

Suite 706
River Oaks Bank & Trust Bldg.
2001 Kirby Drive
Houston, TX 77019
(713) 526-9913

5670 Wilshire Boulevard
Los Angeles, CA 90036
(213) 933-5563

Allegheny Tower
625 Stanwix Street
Pittsburgh, PA 15222
(412) 391-3020

Suite 1760
One Maritime Plaza
San Francisco, CA 94111
(415) 981-7900

Suite 433
606 Madison Avenue
Toledo, OH 43604
(419) 255-1160

Suite 803
815 Connecticut Avenue, N. W.
Washington, DC 20006
(202) 296-6705
*Australia, Belgium, Brazil, Canada, England,
France, Hong Kong, Italy, Japan, Mexico, New
Zealand, South Africa, Spain, Switzerland,
Venezuela

## The Brand Company, Inc

12740 North River Road
Mequon, WI 53092
(414) 242-6203

## Thomas A. Buffum Associates

Two Center Plaza
Boston, MA 02108
(617) 227-4350

## La Societe Caldwell

Suite 2201
1115 Sherbrooke Street West
Montreal, Quebec H3A IH3
Canada
(514) 849-5357

## The Caldwell Partners International, Inc.

Suite 610
Two Houston Center
Houston, TX 77002
(713) 757-1958

Suite 103
50 Prince Arthur Avenue
Toronto, Ontario M5R 1B5
Canada
(416) 920-7702

Suite 1918
500 Fourth Avenue, S.W.
Calgary, Alberta TZP ZVG
Canada
(403) 265-8780

## William H. Clark Associates, Inc.

330 Madison Avenue
New York, NY 10017
(212) 661-8760

Suite 7912
200 East Randolph Drive
Chicago, IL 60601
(312) 565-1300

555 South Flower Street
Los Angeles, CA 90071
(213) 489-2240

One Embarcadero Center
San Francisco, CA 90071
(415) 489-2240

## David W. Cogswell & Associates

Suite 609
400 Montgomery Street
San Francisco, CA 94104
(415) 788-1070

## Thorndike Deland Associates

1440 Broadway
New York, NY 10018
(212) 840-8100

## Devine, Baldwin & Peters, Inc.

250 Park Avenue
New York, NY 10017
(212) 867-5235

Statler Office Building
Boston, MA 02116
(617) 423-1682
*England

## DeVoto & Berry Partners, Ltd.

120 South Riverside Plaza
Chicago, IL 60606
(312) 346-8278

## Eastman & Beaudine, Incorporated

Suite 2150
111 West Monroe Street
Chicago, IL 60603
(312) 726-8195

Suite 2005
437 Madison Avenue

*Denotes Foreign Offices or Affiliates

New York, NY 10022
(212) 486-9655

Suite 940
Two Century Plaza
2049 Century Park East
Los Angeles, CA 90067
(213) 552-6005

Suite 4152
44 Montgomery Street
San Francisco, CA 94104
(415) 788-1666
*Belgium, England, France, Hawaii, Holland,
Japan, Germany, Mexico

## Leon A. Farley Associates
Steuart Street Tower
Suite 1001
One Market Plaza
San Francisco, CA 94105
(415) 777-2888

Suite 1001-E
7315 Wisconsin Avenue
Bethesda, MD 20014
(301) 654-9090

## Foster & Associates, Inc.
Steuart Street Tower
Suite 1115
One Market Plaza
San Francisco, CA 94105
(414) 777-0330

1700 Pacific Building
Seattle, WA 98104
(206) 624-8943

## Haley Associates, Inc.
375 Park Avenue
New York, NY 10022
(212) 421-7860

## Harris & U'Ren, Inc.
1976 Arizona Bank Building
101 North First Avenue
Phoenix, AZ 85003
(602) 257-1072

## Haskell & Stern Associates, Inc.
230 Park Avenue
New York, NY 10017
(212) 687-7292
*England

## Hayman, Hardison & Fowler, Inc.
Suite 1311
8150 N. Central Expressway
Dallas, TX 75206
(214) 696-4000

## Heidrick & Struggles, Inc.
Suite 2800
125 South Wacker Drive
Chicago, IL 60606
(312) 372-8811

100 Federal Street
Boston, MA 02110
(617) 423-1140

1100 Superior Avenue
Cleveland, OH 44114
(216) 241-7410

2728 Republic National Bank Tower
Dallas, TX 75201
(214) 741-9121

2650 Pennzoil Place
South Tower
Houston, TX 77002
(713) 237-9000

Union Bank Square
Los Angeles, CA 90071
(213) 624-8891

245 Park Avenue
New York, NY 10017
(212) 876-9876

600 Montgomery Street
San Francisco, CA 94111
(415) 981-2854
*Belgium, England, France, Germany, Mexico,
Switzerland

## Helmich, Miller & Pasek, Inc.
Suite 280
5725 East River Road
Chicago, IL 60631
(312) 693-6270

1100 Quail Street/Suite 103
Newport Beach, CA 92660
(714) 752-7447

P. O. Box 1448
Green Valley, AZ 85614
(602) 625-6232

## Hodge-Cronin and Associates, Inc.
Suite 904
9575 West Higgins Road
Rosemont, IL 60018
(312) 692-2041

## The Ward Howell/Consulting Partners/TASA Group Ward Howell Associates, Inc. (U.S.)
99 Park Avenue
New York, NY 10016
(212) 697-3730

*Denotes Foreign Offices or Affiliates

One East Putnam Avenue
Greenwich, CT 06830
(203) 629-2994

John Hancock Center
Suite 3350
875 North Michigan Avenue
Chicago, IL 60611
(312) 266-9431

10100 Santa Monica Boulevard
Los Angeles, CA 90067
(213) 553-6638

Three Embarcadero Center
Suite 2680
San Francisco, CA 94111
(415) 398-3900

**\*TASA Inc.—Latin America:**
Douglas Centre, Suite 1001
2600 Douglas Road
Coral Gables, FL 33134
(305) 448-0100
Argentina, Brazil, Colombia, Mexico,
Venezuela

**\*Consulting Partners:**
Europe—Middle East—Africa
Belgium, England, France,
Germany, Italy, South Africa
Switzerland

**International Management
Advisors, Inc.**
485 Lexington Avenue
New York, NY 10017
(212) 490-3858

**Charles Irish Company, Inc.**
420 Lexington Avenue
New York, NY 10017
(212) 490-0040

**Kearney: Executive Search
Division of A. T. Kearney, Inc.**
100 South Wacker Drive
Chicago, IL 60606
(312) 782-2868

29425 Chagrin Boulevard
Pepper Pike, OH 44122
(216) 292-3770

One Wilshire Building
Los Angeles, CA 90017
(213) 627-0721

437 Madison Avenue
New York, NY 10022
(212) 751-7040
\*Belgium, Canada, England

**Kremple & Meade**
1900 Avenue of the Stars
Los Angeles, CA 90067
(213) 456-6451

**Lamalie Associates, Inc.**
13920 North Dale Mabry
Tampa, FL 33618
(813) 961-7494

Tower Place
3340 Peachtree Road, N.E.
Atlanta, GA 30326
(404) 237-6324

120 South Riverside Plaza
Chicago, IL 60606
(312) 454-0525

Central National Bank Building
Cleveland, OH 44114
(216) 522-1650

Olympic Tower
645 Fifth Avenue
New York, NY 10022
(212) 688-0545

First International Building
1201 Elm Street
Dallas, TX 75270
(214) 747-1994

**Lauer, Sbarbaro & Associates, Inc.**
135 South LaSalle Street
Chicago, IL 60603
(312) 372-7050
\*England

**Locke & Associates**
Suite 3145
One NCNB Plaza
Charlotte, NC 28280
(704) 372-6600

**The John Lucht Consultancy, Inc.**
The Olympic Tower
645 Fifth Avenue
New York, NY 10022
(212) 935-4660

**MWS Executive Search**
55 East Monroe Street
Chicago, IL 60603
(312) 726-8730

12860 Hillcrest Road
Suite 105
Dallas, TX 75230
(214) 387-4838

\*Denotes Foreign Offices or Affiliates

1900 M Street, N. W.
Washington, DC 20036
(202) 833-1866

**Management Woman, Inc.**
The Galleria—14th Floor
115 East 57th Street
New York, NY 10022
(212) 888-8100

**McFeely, Wackerle Associates**
20 North Wacker Drive
Chicago, IL 60606
(312) 641-2977

**Moriarty/Fox, Inc.**
20 North Wacker Drive
Chicago, IL 60606
(312) 332-4600

**Oliver & Rozner Associates, Inc.**
598 Madison Avenue—11th Floor
New York, NY 10022
(212) 688-1850

**Parenti & Jacobs, Inc.**
Harris Bank Building
Suite 2525
115 South LaSalle Street
Chicago, IL 60603
(312) 782-9844

**Parker, Eldridge, Sholl & Gordon, Inc.**
440 Totten Pond Road
Waltham, MA 02154
(617) 890-0340

**Pinsker and Shattuck, Inc.**
Suite 501
100 Bush Street
San Francisco, CA 94104
(415) 421-6264

Suite 101
1333 Lawrence Expressway
Santa Clara, CA 95051
(408) 247-5050

**Paul R. Ray & Company, Inc.**
1208 Ridglea State Bank Building
Fort Worth, TX 76116
(817) 731-4111

Suite 1718
400 Colony Square
1201 Peachtree Street, N.E.
Atlanta, GA 30361
(404) 892-2727

Suite 600
1900 Avenue of the Stars
Los Angeles, CA 90067
(213) 557-2828

277 Park Avenue
New York, NY 10017
(212) 371-3431

Suite 1925
100 South Wacker Drive
Chicago, IL 60606
(312) 876-0730

First International Building
Suite 5383
Dallas, TX 75270
(214) 651-9812

3612 Dresser Towers
601 Jefferson Street
Houston, TX 77002
(713) 757-1985
*England

**Robison, Sockwell & McAulay**
3100 NCNB Plaza
Charlotte, NC 28280
(704) 376-0059

**Russell Reynolds Associates, Inc.**
245 Park Avenue
New York, NY 10017
(212) 682-8622

230 West Monroe Street
Chicago, IL 60606
(312) 782-9862

1200 Smith Street
Suite 3350
Two Allen Center
Houston, TX 77002
(713) 658-1776

555 South Flower Street
Suite 3220
Los Angeles, CA 90071
(213) 489-1520

3 Landmark Square
Stamford, CT 06901
(203) 356-1940
*England, France

**Ryan/Smith & Associates**
P.O. Box 253
Westfield, NJ 07090
(201) 232-5720

*Denotes Foreign Offices or Affliates

**Sadovsky, West & Associates**
12700 Park Central Place
Suite 1300
Dallas, TX 75251
(214) 387-8580

**John W. Siler & Associates, Inc.**
5261 N. Port Washington Road
Milwaukee, WI 53217
(414) 962-9400

**Spriggs & Company, Inc.**
John Hancock Center
Suite 4015
875 North Michigan Avenue
Chicago, IL 60611
(312) 751-1200

**Paul Stafford Associates, Ltd.**
45 Rockefeller Plaza
New York, NY 10020
(212) 765-7700

222 South Riverside Plaza
Chicago, IL 60606
(312) 454-0942

888 17th Street, N.W.
Washington, DC 20006
(202) 331-0090

**Staub, Warmbold & Associates, Inc.**
655 Third Avenue
New York, NY 10017
(212) 599-4100

7275 Wynhill Drive
Atlanta, GA 30328
(404) 394-9177

200 East Randolph Drive
Chicago, IL 60601
(312) 861-0900

California First Bank Building
350 California Street
San Francisco, CA 94101
(415) 781-1196
*Belgium

**S. K. Stewart & Associates**
The Executive Building
P.O. Box 40110
Cincinnati, OH 45240
(513) 771-2250

Governour's Square
1193 Lyons Road
Dayton, OH 45459
(513) 434-4311

**Spencer Stuart & Associates, Inc.**
Suite 300
500 North Michigan Avenue
Chicago, IL 60611
(312) 822-0080

2626 Republic National Bank Tower
Dallas, TX 75201
(214) 748-1990

555 South Flower Street
Los Angeles, CA 90071
(213) 620-0814

437 Madison Avenue
New York, NY 10022
(212) 754-1400

Three Landmark Square
Stamford, CT 06901
(203) 324-6333

3773 Redwood Circle
Palo Alto, CA 94306
(415) 493-0340
*Amsterdam, Brussels, Dusseldorf, Frankfurt,
Hong Kong, London, Madrid, Manchester,
Melbourne, Paris, Sao Paulo, Singapore,
Sydney, Toronto, Zurich

**George Sullivan Associates, Inc.**
Rumson Road
Rumson, NJ 07760
(201) 741-4544
*England

**William H. Willis, Inc.**
445 Park Avenue
New York, NY 10022
(212) 752-3456
*Australia, England, France

**Witt & Dolan Associates, Inc.\*\***
1415 West 22nd Street
Oak Brook, IL 60521
(312) 325-5070

**Yelverton & Mace, Inc.**
350 California Street
Suite 1680
San Francisco, CA 94104
(415) 981-6060

*Denotes Foreign Offices or Affiliates
**This firm specializes in the health care field.

# TACTICS FOR GETTING
# THROUGH THE JOB JUNGLE

**Don't quit.** If you have managed to keep your job this long, don't quit before you have secured a new one. As bad as your present position may seem, being unemployed with no immediate prospects for work won't be any better. The statistics show that an employed candidate is more attractive to a prospective employer and will be compensated, on the average, 18 percent more than an equally qualified out-of-work candidate.

**Have a base of operations.** Preferably, your base shouldn't be your home. If you feel comfortable telling your present employer that you are in the market for a new job, then do so and carry out your hunting activities from your own office if it's possible. If not, perhaps you can make arrangements with a friend to borrow the resources of his office.

**Protect your position.** Obviously, the job hunt will be easier if you do not have to be concerned with conducting all related business undercover. If confidentiality is crucial to your current job security, however, be very cautious and discriminating while making your contacts. Even a casual reference to your job-hunting activity dropped at some cocktail party may get back to your office the next day.

**Gear up for a long haul.** Be prepared to put in some time looking for the job. Hunting for big game, you can expect to take three to six months—or much longer. Usually, the bigger the stakes, the more time it takes.

**Have a hunting strategy.** Planning your job-hunting strategy is a process fundamentally like planning a career strategy. An employment campaign is a career plan in miniature and should reflect the same kind of thinking given career planning.

- Update your self-inventory. Each time you change jobs, you will have new experience, new "stock" of which to take account.
- Update your goals. At each state of your career, your employment goals will be different. Establish your pay objectives, your choice of functional area and industry, and your general preferences and priorities.
- Design a strategy for systematically targeting job opportunities.

# ZEROING IN ON THE OPPORTUNITIES

## THE WANT ADS

Want ads are the most obvious source of job leads. Or are they? The experts seem to disagree, as usual. According to an item in *The Wall Street Journal*, a 188-company survey conducted by the Bureau of National Affairs revealed that 80 percent of the surveyed firms used classified advertisements to recruit professional and managerial people. In another article, also in the *WSJ*, Betsy Jaffe, director of programs for employers at Catalyst, a nonprofit career information clearinghouse based in New York, was quoted as saying that 80 percent of available job openings are not advertised. The source of her statistic is not noted. In any event, *some* executive positions are recruited through the classified ads, and you should not discount any available source of jobs:

- Major newspapers, such as *The Wall Street Journal*, *The New York Times* (the Sunday business and finance section), etc., business magazines, and, especially, trade journals in your field all carry classified advertising.
- Some experts recommend that you follow up any ad that advertises heavily for any kind of executive position, even though there is no specific mention of a need for people in your functional area.
- Performance Dynamics International (PDI), a personnel marketing firm, puts out a national weekly directory of classified ads. You can subscribe to the *National Reporter of Job Openings* through PDI, 400 Lanidex Plaza, Parsippany, New Jersey 07054. Subscriptions are $90 per quarter.

Robert Gerberg, president of PDI, claims that "success in job hunting depends 70 percent on personal marketing skills and 30 percent on a person's background and abilities."[*] For $15 you can read up on PDI's self-marketing techniques in a widely read book called *The Professional Job Changing System*. For a larger investment, about $500–950, you can buy from PDI a how-to-sell-yourself miniprogram to work on at home. Contact PDI at the address noted immediately above (see inset, last paragraph).

---

[*] Quotation from William Flanagan, "The Job-Changing Game" (*Esquire*, August, 1979), p. 7.

# PERSONNEL AGENCIES AND JOB COUNSELORS

**WHAT AN AGENCY CAN DO FOR YOU**   Unlike executive search firms, personnel agencies and job counselors are easily approached and geared to serve the individual executive looking for new employment. For this service the executive sometimes pays the fee (as much as 25 percent of a year's salary), although many positions available through these agencies are company paid even at the management level. An agency can offer you:

*Expertise.* A good counselor makes his living by knowing how to conduct a thorough and selective job search. He can save you time, although some experts warn that dealing with go-betweens in a job hunt can also end up wasting your time. Those experts advise that the time you spend looking for a *good* agency might be better spent looking for a job direct.

*Job opportunities out of town.* National Personnel Associates is an international network of 226 independently owned agencies located in 130 cities. These agencies, many of which specialize in management jobs, exchange over 1,600,000 résumés and job listings a year. If you wish to relocate to a specific locale, a member agency can link you with an affiliate in that area, saving you the time and expense of making a blind job-hunting trip out of town. For the National Personnel Associates office near you, look in the local white pages. If no listing appears, call the main office in Grand Rapids, Michigan, toll free, at (800) 253-2578.

*Coaching and insight.* A skilled counselor can help prepare you for an interview by coaching you in general interviewing techniques and by providing information and insight into a prospective employer.

**HOW TO PICK AN AGENCY**   The same survey that revealed that four out of five companies recruit executives through classified ads also showed that three out of four companies recruit through employment agencies.

Stick to the employment agencies that specialize in recruiting for executive positions. For the most part, agencies recruit only for lower or middle level positions. Don't waste a lot of time filing applications with several agencies. Pick one or two of the top agencies and let them do the footwork for you.

Agencies advertise positions in the classified sections. Look through the ads for the names of those agencies that seem to specialize in jobs for your field.

Speak to personnel people or business associates who may be able to direct you to a reputable or outstanding agency.

**HOW TO APPROACH AN AGENCY**   After you have selected a handful of agencies, send a résumé to each one along with a brief cover letter. Follow up with a telephone call and make an appointment for an interview.

Keep the interview short. Prepare to state your case in about 15 minutes. Agencies do a volume business.

If no appropriate job openings turn up immediately, you may be called later on when something comes up that is your field. Agencies do keep extensive and up-to-date files. It could pay to keep your résumé on file with an agency even if you have no real immediate desire to move on. Filing with an agency may give you the first shot at the best opportunities.

If you are concerned with maintaining the confidentiality of your search, give clear instructions to any agency you contact. A good agent knows how to be discreet, and counselors claim that in instances of information leakage, the client's own carelessness is often to blame. Nevertheless, make your position clear to your counselor.

# CREATIVE JOB-HUNTING: HOW TO INVENT A JOB

Classified ads and personnel agencies are by no means the only sources of job leads. They are merely the most obvious and the most easily accessible. Professionals in the field of job hunting claim a vast number of other job openings can be found if you know how and where to look for them.

Conduct your job hunt the way Sherlock Holmes conducts a criminal investigation. Only a lesser sleuth is satisfied with the obvious (e.g., the butler did it) and lets it go at that. Ads and agencies are the butlers of the job market: At first glance, they are the most likely job sources, and they can save you work. However, a more creative approach to your investigation may yield more exciting, creative results—a position tailor-fit to your specifications, for instance. Here are some experts' suggestions on how to best piece together the perfect job solution:

## CULTIVATE CONTACTS

Most experts agree that contacts can produce leads to jobs that otherwise would be inaccessible to you. Your best contacts are your business colleagues and associates—the people you work with, the people you do business with, the people who do business with the people *you* do business with. Build up a network of *meaningful* contacts. Trade association meetings, trade fairs, even cocktail parties can produce a number of good contacts. Beware, however, people don't like to be put on the spot, especially in social situations. So drop only discreet words, if any at all, that you are actually in the market for a job. Keep your inquiries casual at first. A recommended approach: Ask for *advice*, not a job. Pursue any substantial leads.

## BE PERSISTENT

John C. Crystal, a professional noted for his innovative ideas on job-hunting, suggests that you save any formal rejections, wait a month or two, and then recontact the employer with an enthusiastic letter reiterating your interest in working for him or his company.

## WATCH THE NEWS MEDIA

Creative job hunting calls for creative detective work. Learn to anticipate opportunity by learning how to scan the media for clues to *potential* job openings. The newswatchers often monitor and report on the internal affairs of corporations. Keep an eye open for news of corporate mergers, acquisitions, even purges—mass firings and the like. Such reorganization often means jobs open up; make inquiries. Read trade papers to keep on top of the current developments in your field in particular.

## TARGET COMPANIES

Go through the Yellow Pages. Go through any directory that lists corporations according to industry and target the names of any business in which you think your experience might fit. Go back to the trade papers; learn all you can about these key companies. Check *Standard and Poor's Register* for the names of the current top officers. Send a résumé addressed to the appropriate executive (i.e., the one with the power to hire) along with a cover letter stating your great desire to work for that person in that organization and stating your qualifications to do so. Mention in the letter that you will follow up with a phone call on a specific day; then do it.

## START A CORRESPONDENCE

Write to the key person in the one corporation for which you would like to work. Study the corporation and its service or product, do some original thinking, and submit your ideas in a personal letter to the chief executive officer, president, or chairman of the board. This is a creative, but somewhat indirect approach. One expert suggests that you back up your interest in the company by becoming a shareholder, if you can.

## TARGET THE TOP BANANA

This is the principle of the highest first, propounded by maverick thinkers such as Crystal. Find out everything you can about the one executive in your field who is considered to be the most eminent/creative/powerful. Call him. Tell him how much and *exactly why* you admire him. Ask him if you can speak to him in person to get his expert advice about your career. DO NOT mention you are looking for employment. The idea is that if he grants you an interview, you then have the opportunity to impress *him* with your credentials, your enthusiasm, and your drive. Follow up the interview with a thank-you note so he has your name and address on paper for the record.

You get the general idea: If you cannot get the job you want through the obvious channels, then use your ingenuity to create new channels, even new opportunities. For the person who demonstrates ambition and enthusiasm—and the intelligence to use these qualities in unusually creative ways—a top executive with both smarts and authority can *make* an opening where none existed before.

# 25

# THE ONE-TWO PUNCH: RÉSUMÉS AND INTERVIEWS

A market is an arena for exchange of particular goods and services between buyers and sellers. In the job market, as an executive looking for work you are like a salesperson looking for a customer. Your experience and capabilities are the products you proffer for sale to buyers in the corporate hierarchies.

As marketing and sales professionals will tell you, how well you package and present the product is crucial to closing a sale.

## GETTING THROUGH THE DOOR IN AN ENVELOPE: THE RÉSUMÉ

Before you can deliver a sales pitch, however, you do need the proverbial foot-in-the-door. In the job market, your résumé is, as Jill Smolowe wrote on the subject in *The New York Times*, "the calling card that brings job candidates to the attention of employers." A résumé is an advertisement for yourself. Like any advertisement, it should entice the customer to want to know more about the product.

Books have been written on the philosophy and practice of writing the proper résumé. As John C. Crystal expressed it, some experts claim that "the résumé is the soul of the job-application process." Other experts, like Crystal himself, maintain that this is a myth—that most résumés end up in the circular file. Experts aside, it is fair to say that at some point in your working life you will probably have call for a résumé, and you will want to compose one intelligently.

### COPY AND LAYOUT

The form and content of a résumé are for the most part dictated by plain common sense. As to form, you want to use standard paper

| Name | Home phone |
| Address | Office phone |

## JOB OBJECTIVE

**A simple statement that indicates the specific type of work you're interested in and the type of business for which you would like to work.** Example: "General-assignment reporting for a metropolitan newspaper." This should take only one sentence and be tailored to meet a particular opening.

## WORK EXPERIENCE

**1975-present:** Job title, place of employment, city, state.

A one-sentence statement of job responsibilities that avoids use of the personal pronoun. Example: "Covered city politics with an emphasis on budgetary matters."

**Brief summaries of successful projects initiated, accomplishments that benefited the company and awards or commendations received.** Example: "Broke the scandal on kickbacks in City Hall that led to indictments of nine officials."

**1972-75:** **Note that the list is offered with work experience listed in reverse chronological order.** If you have limited work experience, you might want to take a functional, rather than a chronological, approach. Here you would divide your qualifications into categories which stress skills you have acquired in school, organizational activities or part-time jobs that relate to your job objective. Example: "Writing: Wrote publicity releases for the local theatre," or "Gathered and analyzed information for college poll." If you do a functional listing, then list educational experience before work experience.

**1970-72:** **Never apologize for time spent out of work; turn it to your advantage.** Example: "Spent these years in independent enterprise," "Personal needs dictated spending time away from career — will explain at interview," or "independent consultant."

## EDUCATION

**B.A. Journalism, college, year of graduation, grade-point average.**
This list should be in reverse chronological order with all degrees since high school. If you are just out of school, include academic honors and scholarships received. If you paid for a significant portion of your education, say so; it indicates industriousness. Recent graduates can include information about courses, papers written (that might pertain to the job), and any offices or memberships held in school organizations. If you are willing to travel and relocate, say so. List military training, on-the-job training, and results of college-equivalency tests.

## PERSONAL

**Brief statements that include any honors received, and a concise listing of outside interests that might pertain to the job.** Example: "Edited community-group newsletter. Outside interests: photography, reading." You are not required to include the following: age, sex, marital status, and health status. You should not include past salaries or salary desired.

## REFERENCES

**A simple statement, such as "references available on request."** This saves space, and a résumé should never be more than two pages long. Career counselors often stress that "the more you've done, the less you write"; meaning that your job history will speak for itself. If you are just out of school or have been absent from the job market for a long time, you might need more room to explain the skills you've picked up in volunteer jobs and extracurricular activities.

Fig. 46. Sample résumé

From *The New York Times* National Recruitment
Survey, October 14, 1979.
© 1979 by *The New York Times* Company.
Reprinted by permission.

(white, 8½ by 11 inches). The finished product should be neat and carefully proofread—without errors of any kind—just as advertising copy would be. It should be professionally duplicated; photo offset is the recommended method. The résumé should be concise: Two pages is absolute maximum length; one page is preferred. Below, reprinted from Smolowe's article, is an example of a standard résumé format, including generally accepted guidelines for résumé content.

Though most résumés conform in principle to the one shown in Fig. 46, expert opinion differs as to the kind of details you should include in your description. Smolowe maintains that you need not include information about your sex, age, etc.; other professionals point out that any company that would eliminate you on the basis of such data in your résumé would not be any more likely to hire you after an interview for the very same reasons. You might save yourself the frustration of the interview by being candid in your résumé.

Likewise, excluding a statement of salary range or your flexibility regarding relocation, especially in answering "blind" job ads, could result in many pointless interviews. Let your own judgment tell you when it helps or harms to be frank about these issues in your résumé.

## GENERAL POINTERS

*Sell your experience.* Titles in and of themselves are generally meaningless. Industries and individual corporations devise titles for different purposes. Besides, a title provides no in-depth information about the actual responsibilities of a particular executive job.

*Describe your achievements.* Don't just list duties; talk in terms of facts and figures: "Increased departmental profits by 10 percent in eight months."

*Be selective.* Play up the good and learn to obscure the grey areas in your work experience.

*Think like an advertising copywriter.* Use action verbs and eschew use of the first person singular pronoun. "Promoted to vice-president"; not "I was made." "Responsible for"; not "I was given." Don't make up stories; just find the most appealing angle on the truth.

### THE RESUME VS. THE LETTER

Currently, the letter is touted by some experts as the sensible alternative to the résumé. If résumés are commonly disposed of without ceremony, letters, say these experts, at least have some chance of being read. The other side of that argument is that the pertinent information gets lost in the verbiage of a letter and that the résumé makes the point more clearly and simply. Most experts do agree, however, that a cover letter is an essential supplement to any résumé. In a cover letter you can address yourself more specifically to the particular requirements of a position or corporation. Of course, if you are following through on a contact, mention in your letter the name of the person who referred you—if it is a meaningful contact. Make certain that you convey that you are interested in working for the company. Be clear about this, but be subtle.

---

# CLOSING THE SALE: THE INTERVIEW

---

The résumé may get you through the door, but the interview is the forum in which the salesperson gets to show his stuff. If you don't hook your customer at the interview, you have absolutely lost the sale.

## SALESMANSHIP:
## THE DYNAMICS OF AN INTERVIEW

As any good salesperson knows, selling requires a subtle understanding of human psychology. In a sense, you cannot *sell* anything. What you can do is demonstrate in a convincing manner that you have just the item your customer is looking to *buy*. In an interview situation, you begin with a decided advantage from a salesperson's point of view: In most instances, there is no question that the employer is in the market to buy. He has an organizational need, and he is shopping for the particular product that best fills the specified need. As salesperson, your job is to convince him that your product *is* the best of all products of its kind on the market.

In that case, however, it is still a buyer's market, with many salespeople competing for a single customer. Well aware that any salesperson worth his name is going to pitch his goods in superlatives, the wise consumer will use his own techniques to scrutinize the product and the pitch. These are the dynamics at work in a job interview. While you, as applicant, are selling the employer on your assets, the employer, as interviewer, will be listening to pick out your liabilities: Your customer is not interested in buying a defective product and is wary of smooth-talking salespeople.

## BEHIND THE LINES

The best survival handbook for the interviewing applicant is the textbook written for the person on the other side of the desk. In the interest of self-protection, *know thy adversary* and *know what thy adversary knows*. For a definitive look into the minds of personnel professionals, read a classic, *The Evaluation Interview*, by Richard A. Fear (New York: McGraw-Hill, 1978).

This technique for conducting a "patterned" interview is known in the business as the Fear Method. The irony of this name is fully apparent only when one reads Fear's advice to would-be interviewers. On facial expressions: "Raising of the eyebrows, in particular, should take place whenever important questions are posed and . . . a half-smile [should] be permitted to play about the lips, particularly when asking somewhat personal or delicate questions. The edge is taken off a delicate or personal question when it is posed with a half-smile and with the eyebrows raised."*

The Fear Method may seem more comical than fearful, but the point to be learned is this: While the interviewer may seem to exercise the hand of fate over the future of your career, he is, nevertheless, a human being, and, like you, subject to his own foibles, professional as well as personal. Learn the ins and outs of a professional interviewing technique. Knowing a good technique will help you spot the poor one as well; no doubt many a job has been lost by a well-qualified candidate who fell victim to an interviewer unskilled in his art.

## THE BIG TEN QUESTIONS
## INTERVIEWERS LOVE TO ASK

Below is your crib sheet.

Never go into an interview without knowing clearly your answers to these questions. Study them, read the rest of this section on how to protect yourself in the interview, and then prepare your answers to the questions.

1. *The icebreaker question:* So, what do you think of this weather we're having? *Alternative:* I see from your application you enjoy dogsledding. It sounds fascinating. Tell me, how did you become involved in such a unique sport?
2. What was your last job? Why did you leave?
3. What did you like about your past jobs? What did you hate?
4. Those were your duties. What were your *achievements?*
5. Tell me about yourself. *(Watch for raised eyebrows.)*
6. Now I know your best points. What about your shortcomings?
7. If you could describe your ideal job, what would it be right now?
8. What would be your ideal job five years from now? Ten years from now? What are your career goals?
9. Why do you think you are the ideal candidate for *this* job?
10. And how much money did you say you wanted?

---

*From *The Evaluation Interview,* by Richard A. Fear, p. 63. Copyright © 1978 by McGraw-Hill. Used with permission of McGraw-Hill Book Company.

---

## PREPARE. BE CLEAR. BEWARE.

PREPARE The interviewer's task at the outset is to get as much information as possible *from* you while giving up as little information *to* you as he can. If you are blessed with an experienced, well-intentioned interviewer, he will try to accomplish this goal in an amiable manner. Even so, since he is not likely to *supply* you with information, you are best prepared to come to the interview well equipped with your own. Likewise, be ready to supply information about yourself. *What* information you choose to supply will depend on your educated assessment of what is in your best interest to tell. *Knowledge is your best protection against the unknown.* Therefore, arm yourself beforehand with any and all information you can gather.

*Know thyself.* Just as you did when mapping out your career strategy, take an unsentimental look at yourself before the interview. Take stock of your achievements. Recognize your failures. Take an emotional inventory, too: How do you *feel* about your successes and, particularly, your failures?

*Know the position for which you are applying.* Tap every available source. If the interview was set up through a friend or a professional intermediary, don't be shy about questioning him. Your predecessor on the job, if he is accessible, is a good source of information. But be discreet. It's possible he may be unaware of his lame-duck status. If it is inappropriate or impossible to contact your predecessor, try someone close to him within the company. When possible and proper, try to find out from insiders what the job is about and what happened to the one whose shoes you may be filling. If you can't get the inside scoop on the job specs, get in touch with people who hold similar positions in similar firms. Use your contacts.

*Know the corporation.* Read the company's annual report or prospectus, if there is one. This could provide vital statistics about your prospective supervisor as well as about the company itself. It may even give you a clue to company compensation policies. Ask around the industry for any information you can get about the company, its reputation, its relationship with its customers, its suppliers, its competitors. Research the industry itself. Go to trade shows. Read the trade journals. Scan the financial papers for any fact, big or small, that may be valuable for you to know. The more you know, the more you will have to talk about. *If you are interested, you will be interesting.*

*Know the interviewer,* particularly if he will be your boss when the job is yours. Use all available resources to find out his professional reputation, how he relates to his associates, what his personal likes and dislikes are. On the other hand, don't pay too much heed to gossip.

Keep an open mind when you go into the interview and establish an unprejudiced relationship with the interviewer.

## BE CLEAR

*Sleep right. Eat right.* Be fresh and rested. Don't be hungry, but don't be overstuffed, either. You'll want to feel comfortable.

*Dress right.* If you don't know what that means in your particular situation, conservative dress is always safe. If you don't know what *that* means, read one of the many books on the subject of proper dress for the executive. These reminders may seem obvious, but in a preinterview bout with nerves, you may overlook the obvious. (See The Executive Wardrobe section in Chapter 40)

*Establish your priorities.* What do you want in a job? Match your job expectations to your talents. It is not to anyone's advantage, least of all your own, to accept a job for which you are ill-suited. A position that puts too much stress on your weak spots may not be the one you want. Represent yourself accordingly. That the job *could* be yours doesn't make it right for you.

*Be articulate.* You may be truly capable, eager, and right for the job. The trick, however, is to be able to communicate your self-confidence and enthusiasm to the interviewer. Don't just protect yourself. *Sell* yourself.

*Be specific.* Did you mention a preference for performing managerial duties over accounting details? Don't be too casual. Be clear: "It's not that I *hate* accounting work. I'm actually quite skilled at it. I simply *prefer* hands-on management."

*Pay attention.* This is easier said than done when nerves have the better of you:

- Answer the question you've been asked. Answer all parts of the question. On the other hand, be selective. Don't give answers you haven't been asked for.
- Listen for the giveaway word or phrase that may uncover the employer's bias.
- Recognize the calculated pause. It's okay to fill the gap, but don't run on at the mouth.
- Observe your interviewer—discreetly. Bodies have a way of speaking without words. What is his body communicating? Of more importance, what is *yours* communicating?

BEWARE Your store of knowledge is your protection against being caught unaware at an interview. *Beware* means *be aware;* be neither defensive nor off-guard. Be steady and alert.

*The first five minutes of your interview are probably as important as all the rest of the time.* If you find that your interviewer is asking about the weather or some other seemingly irrelevant topic, don't be paranoid. These are probably not trick questions, but simply techniques for generating small talk, commonly believed to be an effective tool to open a relaxed, yet directed interview. But be prepared for a more pointed approach as well. Your interviewer may prefer the prosecuting attorney's method, or the rapid-fire line of questioning. On the other hand, he may take an "unpatterned" approach, which may seem to you like no approach at all. In this case, you take control. This is probably the response he is looking for.

*In a good interview, both sides come prepared.* The skilled interviewer will ask his questions with a purpose in mind. Don't be unnerved if he makes notes while you do most of the talking.

*The interview is your chance to look over the company.* You too are entitled to ask questions.

*Don't assume the interviewer knows what is best for you.* Don't even assume he knows how to do his job. Your interviewer may not have a clear idea in mind of what he wants or needs to learn from you. It's entirely possible he isn't even quite sure what the open position is all about.

*Your interviewer is not your confessor.* Though *you* may recognize your shortcomings, it is not incumbent upon you to reveal them to *him*. As Madeleine Swain, a career consultant with Eaton-Swain Associates (New York), has said, "Whoever said honesty was next to godliness, probably never had to interview for a job."[*]

*An interview that discloses no unfavorable information regarding the applicant is an unsuccessful interview—at least according to Fear tactics.* In the interest of getting to "the real you," the interviewer will couch his comments in euphemisms and phrase his questions in such a way that, as one critic wrote, "the applicant self-destructs without realizing it." Don't be unnerved. If you prepare properly, no question should throw you off-balance.

*Your interviewer's manner of conducting himself may give you some insight into the company that keeps him on its payroll.* The interview is usually your first direct personal contact with the company, and at that time the interviewer is expected to represent to you the corporate image. It is a matter of style. If your style doesn't jibe with his, will it jibe with the corporate image? Perhaps a union here is, after all, not a marriage made in heaven.

---

[*]From Madeleine Swain, "Fired! Recoup, Recover and Re-enter!" (*The Executive Female Digest*, May/June 1979).

---

*When all else fails:* Is the interview deteriorating rapidly? Have you nothing else to lose? Then, as John Berendt suggested in an article in *Esquire* magazine, you may be interested to know that federal and certain state regulations limit the line of questioning that an employer may take at a job interview. Questions concerning race, religion, ethnic background, age, or history of arrest (not *conviction*) are deemed unlawful by the federal government. In addition, New York State, for example, prohibits questions asking for maiden name, place of birth, number of children, social club memberships, and other such facts not directly pertinent to the job. If your rights are being violated, go ahead—stand up for them.

## THE CHEMISTRY TEST

The following anecdotes are based upon real incidents reported in various newspaper and magazine articles. For each interview situation, respond "yes" if you think you get the job, "no" if you think you don't. Compare your answers to the actual outcomes given below.

1. The interviewer takes a cigarette and offers one to you. You refuse politely, but ask if he minds if you smoke a pipe. He says he doesn't mind.
2. You have been flown to town and put up in a good hotel, where your prospective employer meets you for an interview over lunch. It goes very well, and at the end, as he is about to leave, you realize it has unexpectedly begun to rain. You happen to have an extra raincoat in your room and offer to lend the man your spare. Although it is a bit small on him, he accepts the offer.
3. During the interview the fact emerges that you have just moved your family into a new home—a large Victorian house in an exclusive neighborhood. As it turns out, your interviewer shares your fondness for Victorian houses and also has a pretty accurate idea of what such houses sell for. He remarks that, considering your current salary, you must have borrowed to the hilt to buy the house. You frankly admit you did, but add that you didn't feel a moment's hesitation about the decision; you felt it was an excellent investment and, given the inflation rate, decided it was cheaper to get what you wanted today, on credit, than to buy tomorrow with cash.
4. You are a steak-and-potatoes man from way back, but on the interview, your prospective employer takes you to lunch at a continental restaurant where a very limited menu of haute cuisine is served. You allow your interviewer to order for you. The first course is whole artichoke. You are embarrassed to say you have never eaten one before, but you pick up your knife and fork and do your best.

5. You are asked by the interviewer about your family. You tell him enthusiastically about your nine-year-old son's little league team, which you enjoy coaching.
6. You are being interviewed for a job as a personnel executive specializing in industrial relations. Your prospective boss is telling you about his proposal for a change in a particular corporate policy. You tell him frankly that you disagree with his idea and give him your reasons for taking odds.

ACTUAL RESULTS

1. *No.* This interviewer didn't mind pipes per se. However, he associated pipe smoking with the laid-back atmosphere of a university faculty lounge and not with the high-pressured, high-paced life of an executive. He felt someone who smoked a pipe would not fit into his organization.
2. *No.* This interview *had* gone well until the employer put on the raincoat and realized just how *short* the applicant actually was. He himself was a tall man and believed that to be respected in business, you literally had to be looked up to by other people. He did not want a short person representing the corporation.
3. *Yes.* This is a composite of two actual situations. One interviewer admitted favoring a particular candidate who shared his interest in Victorian houses. He felt this reflected a compatibility of styles. In the second interview situation, the employer wanted to hire someone who had personally borrowed to the limit because he thought this act was characteristic of one who was self-confident, aggressive, and unafraid to take risks. This was the kind of executive he needed for the job.
4. *No.* In this situation the interviewer refused to hire someone who didn't know how to eat an artichoke properly. He was appalled at the candidate's lack of what he considered basic etiquette.
5. *No.* The interviewer was turned off by the applicant's animated description of his little-league coaching efforts. He perceived a possible conflict of loyalties between home and office, and he wanted an executive who clearly placed the company above all else.
6. *Yes.* This interviewer was looking to hire a tough negotiator who would not be intimidated easily. The applicant showed the right kind of spunk when he openly disagreed with the interviewer's ideas.

ANALYZING THE CHEMISTRY TEST  If you scored poorly on the test, don't be discouraged. Despite the results of the actual interviews, there are no "right" answers. In each illustration, your answer could have been yes or no with equally sound reasoning. If the "chemistry test" seemed unfair, it *is* unfair. You did not have the benefit of the whole picture—the candidates' overall qualifications or the job specifications—but the fact is that *the employer did not consider the whole picture in making his choice.* That, of course, is the point of the chemistry test. In the final analysis, the reasons by which hiring decisions are made defy common sense and logic.

There are *sensible* reasons why a particular candidate is turned down for a job, such as refusal or reluctance to relocate, inappropriate personality, and high required salary. According to a survey conducted by researchers at Northwestern University, of the 14 reasons given for rejecting job applicants, seven are interview related. The most common of these is the inability to demonstrate self-assurance, enthusiasm, or clearly defined career goals.

According to some experts, however, in more than 50 percent of all cases, the best-qualified applicant *does not get the job.* This is where the "X" factor—personal chemistry—comes into play. It is a variable in the hiring process whose effect is totally unpredictable; yet it is a crucial catalyst in the employer's decision-making.

There have been many attempts to explain the chemistry factor, but the evidence is contradictory. One popular theory holds that like attracts like. In other words, a chief executive officer tends to hire in his own image. This, according to the National Personnel Associates, would explain discriminatory hiring practices against racial and ethnic groups and against women: Most chief executives are white males. Proponents of this theory maintain that a hiring decision may also be made on the basis of perceived shared values and interests—the Victorian house, for example. The applicant who shares such values with the prospective employer will more likely be chosen over the candidate who does not share such values, even though the latter candidate may be equally or even better qualified in other respects.

A 1979 survey conducted by the New York—based search firm of C. Stewart Baeder Associates would seem to refute that theory, however. According to the survey, less than half of the CEOs interviewed expected their successors to have backgrounds similar to their own. The consensus was that in order to meet new corporate challenges, the top executives looked for candidates who offered an operating style different from their own.

The only flat statement most experts are willing to agree upon is that the "X" factor is more than ever a major consideration in the hiring process. The job applicant may be called back for four or five evaluation interviews to meet not only with prospective supervisors, but with prospective peers and subordinates as well. With the growing corporate trend toward participatory management, in which staff is consulted with rather than simply dictated to from above, a compatible "chemistry" among co-workers is vital to operations.

# THE CORPORATE SNOOP:
# PRIVACY AND THE JOB HUNT

### HIS MODUS OPERANDI

Somewhere in Gotham, the details of your life history may be locked into a computer memory bank and available to anyone at the press of a recall button. So warns Robert Ellis Smith in his book *Privacy: How to Protect What's Left of It* (New York: Doubleday & Co., Inc., 1980).

Think back to all the positions for which you have applied and all the jobs you have actually had—and all the forms you filled in to apply for them, to secure them, and to get compensated for them. Think of all the information you have voluntarily supplied to your employers or prospective employers: the psychological tests you may have taken, the forms you filled in disclosing your job history, personal background, medical history, credit record, arrest history. Imagine all the data your employers could have collected on you *without your knowledge:* from information provided about you by people who know you, by people to whom *you gave* formal authorization to disclose as well as to collect information you yourself disclosed in previous questionnaires. You should assume, says Smith, that the record you have provided of your life "will become part of a computerized network and that it will take on a life of its own beyond your control." So the corporate snoop collects the information that goes into your dossier. You have probably done your share to make his job a very easy one.

# YOUR LEGAL RIGHTS

While our laws protect our individual liberty from abuses by the government, the individual has almost no protection at all under law from abuses of these same rights by private business. According to Smith, there are almost no legal restrictions, for example, on information gathering by employers, nor on the disclosure of that information to others, nor on the system of storage and dissemination of that information. In forty-five states there is not even a legal requirement that an employee be allowed to inspect his dossier, and only in Michigan is the employee given the right to amend inaccuracies or unfair statements on the record.

# HOW TO BE A VIGILANTE

The corporate snoop is a serious threat to your right to privacy. The present legal codes offer you inadequate protection against such invasion. However, Smith offers some practical suggestions on how you personally can combat the effect of past abuses as well as protect yourself against the occurrence of future ones:

- As previously mentioned, the law *does* give you the right to withhold certain information from an employer. You can refuse to disclose your race, color, national origin, age, sex, handicaps, possession of a driver's license, or other facts not directly relevant to the job you will perform. Exercise your rights.
- When completing questionnaires, fill in the blanks but learn to "fog" your answers. Use abbreviations such as "N/A" for "not available" or "not applicable," or more obscure abbreviations such as "WBSUE" for "will be supplied upon employment," or "UOQ" for "unsure of question." Where you are asked to provide age, for example, you can be truthful, but vague: "eighteen plus." Most clerks handling the forms will be too embarrassed to admit that they don't understand the abbreviations, or too lazy to pursue the answers any further.
- Proposals have been made to Congress to draft laws giving an employee the right to inspect his records, and many companies, wary of future repercussions, are in some instances voluntarily beginning to comply with individual requests to do so. Take advantage of this option and demand to look at your own files as well as to correct or delete out-of-date or inaccurate information. Also, demand to be notified if any information from these records leaves the company. You have nothing to lose by asking to exercise these yet unprotected rights.
- You do have a right under the federal Fair Credit Reporting Act to request to be given notice of any investigation into your personal life, character, or reputation. The employer has five days to comply with your request by reporting to you both the intent and extent of any such inquiry. In addition, the employer must disclose any adverse action taken pursuant to the findings of the inquiry. If such action has been taken, the employer is required also to disclose the name and address of the investigating firm. You then have a right to learn from the consumer investigation company the matter of information contained on you in their records and also the names of those employers who have been given access to these records in the past two years. If you challenge any of the data in your file, you may request a new investigation or demand inclusion of your version of the story in the record.

# 26

# APPENDIX TO PART V: ACTIVITIES AND RESPONSIBILITIES OF THE EXECUTIVE

The following questionnaire, designed by John K. Hemphill for his study of executive positions, serves as a useful self-test in defining your own job. There is a total of 191 questions in the four-part questionnaire. Follow the instructions at the beginning of each part.

From John K. Hemphill, "Dimensions of Executive Positions"
(Princeton, N.J.: Educational Testing Service, 1959), pp. 27-37.
Reprinted by permission of the author.

## PART I   POSITION ACTIVITIES

Consider each of the following statements which may describe something that
would be done by an individual in your position. If the statement describes
something that does not apply to, or is not true for your position because it
describes something that is delegated by you to a subordinate, it is not a part of
your position. Enter a number between 0 and 7 in the blank before each statement
according to the following scheme.

0.   Definitely not a part of the position, does not apply, or is not true.

1.   Under unusual circumstances may be a minor part of the position.
2.
3.
4.   A substantial part of the position.
5.
6.
7.   A most significant part of the position.

**AN INDIVIDUAL IN THIS POSITION WOULD:**

_____   1.  Plan the analysis of quantitative data.
_____   2.  Forecast the volume of work to be done in the near future.
_____   3.  Maintain personal contact with heads of union groups.
_____   4.  Schedule work so that it flows evenly and steadily.
_____   5.  See representatives of institutional investors.
_____   6.  Assist salesmen in securing important accounts.
_____   7.  Nominate key personnel in the organization for promotion.
_____   8.  Make assignments of jobs to subordinates.
_____   9.  Submit regular reports concerning accomplishment of groups
                 ofemeloyees.
_____  10.  Visit each of the company's major units at least once a year.
_____  11.  Write or dictate at least 25 letters per week.
_____  12.  Verify important facts before they become part of a record.
_____  13.  Edit drafts of special reports.
_____  14.  Make speeches at public gatherings.
_____  15.  Sign documents that obligate the company to the extent of at least
                 $1,000.
_____  16.  Travel at least 30 days each year as a representative of the
                 company.
_____  17.  On the average spend at least one hour per day completing routine
                 paper work.
_____  18.  Approve transfers of workers from one job to another.
_____  19.  Keep detailed and accurate records.
_____  20.  Make recommendations on matters at least as important as the
                 construction of a new plant.

| | | |
|---|---|---|
| _____ | 21. | Advise junior persons on technical matters related to the business. |
| _____ | 22. | Make analyses of statistical reports. |
| _____ | 23. | Approve the introduction of new products or services. |
| _____ | 24. | Have a public speaking engagement at least as often as once every six months. |
| _____ | 25. | Be involved in establishing sales objectives for the company. |
| _____ | 26. | Approve labor contracts. |
| _____ | 27. | Set profit objectives. |
| _____ | 28. | Justify capital expenditures. |
| _____ | 29. | Make suggestions for improvements in company products and/or services. |
| _____ | 30. | Appraise the results of operations. |
| _____ | 31. | Anticipate new and/or changed demands for products and/or services. |
| _____ | 32. | Serve on a committee concerned with appraisal of performance. |
| _____ | 33. | Compute the costs of producing products and/or rendering services. |
| _____ | 34. | Set profit objectives for operating groups. |
| _____ | 35. | Bargain with union representatives. |
| _____ | 36. | Review reports on inventory. |
| _____ | 37. | Analyze expense items involving a gross of at least $5,000. |
| _____ | 38. | Furnish guidance to others in the preparation of budgets. |
| _____ | 39. | Assist sales representatives on large projects. |
| _____ | 40. | Analyze regularly the effectiveness of operations. |
| _____ | 41. | Review budgets for operations. |
| _____ | 42. | Establish effective expense controls. |
| _____ | 43. | Supervise a team of specialists. |
| _____ | 44. | Represent the president outside the company. |
| _____ | 45. | Analyze operating performance reports. |
| _____ | 46. | Devise procedures to properly reflect the results of operation. |
| _____ | 47. | Trouble-shoot special problems as they arise. |
| _____ | 48. | Plan the best use of available facilities. |
| _____ | 49. | Explain divergence between budget and actual expenditures. |
| _____ | 50. | Make use of staff people. |
| _____ | 51. | Consolidate estimates from various sources. |
| _____ | 52. | Evaluate records of production. |
| _____ | 53. | Analyze sales techniques. |
| _____ | 54. | Secure facts and information for others. |
| _____ | 55. | Serve as a member of one or more committees concerned with company policy. |
| _____ | 56. | Set goals for future performance. |
| _____ | 57. | Serve as a consultant in work with branches of the company. |
| _____ | 58. | Brief others on the contents of reports, letters, etc. |
| _____ | 59. | Appraise the results of operations. |
| _____ | 60. | Define areas of responsibility for supervisory personnel. |
| _____ | 61. | Make recommendations for salary increases. |
| _____ | 62. | Serve as a consultant in the interpretation of data and/or other information. |
| _____ | 63. | Keep a constant check upon the activities of subordinates. |

# PART II    POSITION RESPONSIBILITIES

Consider each of the following statements which may describe something with which an individual in your position must be concerned. If your position requires that you be attentive to, worry about, be responsible for, or oversee the matter described in the statement, you are to consider it a part of your position, regardless of how much time you devote to it personally. However, if the statement describes something which is strictly the concern of a superior or of a subordinate you should not consider it a part of your position. Enter a number between 0 and 7 in the blank before each statement according to the following schema.

0.  Definitely not a part of the position, does not apply, or is not true.

1.  Under unusual circumstances may be a minor part of the position.
2.
3.
4.  A substantial part of the position.
5.
6.
7.  A most significant part of the position.


**AN INDIVIDUAL IN MY POSITION MUST BE CONCERNED WITH:**

_____ 64. Long-range objectives of the organization.
_____ 65. Preparation of an annual budget of at least $200,000.
_____ 66. Optimum return on investments of the organization.
_____ 67. Preservation of capital assets.
_____ 68. Capital expenditures.
_____ 69. Payment of salary and/or wages.
_____ 70. Expenditure of sums exceeding $10,000 in routine operations.
_____ 71. Selection of new employees.
_____ 72. Labor contracts.
_____ 73. Definition of areas of responsibility of supervisory personnel.
_____ 74. Payment of company obligations.
_____ 75. Forecasting future trends or events.
_____ 76. Preparation and circulation of bulletins and reports.
_____ 77. Development of new business.
_____ 78. Enforcement of rules and regulations.
_____ 79. Control of inventories.
_____ 80. Improvements in product design.
_____ 81. Protection of company property.
_____ 82. Employee benefit plans.
_____ 83. Preparation of standards and/or specifications.
_____ 84. Reduction of costs.
_____ 85. Pricing company products and/or services.
_____ 86. Promotion of the company's products or services.
_____ 87. Proper handling of other than personal monies.
_____ 88. Compliance of practices with state and federal laws.
_____ 89. Relationships with unions.

_____ 90. Insurance programs and/or policies.
_____ 91. Delivery schedules.
_____ 92. Coordination of certain activities of many subdivisions of the company.
_____ 93. Loss of the company's money and/or property.
_____ 94. Acceptance of the company in the community.
_____ 95. Price trends.
_____ 96. Promises of delivery that are difficult to meet.
_____ 97. Product specifications.
_____ 98. Sales quotas.
_____ 99. Merchandising policies.
_____ 100. Activities of competitors.
_____ 101. Market records five to ten years in the future.
_____ 102. Long-range solvency of the company.
_____ 103. Employee attitude surveys.
_____ 104. Employee vacation and benefit plans.
_____ 105. Interpretation of details of a collective bargaining agreement.
_____ 106. What business activities the company is to be engaged in.
_____ 107. Long-range trends in management thinking.
_____ 108. Taxes (other than personal).
_____ 109. Control of product quality.
_____ 110. Industrial relations.
_____ 111. Opportunities to promote the company before the public.
_____ 112. New competitive products.
_____ 113. Union activities within the company.
_____ 114. Over-or-under staffing of jobs.
_____ 115. Maintenance of proper inventories.
_____ 116. New markets for the company's products.
_____ 117. Engineering standards.
_____ 118. Details of a collective bargaining agreement.
_____ 119. The long-range potentialities of the business.
_____ 120. The effectiveness of a force of 100 or more employees.
_____ 121. Proposed legislation that might affect the company.
_____ 122. Pilot projects.
_____ 123. Sizing up people.
_____ 124. Evaluating new ideas.
_____ 125. Responsibility for products having a value of at least $100,000.
_____ 126. Redesign of products to reduce costs.
_____ 127. Quality control.
_____ 128. Good will of the company in the community.
_____ 129. New markets for future products.
_____ 130. Market conditions affecting the users of the company's products and/or services.
_____ 131. Efficiency of operations.
_____ 132. Preparation of quarterly (or more frequent) reports on operations.
_____ 133. Development of management trainees.
_____ 134. Human relations practices.
_____ 135. Consolidation of data and/or information from numerous sources.

# PART III    POSITION DEMANDS AND RESTRICTIONS

Consider each of the following statements which may describe a restriction, limitation, control or demand upon an individual in your position. Consider that the statement describes a part of your position if it is true when applied to your position and it is likely that failure to observe the matter described would cause others to think you inadequate or unqualified for your position. Do not consider that a statement describes part of your position if it is not true or does not apply or because it agrees with your personal view about what is proper. Enter a number between 0 and 7 in the blank before each statement according to the following schema.

0.  Definitely not a part of the position, does not apply, or is not true.

1.  Under unusual circumstances may be a minor part of the position.
2.
3.
4.  A substantial part of the position.
5.
6.
7.  A most significant part of the position.


**MY POSITION REQUIRES THAT I:**

_____ 136. Refrain from activities that might imply sympathy for unions.
_____ 137. Be active in community affairs.
_____ 138. Avoid identification with political elements that others consider radical.
_____ 139. Even during most relaxed social occasions avoid deviations from generally accepted behavior.
_____ 140. Maintain membership in one or more clubs.
_____ 141. Keep informed about the latest technical developments in a professional area.
_____ 142. Avoid any public comment critical of good customer and/or supplier.
_____ 143. Avoid the use of any kind of profanity.
_____ 144. Be very careful to avoid inadvertent disclosure of confidential information.
_____ 145. Spend as much as 50 hours per week on the job.
_____ 146. Take a leading part in local community projects.
_____ 147. Work with persons whose interests conflict with the demands of my position.
_____ 148. Sit at a desk at least 20 hours per week.
_____ 149. Be capable of performing the jobs of all subordinates.
_____ 150. Participate in outside activities to increase the prestige of the company.
_____ 151. Gain the respect of very important persons.
_____ 152. Work with information of questionable reliability.
_____ 153. Maintain membership in two or more business organizations.

_____ 154. Present the company to the public in its best light.
_____ 155. Avoid publicity associated with personal difficulties.
_____ 156. Refrain from being seen at a place (bar, club, etc.) having other than the highest repute.
_____ 157. Maintain active membership in two or more professional organizations.
_____ 158. Get to know each person under me.
_____ 159. Be an active member of at least one civic organization.
_____ 160. Refrain from public criticism of the company's operations.
_____ 161. Make decisions without consulting others.

# PART IV    POSITION CHARACTERISTICS (Miscellaneous)

Consider each of the following statements which may be either true or false if applied to your position. If the statement is true only because of your particular relationship to your position and would not be true of another incumbent, do not consider it a part of the position. However, if the statement would be true regardless of who holds the position, then the statement describes a part of the position. In this case your task is to decide how substantial a part of the job it is. Enter a number between 0 and 7 in the blank before each statement according to the following schema.

0.  Definitely not a part of the position, does not apply, or is not true.

1.  Under unusual circumstances may be a minor part of the position.

2.

3.

4.  A substantial part of the position.

5.

6.

7.  A most significant part of the position.

## MY POSITION:

_____ 162. Signifies membership in top or middle management.
_____ 163. Offers an opportunity to utilize professional training.
_____ 164. Permits access to information regarding executive salaries.
_____ 165. Involves dealing with persons within the company of substantially higher rank.
_____ 166. Involves first-hand contact with customers of the company.
_____ 167. Assures that the incumbent will be noticed by top management.
_____ 168. Is within the normal path of promotion to higher levels.
_____ 169. Offers an opportunity to work with the more influential people within the community.
_____ 170. Allows great freedom of action.
_____ 171. Involves very frequent contact with the public.
_____ 172. Involves maintaining the highest respect of a few important persons.

## DIRECTIONS SUMMARIZED

0. Definitely not a part of the position, does not apply, or is not true.

1. Under unusual circumstances may be a minor part of the position.
2.
3.
4. A substantial part of the position.
5.
6.
7. A most significant part of the position.

_____ 173. Involves first-hand contact with machines and their operations.

_____ 174. Offers an opportunity to gain experience in management.

_____ 175. Involves the "good will" of the company.

_____ 176. Involves meeting problems produced by factors over which I have no control.

_____ 177. Allows me to make decisions that are not subject to review.

_____ 178. Provides an opportunity for actually managing an important part of the business.

_____ 179. Provides a company automobile for my use.

_____ 180. Entitles me to my own secretary.

_____ 181. Involves sharing in a bonus or profit-sharing plan.

_____ 182. Involves close association with women employees.

_____ 183. Involves many regularly assigned duties.

_____ 184. Carries a personal expense allowance.

_____ 185. Directly affects the quality of the company's products or services.

_____ 186. Involves spending at least 10 hours per week in direct association with superiors.

_____ 187. Involves very few routine activities.

_____ 188. Involves activities that are not closely supervised or controlled.

_____ 189. Provides an office that is located in one of the more desirable areas.

_____ 190. Is considered a staff rather than line position.

_____ 191. Involves working under constant pressure to meet deadlines.

# PART VI

# GETTING YOUR SHARE: EXECUTIVE COMPENSATION

"When a fellow says, 'It ain't
the money, but the principle
of the thing,' it's the money."
Frank McKinney Hubbard

# 27

## WHAT EVERYBODY WANTS

Remember when earned income meant strictly salary, and ordinary income meant interest on your savings? Well, no more. The question of executive compensation has become very complex, and as you advance up the corporate ladder, you will be carrying a more mixed and increasingly hefty bag of compensation benefits.

Compensation packages are largely a reflection of the times. Changes in the work ethic and social values have caused most executives to view compensation not strictly in terms of money but, rather, as an amalgam of alternative compensation forms to accommodate changed priorities. To meet these demands as well as to keep up with corporate needs and the ever-changing rules and regulations of the IRS, executive compensation planners have created a smorgasbord of goodies so abundant and exotic that many an executive has stood before it wondering where to dig in.

To get your share of the compensation smorgasbord, you need to approach the negotiating table with the discriminating taste of a connoisseur, but the appetite of a glutton.

To begin to develop a fine appreciation for what goes into an executive compensation package, ponder the following questions:

- *What are you after?* What are your short-range cash income needs and long-term net worth objectives?
- *What is the company after?*
- *What does Uncle Sam want?*
- *What goes on the table?*

## WHAT ARE YOU AFTER?

When it comes to compensation, every executive wants *more*. That is not the question. The question is, what is the real dollar value of your current income and assets, and how much more cash do you actually need to support yourself and your family in the next year; the next ten years? And, in the long term, how much capital accumulation do you require to maintain your present life-style through your retirement years? The break-even point between your projected family needs and your projected family income and assets will determine your bottom line in compensation negotiation. Any compensation above the break-even amount is gravy—and you will undoubtedly want a hearty portion of that on top of your steak and potatoes.

**How to determine your current cash value and near-term cash needs:** As David McLaughlin suggests in *The Executive Money Map,* *

- you can gather together all your personal financial records and deliver them to a financial consultant, accountant, or other professional and pay a substantial fee to receive a "base case projection," i.e., a ten-year forecast of your annual income based on current data; or
- you can gather together your records, a calculator, and a textbook on the fundamentals of accounting and using work sheets such as McLaughlin has devised (*see* my Chapter 30, Fig. 53), do the forecast for yourself.

**How to determine your net worth goals:** Achieving ultimate financial independence and security requires practical planning. Here again, doing a base case projection is the recommended approach to determine projected net worth goals and a capital accumulation strategy. Also, begin to look over the smorgasbord of compensation alternatives to determine which ones will best fulfill your particular net worth goals. For purposes of capital accumulation, the basic compensation forms available to the executive are pensions, profit sharing plans, deferred compensation, and future value incentive plans.

According to an Urban Institute estimate cited by McLaughlin, as of 1975 only five million Americans had achieved a minimum net worth of $60,000. Of those, only 120,000 were millionaires. Inflation and the tax man's ever growing appetite and stiff control over compensation etiquette make it tougher and tougher for you to walk away from the table with a he-man's share.

*David McLaughlin, *The Executive Money Map,* edited by Jonathan Rinehart (New York: McGraw-Hill, 1975).

# WHAT IS THE COMPANY AFTER?

In determining executive compensation policy, the corporation's objectives are:

- to attract you and keep you
- to reduce or eliminate financial strain to the executive
- to stimulate and increase your interest in company growth and well-being by increasing your financial stake in it, i.e., tieing compensation to performance
- to minimize outflow of corporate cash and minimize cost to stockholders
- to keep a lid on company stock holdings by executives
- to minimize dependence of compensation value on stock market prices
- to maximize tax benefit and minimize tax liability to both you and the corporation

Where your interests and the corporate interests coincide, you and your employer can come to easy terms. Where your interests conflict, *you* will have to drive a hard bargain.

**The view from the other side:** If you want to gain added insight into how compensation decisions are made, you might take a look at *How to Compensate Executives*, by James E. Cheeks and Gordon D. Wolf (Homewood, Illinois: Dow Jones-Irwin, 1979). This is an evenhanded look at the executive compensation issue, although the book is intended for the employer. It emphasizes the true costs of the programs to the employer, and the tax benefits to both employer and employee of the various plans. This straightforward volume will give you insight into how compensation programs are structured and why the employer seems more flexible on some points than on others.

# WHAT DOES UNCLE SAM WANT?

Uncle Sam wants something from everybody. What Uncle Sam wants, of course, is money—money out of the money you make and out of the money your employer makes. He sends around the tax man to collect. The tax man has a guidebook over 40,000 pages long telling him *what* he can collect from whom.

Now, not only you and your employer make money, but money itself has the ability to make money, either through savings or investments. The method by which some money makes *more* money determines the way the tax man collects his share. Indeed, sometimes it seems that the tax man makes off with the most money.

The Economic Recovery Tax Act of 1981 has altered tax treatment of stock options, capital gains, and other aspects of individual and business taxation. Such provisions may affect your compensation plan. It is wise to consult an accountant.

## The tax man's classification of income

- *Earned income* is the money earned as salary or other *current* compensation in the form of cash, stock bonuses, and non-qualified stock options.
- *Ordinary income* is ordinary in the sense that it is subject to ordinary progressive tax treatment vis-à-vis extraordinary or special tax treatment. Ordinary income is money earned from dividends, interest, deferred compensation, or gambling. It is not necessarily income earned in connection with your work.
- *Preference income* comes in eight varieties earned through particular kinds of investments, for example, gains made on the appreciation in value of an exercised stock option. These monies receive "preferential" treatment up to a specified limit.
- *Capital gains* are profits made through sale of an asset whose value has increased since time of purchase.

**Playing favorites:** Uncle Sam's preferences are built into the tax structure. The design of tax provisions "favors" certain forms of compensation and investment income and thereby determines the popularity of particular compensation plans.

- Allowable tax deductions are one means by which the tax man encourages us to play his favorites. As McLaughlin notes, profit sharing plans, pensions, and some perquisites are considered "legitimate deductible business expenses," and, consequently, such forms of compensation are favored by corporations.
- Likewise, the "tax structure favors builders," so both employer and employee tend to look for compensation means that generate income subject to favorable capital gains treatment.
- On the other hand, salary and cash bonuses are subject to progressive tax treatment. An executive whose income is accrued primarily through those means will pay a larger portion of it back to the government.

**Playing the tax man's game:** The complicated tax structure makes it difficult for an executive to evaluate the true dollar worth of a compensation offer and to compare offers made by various companies. However, the greatest difficulty faced by executives and compensation planners alike in playing the tax man's game is keeping up with the tax man's changing rules. A compensation policy that looked rosy under last year's provisions may pale in the light of new and current regulations.

**Don't cheat the system, beat the system:** McLaughlin points out that tax *avoidance, not* tax evasion, is a legitimate means of beating the tax system—or, at least, of making the best of it. The government leaves to the individual the responsibility of formulating a strategy to minimize taxes. You are expected to use established policies to your personal financial advantage: Give yourself every break permitted by law.

Whether or not you actually can *beat* the tax man at his game is a moot question. You do have to keep up with it, though; so unless you yourself are a tax consultant or accountant, you will in the long run do best to seek the advice of a professional when structuring your pay package.

# 28

# HOW MUCH?

In the current economic environment, a buck in the hand is worth two on the books. Salary, delivered *now* in cold hard cash, is still the most coveted prize. The size of the paycheck is predetermined and guaranteed. There is no risk; no cost; no restriction. You can spend it, save it, invest it as you please. From your viewpoint, it's "take the money and run." From the corporate viewpoint, "cash motivates," and that looks good, too.

Even so, when it comes down to the negotiating table, many executives do not know how to determine their fair share of the boodle or how to bargain for what they are worth. The corporate cashier is regarded by the executive with some distrust: his motives are suspect; his decisions arbitrary.

The truth of the matter is that compensation decisions should be, and usually are, quite reasonable, and corporate pay policies are not only accessible, if you know where to find them, but also quite understandable from the corporate point of view. Salary levels are carefully determined by corporate personnel who have to defend their judgments not only to you, the executive, but also to the chairman of the board, company stockholders, and Uncle Sam.

## WHAT REALLY COUNTS:
## SALARY FACTORS

In certain instances, especially those involving top management at large corporations, perks such as stock options and pension plans can be even more important than salary. But in the vast majority of cases, the real bargaining takes place over salary and bonus.

Some careful studies have been made of compensation patterns, and several key factors have emerged:

**Industry.** Some industries tend to pay more than others, across the board. Salary levels tend to be set by intraindustry competition, rather than by the broader corporate environment.

Company size within an industry is also a factor to consider. Some surveys show that larger companies, on the average, tend to pay higher salaries. In cross-industry comparisons, however, there are notable exceptions to this rule.

**Region.** According to studies published by Financial Executives Institute, the highest-paid top executives in 1978 were in the West, followed by executives in the Northeast, Rocky Mountains, Midwest, Mideast, Southwest, and Southeast. However, the study notes, these statistics are "general in nature. Actual regional differences can vary greatly depending upon size of company and industry."

**TOP EXECUTIVES:**
Comparison of compensation by industry

| | RANK | | INDEX | | | | |
|---|---|---|---|---|---|---|---|
| | | | *(All-industry average = 1.00)* | | | | |
| | 1978 | 1976 | Chief Executive | Top Financial Officer | Controller | Treasurer | Top Executives Combined |
| Transportation Equipment | 1 | 1 | 1.52 | 1.43 | 1.47 | 1.47 | 1.48 |
| Financial Holding and Investment | 2 | 3 | 1.38 | 1.22 | 1.24 | 1.15 | 1.29 |
| Chemicals and Petroleum | 3 | 2 | 1.29 | 1.25 | 1.23 | 1.18 | 1.26 |
| Paper Products | 4 | 5 | 1.24 | 1.15 | 1.12 | 1.08 | 1.18 |
| Food Products | 5 | 4 | 1.11 | 1.04 | 1.06 | 1.17 | 1.10 |
| Basic Materials | 6 | 10 | 1.07 | 1.05 | 1.08 | 1.11 | 1.08 |
| Mining | 7 | * | 1.09 | .98 | 1.05 | 1.15 | 1.07 |
| Instruments | 8 | * | .96 | 1.15 | 1.11 | 1.19 | 1.06 |
| Primary Metals | 9 | 6 | 1.13 | 1.04 | 1.08 | .84 | 1.06 |
| Electrical Machinery | 10 | * | 1.01 | 1.13 | 1.11 | 1.03 | 1.05 |
| Construction and Contracting | 11 | 17 | 1.11 | .93 | .83 | .93 | 1.00 |
| Machinery | 12 | 8 | .98 | 1.01 | .94 | .98 | .98 |
| Retail Sales | 13 | 14 | .95 | .95 | .90 | 1.14 | .97 |
| Transportation | 14 | 11 | .98 | 1.01 | .93 | .88 | .96 |
| Insurance | 15 | 19 | .94 | .96 | .95 | .91 | .94 |
| Fabricated Metal Products | 16 | 16 | .91 | .91 | .92 | .93 | .92 |
| Textiles and Apparel | 17 | 13 | .89 | 1.02 | .94 | .80 | .91 |
| Publishing | 18 | 15 | .86 | .85 | .80 | 1.00 | .87 |
| Business Services | 19 | 18 | .82 | .87 | .85 | .97 | .86 |
| Utilities | 20 | 22 | .79 | .87 | .88 | .81 | .82 |
| Banking (Commercial) | 21 | 20 | .81 | .73 | .74 | .75 | .77 |
| Real Estate | 22 | * | .70 | .76 | .72 | .77 | .73 |
| Wholesale Trade | 23 | 21 | .63 | .70 | .70 | .70 | .67 |
| Banking (Thrift Institutions) | 24 | * | .66 | .66 | .64 | .71 | .66 |

*Insufficient data

Fig. 47. Comparison of compensation by industry
Index of the compensation levels of top executives in 24 top industries, with the all-industry average equal to 100.

Reprinted from Edwin S. Mruk and James A. Giardina, *Executive Compensation* (New York: Financial Executives Institute Inc., 1979), p. 55. Used by permission of publisher.

**Tax provisions.** Corporations, like individual executives, are concerned with juggling their compensation plans to minimize costs and maximize tax advantages. The corporation, unlike the executive, faces the additional considerations and restrictions imposed by IRS standards of "reasonableness." Corporations must be able to show to stockholders, as well as to the IRS, that an executive's compensation level is justified in terms of services rendered. As reported by compensation experts James E. Cheeks and Gordon D. Wolf in *How to Compensate Executives* (Homewood, Illinois: Dow Jones-Irwin, 1979), reasonableness is determined by:

- what other executives earn in similar positions in the same industry

---

**TOP EXECUTIVES:**
**Percentage increase in total compensation by industry**

| | Rank | 1977-1978 Increase |
|---|---|---|
| Machinery | 1 | 20.0% |
| Banking (Commercial) | 2 | 18.1 |
| Financial Holding and Investment | 3 | 18.1 |
| Electrical Machinery | 4 | 17.9 |
| Instruments | 5 | 17.3 |
| Mining | 6 | 16.9 |
| Transportation Equipment | 7 | 16.4 |
| Publishing | 8 | 16.1 |
| Fabricated Metal Products | 9 | 14.8 |
| Business Services | 10 | 14.3 |
| Basic Materials | 11 | 13.8 |
| Insurance | 12 | 13.5 |
| Textiles and Apparel | 13 | 13.4 |
| Primary Metals | 14 | 13.1 |
| Food Products | 15 | 13.0 |
| Chemicals and Petroleum | 16 | 13.0 |
| Construction and Contracting | 17 | 12.9 |
| Paper Products | 18 | 12.4 |
| Retail Sales | 19 | 12.2 |
| Banking (Thrift Institutions) | 20 | 12.1 |
| Wholesale Trade | 21 | 12.0 |
| Real Estate | 22 | 11.2 |
| Utilities | 23 | 10.7 |
| Transportation | 24 | 10.3 |

---

Fig. 48. Percentage increase in top executive
salaries 1977-78, by industry

Reprinted from Edwin S. Mruk and James A. Giardina,
*Executive Compensation* (New York: Financial Executives
Institute Inc., 1979), p. 56. Used by permission of publisher.

**Average total compensation by sales volume**
*(Thousands of dollars)*

|  | Bonus Companies | Nonbonus Companies | All Companies |
|---|---|---|---|
| **1978** | | | |
| Under $10 Million | $120.8 | $ 86.5 | $106.6 |
| $10-25 | 115.8 | 73.2 | 103.7 |
| $25-50 | 131.4 | 85.6 | 122.9 |
| $50-100 | 149.8 | 98.7 | 138.8 |
| $100-200 | 177.6 | 126.8 | 167.9 |
| $200-500 | 216.4 | 151.9 | 202.7 |
| $500-1 Billion | 284.7 | 185.1 | 258.7 |
| $1-2 | 351.7 | 222.6 | 329.8 |
| Over $2 Billion | 426.4 | 247.3 | 384.2 |
| **1977** | | | |
| Under $10 Million | $ 95.1 | $ 75.2 | $ 87.8 |
| $10-25 | 104.5 | 65.0 | 95.6 |
| $25-50 | 113.3 | 84.0 | 107.4 |
| $50-100 | 135.8 | 93.1 | 127.2 |
| $100-200 | 158.0 | 108.6 | 149.7 |
| $200-500 | 196.1 | 149.6 | 185.3 |
| $500-1 Billion | 259.2 | 159.0 | 236.1 |
| $1-2 | 296.7 | 214.4 | 278.1 |
| Over $2 Billion | 391.1 | 225.2 | 356.5 |

Fig. 49. Average total compensation by sales volume
Table includes compensation in bonus companies,
nonbonus companies, and all companies, by sales volume.
Figures expressed are for chief executives.

Reprinted from Edwin S. Mruk and James A. Giardina,
*Executive Compensation* (New York: Financial Executives
Institute Inc., 1979), p. 21. Used by permission of publisher.

- the level of experience and credentials of the executive
- the current income level of the executive
- the level of responsibility of the job
- corporate size and organization
- company earnings
- general corporate compensation policy
- size of dividend payouts to stockholders
- prevailing business conditions

To conform to standards of reasonableness, an executive's salary

**TOP FINANCIAL EXECUTIVES:**
**Compensation as a percentage of**
**chief executive's compensation by industry**

| | INDEX _(Chief executive's compensation = 100%)_ | | |
|---|---|---|---|
| | Top Financial Officer | Controller | Treasurer |
| Banking (Commercial) | 43% | 27% | 30% |
| Banking (Thrift Institutions) | 47 | 29 | 35 |
| Basic Materials | 46 | 30 | 33 |
| Business Services | 50 | 31 | 38 |
| Chemicals and Petroleum | 45 | 28 | 30 |
| Construction and Contracting | 39 | 22 | 27 |
| Electrical Machinery | 52 | 32 | 33 |
| Fabricated Metal Products | 47 | 30 | 33 |
| Financial Holding and Investment | 41 | 27 | 27 |
| Food Products | 44 | 28 | 34 |
| Instruments | 56 | 34 | 40 |
| Insurance | 48 | 30 | 31 |
| Machinery | 48 | 28 | 32 |
| Mining | 42 | 29 | 34 |
| Paper Products | 44 | 27 | 28 |
| Primary Metals | 43 | 28 | 24 |
| Publishing | 46 | 28 | 37 |
| Real Estate | 51 | 31 | 36 |
| Retail Sales | 47 | 28 | 39 |
| Textiles and Apparel | 54 | 31 | 29 |
| Transportation | 48 | 28 | 29 |
| Transportation Equipment | 44 | 29 | 31 |
| Utilities | 52 | 33 | 33 |
| Wholesale Trade | 52 | 33 | 36 |

Fig. 50. Compensation of top financial executives
Figures represent percentages of the chief
executive's salary, by industry.

Reprinted from Edwin S. Mruk and James A. Giardina,
_Executive Compensation_ (New York: Financial Executives
Institute Inc., 1979), p. 59. Used by permission of publisher.

need not be justified by each and every one of these determinants, but
only a few. By IRS standards, reasonableness applies to the compensation package as a whole, not to individual elements of the package.
Therefore, as Cheeks and Wolf note, "if a salary of $90,000 and a bonus
of $10,000 is reasonable for a job, then a salary of $10,000 and a bonus
of $90,000 is equally reasonable for that job."*

*From James E. Cheeks and Gordon D. Wolf, _How to Compensate Executives_ (Homewood,
IL: Dow Jones-Irwin, 1979), p. 26, copyright © 1979 by James E. Cheeks and Gordon D.
Wolf.

**Corporate power structure.** Top executives play a role in determining their own salary and in influencing board members who create compensation policy.

**Character of top executives.** Their personal philosophy and views on the work ethic contribute to policy.

**Bargaining factor.** Successful executives are shrewd and tough negotiators with political savvy and innovative, creative techniques. They know how to get what they want.

**CHIEF EXECUTIVE:**
Comparison of average total compensation

| | RANK | | INDEX | |
|---|---|---|---|---|
| | | | (All industries combined = 1.00) | |
| | 1978 | 1976 | 1978 | 1976 |
| Transportation Equipment | 1 | 1 | 1.52 | 1.39 |
| Financial Holding and Investment | 2 | 3 | 1.38 | 1.27 |
| Chemicals and Petroleum | 3 | 2 | 1.29 | 1.28 |
| Paper Products | 4 | 5 | 1.24 | 1.21 |
| Primary Metals | 5 | 6 | 1.13 | 1.14 |
| Construction and Contracting | 6 | 16 | 1.11 | .85 |
| Food Products | 7 | 4 | 1.11 | 1.24 |
| Mining | 8 | * | 1.09 | * |
| Basic Materials | 9 | 11 | 1.07 | 1.01 |
| Electrical Machinery | 10 | * | 1.01 | * |
| Machinery | 11 | 7 | 98 | 1.08 |
| Transportation | 12 | 9 | 98 | 1.06 |
| Instruments | 13 | * | 96 | * |
| Retail Sales | 14 | 13 | 95 | 93 |
| Insurance | 15 | 21 | 94 | 76 |
| Fabricated Metal Products | 16 | 15 | 91 | 86 |
| Textiles and Apparel | 17 | 14 | 89 | 89 |
| Publishing | 18 | 17 | 86 | 83 |
| Business Services | 19 | 18 | 82 | 82 |
| Banking (Commercial) | 20 | 19 | 81 | 80 |
| Utilities | 21 | 20 | 79 | 79 |
| Real Estate | 22 | * | 70 | * |
| Banking (Thrift Institutions) | 23 | * | 66 | * |
| Wholesale Trade | 24 | 22 | 63 | 73 |

*Insufficient data

Fig. 51. Compensation rankings of chief
executives, by industry

Reprinted from Edwin S. Mruk and James A. Giardina,
*Executive Compensation* (New York: Financial Executives
Institute Inc., 1979), p. 19. Used by permission of publisher.

# COMPUTING YOUR COMPENSATION

Wouldn't it be great if there were a simple mathematical formula for determining what a job is worth? Well, there isn't, but not for lack of trying. Every so often, one of these attempts reveals some numerical

**CHIEF EXECUTIVE:**
**Percentage increase in average total compensation by industry**
*(1977-1978)*

|  | Bonus Companies | Nonbonus Companies |
|---|---|---|
| Banking (Commercial) | 24.5% | 14.8% |
| Banking (Thrift Institutions) | 14.6 | 23.2 |
| Basic Materials | 15.0 | 14.9 |
| Business Services | 20.9 | 9.2 |
| Chemicals and Petroleum | 14.0 | 15.0 |
| Construction and Contracting | 10.8 | 8.9 |
| Electrical Machinery | 21.9 | 2.9 |
| Fabricated Metal Products | 18.4 | 10.9 |
| Financial Holding and Investment | 23.4 | 3.5 |
| Food Products | 14.9 | 7.1 |
| Instruments | 23.7 | — |
| Insurance | 13.3 | 22.5 |
| Machinery | 21.9 | 10.7 |
| Mining | 23.6 | 6.7 |
| Paper Products | 11.0 | 11.1 |
| Primary Metals | 11.5 | 20.4 |
| Publishing | 22.9 | 2.4 |
| Real Estate | 15.0 | 12.5 |
| Retail Sales | 16.2 | 12.7 |
| Textiles and Apparel | 12.5 | 10.8 |
| Transportation | 6.8 | 3.7 |
| Transportation Equipment | 15.0 | 25.5 |
| Utilities | 28.2 | 8.6 |
| Wholesale Trade | 14.9 | 3.9 |

Fig. 52. Increase in chief executive compensation
1977-78, by industry

Reprinted from Edwin S. Mruk and James A. Giardina,
*Executive Compensation* (New York: Financial Executives
Institute Inc., 1979), p. 18. Used by permission of publisher.

relationships that help our understanding of the factors involved, even if it is a less than foolproof indicator of dollar value.

Eugene Finkin, writing in *Personnel Journal,* observed that salary is most closely related not to corporate profits, not to division profits or sales, but to *the salary of the CEO* (which is related to corporate sales) and *your level in the hierarchy.*

If you know the sales figure and how many people get paid more than you, you should, says Finkin, be able to arrive at a reasonable approximation of compensation in dollars. He has even proposed a formula for CEO compensation:

$$c = Ax^{B}*$$

wherein $c$ = compensation in dollars, $x$ = sales, and $A$ and $B$ are appropriate constants.

Once the CEO compensation is determined, the senior management salaries are determined as a percentage of that. Finkin found that in 1976 the second-highest-paid executives of Fortune 500 companies received, on the average, 72 percent of the CEO salary. Senior and executive VPs positioned third to fifth in the company got between 52 percent and 54 percent. The next level was in the 35-37 percent range.

The results seem to indicate that it would be better to hold a senior management position in a billion-dollar company than in a 100 million dollar company, and that a promotion in a larger company may be worth much more in terms of dollars than a switch to a smaller company where you would have more potential for advancement. But this is far from a hard and fast rule: It may not apply to closely held or private companies. It doesn't take the dollar value of perks into account. And the value of these figures is questionable due to the effects of inflation and energy costs on profits, sales, and living cost since 1976. In addition, the constants, A & B, may be affected by such factors.

The formula is based on power laws. If you are interested in the math behind all this, see "How to Figure Out Executive Compensation" by Eugene F. Finkin, in the July, 1978, issue of *Personnel Journal,* pp. 371-375.

**Comparison shop.** A general method to estimate a reasonable salary level for a particular position is to determine the "going rate" for someone of your qualifications holding a similar position within the same industry. Good sources for salary information are:

- trade associations
- trade papers and journals, particularly publications for personnel professionals
- classified advertisements

*Reprinted with permission from *Personnel Journal,* Copyright © July, 1978.

- personnel agencies and executive recruiters
- company proxy statements (an excellent source of information on entire compensation policy, not just salary)

---

## THE CASH OR INCENTIVE BONUS

---

The lure of more cash (even if it is paid out in stock, a bonus is taxed like cash) makes this dish an especially appealing and popular one to the executive. From the corporation's perspective, an incentive bonus is a means to tie an executive's compensation to corporate performance and thereby motivate the executive to further the company's career as well as his own.

In the past, the cash bonus has been a staple in manufacturing industries, but in recent years, service companies, especially banks and insurance firms, have begun to join the bonus plan bandwagon. Since 1972, 25 percent more major corporations have begun to offer executive bonuses. Oddly enough, those corporations that offer a bonus plan very often also offer a higher pay scale.

**The bonus formula.** The formula, which varies from situation to situation, identifies a specifically defined corporate or divisional performance goal (commonly related to sales, profits, return on investments, or dividends) as well as the bonus amount (usually a percentage of base salary or profits) to be received by the executive once the goal is met. A divisional plan is preferable, particularly for a division executive, because it is possible for a division to perform well even though overall corporate performance is poor.

Whether the corporate philosophy is to reward the "team" across the board or to reward the "stars," the particular formula applied reflects the corporation's attitude toward its executives on performance standards. If everyone gets the bonus, you may want either your salary level or your bonus formula percentage to reflect your individual performance and visibility.

How the bonus is structured and administered, how performance is to be judged, the timing and form of the payout, and especially how the company bonus plan has worked in practice (not just how it appears on paper) are issues that should be studied carefully when you appraise the value of a bonus offer.

**Discretionary bonuses.** Not linked to a predetermined performance goal, these bonuses may be awarded in recognition of some noteworthy accomplishment by an executive.

---

# 29

# PERKS

The heavy corporate tax burden and the need to manage cash flow have combined to make perquisites an increasingly popular form of executive compensation. At the same time, slower economic growth has resulted in the curtailment of the more extravagant and wasteful fringe benefits enjoyed by top executives during the booming sixties. The important ones have survived, and they are described below. You should be familiar with them, because perks are often as important a part of a compensation package as salary and bonus.

## COMPANY INSURANCE PLANS

Since almost everyone gets company insurance, no one seems very excited about it. As David McLaughlin points out, insurance is bad news, it's boring, and everyone assumes big daddy is looking after it. Nevertheless, properly planned company-paid insurance coverage can represent a hefty "extra" to the executive. Generally the company contribution to executive insurance is not taxable income to the executive and is tax deductible to the corporation, making insurance a tax-favored compensation alternative all around.

From the point of view of the individual executive, however, company insurance plans are often inadequate, because they are usually geared to the group and directed to the needs of the average employee. In addition, group policies are often designed and revised in piecemeal fashion and, as a result, tend to be outdated or to offer poor coverage. Due to the tax-favored status of insurance, however, many corporations are willing to negotiate individual policies geared to meet the needs of key executives. If you cannot negotiate a policy that is suited to your needs, you may be wise to see if you can do better by securing coverage on your own.

The value of any particular company policy is its "replacement" cost to you, i.e., what you yourself would have to pay out-of-pocket for equal coverage. A typical plan for an executive can run several thousand dollars. Of course, if the company coverage is company paid, by all means take it. But if the coverage is insufficient, supplement it with a private plan.

## LIFE INSURANCE

Life insurance is intended to protect your family by providing for its financial needs in the event of your death. For a young executive, especially one with a family and with little opportunity so far to have built up net worth, life insurance is most essential as well as very costly.

The value of the coverage you require will be determined by the number and age of your children, by your spouse's age and and by projected future family income needs, including cost of education for your children and the repayment of outstanding debts. Don't accept the company plan blindly. Beware, not all plans can be taken with you if you leave the firm. Consult an expert. Most of them recommend you carry private protection and that you update your coverage periodically.

## MEDICAL INSURANCE

The great majority of corporations provide medical insurance to most of their employees, and the typical executive is usually covered under the group plan. The problem is that many executives find upon examining the corporate plan that, although the company often pays a high percentage (if not all) of the total premium, coverage is inadequate. To make the matter worse, although insurance premiums themselves are deductible expenses, tax provisions do not allow deductions for any personal medical expenses if total expenses are less than three percent of annual income. An executive earning $60,000 a year would have to run up a considerable medical bill before he could begin to derive any tax benefit. Considering the skyrocketing costs of medical care, this is an unhappy situation for the executive. To alleviate the problem, many corporations have begun to reimburse executives directly for their medical expenses (*see* section on "perks," below).

## DISABILITY INSURANCE

Disability insurance may be paid as sick-leave pay, short-term disability, or long-term disability, depending on the length of illness. Social Security benefits and workmen's compensation are collectible in the event of extended sick leave. Company coverage, however, is usually limited, and you should study plans to determine if sufficient protection is provided. Avail yourself of maximum coverage offered, but if it is limited and your salary is high, consider subscribing to a policy on your own. Amounts earned as sick pay from the company are considered fully taxable income to the executive. However, payouts on a private policy are not subject to tax.

---

# THE COMPANY PENSION PLAN

---

Compensation provisions for retirement are clearly an important part of the pay package. The value to the executive in terms of replacement cost is extremely high, because the coverage provided by most company plans would be a substantial expense if the individual were to carry it alone. In any case, many qualified plans are actually company paid. Nevertheless, you can expect that the company pension plan, which, unlike other compensation forms, cannot by law discriminate in favor of the executive, will be inadequate to meet your retirement needs (usually calculated as some percentage of preretirement income).

## THE STRUCTURE OF A PENSION PLAN

The pension plan is a very complicated arrangement, and even compensation planners are advised not to construct a program without the advice of specialists. Its complexities notwithstanding, you are well advised to carefully scrutinize the provisions of the corporate pension plan long before your retirement is due, and plan ahead if the coverage is inadequate. When reviewing the plan, consider the following points:

ELIGIBILITY REQUIREMENTS   How do you qualify to take part in the plan? Usually there is some minimum employment period before you can participate.

THE FORMULA   Is your payout a percentage of annual earnings, a career average, or some final average (say, total pay over the last several years)? Is there a maximum payout? How is the formula affected by Social Security benefits?

COVERED EARNINGS   Do bonuses count as earnings? IRS guidelines discourage the inclusion of the bonus as part of earnings for the purposes of a pension plan (as this would unfairly discriminate in favor of an executive), but some companies are able to argue the point effectively and include at least a portion of bonus payments as earnings.

CREDITED SERVICE   What periods of your employment are considered "credited" in terms of the pension? Your total years with the company, or only those years in which you actually participated in the company plan? What about leaves of absence? What if there is a company merger? Is there an upper limit on the number of years that can be counted as credited service?

---

WHO PAYS? Is the plan contributory or company paid? If you are required to contribute, how much will it cost you? If employee contributions are voluntary, how much can you contribute?

VESTING You are not automatically entitled to the monies in your pension fund. Depending on your years of credited service, you are entitled to none, a percentage, or all of your pension. In some circumstances, you can lose all or part of your right to the funds if you leave the company.

RETIREMENT AGE If you want to retire before 65, what provisions are there for an earlier retirement age?

PAYOUT Is it guaranteed for life, or at least for a minimum period? What if you become disabled before retirement? If you die before retirement or after retirement, are there special provisions governing the payment of your pension to beneficiaries?

# PROFIT SHARING PLANS

As the name implies, profit sharing plans relate employee compensation to company profitability. In most plans, the employee receives a share of profits determined by a certain percentage of his base salary. There are three common plans:

- *cash profit sharing plans*, commonly used in banking establishments, in which some annual payout is made to the employee
- *profit sharing retirement plans*, commonly used in younger corporations in place of a pension plan, in which payout is deferred to provide retirement income
- *thrift or savings plans*, commonly used as a supplemental pension plan, in which payout is deferred much the same as in a profit sharing retirement plan

### EVALUATING A PROFIT SHARING PLAN

To evaluate a particular plan, consider the following:

CONTRIBUTIONS TO THE PLAN Who makes them? When? What is the rate of contribution? Are contributions based on straight salary, or salary plus bonus? Are employee contributions voluntary or mandatory? Is there an earnings maximum? What is the choice of investment vehicles?

VESTING AND SETTLEMENT PROVISIONS When are you vested in the plan? Do you stand to lose the monies if you lose your job? How is payout made? What will be the tax consequences of payout timing?

VALUE OF THE PLAN   Depending upon the contribution rate, the profitability of the investment vehicle, the period of participation, and the rate of growth of the executive's compensation, a profit sharing plan can be an important factor in net worth growth. As McLaughlin puts it, "profit sharing is a big compounded earnings game. The trick is to get as much money as possible into the tax-sheltered trust in your early years."*

THE INVESTMENT VEHICLE   Should you keep your money in a fixed-income trust fund, a conservative mutual fund, a riskier stock fund, or some combination thereof? One common option is to invest in the corporate stock. The investment results will in large measure determine the real value of your settlement.

WITHDRAWAL PRIVILEGES   The advantage of profit sharing plans over any pension fund is that *some* profit sharing plans grant withdrawal privileges, usually under restricted conditions. Also, since most pension funds allow withdrawal only of contributions made by the corporation, any personal contributions to such a fund must be considered forced savings.

---

## DEFERRED COMPENSATION PLANS

---

### WHY?

Deferring payment of *currently* earned compensation is a means of timing income gains to minimize tax liability. According to the tax principle of "constructive receipt," you are not liable to the IRS until payment is actually made, even though the money was earned at some earlier date. In the typical plan, the payout, usually in cash, stocks, or a combination of both, is made at intervals over a period of years or deferred until retirement, when the executive anticipates a substantial reduction in income and, therefore, in taxes. The latter type of deferred compensation plan is a valuable alternative to the executive who has had to forfeit pension benefits when changing jobs.

### WHY NOT?

For obvious reasons, deferred compensation plans, particularly those that do not invest deferred earnings, have received some mixed reviews from financial advisors.

THE BUCK-IN-THE-HAND THEORY PREVAILS   Deferred compen-

---

*From David J. McLaughlin, *The Executive Money Map* (New York: McGraw-Hill, 1975), p. 11.

---

sation is *current* income intentionally held back for future payout. With double-digit inflation, postponement of payment cannot be justified *unless* the deferred income is invested wisely for the deferral period. If not, you lose not only a percentage of the current dollar value of that income due to inflation, but also potential interest or investment income.

THE TAX SITUATION IS UNRELIABLE   Even if the tax provisions that seem to favor the plan at its inception remain on record as is, deferred income is not taxed as "earned" income and is potentially liable to a 70 percent maximum tax rate. If you are not already in a 60 percent tax bracket, deferring compensation is probably not to your benefit.

YOU RISK PARTIAL OR TOTAL LOSS OF THE DEFERRED INCOME   Corporations are not obliged to put aside actual funds equal to your deferred earnings. Usually their commitment amounts to no more than an entry on a ledger sheet. If the company should go bankrupt, your monies are not guaranteed.

---

## FUTURE VALUE INCENTIVE
## PLANS: TAKING STOCK

---

Herein lie the executive's best opportunities for substantial capital accumulation and net worth growth. Most of these plans have two things in common:

- They give the executive a vested interest in the future prosperity of both the company and its stockholders by relating compensation to the value of company stock; i.e., they "stimulate."
- They tie the value of the compensation to future conditions, i.e., stock market appreciation, company performance, continued employment, or some combination thereof.

These plans are distinguished by whether or not participation requires a cash outlay by the executive.

What plan enjoys vogue at any given time is largely dictated by the current tax rulings. As rulings change, compensation planners invent new wrinkles.

The executive is given an option to purchase shares of company stock at a set price over a period of time, usually five to ten years.

**Qualified stock options.** Effectively killed by the Tax Reform Act of 1976, this plan once enjoyed great popularity. The option could be exercised over a five-year period, but once the shares were purchased, the executive was bound to a three-year holding requirement. The cost of the stock to the executive was set at the market price at date of grant. The "qualified" stock option was so named because it qualified for capital gains tax treatment. (Under a law effective May 21, 1981, any qualified option granted under an old plan converted to a nonqualified option.)

**Nonqualified stock option (a.k.a. unqualified stock option).** This plan follows the basic theme of the qualified option, except the terms are changed: The price is set at current market value *or* at a discount from market price, and the option can be exercised over a ten-year period. The longer life of the award, plus the fact that purchased stock can be turned over after only six months, gives the nonqualified option an attractive advantage over the old "qualified," particularly in a depressed market; however, the profits earned on the nonqualified option at the time it is exercised are taxed at the maximum 50 percent earned income rate. An added advantage of this newer version is that the executive can exercise a new option even if he holds a higher-priced option outstanding.

**Performance option.** Rights to purchase stock can be exercised only when the executive has met predetermined performance goals.

**Variable-priced options.** Depending on certain conditions, such as market appreciation or corporate performance, the option price may drop below the price set at date of grant.

**Tax-offset options.** When the executive exercises his option, the tax liability, incurred as a result of profits made on the appreciation in value of the option since date of grant, is offset by a cash payment made to the executive.

**Formula value option.** The award price is set not at market price, but according to some formula (for example, book value). The company has the right to repurchase shares at the same rates determined by the formula.

**Stock appreciation rights (SARs).** A modified version of the nonqualified stock option plan, SARs entitle the executive to choose to receive the appreciation in market value of the option in cash *or* in stock, or both, in lieu of exercising the option. There is no investment cost to the executive, and gains are charged to corporate earnings. Currently, SARs are in vogue.

**Phantom stock (a.k.a. fictional stock units).** This plan is commonly a simulated option. The executive is granted fictional stock units valued at the actual market price of a company share, and he receives the appreciation in market value over the term of the plan and, in some cases, also the accrued dividend equivalents. Profits can be received in cash, real stock, or both. The unit value is taxed to the executive upon payout.

**Book units (a.k.a. formula value grants).** This plan is like the phantom stock option, but the stock units are granted at book value, not market value, and appreciation is paid on book value as well. The advantage of this plan over phantom stock is that value of the units is independent of market fluctuations, yet the executive benefits from actual gains in profits.

**Stock purchases.** Stock purchase plans grant the executive the opportunity to purchase over a period of time actual shares of corporate stock, usually at a discount from market price and/or with a loan arranged by the corporation. A stock purchase plan differs from a stock option in that the latter plan extends over a longer term.

**Book purchases (a.k.a. formula value purchases).** The executive has the right to purchase stock at book value, not market value, and the stock is subject to repurchase by the corporation at the same formula value.

**Performance shares.** The executive receives a grant of stock units that convert to actual stock contingent upon the achievement of specific and predetermined performance goals to be accomplished over a set time period, typically three to six years. Performance is measured by appreciation in book value, earnings per share, or return on investments. The employee may elect to receive the award in actual stock, cash, or both. This is a popular version of combination-type incentive plans in which both the amount of the award and the value of the award are variable depending upon corporate performance and stock market appreciation. Such arrangements are popular with corporations, because if goals are met, the executive, the shareholders, and chief officers alike are apt to be pleased with results. The executive's profits are taxed at the 50 percent earned income rate, and any subsequent income earned from future sale of stock is taxed at the lower capital gains rate.

**Performance units.** Unlike performance shares, performance units are granted at an assigned dollar value not related to current market price, and if performance objectives are met, the executive earns the value of the award in cash or equivalent shares of stock.

412

**Restricted Stock Plans.** Popular in the sixties, this plan is enjoying a new vogue due to its currently attractive tax and accounting features. A restricted stock plan is an arrangement whereby the executive receives an outright grant of stock at no cost, but contingent upon his continued employment. The restriction: The stock is nontransferable and subject to forfeiture for a set period of time.

# PERKS: THE PRIVILEGES OF POWER

Perquisites are those little extras that can add up to a lot—or to nothing. In many instances, the true value of a particular perk is measurable in status rather than in dollars and cents, but in the hierarchical corporate world, power and prestige are both valuable tools and valued rewards that come with the upper territory.

## THE TAX ADVANTAGE

Beyond the appeal of prestige, the right perks can substantially increase the value of your compensation package without increasing your tax bill. In fact, the rationale for offering most perquisites is that they are legitimate corporate business expenses and, as such, are actually deductions on the company tax bill and virtually tax-free income to you. What constitutes a *legitimate* business expense, however, is open to interpretation by the IRS and these days the interpretations are inclined to be less flexible than formerly.

## THE PERQUISITE PREREQUISITE

To determine what a perk is really worth to you, consider whether it can be converted to a cash benefit and whether it provides you with something that you would purchase for yourself, at greater cost.

## TOP-OF-THE-LINE PERKS

Usually reserved for the top corporate ranks, these perks are particularly valuable in that they are designed to stimulate the growth of net worth.

COMPANY LOANS  A timely low-interest, or even no-interest, long-term loan can give the executive the leverage he needs to make an investment that can in turn yield substantial amounts of capital. The loan may be arranged by the company and financed through a third party, or may be funded directly by the corporation. In either case, be clear on the terms of the loan. It *does* have to be paid back *whether or not* your investment is lucrative.

PERSONAL ESTATE PLANNING AND FINANCIAL COUN-SELING  The personal financial concerns of a successful, busy executive can themselves be quite time-consuming. Recognizing that fact, corporations have begun to provide company-paid financial counseling to those executives whose already sizable incomes and net worth warrant such attention. Of course, the real value of such counseling depends to a large extent upon the quality of the advice—and much of it is less than "expert." Nevertheless, *good* advice can be invaluable, and this particular perk, which is low-cost to the company, is one whose popularity is growing. The tax picture: The cost of the service is considered taxable income to the executive, although about half can usually be legitimately deducted as fees for investment or tax counseling.

THE COMPANY CAR  The number-one transportation perk provides convenience and, if properly packaged—in the body of Cadillac, for instance—a symbol of status as well. Especially for the executive who might otherwise be unable to afford a second car, it can be an attractive part of a pay package. There is no cash outlay for the executive, and any later costs tend to be lower due to the quantity discount rates charged to a corporation on purchase and service. The true value to you of the company car is commonly calculated at 25 percent of what it would cost you to purchase and support a privately owned car.

THE EXECUTIVE DINING ROOM: ALL YOU CAN EAT—TAX FREE  The executive dining room, intended as a place to conduct business over lunch, is another low- or no-cost convenience perk. The company's cost, which can be rather high, is a deductible business expense, and the value of the perk is not imputed as income to the executive. The true value of such services will depend largely upon your personal eating habits. A fine company dining room whose basic fare is prime ribs and potatoes is not worth very much to a vegetarian executive. If you are not a fussy eater, but you do enjoy a good meal, you can probably save yourself as much as $10 a day, or about $2,000 a year by lunching in corporate facilities.

HOUSING  For the commuting executive who often works late into the evening, or for the executive who makes frequent business trips to a particular regional office, the executive apartment or hotel suite is a perk that makes sense. Otherwise, executive housing is not worth much, unless, of course, it can be utilized as a getaway or resort—in which case it is a high-status item.

CLUB MEMBERSHIPS  In suburban areas, the country club usually offers the best facilities for business entertaining, and corporations will pay membership fees for some top ranking officers. In urban environments, membership in the "luncheon" club—university clubs, athletic clubs, or exclusive social clubs—is a popular perk. The higher your status, of course, the more prestigious the club. Here again, the company will foot the bill for the initiation fee and monthly dues, although day-to-day expenses are usually limited. These clubs offer a variety of facilities—dining rooms, libraries, various athletic facilities, exercise rooms, and the like. While the value of the luncheon club membership is usually not taxable income to the executive, country-club memberships and company-refunded expenses are.

EXCESS MAJOR MEDICAL INSURANCE AND HEALTH CARE  With rising costs of medical care, this perk is increasingly popular. The company directly reimburses the executive for all medical (and often dental) expenses not already covered by his existing insurance policy—and there is nothing deductible. Coverage is typically $50,000 per illness or accident, although in some instances there is no dollar limit at all. Many corporations are also offering free medical checkups, vaccinations, and the like. Depending upon the executive's status, the checkups can be very thorough and elaborate, sometimes conducted by private physicians at posh health facilities.

## PRODUCT PERKS

Most companies offer all their employees some privileged access to the corporate product or service. Depending upon the nature of the business—be it discounts on company merchandise to employees of a major retailer, or special traveling privileges to employees of an airline—these perks can be of some genuine value even to the executive.

## MISCELLANEOUS PERKS

- company-paid donations to your personal charitable cause
- company-paid dues to professional and trade associations
- company health club, shoe shine, barber, etc.
- death benefits

Use your imagination: If you can prove its business relevance to the IRS, it's a potential perk.

---

# THE EXECUTIVE EXPENSE ACCOUNT

---

If your position requires a considerable amount of traveling or entertaining on behalf of the corporation, then an expense account is an item well worth negotiating apart from a simple increase in salary. An executive, given the choice between a $50,000 salary and a $45,000 salary plus a $5,000 expense account, is in most instances better off

---

415

going with the second package. Practical tax advantages are derived from this type of arrangement. First of all, reporting business expense deductions on an expense account is a much simpler matter than reporting and *proving* to the IRS those legitimate expenses out of your pocket. Additionally, there is no withholding tax incurred on the amount of the expense account. Needless to say, there are restrictions on what the IRS considers to be legitimate business entertainment and travel expenses, but the tax guidelines are actually quite liberal in this respect. The corporation must distinguish between payment of the executive's personal expenses and business expenses, the former being considered as taxable income to the executive, and the latter usually being tax exempt.

---

# VACATIONS

---

### THE VANISHING VACATION

In the life of a busy executive, the vacation seems to be a dying benefit: Fewer and fewer executives are exercising their option to take time off. A survey by Rene Plessner Associates of 210 executives earning between $50,000 and $75,000 per year revealed that almost 50 percent of them had not taken their allotted two- or three-week vacation time last year. Yet, judging by the high suicide rate among their peers, these middle managers, more than anyone else, probably need to take time off.

### NEW TRENDS

Without a doubt, many executives are suffering from a syndrome that impairs peak performance. Known to the medical community as dysponesis, it's known to most of the rest of us as being burned-out. The traditionally prescribed antidote to the strain of too much activity has been rest, usually taken in the form of a vacation. But in recent times the traditional work schedule—50 weeks on/2 weeks off—has come under scrutiny, and ideas for alternative schedules have emerged:

THE FOUR-DAY WEEK   A number of corporations, particularly in the publishing and advertising fields, have already instituted some form of a four-day work week, an alternative recommended by some experts as a way to provide relief from the increasing stress of daily corporate life. The four-day week generally does not reduce the number of working hours, but redistributes the same hours over a four- or four-and-a-half-day week, thus extending the weekend to two and a half or three full days. Some companies juggle the hours so schedules alternate: five days one week, four days the next. Such extended-weekend scheduling is particularly popular during the summer months, which tend in some businesses to be comparatively slow anyway.

LESS PAY, MORE LEISURE   In February, 1979, *Psychology Today* magazine reported a study in which workers were given the hypothetical choice of receiving a 2 percent pay hike or a reduction in work time (10 minutes less per day, 50 minutes less per week, 5 extra days off per year, *or* 1 week earlier retirement per each year worked). Eighty-five percent surveyed chose shorter work time over increased pay; more than half of those opted for the additional 5 days off per year. When the figures were raised from 2 percent to 10 percent more pay and to 10 percent more time, 41 percent still chose to have more time.*

SABBATICALS   An increasing number of executives are opting to take extended periods of time off (one month; six months; even a year or longer) from work for doing their own thing. In a provocative book by Bernard Lefkowitz, *Breaktime: Living without Work in a Nine to Five World* (New York: Hawthorn, 1979), the author looks into the lives of 100 people who have opted to stop working altogether. While these people do not represent a major shift in social trends, their increasing presence in our society is a further indication of the move toward a new work ethic. For the majority of executives, a permanent vacation is not a desirable option, but for a growing number, the mid-career sabbatical is an important time of rejuvenation and reevaluation.

## WHEN CAN A VACATION BE HARMFUL?

- When it is poorly organized and disappointing as a result
- When it generates a sense of idleness and concomitant feelings of guilt
- When it forces too much unwanted contact with friends and/or relatives
- When it eliminates much-yearned-for privacy

Some psychologists maintain that a vacation under such conditions can actually create, rather than eliminate, stress. A remedy, of course, is to plan a vacation carefully to suit your real needs for rest. At least one writer on the subject maintains that for the genuine workaholic, even a planned vacation is likely to generate dis-ease and discomfort.

---

*Fred Best, "Preferences on worklife scheduling and work leisure tradeoffs" (U.S. Department of Labor: *Monthly Labor Review,* June, 1978), pp. 31-37.

## YOU AND YOUR VACATION

If you happen to cherish your vacation time either as a period of rest and relaxation for yourself or as an important opportunity to be with your family, then be aware of what the corporate vacation policy is—not just on paper, but in actual practice. Find out how many executives are actually taking allotted vacation time off, and if they are not, whether they are at least receiving their vacation pay for their overtime, or whether unused time is accrued in following years.

# 30

## MAKING YOUR BEST DEAL: THE BARGAINING TABLE

Now that you have a taste for what's on the table, go after your desires with a robust appetite.

## WHEN?

Negotiate a new pay package when:

- you accept a new job
- you accept or decline a promotion
- you accept a division transfer
- you are called for a performance review

## YOUR BARGAINING POSITION

The strength or weakness of your position depends upon:

- the uniqueness of your skills and qualifications
- your past performance and visibility
- supply and demand—how much the company needs you
- who sought out whom
- your current employment status

## PREPARE BEFORE YOU BARGAIN

- Establish your income and net worth goals.
- Study company policy.

- Investigate the financial health of the company.
- Investigate existing compensation plans and policies of the corporation.
- Know the corporate operating style and philosophy.
- Investigate the going rate of executive pay for like positions.

---

## BARGAINING PROTOCOL

---

**Timing is important factor in successful bargaining.** Know *when* to bring up compensation issue.

- Establish parameters early, but don't make compensation the big issue. Or:
- Don't bring it up at all, and when the question arises, turn it around: "Now that you mention it, what *is* the salary range for this job?"

*Know when to drive a hard bargain.*

- When you are sure the company wants you, i.e., when the employer has made a commitment, *push.*
- Don't put off for tomorrow what you can negotiate today: Get 'em while they are still smiling.
- Don't accept an offer on the spot: Think it over and push some more tomorrow.

**Once bargaining begins, take an active role.**

**Be a glutton.** Have confidence and shoot for the most. If you doubt you deserve what you want, you won't get it.

**Never demand a plan that is not already part of the corporate compensation policy.** Unless the circumstances are quite unique or unusual.

**The higher the stakes, the more room to negotiate.**

**Compensation planners are, by training, sticklers for detail and tight-fisted.** If they appear stingy, don't mind. They are only doing their job.

**In compensation terms, an executive is defined not by title, but by his perceived value to the company.** What counts is his net effect on corporate success and prosperity.

---

# POINTS WORTH BARGAINING
## FOR IN A NEW JOB

**Salary.** If they recruited you, you are worth a 25-50 percent cash increase; if you approached them, you are worth 10-15 percent more; if you are unemployed, you are not worth much more than your last salary, if that.

**Long-term income plans.** The *key* bargaining issues are capital accumulation plans. Salary range of a position is often predetermined, and beyond a certain latitude salary alone is not a negotiable point.

**Pension and stock options.** If a prospective employer has sought you, and if by leaving your present job you would sacrifice stock option or pension benefits, negotiate to replace them with comparable plans.

**Severance.** Ask for a severance package (one year's salary) *just in case*, especially if the financial future of the company is shaky or if a merger is imminent.

**Company-paid relocation costs.** A must item when negotiating a transfer.

**Employment contract.** A rule of thumb: If you make $40,000 plus, negotiate for a contract. Many experts advise, however, that if you are still in the formative years of your career, you will not want to tie yourself down to any one corporation too long. A two- or three-year contract would be maximum in that case. If a merger is looming on the horizon, then bargain for some formal commitment if that is what you want.

**Company executive bonus plans.** Request *at least* minimum participation for first year of new employment. Review carefully the precise details of the bonus formula, noting how it is applied and how rewards are administered in practice as well as in principle.

**Promotions.** If you are on a fast track, agree now upon a time schedule for your next promotion as well as upon the terms of compensation increase.

**Perks.** Inquire about company policy on perquisites, but *do not push* on this point.

# MAXIMIZE YOUR TAX ADVANTAGE

Having a basic understanding of general tax principles (such as deductions and tax treatment of income types) helps to provide some framework within which to evaluate various compensation plans. Considering the complex tax consequences of the interaction among various classifications of income, you will want to plan your pay package to maximize your tax advantage. McLaughlin suggests you can do this in three ways:

**Combine plans for maximum profit and minimum tax.** Certain fringe benefits are virtually tax free or taxed at lower rates. For example, capital gains income from stock options may be taxed at substantially lower rates than ordinary income.

**Time payout.** Deferred compensation and stock option plans are two available modes that allow you to time receipt of gains to minimize tax liability on large sums of income. Income averaging is another means of minimizing liability on windfall income that has substantially increased your earnings in one year over the previous years.

**Maximize allowable deductions.** You are allowed deductions for charitable donations and medical expenses and the like, but you can also "shelter" additional income through investments designed for that purpose. There may be high risks involved, so get sound professional advice before investing in a tax shelter.

# EYE ON THE BOTTOM LINE

To a great extent, taxes determine the true value to you of a compensation package. Yet taxes are only one part of the picture. Equally important considerations are:

**The true value of the award.** What is the size of the award? What does it cost you in direct contributions, cash outlay, or financing?

**The potential risks.** Does payout depend upon company performance? Are earnings tied to the fluctuations of the stock market? What are the terms of the plan? When are you vested? Do you lose the right to any benefits if you lose or leave your job?

While you may not yet recognize the fine distinctions between two given plans—which investment vehicle best brings out the sweet advantage of capital gains tax treatment, for instance—you should know enough at least to ask the important questions once you sit down at the bargaining table.

## FOR MORE ON COMPENSATION

For a comprehensive, comprehensible tour of executive compensation-land, read David J. McLaughlin's *The Executive Money Map* (New York: McGraw-Hill, 1975). Due to recent tax reforms, a few facts are dated, but, overall, McLaughlin provides valuable information and perspective on executive compensation as an aspect of both personal financial and career planning. I hope that Mr. McLaughlin will revise his book to reflect the tax revisions.

**Form 1**

**TOTAL COMPENSATION SUMMARY FORM**

FOR _____

CURRENT INCOME _____

HISTORY

| Year | Salary | Bonus Award Dollars | Percentage of Salary | Cash Profit Sharing Dollars | Percentage of Salary | Total Cash Compensation | Percentage Change | Comment |
|------|--------|---------|---------|---------|---------|---------|---------|---------|
| ____ | $____ | $____ | ____% | $____ | ____% | $____ | ____% | _____ |
| ____ | ____ | ____ | ____ | ____ | ____ | ____ | ____ | _____ |
| ____ | ____ | ____ | ____ | ____ | ____ | ____ | ____ | _____ |
| ____ | ____ | ____ | ____ | ____ | ____ | ____ | ____ | _____ |
| ____ | ____ | ____ | ____ | ____ | ____ | ____ | ____ | _____ |

PROJECTIONS

| | | | | | | | | |
|------|--------|---------|---------|---------|---------|---------|---------|---------|
| ____ | $____ | $____ | ____% | $____ | ____% | $____ | ____% | _____ |
| ____ | ____ | ____ | ____ | ____ | ____ | ____ | ____ | _____ |
| ____ | ____ | ____ | ____ | ____ | ____ | ____ | ____ | _____ |

SALARY RANGE     Minimum $_____     Midpoint $_____     Maximum $_____

Fig. 53. Compensation planning form
*(above and next page)*
From *The Executive Money Map* by David J. McLaughlin.
Copyright © 1975 by McGraw-Hill. Used with the permission of
McGraw-Hill Book Company.

**SALARY INCREASE POLICIES**

    Merit increases        Size range_____% to____%    Time guidelines_____

    Promotion increases    Size range_____% to____%    _____

**BONUS AWARDS**

    Payout options      ☐ Current    ☐ Over_____ years    ☐ Deferred_____

    Comments:_____

_____

| Projected Bonus | Dollars | Size<br>Percentage of<br>Salary | Assumptions/Requirements |
|---|---|---|---|
| Minimum | $_____ | _____% | _____ |
| Most likely | _____ | _____ | _____ |
| High | _____ | _____ | _____ |

**PERQUISITES/INCOME EQUIVALENTS** _____

| Type | Estimated<br>Value | Imputed<br>Income | Comment |
|---|---|---|---|
| Company car | $_____ | $_____ | _____ |
| Parking | _____ | _____ | _____ |
| Personal financial counseling | _____ | _____ | _____ |
| Tax preparation assistance | _____ | _____ | _____ |
| Excess medical | _____ | _____ | _____ |
| Luncheon club | _____ | _____ | _____ |
| ----------------------------- | _____ | _____ | _____ |
| Country club | _____ | _____ | _____ |
| ----------------------------- | _____ | _____ | _____ |
| Executive physical | _____ | _____ | _____ |
| Company dining facilities | _____ | _____ | _____ |
| Housing benefit | _____ | _____ | _____ |
| Spouse travel | _____ | _____ | _____ |
| Tuition reimbursement | _____ | _____ | _____ |

**PROTECTION** _____

| Type | Coverage | Personal<br>Contribution<br>Required | Imputed<br>Income |
|---|---|---|---|
| Basic group life | _____ | $_____ | $_____ |
| Supplemental life | _____ | _____ | _____ |
| Accidental death and dismemberment | _____ | _____ | _____ |
| All-risk accident | _____ | _____ | _____ |
| Travel accident | _____ | _____ | _____ |
| Comprehensive personal liability | _____ | _____ | _____ |
| Long-term disability | _____ | _____ | _____ |
| Hospital/surgical | _____ | _____ | _____ |
| Major medical | _____ | _____ | _____ |
| Dental | _____ | _____ | _____ |

# PART VII

# THE OFFICE ARSENAL

"Civilization advances by
extending the number of important
operations which we can perform
without thinking about them."
 Alfred North Whitehead

# 31
# THE OFFICE OF THE FUTURE

One of the hottest buzz words in managerial circles these days is "the office of the future." Trouble is, the office in question is here—if not in your work space, perhaps in that of your competitor. Office automation has fallen prey to a paradox that is common in our technological society: The technology is often available before there is sufficient market for it—before people are ready to accept it, or are even aware of it.

Almost every office function can be improved through the use of some form of machine or computer. And almost every one of these machines involves microprocessors, microcircuitry, or some other form of electronic wizardry such as "ink jet nonimpact printing" and fiber optics. In the last decade, industrial productivity was up 90 percent, while office productivity rose only 4 percent. The office remains a holdout to space age technology.

## WHAT IT IS

An office is essentially a work site where people go to interact with each other and with the information network. Productivity involves the use of analytic, creative, intellectual, and communication skills.

The office of the future is a *concept* that involves the introduction of sophisticated new technologies to improve office communications, increase productivity, and motivate workers by increasing job satisfaction.

The office of the future is also a *tactic*. Used properly, it can provide a means for a company to get the jump on its competition.

Unfortunately, your first contact with "the office of the future" is not likely to include the above considerations. The term is most commonly used to describe a confusing and ill-defined collection of high-tech office machines currently being hyped by their vendors as every office worker's dream come true. In other words, "the office of the future" lives, in our minds and in the brochures, primarily as a *sales pitch*.

# CAN YOU AFFORD TO IGNORE IT?

No way. All the hype aside, the introduction of automation in the office environment is an extremely significant development that will affect your job in several different ways, ranging from your specific responsibilities to methods and procedures—and, ultimately, to your overall performance and its relationship to the company's profits.

For those who can see through the fog generated by the hardware/software hard sell, the office of the future is a concept of major importance in modern management techniques. It doesn't take much technical training or vision to see the potential value of the new technologies, especially since we have been using them already in our homes, at the bank, etc. The question is when and how to implement these advances.

You'd better get with it. Sooner or later, everybody else will. There is no doubt that a well-planned and well-implemented move to office automation can give a firm a clear competitive edge over the nonautomated firms. And *the manager that spearheads such a move will probably score a few extra points when the office begins to hum with the sound of automatic printers and glow in the pale green light of video display terminals.* If the thought of that ambiance doesn't turn you on, then visions of reduced paperwork, fewer errors, lower costs, and swifter communications certainly should.

# WHAT'S BEHIND THE RAPID GROWTH OF OFFICE AUTOMATION?

**The lag in office productivity.**

**Technological innovation.** We are used to seeing microprocessors and microcircuitry in consumer products and scientific equipment. But recently, competition for a share of the booming office equipment market has led to an astounding level of sophistication in design of such products.

**Mounting economic and competitive pressures.** Rising costs of goods, services, and labor have forced managers to look to previously unexplored regions for ways of cutting costs and staying competitive. The office, with its poor productivity, is prime territory for reducing costs.

**The American love affair with gadgetry.** If it beeps, buzzes, talks back, or makes pictures on the TV screen, it's simply irresistible. For many of us, price and cost-effectiveness just don't matter when we are faced with the chance to make our desks look like the flight deck of *Starship Enterprise*.

---

# WHY IT'S NEEDED

---

Although the office of the future will initially cost companies a lot of money, it makes good sense, for several reasons.

**The bulk of a manager's time is spent communicating.** Phone calls, conferences, and originating and receiving correspondence eat up over 70 percent of the typical manager's day. Many of the executive time-wasters are related in some way to the communication function. For example, the majority of phone calls are essentially one-way conversations made to convey information, requiring no immediate interaction with the person on the other end; still, many executives engage in chitchat. And about 70 percent of all business calls are not completed on the first try. Then there is the time it takes to travel to and from a meeting. The rapid, efficient management of information and communication strikes at the heart of what the office of the future is really about.

**Offices are not very productive.** The office is the last holdout to automation. Automated machinery is common in manufacturing plants. And kitchens across the nation are equipped with microprocessor-controlled microwave ovens. So how come you are still using that old adding machine and that awful file cabinet?

The office productivity situation has become very serious as a result of rising costs. An average business letter costs over five dollars to dictate, transcribe, and send. Reaching a business executive by phone during business hours will set your company back between $3.50 and $6.00. Filing (including misfiling) is a multimillion-dollar business. The average misfile costs $75. The misfile rate? One estimate is 3 percent and some experts put the rate as high as 20 percent. American business and governmental organizations are currently being drained by a "productivity leak" that is estimated to cost hundreds of millions of dollars each year.

Office equipment salespeople love to fire these numbers at you, then whip out their pocket calculators and show you how their gizmos will save you money by increasing productivity. In most cases they are on solid ground. Automated equipment can contribute significantly toward an improvement in office productivity.

---

**Many white-collar workers don't like their jobs.** Can you blame them? So much of the work is tedious. Repetitive. Routine. Dull. Rather than stimulating the workers, it creates sluggishness. And little time is left for the challenging and idea-oriented tasks that provide success and satisfaction.

With computers to take over a good deal of the tedium, much of the white-collar legion will be able to play it a bit more fast and loose. And to show more initiative.

This will work out fine, provided upper management cooperates and workers don't feel threatened by computers that do what *they* once did. The jury is still out on this one.

**Office automation can be used as a tactical weapon.** With gloves-off competition in the marketplace coming not only from other domestic firms, but from Asia and Europe as well, it's kill or be killed. And the battles are being fought in the fields of marketing, price cutting, and distribution. Managers are scrambling to force even a slight advantage. One way we can do that is to exploit the slight lead in computer technology enjoyed by American business. Here are a few strategies:

*Accelerate new-product development.* Automation allows such projects to be tightly coordinated between engineers, factory personnel, marketing and sales; everyone has instantaneous access to pertinent information.

*Increase the return.* An automated office can more accurately and rapidly monitor the marketplace and better estimate demand, competition, and the economic and regulatory environment.

*Use heavy equipment more efficiently.* "Smart" information systems can monitor and control machinery 24 hours a day so that they run more efficiently.

*Improve inventory controls and investment.* With computer monitored inventory, you always know what you've got, what you need, what you will need, and where to find it.

*Improve control of sales and service costs.* For example, the sales force can use the information system to zero in on the most profitable customers and be prepared to discuss the most appropriate product. Order entry and paperwork, as well as service histories, can be handled more efficiently.

*Market for less.* If your office is automated, you stand on the threshold of the next revolution in sales and marketing: The customer will be able to view, order, and pay for products and services—all electronically, by conversing through his own terminal with the vendor's computer. In some areas, it's already possible. Customers of New York's Chase

Manhattan Bank can request that the bank's computer pay bills direct.

*Distribute faster, more accurately, and less expensively.* You do it with computer-assisted dispatching, delivery mode selection, cost computation, etc.

*Control cash better.* Institute computerized cash flows, forecasts, and linkups with banks and customers.

*Improve compliance with rules and regulations.* Getting through the maze of government rules and regulations is a colossal task. And if you are challenged by a government agency, you had better be ready with records, test results, quality control data, and other documentation. Automation is a godsend in this area: you can order up this data faster than you can get a BLT from the corner deli.

---

# WHAT YOU NEED TO KNOW ABOUT OFFICE AUTOMATION

---

Dealing with the changes brought on by the office of the future will soon be a critical part of your job. *If you get involved in the design and implementation of an automated system,* it could be a major career coup—or a nightmare. The office revolves around people, and *concern for the staff's feelings and needs is vital.* Equipment should fill needs, and one must be on guard against pushing solutions that don't have problems—office equipment overkill.

The flip side—learning to adjust to a job redefined by automation—is an even greater challenge. Managers and executives are especially threatened, since they regard computers and the like as tools used by clerks, secretaries, and the data processing people—not by the "decision makers," or "strategists," or managers. *However, if you know your way around, you can learn to exploit the equipment that's been laid before you* in order to free your mind to do the kinds of things that will place you on the cutting edge—to think, create, plan, and innovate.

That's why you must learn the basics regarding the *structure, function,* and *hardware* of the office of the future.

### OFFICE AUTOMATION EQUIPMENT MAKES USE OF FIVE BASIC CAPABILITIES:

PROGRAMMABILITY  The set of instructions that tell the machines what to do and how to do it. Programs or sets of programs are usually referred to as software, i.e., a computer product other than hardware.

---

PROCESSING   Manipulation of the information the machine receives. Examples: mathematical computations, sorting, alphabetizing.

STORAGE   The capability of a computer to retain information in its memory, or to read information stored outside the machine (usually on tape or magnetic disc).

INPUT/OUTPUT   The capability of the machine to receive and send instructions and information. This is the phase that involves converting human logic and language into instructions understood by a computer, and vice versa.

ELECTRONIC TRANSPORT   The transmission of data by electronic methods. The form of the data may be impulses understood only by computers; or it may be the human voice, still images, or video. Means of transport include cable, telephone lines, microwaves, fiber optics; even satellite hookups may be involved.

## HOW AUTOMATED OFFICE EQUIPMENT
## USES THESE CAPABILITIES
## TO SOLVE BUSINESS PROBLEMS

ELECTRONIC CONFERENCING   There are already several viable electronic alternatives to the face-to-face meeting. In addition to the telephone conference call, which is already commonplace, *closed circuit video conferences* are within reach. The simple telephone call can be electronically enhanced through the *simultaneous transmission of documents, graphics, photos, and other data.* Microwave and satellite transmission makes it possible to conduct such conferences involving a large number of people in many different locations worldwide.

DATA TRANSMISSION   We've come a long way from the pony express. In the 1980s virtually all information will be transferred at the speed of light. But speed is only one aspect of effective information transfer. Computers have made the process more reliable than ever before. Miniaturization has brought input/output capabilities to the desk top. And since the entire transmission process saves labor through reduced time and errors, it can actually cut costs.

INFORMATION RETRIEVAL   Retrieval of important documents and data relating directly to productivity is now potentially a push-button affair. Managers need not spend hours tracking down problems and tracing errors, clarifying policies and regulations. Computerized external data bases make it possible for executives to access a wide range of specialized and general information from journals, news services, and statistical publications.

TRANSACTIONS   You are part of this process every time you use a charge card. The purchase or sale of goods and services is processed

432

electronically and recorded in the appropriate place, with the appropriate parties receiving notification. This marshaling of automation is rapidly becoming the modus operandi for virtually all types of consumer-related business transactions. It has resulted in a reduction in the paper flow that clerical workers are required to handle, and thus has increased their potential and their accuracy. It's no secret that because a credit card can input to a computer, plastic money is rapidly replacing paper.

PERSONAL COMPUTING   The manager's work is not primarily of a procedural or transactional nature. But the manager can use the automation at his disposal to aid in analysis, problem solving, research, and even decision making, planning, and implementation. With the advent of portable terminals, salespersons, too, have been able to utilize the electronic resources of the home office by simple access over the phone. Even such routine managerial functions as dictation and editing of correspondence have benefited from automation through the introduction of advanced dictation equipment.

WORK AND ACTIVITY MANAGEMENT   One of the most difficult managerial functions involves monitoring the progress of employees and projects. Office automation expands this capability in several ways:

*Time management.* Access to each other's calendars (stored in the computer) allows for more efficient scheduling of meetings and avoids conflicts.

*Monitoring of projects.* The manager can assess the relevant data to see how the project is proceeding on a step-by-step, or even a daily, basis. The manager can then help solve problems and even input pertinent comments, information, and reminders.

*Monitoring of facilities.* Energy. Security. Machinery. And more.

---

## WHAT WILL YOUR OFFICE NEED?

---

Unfortunately, most executives have little or no say as to how their offices will be equipped. Large corporations utilize purchasing agents and productivity experts to determine what kind of equipment to acquire. In smaller firms the situation is often worse, because this area is easily neglected. Often, the boss will buy a computer because the competition has a computer. Or because his buddies at the country club have computers for their businesses.

Then there are the old-timers, who believe that modern office technology is an elaborate hoax, designed primarily to separate the

---

hard-working entrepreneur from his money. After listening to some of the salespeople in this business, I've come to believe that the old-timers are not totally wrong.

The key to intelligent purchasing is to determine just how much technology you really need, and how much is cost justified. Using seven low-paid file clerks and an adding machine, instead of a computer, could be costing you dearly. But so will an office full of gadgets that are rarely, if ever, used. There are many firms out there eager to sell you everything but the electronic kitchen sink.

What follows is a very basic guide to the state of the art in office equipment and gizmos. We have reached the point in our civilization where it often takes longer for words to go from the writer's hand to the bookstore shelf than it does for a new product to go from designer to retail store. This means that practically all of the information regarding prices and models that I have before me will be severely out of date by the time you read this. For this reason I have decided not to review the specific makes and models. Instead, I have listed and described the major categories, all the while keeping an eye toward the future so you will know what to expect in the way of innovation.

# 32

# THE COMPUTER

"By 1990, as much as 90 percent of all managers as well as clerical/administrative personnel in large organizations will be using computers and/or computerized devices." Or so predicts The Diebold Group, Inc.

The computer is the foundation of the office of the future. Saying that a piece of office equipment has been automated is almost always just another way of saying that it has been computerized. Computers, besides being able to accept, store, manipulate, and output information that you provide, can control other devices.

In many cases, the computer circuitry is built into the machine. For example, several new copiers have their own microcomputers to tell them when to stop or start, and whether to lighten or darken the copies. In other cases, computers control from the outside, as with heat and lighting systems that are kept at certain levels by a central computer. Virtually every modern office will have a computer lurking somewhere.

With the possible exception of several specialized executive positions in a small number of industries, it is not necessary for the average manager to become so intimate with a computer that he can pull it apart and put it back together. In most cases it is not even necessary to learn how to program one. But since most of us will be using computers (if we aren't already), there are a few things about them that it wouldn't hurt to know.

## THE COMPONENTS

Virtually any computer can be divided into five basic sections, which are described in terms of the functions they perform.

**Input.** Information from a variety of sources—such as letters, numbers, voice, magnetized ink, and sounds—is "translated" into patterns of electronic pulses that the computer is capable of understanding and utilizing.

**Memory.** This is the section that stores the information until needed. There are two basic types of memory facilities: *Primary storage* is an essential section of the computer that uses ferrite metal cores or semiconductor devices to hold programmed instructions, data to be processed, the results of intermediate calculations, and data to be "output." *Secondary storage* is located outside the basic computer. Information is often stored on magnetic disks, magnetic tapes, or paper tapes. Secondary storage media hold data not immediately needed by the computer. When it is needed, the data from secondary storage is inserted into the primary storage for use.

**Arithmetic and logic.** This is where the actual electronic manipulations, which allow the computer to add two numbers or compare several quantities, takes place. This activity is often referred to as "number crunching" and data manipulation.

**Control.** The control unit regulates the activities of the system. It regulates the flow of information to and from the memory and arithmetic/logic sections, interprets and executes each step of the programmed instruction, and keeps track of the current status of the system and its components.

Taken together, the *primary storage, arithmetic/logic,* and *control* sections comprise the central processing unit, or CPU, of the computer.

**Output.** Here the processed data is converted to electrical impulses capable of controlling many different devices. Thus the output can be used to operate other machinery, or even to feed information to another computer. Most commonly, output refers to the process of converting those impulses into information understood by humans: words and numbers on a video screen, printed out on paper by a printer, or "spoken" by an artificial voice.

---

# THE PROGRAM

---

The program is simply a series of instructions that the computer stores for future use. Programs are designed to solve problems and control procedures and processes, and fall under the heading "software." Software comes in two basic types:

**Applications programs** are those written to solve specific problems or perform specialized tasks for the user. Common examples include calculation of payrolls, loan interest, sales commissions, etc.

---

**Systems programs** allow the user to give some additional instructions on the basic operating procedure of the computer system. Systems programs include troubleshooting, text editing, procedures for loading, writing, and executing an applications program, and many more.

Here is where software begins to get hairy for the layperson. You should know that special programs exist, called *assemblers*, *compilers*, and *interpreters*, which employ a variety of methods to convert the source language (the language the user employs to input data) to machine language (the language the computer understands). This allows the user to operate the computer with a simple language that resembles English.

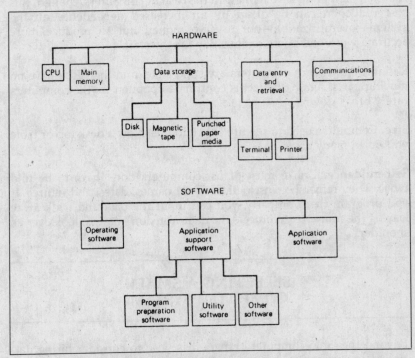

Fig. 54. Basic elements of computer hardware and software.
A simplified schematic representation.

From Robert Allen Bonelli, *The Executive's Handbook to Minicomputers* (New York: Petrocelli Books, 1978), p. 14.
Reprinted by permission of Petrocelli Books.

# THE BASIC ADVANTAGES
# OF A COMPUTER

**More speed.** Computers can calculate, sort, search, compile, and print out at blinding speeds.

**Accuracy.** All the jokes aside, computers rarely make errors. In many systems, millions of calculations are executed without a single mistake.

**Reduced costs.** Any device that can reduce labor costs and save time has the potential to save money. In the case of computers, though, this cost reduction can be offset by an increased dependence on the system—overutilization—not to save money, but to produce more accurate work and a less tedious day for the staff.

**Reliability.** Modern computers are solid state, and the CPUs have no moving parts. Again, the fact is contrary to popular myth: Computers rarely break down.

**Size.** Computers used to require entire rooms. Now a desk top or table will do in many cases.

**Self-guidance.** Unlike most of us, computers don't have to be told twice. They remember instructions. And names, dates, and figures. If you program them properly, you can input the data and walk away leaving the computer to process the data. You don't have to look over its shoulder.

# SELECTING A SMALL
# COMPUTER SYSTEM

Beyond the "minicomputer" range, it is wise to consider hiring data processing professionals or using outside consultants. But if your needs are modest, you may find that much of the responsibility is on your shoulders, or those of colleagues with limited experience.

**Determine what your needs are.** Don't depend on the salespeople. Begin by isolating the critical parts of your business. One way of arriving at this is to ask, What sets us apart from the competition?

Once you determine these critical areas, outline what procedures are necessary to make these areas more effective and efficient.

**Gather the numbers.** Compile statistics on all aspects of your business that might have some bearing on computer selection.

**Get everyone involved.** Their feedback will prove surprisingly helpful. It will also help to alleviate any xenophobia that might result from computer installation.

**Keep it simple.** Now that you know what you want the computer to do for you, make sure that the procedures involved are in their simplest form. This is very important, because the simpler the computer's operation, the fewer the hassles and the lower the costs.

**Write it up.** The best way to deal with computer vendors is to be perfectly clear. It helps to put it in writing. This insures that all the vendors have the same specs to work from—and that makes for more nearly accurate bids. Written specifications also serve to crystallize things in your mind.

A suggested format would include:

- a short introduction to your business—what it does, how it operates; a bit about your industry, and your thoughts about the future of the industry as it may affect your business
- a clear and logical description, in some detail, of the procedures you would like the computer system to perform
- a list of what the bid should include. Request that the vendor state how the system will meet your requirements, the kind of software to be used and whether it is to be packaged or custom, and of course, the itemized costs of each item, including service.

**When evaluating bids, avoid putting too much emphasis on price.** Any vendor can lowball if he knows that's what it'll take to get the job. You want the vendors to believe that getting the job means delivering far more than the lowest price. Don't let them convince you that you don't need a certain feature if you feel you do need it. Cutting corners to bring the price down is a common vendor strategy. And remember that programming is critical. Programs vary greatly. This can affect price significantly, but, if you choose wrong, could cost a great deal more in the long run.

Note that we are talking in terms of bids, and bids are, at best, only promises. They are often overstated, overoptimistic, and just plain too low.

**Don't accept the system until you are satisfied.** Make sure that the system is expandable, so it can grow with your needs. Are the hardware manufacturers financially sound, with good warranties and service records? You don't want a manufacturer who is here today and

439

gone tomorrow. Avoid the gizmo trap. Don't buy appearances, or more than you need.

When the system is installed, pay less attention to how the computer does all the wonderful things that vendors like to demonstrate, and more attention to what you want it to do for you. One way of doing this is to make sure that the program is not written until you have approved a written, detailed description of the program's specs. Make certain that the system will be easy to operate and control for all the users, and that data can be entered easily and will be spit out in a desirable format.

Finally, ask yourself these questions: Now that the system is installed, am I beginning to see an increase in productivity? Can I forecast more accurately? Have clerical errors gone down? Is there a general improvement in efficiency? These questions represent common benefits resulting from the installation of a computer system; you should be able to answer yes to all or most of them.

## CHOOSING A VENDOR

It is a waste of time for all concerned to ask for bids from more than three to five vendors. Before even considering a vendor, consider these points:

**What's the reputation?** Make a few phone calls to friends and associates. Ask for references from the vendor himself. And check them out.

**How many systems has the vendor installed in your field?** Are you the guinea pig? If the vendor says he has sold many units to your industry, find out if that included the software.

**Make sure that the vendor is willing to agree to the most important points in the contract.** Such requirements might include a specific time frame for installation, the system's specs, a trial or test period, etc. Sure, everything's negotiable, but you will certainly want to be unyielding on certain matters. If you can't agree on the basics right at the start of the project, forget the vendor and try another.

## TURNKEY OUTFITS

Turnkeys are firms that perform a valuable service: They connect manufacturers with users by putting packages together and developing software for specific needs. Ideally, turnkeys develop packages and software tailored to a specific market segment and then turn large profits by selling the package many times.

This approach can be of great value to the user who can't afford the time, labor, or money for custom designing, but would like some of the benefits of a system that meets the special needs of his field. An added advantage is the ease of working entirely through one source.

Before giving a turnkey firm the go-ahead, make certain that the package it offers is right for you. Will you have to adapt some of your own procedures in order to get the most out of the package? If, on the other hand, the package offered must be modified to meet your needs, with substitutions in hardware or changes in software, the additional costs could eliminate the benefits of going turnkey in the first place.

# SUGGESTED READING

*Small Computer Systems for Business,* by Gerald A. Silver (New York: McGraw-Hill, 1978)

An excellent, well-balanced introduction. Silver skillfully explains the basics of small computer systems and their applications in business, while avoiding the pitfalls of both the oversimplistic explanations and the technically obscure. The book is profusely illustrated with clear and pertinent diagrams and photographs.

*A Manager's Guide to Profitable Computers,* by Norman Sanders (New York: AMACOM, 1979)

This book is particularly notable because it is well written. In clear, down-to-earth language, Sanders explains why we should bother with computers in the first place, and goes on to provide valuable insights into the process of installing your system. Sanders covers costs, selection, and the legal aspects of the computer system.The book is illustrated with cheerful cartoons and a few charts. Chapter 5, "Almost All You Need to Know about the Computer Itself," is a mere eight pages long, but is one of the best general introductions to computers that I've seen.

*The Executive's Handbook to Minicomputers,* by Robert Allen Bonelli (Princeton: PBI-Petrocelli Books, 1979)

Intended for the executive who may be faced with the task of selecting a minicomputer and supervising its installation and use within the company. It is an excellent book, written in a question-and-answer format. Bonelli provides the reader with an in-depth description of the minicomputer components and how they work, as well as a good background in software and peripherals. A "Selection Criteria" section at the end of each chapter discusses the guidelines and makes recommendations for choosing equipment.

*What Is a Computer?* by Marion J. Ball (Boston: Houghton Mifflin, 1972)

This short, colorful picture book is obviously intended for young adults. However, it does offer a clear, if very basic, introduction to the computer. If you are totally ignorant about computers, give this book a quick read. It won't take long, and it'll put things in perspective, because you'll see that the basic idea behind computers is really quite simple. This book is also excellent for those clericals in the office who may feel intimidated by the computer, but who are unable or unwilling to read anything very complicated.

# 33

## WORD PROCESSORS AND SMART TYPEWRITERS

Among the most significant advances in office technology is the automation of business communication. Communication begins with words, and words can now be recorded, manipulated, stored, and transmitted in ways that were inconceivable to most executives just ten years ago. Spearheading this business communications revolution are the electronic typewriter and the word processor, which are already the workhorses of the modern office.

---

## THE SMART TYPEWRITER

---

This is a good place to start, because you are talking relatively cheaply when you talk electronic typewriters. Chances are your firm will have a few soon; perhaps you have one already. They are also relatively easy to fathom, since they are, in the final analysis, souped-up electric typewriters. They are given some intelligence by silicon chips, microprocessors, etc.

Like a standard office electric, they are self-contained units (not hooked up by cable to some electronic brain somewhere in Colorado, or to your firm's "data processing section"), and they are designed for the secretary's desk. They also look and feel like ordinary electrics (which, in turn, have all mimicked the "feel" of the keyboard, of the ubiquitous IBM Selectric. Best of all, these babies require no special training—there are just a few extra controls and procedures, and they can be learned in a few hours.

There's your basic *electronic typewriter*, and then there's the smarter and more costly *"memory typewriter."*

# THE ELECTRONIC TYPEWRITER

This is, in its most basic form, an upgraded office electric, intended to do what any ordinary electric can do, only faster, easier, and with fewer errors. Functions that are manual on the electric are automated on the electronic. Here's a list of features found on most of them:

ONE-LINE MEMORY   The built-in electronic memory retains all the material on the line as you type it. This function aids in correcting errors and formatting the typing on the page.

AUTOMATIC ERROR CORRECTION   Since the machine can remember what you typed, a single keystroke will send it back over the material on that line, the memory guiding the typing element so that you can erase anything up to one line.

FORMAT STORAGE   Frequently used formats can be stored and accessed so that there is less fiddling and lining things up.

AUTOMATIC CENTERING   The intelligence is smart enough to calculate the center and send the typing element to that point.

ELECTRONIC MARGINS AND TAB STORAGE   Margins for business letters, columns for financial work, special settings for scripts can be stored so that the operator can get the right settings for the job in seconds.

NUMBER ALIGNMENT   This feature is a great help when you've got rows of figures, because the machine will automatically align on the decimal point.

AUTOMATIC INDENTING   This could increase typing speed a bit by eliminating the need to count out spaces for indenting. But so can a conventional tab setting.

PHRASE STORAGE   Conjure up your favorite greetings and/or salutations, closings, and routine wordings in seconds. Hit the code for "As per our conversation" and the machine spits it out.

AUTOMATIC CARRIER RETURN   This is one of my favorite features. When the carrier enters a "hot zone" (usually 5-7 characters before the right margin), it automatically hyphenates the word and heads for the next line.

CHARACTER PITCH/TYPE STYLE   You don't need to go electronic to have the advantage of the changeable pitch and type styles. Nevertheless, all the electronics have this feature. The most common typing elements are the "golf ball," pioneered by IBM, and the "daisy wheel," which is used by Olivetti and several other vendors.

AUTOMATIC UNDERLINING

A few of the units have:

PROPORTIONAL SPACING   Will adjust the pitch to fill the page.

RELOCATE   The carrier returns to where the typist left off before he stopped to correct something.

## THE MEMORY TYPEWRITER

What basic electronic typewriters don't have is text editing capability. They cannot insert, delete, or rearrange blocks of type.

As you may have guessed, "memory" typewriters do possess some text editing function. But the most basic distinction between the simple "electronic" and the "memory" is that the "memory" has *more* memory. Much more. Some units have internal "sealed memories"; others have unlimited storage capacity through the use of separate storage media such as cassettes or minidiskettes, which can be removed and filed away. These units are at the high end of the category, and some are equal in price to many word processors. Some units have memories that can be boosted by adding additional accessories. As far as features are concerned, memory typewriters have everything that the electronics have, *plus:*

MORE MEMORY   They can store from four pages to one hundred pages, depending on the unit.

AMOUNT CONTROL   This is a text editing function. One can move type in memory, by word, sentence, paragraph, line, or character. So you can add something new (a word, a sentence, a paragraph, etc.); or you can delete.

SAVE/RECALL   Save a segment of type, and recall it at will without retyping it manually.

CHARACTER STRING SEARCH   What's a character string? A sequence of characters—high-tech lingo for a word or part of a word. If you're looking for a word or series of characters (abbreviations, numbers, initials) and it's in the machine's memory, it will be found.

FILE   These machines have two kinds of memory: storage memory, which holds information for future use; and working memory, which is the memory that can be manipulated—what you're working with. When you've finished with a document, you can "file" it, i.e., transfer it from the working memory to storage. Automatically, the machine will assign it a file number, making the document easy to call forth again when needed.

RIGHT-HAND MARGIN JUSTIFICATION   This feature really makes a difference. The visual impact is very professional, especially if you type newsletters and material that will ultimately be printed.

GLOBAL SEARCH AND REPLACE   Global search is just like character string search, except that after it finds the string in its memory, it continues searching the whole document automatically for that string. Suppose you typed a report on Ronald Reagen and, later on, discovered the misspelling. This feature allows you to find all the *Reagen*s in the document and change them to *Reagan*s. Some machines will correct every *Reagen* automatically once you enter the right spelling.

SWITCH/MERGE   This is the switching or merging of two memories (two tracks, diskettes, etc.). Suppose one contains a standard letter, and the other a list of names and addresses. Merge the two so you can get that letter automatically typed with each of the names and addresses on the list.

Okay. So some of these features seem stupid to you. But others do seem worthwhile, don't they? You'd be surprised how little agreement there is on what is an important feature and what is mere gimmickry. That's because the manner in which these machines are used is dependent on the kind of office in which they work. A mailing house may have a different use for such a machine than a law office. Obviously, then, you shouldn't be swayed by features that are of little value to you. *Don't buy (or pay for) what you don't need.* This rule applies to all the hardware listed here. *On the other hand, if you don't see what you want, ask for it.* (And if they tell you they don't have it, look elsewhere.) You may have a need for some very special feature. Use your imagination. Dream it up. The chances are good that one of the eggheads who designs these things has already dreamed it and some model, somewhere, has that feature.

This may come as a shock to some of you, but none of this is really new. Machines called word processors have been doing this kind of work for years now. *What is new is the price and portability* at which such amazing capabilities are available. So it's really a step forward and backward at the same time, since these machines are not quite word processors in power and capabilities, but *as typewriters* they represent a huge advance.

## WHO BUYS SMART TYPEWRITERS?

It's hard to say. But we do know who the vendors are *after:* the small office, which can't afford the larger scale commitment to word processing, or which doesn't have the volume to justify it. And the reluctant executive, who wants to hold on to a personal secretary, not give letters to a "word processing operator." Word processing, as we shall see, disrupts this relationship because it is a system. The memory typewriter is a good compromise, because it makes the secretary faster and more efficient without having the effect of replacing him or radically altering his job. He needn't be moved to a word processing work station. The secretary remains loyal to the boss, doing his work on a futuristic new machine that looks and feels much like the old one.

## MAKES AND MODELS

The big names in the field are IBM (What else is new?), Qyx (made by Exxon), and Olivetti. IBM and Olivetti make both electronic and memory typewriters; Qyx is system oriented—there are levels one through five. Level one is purely in the "electronic" class, but you can upgrade it—no need to buy a new unit—through five levels, and levels two and up are in the "memory" class. Levels four and five are almost word processors. Olympia, Adler, and Silver Seiko have memory machines as well, and a company called Transaction Data has a device that will upgrade any IBM Selectric to the status of a memory typewriter.

---

# WORD PROCESSORS

---

Word processors ("WPs") are the fastest-growing segment of the office equipment industry. "WP" encompasses a great many functions and several classes of equipment. Originally, word processors processed words: They stored, manipulated, and automatically typed text. Nowadays these basic functions can also be performed by the less costly and more compact electronic memory typewriters. This is, of course, no accident. Electronic typewriters came into being because word processors grew far beyond the basic text editing functions and something smaller and cheaper was needed to sell to those who wanted just the bare basics of word processing.

*An updated definition of the word processor's function:* to utilize people, procedures, and machinery in a very efficient manner, in order to convert ideas into electronically readable, storable, retrievable, and transmittable form. WPs can be terminals, which derive their computing power from a separate computer, or they can be "stand-alone" units, with their own logic, storage, and control (central processing unit).

*Word processors are the heart of the automated office.* This is where the work originates. At the WP station, ideas are converted from human thoughts and notes into a form that can enter the electronic information network.

*The word processor is an electronic linchpin.*

- *WPs can connect with various add-ons,* called peripherals, or other automated office equipment. This enables the WP to do so much more than just flip-flop words and spit them out.

---

- *WPs can share.* Several WP terminals can be linked via one central storage unit.
- *WPs can communicate with each other.* A document can be transmitted from one WP's memory and typed by another.
- *WPs can communicate with a computer.* Sophisticated "number crunching" done by an advanced computer can be sent to a WP for storage and/or printout.

Word processors communicate via wire, telephone lines, computer services, common carriers, and, in the near future, microwave and satellite.

## THE BASIC COMPONENTS

THE KEYBOARD   The input part of the WP, this is the component that makes direct physical contact with the operator. We "talk" to the WP with the keyboard, using it to "type" commands and data.

The latest trend is away from special buttons that tend to clutter up the keyboard and make it unfamiliar to an operator accustomed to a conventional typewriter. Recently, vendors have made it possible for the users to put the machine through its paces using the standard keyboard. Special functions are entered by combinations of ordinary keys rather than special ones. Thus, someone trained on a standard typewriter can adjust to a WP very quickly. This saves training time and money.

The touch of the keyboard and the shape of the keys appear to be standardizing along the lines of the mighty IBM Selectric. As vendors wisely concluded, virtually every operator is used to this type of keyboard, and that familiarity increases acceptance of the standardized WP.

LOGIC   In order to operate a WP, you must be able to follow the logic upon which it operates. When WPs were introduced, the logic was second nature to a data processing expert, but incomprehensible to the average office worker. But the vendors have seen that their future lies in making WPs easy to operate by anyone with a minimum amount of training. So the logic and language and software have been designed with the user in mind, in a way that makes sense to the typist or clerical worker. In the words of the salespeople, this produces "shorter learning curves"; that is, it takes less time to master WPs nowadays. The logic is the home of the "number crunching" and data manipulation.

STORAGE MEDIA   This is the means by which you store encoded data. Information is stored on the storage medium magnetically, in much the same way you store musical information on magnetic tape when you use your tape recorder. In fact, one common method of storing WP information used in less advanced machines is magnetic tape cassette. But tapes are rapidly being replaced by flat storage media resembling small records, called floppy disks and diskettes. They are easier to file away, and they hold much more information than cassettes. Recently, smaller, more efficient minidiskettes have been introduced.

## PERIPHERAL COMPONENTS

You can accomplish basic word processing functions without the following units. But because of their tremendous advantages, these "peripherals" greatly expand the capacity of the WP, so they are usually included in a WP purchase. Since many WPs are purchased on a component basis, like a stereo system, the buyer might wind up with WP components from several different manufacturers.

DISPLAYS    This is a video screen that displays the text, chart, or other graphic material that you are working with. It allows you to see what you are doing, and what the material looks like as you manipulate it. Another advantage is that the display enables you to verify the data and commands as you enter them on the keyboard; it visually represents them on the screen. Therefore, you can catch errors before the material is transmitted or printed or stored in an electronic memory. Documents that are displayed before being printed can be corrected without the need for new page generation (starting over) or other mechanical correcting measures like "whiting out."

Displays are of the CRT (cathode ray tube) type, and, unfortunately, most of them display less than the visual equivalent of an entire page of text. Most are sold with a WP as part of a package. In many cases, the CRT is manufactured by the WP maker or an associated firm, but there are many CRT models on the market that interface with the major WP units.

In the future, we will see CRTs with larger display capabilities, and new displays using light-emitting diodes (LEDs), liquid crystal displays (LCDs), or gas discharge technologies. Prices should come down.

PRINTERS    WPs are not typewriters. That is to say, they have keyboards, but they are not connected to type and therefore cannot produce printed matter. A mechanical accessory, or printer, is needed to do the job of making "hard" copies.

Printers are not built into the WP because there is a wide range of decisions that the user must make with regard to the kind of printing desired and the speed at which it is done. Treating a printer as a peripheral (as opposed to the built-in approach of electronic typewriters) allows you to make those choices for yourself.

*Speed.* Printers range from the *impact type*, in which the printing element touches the paper, such as an ordinary IBM Selectric modified for WP use, to the more expensive *nonimpact printers*, in which nothing touches the paper but the ink. Nonimpacts are much faster and more expensive. New ultra-high-speed ink jet printers use electrostatically charged ink to attain speeds up to 92 characters per second. New technologies from IBM and Xerox employ laser or xerographic imaging to go at speeds of up to 18,000-20,000 lines per minute.

Naturally, if you've got a great deal of printing to do, faster printers make sense. The quicker the job is done, the more time is available for the WP to do other things. The ultra-fast printer provides an alternative to the one WP/one printer formula, because its blinding speed allows it to handle the work loads of several WP terminals.

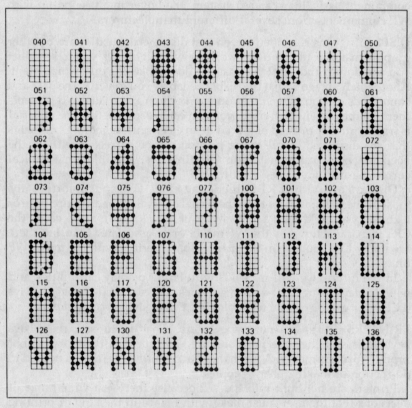

Fig. 55. Matrix pattern
One can see how a matrix printer forms characters using
a series of dots. This is what gives computer-generated
printing its distinctive look.

From Gerald A. Silver, *Small Computer Systems for Business* (New
York: McGraw-Hill, 1978), p. 96. Used with the permission of
McGraw-Hill Book Company.

*Quality.* Ideally, a printer should be of a quality approaching that of the best impact-print typewriter. Among the best are the Xerox Diablo printer, the IBM heavy-duty input/output Selectrics, and Qyx, which many feel exceeds even the Selectric in quality. (The Qyx print wheel has its own motor that moves along with it.)

Making the print quality decision has a great deal to do with your needs. For example, matrix (impact) printers use a series of dots, or "pins," arrayed in a rectangular format to make the alphanumeric characters. The printing, made up of little dots, looks like it came out of a computer; it's very common on invoices these days. This may turn off your clients when used in correspondence.

OCRs (OPTICAL CHARACTER READERS)   The Achilles heel of the word processor is that it requires input; and that is provided by an operator sitting at the keyboard. Thus, the speed and efficiency of the WP is limited by the speed and efficiency of that operator. Often, the advantage of having a WP is wiped out by the waiting time required to get your document inputted into the WP for editing and printing; you have a WP "bottleneck"—work from all over the office converging on this little machine, which, unless you've installed "distributed" WP, has a single keyboard. A solution: Turn every typewriter into a work station. This is accomplished with an OCR, a device that optically scans a page typed on an ordinary typewriter and instantly enters it into the WP storage. This means that the WP can be devoted to output rather than "rekeying" a document that has already been typed. The typed rough draft is put into the OCR, which inputs it at a rate of 10 to 25 times faster than the operator could input it manually, at rates of 500 to 1,100 words per minute (vs. the operator's average of 60 wpm). The person who operates the WP usually spends between 35 and 75 percent of time on input. Obviously, an OCR will increase productivity of the operator tremendously and go a long way in eliminating that bottleneck. Another plus—any person who can operate a typewriter can input to the WP; no laborious training is needed to learn how to put the page into the WP. This device makes sense if your WP is overloaded, or if you feel that not enough people in your office have a chance to take advantage of the benefits of the WP.

OTHER PERIPHERALS   As mentioned earlier, the newer WPs have tremendous interface and communication abilities. Therefore, almost any piece of automated office equipment that can understand WP output (or send it meaningful input) is potentially a peripheral. Such equipment includes intelligent copiers, micrographics, and small computers. But since these items perform quite well on their own, I treat them individually elsewhere, in Chapter 34, rather than as components of the WP.

---

# THE CASE FOR WORD PROCESSING

Word processors do lots of things well. Ultimately, the decision whether or not to purchase one depends on the office procedures and needs of your operation. But it's also a matter of deciding whether the implementation of a WP is worth *altering* your office procedures to come up with an overall improvement. Here's a list of some of the things WPs can facilitate:

FASTER DOCUMENT ORIGINATION   The average secretary can type 60 wpm, but mistakes resulting in "whiteouts" and retyping can bring the real average down to 3-4 wpm. With WP, trained operators average 15-30 wpm, including setup, referencing, and other button-pushing time.

FORMATTING   Legal documents, marketing and sales letters, thank-you notes, and letters to your mother-in-law are filled with standard "boilerplate" paragraphs that get used over and over. With WP, these paragraphs (and "boilerplate" sentences, phrases, and words as well) can be stored in memory. They can be retrieved at will and merged or linked to create new documents or letters.

"CUSTOMIZED" CORRESPONDENCE   A standardized document can be customized by inserting new text in any location, and by changing names, dates, and personal pronouns as needed.

PRODUCTION OF FINAL DRAFTS   Under the old system, every time there is a revision, even a minor one, the document has to be retyped. With WP, the corrections can be made on the display, proofed and reproofed before the final draft is automatically printed—in as many copies as you desire. And the final draft can be stored electronically for later use and/or printout of additional copies.

PRODUCTION OF FORM LETTERS   Form letters sent to a large number of clients can be cumbersome. Offset printing has an impersonal feel, and you may wish to avoid that. This means that, lacking WP, the typist has to type the same letter over and over. And then there's the address: Gummed labels shout "junk mail," but the alternative is typing them by hand.

Some WP printers give a "billing statement" look that can be worse than offset—little dots (matrix printers) and no curved lines.

A WP equipped with a special typewriter printer can turn out individually typed, personalized letters quickly and efficiently.

MAILING LIST HANDLING   Form letters and mailing lists can be stored in the WP memory. The WP will merge any mailing list with any form letter, so you can pull a number like, "Send our overdue payment letter to every company on our aerospace client list, but hold back a week before sending the 'we must take legal action' letter to our automotive clients."

SORTING   In order to get bulk rates from the post office, you've got to sort the mail by ZIP codes. The WP will play virtually any sorting game you like, from alphabetizing to ZIP coding to alphabetizing *under* each ZIP code.

FILING   One of the biggest problems with filing is the decision of what heading to file under. Should you classify the record by client name? By subject? By industry? By geographic area? By numerical code? Once you decide, will other members of the staff be on your wavelength and be able to retrieve the file? As we have seen, the cost of locating a missing file is quite high, as is the cost of duplicating files.

All the relevant information can be stored in "digest" form in a WP's memory. But the real WP edge comes in retrievability. You can classify a single file in many different ways and retrieve it instantly, *without removing the information from the file*. This means that, unless the floppy disk or storage medium itself is lost, the information in the file cannot be misplaced. The user never takes it with him or her, but makes a hard copy if it's needed.

The user also has some control over format of the file output. For example, a file of customers in New York State could be displayed either alphabetically or in order of annual sales (if that information is available to the WP).

UPDATING   Everyone hates the chore of going through files and updating them. With WP, it's easy. Call the record up from memory and review and edit selectively, making additions, deletions, corrections; altering formats. In some machines, a file can be transferred from the WP's "active" memory, where it stays for continuous access, to the "archival memory," usually on tape or floppy disk or diskette, which can be removed or stored until needed.

COMPILING OF LISTS AND DIRECTORIES   Store and sort lists of hundreds of names for easy access. Be able to create and compile an "instant directory" custom made to specifications.

COPY PRODUCTION   Take the load off the reprographics department. The WP can produce hard copy as needed and also allow instant access, thereby, in many cases, eliminating the need for extra copies, since any authorized colleague at any terminal can have a look.

SCHEDULING   Suppose there are several terminals, or, ideally, one for each key staff member. If everyone were to enter his schedule into the WP, it could be checked by anyone with authorization. That means you can always be up to date on meetings, conferences, cancellations, rescheduling, etc. In addition, one is less likely to forget a given meeting or task, since it can be placed on the itinerary for a future date and will appear when that schedule is examined. Some executives program their WPs to remind them a day or a week beforehand of an upcoming important meeting, so they can prepare.

PHOTOTYPESETTING WPs can interface with phototypesetting equipment, providing several advantages. The reduction of time and costs is often one of them, depending on the volume of type your firm uses. You will save time because you can typeset at will, as opposed to what often happens when you send work out for setting. More important, you have more control, because the operation is totally in-house and the material can be stored in memory for future use and revision.

## INCREASED FLEXIBILITY

*Personnel.* How many times have you passed up a real go-getter? Bright. Aggressive. One who would be loyal and efficient. The problem? He can't type, and the job calls for some typing. Enter the WP. Now the person with other redeeming characteristics, presumably intelligent, will master a WP in no time and can use it to compensate for slow or poor typing.

*Productivity.* In an article in the April, 1978, issue of *Administrative Management*, findings from a survey by consultant Robert Schiff were reported: Fifty-three non-WP secretaries said they spent 14 percent of their time waiting for work; the rest of the day was divided between essentially "go-for" and clerical duties. These secretaries are not as efficient as they should be because their attention is too diffused among many small jobs. They are unable to concentrate on any one job for very long.

WP is changing all this, because it allows for a difference in job organization. There's the typist or WP specialist who handles typing and related skills, and the administrative assistant who functions more in support of the superior's special needs.

"HIDDEN" BENEFITS  Finally, there are those benefits of WP that cannot be measured, but are nevertheless quite real. If a firm uses its WP equipment properly, it should produce neater, more detailed and thought-out correspondence, reports, and other printed material—and produce it more promptly. The bottom line is that the image of the company, as it is viewed from the outside, will be enhanced. And how can you put a dollar value on that?

## WHO NEEDS WP?

Everybody, say the vendors. One tried to sell *me* a word processor. His pitch? "You can store an entire book manuscript on diskettes, then go back over it, editing the text on a CRT. When that's done, have the printer spit it out." I must admit that the idea was appealing.

FAST-GROWING COMPANIES  WP means people can work faster—in some cases, two to three times faster. And since peripherals can be added, the WP can grow with you.

COMPANIES WITH A HEAVY CORRESPONDENCE LOAD  You can personalize those form letters. WPs are three times faster than mag card and four times faster than a 100 percent accurate typist.

THOSE THAT REQUIRE 100 PERCENT ACCURACY, AND RAPID-CHANGE CAPABILITY  For example, law firms, insurance firms; anyone with a lot of contract work, advertising production, etc.

## TRENDS IN WORD PROCESSING

Word processing is the fastest growing segment of the office equipment industry.

Its growth is tied to the realization that office productivity has been one of the last battlefields to feel the sting of the automation revolution. Managers have started looking around for ways to cut the fat and reduce wasted time and wasted paper.

JOB DESCRIPTION  Two devices provided the vanguard for word processing: the text editing typewriter and the dictation unit. These two units allowed the job of secretary, with its frustrating lack of structure and challenge, to be divided into two different, more efficiently structured jobs:

*The word processing typist*, who concentrates on typing of all kinds.

*The administrative assistant*, who handles nontyping tasks like phone calls, filing, etc. This job often has no predictable or steady work flow. Rather, the worker is expected to "switch gears" on a moment's notice—and can be hired for being able to do just that, without regard to typing ability.

The result: New equipment and specialized operators have proven cost effective. Work gets done more efficiently, in less time, with fewer mistakes, by a professional word processing typist.

Eventually, the nondisplay and single-line display standalone units will be phased out. That doesn't mean they will disappear from the office. The ones that are in place will probably continue to function quite well for some time to come. But the vendors will put their marketing bucks into the more sophisticated equipment, and for most companies these will represent the better buy.

Certainly, the trend will be toward compatibility. WPs are not an end in themselves; they are only a logical starting point. They will be part of configurations, or networks built around them. Therefore, they are being made to interface with other vendors' equipment so as to increase flexibility.

Actually, the term *word processor* is on its way out, at least as a designation for a particular piece of equipment. Word processing and data processing are moving closer together, and what will result is a multi-function terminal that does number crunching, word processing, electronic mail, and the entire repertoire of automated office feats.

## THE OTHER SIDE OF THE STORY

Word processors are clearly part of an irreversible trend, but don't necessarily rush right down and buy one. The timing may not be right. Take it from one that knows—the U.S. government. David Larkin of the Office of Administrative Services and Procurement, U.S. Department of Commerce, says that few federal agencies have been able to recover their investment costs on WPs.* Some of the blame goes to the equipment, and some to the users:

DOES A WP OR AUTOMATIC TYPEWRITER REALLY SAVE TIME?   The added costs of an automatic typewriter or WP may not be justified by the reduction of typing time. Since the typist must type the original material, the only real savings comes if there is a large volume of "auto typing" of previously keyboarded material. In actuality, claims Larkin, some automatic typewriters *increase* the time required to type an original.

More important is the way WP typing time is measured—words per minute. The vendors claim that a typist will type such-and-such a percentage, or hard numbers, of words per minute. However, office personnel aren't paid by piecework—5 cents per word, or something like that; they are paid by the hour or week. And it is very tough to accumulate enough saved time in "words per minute" to eliminate even a part-time helper, or give a secretary a significant amount of additional work.

LET'S ASSUME THAT THE AUTOMATIC, OR WP, DOES SAVE REAL TIME—DOES THIS RESULT IN INCREASED PRODUCTIVITY?   That depends. Is the typing work load a limiting factor in your office productivity? If you freed the typists to some degree from such chores, would they be able to do other significant work, such as follow up phone calls, inventory, etc.? What good is saved time if that time cannot be converted to productive work? Chances are that if a typist finishes an hour typing job in forty-five minutes, the time won't get filled with an additional fifteen minutes of typing. It might even mean an extra personal phone call to a friend.

---

*From David Larkin, "The government takes a new look at word processing" (*The Office*, January, 1979), p. 81.

---

More food for thought. Larkin points out that early WP vendors, recognizing this problem, reintroduced the concept of typists and machines clustered in work pools, thereby producing the "WP center," which benefited from the so-called "economy of scale." Multiply these fragmented bits of saved time and increased efficiency and you will get savings in terms of hours rather than minutes. But, says Larkin, the real benefits come from the concept of the pool, not from the automatic typewriters. In any event, if you don't have enough personnel or volume to justify such an approach, the "economics of scale" notion is out of reach.

THE GLAMOUR BIT  Even in our austere and dedicated federal agencies, WPs have been acquired as "status symbols" or "morale boosters" for execs and their secretaries.

## THE BOTTOM LINE

Economically, a word processor is generally a bad buy if it replaces a standard typewriter in a one-to-one work situation without increasing the work load of the typing station. However, if you and/or the potential WP operator feel that such an acquisition will make correspondence and other typing production more accurate, more attractive, less monotonous, and speedier, and if you are willing to pay for those things that will enable you to achieve greater effectiveness (even if there is no increase in efficiency), then, by all means, go ahead. And, incidentally, for those of you who do not work for the government: A status symbol or conversation piece that will impress people and communicate that you are up to date can very often be justified. Even the lowly writer can culture an image of success when a visitor sees his little office equipped with a Qyx typewriter and a sophisticated dictation system, even though an argument can be made that all you need is a portable Smith-Corona and a cheap cassette machine.

Finally, Larkin admits that things may be changing. Self-correcting typewriters appear to be cost-effective for most government agencies. The development of new equipment, such as the OCR, can eliminate some of the problems and allow the WP to pay its way.

# 34

# ELECTRONIC DUPLICATION AND STORAGE: DICTATION MACHINES, COPIERS, MICROGRAPHICS

Copiers. Dictation machines. Microfilm. Having been around for years, these three devices are familiar to most executives. But the introduction of microprocessors and advanced optics and circuitry have transformed these machines; in many cases they bear little or no resemblance to their unautomated predecessors.

## DICTATION MACHINES

Dictation machines are a strange breed of device. Almost every businessperson sees their value; but not everyone wants to *use* them. There are many who are still resisting the purchase of even the simplest dictation machine. Stranger still, studies indicate that many desk top units, even when purchased, are rarely used, because executives are easily intimidated by them. Personally, I think dictation machines have an image problem. They are to some a symbol of the impersonal, autocratic manager who is out of touch with his staff—the opposite of the "sleeves rolled up" type that many managers would like to be. Besides, the joy of human contact can flow up as well as down: The executive can do with the nod of the head, the encouraging smile, and the admiring glance often provided by the secretary as the letter, memo, or speech is dictated. You can't very well ask a machine, "How am I doin'?" and expect a meaningful reply. Not yet, anyway.

However, it's incontrovertible that the new dictation machines are incredibly efficient; and designers have gone out of their way to construct the units according to the principles of human engineering. It seems they have finally realized that we will work only with machines we like, especially when it involves a task that has been done "the old way" for years.

## PORTABLE UNITS

Sometimes called notetakers, these are modified and improved portable tape recorders.

*New features include:*

- end-of-tape signal
- recording circuits that act to block out excess noise
- optional foot pedal or special adapter for standard transcribers
- separate, larger playback speakers
- audible fast forward
- extra-fast rewind

These units are carried around, so work can be dictated at any time in any place, for later transcription.

*Standard features include:*

- start/stop/rewind/play/record/fast forward modes
- cueing button. This is what separates the portable dictation unit from the simple notetaker pocket recorder. If it doesn't have a cue button, it's not intended for dictation, no matter what the salesperson tries to tell you.
- other warning devices: "end of tape," "no tape in machine"—to prevent the loss of valuable dictation

## DESK TOP UNITS

Obviously, these are designed for the desk. They perform essentially the same functions as the portables, but they feature paper index strips and have a few operational advantages.

CONTROLS   Some have controls on the machine itself; others have controls on the mike, which is better if you move around while dictating.

MEDIA   There are two basic types. One is the endless loop of tape, which is a lot of tape sealed in the dictation unit. The second type is the discrete media, in which the medium, usually a cassette, can be moved about separately and changed after one use or several dictations.

## CENTRALIZED SYSTEMS

The microprocessor worms its way into yet another piece of conventional office equipment. Here's what these centralized systems can do:

REMOTE ACCESS   "Centralized" means that the user can be some-where far away from the dictation station where the actual recording and transcribing takes place. Centralized systems can be used by several people at the same time:

- from outside telephones
- from inside phones to central dictation areas

A number of recent advances in dictation have been made possible with the microprocessor-controlled central units:

INSTRUCTIONS   Some machines feature a special recording that tells you how to use the machine. Naturally, this little piece of news could get rather tiresome after the tenth time or so. But it's great for organizations with a large turnover and/or particularly slow learners. To be fair, the recorded instruction is a good idea, because it prevents the callers from screwing things up and therefore makes it easier on the transcribing secretaries, who would be reluctant to say, "You nurd, when are you going to learn how to use the Dictaphone!" Because instructions will assist those who are intimidated by the complexity of the system, they will tend to use the system more often.

END-OF-TAPE WARNING   At three minutes and one minute before the end of the tape, a signal lets you know.

"WAIT" NOTICE   This is another feature to prevent dictation loss. You are notified to wait while the cassette is being changed.

AUTO TAPE EJECTION   When the tape has been played, out it pops.

"AUTOMATIC CASSETTE CHANGE"   Cassettes are changed automatically, and the machine will reject broken, jammed, or improperly inserted cassettes. Wouldn't it be great if your stereo cassette deck did that?

INPUT DATA RECORD   The machine keeps a record of all incoming messages: the author's identification number (yes, friend, 1984 is upon us), the time of dictation, the time the cassette was ejected, special instructions, and the name of the intended recipient. With this information, the messages can be prioritized, instead of handled only in the order that they come in.

THREE-WAY FOOT PEDAL   Now, you can go into fast forward, rewind, or play, just by using your foot. Not even your car can do that.

INDEXING   Simple problems have always plagued the dictation unit user. Looking at the tape, we ask, where does the message begin and end? How long is it? (How to format the transcription page unless one knows the length?) What about special instructions?

The vendors have attempted to solve the problem using paper index

---

strips. But the electronic age has ushered in new approaches: Visual cueing, employing light emitting diode (LED) readouts, tell the transcriber where the message starts and ends, the location of special instructions, if any, and who the message is for. There's also an *automatic search*, in which the machine actually locates the desired point on the tape for you.

---

# COPIERS

---

Copiers generate 100 billion pieces per year. Didn't you just love them when you were in college? Funny how simple they seemed when they first came out: Place original face down, press button, out comes copy. And, of course, in the beginning there was only Xerox. Today there are so many makes and models and features and complex controls that many firms employ "reprographics" managers—copy experts. In lieu of that, here's this:

**Fiber optics.** This is the major new advance in copier technology. It replaces the standard lens/mirror optical system with light-conducting fiber. What this means to you is a reduction in production costs, and so also a reduction in price over comparable lens/mirror machines, more compactness and less weight, and sharper, crisper, more consistent copies.

**Single element toners.** Dry copiers, with no liquids. Unfortunately, these copiers have a drawback—"special" plain paper (i.e., not really plain) is used, and it is somewhat shiny.

**Automatic document feed.** This is a real plus, a real time-saver. The document is fed automatically and, through the automatic registration feature, aligned for a perfect copy. It works so well that it will handle even paper that has been wrinkled or crumpled. (Of course, you've got to straighten it out somewhat—the machine that will take a ball of paper has not been invented yet.)

**Dual cassettes.** Many copiers store the paper sheets on cassettes or trays. The newer ones have two, so that two sizes and/or types of paper are available to you while you operate the machine, eliminating the need to change and/or empty cassettes or trays while you are in the middle of a copying job.

**Sorters.** Machines that sort or collate copies have been around for a while. But sorters have become an integral part of new models.

---

**Smart copiers.** The introduction of microprocessor technology into copier design has allowed for smooth operation of internal controls. The reproduction process is regulated by microprocessors, and this cuts down on "downtime" and mechanical foul-up.

**Very smart copiers.** Soon we will be using a hybrid of the copier and word processor; several are being tested.

**Intelligent copiers.** These copiers don't have to "see" what they copy. They can copy without conventional originals, working from WP instructions. They can store over 1,000 pages in a storage memory and make copies in several different type sizes, faces, and graphic styles. They can create charts and photos from information typed on a keyboard. These machines rely on laser optical systems or fiber optics. Welcome to the future.

**Peripherals and software.** Electronic copy control systems arose to fight the copyholism epidemic. At least 20 percent of all copies made are unnecessary. About 30 percent are made on the wrong machine for the job. These two sins can cost a firm 50 percent or more of its total copy expense in unnecessary copy charges. Copy control simply keeps a record of who is making the copies and how many they are making, broken down by client, job, etc.

## The economics of copiers.

*Unit purchase prices.* The bottom line is *the desk top copier*, which runs about $1,500-2,000 for coated-paper models and $3,000 for plain. The trend here is clearly up.

*Outright purchase.* This is the hot trend in machines in the $5,000-6,000 range; 75 percent of this market opt to buy.

*Factory reconditioned.* It pays to look into this. Such machines are almost as good as new ones, and they sell 40-60 percent cheaper.

*Rentals.* The charge is monthly; it includes a copy allowance. There is a surcharge on copy work exceeding the allowance. This is akin to some kinds of auto rental: so much a day, so much a mile after the first 100 miles.

*Service contracts.* These are keyed to usage or a specified time, whichever comes first, like the "5 year or 50,000 mile" warranties on cars—except that you must pay for a service contract, while a warranty is free.

*Brands.* Xerox once had a virtual monopoly. But now it's getting hit from two directions: high-end competition from Kodak, 3M, and IBM;

low-end from Savin, Sharp, Saxon, Toshiba, Canon, and others. And these johnny-come-latelys are good.

**What to look for in a copier.** According to a recent survey conducted by *Administrative Management* magazine, users of large copiers rated high reliability and good service the number-one desirable features of copiers, followed by reasonable costs. For users of smaller machines, reliability and service also finished at the top, but copy quality was next on the list. This difference is easy to explain. All copiers have their share of downtime in which they chew, smudge, and otherwise destroy paper—but among the larger machines, which are more expensive, copy quality is almost always good; with smaller ones, it's catch-as-catch-can, especially when dealing with coated paper.

Here are the results of the survey in a nutshell:

### USERS OF LOW-END COPIERS

| *most wanted features* | *least wanted features* |
|---|---|
| 1. prompt response to service calls | 1. mobility, portability of unit |
| 2. reduced frequency of paper jams | 2. erasability on copy |
| 3. service with expertise | 3. sheet bypass |
| 4. reduction of downtime | 4. service code display cards |
| 5. frequent scheduled service calls | 5. stream-feeding of originals |
| 6. consistent copy quality | 6. copying on offset master stock |
| 7. smudgeproofness of copy image | 7. copying on colored paper |
| 8. uniform quality across page | 8. duplexing |
| 9. minimum quality fall-off between scheduled maintenance calls | 9. trade-in allowance |
| 10. copy counter that clears to zero after run | |

# USERS OF HIGH-END COPIERS

| *most wanted features* | *least wanted features* |
|---|---|
| 1. servicemen's expertise | 1. feeding unburst computer printout |
| 2. prompt response to service calls | 2. copies on offset master stock |
| 3. net uptime | 3. enlargement capability |
| 4. reduced frequency of jams | 4. dedicated electric line |
| 5. reasonable out-of-pocket costs | 5. machine resale value |
| 6. frequently scheduled service calls | 6. trade or rental credit allowance |
| 7. reduced job turn-around—time in to time out | 7. ADH for 11" x 17" originals |
| 8. replacement parts availability | 8. copies of film transparencies |
| 9. reasonable consumable supply costs | 9. reproduction of colored images |
| 10. automatic document handler (ADH) | 10. no image edge skip |

If you are puzzled by the wide range of machines and features, take a careful look at this list before you make your final decision. If you are going to look at equipment, take the survey with you. If you don't want to carry this book, you can always . . . well . . . make a photocopy of the survey.

## A COPIER CHECKLIST

This checklist* is designed to help evaluate your office reproduction system, to assess its needs and special problems. It will be useful in deciding what equipment is best.

1. How long have we had our present copier(s)?
2. If leased or rented, what kind of lease or rental agreement is involved? How long does it run? When does it expire? What are renewal arrangements? What are the penalties, if any?
3. How many copiers do we have? What type of copiers are they? Are they centralized or decentralized?
4. What type of copier do we have—plain paper or other? Dry toner or liquid toner?

---

*Reprinted by permission of Toshiba America, Business Equipment Division, Wayne, New Jersey.

5. Are different supplies—papers, toners, developers—used for each, or are special supplies needed?
6. Can we copy onto all types of material: letterheads, self-adhesive labels, transparencies, offset masters?
7. Do we have any policy to control length of runs on each unit and/or to prevent unauthorized copying?
8. Do we have any other duplicating machines?
9. What is the monthly volume of copies for each machine we have? What is the manufacturer's recommended usage for each model?
10. What is our cost per copy? In the case of rental equipment, does this cost include all supplies?
11. What kinds and sizes of documents are we copying on a regular basis?
12. Do we get consistently good copy quality, with solid black tones in both text and artwork?
13. What is our experience with misfeeds and breakdowns?
14. Is our principal copier rated as high-speed or medium-speed? Do we have any other copiers available?
15. How fast a copying speed do we need for our copy volume?
16. What is the average number of copies run per original?
17. What special copier requirements do we have, for example, two-sided copying; transparencies; book copying; reduction; ability to copy from a wide range of different types of originals?
18. Are disadvantages to our having high-speed copiers inherent in the electrical requirements; the question of centralized vs. decentralized copying; size; reliability (the higher the speed the greater the possibility of jam); availability of backup equipment in case of downtime?
19. Are we using our copier for reproduction that would be substantially cheaper if it were done on a printing press or a duplicator?
20. In computing our indirect copying costs, do we figure in such factors as supervision, personnel time (waiting, walking, operation), waste, and downtime?
21. Are major multipage documents being reproduced unnecessarily when a few routing or file copies would be sufficient?
22. Are the reasons we selected centralized or decentralized copying still relevant to today's requirements?
23. Are there budget benefits in departmentalizing copiers for accurate allocation of costs?
24. Is there a benefit in having more than one copier available for use in case of breakdowns, elimination of travel time, queuing time, etc.?

FOR MORE INFORMATION   For a detailed report of the results of this survey, contact:

> Richard Hanson & Associates
> Box 353
> Setauket, New York 11733

Richard E. Hanson is a recognized authority in the field of copying and duplicating. His user-oriented report, "Hanson's Guidelines...Best Copier Buys for the Small User," discusses prices, user experience, and new models and features. It is updated quarterly. Another helpful publication from Hanson is his book *A Manager's Guide to Copying and Duplicating.*

For more detailed information on copiers, The Buyer's Laboratory puts out "Copier Review," which includes a monthly newsletter on the industry, test reports on copiers, dry toners, and duplicating systems, a 28-page guide to copiers, and information on controlling copier costs. This material is obviously intended for purchasing agents in large companies, but you can obtain the reports on a one-time basis, as opposed to a subscription. The reports are Consumers Union style, unbiased and bench-tested.

> Contact:
> Buyer's Laboratory, Inc.
> 20 Railroad Avenue
> Hackensack, New Jersey 07601
> (201) 488-0404

---

# MICROGRAPHICS

---

The technology around which micrographics is built is a product of the nineteenth century. For a while there, the computer community looked upon it as easy prey, since it seemed easier to store and access records in a computer. They soon changed their minds:

1. *What happens when a computer loses power?* Often, the memory is erased. And what happens if some dodo erases something by accident? Even with checks and balances, it still happens. *Microfilm or microfiche is an inexpensive, space-saving way of keeping a backup record.*
2. *Micrographics is actually less expensive than digital storage.*
3. *Hard copies are very easily generated.*
4. *Micrographics can be easily handled and filed.*

# TYPES OF MICROFORMS

Micrographics involves the use of microforms, a generic term for any microphotographically produced printed matter. Microforms cannot be read without the aid of a reader that magnifies the microform and usually projects it onto a screen. There are several formats:

MICROFILM   Microform in 16mm or 35mm roll format, microfilm is the granddaddy of microforms, developed as a space saver for copying newspapers and magazines.

MICROFICHE   The format is a 4" x 6" film card that carries reduced images, assembled in rows. Fiches may be either black-and-white or color, and the conventional fiche can hold up to 98 pages of text.

MICROBOOK FICHE   The microbook holds page reproductions that have been greatly reduced (between 55 and 90 times), allowing them to hold up to 1,000 pages.

Other forms include microprints and microcards, which are gradually being replaced by microfiche.

# PRINCIPAL USES OF MICROGRAPHICS

1. as protection against information loss
2. as insurance against the deterioration commonly associated with paper
3. as a rapid, inexpensive means of duplication
4. as an efficient means of storage and retrieval

The microforms used in the modern office are almost always *microfilm* or *microfiche*.

# WHAT MICROFILM CAN DO

Microfilm can file information in as little as 10 percent of the space required by paper. Microfilm storage can be extremely cost-effective. Some experts have estimated that even with the cost of converting to microfilm, the first year's expense would be half that of maintaining an equivalent amount of paper files.

# WHAT MICROFICHE CAN DO

It occupies less than 1 percent of the space required by paper. It is cheaper than paper. A microfiche report costs between 7 percent and 30 percent less than a copy of the same report on paper. A new fiche system utilizes fiches that can be added to, erased, and even written on.

# COM (COMPUTER OUTPUT MICROFILM)

Micrographics is hot. So rather than go head to head against it with electronic storage, computer engineers opted for a marriage. Apparently it worked, because the result, COM, is the fastest-growing segment of the micrographics industry. Simply stated, data from a computer is flashed on a CRT and then reduced by a lens system and recorded on film or fiche. The next step is processing and, if necessary, duplication of the film.

## COM ADVANTAGES

1. *COM printing is 10-20 times faster* than an impact printing interface with a computer. COM can convert computer output into readable text at up to 342 standard computer pages per minute.
2. *COM, of course, provides all the advantages of microfiche.* Cost per 500 pages is 30¢ for fiche, versus approximately $9 for paper. One pound of microfiche is the storage equivalent of 300 pounds of paper. One can store in one filing cabinet the COM equivalent of 50 filing cabinets of output paper.
3. *Off-line recording* allows the computer to be used for other tasks while the COM is being recorded—which means better use of computer time.
4. *Form flexibility.* Picture this. You have custom forms. And you have your data. When making the fiche, you can superimpose a custom form over the computer generated data; the microfiche will be produced as a completed form just as if you had filled in the blanks on the custom forms. You make them on the spot.

COM TRENDS   It's not hard to see why COM is growing 35 percent annually. And new technology such as dry processing is making the process even simpler. Some vendors have already succeeded in merging WP with COM and are using the WP output and COM input. In addition we can expect on-line COM, laser COM, and a host of other innovations.

- *CAR* (computer assisted retrieval). The biggest complaint about micrographics is that retrieving it can be a big hassle. CAR solves this problem, with a computerized index to help locate a microform.
- *CIM* (computer input microfilm). One such system uses OCR (optical character recognition) to scan a microform, convert it to bits, and put it on a screen or even transmit it. Thus, in CIM, the computer "sees" the microfilm and, therefore, accepts it as input.

*Computers have done a lot for microforms.* Not only is the micrographic alternative more viable and efficient; *it has gone from just an archival storage system to an operational storage medium.*

# 35

# TELEPHONES

I don't have to tell you that there is a major telecommunications revolution taking place. The business sections of the news media detail the lawsuits coming at Ma Bell like heavyweights used to come at Muhammad Ali. Then there are the ads for stores like Phone City, Phonetique, and hundreds of mail-order pitches for the latest in telephoning.

The kinds of equipment and services that are offered are so extensive, so diverse, and so individualized that all I can offer are some basic guidelines. Do you need any of this stuff? If you think you do, I guess you do. All these gadgets do things that have some value. But whether they are worth their price is difficult to assess across the board. It's a very subjective thing. For example, I like having a telephone amplifier, because I am able to file, take notes, even type while talking on the phone. For an executive who needn't bother with any of this and doesn't require hand-free operation, this device may not be important. On the other hand, he may wish to have one in the conference room, so that others outside the room (or the country) may take part in meetings held within.

## THE PRINCIPAL DEVICES

**Automatic Dialers.** They do just what you'd expect. You program the most frequently used numbers into the dialer's memory and label a series of buttons with the parties' names. Push a button, and the number is dialed almost instantly, with nary a misdial. Purpose? Well, it saves money on misdials and may save you a little time in looking up the numbers. But so would a card that holds the same numbers and sits on your desk next to the phone. Will it save you time in dialing? Come on. The one exception is the case of those who have poor vision or are blind, since it's easier for them to locate the proper button than to dial.

The major difference in machines is in the number of phone numbers they can store. Some of the flashy features include a "last number dialed" redialing feature, so you can keep trying if you get a "busy" the first time. I suppose that any machine that saves you the trouble of redialing a busy number is worth the price in saved aggravation when calling a government agency, a movie theater for times, or any teenager. At least one unit has a special dial speed sequence for use in offices where you have to dial a single digit before the number in order to get a dial tone. Some have built-in "speaker phones," and dials that double as calculators.

**Telephone answering devices.** These machines are unquestionably the most popular of the accessories on the market, and if you haven't made contact with one yet, pinch yourself—you're probably dead. They are everywhere, and as much as we dislike them, they are often more reliable than human answering services. And they don't talk back. The major problem is that a calling party will rarely hang up on reaching a service, but many, many people hang up the minute they hear the wow and flutter of your voice on tape. Originally these machines were very simple. After a number of rings, they would greet your caller with a taped message and signal him to leave a message on the machine, usually on a special message tape for recording these messages (the two-tape system is better and more costly than a single-tape).

Lately, these machines have become much more sophisticated, with an eye toward the business market. Several models can carry on a simulated conversation with callers, allowing it to take orders and the like. Several can be programmed to take a survey by asking the caller a series of questions and pausing for a reply. Voice activation allows the machines to "know" when the caller is through speaking and move on.

Most answer-and-record units allow you to vary the number of rings required to trigger the answering machine, to limit or allow for unlimited message lengths, and to retrieve your messages by phone from outside by using a pocket remote unit. Other advances include automatic call diversion, which diverts your call to the number where you can be reached, and machines that can handle up to 12 lines simultaneously. Most units allow you to monitor the caller's voice and decide if you want to pick up the call as it comes in or tend to the matter later.

Some problems exist with these machines. They are dependent on voltage levels and other electronic cues from the telephone system, and little glitches in the phone lines may cause them to malfunction. The endless loop tapes stretch easily, thus, after a time, the voice on the message will be distorted. Many of the machines do not incorporate high-quality play or record heads, so you get fuzzy reproduction, poor tape quality, and even some static. A few industry experts I talked to rated Sanyo and Sony among the best on the market.

Good quality machines range from $150 to $300. Commercial units go from $900 to around $1,500. They offer better tape mechanisms and recording quality, but most of the same features are also found in the better consumer models.

**Telephone amplifiers.** These devices enable you to hear phone calls without putting your ear to the phone's receiver. Some devices also allow you to respond in the same fashion. How they work: They employ small speakers and condenser microphones, and the circuit amplifies the phone signal and throws it into the room via the speaker. The condenser microphone, similar to the one in your portable cassette recorder, picks up speech in the area and transmits it to the phone unit. Thus, you can walk, pace, organize your desk, take notes, or make love while talking on the phone. No hands needed (at least not for the phone). Panasonic's KX-1030 has a built-in LED (light-emitting diode) clock/timer.

**Timing devices.** Timing devices are added features that can be found on anything from auto phone dialers to amplifiers to answering machines, since they are not central to the function of the device, but are just clocks, built in as an add-on.

**Telephone security devices.** There are three basic types: *locks*, which prevent dialing and/or summoning the operator; *code devices*, which require the phone system to respond to codes before allowing calls to go through—all calls, if you prefer, or only calls to a specific party; and *"de-bugging"* devices, which let you know when someone is listening in, or (so goes the manufacturers' claim) prevent bugging from taking place.

**Wireless phones.** They've been around for quite some time, in automobiles, where the phone message was transmitted by radio to a nearby phone company receiving station for transmission over telephone lines. It used to be that you had to go through an operator. Now direct dialing is available, and wireless phones come in attaché cases that can be used as regular telephones. These phones work only in selected cities that have the special setups needed.

Then there's the home hobbyist's wireless phone. This device consists of a "base station," a gizmo that gets plugged in at the phone outlet. Then you've got the handset, which is a phone equipped with a radio transmitter and an antenna; it transmits the call to the base station, which in turn feeds it over the wires. This is a great item for your backyard, pool, or tennis court. The range varies, but it is not meant for great distances. Business applications appear very limited in this case, although I know of one retailer who has chosen to equip his premises with one base station and several phones near the registers, rather than to wire the store for regular phone extensions.

**Souped-up phones.** Since the FCC and court rulings have sanctioned competition in the phone equipment market and the specifications have been standardized, you can walk into a "phone store," or "boutique," and buy any phone you like, take it home, and hook it up. Essentially, this makes a phone available just like any other household appliance or piece of office equipment. And all the laws of the marketplace prevail. There's a collection of "designer" phones, "antique look" phones, even Mickey Mouse phones (AT&T itself thought that one up). And the microprocessor freaks have struck again; they got hold of the phone, pulled it apart, and started adding things. When I was a kid, we used to customize cars; today that's too simple (and gas costs more than phone calls). Some examples are phones that act as calculators, alarms....

## MISCELLANEOUS GADGETRY

You can purchase computerized units that monitor every phone call: where to, who from, time and charges. These devices are becoming popular in hotels (which pass the phone charges on to their guests and need reliable records), in businesses that are trying to control costs, and in service businesses like law offices, where the client is billed for phone expenses.

On the more mechanical side, for the phone on your desk you can purchase brackets that allow you to move it around to a convenient position somewhere in midair. Program music into "hold" units, if you like (and frustrate callers who have different tastes in music). Install silencers to cut off the ring, "bell extenders" to make the ring louder or more remote (I'd love one for my shower), 150 feet of extra cord in case you want to take your phone with you to the deli across the street (there are take-up reels too, so the phone will snap back when you let go of it), extra-large buttons and numbers for easier dialing, noise filters to cut out cross-talk and other annoying sounds.

## THINGS TO REMEMBER
## ABOUT TELEPHONE SERVICE

**Check your bills carefully.** Look for calls improperly charged to you each month. Every six months, check your monthly statements for service and miscellaneous charges.

**Talk telephone with your accountant.** Equipment rental is tax deductible. Purchase gives you investment tax credit plus accelerated depreciation.

**Remember WATS lines are not free.** And long conversations defeat their purpose and cost effectiveness.

**Analyze your service deal and configuration.** You often have more service than you need, or the wrong kind of service. You'll pay dearly for it.

**If you have a switchboard, consider the computerized option.** Such devices can perform faster and better than an operator. By one estimate, you'll enjoy up to a 30 percent return on investment per year through use of such equipment.

**Use credit cards only when you can't dial without operator help.** They are often used simply because they provide you with a record of calls made from the outside. But credit-card calls are operator-assisted and, therefore, very expensive. There are better and cheaper ways to record your phone calls and costs. Try a little phone log or the expense section of your pocket diary.

When you're in a hotel or motel, however, the telephone charge may be less if you use a credit card than if you use the hotel switchboard services for intrastate calls.

**Do not ignore abuse and misuse of telephones.** The amount of time and money devoured by employees on the phone is incredible. Executives have a number of options. Obtrusive methods involve asking people to cut down, log their own calls, etc. There are also unobtrusive computerized devices that will restrict and/or log calls automatically. The return on investment on these is very rapid. Don't supply company phone credit cards. Rather, reimburse employees for personal credit card use; this method protects the company if an employee quits or is fired.

**Reassess your equipment periodically.** There are many new options and suppliers to consider. Besides, inappropriate or outdated equipment often wastes money. Take a good look at least every two years—more often if your company is growing very fast. And keep an open mind toward alternatives.

**Learn how to work with consultants.** As in the computer business, telephone system options get so complicated that, often, you must rely on consultants to lead you through the maze. Ideally, consultants will make a thorough study of your office and then recommend ways to cut costs and improve service. If they suggest new equipment, they should provide several options.

Be careful when you choose a consultant. Many "consultants" are simply former salesmen who've gone out on their own, but maintain ties to their old company. Others may receive a kickback under the table. How to protect yourself: Ask for the names of the last ten jobs and check to see who the vendors were. If it's the same in all or most of the cases, you just might have a problem.

Ask for a statement in writing that the consultant is in no way affiliated with any vendor and that he receives no sales commissions on any equipment purchased.

Don't pay on the basis of percentage of savings in phone equipment or service costs. Any fool can save you money by buying inexpensive equipment or downgrading your service. Pay a per diem or a fee for the entire job.

---

## SUGGESTED READING

---

*How to Cut Costs and Improve Service of Your Telephone, Telex, TWX and Other Telecommunications,* by Frank K. Griesinger (New York: McGraw-Hill, 1974).

This is an excellent book, written by one of the true authorities in the field. It is very thorough and will undoubtedly save you some money in the long run. It is a bit outdated, though, with respect to rates and the latest equipment.

---

# 36

## ELECTRONIC MAIL

Another one of those fancy marketing buzzwords, *electronic mail* can mean one specific service or an entire field, depending on who you're talking to. The safe way is to take the broad approach and use the term to apply to any electronic means of transmitting data or messages. Here are the principal ones:

- communicating computers
- communicating WPs
- telex and TWX
- facsimile
- mailgrams
- telegrams
- message switching
- *new carriers coming up:* satellites, microwave, optical, teleconferencing

## COMMUNICATING COMPUTERS AND WORD PROCESSORS

At high levels, word processors and computers are difficult to tell apart, since they do so many of the same things. Computers that transmit data to each other have been around for years and are very helpful in keeping records in industries such as banking and travel. Currently, it is more difficult to get WPs to communicate with each other (there are interface and other problems); the potential applications are great, but most of them have yet to be realized.

Let's say an executive in the main office receives a letter from a field salesman in the Orient. He wants all the branch offices to see the letter immediately, but with a few additions and comments. So he has it put in the OCR, edited, annotated and sent to WPs in all the branch offices, where it is printed. But, you say, couldn't he have used a "fax" (facsimile) machine or sent a telex of the main points of the letter? Sure, he could've. He even sent diagrams by telecopier. And this is where the various kinds of electronic mail systems may cannibalize each other. *It's not what they do that is so different, but how they do it.* Volume, cost, the final form of the data that's needed, and speed are just a few things that will determine which method your company will use. You must also consider the terminal capabilities of the receiving party.

# TELEX AND TWX

These are the primary "wire services." Technological first cousins of the telephone, they use teletypewriters instead of phones to send printed messages. Both are owned and operated by Western Union, and although telegrams are obsolete for business uses, telex and TWX are certainly not. These systems are fast, and they are *cheaper than phone.*

## ADVANTAGES OF TELEX AND TWX
## OVER OTHER TRANSMISSION MEDIA

- *fast.* Transmission speed is less than 15 seconds.
- *excellent for one-way messages.* Use of wire services eliminates the salutations and small talk involved in phone calls; eliminates being placed on hold.
- *less time spent in sending messages.* And operator time costs less.
- *less executive time consumed.* It takes much less time for an executive to write a telex or TWX message than to phone or to compose a letter.
- *widely used abroad.* There is the cost advantage; and a hard copy is produced, which is easier to understand and translate than a voice message.

## MAKING THE CHOICE BETWEEN TELEX AND TWX

CONSIDER YOUR DOMINANT INDUSTRY Who will you be communicating with? Some industries have a "standard" wire service. Don't get a telex if everyone else is on TWX.

MESSAGE LENGTH How long will your messages run? In general, lengthy messages sent at 100 wpm on TWX are cheaper than those sent at 66 wpm on Telex. But if the messages are short, telex might be the cheaper of the two.

WANT RECORDS FOR ACCOUNTING? Telex gets the nod. You can get detailed itemizing of each message sent. This costs more. If you can maintain these records yourself with careful operators, you may be better off with TWX; you can save dollars and still have the telex option open.

INTERNATIONAL COMMUNICATIONS   Go with Telex. It's dominant abroad.

DOMESTIC COMMUNICATIONS   Consider the location of most frequent message destinations. *Telex used to compute charges by zone rates* (not unlike the Postal Service), and *TWX used to go by airline mile rates.* Recently, Western Union announced a plan to establish uniform usage rates of 33.75 cents per minute for Telex and 41 cents per minute for TWX. Western Union is also seeking to establish uniform rates for Canada and Mexico. Telex has exchanges in principal cities, and there is an extra charge if the message is going to a locality that doesn't have an exchange. The TWX uses phone lines and can go where the phones go, but there is an extra charge in remote areas.

### INFOMASTER

Western Union introduced telex, a message oriented system, in 1958. In 1971 it picked up TWX, a message and data oriented service pioneered by AT&T in partnership with Telcos. Western Union then found itself with two incompatible systems. A year later it came onstream with Infomaster, a computer center that allows Telex and TWX units to communicate with each other.

---

# FACSIMILE ("FAX")

---

The most typical facsimile machines use a light-sensing device to scan the page and transmit the pattern via telephone lines to another transceiver, where it's reproduced. Such systems have actually been around for years; they have been in use since the 1920s in the weather bureaus, news services, and law enforcement agencies. But it wasn't until 1966 that the "fax" entered the business market.

There are three basic classes of business fax equipment:

- *low-speed:* transmission speed of 4-6 minutes per page
- *medium-speed:* 2-3 minutes per page
- *high-speed:* under one minute per page

Low-speed equipment dominates the market. About 90 percent of all faxes in use are low-speed. Xerox has the dominant share of the market, with Exxon's Qwip coming on strong and 3M and Graphic Sciences bidding for a piece of the action.

The trend is toward medium-speed equipment as its price comes down. The user will pay no more for medium-speed equipment than for low. With low-speeds now at $150 per month and mediums predicted to cost $40-50 by 1985, experts expect that about half of the fax units will be medium-speed. Their use is growing: The projection is half a million units by 1985.

ADVANTAGES

- *exact copy.* What you see is what they'll get: words, numbers, and pictures exactly as they are on your in-house copy of the fax. Useful for transmitting charts, graphs, ads, etc.
- *speed.* Transmission is immediate, and reasonably fast.
- *virtual error-free transmission*
- *no "rekeyboarding"*
- *no special training needed to operate*
- *easy to install*
- *sender keeps original*

DISADVANTAGES

- *cost.* You've got to rent the equipment and pay for phone lines. When you talk fax, you talk phone charges. And when you are sending a three-page report on a low-speed machine, that's a phone call of around fifteen minutes. Compare that to the cost of mailing the report and, well, it's expensive. A few insiders say that the phone companies make more on the fax systems than the fax manufacturers make.
- *two machines required for each message.* You can't send a message to someone who isn't equipped to receive. And there are relatively few fax units around. Many companies arrive at a decision jointly with a client or associated company to install a telecopier; for example, a Madison Avenue ad agency and a midwestern food processor may agree that "faxing" ad and other promotional material for approval and revision will be cheaper than overnight package services and other methods of meeting deadlines.
- *no intelligence.* A few faxes have simple chips for limited storage, but most are dumb; they only scan and transmit.
- *incompatibility.* Most machines can't communicate with those of other manufacturers, or even with those of the same make that have different speeds. But look for some changes. Graphic Sciences has a model that can switch speeds, and Xerox has come out with a machine that can communicate with most other models.

  A committee has been set up to create an *international standard.* But as of this printing, about 80 percent of the machines are low-speed models, such as the Telecopier 400, and don't meet the proposed standard.
- *scanner method.* The fax machine scans the entire page, transmitting information in black-and-white. It looks at between

67 and 200 spots per inch. That's a lot of information to transmit—much of it about blank space.

IN THE FUTURE  The vendors are working on ways to reduce the scanning process so fewer "spots" are required. More speed should mean lower cost. Future users of faxes will tend to be smaller firms, or smaller offices of larger firms. Communicating WPs and other computer based message systems (CBMS) will replace them in larger firms, where more sophisticated equipment makes sense economically.

---

# MAILGRAM

---

Quicker than mail, cheaper than phone, this is the granddaddy of electronic mail; you've probably sent or received at least one Mailgram in your time. Mailgram is a joint venture by Western Union and the Postal Service. Messages are received by Western Union's Infomaster computer centers in Missouri and Virginia and sent via land lines or satellite to a post office center (there are 141 in the United States). There the message is printed out and delivered by carrier the next day.

APPLICATIONS  Excellent for all types of one-way messages, Mailgrams are widely used for price change announcements, political party mailings, sales promotions, publicity and PR, and just about anything that requires impact. *Mailgrams get opened right away.*

SEND A MAILGRAM MESSAGE VIA:

- "800" telephone number
- telex or TWX
- Western Union office
- computer or communicating WP
- magnetic tapes or other standard computer generated input

DELIVERY  Mailgrams are deliverable in the first mail delivery on the following business day. (Although this is not guaranteed by the Postal Service or Western Union, the service is monitored, and reliability is generally high.)

OTHER MAILGRAM SERVICES

*Stored Mailgrams.* Texts and lists that are frequently used can be stored for access from a terminal. Formatting and editing capability is also available, so you can alter and update a "boilerplate" mailgram.

*Redilist.* Western Union will store your mailing list in its computer, to be used on demand for transmission of any message requiring Western Union services.

---

*Confirmation copies.* A copy of the Mailgram goes to the sender.

*Certified Mailgram.* Signed receipt is returned to sender.

*Business reply.* A response form and window envelope are delivered with the Mailgram.

*Datagram.* If you are really in a rush for a reply, you can include a special Datagram "800" telephone number. The recipient phones in the reply, which is then transcribed and delivered instantly to the sender via Telex or TWX.

*Money order.* You can use the Mailgram service to wire money. But first you have to open an account with Western Union or use a charge card. Western Union will then redeem the money order sent by Mailgram.

*Graphnet.* This is an over-the-counter service providing same-day delivery. The message is sent via telephone tie lines or telex or TWX. It is sent on a "store and forward" basis and provides delivery in less than two hours. The recipient can get the message through a fax terminal, first class mail, messenger delivery, pickup, special delivery, or telephone delivery (a confirmation is mailed after the call). If you need to send something in a big hurry and you have no wire service or fax equipment of your own, this is a good, speedy alternative if you are near a Graphnet office.

## DISADVANTAGES

*Little personalization.* A Mailgram is not a letter. It is meant for succinct communication, and if it is being sent to hundreds of people, you can forget the "How's your sick mother?" bit.

*Limited intelligence.* Storage, editing, merging, etc. Most of the things that communicating word processors and computer based message systems can do, Mailgrams can't.

*Privacy.* Forget it. It's almost impossible to send a confidential Mailgram, because it passes through so many offices and hands.

---

# COMPUTER BASED MESSAGE
# SYSTEMS (CBMS)

---

This special form of electronic mail allows the user to be alert to the flow of messages—and to control the flow. For example, you can access incoming messages at your convenience. Once received, a message can be disposed of (erased) electronically, filed, or passed along. CBMS

---

leave tracks—they can be traced back to the source or forward to the last person to see the message. Obviously, such a system reduces filing tremendously. The biggest disadvantage is that the system usually requires executives to be near the terminal and operate the keyboard. Do not be shy about learning to use the terminal. A computer is not a piece of secretarial support equipment. It can be, and often is, a strategic device that aids in decision making. Status should come with the introduction of a terminal to your desk territory. This is one area where you shouldn't be afraid to buck the system. Be the first one on your block to have a cathode ray tube on your desk top. It's the wave of the future.

Computer based message systems are now available from Compuserve and Umex, with systems on the way from ITT (Compak), and Bell (Data Network).

## CBMS ADVANTAGES

SPEED AND EFFICIENCY   These systems can handle up to 30 pieces of routine correspondence per hour. Compare that with the five or six phone calls you could make during that time; the three letters you could write; the one, maybe two meetings you could engage in.

NONSIMULTANEOUS TIME   Use your time the way you want to. Solve problems when you want to. In the case of a completed phone connection, both you and the other party must be "tied up" at the same time. Chances are that one of you is being pulled away from another high-priority task. With CBMS the sender can lay down the message at his convenience, and you can receive it at yours.

PRIORITIZING   The beauty of this system is that you do not have to deal with messages on a chronological basis. The first message of the day may be the last one you actually read. The computer provides a list of all the messages on tap; you pick and choose. Some systems even allow a high-priority signal, which lets you know that an important message is coming in.

INTERRUPTIONS   Really cuts them down, especially those that are phone related.

COSTS   CBMS are not cheap. They run from 75¢ to $1 per message, or a minimum of $500 per user per year. But, as I've pointed out throughout this section, the most expensive part of the office budget is labor, and the most expensive part of that is executive time. Used correctly, the CBMS could save an exec hours each day.

# TRENDS IN ELECTRONIC MAIL

Everyone is getting into the act, offering or planning to offer some form of electronic mail or transmission service.

**ECOM.** This is the Electronic Computer-Originated Message Service, brought to you by the United States Postal Service. It's really a souped-up version of the Mailgram. Although it is marketed by the Postal Service, Western Union computers are involved. It's aimed at high-volume users with high-level computer setups. This system guarantees overnight delivery for first class mail. The messages come into the post office terminals, where they are printed, put in envelopes, and shot into the normal mail flow.

**SBS, or Satellite Business Systems.** This system is a joint venture of IBM, Comsat General, and Aetna Insurance. It uses satellite communication networks to provide extremely high-speed transmission of data, voice, facsimile, and conferencing, all on a multiple access setup. Big stuff.

**XTEN.** The Xerox Telecommunications Network, a microwave transmission service.

**ACS, or Advanced Communication Service.** This service, from AT&T, will be compatible with the five types of terminal protocols that are used in 75 percent of the terminals now on the market.

**GE MARKLINK** will utilize GE's existing time-sharing system.

**BNA** will link Burroughs computer systems with each other and several other suppliers' computers, so that smaller units will be able to tap the capacity of larger ones.

## TELECONFERENCING

Video was once the sole property of television networks. Then came the cable systems. Now comes the business community. In the near future, many of the electronic transmission networks will be able to set up a conference in which people interact via voice, video, or pure data, without the necessity of shared physical proximity. Recently, a special report in *Fortune* magazine cited an SRI report done for the National Science Foundation. It found that about 50 percent of all business travel could be obviated by electronic alternatives. The same *Fortune* report also quotes George Gantz, of the New England Energy Congress, who claims that even by the year 2000, this replacement of travel with electronic communication will conserve only about 1 percent of the total American energy bill.

That's a problem, because energy savings could have provided a great incentive to switch to teleconferencing. Things will move slowly, because it will take time for the facilities to become widespread and for executives to alter old patterns and get used to newer means of doing business. Nevertheless, we're more familiar with teleconferencing than we probably think. For years now, news programming has resorted to interviews via video transmission. Watching Rather in New York interviewing Mitterand in France live, no longer seems strange. So when the time comes for you to have a teleconference with a J.B. who's a thousand miles away, you shouldn't be too rattled.

Upper management spends approximately 80 percent of its time communicating. Middle management spends 60 percent. So electronic mail is not to be taken lightly.

## ADVANCED PRODUCT TESTING TECHNIQUES

With electronic mail, companies will be able to gather information about their goods and services from test markets and analyze them much more rapidly. Thus, products will fly—and die—at a much faster pace. This eventuality will also mean further market fragmentation, with vendors appealing to more specific and numerous market segments—resulting, in turn, in more choice for consumers and more alternatives for vendors. And this should (with heavy emphasis on the "should") be a very positive development for the free market system, since smaller companies can thrive by zeroing in on a small, but specific market. On the other hand, the huge corporations, usually slow as elephants in capitalizing on small markets, will have the equipment and facilities to move more rapidly. For example, will the large appliance manufacturers be able to generate millions of "one of a kind" models and cut into the market of the prestige manufacturers that are selling to the small numbers of people who are willing to pay for something different?

## IN DEFENSE OF PAPER: A PERSONAL TRIBUTE

I have used them all...CRT terminals to edit and retrieve vital information, facsimile machines to transmit a brilliant ad to a client's home office for approval; I have searched out little-known articles in obscure journals by scanning microfilm and microfiche; I have sent telexes, TWXes and Mailgrams, and stored manuscripts in the memory of standalone WPs. In every case, one is working with electrons, magnetic charges, bits of celluloid, or sophisticated optical manipulation of characters. But there is no question—and the experts in the industry bear me out on this—that plain old paper is here to stay.

Perhaps I'm sentimental; I don't think so. Paper is personal, and it has purpose. It may be the only medium that we will be able to command better than computers in the years to come. More important, a close examination will reveal that it is not as primitive as the tech boys and girls would have you believe. In fact, it'll probably take decades for the new office technology to catch up to ordinary paper.

You can do things with paper that are far beyond the capabilities of primitive information tools like CRTs, microfiche, and microfilm. You can fold it and stick it in your pocket. You can get it copied "on the street," in thousands of copy centers, or at a coin-op in any library. You can curl it, or curl up with it—in bed, in the sauna, by the pool, on a plane. No terminal is necessary. You can write on it. And it costs very little. It will not erase during a power failure. You can doodle, draw diagrams and little pictures. You can show it to your spouse, your kids, and your parents, so they can swell with pride over your work. And they can show it to their friends.

- FACT: Approximately 82 percent of all correspondence is still originated by some writer, somewhere, putting pen or pencil to a piece of paper.
- FACT: Office paper sales are still growing, currently at a respectable 7 percent.
- FACT: The reading or recording of information on cathode ray terminal displays has been shown to be significantly more fatiguing than reading or writing on paper. And some rumblings about unsafe radiation emitted by CRTs are heard now, too!
- FACT: When was the last time you received a perfume-scented computer-originated letter?

# 37

## OFFICE SECURITY

Before we enter the world of vibration sensors, vaults, and hidden microphones, let's consider a few basic points:

**There is no such thing as a totally secure office.** A security system can reduce vulnerability, but not eliminate it. The difference in the type of protection is measured in the extent of vulnerability of the office. As you learned on "Mission Impossible" and "It Takes a Thief," there is no such thing as an impregnable office.

**Security is not an industry with a large discount market.** Bargains are few and far between. And there are even fewer exceptional values. A good security system that is also cheap is a contradiction in terms; such systems don't exist.

**A security system is a system.** What isn't a system these days? Each piece of equipment must be viewed as part of the whole.

**Once installed, the stuff must be used.** Professional burglars know that security systems are often not turned on. And these guys are great at playing the odds, picking the office with the switch box that hasn't been opened in weeks.

---

## EQUIPMENT

---

**Locks and keys.** Locks have been used for over 4,000 years. And for 4,000 years, the bad guys have been trying to pick them. It's a little tougher nowadays. Some of the newer locks, such as those by Medeco, Illinois Duo, Sargent, Keso, Eagle Three Star, Mela, Fichet, and Miracle Magnetic are highly pick resistant, because they use special keyways and keys. A good lock will insure that it takes a long time for the intruder to gain entry by breaking the lock through mechanical means. If he decides to blow the door, how long it'll take depends on how tough the door frame is. Many locks have a registered key system that prevents duplication by unauthorized personnel. This is a good idea, but it can be quite a nuisance. Some locks have a built-in alarm, which sounds when tampered with.

**Glazing.** Glass doors, windows, and showcases have always been a problem, because it's one thing to prevent them from being opened, quite another to prevent them from being smashed or broken. One way to deal with that problem is to tape *foil strips* to the window. They conduct electricity and act as a continuous circuit. Presumably, when the glass is broken, the tape and, simultaneously, the circuit is broken, and this triggers the alarm. However, if the burglar has a simple glass cutter, he can cut a hole without breaking the tape, stick his hand in, and release the latch. Or wriggle through the hole. A better solution is the *vibration sensor,* now being touted by Honeywell and others. This, as the name implies, is triggered by excess vibration. Laura Payerlee, of Honeywell, told me that even the slightest pressure on the glass will trigger the sensor, so that no tampering is possible. I hope that birds can't trigger it, or moths flying toward the light. Certainly, if you work in a neighborhood where lots of baseball and football is played, a four-bagger or an incomplete pass could have the whole PD down on the backs of the kids.

Another modern form of glazing protection is surprisingly unelectronic—*tougher glazing material.* Unbreakable, polycarbonate transparent materials have been developed. They look like glass, but are difficult to break, because, among other things, they are less brittle. Plexiglas has been eclipsed by GE's Lexan, which is guaranteed unbreakable. It costs two to three times as much as glass and scratches very easily. Lexan MR-400 is still more expensive, but it won't scratch as easily. The container of my food processor is made of Lexan, and it is certainly tough. Another tough glazing product is similar to auto safety glass. It consists of two pieces of glass bonded together by a layer of tough, transparent vinyl. It can be broken, but the effort takes quite a while and creates lots of noise.

**Lighting.** Lighting should be sufficient to heighten the chance of detection of an intruder. You don't have to light the entire office, just key points of possible entry so the security personnel can have a clear view. Lighting must be able to operate for an extended period of time in a blackout, brownout, or emergency.

**Safes.** There are two types of safes, and both, like door locks, are intended to *resist* burglary, not prevent a determined, expert assault.

**Money chests.** For cash, jewels, and other valuables. These chests will resist burglary tools for one hour or more. Most are suitable for mounting, or anchoring, in a concrete floor. They won't protect against heat or severe temperature change.

# TYPES OF SECURITY SYSTEMS

**Access control systems.** These systems use cards or special keys inserted into a slot, allowing access by electronically releasing the locks, unlatching doors, or activating elevators. Such a system can be a real science fiction gadget: Some of the newer ones will respond to identification of a profile of the hand, fingerprints, even signatures, the patterns of which are stored in the computer for recognition. Texas Instruments has developed a voice-activated device that is now in use at the Department of Defense. (It is rumored that beeps sound in a guardhouse when the device detects a Russian accent.) Some systems keep a record of who entered, at what entry point, and at what time.

However, these security access systems are only as good as the lock and alarm system they are built around. If the access is wired to some cheapo lock that can be picked with a paper clip or a Visa card, it won't keep an intruder out just because he doesn't have a special entry card, a key, or an authorized set of fingerprints.

**Surveillance/intrusion systems.** These systems will detect the presence of an intruder. The critical element is what the system does when the intruder is discovered. Some merely sound a built-in alarm. The assumption is that it will frighten off the intruders, or that someone, upon hearing it, will phone or otherwise summon the police. Not a good idea. We buy security systems to protect us from, alas! human nature. What good is an intrusion system that relies on that very element? Too often, no good at all. Any good system should be connected to a remote monitoring site, such as the police station or a private security service.

**Intrusion detection methods.** *Contact devices* act as mechanical switches, breaking a circuit when disturbed. The foil strips mentioned in the glazing section are one type. Another is the *common contact plate*—one element on the door or window, the other on the frame. The device is triggered when the plates are separated. A *string-pull alarm* does the same thing with a string—for example, one stretched across an air conditioner. If an intruder tries to push the air conditioner back into the building from the outside (so he can enter through the hole), he will push against the string, which will be pulled and go off. The key issue: How reliable are the contact switches, and how sensitive? Will they stick, rust, break, crack? Can a burglar outfox them with a light touch? *Pressure-sensitive pads* or mats can be placed under carpets or mats and will go off when triggered by the weight of the intruder.

More sophisticated intrusion detection systems may use:

- *microphones* that detect noise
- *microwaves* or *ultrasonic waves* to detect movement
- *infrared heat sensors* to detect body heat radiation
- *vibration sensors* to detect vibrations
- *intelligent closed circuit TV* specially equipped to digitalize image and detect changes in the grey scale. In other words, this system senses the presence of an intruder by the change in light value. The cameras are of the low-light type, and a time-lapse videotape recorder can be added that will record any incident.

Again, it is worth noting that these systems *detect* the intruder. They don't capture him, or, necessarily, even scare him off. So it is up to people to respond. If your premises are monitored, make certain that the security service or local police are prompt and professional. Go to great pains to avoid false alarms: Never rule out the "boy who cried wolf" syndrome. Some systems use a recorded tape and phone line system, which, when triggered, dials the police number and plays a tape providing the location of the intrusion.

**Integrated security systems.** Larger corporations and office complexes increasingly are linking security systems together so they can be coordinated from a single security command post, or "war room." The integrated systems can provide controlled access, fire detection and suppression, intrusion sensing, closed circuit TV monitoring, communication with security guards walking a beat and with sentries.

**"Bug" detection.** There are firms that will periodically "sweep" the premises to uncover any hidden microphones or recording devices. Bug detectors can be useful if you are in an industry rife with corporate espionage or attempts to uncover "blind bids." You can purchase a portable model for your own use.

---

# FIRE DETECTION/SUPPRESSION

---

**Sprinklers.** Sprinklers are the most common; the valve melts under heat and the water sprinkles out. They can also be connected to an audible alarm.

**Smoke alarms.** These are becoming very popular because they provide an early warning: Often, smoke forms before blazing heat and fire. Besides, they avoid the water damage caused by sprinkler systems. They use photocells to detect particles in the air. Beware, however:

**Intrusion Detectors**

| Device | Operational Mode | Pattern | Approximate Range | Comments |
|--------|------------------|---------|-------------------|----------|
| Acoustic | Listens to sounds | Omnidirectional | 25-foot radius | Basically open microphones placed in the protected area. Filters out extreme high- and low-frequency noises; discriminators cancel some sounds. These sensors work best in protected areas with background noises low and continuous. Systems can have listening monitor and two-way communication (talk-back) capabilities. |
| Sonic | 4,000-8,000 cycles transmitted and reflected Doppler signals | Omnidirectional | 25-foot radius | Sensor triggered by object moving toward or away from the sensor. May be set off by moving objects such as curtains, doors, etc. |
| Ultrasonic | 18-45 kHz. Transmitted and reflected Doppler signal | Omnidirectional | 15-30 foot radius | Does not go through walls or building materials. Best used indoors because of extreme sensitivity to motion. |
| Microwave | 2.5 to 10.5 gHz. Transmitted and reflected Doppler frequency shift principle | Fan-shaped, sausage, and cigar-shaped beams. | Varies with antenna configuration. May cover up to 10,000 sq. ft. | Goes through many building materials; can be set off by moving objects and interfering radar systems. |
| Infrared | Passive detector senses change in radiated heat | Omnidirectional, fan or cone shaped | 20-foot radius | Will not go through walls or other construction materials. May be set off by hot objects such as radiators, heaters, incandescent lights, and the sun. |
| Infrared/ laser | Electro-optical Pulsed beam | Line of sight | up to 10,000 ft. | More advanced laser systems are not troubled by adverse weather conditions. "Fence" capability with stacked transmitter/receiver set up. |
| Capacitance | Electrical capacitor creates protective field, change in capacity signals alarm | Omnidirectional | Inches-10 feet | Unaffected by noise; good short range protection. Often difficult to tune or set up. Self-tuning, self-adjusting devices best. |
| Vibration | Vibration conduction | Omnidirectional | 30-foot radius | A specialized type of contact microphone attached to walls, floors, ceilings, or protected object and senses attempts to penetrate the protected surfaces by force. |
| Photoelectric | Light beam-photocell | Straight line | Up to 1000 ft. | Beam can be pulsed and modulated. Use of mirrors can create angled and criss-cross patterns. |
| Video | Change within detection of motion zone | Omnidirectional | Varies with camera and lens | Not affected by noise, heat, etc. Senses change in existing static pattern, such as brightness. Needs lighted area. |
| Seismic | Low frequency vibration in the ground | Omnidirectional | 25-50 ft. | Disturbances on the surface, when they exceed a preset amplitude, are sensed by a geophone and an alarm signal is activated. Subject to triggering by ground tremors caused by trucks, noise, etc. |
| Stress | Flexing in structural members cause changes in resistance of sensor. | Omnidirectional | 15-ft. radius | Sensor is affixed to structural beam which flexes. Unaffected by noise, heat, outside signals. |
| Electro-mechanical | Shorting or opening of a continuous circuit | According to device | Determined by protected surface | A simple system of a continuous circuit around walls, ceilings, doors, and windoes. Includes metal foil, switches, and pressure mats. Simplest and cheapest of all alarm systems. |

Fig. 56. Intrusion detection systems
From Jan Reber and Paul Shaw, *Executive Protection Manual*
(Northbrook, IL: MTI Teleprograms Inc., 1976), p. 122.
Reprinted by permission.

**Access Control Systems**

| Type | Description | Features |
|------|-------------|----------|
| ID cards | Usually a laminated card with the name of the individual plus signature and photograph | Basic cards use photographs and signature plus data on ordinary paper; the card is sealed by lamination. More advanced cards provide security and forgery resistance in the following ways: use of watermarked papers; photograph printed on special paper; fine line, two color overprinting from engraved plates; fluorescent overcoating detectable by black light; optically readable codes; hidden data printing; magnetic stripe coding; and backside two-color overprinting from continuous fine line patterns not registered on the front of the card.<br>  Purposes, or classes or card holders, can be distinguished by graphic design or use of different colored coding bars, letters, etc. |
| Card/card-key | Electronic access readers: system employ various coding elements including lettering, mechanical hole position, optical or magnetic tape, radio frequency signals. Card must be inserted into a compatible reader; the reader will examine the card and validation will activate the access controlling mechanism. | Access is limited to a "valid" card. Some systems have multiple-mastering features, enabling a quick change of access control codes. |
| Coded units (for electric door strikes and door operators) | A keyless, coded push button control device which supplies the proper voltage to the locking (electronic) mechanism. | Code must be in the proper sequence to open access control mechanism. |
| Cards/codes | These are combinations of card readers and coded units. Both the card and a memorized code are needed to gain access. The card is inserted in the reader and a "password" code is entered on a touch keyboard. | Since two elements are involved, a greater degree of security is provided.<br>  "Passwords" or codes are usually a four-digit memorized series of numbers which must be tapped on the touch keyboard. |
| Hand geometry/card reader | Verification using an individual's hand geometry characteristics which are measured and compared by a machine; these measurements are compared against data previously encoded on the individual's card — also read by the machine. | This technique is based on a computerized statistical analysis of glove measurements for Air Force pilots.<br>The study concluded:<br>— Hand geometry is a distinct human, measurable characteristic that can be related to individuals.<br>— Tolerances can be established so that the probability of a particular individual cross-identifying can be reduced to one out of thousands. |
| Signature verification | A measure with respect to time of the pressure applied to a writing instrument when one signs his own name. | Statistics show that each person's "pressure pattern" is unique to the individual and remarkably constant from one signature to the next. Since the technique is only indirectly related to signature appearance, the "pressure pattern" of a forgery is totally different from the genuine signature. Each "pressure pattern" is a distinct personal characteristic which is virtually impossible to duplicate and relatively easy to measure.<br>  To enroll in the system a person taps out an assigned identification number on a keyboard and then signs his name several times with a special ball point pen. Signature data are transmitted to a central processing computer which develops a signature "standard" data base for the individual. The standard is then stored in the system's memory. |

Fig. 57. Access control systems

From Jan Reber and Paul Shaw, *Executive Protection Manual*
(Northbrook, IL: MTI Teleprograms Inc., 1976), p. 128.
Reprinted by permission.

These alarms are sensitive. A very prestigious Wall Street brokerage firm hired a young whiz-kid analyst. This guy turned out to be the office guru, who spent his idle time meditating. He had a habit of lighting incense, and since his desk was directly under a smoke detector (he said he didn't smoke), he started a minor panic (brokers are used to panic) when he lit up a stick of Mysore sandalwood.

**Portable extinguishers.** Good investments. Keep them charged. Also good for office Christmas parties, when someone always makes a jackass of himself by squirting someone.

**Record cabinets.** More accurately described as insulated filing cabinets, protect records against prolonged exposure to heat. They are not burglar resistant, so they are not for cash. There are two types of cabinets, one for paper and one for magnetic records. *Paper* cabinets will keep their contents unscathed in temperatures up to 350° F. *Magnetic media* cabinets will protect up to 1700° F for several hours, and are also good for film and fiche records.

---

## BUYING SECURITY EQUIPMENT

---

**Watch out for the "Watch Mr. Wizard" syndrome,** in which you might be led down the garden path by a deep-rooted fascination with gadgets, gizmos, mojos, any metal box with a black matte finish, LEDs, LCDs, and alarm noise that sounds like it's notifying you of a reactor malfunction on the Bàttlestar Galactica. The Mr. Wizard syndrome attacks the part of the brain known as common sense and twists it until you've made a foolhardy purchase in which you've overpaid, gotten more than you need, or, worse, gotten something that is not adequate to your needs.

**Play Show and Tell.** Make sure that the salesperson shows you the equipment in operation, on an actual site if possible. The "tell" part alone is not enough.

**Conform to Underwriters Laboratories standards?** More important than you might think.

**Do a little research.** Get the names of some of the users. Talk to them about the equipment and find out how they feel about it. See if you can arrive at an estimate of the average time between failures and average downtime, or time it takes to repair.

---

**Check out the vendor.** Word travels fast; it is not that tough to find out about a vendor. Has he got a reputation for reliability? Competence? How well are the technicians trained? Does he stock a ready supply of spare parts? And—very important—does he offer 24-hour maintenance service? "I'll send someone over in the morning" may be too late.

**Shredders.** This is a simple (but final) security device that protects against privileged documents falling into the wrong hands. Shredders do exactly what the name tells you—they shred paper sheets so that they come out in a form reminiscent of shredded wheat cereal. Nobody can read or photograph or reassemble a document or computer printout that has been through this process.

Shredders come in several sizes, depending on capacity and power. Many are designed like wastebaskets, so shredding and disposing are accomplished in one motion.

Electric Wastebasket, of New York, makes models that can take two or three sheets at a time and shred up to 2,500 pounds an hour. Many will shred plastic cards, blueprints, and even light metals, and most will take staples and clips. Shredded paper can be sold for recycling.

---

It's only natural that security people would associate to share information, resources, and professional contact. Today many associations have committees, divisions, or specialists concerned with protection of assets from loss. They are found in such fields as banking and finance, airport management, retailing, the pharmaceutical industry, truck transportation, and many more. But the following list is of organizations primarily organized for security or security-related purposes. Membership, when given, is provided by someone associated with the organization.

*Airport Security Council,* 97-45 Queens Blvd., Forest Hills, NY 11374. 212-275-9300. Founded in 1968 to deal with airport crime in the NY/NJ Port Authority area. Exec. Dir.: Edward McGowan.

*American Polygraph Association,* 3105 Gumwood Dr., Hyattsville, MD 20783. 301-779-5530. Members: 1,300. Exec. Dir.: Walter F. Atwood.

*American Society for Industrial Security,* 2000 K St., NW, Washington, DC 20006. 202-331-7887. Members 12,300. An international organization of security people from all aspects of commerce and industry. Exec. Dir.: Ernest J. Criscuoli, Jr.

---

Fig. 58. Guide to security and security-related organizations
(*through page 496*)

Reprinted with permission. © 1980, Security Letter, Inc.

---

*Association of Credit Card Investigators,* Box 813, Novato, CA 94947. 415-897-8800. Members: 1,000. Exec. Secy.: Eve D. Wydajewski.

*Association of Federal Investigators,* Suite 824, 815 15th St., NW, Washington, DC 20005. 202-347-5500. Members: 2,000. Started as an association for Civil Service Investigators. Exec. Secy.: Louis T. Williams.

*Association of Former Agents of the U.S. Secret Service,* Box 31073, Washington, DC 20031. 301-894-2115. Members: 300. Exec. Secy.: Floyd M. Boring.

*Canadian Association of Chiefs of Police,* Suite 1002, 116 Albert St., Ottawa, Ontario K1P 5G3. 613-233-1106. Exec. Secy.: J. W. Paul Laurin.

*Central Station Electrical Protective Association,* 1000 Vermont Ave., NW, Washington, DC 20005. 202-628-4634. Members: 50 companies. Manufacturers of alarm systems and supplies. Exec. Dir.: Raymond J. Lloyd.

*Computer Security Institute,* 5 Kane Industrial Dr., Hudson, MA 01749. 617-562-7311. Members: 1,700. For managers with an interest in EDP security. Exec. Dir.: John C. O'Mara.

*EDP Auditors Association,* 7016 Edgebrook Lane, Hanover Park, IL 60103. 312-837-5739. Members: 3,000. Admin. Sec.: Marian King.

*Harnass Tracks Security,* 150 E. 42nd St., New York, NY 10017. 212-682-7074. Members: 40 tracks. President: John L. Brennan.

*Independent Armored Car Association,* Rapid Armored Truck Corp., 254 Scholes St., Brooklyn, NY 11206. Members: 35 companies. Secy.-Treas.: Ernest W. Moreau.

*International Association for Hospital Security,* Box 3776, Merchandise Mart Sta., Chicago, IL 60654. Members: 1,000. President: Thomas Kramer.

*International Association of Arson Investigators,* 97 Paquin Dr., Marlboro, MA 01752. 617-481-5977. Members: 4,600. Exec. Sec.: Robert E. May.

*International Association of Chiefs of Police,* 11 Firstfield Rd., Gaithersburg, MD 20760. 301-948-0922. Members: 11,000. Conducts tests of security equipment and other services. Exec. Dir.: Glen D. King.

*International Association of College and University Security Directors,* Box 98127, Atlanta, GA 30359. 404-261-8136. Members: 500. Exec. Sec.: James L. McGovern.

*International Association of Credit Card Investigators,* 1620 Grant Ave., Novato, CA 94947. 415-897-8800. Members: 1,000. President: Robert E. Hoskey.

*International Association of Security Services,* 188 W. Randolph St., Chicago, IL 60601. 312-332-2257. Members: 325. Exec. Dir.: Howard Ross.

*The Jewelers' Security Alliance of the U.S.,* 6 E. 45th St., New York, NY 10017. 212-687-0328. Members: 4,800. President: James B. White.

*National Armored Car Carriers Division,* Suite 200, 6165 Barfield Rd., Atlanta, GA 30328. 404-394-7120. Members: 20. Secy.-Treas.: James Campbell.

*National Association of School Security Directors,* 310 102 Ave., NE, Bellevue, WA 98004. 206-455-6000. Members: 250. Exec. Sec.: Harry W. Wilson.

*National Automobile Theft Bureau,* 390 N. Broadway, Jericho, NY 11753. 516-935-7272. Members: 425. Bureau maintains data related to theft and damages related to automobiles. President: Paul W. Gilliland.

*National Burglar and Fire Alarm Association,* 1101 Connecticut Ave., Washington, DC 20036. 202-857-1130. Members: 550. Exec. Dir.: Garis F. Distelhorst.

*National Council of Investigation and Security Services,* 1101 Connecticut Ave., Washington, DC 20036. 202-857-1157. Members: 120. Founded in 1975, later incorporating members of the National Association of Private Security Organizations. Managing Dir.: Brian R. Cassedy.

*National Crime Prevention Association,* 985 National Press Bldg., Washington, DC 20045. 202-393-3170. Members: 400 individuals and corporations. President: Wilbur Rykert.

*National Security Industrial Association,* United First Bldg., 740 15th St., NW, Washington, DC 20005. 202-393-3620. Members: 250 companies. An organization concerned primarily with national security. President: Lt. Gen. Wallace H. Robinson.

*Security Equipment Industry Association,* 3310 Airport Ave., Santa Monica, CA 90405. 213-390-8756. Exec. Dir.: Donna H. Joseph.

*Society of Former Special Agents of the Federal Bureau of Investigation,* Suite 2754, 370 Lexington Ave., New York, NY 10017. 212-687-6222. Exec. Secy.: Fran Keogh.

*World Association of Detectives,* Box 5068, San Mateo, CA 94402. 415-341-0060. Members: 450. Secy.-Treas.: Vance I. Morris.

# 38

# THE OFFICE ENVIRONMENT

As an occupant of an office, and as a person who may one day have to take on the responsibility of "office planning," you should know at least something about the raging debate that has polarized people and resulted in factions being formed on both sides of the partition—or the office door, as the case may be.

## OFFICE SPACE PLANS

### THE CONVENTIONAL OFFICE

This is the kind you played in when you visited Dad fifteen years ago, and the kind you probably fidget in when you visit your accountant or lawyer today. This is an office with a strict quadrangular configuration. The outer offices run along the periphery, and that means they have windows. These are sometimes called "perimeter offices." Then comes some hall space, and an inner row of offices parallel to the window offices. In the center is an open area, often called the "bull pen."

THE CONVENTIONAL OFFICE PECKING ORDER

- *The perimeter offices are for the honchos.* And if you've got *two* windows, you're really special. This is the senior executive turf. A corner office with windows on two walls is usually claimed by a chief executive officer or a partner.
- *The inner offices are for the junior executives.* No windows, but at least there's a door, and an area you can call your own.
- *The bull pen is for the lower echelon and support personnel.* It's like having your desk in the hallway. No privacy. It's tough to swear or sulk out here, because you are utterly visible.

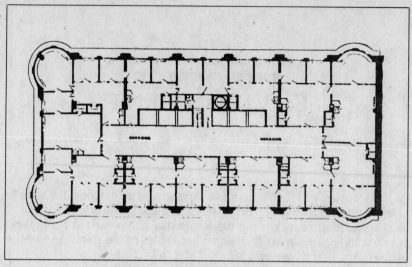

Fig. 59. Conventional office layout
This floor plan shows the design prevalent in older office
buildings with individual offices constructed as part of
the building. This plan is of a floor of the Old
Colony Building in Chicago, built in the 1890s.

Reprinted in John Pile, *Open Office Planning* (New York:
Watson-Guptil, 1978), p. 15.

## THE OPEN PLAN

The open plan, or OP, is a catchall term for several approaches. The oldest and most radical of these is often called the office landscape. Here it is, in theme and variations:

OFFICE LANDSCAPE   This plan was formulated in Germany in the late 1950s and, thanks to some well-staged seminars and support from designers, found its way to the United States in 1968, probably on the heels of the hula hoop of furniture styles, Danish Modern furniture. Instead of enclosed offices, there are free-form groupings, or work clusters. (In their brochures the vendors use lots of terms that sound like they were lifted from a scientific monograph on beehives.) These clusters are not arranged in rows, but, rather, fill the space in a way that is optimal for the work flow and the flow of human traffic. To avoid a surfeit of eye contact, the clusters are bounded by free-standing screens, partitions, or plants (sometimes they're real). The furniture units are the epitome of sleek: no "desks"; rather, simple drawerless tables. Some of the units are so sterile, they could double as operating rooms.

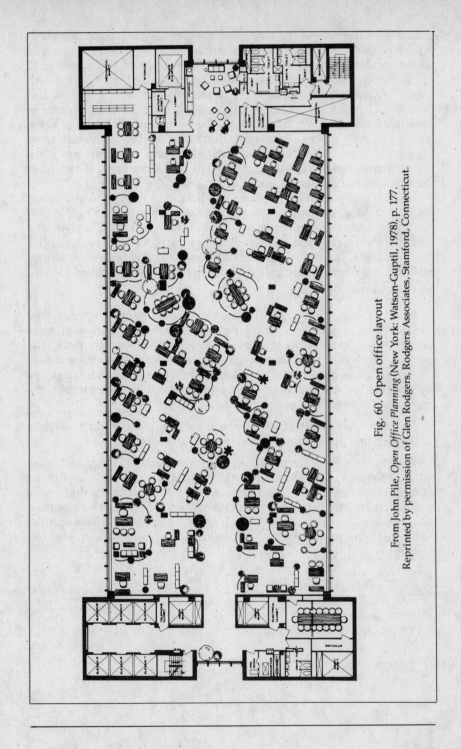

Fig. 60. Open office layout

From John Pile, *Open Office Planning* (New York: Watson-Guptil, 1978), p. 177.
Reprinted by permission of Glen Rodgers, Rodgers Associates, Stamford, Connecticut.

499

The thinking behind the landscape concept seemed sound. Research has shown that employees work better when there is more sunlight, a feeling of contact with the outside environment, and some feeling of territoriality. The office landscape delivers these conditions, along with flexibility that allows the office to be designed according to flow and function. Besides, it seems to fit in with our thinking about the American way of doing things. Since the open plan has no fixed walls and no closed offices, there is no imposing feeling of hierarchy or status. A "team" psychology is fostered by this environment. It's a more "democratic" approach. And what are Americans, if not team players and democrats, lovers of football and the Constitution?

You can easily see why the firms that first went with open offices felt they were doing something special. But the officers couldn't quite part with their status offices. For much though we love team spirit, we love being rewarded even more. And we are, of course, rugged individualists. Today, management continues to cling to its own offices, pleading for privacy. The office landscape had to be modified.

DESIGN APPROACHES

*Panel or Component Systems.* These systems are "hard" versions of the landscape, in which work areas are clustered around partitions that are sturdy enough to support various hanging *components*—desk, file cabinets, shelves, phone stand, etc.—in almost limitless configurations. This type of system has almost totally replaced the pure landscape approach. It's more system oriented and locks you into the components made by the vendor of the partitions.

*Modular (Work Station) Systems.* These are groupings of units, usually L-shaped, that are made of wood, metal, or plastic.

*The American Plan.* Here's the stroke of real genius. Henry Kissinger, in his memoirs, characterized American diplomatic style as that of compromise. And where the changed imperatives of office diplomacy and office formatting converged, compromise we did. Why not have the best of conventional and open plan? Why not have private offices for the upper level execs, a few conference rooms, and an open plan for the rest of the office?

|  | Con | Pro |
|---|---|---|
| Personal Offices | The people in the middle get screwed, as usual. They lose their modest 9′ x 12′ with walls and a door. | The open office offers something for everybody. The biggies still have their inner sanctums, but the support personnel wind up with an area they can call their own. Everybody gets some personal turf. |
| Privacy | In a conventional office, you have the option of closing your door. Many experts feel that the open office may actually impair the performance of high-powered, tough, shrewd employees. Without an office to shut them in, they feel inhibited and less likely to take risks or to "do it their way." | In a conventional office, privacy is just another way of saying that the door closes. Most people either don't want that closed-in feeling or don't want to seem standoffish, so they keep the door open most of the time, and this practice encourages socializing. In this situation the only way to counter interruptions is to position your desk so your back is toward the door. This is creepy and uncomfortable. With an open plan, you can create an L-shape, which gives you a side opening: People don't approach you head-on when they walk by, but will face you if they walk in. Such entrances are difficult and costly to design in a conventional office. |
| Noise | The conventional office insures quiet working | An open office has many "personal privacy |

environment, free of distracting outside noise. When someone is in your office, he hears you, rather than the person in the next work station. In the open office, sounds and speech travel over the panels.

zones," which actually provide greater opportunity for quiet, clear communication. The noise problem can be solved with careful placement of panels to deflect the path of noise. And the newer sound panels are very sound absorbent.

Some people hate "white noise"—they find it distracting.

Artificial white noise can also be used. It blocks out sound without interfering with work. Portable units can be set up as needed.

*Psychological Aspects*

The closed office system sets you apart from the rest of the office. It is conducive to concentration. Closing the door says to others, and to you yourself, that you mean business. It's a great tonic for turmoil. When you have no door, you feel powerless against the raging storm outside your cubicle.

We are an adaptable lot. Before long we will look upon our work stations in much the same way as we look upon our closed offices. Ensconced in them, we will feel removed from the turmoil and very private.

*Productivity*

Improvement in productivity isn't really attributable to the open office. It's merely a coincidence: Open office plans are usually implemented in conjunction with a new office or location, which in itself usually boosts morale and generates a "start-fresh" feeling. New offices also mean better lighting, better color,

The open plan improves productivity.

and more sensible layouts.

*The future?*    The jury is still out. Many of the innovators are going back to basics.    According to a Harris Survey of office environments, conducted in 1978 and polling over 1,000 workers, 87 percent of the business executives and 91 percent of the architects in the sample believe that the open office concept will continue to grow.

This, in a nutshell, is the state of the current controversy. The proponents of "OP" are gaining. About ten thousand offices have gone to open plan in the past five years, with predictions that put American business at about 45 percent open as of this printing. Why? The atmosphere is democratic, humane, and individualized for the majority of office personnel. There are increases in communication, flexibility, and, some say, in productivity and efficiency.

Studying extensive surveys and arguing the pros and cons rarely convince anyone to enjoy the OP environment. If you like it and feel that it works for you, it does. Some find it quieter to work behind partitions and feel that they function more efficiently in the open system. Some of the support workers feel that the system is designed to discourage their talking to each other while they work. But it doesn't seem to work that way. A typist employed in a newly converted office in Manhattan's McGraw-Hill building told me, "It used to be that I could talk to my friend while we both typed, or opened and sorted mail. Now, we go around the partition to deliver something and wind up talking just the same. The only difference is that we can't work *while* we talk."

REASONS FOR THE GROWTH OF THE OPEN PLAN    As usual, it all comes down to dollars and cents. The top-of-the-list advantages of open office cited by the Harris survey respondents were:

*The flexibility factor.* Office layout can be changed quickly and cheaply, so office "downtime" is reduced. Changes can be made in layout over a weekend; it used to take months. True, but such changes aren't made often, and since office physical plant costs are such a small part of overhead and labor is such a large part, shouldn't the worker preference carry a higher priority? That depends....

*Greater adaptability of office space to individual job functions.* Very true.

503

If you get a CRT for your desk, your area can be redesigned around it in a jiffy. Got a word processor or a centralized dictation unit coming in? You can make a WP or dictation center and have it waiting for your new gizmo.

And then there are these other possible cost savings under the open plan:

*Installation.* Although many claim OP units cost less to install than drywall, it has proven difficult to generalize. No clear pattern has emerged.

*Space.* There are claims of savings at 20-25 percent of floor space. Such claims are hard to evaluate, because open office usually coincides with office reorganization—which almost invariably means better use of space and sometimes also means a reduction in the work force. There is no doubt that OP increases the utilizable *vertical* space: The sheer number of partitions increases the possibility for shelves, cabinets, and other add-ons.

*Energy.* Open office allows for "task lighting" instead of inefficient overhead. The general illumination in the office can be lower, with individual lighting requirements attended to as needed. A CRT reader may want lower light or indirect light so that the screen is easier to read. Someone who handles lots of paper may wish more light. The task lighting is fixtured to the partition of the component system. At present such lighting equipment is rather costly and a bit too weighty to move around.

HOW TO SET YOURSELF UP IN AN OPEN OFFICE   In your office, OP may be a fait accompli. If so:

*Try to get a spot near the back.* All considerations of work flow aside, you don't want a visitor to see you peering out from behind your screen just as he gets off the elevator. You want an insulated feeling that conveys status.

*Keep your area absolutely immaculate.* Work spaces are designed to facilitate work. They have lots of shelves and drawers and desk area—spaces that are meant to be used. But since such work stations are not offices, people don't treat them with the same care that they would afford a room. Shelves tend to get untidy, and papers are left on the desk. This is okay for sleeves-up kind of work. But you want to impress upon your visitor (and your boss) that you are a decision maker, not a paper pusher. So an aesthetically stark look—clean, empty desk, neat notebooks and binders arranged artfully on the shelves, pen-and-pencil set, pictures of the family—will make your spot stand out.

*Try for a good space allocation.* The current average is 125 square feet per worker. That's not bad. It's a little larger than that 9 x 12 area rug at home. But the hitch is that, as with all averages, some workers get more, others less. Make sure you get more—maybe even enough for a bric-a-brac shelf or a coffee unit or something totally useless.

## IF THERE IS NO OPEN PLAN, BUT ONE MIGHT BE COMING

*As soon as you hear the news, begin building a case for getting one of the perimeter offices that will be left.* One junior executive I know at an ad agency started having lots of meetings with clients at the agency rather than at the client's office. He tried everything: ordering up breakfast for the client; showing him particularly scrofulous video cassettes on the office machine. Soon he had the client hooked; he loved to come there, and the exec always told his secretary to hold all calls during the client's visits. Now, I might add that this fellow was first-rate—he did a bang-up job. When the office went OP, it was decided that the juniors would get partition space, but would have several conference rooms to use as needed. Our friend very graciously pointed out to upper management that he had a very heavy meeting schedule (he even submitted his daily record for the past several months) and suggested that he didn't want to hold back his co-workers by monopolizing conference space to meet with a single (but very important) client. The brass decided that it made more sense to give the guy his own fixed-wall office. The idea was that whoever had that account would get the office, so no favoritism would be shown. But the junior exec has an even larger office now. He is a senior exec.

*If they ask for office-renouncing volunteers, don't do it.* You might be tempted because you'd like a change. Or because you want to show that you are "with it" and very adaptable. But once you give up your office, there is usually no going back. Possession is nine-tenths, and all that. If you want a taste of OP, there are other ways of getting it. If you are curious, spend a few hours in your secretary's cubicle when she is out sick.

*Don't get uptight.* OP may be an irreversible trend that will put everyone in the same boat. Thus, a fixed-wall office, if you've got one, will be a real status symbol, because they're so rare, but the lack of one won't be a negative. And with the current trend in freewheeling, "hands-on" management, maybe even the CEOs, in a fit of team spirit, will abandon their corner offices, just as some answer their own phones or open their own mail.

The current "final word" on OP is the Louis Harris survey on the office environment, commissioned by Steelcase, the world's largest manufacturer of open office systems. Steelcase obviously hopes that the results of this survey will help gain acceptance of its products. In any case the firm should be commended, because the study is well balanced and fair, and although the suggestions are somewhat bland, the findings are not. To obtain a copy, write:

Steelcase
1120 36th Street S.E.
Grand Rapids, Michigan 49501
Ask for "The Steelcase National Study of Office Environments."

YOUR NEEDS VS. THE COMPANY'S  The office environment is another case of balancing your own needs and desires with those of the corporation. If you are too selfless, you will quickly become part of the furniture...a component. If you assert yourself too much, you'll become known as the person who is only out for himself. The power-tripper philosophers, like Michael Korda, while accurately pointing out the potential pitfalls of the open office plan and how it can impede your rise to the top, are a bit aristocratic in perspective.

A bad spot in the office is like a sand trap in a golf course. Tricky, and tough to get out of, but how big an obstacle it is depends on how well you play the game.

TO LEARN ABOUT OPEN OFFICE PLANNING  The very best book on the subject is *Open Office Planning*, by John Pile (New York: Whitney Publications, Watson-Guptill, 1978). Intended for interior designers and architects, this extremely readable and profusely illustrated book examines the various approaches to OP. It is plainly biased against the conventional office, but attempts to examine the various types of open offices with an open mind.

Contact:
Watson-Guptill
1515 Broadway
New York, New York 10036

---

# THE BUSINESS LIFE OF PLANTS:
# OFFICE GREENERY

---

Indoor plants are all the rage these days—and the dead and dying are in evidence everywhere. Plants require care and attention. As a result of the plant boom, a new vocation has been created: the plant doctor, who, for a fee, will make house calls, either to heal the sick ones or to administer routine physicals or preventative care, which usually consists of examining the underside of leaves for plant acne or some such thing, making sure the soil is not too wet or too dry, checking on the location of the plants vis-à-vis sunlight, trimming, cutting, replanting, root untangling, etc.

Plants are still selling healthily. And although it is not crucial for any reason whatever to have plants in your office, there are many good reasons to have a few around:

---

- *Plants fight sterility.* Many offices lack sufficient windows, fresh air, and/or warmth of design, and plants add color, character, and a touch of nature to the environment. If the effect on your mood is positive, then why not go ahead?
- *They can serve a design function.* Well placed and arranged plants can serve as visual screens that can be employed to obscure the view of the executive's desk when the door is open, or to divide an office or work space into two separate areas with two separate functions, for example, work area and meeting area.
- *They enliven the air.* Some will tell you straight out that their plants make the air in the office fresher, cleaner, more "lively" and humid. Such benefits have yet to be proved. And there aren't enough plants in most offices to have any significant effect on the air.

## CHOOSING PLANTS FOR THE OFFICE

- *Light.* Where is it? How much have you got to work with? Include both window and electric light. Fluorescents can actually benefit certain plants.
- *Temperature.* Consider the overall temperature levels and, more important, the levels in the places you've singled out for the plants. Placing them near ducts is usually a no-no, because blasts of warm or cold air or sudden changes in temperature will harm most plants. High-heat areas will naturally be better for succulents, which like it hot and dry.
- *Humidity.* Central heating usually means dry air, which is bad for most tropical plants. If the air in your office is dry, get a humidifier or go with the old tray-of-water-under-the-pot approach.

Once you've considered the three variables mentioned above, find a knowledgeable person to recommend plants for your office conditions. Several books are very helpful, but so are the proprietors of reputable plant nurseries and stores accustomed to dealing with office gardening.

Buy from a reputable source. Stay away from florists; they know less about plants than specialists, and they often charge much more, because they are gift-oriented. Find sources that offer advice free of charge, and see if you can get a guarantee. Some sources will give cash credit if a plant dies before the guarantee elapses. If you must have a specific plant that is less than ideal for your growing environment, be prepared to make the necessary adjustments, using humidifiers, grow lamps, etc.

Your first plants should be of the smaller, green foliage variety (examples are philodendrons, dracaena, and ivy). These are the most hardy, and they are less likely to die from your mistakes. The spider plant and cast iron plant do especially well under fluorescent light. Once you have the hang of it, you can go on to trees, shrubs, and even flowers.

## THE CARE AND FEEDING OF PLANTS

USE TEPID WATER   Water from the office cooler is often too cold, or, if from the red spigot (perish the thought), much too hot. Go to the john, where you can regulate the water temperature, or to the kitchen if you have one.

ROTATE PLANTS FOR EVEN GROWTH   Especially if a plant is by the window. Since plants grow toward the source of light, a plant kept in one position will lean.

WASH YOUR PLANTS   Using warm water and a damp cloth, wash the leaves carefully. Do this several times a year, or have someone else do it several times a year.

USE FERTILIZER WITH CARE   "The more, the better" is a myth. Your goal is a healthy plant, not a dress rehearsal for "Jack and the Beanstalk." Too much fertilizer can harm a plant, or weaken it with too rapid growth. Keep fertilization down in winter.

GROW LIGHTS   Office light is often sufficient for sustaining plants. When there appears to be a problem, it's often the result not of insufficient light, but of poor positioning. Sometimes a grow light with a timer is necessary. Get some advice on this.

DON'T SPOIL THE PLANTS   Some businesspeople tend to treat plants like neglected kids—give them lots of anything but care. Don't overwater, overfeed, or overcrowd plants. They have different requirements and should be fed and watered accordingly. Don't crowd them together; it's unhealthy. If it's too much trouble to keep up a consistent watering schedule, get fewer plants, or get someone else to help.

## PLANTS AND APPEARANCES

A few attractive, well-positioned plants will spruce up your office and enhance its appearance. But don't overdo it. An office that looks like the Amazon or Tarzan's digs won't do. And forget growing herbs or tomatoes in your office. You do not want to come across as Farmer Grey.

An overabundance of plants signals that you are trying too hard to be with it. Or that you have a certain revulsion for the work space and are trying to bury the business environment with some kind of "Garden of Eden" overkill.

Even worse is allowing sickly plants to remain untended in your office. This signals neglect; better to have no plants at all.

# 39

# THE AUTOMATED OFFICE: SURVIVING IN STYLE

Offices are automating so rapidly that most of you will already have had some contact with much of the equipment mentioned. The methods of introducing office automation are as diverse as the number of firms involved, and the same holds true for the executives involved. This chapter is an attempt to help you meet the challenge of the office of the future, and to anticipate some of the problems you may encounter.

## CONVINCING YOUR BOSS: WHAT YOU MAY BE UP AGAINST

Bosses always like people who have new ideas, who keep pace with the times. As long as those new ideas don't cost them too much money. The key to convincing your boss to automate or to purchase some otherwise wonderful piece of office hardware is not to show that it won't cost much, but that *it won't cost anything!*

**Know your stuff.** Find out everything there is to know about the equipment in question. Get some price quotes and comparisons. Check out competitive models and service.

**Compute the costs.** Not just the costs of the equipment, but of the current situation. Include the cost of equipment, supplies, space, manpower. The idea is to demonstrate that this is the new approach, a sound investment that will enhance the company's competitiveness and general economic well-being. Only you can judge how far and how detailed you'll have to go in your analysis. Maybe you'll have to run time/motion studies. Evaluate work procedures and show how they can be improved. Remember: The biggest attraction of office automation is reduced manpower. This doesn't necessarily spell layoffs. It can mean *fewer people* doing the same work done at the same level of service; or it can mean *more work*, increased level of service with the same people. If it's not one of these two, you're going to have problems. *For the only way to cut costs significantly in a modern office is by saving employee time, which saves money.* (One exception—a file system that goes micro can save a good deal in square footage; but unless the office has tens of thousands of files, the saving is not significant).

**Make the presentation.** Remember those numbers about industrial productivity (up 90 percent in the last decade) vs. office productivity (up 4 percent). Now, the only way to effectively increase office productivity is to (1) eliminate jobs and nonproductive work and/or (2) make workers more efficient and effective.

Give the boss a complete economic evaluation, covering, essentially:

- *the cost of the present system.* How it works.
- *the cost of the new system.* How it will work.
- *the value of time to be saved by the new system*
- *the expected rate of return on investment.* Example:

$$\frac{\text{total investment}}{\text{daily savings}} = \text{days required}$$

Convert to months and apply a rule of thumb: It should pay out in 12-18 months, unless it's a giant computer or something of that magnitude.

After you get the go-ahead, you'd better make it work. The boss goes on the line for the money allocated from the budget on the strength of your argument. If your theory does not transfer to reality, it'll look bad for him—and for you. So if you are in doubt, hold back. Or if you think it can't wait, but you aren't 100 percent certain, say so, thus transferring at least part of the risk to the person upstairs.

---

## A BASIC PLAN FOR
## INTRODUCING OFFICE AUTOMATION

---

**Generate some paper.** Prepare a report that discusses the purpose and objects of your program. Include a schedule for your plan and a sample questionnaire for an evaluation survey. Surveys and polls are "hot." They are often used as a basis for an office automation plan.

**Arrange a trial run for equipment.** If you can pretest the equipment, so much the better. In some cases, you might wish to hold off on introducing any equipment until you've made a strong case "in theory," based on your survey.

---

**Spill the beans.** Tell everyone what you are going to do. Use a memo or meeting to describe the survey and smooth out a few feathers before they get ruffled. You want as many of your colleagues as possible on your side. Fear of office automation can usually be equated with fear of the unknown.

**Take your poll.** Give out the survey; collect the survey. You can also use work sampling techniques—for example, look at workers' logs with an eye toward production, or the number and types of documents generated. Personal interviews are valuable too. You'll get some juicy quotes and a more "grass roots" idea about how things are going.

Vendors can be very helpful in structuring surveys and helping your personnel understand the machines. But be wary. They can structure your survey in a way that skews the results in favor of their own objectives.

**Perform data reduction and analysis.** Collate results and prepare a statistical analysis.

**Generate some more paper.** Summarize the results of the survey, and draw conclusions from your findings. But please: Make your summary short, to the point, succinct, comprehensive.

**Your big moment: Present the results.** Don't sell so hard that it looks like you are being greased by the vendors. Just present the facts, projections, advantages, cost analysis, cost effectiveness, return on investment; etc.

---

# ADJUSTING TO THE OFFICE OF THE FUTURE

---

We've all known for quite some time that technology is accelerating change at a rate that is just barely tolerable by human consciousness. The problem is, no executive wants to flip out his staff with a "Buck Rogers" desk and filing cabinet, but no executive wants to be left behind, either. As a manager, your job is to balance the two concerns—human and technological—to produce the optimum effects.

The modern executive himself has to do a bit of adjusting. Office machines are no longer just for the underlings. The notion of having a desk top so sleek and so empty of working tools that it resembles the top of a coffin is going by the wayside. Instead, your desk might look like mission control at the Houston Space Center or something off the set of *Dr. Strangelove.* But what is required is more a cognitive change than a change in personal habits or methods. We must be able to package information so it can be utilized by machines with electronic intelligence. Even more important, we must learn to accept and use whatever data the machines spit back, converting it into the kind of information our brains can use. Personnel changes mean making certain adjustments, so why not look at learning to interact with automated office equipment as learning to adjust to—and exploit—a particularly weird set of friends and co-workers?

---

# TRENDS TO WATCH IN
# OFFICE AUTOMATION

---

There are three primary factors affecting the future development and availability of office technology:

**Advances in technology.** Each year, improvements in manufacturing techniques and new breakthroughs *drive costs down*. According to the International Data Corporation study in *Fortune*, October 8, 1979, the cost of communications is shrinking at a yearly rate of 11 percent, computer logic at a rate of 25 percent, and electronic memory at an astounding 40 percent.

The cost of data processing will be cut by more than a factor of ten during the eighties. The price of storage will decline 80-90 percent. The cost of transfer will shrink with the advent of satellites, fiber optics, microwave and other technologies. Now, more efficient forms of input/output, such as ultra-high-speed printing, are cutting costs.

Everything in the industry has succumbed to the "small is beautiful" psychology, and increased miniaturization is making each generation of WPs and other equipment more intelligent without making them larger.

As electronic parts replace mechanical ones, maintenance becomes easier and cheaper and the fabrication costs go down.

All this adds up to lower prices, or, at least, more for your money. But this advantage is offset by another factor. (No, it's not greed this time, although that was a good guess.)

**Marketing costs.** The gremlin here is marketing costs. They remain high. This is a very tough, ultracompetitive marketplace, with every guy more than three years out of M.I.T. going into business with his wedding stash or his rich friend's trust fund.

The companies that get ahead must do it one of three ways: by advertising a lot (difficult for companies on limited budget) or by price cutting (which reduces profit margin) or by designing in some unique feature. Quality in this industry is generally quite high, so it's difficult to rely simply on building a superior product.

Another cost problem is operator training. When you sell a machine, you've got to train the staff how to use it. That means instructional manpower and materials. And they cost money.

In the future, look for an increasing trend toward user-engineered items, programmed so the training costs can be reduced substantially. Firms will also take a more sophisticated look at "positioning" and designing products for a segment of the market, rather than the market in general, thereby reducing competition to a manageable amount. This will work only if office automation spreads across the board. If it remains heavily concentrated (within communications, banking and finance, and mail order industries), positioning won't work. You can't design for a market segment that isn't interested in buying your stuff.

**User awareness.** A product is more difficult to sell when the potential buyer is more sophisticated. The managers who buy office equipment are much hipper today than five years ago. Managers should know at least the basics about what a machine is supposed to do, and what their own needs are. Vendor salespeople can no longer do a "quickie survey" in the office or try some demo-and-fast-talk roadshow and expect to sell. No one is interested in gimmicks. Everyone wants features that they can use, not the option of playing computer battleship during the coffee break, and having the office lights blink and the dictaphones playing "Rule Britannia" every time a ship is sunk.

Salespeople realize this and are changing their approaches, so you can expect a bit more straight talk in the future. Nevertheless, keep your guard up.

Another thing. More data processing people are getting involved in office automation designs and purchase. They see that a marriage is inevitable, so they want to have a hand in choosing the best equipment for their purposes. Unlike the average manager, the data processing people understand how these gizmos work.

## THE TREND TOWARD COMPONENTS

Used to be that the central processing unit was the most expensive part of the automation system; so peripherals were designed as slaves to the central processing unit. Now, intelligence is cheap. As a result, the peripherals themselves have built-in-microprocessor intelligence, making them more flexible and independent so that more sophisticated configurations are possible.

According to John J. Connell, of The Office Technology Research Group, "The Office of the Eighties will consider the human equation first and tailor the machinery accordingly. Technology must be humanized, adapted to different styles and capabilities. It cannot be developed as the computer was, with emphasis on bits, bytes, bauds and other technological terms."

---

## WHAT IT WILL ALL MEAN

---

The best study of the implications has been done by The Diebold Group, a New York based consulting firm. Some of the more important conclusions:

**We will be able to "pick and choose" our work.** What Diebold calls "the entrepreneurial work force" will become a reality. With highly advanced methods of telecommunication, electronic mail, data storage and computation, executives can be more selective, doing the kinds of things they want to do and having other work parceled out to others or to a machine.

Since the automated office can serve to interface the work of one executive with the work of others, it will be less crucial that the executive be in the office often, or simultaneously with other members of the staff. Imagine that a car could be designed by a team of designers, draftsmen, and engineers in different parts of the country. Each member of the team could assess all or any blueprints, sketches, or specifications and send an inquiry or a suggestion from a terminal. Obviously, a few brainstorming sessions would be in order. But that's just the point: *The executive, freed from the tedium, will have more time to devote to creative activity.*

Years ago, executives could get ahead on the strength of things like "reliability," accuracy, and long hours worked. In the future, wits will count more, because the computer will be a great equalizer in the area of office routine—everyone will be more accurate and thorough. You'll need more than that to earn a promotion.

The "knowledge workers" of the future will be more independent and, therefore, more able to keep up with their own specialties. They will have more time to devote to maintaining a "state of the art" expertise.

**The executive work space will become a communications center.** You'll be equipped to assess information from computers, construct models, even engage in teleconferencing. You will be able to do things that only a few years ago were the domain of NASA and its billion-dollar budget—such as communicate via satellite.

---

514

**The real estate broker will take on another function—that of information broker.** All this automation requires very sophisticated and complicated hookups and access and configurations. Office buildings will be equipped with a variety of services, such as advanced phone circuitry with a computerized exchange and switching that will serve the entire building, connection to major info networks and electronic mail, and even a dish antenna on the roof to assess the satellite based services. Thus, the real estate agent will be a retailer offering a wide variety of information services. It is very likely that such an approach will allow the realtor to purchase the services at wholesale rates and/or commissions and then mark up the costs to the individual tenants.

**Workers will be more flexible and independent.** Especially in the white-collar area, automation will bring an increase in flexibility in hours, compensation plans, job descriptions, and salaries. Although this will make payroll much more complicated than it already is, the computer will make that job easy to manage.

**The home office will probably be commonplace.** With all this talk about independence and remoteness from the workplace, it is natural to conclude that you could place a terminal in your home and work from there. Many executives have already done so, if only to supplement their office activity or to provide themselves with a way of staying in touch if their preferred residence is in a rural area or in a city other than the one in which their office is located.

Almost every piece of equipment mentioned in this chapter can be assessed, communicated with, or otherwise instructed from your home, assuming the proper equipment is in place. Lots of experts, including The Diebold Group, believe that the advent of the home-office configuration is just a matter of time. But a few disagree. Success in business, they say, demands a creative and dynamic environment, with the constant interaction that is provided only by continuous presence in the workplace. Company politics, power games, one-upmanship, and all the subtler aspects of the business success game would be hard to play on a computer terminal. Thus, some pundits go halfway and predict that the remote offices will be set up wherever businessmen tend to gather—and that could mean a country club, corporate "club," etc.—anyplace but the home, which is the one environment that the executive wants to keep relatively off-limits from the demands of his job.

Personally, I tend to agree that a "change of scene" is psychologically essential for effective work. But I don't think that we know for certain how that will be accomplished in the future. Some experts have suggested that there will be "office rooms" in dwellings, designed specifically as such by home and apartment builders. Others believe that shared offices will spring up—several friends will pool their resources and take an office to their liking, even though they all work for different corporations.

---

### IN A "CLASS" OFFICE...

Whether in the office of the past or the future, some values remain constant:

- Coffee is served with milk instead of "nondairy creamer."
- The magazines in the waiting room are up to date.
- There's a place to hang your coat apart from the hook on the inside of someone's door.
- You don't have to be an electronics expert to get an outside line on the phone.
- When you need a photocopy, you don't get the same reaction as you would if you wanted access to the company safe.
- Last year's calendar isn't left on the wall until May.
- When you call, they don't play Muzak while you are on hold, so at least you can speak to someone in your *own* office without hearing a plastic version of "Yesterday" going in the background.
- You can obtain entry to their bathroom without having to call an impromptu general staff meeting to find the key.
- You are served tea in a real (nonplastic) cup, and you are given a place to put the teabag.
- Care has been taken not to hire a receptionist who tells you that Mr. Jones's office is the last door on the left when it's last door on the right.
- There are always enough chairs.

# 40

# PERSONAL ACCESSORIES AND APPOINTMENTS: EXECUTIVE STYLE

Ever since primitive man picked up a rock and a stick, tools have been vitally important. Modern man has perhaps added a new dimension: No longer is the usefulness of the tool the only thing that counts. The *look* and *feel* of one's possessions can convey a great deal about who one is and how one thinks. Let's look at a few personal items that every executive should own, paying careful attention to form, function, and the image conveyed.

## THE FIRST IMPRESSION: STATIONERY

In many cases, your initial business contacts are made by mail. Stationery can say a great deal about you and your company.

**Paper.** The *composition* of paper is wood pulp and cotton—the more cotton, the better. So the cheapest paper is all wood pulp, the most costly all cotton; and in the middle are various wood/cotton blends. Invest in all-cotton paper, or something very close to it.

The *weight* of the paper is also important. The rating in pounds is the weight of 2,000 8½" x 11" sheets of that paper. The higher the weight, the thicker the paper. Go with paper in the 20-24-pound range.

A translucent symbol impressed during manufacture, the *watermark* is usually the name or logo of the paper company. All fine papers have watermarks.

**Letterhead size.** *Letter size* (8½" x 11") is the most commonly used format in business. But there is also *monarch* (7½" x 10½"), usually reserved for the personal letterheads of upper level executives. Monarch carries prestige. But if you have some monarch made up before your time, don't send it to people who know your status. You'll just look silly.

**Printing.** There are several methods:

- *offset.* Cheap, and looks it. Avoid.
- *thermography.* Glossy letters with a raised feel. Thermography produces an engraved look for less money than true engraving. It's acceptable in most cases.
- *engraving.* The cleanest, sharpest, and best. Your stationery will impress, provided the recipient can tell the difference. Expensive.

**Color.** White or off-white—go no further. You can jazz it up with tasteful colored inks—blues, browns, greys.

**Logo.** This requires a great deal of thought. While you needn't spend hundreds of thousands, as many Fortune 500s do, it pays to hire a designer. Whenever I see an inappropriate or unattractive logo, I ask who is responsible. The results of my survey to date: 75 percent of those logos were done by the spouse of a key executive. The logo should convey something about your company. If you don't want to commit the time or the funds, go with your name and address only, set in a simple type style.

---

## THE BUSINESS CASE

---

The function of a business case is to transport important papers and small items from one place to another. But in the current climate of first impressions, the case you carry your papers in says as much about you as what's inside. Well, almost.

If the contract is a good one, you should be able to bring it over in a knapsack and still make the deal. But since every executive chooses a business case at least once every couple of years (if not more often), you should consider what goes into making the right choice:

**Try to stay thin and light.** You should not carry lots of work around with you. The successful executive is not snowed under by paperwork. He's a decision maker. And final decisions don't take up reams of paper. The one exception is a lawyer. But even lawyers are succumbing to the "thin" look. For trips to and from home, many lawyers use a briefcase with capacity for several law books and large briefs; but they carry a thin portfolio or attaché to client meetings during business hours.

Portfolios have become very popular in recent years, because they are light and elegant. They hold about as much as a large manila envelope. But you can't very well carry a fifty-cent manila envelope around;

you'll look like a messenger. You can spend over a hundred bucks on a deluxe leather portfolio, and everyone will know that you can afford to spend that kind of dough to carry five sheets of paper.

There are underarm cases that are larger than portfolios, but they are in no-man's land—too bulky to have the status of a portfolio and not as elegant as a good attaché.

**If you're buying an attaché, listen to the locks.** A nice clean sound indicates a well-made lock. Also, it makes for high drama when you enter the room, place your attaché on the table, and "click" into action. (Just make sure that you don't open your case upside down.)

An insider's tip: The snap of the locks closing is a sign that you are about to leave. You can use this as a negotiation tool. One lock snapped shut says "I'm ready to leave." Two locks shut says "I'm leaving." You can always open the locks again should your adversary change his mind or his offer. Or if you back off on a bluff.

**If you use an ID tag on the outside, it should be tasteful.**

**The handle should be comfortable.**

**Initials should be very discreet.** Initials on a business case are like initials on a shirt; you don't want to advertise. If initials can't be embossed or otherwise affixed in a tasteful, expensive-looking manner, forget them. Stick-on metallic letters are out.

**Choose leather if you can afford it.** High-quality vinyl looks okay for a while. But it doesn't age gracefully, as leather does. Recently, other natural fabrics have become acceptable in certain situations. Wood such as rosewood or teak attachés and linen or high-quality canvas envelopes are becoming more common.

**Consider your business case to be part of your wardrobe.** You can ruin the look of an expensive suit with a cheap or tasteless case. Embossed designs—eagles, stars, etc.—are out. Tacky.

**Stitching should be unobtrusive.** Thread should match the case color. Contrasting stitching is a no-no.

### WHAT TO LOOK FOR

IN ATTACHÉS   They all have hard sides and a frame, or they achieve the same effect through molded sides.

- *Good quality leather*
- *Sound overall construction*

- *Hardware* (locks, handles, snaps, etc.). Metal should be brass with a brushed or satin finish. This includes the lid stays, which hold the top open.
- *Lining.* A "status" case is lined with leather, suede, or linen.
- *Interior features.* Two or three organizing file compartments.
- *Lock.* If you are concerned about security, a combination lock is preferable.
- *Color.* Men should choose black or a brown. Avoid grey and other neutral colors. Women are safe with the same rules, but can also go with a burgundy or a tan. Stay away from blues, reds, greens, etc. They are not for business.
- *Price.* Expect to spend $200-plus for a good one.
- *Width.* The two-inch model is okay for women, but men should use a portfolio instead if a slim case is what they want. The 3½ inch model is best. Five-inch models can hold a great deal, but they are short on status. After that, the attaché becomes a sample case.

IN PORTFOLIOS   Portfolios are made like handbags. Their leather is softer, and they are lighter in weight than either attachés or briefcases.

- *Handles.* You have a choice of fixed handles, retractable handles, or none at all.
- *Hardware.* Brass.
- *Lining.* Suede, smooth leather, or high-quality fabric.
- *Pockets.* Some portfolios have outside pockets for quick access to items such as a folding umbrella or newspaper.
- *Zipper.* Should be brass, very high quality and heavy duty.
- *Price.* $85 and up.

IN ENVELOPE PORTFOLIOS   Very thin and simple, envelopes have a flap closure or top zipper. The emphasis should be on the quality of leather and the construction. The stitching will be very conspicuous, so it should be of high quality.

Because of the popularity of envelope portfolios, many of the better attachés come equipped with a snap-out envelope.

IN BRIEFCASES   Briefcases have the advantage of expandable sides and top loading. They are also very rugged.

- *Compartments.* You'll find up to four compartments inside.
- *Lining.* Usually, none. If the manufacturer does bother to put in a lining, it's of high-quality fabric.
- *Price.* $100 and up.

# CALCULATORS

## SELECTING A CALCULATOR

Choosing the right calculator for your needs has become almost as complicated as the calculators themselves have become. There are hundreds of models available in a wide range of sizes, shapes, displays, weights, and power sources. And the combinations of functions and features are endless. Tough competition and price cutting practices have led manufacturers to concentrate on specialized calculators, their features designed for specific life-styles and occupations. Executives usually select calculators from one of three basic categories:

GENERAL PURPOSE  If most of your computations involve only simple arithmetic, you need go no further than a general purpose calculator. These models emphasize the four basic arithmetic functions—add, subtract, multiply, and divide. Most of them come with a simple memory, which will store a figure for later use while you continue with another computation. Many have percent keys. Some compute square roots and/or minus numbers.

Besides the advantages of simplicity and a generally lower price, general purpose calculators offer the greatest choice in models. They range in size from "office printing" to ultrathin, "credit card" size. Some come with special add-ons, such as clocks, stopwatches, alarms, and radios. General purpose calculators are built into pens, cigarette lighters, wristwatches, portable cassette recorders, and other devices. Since the basic calculator circuitry is so inexpensive, this trend is likely to continue if the addition of a calculator helps move the product. You'll be seeing them built into attaché cases and appointment books.

Keep in mind that a job change, a new responsibility, or a new investment strategy can render a general purpose calculator obsolete. You might find yourself in need of a more advanced or specialized calculator. But many executives own two—a general purpose for home or travel use and an advanced model for office or den.

SCIENTIFIC  Intended primarily for engineers, technicians, chemists, and others in the sciences, these calculators feature a large number of advanced scientific operations, such as trigonometric functions, logarithms, and metric conversions, and statistical functions such as standard deviation and correlation coefficient. In general, a scientific calculator is not ideal for most business calculations unless (1) it is programmable, allowing you to use business and financial programs, or (2) it is one of the few higher priced, advanced models that feature both financial *and* scientific functions. However, the statistical section of most scientific calculators can be used to solve problems in business statistics. And in cases where business and engineering go hand in hand, a scientific calculator may actually be required to figure costs and profits and perform other business-related calculations.

FINANCIAL   Financial calculators are designed specifically for business executives, financial analysts, and managers. If you often prepare figures, compute interest rates, salary analysis, or projections, or employ technical analysis for investments, a financial calculator can save you lots of time and minimize the possibility of errors. You can also do sophisticated figuring on short notice, which can be a godsend when quick decisions are required. A financial calculator can be especially useful in real estate, insurance, securities, and tax accounting.

The range of available financial calculators is much more limited in size, functions, and design. The manufacturers make models that are quite similar to one another in each price range. But in my calculator survey, Texas Instruments and Hewlett-Packard were singled out by executives who owned financial calculators. "The Hewlett-Packard," says Anthony Candido, of Manhattan Office Products, "is considered the 'Cadillac' of calculators among businessmen," because of its rugged construction and sophisticated features. Both TI and HP claim to have surveyed businessmen for their preferences and incorporated these preferences into the design of their calculators.

## PROGRAMMABILITY

PREPROGRAMMED   Selected, commonly used programs involving complex calculations are permanently built into the calculator. For example, most financial calculators are preprogrammed to compute *compound interest*: All you need do is press the appropriate keys and the computer automatically determines the interest rate, present or future value, or time period. Preprogrammed calculators are less expensive than those you can program yourself, but they are also less flexible. However, if your work involves only standard financial and business computations, you may find a preprogrammed calculator with programs that suit your needs.

KEYSTROKE PROGRAMMABLE This calculator allows you to "command" it to carry out a specific sequence of functions in a specific order; you program the calculator to do so by pushing keys. Then you enter the numerical values and the calculator runs through the sequence, performing the step-by-step operation as indicated in your "program." This feature is a tremendous aid in performing complex and repetitive calculations, and it prevents human error caused by fatigue and the confusion that can result from repetition. However, until you get the hang of it, programming the calculator, in itself, can be tedious, time consuming, and somewhat confusing. Another catch—the "program" you've written will be erased when you turn the power off. So if you spend 15 or 20 minutes keying in the program and you wish to use the same program the following day, you'll have to leave the power on (unfortunately, some have auto shut-off) or program it again. HP makes a "continuing memory" feature and TI a "constant memory" on some models. This solves the problem: The feature will hold the program even when the power is off. Some models are keystroke programmable, but feature preprogrammed computation formulas for the commonly used formulas. Such models are ideal, since most of the time you can get along with preprograms, but you can always write your own when the going gets tough.

FULLY PROGRAMMABLE   The most advanced, powerful, and flexible of the calculators. Fully programmable calculators defy classification as scientific or financial, since they can be whatever you want them to be. In addition to keystroke capability, complex programs are stored on magnetic cards or, in some cases, solid state modules. You can choose from the fantastic library of program cards from the manufacturer; there are literally thousands of programs available. Or you can insert a blank magnetic card and then write your own program. You then have the program stored permanently for whenever you need it. Imagine your calculator computing depreciation, payroll, and inventory, and, a few minutes later, doing your astrological forecast. These machines cost much more money, but they are not likely to become obsolete for some time. And they are extremely versatile, usable as a professional or personal calculator and as an adult toy.

The next generation is more aptly called "portable" or "pocket computers." They are so powerful and so flexible that, as they decline in price and size, are expected to eliminate calculators altogether.

## SIZES

THE HAND-HELD   Quite simply, this is any calculator that you can operate while holding it in your hand. This category excludes only the desk-top calculators and the larger portables, which, although still small enough to put in your attaché case, are not the kind of machine that you would pull out in a restaurant. Most of the hand-helds are plenty small enough—around 6-7 inches high, 3-4 inches wide and 1-2 inches thick. The weights range from 6 to 8 ounces. The printing portables weigh around 12 ounces. All can be powered by rechargeable battery packs or AC. This size makes the calculator quite convenient to keep with your books and papers, and no problem at all to use on the run. However, if you travel light and like to conserve space, you might consider the next category, the palm-size calculators.

THE PALM-SIZE   Here we are talking about calculators 3-5 inches long, 2-3 inches wide, and around ½ inch thick. They are extremely light in weight—3½-4 ounces. This is really a "middle ground" category—smaller than hand-helds, but larger than the latest credit card variety. If you are interested primarily in compactness, these are obsolete. But some in this size range have more functions and larger display capacities than the credit card size. And some will accept AC adapters and/or are rechargeable. Although they are small enough to carry with you in a coat or shirt pocket, you must remember that you'll also have a wallet, appointment book, and perhaps a checkbook and a pen. In such circumstances the palm-size calculator may not seem so small, and you may wind up carrying it in your briefcase after all.

SLIMLINE

*The credit card.* This is the latest craze. Incredibly thin (most slimlines are under 5 millimeters, or 3/16 inch), light (under 2 ounces), and roughly the dimensions of your credit card; hence the name. The slimline is not as flexible, though, so don't try to stuff one into your hip wallet—you might find it bent or broken after you get up from a big meal. This is the calculator to carry with you. Slip it into your jacket hip pocket, even into your vest; it goes virtually undetected. All have LCD readouts, and the batteries, like electronic watch and hearing aid batteries, are small and last a long time. The Canon LC-7 can go 2,000 hours on one battery. The Sharp 8145 is perfectly flat—no protruding buttons. It stores numbers while the calculator is turned off and shuts itself off after a few minutes of nonuse. The big names in this type are Casio, Canon, and Sharp. Casio has gone into it in a big way: Its amazing fx-58 Super Math Card features 31 essential scientific functions, a clock, two alarms, a stopwatch. It runs for 600 hours on two small batteries.

*"Pencil shape" calculators.* These are designed to fit into a breast pocket. About as wide as a few pencils and a little shorter than one, they are favored by those who work in lab coats. Many engineers like them simply because their shape is reminiscent of that primitive tool, the slide rule. Sharp and TI make them in general purpose models; Sharp also has a scientific version.

## FEATURES WORTH LOOKING FOR

- *Automatic shut-off.* The calculator cuts off its own power after a few minutes of nonuse. This saves the batteries.
- *Continuous, constant, or storage memory.* Three different ways to say the same thing—that the calculator will hold a number in its memory even while the power is off. Most calculators erase themselves when turned off. But this feature means that you can store a number as long as the batteries remain good. It's a help if

you have a checkbook balance in the memory, or a figure that you know you'll be using later in the day. Some will even store whole programs for later use.

- *Beep tone and flat keys.* These features are listed together because, at the moment, only Sharp offers them. Sharp's line of thin calculators all have nonprotruding keys, so they are thinnest. This makes it a bit more difficult to tell by touch if you've made the entry. Sharp solved the problem by designing the calculator to emit a pleasant beep with each entry. You can turn the beep off if you wish.

- One of these equipped with a *chronographic device* (alarms, timers, stopwatches, clocks) will be helpful if you are a clock watcher, or should be.

- *"Memo."* With the flick of a switch, the numbers become letters, and you can spell out simple messages on the display. Hit your memory, and they are stored. Useful? Perhaps, if you dislike making notes or tend to lose those little pieces of paper.

### PRICE

A calculator's price may remain fixed for a while, especially if it is unique. But as competition hits the market and the manufacturers recover the initial tooling costs, *they tend to bring the price down.* The cost of materials is not high, so prices can fall pretty far. There are some general purpose calculators available at under $10. They sold for over $50 a few years ago! Shop around. Some stores do break list prices; some have models that are being phased out at fantastic savings. Even the more exclusive stores will run manufacturer authorized "sales." In general, timing is the key. Buy a calculator that's new on the market and you'll pay the highest price. A model that's been around for some time costs less. Prices for calculators sold through the mail, such as airlines gift catalogs, mail-order ads, etc., are generally full list price. Ordering from them may save you time, but not money. Occasionally, mail-order ads, such as those run by JSA in *The Wall Street Journal* and other publications, will feature a calculator yet unavailable in stores. These mail-order houses have made fortunes catering to the gadget buffs who want to be "the first on the block to own...."

## HOW TO CHOOSE A PEN

**Feel.** Never buy a pen without trying it first. It should be well balanced, of the right size and weight for you, and comfortable to write with. The pen should write smoothly at the angle you are accustomed to.

**The nib.** If you're buying a fountain pen, the nib, or point, is the most important part to consider. First decide on a nib size. They are typed according to the writing line they produce, usually double broad, broad, medium, fine, or extra fine. This is largely a matter of taste. With the possible exception of those who require a fine line for ledger entries, men tend to prefer a broader stroke for general writing purposes, and women a finer line.

Most better pens have gold nibs, as opposed to steel. Some experts claim that a gold point provides freer and smoother writing and ink flow. Gold nibs retain their shape and point longer. Practically speaking, though, the chances of wearing out a nib—either gold or steel—are relatively slim. Most people lose their pens or drop them on their points long before they wear them out. And once the point is bent, it almost always has to be replaced.

**Eye appeal.** Pen designs range from the old-fashioned, bulky pens to modern, sleek, understated designs. They come in a number of metallic finishes—gold or chrome, and the now popular "high tech" black matte finish. Plastic cases, of course, come in a wide variety of colors. And recently, Chinese lacquer-coated pens have been introduced in blue, brown, green, and black.

A pen is a personal item, and its appearance should please you above all others. However, since it is also a piece of jewelry, you might consider how it looks on you. Try it on. See how it fits and looks under your jacket. If you tend toward traditional clothing or deal with conservative clients, you might wish to shy away from the avant garde. On the other hand, an advertising agency or engineer might find an innovative design to be just the thing. Indeed, Isabelle Flax, of Sam Flax, Inc., one of New York's largest pen dealers, reports large sales in a pen that is almost completely flat and, therefore, hard to hold and difficult to write with. But, so many executives like the way it looks that they are willing to put up with the discomfort. One such flat pen can be found in the Museum of Modern Art in New York.

**Status.** "Under no circumstances should a man use a cheap pen or pencil in the presence of other men," says John Molloy, author of *Dress for Success.* Your pen is part of your wardrobe. Why wear an expensive suit to an important closing and then take a 29-cent Bic pen out of your inside pocket to sign a million-dollar contract? Gold or sterling silver pens are always somewhat impressive, although gold has become a strong favorite.

There are many "prestige" pens on the market, but experts agree that the Mont Blanc Diplomat (about $185) or its smaller brother, the Classic (about $20 cheaper than the Diplomat), is *the* pen to be seen with. Both are great favorites of professional people. The Mont Blanc comes with a lifetime guarantee and a hand-crafted nib of white and yellow gold that makes it one of the smoothest-writing pens made. The jumbo design is unmistakable, and few will fail to notice it.

Other "status" pens include the Dupont de Paris Chinese lacquer coated pens. The imported Chinese lacquer is applied in France, by hand, in 13 coats (100 hours of drying time between coats), onto a sterling silver casing. The finish is hand rubbed. This pen costs over $200, the exact price varying with the color. Warren Brown notes that the Duponts have become so popular that Sheaffer and Parker have followed suit, offering their own Chinese lacquers. They are less expensive—about $150 for the Sheaffer and $100 for the smaller Parker. Incidentally, Dupont de Paris also makes matching Chinese lacquer cigarette lighters.

**Price.** The price range in pens is enormous. You get what you pay for, up to a point. Gold ballpoints start at $25. Good fountain pens range from $50 to $135. You can't get a fountain pen with a gold point for less than $30. Beyond that you are paying almost strictly for the precious metals in the casing and for unusual design. But if it isn't important to you to have a pen of solid gold or silver, you can get a fine instrument in stainless steel for much less. And there is little difference in the inner workings.

**Use.** Obviously, if you are going to use your fountain pen only to sign your name, you can afford to be less concerned about its "feel." But if you like to write a lot of personal notes, comfort will be important. So the manner and amount of use will affect your choice. If you must sign many carbon forms, you will need a good ballpoint or rolling marker, because you simply can't bear down upon a fountain pen.

BALLPOINT, FOUNTAIN PEN, OR ROLLING MARKER?   The ballpoint has certain advantages over the fountain pen. Its paste ink dries faster; it's retractable; it rarely leaks; and, as just mentioned, it can write through several carbon sheets.

Recently, however, fountain pens have been making a comeback. They have character, both in design and in the way they write. They give your penmanship a distinctive look, and your signature becomes truly personal. Thus, in signing a contract, a check, or other important document, a fountain pen carries more prestige. A fountain pen will write at any angle. A ballpoint is much more limited. Usually you must hold it closer to the vertical than you would have to hold a fountain pen. As a result, many people find fountain pens more comfortable. Improvements in design have all but eliminated the problem of leakage.

Rolling markers are really just another type of ball pen, utilizing a ball that "floats" on a cushion of liquid ink. Conventional ball pens use paste ink. But the thinner liquid ink flows more freely, approximating the feel of a fountain pen. It's something of a cross between a ballpoint and a fountain pen. Rolling markers are good for people who write a great deal, because you don't have to exert as much pressure. Hence, you can write faster and with less effort. And rolling markers will make clear carbon copies. The ink has a slower drying time than that of a ballpoint, but it's faster than fountain pen ink.

Recently, some manufacturers have introduced convertible models. The pen casing will accept both ordinary ballpoint refills and rolling-marker refills, as well as soft-tip refills (the artsy, artifical-fiber tips, like those found in Flair and Bic Banana pens, more suited to doodling or note taking than to business communication). These convertible systems are very popular, their versatility and well-designed outer cases being the primary reasons.

TIPS FOR LEFT-HANDERS   Writing for left-handers is often difficult, and this minority has invented countless methods for holding a pen in order to get the letters to slant toward the right, as our schoolteachers all taught us they should. In order to write in a conventional manner, lefties have to adopt uncomfortable ways of holding a pen.

An *oblique point* is cut on an angle that makes it easier for the left-hander to write smoothly. Parker makes one for its "75" series. Most other pen makers do not supply them. But check some of the older pen shops; many still have some in stock.

Warren Brown, of Arthur Brown & Bros., New York's largest pen shop, has a suggestion for left-handers: If you've already decided on a make or model, ask to try a few pens in the model of your choice. They look identical, of course, but since most better quality fountain pens have a gold nib that is hand finished, the nibs will vary slightly from pen to pen. Keep trying until you find the one that is comfortable. Mr. Brown says that his salespeople will let left-handers try as many as they need to find satisfaction. Most other better stores also adhere to this practice.

## PENS AS COLLECTIBLES

Save Grandma's old fountain pen. It has value as a collectible, and it is likely to increase in value. If it no longer works, repair it soon: Parts are no longer made for older pens, and they are becoming more and more scarce. It might take quite awhile to locate the proper part.

One of the nation's leading pen experts is Cecil (a.k.a. "Dr.") Brown, at M. C. Flynn Stationers, in New York. By his count, he is one of the 14 remaining experts in the United States. Manufacturers refer customers to him when they are unable to fix a pen. He keeps a collection of parts on hand and, often, can make a part if it isn't available. Brown has been repairing pens for over 40 years, and he receives them from as far away as Africa (he will service pens through the mail). Says Brown of his passion for pens, "If you cut me, you'd find ink coming out instead of blood."

Contact:
M. C. Flynn, Inc.
43 East 59 Street
New York, New York 10022

---

# THE EXECUTIVE WARDROBE

---

Who should you listen to when it comes to selecting business clothing? Two arbiters have something meaningful and original to say on the subject and understand the unwritten rules of the business community: John Molloy, who has approached the subject as if he were preparing a PhD dissertation; and Michael Korda, who has brought his typically heavy but experienced hand to bear.

Korda and Molloy differ very little from one another in their advice, except that Molloy is interested mainly in what will gain acceptance and avoid negative reactions, while Korda tells you what successful people wear. In both cases, the message is the same: Stay with a conventional look that will not offend other people, but will make them notice your good taste, your understated elegance, and your appreciation of fine quality. Both implore you to save the Beau Brummel act for after-hours activity. Korda adds that an objective of the "success look" is to look as good at five as you do at nine; to appear unaffected by the elements that may tend to ruffle and undo ordinary folk.

Below you will find a distillation of the advice of Molloy and Korda. If you follow their guidelines, you will have little room to maneuver, but it is unlikely that you will ever wear the wrong thing for business. Still, you should not forget that, in the final analysis, you are the best judge of what to wear. Give your choice of clothes some time and thought: Good taste usually requires some education. In general, if you feel comfortable in a particular style and it is well made and suits you physically, you will look good, no matter the fashion. But remember: Clothes are a statement, a means of expression. If you wear the latest Italian fashions on Wall Street or in the Midwest, you will certainly stand out. If that is your intention, fine; many do this with good results. However, if you feel that a flamboyant or flashy appearance is a risk you'd rather not take, stick to the guidelines.

| | *Molloy* | *Korda* |
|---|---|---|
| HATS | Generally unnecessary. If you must wear one, make sure it's conservative. | Don't wear them. Buy an umbrella. |
| HAIR | Pick a cut that flatters your face. Make sure that your hair is neat at all times. If your ears are big, wear your hair long enough at the sides to cover them a bit. | Get it styled. Try to tone down big ears. You are after the natural look: Avoid too much spray or creams. If you are bald, better to flaunt your immaculate pate than to use any hair replacement method that has even the slightest chance of detection. |
| FACE | Most men should avoid growing facial hair. However, in some cases a beard can convey power or authority. If you decide to wear a beard, make sure it's a full one—no goatees. Keep it well trimmed and shaped, never heavy. Do not wear handlebar mustaches. | Your face should project vigor, health, and energy. Shave carefully and often, even at the office if you have a heavy beard. Get enough rest; and to help eliminate bags under the eyes, bloodshot eyes, and a puffy face, avoid alcohol. |
| GLASSES | Wire rims look better on younger men; plastic or horn rims make you look older. Pick a frame color that complements your hair color. Frames should be heavier if you have a large jaw and facial structure, lighter if jaw and cheekbones are less prominent. | Keep the frames simple. Avoid decorations. Korda likes gold metal frames. |

SUITS

*Style:* Avoid European styling and very fitted suits for business. Never buy a new style the first year it appears; see if it catches on. Do not wear suits with any ornamentation. If you have a large rear end, suits with double vents are preferable. Heavy men should avoid double-breasted suits.

Avoid suppressed waists. Left lapel should have a buttonhole, and there should be 3-4 buttons on the sleeve. Do not wear suits with flared-bottom trousers. Since the object is to appear unruffled at all times, it is wise to avoid sweating unnecessarily—don't wear heavy fabrics, even in winter. Inside, you won't need the extra insulation, and you can wear a heavy overcoat over a lightweight suit to keep warm out-of-doors. Double knit fabrics are acceptable for travel, if in dark colors. Avoid textured patterns, contrasting stitching or piping, or pockets with buttons.

*Color:* You are safe with blues, greys, and beiges, but browns and blacks are not always acceptable.

You can't go wrong with dark blues or dark greys.

*Fit:* Remember that ready-to-wear suits are proportioned for the average man. If you are not "average," the waist, seat, or shoulders might not fit properly. If the fit can't be corrected, don't buy the suit. Measurements should be marked with pins, not merely chalked, unless the alteration is a simple

Custom made suits always fit better, but few will notice unless they wear customs too. Alterations are very important: Don't pay in full until they are done to your satisfaction.

hemline. It is wise to tip the tailor five to ten dollars—it'll help you get some extra attention and care.

*Patterns:* Solids are always acceptable, as are pinstripes, chalkstripes, and subtle plaids. Stay away from gaudy stripes and wide or loud plaids. Donegal tweeds and herringbones, common in fine English suits, are also acceptable.

*Sport jackets and blazers:* Sport jackets and blazers are not a good choice for business. If you wear one, make sure that it is a classic or "status" jacket—for example, a camel's hair jacket paired with simple blue trousers.

Sport coats are acceptable in some businesses, but choose a subdued pattern, such as a lightweight tweed or a small check. Do not wear blazers with badges or coats of arms.

*Miscellaneous:* Keep a fresh, pressed suit in your office for emergencies. Have a sufficient number of suits so that you needn't wear one after the pants have lost their crease.

SHIRTS

*Fit:* Make sure that the shirttail is long enough and that the shirt has a six- or seven-button front so that it will stay tucked neatly in the pants. The waist should fit; fabric shouldn't bunch around the waist. The collar should not be so tight that it wrinkles, and it should have removable stays unless it is a button-down. The height of the collar should be right for the length of your neck—higher for longer necks, lower for shorter ones. Custom shirts are clearly the best; semi-customs are next best.

*Fabrics:* Cotton is the fabric of choice. Cotton/polyester blends have their advantages: They are more wrinkle resistant, and they will look better after a day's wear. However, they don't "breathe" as well and aren't as absorbent. Silks, see-through fabrics, and knits are all unacceptable for business. Avoid shiny fabrics of any kind.

One hundred percent cotton is best.

*Colors:* White is still the safest and the best. Light blues and beiges are also good. The shirt color should always be lighter than the suit you are wearing, and the tie should always be darker than the shirt.

Whites are best. Blue is also worn by successful men.

*Patterns:* Besides solids, crisp thin stripe patterns are desirable; so are subtle plaids. Ginghams, glen plaids, ribbons, florals, etc. are not.

Narrow, muted stripes.

**TIES**

*Pockets:* Shirts without pockets are better. If the shirt does have one, it should be a simple patch style without button or flaps.

Do not put anything in your shirt pockets.

*Miscellaneous:* Short sleeves are out.

*Length:* Usually, a better quality tie is longer. When tied, the tie should fall to the belt buckle—no longer, no shorter. When buying a tie, always keep in mind the kind of knot you prefer, and your height. These factors will affect the length of the knotted tie.

*Fabrics:* Silk is without question the fabric of choice in ties. However, one should avoid cheap or shiny silks. Polyesters are acceptable if they look like silk. Cotton is permissible in the summer and year round in the South. Wools are not good for men with large necks, because the knots are large. Whatever the fabric, you should be able to tie a knot easily, and they should look well with the shirt collar you prefer.

*Patterns:* Solids, small polka dots, diagonal stripes, small repeating shapes, subtle plaids and paisleys are all acceptable. Never wear gaudy ties, picture pat-

The less conspicuous or flashy, the better. Stripes, checks, polka dots, and paisleys are fine. Stay with quiet patterns—no geometrics or sunbursts.

terns, or unusual patterns that are trying to look upon. You *can* go all-solid—shirt, suit, and tie.

*Colors:* Beiges, blues, maroons, and greys. Pastels for summer. Never wear purples or blacks, except as a small part of a paisley.

*Miscellaneous:* Tie clips are no longer needed. Tie should be middle-of-the-road in width—not too wide or too narrow.

**BELTS**

Belts are rarely the problem—usually, it's the buckle. Large, bulky, heavy, or ornate buckles are not good. Stick with traditional, smaller buckles with squared lines.

Belts should be plain, unless you are a real Western style dresser à la J. R. Ewing. In such cases, a belt design is okay. Suspenders are acceptable, especially on lawyers, but wearing a belt and suspenders at the same time is not.

**SOCKS**

Avoid ankle-length or droopy socks. Socks should be dark in color.

No skin should show when you sit down. Over-the-calf socks do the trick. Black is always a safe color.

**SHOES**

Gucci loafers and tasseled shoes are acceptable only in ultra-sophisticated cities. Avoid shoes with too much metal. Wingtips are always safe. Plain laced shoes and simple slip-ons are acceptable. Colors for business are black, brown, and cordovan. Patent leather only works in glamor businesses.

Wear elegant, finely crafted shoes. This shows others that you never have to "rough it," i.e., slosh through the rain and mud to get to work. If necessary, wear hiking boots and change in the office. Shoes should be free of ornamentation or fancy stitching, and they should be shaped like your foot—not too pointy or too rounded. Black is the most useful

color, because it goes
acceptably with every-
thing.

## THE EXECUTIVE WARDROBE FOR WOMEN

Women have much more flexibility than men when it comes to
business dress. Perhaps this is because they are relative newcomers to
the executive ranks and are therefore not constrained by so many
conventions. However, women should keep in mind that there is a
distinct difference between what is worn at the office and what is worn
in the evening or in casual situations.

The most important rule is to dress in a tasteful, understated manner
that acknowledges your femininity, but does not exploit it. Many men
rather like alluring outfits on their secretaries and female support
personnel: It enhances the feeling of male dominance and makes it
easier to avoid taking these women seriously. But who wants to take
orders from a gal in a low-cut sweater and tight pants? In the long run,
men react negatively to overtly sexual outfits at the workplace. They set
the wearer apart and make it difficult for her to compete and be treated
equally.

Simple shirtdresses, suits, and blazer and skirt combinations are
usually safe. Don't wear short skirts, blue jeans, or low-cut outfits.
With many women entering the work force, magazines catering to this
audience have appeared. They can be helpful in guiding you on what
the well-dressed executive woman is wearing. Among them, *Working
Woman* and *Savvy* are particularly good.

## PART VIII

# ON THE ROAD: WHAT THE TRAVEL GUIDES DON'T TELL YOU

"People who develop the habit
of thinking of themselves as world
citizens are fulfilling the first
requirement of sanity in our time."
Norman Cousins

# 41

# GETTING THERE BY AIR

Business travel is often one of the most exasperating aspects of executive life. But it needn't be, if you take the time to understand how the travel industry operates, and how you can use the system to meet your own needs.

## IS THE TRIP REALLY NECESSARY?

True, the world is shrinking. Jets ply the air corridors, and Concordes whisk us to London in under three hours. At first glance, jet aviation seems like a big boost to business, because you can attend a conference or clinch a sale in Chicago and be in New York for the evening. But more often than not, you find yourself in an orbit of bad coffee, jet lag, wrinkled suits and ripe T-shirts, too much booze and too little sleep. Yes, the world is getting smaller; but in the 1980s, telecommunications will be the main shrinking agent. So before you plan that Marco Polo itinerary, consider the many ways you can get the job done without leaving home and hearth—or office.

**Conference calls.** Commonly accepted in business today, this approach can actually enhance your status. If handled with finesse, a reluctance to travel can be a sign of a very busy executive whose time is at a premium. Naturally, it's easier to take part in conference calls with people you already know well.

Maybe you're the type that makes a dynamite impression when you appear in the flesh. Obviously, you'll want to use that personal charisma to your advantage. But don't *overuse* it. Always be aware that you have other options besides "the next flight out."

**Electronic conferences.** Some of the megafirms already have the capability of staging electronic conferences. Get used to them. They save time and money, so they are bound to become more popular as the cost of air travel rises with the cost of fuel and inflation.

**Electronic mail.** Take advantage of the wide variety of alternative ways to communicate. There is bound to be a form of electronic mail to suit your needs (*see* Chapter 36).

*Caution:* In some companies, business travel is the mode of the executive who is not afraid to get his hands dirty—like the field commander, as opposed to the desk captain, in the army. Don't allow yourself to be confused with those who eschew travel because they don't want to be away from their families or don't want to miss their golf game. Keep everything on the cost-effective, business-wise level.

**What to do when they start cutting down on business trips, and wield the knife on your travel budget.** *Don't fight it.* Those who resist the demise of shuttle capitalism will be tagged as people with weak egos who *fear the loss of status* because they were discouraged from making the trip to Dallas. They'll take this as an indication that their bosses think they haven't been doing a good job, or just aren't needed in those crucial field meetings. *Do not see business travel as a form of ego boost. It either helps you do business or it doesn't. That's the bottom line.*

Some people get lonely on the road. But many others see travel as an opportunity for renewed freedom: Nobody knows you; there are big gaps of time that needn't be accounted for. Whether those hours are spent reading, at a pool hall or at the opera, many members of the business community cherish this time. Enjoy it when you can. But remember—*the company is not obliged to help you live a double life.* And if you fight for more business trips with the lust for going incognito as your primary motive, you'll be on shaky ground. You know when a trip is called for. And when it's a sham.

*Jump on the bandwagon.* Eliminate wasteful trips on your own initiative. Learn how to be effective in a conference-call situation. You'll be under less pressure and will gain time. Let those factors work for you. And *when you feel you must take a trip, don't be nonchalant about it—make a good case for going.*

---

# PLANNING A BUSINESS TRIP

---

### WORK WITH A TRAVEL AGENT

A good one will save you time, money, and headaches. A bad one is the quickest way to an ulcer. In many cases, you'll have no choice in the matter—the firm has already gotten very cozy with a travel agency. In other cases, the large firms have a convenient in-house setup. This approach is dying out, because it is expensive.

If you don't have a choice, *get close to one or two of the agents* so that they will pay special attention to your needs. When they bend over backward to help you, or act very promptly, show your appreciation (how you do it is up to you).

*Be patient,* even if it is in the face of utter incompetence; if the relationship is a lengthy one, it is unlikely that the boss will switch agencies on your say-so. Don't allow yourself to be pushed around, and don't be afraid to take an agent to task. But be polite and respectful.

*Listen.* The travel biz is so confusing, almost nobody gets it right the first time anymore. But if you listen carefully, you will finally figure out where you are going, when you are leaving, where you are staying, and how much it will cost.

## HOW TO CHOOSE A TRAVEL AGENCY

*Decide whether to go with a generalist or a specialist.* This depends on how you travel. And where you go. Some agencies service primarily businesses. This can be a plus. They don't deal with Grand Canyon Tours and the like, but they can get you a seat on the morning flight to St. Louis and reserve a car 30 minutes before flight time. Some specialize in certain locations, so if you do lots of business in the developing nations, the Third World, or the communist bloc, it may be wise to use a specialist. Some agencies specialize in a particular mode of travel. This is not really an issue for business, since you will almost always be taking a plane rather than going by boat or rail. Stay away from agencies that deal primarily with tour packages.

*Case the joint.* If the agency looks like a dentist's office or a bookie joint, beware. It should be somewhere in between: not excessively neat, since any successful travel agency generates a lot of paper; but not sloppy, either. That piece of paper serving as a coaster for some guy's coffee cup could be your ticket. The agents should have within easy reach such tools of the trade as the *Official Airlines Guide (OAG)* and the *Hotel and Travel Index.* A computer terminal is also a good sign.

*ASTA member?* The American Society of Travel Agents is the largest industry trade organization. You have to be in business at least three years to join. It doesn't really mean that much, except that ASTA will act as a mediator in the case of a dispute between an agency and its customers. ASTA also offers seminars and conferences to keep its members up to date on changes within the industry. All this might make you feel better if you are going in cold, without a referral.

*Certified Travel Counselor?* The PhD of the travel biz. You need five years' experience and an 18-month course. The CTC should know considerably more than your average ticket pusher. On the other hand, there are many very good agents who don't bother with things like "certification."

*What is the agency willing to do for you?* Will its personnel assist you with visas and passport renewals? Are they able to respond quickly? Does the agency have correspondent agencies in other countries and cities to serve you when you are away? Are its billing and credit terms favorable? A good agency is one that is looking to build its business on a repeat basis, not a one-shot fleecing. Agents that want you to come back again and again will try to accommodate you.

*Learn to speak their language.* When you want a reservation or a quote, give agents the info they need—where, when, class of service, room size, class of hotel, type of car, etc.; and method of payment if the costs are not to be charged to your account. If you want a special meal or specific seat location, or if you plan to take along a pet or some weird baggage, say so. The more they know, the more they can help you. If you get familiar with terms like "wait-list," "standby," "CTO" (city ticket office), "ETA" (estimated time of arrival), so much the better.

*Don't be afraid to shop around, even if you have a regular agency.*

*Get the lowdown on the charges before you book.* Fees? Service charges? Telex and/or long distance phone charges? Policies on out-of-pocket expenses vary from agency to agency.

## KNOW THE GROUND RULES FOR AIR TRAVELERS

### FARES

*Pay as far in advance as possible.* This almost always *can* mean cheaper fares. But make sure you find out all the options. You may qualify for a cheaper fare, but the reservation agent doesn't always make you aware of it.

*Shop around.* Fares are no longer set by an industry cartel. So one airline's fare may be much more than another's.

*Don't trust anybody.* Reservation agents—whether by intention, by mistake, or by their inability to unravel fare structures that do often seem more complex than the special theory of relativity—are notorious for their inability to provide you with the same fare quote twice in a row. Some people, including yours truly, have been known to keep calling the airline for quotes, rebooking when they get an agent who comes forth with a lower quote; think of it as a kind of airfare auction. Even travel experts who write for national magazines have been quoted several different fares for the same trip.

*It's cheaper to fly midweek than on weekends.* The exception is the "business run," such as New York to Chicago and New York-D.C. They can be cheaper on weekends, when airlines want to increase ridership on a route that is more profitable weekdays.

*It's cheaper to fly at night than during the day.* This doesn't always apply to transatlantic flights, because scheduling demands determine what time the flight leaves. A great many peak-traffic transatlantic flights are evening departures.

*Bargain rates usually take a vacation during holiday periods.* Bargain rates and discounts are essentially off-season sales. When the demand is high, so are the fares. If you are looking to save money, don't travel around Christmas. Some "super savers" or other discount fares are relatively cheap because one pays well in advance and will have some difficulty canceling. While these are sometimes available for holiday periods, there are far fewer seats allocated for these special fares.

*Package deals can be cheaper, but there are almost always strings.* Package deals include air fares, lodging, meals, even car rentals. But they often require advance purchase and have minimum and maximum stays.

- Limited seats are available.
- Often, no changes in itinerary are allowed without a penalty. However, for a nominal fee you can get trip cancellation insurance that will cover the penalty on an involuntary cancellation.

*What to ask the airline or travel agent*

1. *When are the fares lowest?* Get specifics—days, times, dates.
2. *What about stopovers?* Are they permitted? In one direction? In both directions? How many? Extra costs?
3. *Which fare is cheaper, a round-trip ticket or two one-ways?*
4. *Are there special rate structures?* Such as family plans, take-along-your-spouse-for-half-fare, etc.?

## RESERVATIONS

*Make them ASAP.* You'll avoid the businessperson's trap: book last minute, pay full fare. And don't forget to get your seat assignment and line up special meals, etc.

*Reconfirm.* This is important, because mistakes are often made. If an agent pushes one wrong key on the computer, you could wind up with a special Stillman water diet meal, or something else you didn't want. Or, more commonly, you'll be seated next to a chain-smoker when you're just beginning to think you've kicked the habit.

THE OFFICIAL AIRLINES GUIDE (OAG) This is the industry bible. Published in two volumes (North American and international), it lists all the flights on every airline and specifies type of equipment, meal service, flight time, fares, airports, and connecting flights. The *OAG* is available as either a bi-weekly or a monthly and is a bit too detailed and cumbersome for you. Also, it's $62 per year for the monthly North American edition alone, $85 for the bi-weekly. But the *OAG* people (they are owned by Dun & Bradstreet) got hip to the fact that jet-set executives were going nuts trying to get through to understaffed airline reservations offices and lethargic travel agents. So they put out the

NORTH AMERICAN OAG POCKET FLIGHT GUIDE *Pocket* is the key word here; this is a mini version of the regular *OAG*, containing information on the most frequently flown flights (about 27,000 are listed). The listings, by destination city, provide you with information about stops en route, meals, airline phone numbers for every city shown, and other useful information. This book is a godsend when your entire itinerary falls apart, whether because of a snowstorm or because of a snow job by a client, or when your car or business negotiations break down unexpectedly. The *OAG Pocket Guide* makes it easy to see all the alternatives at a glance. Even though every airline agent has virtually the same information in the computer on the desk, he may be reluctant to tell you about every single flight to Des Moines from 2:00 P.M. on. So you'll get just one or two alternatives—or get put on hold while the agent checks. Besides, sometimes there are exotic ways of reaching a destination that wouldn't even occur to an agent with several calls waiting. Sometimes you can go via another city that you have business in, and catch Des Moines on the way back home. If you travel a great deal, this book is worth the $30 per year for 12 monthly issues. Curiously, mail delivery is extra.

Contact:
OAG Publications
2000 Clearwater Drive
Oak Brook, Illinois 60521

# THINGS THAT GO BUMP
# ON THE FLIGHT

## OVERBOOKING

Airlines engage in a practice, known as overbooking, that helps them keep the flights as full as possible. Their computers track passenger patterns and determine that a certain percentage of travelers who make reservations on a given flight never show up. Rather than letting the seats of these no-shows go empty, the airlines book more passengers than they have room for, figuring that the no-shows will bring the flight back in line. You really can't blame them for doing this: It makes good business sense, and prices would be even higher if airlines didn't overbook.

Most of the time the airlines guess right. But sometimes a flight has more people than seats. Who stays behind in that case? The airline offers anyone who gets bumped a cash bonus plus the next flight out. The bonus ranges from $37.50 to about $200, but usually it is around a hundred bucks. With this as an incentive, the airline agent will ask for volunteers who wish to take the money and wait. Usually, enough people step forward so you won't get bumped against your will. If you volunteer or are bumped against your will *and* they can't get you on a flight within two hours (this happens less than one percent of the time), the CAB says you go free.

## WAIT-LIST

This is the list you get put on when you want a seat on a flight that is sold out. When you are "wait-listed" for a flight, don't expect to hear from the airline unless you are "cleared" for the flight—that is, unless a seat opens up for you. It doesn't hurt to check with the airline periodically; sometimes such persistence improves your chances of getting a seat. According to the rules, the wait-list clears on a first come, first served basis.

It is important to remember that being on the wait-list has no connection with standing by at the airport. If you haven't been cleared for a reservation by the day of the flight, consider it a whole new ball game.

## STANDBY

You're on standby when you arrive at the airport without a reservation and "stand by" for the flight, hoping that someone who is booked on the flight won't show up and you'll get the seat. Being wait-listed for the flight won't mean a thing; being first in the standby line *will*. So when you arrive for standby, have the time of check-in and the agent's sign (identification) stamped on your ticket. This will establish priority at the gate.

The rules state that in standby, full fares have priority over the discount standby fares—students, special promotion fares, military personnel, and airline employees. But it ain't necessarily so. Popular employees and airline execs, VIPs, and soldiers on special orders sometimes get seated first. However, on balance, those willing to pay list price will rarely get left behind. In these times of poor fiscal health, the airline biggies have given the word to the gates: Heads will roll if anyone seats a cheapo or a freebie ahead of a full fare.

# ON-BOARD OPTIONS

### FIRST CLASS

When it comes to arriving fresh and well rested, first class is the only way to go. A recent survey indicated that most business travelers still fly coach, but the number of first-class travelers increases with the length of the trip. This shows that the average American business traveler is pretty smart: He travels first class not for its snob appeal, but for its comfort.

In first class, the food and beverage selection is better, the service is better, and, best of all, the seats are bigger. Sometimes there is special check-in for first class, and luggage priority (your luggage is last on, first off); so your waiting time is reduced. The first-class section is smaller than coach. And nothing can drain you faster than being surrounded by rude, loud, and inconsiderate fellow passengers.

First class costs more money, but this surcharge is deductible: As far as the IRS is concerned, first class is no different from coach. The fares have been reduced to about 20 percent above coach, and as a result, the first-class sections are fuller than they used to be. But it is *still* worthwhile to fly first class for comfort.

### IN-FLIGHT EXTRAS

First came the stewardess, then the steward, and now the service director. This person is the maitre d' of the flight and can do some special things for you. For example, the service director can make hotel, airline, and rent-a-car reservations, reconfirm flights, and, in certain cases, get seat assignments—all while in flight.

### SPECIAL MEALS

Unfortunately, special meals are usually not very special. But then again, neither are the regular meals. And if you have a restricted diet, a little knowledge and a phone call can keep you from starving. A commonly held belief is that there are only four or five special meals. This is wrong. United has about 13; Pan Am, 19. And although the basic classifications appear to be industry-wide, each airline has its own interpretation. A couple of sample lists are included here to give you an idea of the range of meals available. If you don't see what you want, ask for it. You may be pleasantly surprised. Just get in your meal request 48 hours in advance. If you can't do that, request your choice anyway. Sometimes an airline can rustle something up on short notice.

## DIETARY MEALS

Special meal service may be ordered through local reservations offices. Hindu, Kosher, Muslim, Oriental, Soul Food, Weight Watchers and children's meals require confirmation from United's flight kitchen and catering locations if less than 24 hours notice. All other type meals require up to 4 hours notice prior to departure. Dietary meals will be provided using a variety of the components as shown. Specific items (for ethnic, religious, medical or dietary restrictions only) may be requested and will be served as available. Personal preference requests are *not* to be accepted.

**NOTE:** Passengers traveling with children on flights scheduled for meal service should inquire about children's meals at the time of reservation. These meals are no longer available in-flight if not specifically requested prior to flight departure.

The items listed are only a guide, do not treat them as exact meal components.

| DIETARY MEAL | BLAND | CHILDREN'S | DIABETIC |
|---|---|---|---|
| **LEAD TIME REQUIRED** | 4 hours | 4 hours | 4 hours |
| **CODE** | SPML | CSML | SPML |
| **RESTRICTIONS AND REMARKS** | Dried beans and peas. Corn, broccoli, brussel sprouts, cabbage, onions, cauliflower, cucumber, green pepper, rutabaga, turnips, sauerkraut. Any fried and highly seasoned item including snacks such as chips or frankfurters, sausages and luncheon meats. Chunky peanut butter Any item containing nuts or coconut. | Listed below are meals available. If any other meal is specifically requested, it may be confirmed with 24 hours notice to appropriate kitchen or catering location. | Commercial hot chocolate Sweetened fruits and juices Pastries, sugar coated cereals. Sugar, syrup, honey, jelly, jam, preserves, marmalade. All candy including dietetic candy. Cakes, cookies, pies. Sweetened soft beverages Sweet pickles. |
| **FOODS RECOMMENDED OR AVAILABLE** | Milk and milk drinks. All vegetable and fruit juices. All cereals, breads, rolls, crackers. Fruits Non-fried starches Meats and substitutes not fried or highly seasoned Butter/margarine and mild salad dressings. Smooth peanut butter Decaffeinated coffee and non-cola beverages. | Hot dog and bun Assorted cold sandwiches Franco-American spaghetti and meatballs. | Milk All vegetables Fruits and juices with no sugar added All bread products Potatoes and substitute starches. All meats, eggs, cheese. Peanut butter Butter, margarine, salad dressings including mayonnaise. Soups Artificial sweetener coffee, tea, dietetic pop Spices, nuts, gravies. |

---

Fig. 61. Typical airline guidelines on special meals
(*through page 551*)
Reprinted by permission of United Airlines.

---

| DIETARY MEAL | GLUTEN FREE | HIGH PROTEIN | HINDU |
|---|---|---|---|
| LEAD TIME REQUIRED | 4 hours | 4 hours | 24 hours |
| CODE | SPML | SPML | HNML |
| RESTRICTIONS AND REMARKS | Commercial chocolate milk, malted milk<br>Any creamed or breaded vegetables<br>*Any wheat, rye, oats, barley, buckwheat product.*<br>Cold cuts, sandwich spreads, canned meats prepared with wheat, rye, oats, barley, or buckwheat.<br>Processed cheese<br>Commercial salad dressing<br>Chili sauce, soy sauce, bottled meat sauces with wheat, rye, oats, barley or buckwheat. | General diet with increased protein of high biological value. | Vegetarian Hindu:<br>— Three types<br>  eat all vegetables except parts of roots<br>  eat only fruit and milk<br>Non-vegetarian Hindu: no beef or veal but will eat all other meat, poultry, fish. |
| FOODS RECOMMENDED OR AVAILABLE | Milk and milk products other than above.<br>Fresh vegetables<br>All fruits, juices<br>Corn or rice cereals, gluten free bread, breads and rolls made from arrowroot, rice, corn, potato, soybean flour.<br>Potatoes, rice<br>All meat, poultry, fish, shellfish<br>Eggs, nuts, natural cheese, peanut butter<br>Butter, margarine<br>Sugar, cake, ice cream. |  | Milk and milk products, yoghurt.<br>Fruits<br>Whole grain products, rice.<br>Cheese, eggs, peanut butter.<br>Tea, coffee.<br>Spices, nuts. |

| DIETARY MEAL | MUSLIM | ORIENTAL | SOUL FOOD |
|---|---|---|---|
| LEAD TIME REQUIRED | 24 hours | 24 hours | 24 hours |
| CODE | MOML | ORML | SMPL |
| RESTRICTIONS AND REMARKS | Diet avoids pork products, shrimp, lobster, scavenger fish and shellfish. | Diet typically favors stir fried or slightly undercooked vegetables. | Diet typically favors home cooking and the addition of hot sauce or Tabasco with meal. |
| FOODS RECOMMENDED OR AVAILABLE |  |  |  |

| DIETARY MEAL | HYPOGLYCEMIC (Low Carbohydrate) | INFANT | KOSHER |
|---|---|---|---|
| LEAD TIME REQUIRED | 4 hours | 4 hours | 24 hours |
| CODE | SPML | BBML | KSML |
| RESTRICTIONS AND REMARKS | Chocolate milk, hot chocolate. Any breaded vegetables Sweetened fruits, juices Pastries, quick breads, sugar, syrup, honey, jam, jelly, preserves, molasses. All candies, cakes, cookies, pies, pudding, ice cream, sherbet, jello Sweet pickles, gravies Cola, coffee, tea, soft beverages. | Special diet for infants 8 months to 2 years of age. | Kosher breakfasts, lunches, dinners and snacks prepared for United Airlines by an approved Kosher caterer. Contains no pork, shellfish or scavenger fish products; milk and meat products prepared separately. |
| FOODS RECOMMENDED OR AVAILABLE | Whole, lowfat, skim, or buttermilk. All vegetables Unsweetened fruits, juices Breads and cereals Potatoes and substitutes Meats and substitutes Fats Soups Decaffeinated coffee, dietetic soft beverages Nuts. | Typically strained or finely chopped fruit, meats and vegetables. | Reservations should specify "beef" or "chicken" on passenger meal request for lunches or dinners. |

| DIETARY MEAL | LACTOSE RESTRICTED | LOW CALORIE | LOW CHOLESTEROL |
|---|---|---|---|
| LEAD TIME REQUIRED | 4 hours | 4 hours | 4 hours |
| CODE | SPML | SPML | SPML |
| RESTRICTIONS AND REMARKS | Milk and milk products served or used in preparation of any foods. | Chocolate milk or commercial hot chocolate Sweetened fruits and juices. Sugar, jelly, jam, preserves, syrup, honey, molasses, candy. Cakes, pies, puddings, cookies, ice cream, sherbet Sauces, gravies. Regular sweetened pop. | Whole milk and products made from whole milk. Egg breads, butter rolls Breads and cereals made with egg yolks, butter, whole milk, or cream. Fatty meats, duck, bacon, corned beef, spareribs, sausages, canned meats, shellfish. Ice cream, ice milk Chocolate, coconut. Cashews, macadamia nuts. |
| FOODS RECOMMENDED OR AVAILABLE | All food items which do not have milk or milk products as an ingredient Fortified margarines marked "Kosher" or "Pareve." | Milk, all vegetables, unsweetened fruits, juices. Meats, poultry, fish Cheese, eggs, peanut butter Nuts. Potatoes and substitutes Soups Dietetic pop, coffee, tea. | Skim milk All vegetables Fruits Whole grain breads Potatoes, rice, barley Lean meats, poultry without skin. Corn, safflower, soybean oils, polyunsaturated margarine Sweets made with skim milk, egg substitutes. |

| DIETARY MEAL | LOW FAT | LOW PROTEIN | LOW SODIUM |
|---|---|---|---|
| LEAD TIME REQUIRED | 4 hours | 4 hours | 4 hours |
| CODE | SPML | SPML | NSML |
| RESTRICTIONS AND REMARKS | Whole milk, 2% milk, low fat milk, chocolate milk, evaporated and condensed milk and their products. Broccoli, brussel sprouts, cabbage, corn, cauliflower cucumber, garlic, dried beans and pies, onions, green pepper, rutabaga, turnips, sauerkraut Avocado Breads with large amount of fat Fried potatoes, meats Bacon, sausages, luncheon meats, duck Poultry skin, high fat cheeses, cream cheese Gravies Ice cream, nuts. | Buttermilk Artichokes Glazed fruits Commercial waffles and pancakes Brains, kidneys. | Buttermilk Vegetables prepared with salt Frozen peas, lima beans, mixed vegetables, corn. Sauerkraut, pickles and other items in brine Instant cereal and other dry cereals Salted butter, margarine Any item with salt as an ingredient or has salt needed for preparation. All candies made with chocolate, nuts, coconut. |
| FOODS RECOMMENDED OR AVAILABLE | Skim milk Vegetables other than above All fruits except avocado Potatoes and substitutes. Lean meat, poultry, fish, shellfish broiled, baked, roasted, stewed. | Milk and milk products other than above. All vegetables All fruits and juices Breads and cereals except quick breakfast breads Meat, poultry, fish, shellfish Cheese, eggs, peanut butter. | All milk and milk products Low salt/sodium items including fruits, juices, whole grain or enriched bread, potatoes, meat, poultry, fish, shellfish. |

| DIETARY MEAL | VEGETARIAN: LACTO-OVO | VEGETARIAN: PURE | WEIGHT WATCHERS |
|---|---|---|---|
| **LEAD TIME REQUIRED** | 4 hours | 4 hours | 24 hours |
| **CODE** | VGML—Dairy Eggs OK | VGML | SPML |
| **RESTRICTIONS AND REMARKS** | Diet eliminates all meat, fish, poultry, but includes eggs, milk, and other dairy products. | Diet excluding all sources of animal protein. | Diet approved for use in Weight Watchers Program and features breakfasts, lunches, dinners and snacks. Prepared for United Airlines by approved caterer following Weight Watchers, Inc. standards. |
| **FOODS RECOMMENDED OR AVAILABLE** | | | Typical meals might be: <br>—Breakfast: Spanish omelette <br>—Lunch: Chicken Chasseur <br>—Dinner: Braised Beef Tips <br>—Snack: Cold breast of Turkey Sandwich |

## UNITED FOOD SERVICE CODES

**MEAL CODES**
- **B** Breakfast
- **C** Brunch/Deli Service
- **D** Dinner
- **L** Lunch
- **P** Purchase Snack (Price varies depending upon flight segment)
- **R** Brunch
- **S** Snack

**FLIGHT THEMES**
- **F** Four Star Service
- **O** Ocean to Ocean Service
- **R** Royal Hawaiian

**LIQUOR CODES**
- **Q** Cocktails/First Class and Coach
- ***** Cocktails/First Class only

## SPECIAL MEAL CODES (SIPP Codes)

| | |
|---|---|
| BBML | Infant Meal/Baby Food |
| HNML | Hindu Meal |
| KSML | Kosher Meal |
| MOML | Moslem Meal |
| NSML | No Salt |
| ORML | Oriental Meal |
| SPML | Special Meal (Followed by details) |
| VGML | Vegetarian Meal |

## UNITED ONLY SPECIAL MEAL CODES

| | |
|---|---|
| CSML | Child's Meal |

# SEATING

Anyone who travels by plane knows that getting a good seat can make the difference between a pleasant trip and an unpleasant one. What many people don't know is that seating needn't be left to chance.

Lately the airlines have been engaging in a practice known as "reconfiguring"—a euphemism for adding more seats. How do they do it? They reduce or eliminate lounge space, move the seats closer together, and, in some instances, narrow or eliminate aisles.

You can fight back:

REQUEST A SEATING PLAN   Every airline prints up seating charts for all the planes they fly. Sometimes there are several configurations for each type of aircraft.

WHEN YOU BOOK THE FLIGHT, ASK ABOUT THE TYPE OF AIRCRAFT AND THE CONFIGURATION   It's rather like going to the theater. When you request a seat assignment, you've got a chart in front of you so you have a good idea where 18C is located.

MAKE SURE THAT YOU ALLOW SUFFICIENT TIME TO REQUEST THE SEAT ASSIGNMENT   It's first come, first served. The sooner you request, the greater the choice.

DOUBLE-CHECK   Seat assignments are often incorrectly entered in the reservation computer. They seem to get lost often. My guess is that a besieged reservations agent will sometimes juggle seat assignments to mollify an irate passenger who simply will not book on the flight unless promised a particular seat, say, by the emergency exit. The agent plays the odds and figures that you won't gripe too much about the loss of a little extra leg room. *Is it worth the trouble?* You bet! You'll be in the air for quite a while. If you don't want to hassle with this, get your travel agent to do it.

SMOKING/NONSMOKING SECTIONS   The smoker/nonsmoker feud really heats up on planes. There have even been a few punches thrown over a lit cigarette in the wrong row. The CAB has cracked down hard: The airlines and each cabin crew *must* enforce the restrictions. A new rule says that a nonsmoking seat must be provided for anyone who wants one, even if the whole plane has to be given over to nonsmokers.

*If you get bumped from your seat in the smoking or nonsmoking section and the flight attendants are uncooperative,* file a written complaint with the CAB and the airline. Announce your intention to do so. The airline could be fined (you won't get a refund), and it might try a bit harder to accommodate you in order to keep you from sending the letter.

*If you are a hardcore nonsmoker, try for a seat at least five rows away from the smoking section.* Ever try sitting in the row directly behind the smoking section? It's not much of an improvement.

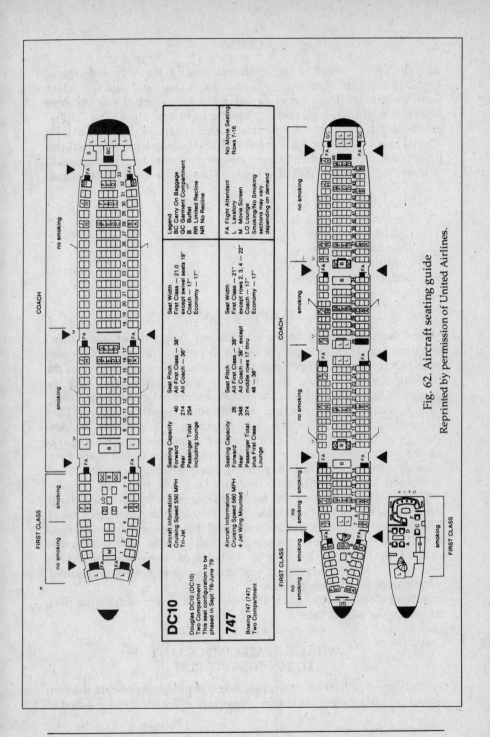

Fig. 62. Aircraft seating guide
Reprinted by permission of United Airlines.

**DC10**

Douglas DC10 (DC10)
Two Compartment
This seat configuration to be
phased in Sept '78–June '79

**747**

Boeing 747 (747)
Two Compartment

| Aircraft Information | | Seating Capacity | | Seat Width | | Seat Pitch | |
|---|---|---|---|---|---|---|---|
| Cruising Speed 550 MPH | | Forward | 40 | First Class — 21.0 | | All First Class — 38" | |
| Tri-Jet | | Rear | 214 | except swivel seats 19" | | All Coach — 36" | |
| | | Passenger Total | 254 | Coach — 17" | | | |
| | | Including lounge | | Economy — 17" | | | |

| Aircraft Information | | Seating Capacity | | Seat Width | | Seat Pitch | |
|---|---|---|---|---|---|---|---|
| Cruising Speed 560 MPH | | Forward | 26 | First Class — 21" | | All First Class — 39" | |
| 4 Jet Wing Mounted | | Rear | 348 | except rows 2, 3, 4 — 22" | | All Coach — 36" except | |
| | | Passenger Total | 374 | Coach — 17" | | rows 17 thru | |
| | | plus First Class | | Economy — 17" | | 48 — 38" | |
| | | Lounge | | | | | |

**Legend**

| BC | Carry On Baggage | FA | Flight Attendant | | No Movie Seating |
|---|---|---|---|---|---|
| GC | Garment Compartment | L | Lavatory | | Rows 7-16 |
| B | Buffet | M | Movie Screen | | |
| RR | Limited Recline | LO | Lounge | | |
| NR | No Recline | | Smoking/No Smoking | | |
| | | | sections may vary | | |
| | | | depending on demand | | |

## CLUBS

Airline "clubs" began as an exclusive service for VIPs only. Now, anybody can join. Membership is only $30-40 per year, and it's a darn good investment if you travel a great deal on the same airline. At these prices, it might serve you well to belong to several clubs. The "clubs" are located at the airports, and most have bar service, free soft drinks, special check-in (the best feature of all), and business meeting facilities (they come in handy when two out-of-towners want to meet in transit).

Major airline clubs are listed below. They all have very silly names:

TWA Ambassador Club
Pan Am Clipper Club
United Red Carpet
American Admiral
Continental Presidents
Eastern Ionosphere

## BUSINESS CLASS

When the air carriers began introducing "super saver" and other discount fares, business people began to revolt. The business traveler pays full coach fare and gets exactly the same service and seating as the discount traveler paying two-thirds or one-half the fare. And the executive has little choice in the matter, except to opt for first class.

Somewhere, some marketing wizard came up with a solution. They call it "business class," which, in my opinion, is a lot of BS. Business class offers travelers first choice of meals, a special counter for check-in, maybe free drinks and/or a headset, access (sometimes) to the first-class departure lounge, and a reserved seat in a "special coach section." Is it worth twice the price of a discount fare? Definitely not.

First of all, the size of the seat is the same as in standard coach. Second, the size of this "special section" is fluid; it depends on demand. The section could be so small (a few rows) that the entire business-class benefit disappears. Booking a seat in a small business-class section may actually hurt you, by limiting your choice of seats—fewer windows and aisles. Since separating of smokers and nonsmokers is required, your choice is cut even further.

Sure, the business class is at the front of the coach section. Big deal; some say the rear is safer.

## WHAT IS REALLY IMPORTANT
## TO BUSINESS PEOPLE?

A study by *Business Week* magazine asked respondents to rate thirteen aspects of airline travel as to their importance. Then they were asked to select the single most important aspect. The eight aspects most often selected:*

|  | Very important | Most important |
|---|---|---|
| Schedule convenience | 81.8% | 30.9% |
| On-time performance | 81.6% | 33.7% |
| Past experience with airline | 59.9% | 16.3% |
| Cabin cleanliness | 52.5% | 1.7% |
| Flight attendants | 51.8% | 3.1% |
| Baggage handling | 47.1% | 1.8% |
| Reservations personnel | 43.7% | 2.1% |
| Airline reputation | 34.2% | 3.6% |

## THE CONCORDE

The Concorde is flown by rich people and business people. The business people deduct the expensive fare, and the rich don't care. Don't fly it for the thrill of breaking Mach 1; there's not much to it. Certainly, the Concorde will save you time. And supersonic travel reduces jet lag, thanks to reduced travel time and better cabin conditions (higher pressure and better temperature and humidity control). But the real reason for flying Concorde is the contacts you might make. As a spokesman for British Airways told me, "Concorde passengers are already successful, so they don't need your book." Let's just say that those who fly this plane place a high premium on their time.

## FUTURE CLASS

Although the airlines may be caught in a profit squeeze, there will never be a shortage of people willing to pay for an extra bit of comfort. In fact in air travel, as in automobiles, as the gap between the rich and the middle class widens, there are more and more people willing to pay bigger bucks for more luxury. The airlines want to avoid getting into an "extras war," as they did in the sixties, with each trying to outdo the other by offering unprofitable come-ons to increase ridership. This time, it's different: The engineers and designers have come up with a host of meaningful extras that well-heeled passengers will willingly pay more for. Some of them are already available:

SLEEPING BERTHS What a pleasure on a long night flight! JAL already has them on certain flights. See Fig. 64 for a sketch of the berth's layout.

*From "A Study of Recent Air Travelers" (New York: *Business Week*, 1979). Reprinted by permission.

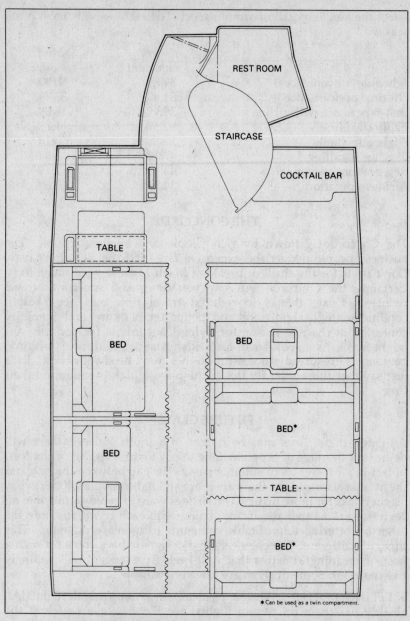

Fig. 63. The sleeping berths currently available in the
upper deck of Japan Air Lines 747 Garden Jets on
trans-Pacific flights and on the airline's
Japan-to-Europe polar flights

Reprinted by permission of Japan Air Lines.

IN-FLIGHT TELEPHONES   You can already place a call while aloft on certain flights. The charge is about $6 plus the regular toll charge. Sometime later, via fully automatic direct dialing service, you'll be able to receive calls as well as place them while in flight.

DRESSING ROOMS AND SHOWERS   Boeing already has these on the drawing board and is no doubt awaiting the go-ahead from the carriers.

OFFICE COMPLEX   This will include photocopy machine, stenographer, and dictation machines, as well as other important office equipment.

GYM   Exercise bikes; treadmills; maybe even a sauna. Their use will have to be supervised, though: Exercising at 30,000 feet could be tricky.

CLOSED CIRCUIT TV   Both standard fare and special programming will be offered.

LIVE ENTERTAINMENT   It's been tried before, but there are signs that the airlines are willing to have another go at it.

## SHOULD YOUR COMPANY
## OWN ITS OWN PLANE?

### THE PROS

- *Airline service to suburban areas and small cities is decreasing.* Ironically, more and more corporations are shunning the metropolitan areas and setting up headquarters in rural areas.
- *Your company can get investment tax credits.*
- *A corporate jet is an excellent "image builder."*
- *You can hold business meetings in the air.*
- *The cabins are very comfortable, so you arrive fresh and well rested.*
- *You are not limited by airline schedules and routes.*
- *You can offset costs by renting out the plane.*
- *Security can be tighter.*
- *Maybe, just maybe, you'll save some money.*

### THE CONS

- *There is a serious shortage of airports and parking space.* At present this is a sellers' market. Demand is very great, so you probably won't find any bargains.
- *You can never completely eliminate airline travel.*
- *A corporate jet increases "executive visibility."* Some stockholders

are extremely sensitive to what they consider abuse of company funds. A jet might increase the level of scrutiny.
- *When a firm owns its own plane, employees tend to use it because it's there.* Not because it makes sense.

When making a decision involving such a large expenditure, careful analysis is obviously required. A plane can cost you anywhere from $35,000 (for your basic single-engine Cessna Skyhawk prop) to a cool $7.6 million (for a Canadair Challenger, powered by turbofan engines and capable of a nonstop transcontinental trip). Now, which one is for your firm?

## HOW TO DO A CORPORATE JET ANALYSIS

TALK TO THE VENDORS   Piper and Cessna offer feasibility studies that can be quite helpful. Of course, they are sales come-ons, but they aren't greatly misleading. These aircraft companies depend heavily on reputation. A good feasibility study by a vendor will:

- help you determine whether you really need a plane
- suggest an appropriate model (built by the vendor)
- compare the cost of outright purchase with that of leasing
- estimate operating costs
- analyze the benefits to your company

YOUR FIRM SHOULD ENGAGE IN ITS OWN ANALYSIS   Look not only at the costs of owning a plane, but also at the costs of the entire corporate travel operation. Questions to ask:

- Who does the traveling in your company?
- How often?
- Where? What are the most frequently visited and most common destinations?
- Do these executives travel alone? With each other? With clients, attorneys, or others?
- How far (in air miles) are these journeys?

Now pull all the travel vouchers. Look carefully at the travel patterns of the staff, and the total costs. Be sure to include surface transit to and from the airport, meals and lodging, and the value of the executive's time. Many firms decide on the corporate jet option, not so much because the airport-to-airport fare is cheaper than that of a commercial airline, but because the company plane can save enough executive travel time to make it cost-effective. Just compute (with base salary, benefits, and incentives) what an hour of senior management time is worth. It'll make you a believer.

The next step is to compare this with an analysis of what it's going to cost to own a plane. The costs can be divided into two categories:

- *fixed.* Includes the purchase price of the plane and finance charges; the cost of the hangar space; the pilot's salary; insurance and depreciation. Fixed costs per hour are reduced as usage increases.
- *operating.* Landing and parking fees; fuel and oil; maintenance. Operating costs increase as usage increases.

At this point it is a good idea to figure out just how much airline travel you can eliminate and how efficiently the corporate jet would operate. Can you fill the seats regularly? Sometimes, efficiency means flying a planeload of executives to a centrally located airport, where they connect with scheduled airlines, and picking them up in the same manner.

Before you buy, you might try chartering a plane in order to gain some hands-on experience. You can either charter on a pay-as-you-go basis or purchase a block of time (so many hours per year or per quarter).

## RENTING A PLANE

This alternative is becoming increasingly popular, especially when you've got to get to a place not served by a scheduled airline or want to avoid a stopover, change of plane, or flying out of your way. Prices run from $50 up, for a small one- or two-seater (in addition to the pilot's seat), to $400 per hour and up, for the top-of-the-line six-seat turboprop. A few tips:

CHECK OUT THE RENTAL OUTFIT  If it doesn't come recommended, you can call the FAA to check on its license, safety record, and classification (some charter companies are licensed for photo and sightseeing excursions only).

SPREAD THE WORD  All pilots need to log flight time in order to qualify to operate aircraft. There are always a few around who are in the process of qualifying for a certain type of aircraft. So eager are they that they will often take you where you want to go if you pay only aircraft rental and fuel expenses. Sometimes you'll run into pilots with their own planes who will get you from here to there for just fuel and landing fees—a good way to travel on the cheap.

## FEASIBILITY STUDIES

TRANSPORTATION ANALYSIS PLAN (TAP)  From Cessna Aircraft and available through Cessna dealers, the data is then sent to Cessna's headquarters, in Wichita, Kansas, for analysis. Your comptroller might take issue with some of the estimates and figures, but with a little extra work, he should be able to tailor them to your own requirements.

Contact:
Cessna Aircraft Company
P.O. Box 1521
Wichita, Kansas 67201

PIPER AIRCRAFT TRAVEL COST/BENEFIT ANALYSIS AND CASH FLOW   Available free through Piper dealers, this analysis is computer generated and written in accountantese. As with Cessna's TAP, the analysis is worthwhile.

Piper also offers a detailed lease back cash flow analysis program that generates both cash flow and income projections for an individual lease back package.
Contact:
Piper Aircraft Corporation
820 East Bald Eagle Street
Lock Haven, Pennsylvania 17745

BUSINESS AND COMMERCIAL AVIATION FEASIBILITY/JUSTIFICATION STUDY   This study is essentially a do-it-yourself travel analysis kit. Even if you don't buy a plane, this kit will provide you with invaluable information on just how the staff gets around. Prepared in 1975, the cost estimates are out of date, but a little arithmetic can remedy that.
Contact:
Business and Commercial Aviation Magazine
Hangar C-1
Westchester County Airport
New York, New York 10604

---

# HOW TO SURVIVE A PLANE CRASH

---

*It is possible to increase your chances.* Consider these facts: Most crashes occur on takeoff or landing. The majority of people die not because of impact, but because of failure to get out of the plane.
*You must learn to:*
(1) survive the impact
(2) evacuate as quickly as possible

## PREPARATION

ACCEPT RESPONSIBILITY   You have no control over the flight, nor can you even see where you are going, so there is a tendency to simply put yourself in the hands of the flight crew. But when there is trouble, how much can several hostesses and stewards do for 75 or more passengers? You'd better be prepared to take matters into your own hands.

---

READ THE LITTLE PLASTIC CARD AND LISTEN TO THE TAKEOFF SPEECH   Don't assume you know the layout because you've taken this kind of plane before; the configuration does change often. Find your seat on the diagram and locate the nearest exits and an alternate. Find the closest exits—two front and two rear. Take some time to examine the doors to see how they work.

BE ALERT DURING TAKEOFFS AND LANDINGS   And do put those seat backs and tray tables "in their original, upright positions." This minimizes the possibility of injury and keeps the aisles and rows clear.

LOCATE FLOTATION EQUIPMENT   Longer overwater flights have life jackets that the attendants will demonstrate. Otherwise, a part of the seat acts as a flotation device.

WEAR YOUR SEAT BELT   Make sure you know how to work it, and wear it tight and low. Erect posture is safer.

DON'T BE UNCOOPERATIVE ABOUT CARRY-ONS   The temptation is to stick something heavy, like a camera or a bottle of Scotch, in the overhead compartment. Don't. When they say that the carry-on should fit under the seat in front of you, don't flimflam. If it blocks the aisle, it may kill you and the person next to you.

## SURVIVING THE IMPACT

ASSUME BRACE POSITION AT THE SIGN OF ABRUPT CHANGE IN ALTITUDE, FIRE, TWISTING OR BREAKING METAL   This position will give you some protection against debris: Bend over, placing your arms around your ankles, and your head between your arms against your legs. Or, cross your arms in front of your head, folding them against the seat in front of you. Then lean forward, with your head against your arms.

## EVACUATION

GET OUT AS FAST AS YOU CAN   Undo your seat belt. Leave everything behind and head for the exit.

*At the exit.* Open the door and look out. If you see fire, go look for another exit. If not, you want out:

- *Inflatable slide?* Inflate, pull handle, and jump.
- *Escape rope?* Hand over hand, lower yourself until you are low enough to jump.
- *Stairs?* Run down them.
- *Window over wing?* Exit feet first, move toward the back of the wing, and slide off rear wing flap.

GET AWAY FROM THE PLANE   Go for a good, safe distance, but don't hail a cab for the nearest Holiday Inn. Stay around. Your assistance will be of immense importance to the authorities. And if you are not there when the head counts are done, your next-of-kin might be in for a pretty distressing phone call.

IF THERE IS SMOKE   Smoke, especially from burning jet fuel, is the killer.
   *Crawl toward the exit, on all fours, but not with your belly on the ground.* The crawl should put you under the rising smoke; but if you go too low, you might get your lungs full of some toxic gases that tend to sink rather than rise.

IF THERE IS FIRE   Never run into it, unless you absolutely have no other choice. If you know the alternate exits, you have a much better chance to avoid performing a "wall of fire" trick.

WHAT ABOUT EXPLOSIONS?   Nothing looks better on film than an explosion, so most of us have seen Hollywood blast a few planes now and then. But the truth is, planes rarely explode. They rely on kerosene, not gasoline, and kerosene is much less explosive. What people often mistake for an explosion is the fire flaring up as the result of being fed by more fuel from ruptured tanks. Airplane survival expert Sarah Uzzell-Rindlaub* compares this flare-up to the one that occurs when we throw another log on the fire. Worry about fire, not explosion. It means that running clear of the plane is worth the effort. Some people think that they will be vaporized by a gigantic explosion just slightly smaller than Hiroshima and never bother to run the hundred yards that could make a difference.

THE HUMAN FACTOR: PANIC   *Negative panic.* This occurs when, in a crisis, people just freeze: no screaming or struggling, just sitting or standing motionless. These people fail to leave the plane in time and often succumb to smoke inhalation.
   *Regular panic.* Not as prevalent as negative panic, but equally deadly, because screaming can cause you to engulf large amounts of smoke and waste your breath. Also, the panic contributes to confused and illogical thinking and action—for example, trying to get off the plane with the stuffed animal you bought for your niece.

PLANES ARE DESIGNED FOR EASY EVACUATION   In order to pass the FAA regulations, the airplane manufacturer must demonstrate that a full load of passengers can get out of the plane within 90 seconds, even with half the exits blocked. Theoretically, this means that you should be able to get off within 90 seconds, provided you know where you're going.

---

*For more on this subject, read Sarah Uzzell-Rindlaub's article "Getting Out in 90 Seconds," *Quest*, September, 1979, pp.18-20.

---

## BEWARE OF THE
## CHARLES LINDBERGH/AMELIA EARHART
## SYNDROME

The syndrome manifests itself when reading the seat card, listening to the flight briefing, and examining exits is regarded as inconsistent with one's image of the sophisticated traveler totally at home in the sky, the jet-setter with no fears. You may not impress the folks next to you if you appear concerned about how to open the exit door, but think of how impressed they'd be if you led them to safety when the plane landed in Shea Stadium instead of JFK.

Now relax and enjoy your flight. Up, up, and away.

---

# YOUR PAPERS, MONSIEUR?

International travel is becoming physically easier, but bureaucratically more complex and difficult. In some countries, governments change faster than the weather; visa requirements appear to be authored by the Marx Brothers.

**Plan ahead.** Give yourself lots of time to get the necessary shots and applications in order, especially when traveling outside Western Europe or the industrialized nations of Asia.

**Double check.** If you have acted in advance, don't assume that your visa is irrevocable. It isn't. Make sure that, in the interim, regulations haven't changed; check just before you go.

**Consider using a visa agency.** Things have gotten so crazy that a hot new service has emerged for travelers—visa agencies. They share the same basic premise of the travel agencies—save the customer the hassle. Of course, visa agencies do not get a commission from the country granting the visa (wouldn't that be a twist); they make their money by charging you.

*What visa agencies do.* They do the running around. They take care of getting you the visas and passport renewals and extra pages. In some cases, they arrange for vaccinations and/or vaccination certification. And they handle a few quirks. For example, if you want to go to Libya or any other Middle Eastern country of the rabid anti-Zionist persuasion and you have an Israeli stamp on your passport, you are advised to stay on the plane. And Taiwan doesn't want you if you have been to Peking, etc. Any good visa agency is hip to this and will get you

---

a second, "restricted," passport for use in countries that are into this sort of thing. Or it can get you additional passport pages that you can use for the Israeli or South African stamp or that of any other "ostracized" nation; you remove the offending page before you hit the Baghdad airport. Of course, you can do this yourself: Any holder of a valid passport can apply for a "restricted" one or get extra pages. Another bit of weirdness is the requirement by some Arab nations (you guessed it—Libya's in this group too) that your visa application be submitted in Arabic. Unless you took Arabic 101 in college, this means a translation. The visa agencies will provide it for a fee.

Perhaps a visa agency can be most valuable to you by virtue of its location. Most visa agencies are in Washington, D.C., and since a surprisingly large number of countries won't allow you to apply for a visa through their missions or consulates around the country, it can be handy to have a person in Washington, where the embassies are.

*Watch out.* Visa agencies are not licensed. Try to get the name of one from an associate. Or check with the embassy of the country(ies) you wish to travel to and see whether it has dealt with the agency and found it kosher (don't use that term at the Libyan Embassy).

### Countries requiring a business visa (but not a tourist visa)

| | |
|---|---|
| Dominican Republic | Philippines |
| Jamaica | Sri Lanka |
| Mexico | Trinidad/Tobago |
| Pakistan | Venezuela |

### Countries not requiring business or tourist visa

| | | |
|---|---|---|
| Argentina | Great Britain | New Zealand |
| Austria | Greece | Nicaragua |
| Bahamas | Grenada | Norway |
| Barbados | Guyana | Panama |
| Belgium | Haiti | Paraguay |
| Botswana | Iceland | Peru |
| Canada | Ireland | Portugal |
| Chile | Israel | Singapore |
| Colombia | Italy | Spain |
| Costa Rica | Lesotho | Surinam |
| Cyprus | Luxembourg | Sweden |
| Denmark | Malawi | Switzerland |
| Ecuador | Malaysia | Tunisia |
| El Salvador | Malta | Turkey |
| Fiji | Morocco | Uruguay |
| Finland | Netherlands | West Germany |
| France | | |

Regulations concerning currency can be rigorously enforced and failure to comply with them can cause travel delays and severe penalties. Many countries allow free import and export of foreign currency and traveller's cheques, but have strict laws regarding local currency. Other countries allow unlimited import of foreign currency on condition that it has been declared at the point of entry. Usually the amount taken out must not exceed the amount brought in. Even when a country fails to list restrictions on currency, it will rarely permit the unrestricted flow of gold coins or bars.

The phrase "unrestricted if declared" should be interpreted to mean that the import of foreign currency is unrestricted and the amounts declared upon entry may be re-exported.

In some countries it is difficult to cash large traveller's cheques, thus cheques of small denominations are recommended.

The following currency prescriptions were in effect at the time this directory went to press and apply to travellers only.

   * The Won is not an international currency and cannot be exchanged outside Korea.
   **Visitors are advised to use traveller's cheques.

| Country | Local Currency Import | Export | Foreign Currency Import | Export |
|---|---|---|---|---|
| Afghanistan | Af. 500 | | unrestricted if declared | |
| Albania | prohibited | | unrestricted if declared | |
| Algeria | prohibited | | unrestricted if declared | |
| Angola | prohibited | | unrestricted if declared | |
| Argentina | unrestricted | | unrestricted | |
| Australia | unrestricted I A. $100. | | unrestricted if declared | |
| Austria | unrestricted I Sch. 15000. | | unrestricted | |
| Bahamas | unrestricted | | unrestricted if declared | |
| Bangladesh | Taka 25 I prohibited | | unrestricted if declared | |
| Barbados | unrestricted | | unrestricted | |
| Belgium | unrestricted | | unrestricted | |
| Benin | unrestricted | | unrestricted | |
| Bermuda | unrestricted | | unrestricted if declared | |
| Bolivia | unrestricted | | unrestricted | |
| Brazil | unrestricted | | unrestricted | |
| Bulgaria | prohibited | | unrestricted if declared | |
| Burma | prohibited | | unrestricted if declared | |
| Burundi | unrestricted if declared | | unrestricted if declared | |
| Cambodia | prohibited | | unrestricted if declared | |
| Cameroon | unrestricted I CFA Fr 25000. | | unrestricted if declared | |
| Canada | unrestricted | | unrestricted | |
| Central African Rep. | unrestricted | | unrestricted if declared | |
| Chad | unrestricted | | unrestricted if declared | |
| Chile | unrestricted | | unrestricted if declared | |
| China | prohibited | | unrestricted if declared | |
| Colombia | unrestricted I Pesos imported | | unrestricted | |
| Congo | unrestricted I CFA. Fr. 50000. | | unrestricted if declared | |
| Costa Rica | unrestricted | | unrestricted if declared | |
| Cuba | prohibited | | unrestricted if declared | |

Fig. 64. International currency regulations
Check with the embassy of the country of destination
before you go for any revisions.
(*through page 567*)

From *The Multinational Executive Travel Companion* (Cambridge, MA:
Guides To Multinational Business Inc., 1979), pp. 51-53.

| Country | Local Currency | | Foreign Currency | |
| | Import | Export | Import | Export |
| --- | --- | --- | --- | --- |
| Cyprus | unrestricted | | unrestricted | |
| Czechoslovakia | prohibited | | unrestricted if declared | |
| Denmark | unrestricted I Kr. 3000. | | unrestricted | |
| Dominican Rep. | unrestricted | | unrestricted | |
| Ecuador | unrestricted | | unrestricted | |
| Egypt | E. P. 20 /prohibited | | unrestricted if declared | |
| El Salvador | unrestricted | | unrestricted if declared | |
| Ethiopia | unrestricted I E. $100. | | unrestricted if declared | |
| Finland | unrestricted I Markka 3000. | | unrestricted if declared | |
| France | unrestricted I F. 5000. | | unrestricted if declared | |
| Gabon | unrestricted | | unrestricted if declared | |
| Gambia | unrestricted | | unrestricted if declared | |
| Germany (East) | prohibited | | unrestricted if declared | |
| Germany (West) | unrestricted | | unrestricted | |
| Ghana | unrestricted | | unrestricted if declared | |
| Great Britain | unrestricted I PStlg. 25 | | unrestricted if declared | |
| Greece | Dr. 750. | | unrestricted if declared | |
| Guatemala | unrestricted | | unrestricted if declared | |
| Guinea | prohibited | | unrestricted if declared | |
| Guyana | unrestricted | | unrestricted if declared | |
| Haiti | unrestricted | | unrestricted if declared | |
| Honduras | unrestricted | | unrestricted if declared | |
| Hong Kong | unrestricted | | unrestricted | |
| Hungary | Ft. 400. | | unrestricted if declared | |
| Iceland | Kr. 500. I Kr. imported | | unrestricted if declared | |
| India | prohibited | | unrestricted if declared | |
| Indonesia | prohibited | | unrestricted if declared | |
| Iran | unrestricted I Rl. 3000. | | unrestricted if declared | |
| Iraq | Din. 25. | | unrestricted if declared | |
| Ireland (Eire) | unrestricted P. 25. | | unrestricted if declared | |
| Israel | IL. 200. | | unrestricted if declared | |
| Italy | LIT 35000. | | unrestricted if declared | |
| Ivory Coast | unrestricted I CFA. Fr. 75000. | | unrestricted if declared | |
| Jamaica | unrestricted I J. $20. | | unrestricted if declared | |
| Japan | unrestricted I Yen 30000. | | unrestricted if declared | |
| Jordan | unrestricted | | unrestricted if declared | |
| Kenya | prohibited | | unrestricted if declared | |
| Korea (North & South)* | prohibited | | unrestricted if declared | |
| Kuwait | unrestricted | | unrestricted if declared | |
| Laos | unrestricted | | unrestricted if declared | |
| Lebanon | unrestricted | | unrestricted | |
| Lesotho | unrestricted | | unrestricted if declared | |
| Liberia | unrestricted | | unrestricted if declared | |
| Libya | L.D. 20 | | unrestricted if declared | |
| Liechtenstein | unrestricted | | unrestricted | |
| Luxembourg | unrestricted | | unrestricted | |
| Madagascar | unrestricted | | unrestricted if declared | |
| Malawi** | unrestricted | | unrestricted if declared | |
| Malaysia | M. $500. | | unrestricted if declared | |
| Mali | unrestricted | | unrestricted if declared | |
| Malta | unrestricted I P.M. 20 | | unrestricted if declared | |
| Mauritania | unrestricted | | unrestricted if declared | |
| Mexico | unrestricted | | unrestricted | |

| Country | Local Currency | | Foreign Currency | |
| --- | --- | --- | --- | --- |
| | Import | Export | Import | Export |
| **Monaco** | unrestricted | | unrestricted | |
| **Morocco** | prohibited | | unrestricted if declared | |
| **Mozambique** | Esc. 2500. | | unrestricted if declared | |
| **Nepal** | unrestricted | | unrestricted | |
| **Netherlands** | unrestricted | | unrestricted | |
| **New Zealand** | NZ. $10. | | unrestricted if declared | |
| **Nicaragua** | unrestricted | | unrestricted | |
| **Niger** | unrestricted I CFA. Fr. 75000. | | unrestricted if declared | |
| **Nigeria** | prohibited | | unrestricted if declared | |
| **Norway** | unrestricted I Kr. 800. | | unrestricted if declared | |
| **Pakistan** | P.Rps. 20. | | unrestricted if declared | |
| **Panama** | unrestricted | | unrestricted if declared | |
| **Paraguay** | unrestricted | | unrestricted if declared | |
| **Peru** | unrestricted | | unrestricted if declared | |
| **Philippines** | P.Pesos 100. | | unrestricted if declared | |
| **Poland** | prohibited | | unrestricted if declared | |
| **Portugal** | Esc. 1000 | | unrestricted | |
| **Rhodesia** | R. $10. | | unrestricted if declared | |
| **Romania** | prohibited | | unrestricted if declared | |
| **Saudi Arabia** | unrestricted | | unrestricted if declared | |
| **Senegal** | CFA. Fr. 75000. | | unrestricted if declared | |
| **Sierra Leone** | Leone 20. | | unrestricted if declared | |
| **Singapore** | unrestricted I Sing. $1000. | | unrestricted if declared | |
| **Somali Rep.** | unrestricted | | unrestricted if declared | |
| **South Africa** | Rand 50. | | unrestricted if declared | |
| **Spain** | Ptas. 50000 I Ptas. 3000. | | unrestricted if declared | |
| **Sri Lanka (Ceylon)** | Rps. 50 | | unrestricted if declared | |
| **Sudan** | prohibited | | unrestricted if declared | |
| **Surinam** | unrestricted | | unrestricted if declared | |
| **Sweden** | Kr. 6000. | | unrestricted | |
| **Switzerland** | unrestricted | | unrestricted | |
| **Syria** | S.100. | | unrestricted if declared | |
| **Taiwan** | N.T. $4000. I N.T. $2000. | | unrestricted if declared | |
| **Tanzania** | prohibited | | unrestricted if declared | |
| **Thailand** | Baht 500. | | unrestricted if declared | |
| **Togo** | unrestricted I CFA. Fr. 75000. | | unrestricted if declared | |
| **Trinidad & Tobago** | unrestricted | | unrestricted if declared | |
| **Tunisia** | prohibited | | unrestricted if declared | |
| **Turkey** | TL. 1000 | | unrestricted if declared | |
| **Uganda** | unrestricted | | unrestricted if declared | |
| **Upper Volta** | unrestricted | | unrestricted if declared | |
| **U.S.A.** | unrestricted | | unrestricted | |
| **U.S.S.R.** | prohibited | | unrestricted if declared | |
| **Venezuela** | unrestricted | | unrestricted if declared | |
| **Vietnam** | prohibited | | unrestricted if declared | |
| **Yugoslavia** | Y.Din. 1500./Y.Din. 1000 | | unrestricted if declared | |
| **Zaire** | unrestricted | | unrestricted if declared | |
| **Zambia** | Kw 10 I Kw imported | | unrestricted if declared | |

**State Department list of countries considered dangerous for Americans** (as of February, 1980)

Check with the State Department before going to a country of questionable safety. U.S. intelligence may have gone downhill in recent years, but it can still call a dangerous situation. The list:

| | | |
|---|---|---|
| Afghanistan | Iran | Oman |
| Algeria | Iraq | Pakistan |
| Bahrain | Kuwait | Qatar |
| Bangladesh | Lebanon | Syria |
| Chad | Libya | United Arab Emirates |
| El Salvador | Nicaragua | Yemen |

Limited warnings have been issued for Uganda and Zimbabwe-Rhodesia. The State Department also puts out bulletins on special situations—a crime wave, a ring of passport thieves, etc.

---

# GUIDES TO MULTINATIONAL BUSINESS

---

This company, in Cambridge, Massachusetts, issues several travel guides that rank among the best available for businesspeople. Cheap they are not, but they have the kind of information that matters when you mean business. Most other travel guides are concerned primarily with restaurants, museums, and other diversions.

Take, for example, the *Multinational Executive Travel Companion.* It has information on over 160 countries and features in-depth information on 115 international business centers. Besides the expected data on airlines, cars, embassies, hotels, etc., there are entries for business hours, business customs, trade fairs, holidays, currency regulations, and even important business statistics, such as key market indicators, balance of payments, and the performance of over 1350 companies worldwide.

The publishers mean for you to take this book with you, so it is very small. Even at 624 pages, it is quite light and slim. They do this by making the print very, very small, and the paper is very thin—that's the trick.

The book is updated annually, and it costs $35, $45 if ordering from abroad.

Another useful guide put out by this publisher is the *Businessman's Guide to the Arab World.* This book is intended to aid westerners' perspective on countries that are culturally, politically, and economically very different from our own. Although this book won't give you any real insight into the Arab mind, it'll keep you from committing gaffes

---

like making cornball remarks about Cleopatra when in Egypt. The primary value of the book is its statistical information. It's $35 domestically, $45 abroad.

Rounding out the selection is *Business Travel Costs Worldwide*. This is a book about what things cost—transportation, accommodation, dining, entertainment, personal items and services, and business services. Average costs are not very reliable, but a few specific quotes allow you to see and assess value. However, as the editors point out in their Introduction, the book is meant to serve only as a *guide*. Despite its shortcomings, this book is helpful, and it's one of the few expense guides available. $100 domestic. $125 abroad.

Contact:
Guides to Multinational Business
Harvard Square
P. O. Box 92
Cambridge, Massachusetts 02138
(617) 868-2288

If you are ordering, you must enclose a check or money order.

---

# HOW TO GO TO A TRADE SHOW

## IF YOU ARE ATTENDING AS A VISITOR

Trade shows are an important medium for companies to make contacts, write business, and show their goods and services to the business community and the press. But often, the difference between being "the talk of the show" and being lost in obscurity has little to do with the quality of the product on exhibit; there is an art to setting up a booth at a show.

Attending a show can be a colossal waste of time if you wander aimlessly, picking up brochures and chatting with ladies in bathing suits or half-drunk glad-handers in polyester suits. Make a game plan based on the size of the show, its duration, and the amount of time you are prepared to commit.

CASE OUT THE SHOW  If it's one you've never attended, talk to someone who has. Find out its primary purpose. Some shows are mainly for writing business. Others are strictly showcases. Still others are merely a chance to trade business cards, talk shop, and gossip. Is the show "to the trade only" or open to consumers? Whatever the case, it's up to you to decide whether the show will justify your time and expense. One ambitious young junior executive working for a major communications conglomerate convinced his superiors to retain the services of an outside consultant whose job was simply to advise them on what shows to attend, what shows to place booths in, and what shows to skip. It paid off. The junior executive claims he doubled business in his division simply by following the "road show" schedule proposed by the consultant.

Speak to colleagues who have attended the show in the past. Call the show manager and ask questions about who attends, and for what purpose. Ask for data to be mailed to you. Also, find out how "new" the show is: Shows often take several years to get organized and gain credibility in the industry. The first few computer industry shows were sheer pandemonium. Many are no longer held, but the ones that survive are well attended.

PRIORITIZE  Some exhibitors are musts. Know who they are and where they are. You don't necessarily have to hit them first, but hit them with enough time to do what you have to do. Some of the larger exhibits maintain "hospitality suites," which offer a more intimate setting. Since the shows usually run about three days, that leaves only three evenings—and three dinner engagements. Try to lock the key people into dinner at the start of the show, before the others get to them. Don't be surprised, however, if the exhibitor cancels because there is someone else he wants to have dinner with (someone who has more clout than you have). *C'est la guerre.*

GET A COPY OF THE EXHIBIT DIRECTORY AND SCHEDULE, AND STUDY IT BEFORE EMBARKING  This will help you avoid skipping from floor to floor or searching endlessly for your destination. Exhibition centers are huge.

DON'T BE SUCKED INTO TOO MANY SEMINARS  Seminars given at trade shows are more for insiders than for outsiders. Often, they are PR vehicles for the speakers of the sponsoring companies. But if the idea of a given seminar grabs you, by all means attend. You'll be able to tell after the first few minutes whether you will learn anything worthwhile. If your reaction is negative, don't be embarrassed; get up and leave. Another approach is to have someone tape the seminar for you; then you can listen to the proceedings while soaking in a tub or driving home.

DON'T TRY TO GET FREE MERCHANDISE  It makes you look like a nickel-and-dime merchant. Don't drool; be subtle. If it's a big item and you are not giving the company a big order, the best you can expect is a chance to buy at cost. Selling merchandise out of a booth is usually banned at trade shows, but the exhibitors would rather not pay the shipping charges of returning the stuff to home base. So on the last day of the show, they'll try to get rid of it by selling it to attendees or to a local store that can pick it up. Sometimes you can get them to promise the stuff to you right at the beginning. But don't bug them throughout the show; this is not the primary reason you are there.

PLAN A STRATEGY TO SHOP THE SHOW  Most shows are organized with the larger and more established lines on the lower floors, the newer and often smaller lines and firms on the upper floors. Some buyers refer to "working the show backward" when they are interested primarily in seeing what's new and who's new.

## IF YOU ARE AN EXHIBITOR

PLAN WELL IN ADVANCE  There are always problems. And it takes a good 60-90 days to build a display. Beginning a year in advance is not excessive. Talk to the show management for all the details.

FORMULATE OBJECTIVES  What do you hope to accomplish? Are you going to the right show for that purpose? Get demographic and marketing data from the show management before making a final decision. Shows can be quite expensive, with costs encompassing booth rental space, display construction, and the travel and living expenses of personnel.

BUDGET  Decide in advance how much to spend.

DECIDE ON A THEME  You are competing for the attention of the attendees, so the tenets of advertising apply—you've got to get your message across, convincingly, forcefully, and memorably. Don't be afraid to go to your ad agency. And once you have a basic theme, a design consultant can be very helpful in translating it into a display with impact.

GET THE ENTIRE FIRM BEHIND YOU  It helps to have enthusiasm from top management. Since your exhibit will both represent and influence the image of the firm, it should not be regarded as strictly a project of the sales department. Bring in the advertising and PR people. Even product design people benefit, because feedback from buyers about what they want is priceless.

Make sure your booth will be manned by informed, well-mannered personnel. Too often, this is left to the last minute and you wind up with people who can't talk shop and, all too apparently, are just minding the store. Don't let this happen. And don't skimp on personnel: The booth must be attended at all times, and you may want to slip away to talk privately with a client. Some exhibitors rely on the crude method of using bikini-clad or seductively dressed models to lure potential customers to the booth. There is no denying that it sometimes works, but the practice is offensive. (Many women are now buying, and you could lose business.) My advice is to hire intelligent, well-qualified people. Women should wear fashionable business dress.

PUSH  Promote the show and your exhibit *before* as well as during the show. You want to reach the out-of-towners who are here for the show.

Take ads in the local papers, and, if you have the bucks, try radio (ideally, run your ad during business news and the stock market report). Other approaches include billboards along main routes (especially to airports), ads in trade papers, and, of course, the exhibitor's stock in trade—premiums, ad specialty items, gimmicks, and other giveaways. Check with exposition management for the rules regarding this.

GO FOR IT   Go after business, whether you are out for orders, looking for contacts, or just desirous of spreading the word.

## WHERE TO LEARN MORE ABOUT TRADE SHOWS

The most complete listing of trade shows is the *Exhibits Schedule, the Annual Directory of Trade and Industrial Shows*, published by *Successful Meetings* magazine in cooperation with the Exhibit Designers and Producers Association. It classifies trade shows in three ways: by industry, by geography (city, state, and nation), and by chronology. The listings include the name of each show, its frequency, site, and dates; the names of the exhibition manager and the sponsoring organization; the exhibition's size and number of booths, the location of the sponsor's headquarters, and an estimated attendance for each show. It is invaluable for planning your show schedule, whether you are an exhibitor or an attendee.

> Contact:
> Exhibits Schedule
> 633 Third Avenue
> New York, New York 10017

The U.S. Department of Commerce publishes the *Overseas Export Promotion Calendar*, which lists U.S. trade promotion events held abroad. The calendar is organized by product classification and gives the name, location, date, and American-based contact for each exhibition, mission, or seminar included.

> Contact:
> Overseas Export Promotion Calendar
> Industry Participation Division, Room 4012
> Office of Export Promotion
> U.S. Department of Commerce
> Washington, D.C. 20230

*The Dow Jones-Irwin Business Almanac* also lists some of the principal international trade shows and fairs.

> Contact:
> The Dow Jones-Irwin Business Almanac
> Dow Jones-Irwin
> 1818 Ridge Road
> Homewood, Illinois 60430

# 42

# TRAVEL BUMMERS

A vacation spent in a sickbed can leave you depressed. But a business trip thrown out of kilter by an unexpected, unpleasant occurrence can cost your firm a great deal of time and money—and cause a setback in your career.

## AIR SICKNESS

Your personal experience may tell you otherwise, but air sickness is much rarer these days. Planes fly higher, and cabin conditions have improved. Still, the presence of turbulence, or just your own natural tendency toward queasiness may result in your being fixated on the air sickness bag in the pocket in front of you.

### PRECAUTIONS

- *Loosen tight clothing, or remove it.* Especially tight things—stockings, girdles, garters, neckties, shoes.
- *Stand and stretch periodically.* This is especially important for those who are older or obese, or who suffer from a bad heart or varicose veins.
- *Try to get a seat on the right-hand side.* In holding patterns and approaches to domestic airports, more left turns occur than right.
- *If you anticipate a problem, you might want to take a pill.* Bonamine, Dramamine, and Marezine are very effective. *Caution:* They make you drowsy. You'd better keep this in mind if you'll be driving after you leave the plane, or if you have to be sharp for a business meeting.
- *Sit in a reclining position and keep your eyes closed.* Relaxing this way will help stave off the onset of air sickness.
- *Don't eat anything that is new to you or that you tend not to digest easily.*

# JET LAG

## JET LAG IS REAL

It is now generally regarded as a disease called circadian dysrhythmia and desynchronosis. This simply means that the body's natural rhythms and cycles—such as sleep, digestion, hunger, and sex—become out of phase with the external world and out of synch with each other. Jet lag can cause insomnia, headaches, irritability, diarrhea or constipation, muscle aches, and excessive fatigue, to name just a few of the more common disorders.

## THE PROBLEM

Adjusting to a new time zone takes time; unfortunately, we don't usually have the time we need. Although some rhythms can adjust within 48 hours, the digestive system usually takes about one day to normalize for each time zone crossed (New York to Rome crosses *seven* zones). The heart rate takes five and a half days to normalize; body temperature, seven; urine output, ten; and sleep patterns, up to fourteen.

## THE BEST REMEDY IS REST

The International Civil Aviation Organization has come up with a formula for determining the rest (in tenths of days) needed to overcome the effects of jet lag:

$$\frac{\text{travel time (hrs)}}{2} + \text{time zones in excess of 4} + \text{departure time coefficient} + \text{arrival time coefficient} = \text{rest period (tenths of days)}$$

*To determine arrival and departure coefficients:*

| period (hours) | departure time coefficient | arrival time coefficient |
|---|---|---|
| 0800-1200 | 0 | 4 |
| 1200-1800 | 1 | 2 |
| 1800-2200 | 3 | 0 |
| 2200-0100 | 4 | 1 |
| 0100-0800 | 3 | 3 |

*Example:*   New York to London:   travel time = 6 hours
time zones crossed = 5
departure time = 1800 (New York time)
arrival time = 0500 (London time)

Formula: $\frac{6}{2} + 1 + 3 + 3 = 10$ (tenths of a day) = 24 hours' rest

## HOW TO MINIMIZE JET LAG

Plan ahead. A few simple maneuvers can make all the difference in how you feel at the end of your trip.

PREPARE YOUR RHYTHMS IN ADVANCE   Several days before departure, begin gradually to change your eating and sleeping schedule in the direction of the time zone you are traveling to.

CHOOSE YOUR FLIGHT   Consider:

- *travel time.* Minimize lengthy stopovers.
- *departure and arrival times.* It's better to leave in the morning and arrive at your destination when it's time to rest, than to fly all night and arrive during early-morning activity.
- *flight load and configuration.* The more space, the better; if it's a long flight, opt for a wide-body craft, and a first-class seat if it's in the budget.

SELECT YOUR SEAT   Seats opposite emergency exits, hatches, or bulkheads have slightly more room. Try to stay on the aisle or at the window; middle seats offer the least room. Arrive early so you can choose the "best" seat. Ask about the load: If it is light, request a seat next to two empty ones so you can stretch across them (the arms of the seats fold up and back) and sleep.

TRY TO AVOID TRAVELING ALONE   Believe it or not, studies show that jet lag is lessened when you travel in a group or with a companion.

DRESS CASUALLY   Wear loose clothing; allow circulation to be free. Tight neckties and tight shoes are out. Better yet, take a carry-on with you and keep your necktie there—you can put it on just before landing, if necessary. Some airlines provide soft slippers. Use them, or bring your own. On a very long flight, it would be wise to bring along your favorite comfortable "dress down" clothing—soft jeans and a sweat shirt, maybe?—and change on the plane, and then back again if you've got a meeting upon landing.

KEEP "FRESHENERS" WITH YOU   Toothbrush and paste, razors, after-shave, mouth wash, eye wash, deodorant, moisturizer (to combat the desert-dry atmosphere aloft). You'll be surprised at how much better they can make you feel.

---

DON'T DRINK   Okay, okay; if you must drink, drink moderately. The notion of "I had a few drinks, and didn't feel a thing the whole flight" is, for most people, a big mistake. Remember—the higher you are, the higher you'll get. At only 10,000 feet, two or three martinis are as potent as four or five imbibed at sea level. And hangover from in-flight drinking lasts much longer, too. Because the oxygen supply in the planes is reduced, the cells of the body get less of it, and lack of oxygen aggravates the effects of alcohol.

KEEP SMOKING TO A MINIMUM   Excessive smoking in a poorly ventilated area can contribute to nausea, especially when supplemented by the effects of the altitude, turbulence, and lack of exercise and sleep associated with air travel. In addition, the cabin air is not only short on oxygen, but also virtually free of moisture. The dryness and lack of oxygen increase the amount of carbon monoxide absorbed into the blood by the smoker, and this may increase the work load of the heart.

EAT RIGHT   Eat lightly and never at odd hours. It may be lunchtime on the plane, but if your body is set at 3:00 A.M., a steak is hardly the thing. Odd-hours munching will throw your digestive cycle out of whack. And remember, *a plane is not the place to try something new.* Most airline food is extremely predictable. When in doubt about a particular dish, choose the simplest or most familiar one on the menu.

EXERCISE   From time to time, take a walk down the aisle. Some airlines provide suggestions for exercises you can do in your seat. Stretch those muscles. Prolonged sitting is a bigger problem than you might think—the muscles are weakened, the joints get stiff, circulation is hampered—and you notice these effects in the form of tension, fatigue, backaches, cramps, and other annoyances. It is amazing how many of us never miss a day of jogging or pushups at home, and then go on a trip and skip all exercising for days at a time. It may be socially awkward to do some simple calisthenics on a plane or in a flight lounge—but do them. You'll see Japanese and Chinese tour groups doing them wherever you go.

TRY TO AVOID SCHEDULING YOURSELF TOO TIGHTLY   If you want to rest after the flight, you should be able to do so.

CONTINUE WITH PRESCRIBED MEDICATION   Get advice from your doctor concerning timing. For example, if the pill bottle says "before bedtime" and you are traveling, does that mean you take the pill before you go to bed in Hong Kong, or when it's bedtime according to your home time zone? Some medication works better before sleep; in other cases, it's the time between dosages that is important. Get it straight.

AVOID PROLONGED FLYING   The biggest danger is from *accumu-*

*lated sleep debt.* Then there's the *excessive dryness* in the cabin. Prolonged exposure can cause scratchy throats, itchy eyes, dimming vision, and other signs of dehydration. In extreme cases, cabin conditions, when coupled with alcohol and smoking, can produce brittleness of hair and nails, and hypoxia (oxygen deficiency) leading to temporary anemia and subpar mental ability and perception. So remember to plan your trip to allow time for rest.

A NOTE OF CAUTION   The change in air pressure during landing can cause discomfort in the ears and, in some cases, lead to permanent damage. If you notice a problem, chew gum or open your mouth to equalize the pressure in the inner ear with that on the outside. Avoid traveling with a bad cold. If you feel a need for it, take a decongestant about a half hour before landing to clear your respiratory passages. Some people have a chronic problem with their ears at high altitudes. If your ears bother you during a long elevator ride or at the top of a tall building, get them checked before you fly. It's a more serious problem than the airlines are willing to admit.

---

# WATER

---

You've got to be careful about drinking water overseas. But don't overdo your concern. "I have had patients who have become so obsessed with precautions about water or disease that they have actually filled their bathtubs with bottled water," wrote noted tropical medicine expert Kevin Cahill, MD. "This is asinine." Here, in a nutshell, are the rules to follow:

- *In the large cities of industrialized nations, tap water is safe to drink.*
- *Tap water is often safe in many developing countries, but it is advisable not to depend on its potability.*
- *When drinking bottled water, make sure that you or one of your companions breaks the seal.* A common trick of locals is refilling mineral water bottles with the local stuff. Usually, such a bottle will be poorly sealed.
- *Although it seems logical that using locally made ice would defeat your purpose, small amounts of contaminated water almost never do any harm.* So an ice cube or two won't hurt you. Neither will a little water for brushing your teeth or douching. Still, it's a good idea to check first with local health officials, because there are local outbreaks during which the water could become severely contaminated.
- *When in Africa, Asia, or South America, do not swim in inland bodies of water or canals.* They are usually filled with parasites and infectious amoebas.

---

**Water Purifiers.** Recent interest and technological advances have made possible the development of portable water purification units. Actually, typical American tap water is quite good, but fears of contamination by everything from nuclear fallout to defoliants have become regular media fodder.

Unfortunately, it is unlikely that water purifiers intended for home use can be of much help in filtering out carcinogens and dangerous chemicals. But the smaller purifiers, designed for travel, can be of some value abroad.

Among the best models are the *Walbro Water Purifier* and the *Minisilverator Water Washer.* Both units involve pouring the water through a filtration unit. The Walbro uses a chemical filter that contains iodine, but the Water Washer uses activated charcoal and silver.

As a result, the Water Washer is much better at removing sediment and chemical residue, but not as effective in killing bacteria. The manufacturer is well aware of this, so it provides a "mini booster," a bottled sodium hypochlorite solution that is effective against bacteria.

The Walbro's iodine filter kills bacteria, so there's no need for additional treatment. But, believe me, you can taste the iodine in the treated water—not that water treated with the Water Washer tastes that great, either.

Both units are small, but the Walbro is much smaller and lighter. The Water Washer weighs 20 ounces; the Walbro weights only 3½.

> Contact:
> *Walbro Water Purifier:*
>> Water Pollution Control Systems, Inc.
>> Subsidiary of the Walbro Corp.
>> 3001 South State
>> Ann Arbor, Michigan 48104
> *Portable Water Washer:*
>> American Water Purification
>> 1990 Olivera Road
>> Concord, California 94520

*A note of caution.* Don't become overconfident because you have one of these purifiers. Rely on it only to make safe, but unpleasant water more pleasant. Both units are helpful in an emergency, when you have no choice but to drink contaminated water—but they are not totally effective.

# OTHER LIQUIDS

**Beer.** When you are hot and thirsty, beer can be a good, safe way to quench yourself. Although beer is better than hard liquor, keep in mind that one gets drunk easier while sweating.

**Soft drinks.** Stay away from the local stuff when in the tropics. Sugar in liquid provides an excellent culture for bacteria. Imported soft drinks are usually okay. And some soft drinks, such as Coca-Cola, are prepared according to strict standards. Again, watch out for Coke bottles that have been filled with something else.

**Wine.** Wines do not travel well and are usually not good in the tropics, except in the most plush hotels or industrialized tropical nations.

**Milk.** Milk is dangerous in many places. Pasteurization is still uncommon in developing nations, and even where it does exist, sterilization is sometimes poor. You could boil your milk first, but boiling also destroys the protein. Another alternative is powdered milk, provided you mix it with safe water.

# FOOD

Americans often claim that they got sick from the food in a given country. Very often, it's simply a matter of eating something that didn't "agree" with them. Doctors cite four main factors that contribute to food-related sickness:

**Insects.** In tropical climates, it is very difficult to keep insects away. Stay away from food that has been sitting out in the open.

**Proper hygiene.** You must be especially careful when abroad. Wash thoroughly, especially after a visit to the lavatory. This also applies to the domestic help, so you should be conscientious in finding a hotel that has high standards of cleanliness.

**Lack of good judgment.** If you are the type that likes to do as the locals do, you might get a bit too fearless. Don't eat in dirty places or from dirty dishes, and be sensible when it comes to trying exotic fare.

**Contaminated food:**

- *vegetables.* Fresh vegetables are usually safe when freshly cooked. Reheated vegetables are a no-no. Stay away from the leafy green variety in the tropics.
- *fruit.* Fresh fruits with unbroken skins are usually okay. Fruit compotes must be fresh, or forget about them. Always wash and peel fresh fruit yourself. If the skin is broken, throw the fruit away.
- *fish.* Avoid clams in strange places. They are hepatitis carriers. Fresh fish is usually safe if well cooked. Be careful with raw or smoked fish.
- *meats.* Should be well cooked and hot.
- *duck.* A poor choice, because it takes a long time to prepare and is often reheated.
- *lamb.* A very safe bet, if freshly killed and cooked on charcoal, as it is in the Arab nations. If you can watch your meal being prepared, you can feel safe even in a dirty restaurant.
- *cold plates, custards, pastries—or anything prepared long in advance.* Watch out; flies can carry disease.

---

# MEDICAL CARE

---

If you are abroad for a short stay, avoid seeking medical treatment unless it's absolutely necessary. When you begin treatment, you are opening yourself to the possibility of complications, infection, and lack of proper follow-up. Besides, in general, the quality of medical care abroad is far below that available in the United States. Possible exceptions include England, Switzerland, Germany, Scandinavia, Japan, and the Soviet Union. If you are planning to stay around for a while or take up residence, of course you'll have little choice. The best thing to do is get the name of a good doctor *before* you need him. Get a referral from someone you trust. It pays to drop by for a preliminary visit and to provide him with a medical history. This precaution is especially important if you have kids with you.

If you don't know anyone in town, try the American Embassy, British Embassy, an American airline or cruise line, or an American or British missionary organization. All of these groups keep lists of English-speaking doctors.

**International Association for Medical Assistance to Travellers (IAMAT).** This directory provides information on "western style" medical services in 450 cities around the world. All the doctors cited in the directory speak English and have fixed rates for office visits, house

---

calls, and Sundays or holidays. In addition to the directory, IAMAT will provide you with a membership card, a "Travellers Clinical Record," and a "World Immunization and Malaria Chart." You can also gain access to IAMAT's "World Climate Charts," which also feature information on food, water, and milk in 1,440 cities around the world.

The IAMAT membership is free, although I recommend a donation. A fixed minimum donation for membership is required if you wish to gain access to the climate charts. Corporate memberships are accepted. You may request as many applications as you like for your traveling employees, but then a donation must be included.

    Contact:
    IAMAT
    350 Fifth Avenue, Suite 5260
    New York, New York 10001

**Intermedic.** A subsidiary of the Executive Health Examiners Group, Intermedic is a very reputable organization that provides health services to corporations, unions, and other organizations. For a modest fee (currently $6 per year per person, $10 per family—spouse plus kids), you get a directory of participating physicians in over 200 cities who subscribe to the service. They have agreed to a "fee ceiling," they speak English, and they have pledged to respond promptly to calls from Intermedic members. The directory also includes space for your medical records, and upon request Intermedic provides a service which gives you important travel information before you go. The directory does not list the specialties, but all physicians' credentials are scrutinized by Executive Health Examiners' Medical Director, before they are accepted and listed in the directory. Their qualifications are on file at Intermedic in New York. Still, the service is pretty cheap, and judging by the folks who run it, pretty reliable.

    Contact:
    Intermedic, Inc.
    777 Third Avenue
    New York, New York 10017
    (212) 486-8974

**Returning home.** It is always a good idea to get a checkup upon returning home from (a) the tropics, (b) developing nations, (c) any long trip, (d) any trip during which you have been sexually adventurous. Or if you have done something risky or simply have a hunch that you might have been exposed to disease.

The world is full of weird strains of VD; even doctors misdiagnose them. So watch out. Most developing nations have VD epidemics. And even in the advanced nations, VD is still very easy to pick up. Why, just look at the situation in the United States. See a doctor at the first sign of any possible symptoms.

Tropical diseases are also easily misdiagnosed. And they can linger in a dormant stage for months after you return. If you have been in a tropical or underdeveloped nation, ask your physician to do a blood count, tuberculin test, urine analysis, and stool analysis. Depending on the indications, the doctor may wish to run a liver function test, chest X ray, proctoscopy, serologic test, and/or skin test.

---

## WHAT TO TAKE WITH YOU

---

YOUR BASIC KIT

- *an extra pair of eyeglasses.* Your eyeglass prescription.
- *extra medication,* clearly labeled, and a renewal prescription that gives the generic name and dosage of the medication
- *a brief medical record,* noting blood group, Rh factor, etc., and any drug-related allergies
- *sleeping pills.* These are not recommended for regular use, but if jet lag really throws you out of whack, they might help you get on track again.
- *an antihistamine,* such as Chlortrimeton or Benadryl. Relieves itching from bites or rashes.
- *an antibiotic, such as tetracycline*
- *an analgesic, or painkiller.* If you are ever in a great deal of pain, these could save your life by allowing you to function.
- *a decongestant,* if you suffer from clogged ears on plane flights.

WHEN VISITING TROPICAL OR DEVELOPING COUNTRIES

- *insect repellent.* You can usually buy this locally.
- *water purification tablets.* They often make the water taste awful.
- *chloroquine.* The old standby antimalarial.
- *paregoric.* An antidiarrheal agent, but it is an opiate. Use only if you really have it bad. Otherwise, stick with Kaopectate or Lomotil.
- *snakebite kits.* Well, maybe if you plan to stomp around in the desert or high grass. It is more important to be careful and wear proper footwear where snakes are known to hang around. But snake bite kits don't weigh much or cost much, so what the heck.

# LOSING THINGS

The best advice—indeed, the *only* general advice that makes sense—is to prepare for the possibility that you will lose something, somewhere:

**Have enough of the right kind of insurance.** Make sure that your policy covers luggage. The airlines have limited liability, and it usually isn't enough to cover the full value of the contents of the luggage. Does your policy cover the *loss* of property, or only what's missing as a result of a crime? Is the policy in effect abroad as well as in the United States?

**Make copies.** When you are away, the only really critical things you can lose are things you need to get back home. Valuables such as jewelry can be insured, but all the insurance in the world won't help you if you lose your passport in Bulgaria. Do this now:

*Get your wallet in order.* Notice the discrepancy between what is in it and what you *thought* was in it. When you are satisfied that the wallet carries the items you require to be kept on your person at all times, go to the nearest copier. Remove all papers and cards from the wallet and make copies of them. Some copiers will reproduce credit cards and IDs. If yours doesn't, write all the numbers on a piece of paper. File the copies and other records.

It's a good idea to make *two* copies of what's in your wallet: Take the extra copy with you on the trip. This copy will not only aid you in retrieving a lost wallet, but might also serve as ID in the absence of the real thing.

*Before you go.* Make a record of traveler's cheque numbers. File it. Take on your trip the record that the issuer gives you, but keep it apart from your traveler's cheques—you don't want to lose both your cheques and your record of their numbers.

**Carry your plane tickets separately.** They are very tough to replace. Overseas, it's more difficult for a thief to cash them in or use them, because he'll need your passport: So don't keep your tickets and passport in the same place. It's also wise not to put them in your wallet.

**Guard your passport.** A U.S. passport is a super-hot black market commodity. If you lose it, chances are you'll never see it again. Call the American embassy, mission, or consulate immediately. Life without your passport can be a big hassle if you are in a remote area, far from a government office. In some countries, you *are* your passport. Without it, you simply don't exist. And it's not only in the Warsaw Pact nations or the developing countries that you might encounter this attitude. Try losing your passport in Switzerland sometime.

**Consider joining a credit card bureau.** For a small annual fee, it will insure you against misuse of stolen credit cards, keep on file a record of all your cards and numbers, and notify all the card issuers for you; you just phone the bureau. Some credit card protection services also offer emergency cash advances.

# 43

# ARE YOU A TARGET? TERRORISM AND THE AMERICAN EXECUTIVE

In 1978, American businesses spent more than $7 million on anti-terrorist security. Even that wasn't nearly enough. This chapter should be taken quite seriously, because terrorist activity against you or your firm may be a very real threat. Naturally, some will chide you for taking an alarmist or paranoid attitude. Better to appear slightly foolish than dead.

Several basic facts about terrorism help explain why it has become so widespread:

- Terrorism is a tactic used by small groups to call attention to their cause and, sometimes, to force capitulation to their demands and goals.
- For terrorists, the ends justify the means.
- They generally accept the loss of life (both theirs and that of their victims) as a part of the struggle.
- Terrorists are aware that attacks on high-profile individuals and institutions (and their representatives) will bring publicity.
- Terrorists have a stake in demonstrating that the "establishment" doesn't work—that it is incapable of protecting its citizens against terrorism and that it is disorderly and weak.
- Terrorists generally run in small groups, but they are often very well organized, well trained, and good at what they do. They may be fanatics, but they are not dumb. More often than not, they outsmart local law enforcement officials.
- Terrorists do operate inside the United States as well as abroad, although their activity here appears to be more clandestine and less headline-grabbing. In 1976, 26 percent of all bombings in the U.S.A. were against domestic corporations; 12.5 percent were against banks. And 18.3 percent were against foreign companies. That means that over half were directed against private capitalist institutions. Only a small number were against political factions and individuals. And only 26 percent were

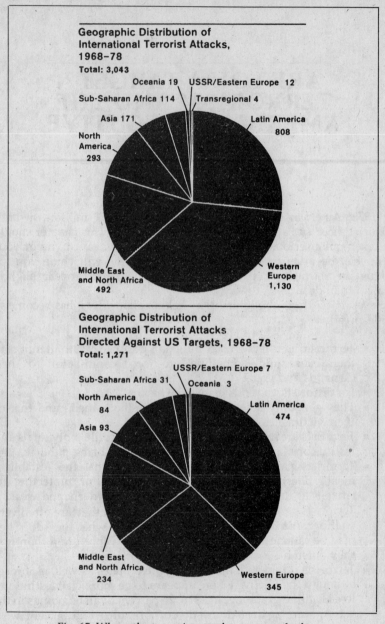

**Geographic Distribution of International Terrorist Attacks, 1968–78**
Total: 3,043

Oceania 19    USSR/Eastern Europe 12
Sub-Saharan Africa 114    Transregional 4
Asia 171
North America 293
Latin America 808
Middle East and North Africa 492
Western Europe 1,130

**Geographic Distribution of International Terrorist Attacks Directed Against US Targets, 1968–78**
Total: 1,271

USSR/Eastern Europe 7
Sub-Saharan Africa 31    Oceania 3
North America 84
Asia 93
Latin America 474
Middle East and North Africa 234
Western Europe 345

Fig. 65. Where the terrorist attacks occur, and where they are directed against American targets

From "International Terrorism In 1978," National Foreign Assessment Center (Washington, DC: Central Intelligence Agency, 1979), p. 2.

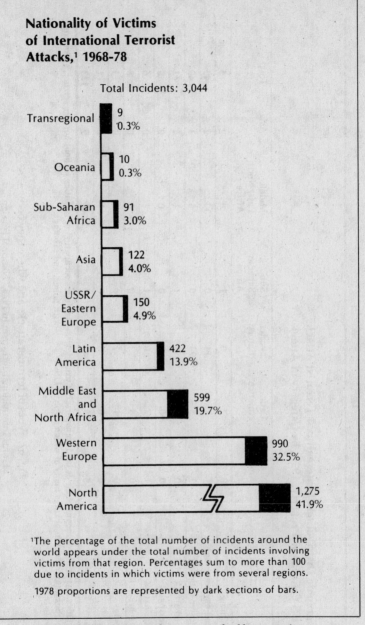

**Nationality of Victims of International Terrorist Attacks,[1] 1968-78**

Total Incidents: 3,044

| Region | Incidents | Percentage |
|---|---|---|
| Transregional | 9 | 0.3% |
| Oceania | 10 | 0.3% |
| Sub-Saharan Africa | 91 | 3.0% |
| Asia | 122 | 4.0% |
| USSR/ Eastern Europe | 150 | 4.9% |
| Latin America | 422 | 13.9% |
| Middle East and North Africa | 599 | 19.7% |
| Western Europe | 990 | 32.5% |
| North America | 1,275 | 41.9% |

[1]The percentage of the total number of incidents around the world appears under the total number of incidents involving victims from that region. Percentages sum to more than 100 due to incidents in which victims were from several regions.

1978 proportions are represented by dark sections of bars.

Fig. 66. The victims: who gets attacked by terrorists

From "International Terrorism In 1978," National Foreign Assessment Center (Washington, DC: Central Intelligence Agency, 1979), p. 4.

**Geographic Distribution of International Terrorist Attacks On US Citizens or Property, 1978, by Category of Attack**

| | North America | Latin America | Western Europe | Sub-Saharan Africa | Middle East/North Africa | Asia | Total |
|---|---|---|---|---|---|---|---|
| Kidnaping | 0 | 2 | 0 | 1 | 0 | 2 | 5 |
| Incendiary bombing | 1 | 1 | 15 | 0 | 30 | 2 | 49 |
| Explosive bombing | 3 | 5 | 23 | 0 | 6 | 3 | 40 |
| Armed attack | 0 | 3 | 4 | 1 | 1 | 2 | 11 |
| Hijacking[1] | 0 | 0 | 0 | 0 | 0 | 0 | 0 |
| Assassination | 1 | 2 | 0 | 1 | 2 | 0 | 6 |
| Theft, break-in | 0 | 5 | 3 | 0 | 0 | 0 | 8 |
| Sniping | 0 | 1 | 2 | 0 | 0 | 0 | 3 |
| Other[2] | 0 | 0 | 0 | 0 | 1 | 0 | 1 |
| Total | 5 | 19 | 47 | 3 | 40 | 9 | 123 |

[1] Includes hijackings of means of air or land transport, but excludes numerous nonterrorist hijackings many of which involved US aircraft.

[2] Includes occupation of facilities without hostage seizure, shootouts with police, and sabotage.

Fig. 67. Types of terrorist attacks and where they occur
From "International Terrorism In 1978," National Foreign Assessment Center (Washington, DC: Central Intelligence Agency, 1979), p. 11.

against federal and state government domestic offices. (Are you squirming yet?)

The terrorist activity around the world is all the more unnerving when one realizes that there are probably fewer than 3,000 hard-core terrorists in fewer than 50 terrorist organizations. The primary threat comes from four or five groups with a total combined membership of about 200. Increasing economic and political instability worldwide could indeed swell the numbers of active terrorists. *American business-people are extremely vulnerable, especially when traveling abroad.*

---

## CHECKING OUT THE BASICS

---

**If you work for a large corporation that regularly sends people abroad, find out if it has taken any preventive measures and/or has developed some kind of organized response capability to such a crisis.**

Lloyd Singer, Jan Reber, and Paul Shaw, experts on terrorists and terrorism, suggest the formation of a *Crisis Management Team (CMT)* that will be trained in how to handle a crisis generated by terrorists—and any other unforeseen disaster, man-made or natural.

In addition to establishing a mechanism to handle such problems effectively (this may save your life if it's a matter of delivering a ransom in 48 hours—the CMT will have thought it out in advance):

**See to it that appropriate defensive measures are taken to protect you and your family.** The days of the muscle-bound bodyguards have long been over. What good is a black belt in karate when you're confronted by a student terrorist armed with a Kalashnikov machine gun?

Terrorist groups, financed by Libya, the Soviet Union, and booty from bank robberies and kidnap ransoms, buy the best equipment they can. The protection program should be realistic and in line with the risks involved.

If you work for a Fortune 500 company, it is fair to request the facts regarding the executive protection program. Often, you will be briefed by a security expert on counterterrorism measures. If you are an entrepreneur, or an executive for a small company, you may be on your own. So here are some basic points to consider before making that swing through Italy (over 2000 terrorist attacks in 1978) or Latin America (nobody knows how many terrorist incidents take place there).

---

# ARE YOU A POTENTIAL VICTIM?

This checklist was compiled with the assistance of Carmine Pellosie Jr., vice president of Communication Control Systems, a New York based firm specializing in countersurveillance and protection equipment.

1. *How visible is the corporation you represent?* Is it known nationally? Internationally? Is it familiar to the public, or to the trade only? Has it been involved in any well-publicized or controversial ventures? How are relations with local and national governments, and the community? What has been the extent of the press coverage it has received: general and trade press? radio? television? Do terrorists consider your firm exploitive? What about its products? Does the company make a point of appearing to be tough on security? Is this provocative behavior, or does it seem to be a deterrent? Does the firm publicize its wealth?

2. *How visible are you?* Do you have a high or a low profile? Are your movements noted in the general or trade press? Do you "make a splash" among colleagues or in social circles? Are you known to be well-to-do? Are you considered by many to be a key executive in your firm? Are you the subject of coverage daily? Weekly? Just occasionally?

3. *What countries will you be in?* Some countries carry higher risks than others. In each country you'll visit: How stable is the government? How competent and cooperative is the law enforcement? Is there much terrorist activity there?

4. *How desirable are you as a target for terrorism?* A morbid question, but consider what the terrorists could gain by kidnapping you. The types of people terrorists consider victimizing vary, depending on the cause and the country. For example, women and children are prime targets in Israel, a nation struggling to preserve an ethnic group that was very nearly wiped out by the Nazis. A major target among the English is royalty, because of the "symbolic" importance. Attacks against U.S. "imperialism" by leftists often involve American multinational corporations, which are the most visible signs of the American presence abroad.

5. *Consider the motives of the terrorists.* Are they primarily monetary? Political? Religious? Or purely tactical? Often, the motive is a combination of several of these factors.

6. *How available are arms and weapons in the country?* In some countries, one can buy a heat-seeking missile, which can be fired from the shoulder, for a mere $15,000. Not much when

you consider that the PLO has a budget of $1 million per day. Such a missile could turn your Learjet into a crash statistic. And what about AK-47s, Uzi submachine guns, etc.? In some countries, possession of a handgun is enough to put you behind bars. In others, don't be surprised to see twelve-year-olds armed with high-powered rifles.

7. *How available is information about you and your movements?* Terrorists need information in order to operate. Unless you take precautions, it is easy to discover your personal and business travel plans, mode of travel, movement patterns, and general life-style, as well as facts about your firm and its security measures.

8. *Will your company protect you? To what extent?* What is the nature of insurance coverage for you and your family should something occur? How much is the company willing to do to insure your safety? This usually translates to "How much is it willing to spend?" As with any other business expense, your company will use some type of criteria to determine what amount of cash constitutes a reasonable security expense, given the situation. Just be sure that it has some means of taking into account the risks involved. It is true that the lower level executive is less likely to be a target and, therefore, does not usually require extensive security protection; but that same lower level executive, when traveling abroad, might be the highest ranking executive within striking distance of a terrorist organization. Even salesmen have been targets of terrorism and kidnap over the years.

9. *What is your primary mode of transportation?* Public? Train, bus, or plane? Private? Automobile? What kind—company limo or rented Fiat? Will you have a driver?

10. *Will you have an entourage?* Perhaps a local business associate will be at your side constantly. Or maybe you will be followed by publicity hounds, journalists, and paparazzi. If the entourage includes business people or government officials, consider whether they might be targets.

11. *How will you be transmitting information?* Phone? Telex? What is the possibility that your communications will be monitored or bugged?

12. *Where will you be working?* Will you be spending your time at the local offices of your firm, or those of a subsidiary? At the offices of a firm with which you are doing business? Or at a hotel conference room or trade show? It is difficult to generalize about which site is safest. In a nation being torn apart by leftist agitators and rioters, a building owned by Ford, GM, IBM, or ITT might not be such a safe place. But if it's a small group of terrorists that you are concerned about, such

buildings, equipped with excellent security, might be much safer than your hotel room, where the complicity of one clerk or chambermaid could place you in danger.

13. *Where will you be staying?* Consider the section of the city and the security at the hotel, home, or apartment. Again, how safe a place is depends on the situation. Sometimes the downtown areas are where law enforcement is most efficient and heavily concentrated, while the outskirts of town are danger zones. In other cases the relative obscurity of a rented suburban home or apartment with good protection systems might be more desirable.

---

# REDUCING THE RISKS

---

Security experts divide "protection strategies" into two basic approaches. The "low profile" approach seeks to eliminate all forms of attention-getting behavior and property. No flashy limousines, luxurious hotel rooms, or corporate aircraft.

The opposite strategy is sometimes called the hard-line (maximum security) approach. This involves providing the highest degree of protection available for the executive and family. Naturally, the armored vehicles and fortified residences involved will attract attention, but the sheer thoroughness and defense capability of the system is thought to serve as a deterrent. The hard-line strategy costs money and is usually used only by large corporations and wealthy individuals. Besides expensive hardware, it calls for specially trained security personnel who will brief the parties to be protected on what to do and what not to do.

The low-profile approach is within the reach of every executive. It just means being aware of the potential dangers and taking precautions to minimize the risks. But even the low-profile approach should be coordinated with a crisis management team in the home office, so that if something does happen, someone, somewhere, will know what to do.

*Remember, when you travel abroad, the U.S. Constitution doesn't travel with you.* So you might not get the kind of fair treatment and protection you are used to from local law enforcement authorities.

Here is a regimen of preventive measures generally agreed upon by most security and law enforcement experts:

**Limit information.** Terrorist activities are usually well planned. Attackers must know a great deal about their potential victims. Don't make it easy for them. Control and conceal information regarding:

---

- your patterns of movement, and your general life-style and that of your family
- business and personal travel plans, itineraries, and modes of travel
- the location, physical layout, and other details about your office or work site and your residence
- facts about your firm, its subsidiaries, and your personal duties and responsibilities
- details concerning security measures and procedures to protect you, your family, and your residence

Be reticent about such details when filling out hotel registration cards, conversing with strangers, filling out forms, and talking on the telephone.

**Vary patterns and habits.** Terrorists and other criminals are, by necessity, trained observers. The more you fall into daily routines and patterns of behavior, the easier it is for a crime to be planned and executed against you. Some of the most common patterns are:

- your departure time, travel time, and route to work—or, in the case of your family, to school, social activities, and shopping
- children's play patterns
- your work patterns and the times, frequency, and duration of periods you spend alone

Vary these patterns as frequently as possible. Take care that your variation is not a pattern in itself: Monday you leave for work at 9:00, Tuesday at 8:30, Wednesday at 9:15. An observer will quickly catch on, and know what to expect.

**Be alert.** People who want to observe you or your family on a regular basis risk making themselves conspicuous. Of course, they will attempt to be discreet, but if something seems strange to you, don't be so quick to dismiss your observation as paranoia. Common surveillance techniques used by terrorists include these phenomena:

- a cruising vehicle (car, bike, scooter, truck) passing in front of your residence or office several times a day or night
- a vehicle parked nearby that looks out of place. If it often has occupants who just sit there, be even more suspicious.
- attempts to case out your home or work site using clever disguises—mother with baby carriage, young couple with children, repair crews, etc.
- frequent phone calls in which the caller asks personal questions, or frequent phone hangups
- survey takers, door-to-door salespeople, bellhops, chambermaids, and waiters

- someone tailing you by car or other vehicle, or on foot. This is done while you are riding, walking, or engaged in recreational activity.

**Take precautions when you travel.**

- Inspect your car.
- Drive a car commonly used in the host country. And make sure that it has common plates.
- If it is a rented car or a company car, change the car frequently. If you own it, switch often with another executive.
- Vary your routes to work. This holds true even if you travel by bus or train.

**Make sure your work site is secure.**

- If it's an office, be sure that access is limited, that there is an adequate protection system, and that packages and deliveries can somehow be screened.
- Never work alone after hours.
- If you are working in a hotel, leave specific instructions with hotel security: Make sure that neither your name nor your room number is given out, and give the clerks and security guards a list of expected visitors.
- Do not attend meetings in unfamiliar places, especially when the meeting is arranged by someone you don't know well.

**Limit information concerning trips.**

- Don't buy tickets too far in advance. Get them at the airport or train station on the day of departure, if possible.
- Don't give affiliations and position to hotel check-in people or to travel agents.
- Most of the problems occur during transit to and from airports or train stations, so get there several hours early. This is not the kind of behavior expected of a busy executive.
- Don't have a chauffeured limousine waiting to meet you upon arrival. Take a cab instead.
- If you have a company plane, don't advertise the fact. Make sure the markings on it are discreet and that you have adequate preflight security. When the plane is parked, make sure that it is sitting in a secure hangar in an area that is well patrolled; or see to it that the plane is equipped with a perimeter alarm system.
- If you travel by train, lock your compartment.

**Keep your mouth shut.** Do not boast, broadcast information about where you are staying, or say why you are visiting, etc.

## Prevention Checklist 1: General

1. Instruct family and business associates not to provide strangers with information concerning executive or family.

2. Avoid giving unnecessary personal details to information collectors in response to their inquiries on behalf of publications such as business directories, social registers, or community directories.

3. Review organization's security plans to determine its effectiveness. Make certain all employees are aware of these plans.

4. Establish simple, effective signal systems which, when activated, will alert business associates, chauffeur, or family members of danger.

5. Be alert to strangers who are on business property for no apparent reasons.

6. Vary daily routines to avoid habitual patterns which kidnappers look for. Fluctuate travel, times, and routes to and from the office.

7. Executives should refuse to meet with strangers at scheduled or unknown locations.

8. An executive should always advise a business associate or family member of his destination when leaviing the office or home, and intended time of arrival.

9. Do not accept delivery of packages from unknown persons unless they have been cleared by security.

10. Do not open doors to strangers.

11. Do not hire domestics without a thorough background check.

12. Try to know where every member of the family is at all times, or where they will be.

13. Know all phone numbers — office, home, police, security headquarters.

14. Set up regular telephone check-in contacts between: Executive and family; executive and office; and executive and security base.

15. Use simple code words to confirm that everything is all right. Code words can be used for executive, family, security officer, parts of the city, etc.

16. Be cautious about giving out information regarding family, travel plans, or security measures and procedures. Use the phone with caution.

17. Report all suspicious persons loitering near the residence or the office, with a complete description of the person and/or vehicle to the police or security.

18. Know enough of the language of a foreign country to ask for a policeman or a doctor. Know how to use the telephone, especially pay phones.

19. Corporate press releases announcing promotions of executives should not list the executive's home address; other information releases should not discuss upcoming travel plans or other activities that might provide useful information to terrorists on where an executive might be at a given time, or on his pattern of living.

Fig. 68. Three antiterrorist and security surveys
(*through page 597*)

From Jan Reber and Paul Shaw, *Executive Protection Manual*
(Northbrook, IL: MTI Teleprograms Inc., 1976), pp. 111a-111b,
143-144. Reprinted by permission.

20. Press releases should be either without photographs of the executive, or else should not show the executive in his office or work location. Use a grey or a neutral background for all photographs.

## Prevention Checklist 2: Vehicle Protection

1. Inspect the car before entering. Look for:
   a. Evidence of entry
   b. Tail pipe blocked with explosives
   c. Material in the tire wells
   d. Check the back seat
   e. If packages are found near the car, do not move them. Call authorities.

2. Whenever possible, do not park the car unattended or unlocked.

3. Do not have the company or the executive's name on the car.

4. Park the car in a locked garage; never leave it parked on the street.

5. Park in general reserved areas, not in reserve stalls with executive's name.

6. The hood latch should be controlled from inside the car. The hood should also have a lock. The gas cap too, should have a lock.

7. The executive car should always have at least a half tank of gas.

8. Tamper alarms should be installed on the car.

9. The car should be serviced by the organization or by a local service station that has been given a thorough background check.

10. Never leave keys, other than the ignition key, with a service station or parking garage.

## Executive Biographical File Checklist

1. Does file contain full name and any nicknames?

2. Are home address and all telephone numbers (home, office, marina, etc.) included?

3. Are names, addresses and telephone numbers of all neighbors included?

4. Are five sets of photographs, fingerprints and palmprints included in each file? (Two photos should be black and white and three should be color.) Are copies of dental charts included in the file?

5. Are blood types, commonly-taken drugs, and sources of supply for both listed?

6. Are names of school, school officials, location, and school schedules for dependents included?

7. Are profiles of special activities (sports, etc.) included as well as location of usual indulgences?

8. Are written physical descriptions included?

9. Are descriptions of favorite articles of clothing and accessories (sunglasses, cane, etc.) included?

10. Are all regular activities such as church listed with schedules and locations?

11. Are all details of vehicles (cars, bicycles, motorcycles, etc.) listed? (Details should include make, model, year, color, license plate, accessories, serial number, etc.)

12. Are full details and photos of servants and drivers included? (Name, address, telephone, photos, schedule, fingerprints.)

13. Are names, addresses, telephone numbers of family and friends noted?

14. Are names, addresses, telephone numbers and schedule of employment for any working dependent included?

15. Are the names, addresses and telephone numbers of personal lawyer, physician, psychologist, and all other professionals included?

16. Are the names, addresses and telephone numbers of relatives included?

17. Are details of all forms of personal insurance included?

18. Are details of all forms of duress signals and codes included?

FOOTNOTES

1. Arthur A. Kingsbury, *Introduction to Security and Crime Prevention Surveys*, C. C. Thomas, Springfield, 1973, p. 6.

2. Adapted from *ibid.*, pp. 24-25.

**Harden your heart to hitchhikers.** This is tough, especially if you hitched your way through Europe as a student. But times have changed. And don't be victimized by giving into the temptation of having an attractive traveling companion. There is no law that says terrorists have to be ugly.

**Don't leave valuable documents in your car or in your hotel room.** Remember that U.S. passports are worth cash on the black market.

**Believe your eyes and ears.** Cops and soldiers in riot gear are a bad sign: Get the hell away from the area. Chances are they are not shooting a movie. You don't rubberneck in Italy, Turkey, or South America.

**Foreign cops are often not nice people.** They can tend to be trigger-happy in riot-prone or unstable cities. Imagine being an English soldier in Belfast. To them, all rented cars are suspect, and when they ask you to stop, OBEY.

**Dress like a native.** You don't have to overdo it, especially in the Middle East. Just don't look like a rich American or dress in any way that will offend the sensibilities of the locals. If you can blend in with the crowd, so much the better.

**Stay in touch with someone at home on a regular basis.** Keep that person abreast of your plans, and say when you will be calling next.

**Make sure that your company maintains a complete, up-to-date biographical file on you.** This file should include:

- *all important names, addresses, and phone numbers,* including those of friends and neighbors, relatives (both at home and abroad), people at the office, country club, marina, etc., and doctors and lawyers
- *several sets of fingerprints, palm prints, photos, and dental records for you and your family*
- *physical descriptions and information on hobbies and special activities*
- *medical info,* including blood type and drugs taken
- *activities you engage in regularly.* Sunday mass, etc.
- *insurance records*
- *duress signals.* Code words that you will use to indicate various types of emergencies

**Insurance.** At least 25 percent of the Fortune 500 companies carry kidnap insurance. It's maintained strictly on the q.t., because if terrorists or other criminals were to get wind of it, it would surely increase the likelihood of a kidnap attempt. The perpetrators figure that their chances of getting a ransom are better if the payment is covered by an insurance company.

Nevertheless, a quiet inquiry with regard to insurance is a sound idea.

# HARDWARE: JAMES BOND IN PINSTRIPES

For those individuals or companies opting for the hard-line approach to security, there is almost no limit to the number and sophistication of security devices available. That is, of course, if you have the cash. Carmine Pellosie, of Communication Control Systems, tells of a certain gentleman who wanted an absolutely burglarproof, snatchproof, fireproof, bombproof attaché for some papers. He called in the morning, and CCS had one ready, custom made, by the afternoon.

For the more typical executive with more modest requirements, CCS also carries a large in-stock selection of protection devices.

**Armor for the automobile.** Ninety percent of all kidnappings involve an automobile. It is considered a prime target by terrorists because it contains the victims in a small space, is easy to identify, and offers them a wide choice of time and location of attack.

Any car can be armored, even VWs, Toyotas, and Fiats; so you can choose a commonly used car instead of a huge, gas-guzzling American car if you want to keep a low profile. However, as some experts point out, in order to protect against high-powered rifles or explosives, you need a car with additional weight, such as a Mercedes, a large Peugeot, or perhaps a Catalina or a Bonneville (not so uncommon in Latin America). Some security experts prefer working with a car that is two or three years old rather than brand-new, because it has a lower profile. Armored cars have several basic elements: power steering, automatic transmission, high performance engines, air-conditioning, stronger chassis, suspension brakes, four doors, automatic locking, special bolts that won't fly off when hit. Advanced communication equipment is a must. The specifics of armoring include:

- *bullet-resistant glazing.* Bulletproof glass. Recent advances have made certain types resistant to common projectiles such as bricks, rocks, hammers, and steel bars.
- *vehicle armor.* There are several ways to go, depending on costs, allowable extra weight, and degree of protection. Fiberglas and ceramic composites have become popular, because they are lighter than plate steel. A new lightweight steel plate adds only about 600-900 pounds to the car

- *other measures.* There are gas tanks equipped with self-sealing foam that will not only repair leaks, but also prevent the tank from igniting when punctured; special bullet-resistant tires that are treated with foam (a problem at high speeds), steel lines (not a very smooth ride), or plastic (light, absorbs shocks). Then, of course, you can get really heavy by installing a device that squirts a slippery, oily goo from the rear of the car to slow down pursuers. Or you could add a smoke screen device. Or build in machine guns.

Armoring a vehicle is only part of the battle. Your driver should be trained in evasive and defensive driving techniques. If you are doing the driving, it would be worthwhile to take a course on such techniques.

**Armor for the home and office.** Hardware for this purpose is usually standard, involving the more sophisticated burglar, fire, and intrusion alarms systems, as well as access control. These systems usually employ a motion detection unit (sensitive to sound, light, vibration, heat), a closed circuit TV system, and smoke and heat detection for fire. Companies often issue special cards that must be used to gain access to its premises. In a nation with lots of violence, "site-hardened" residences often are equipped with bullet-resistant windows and security fences with built-in intrusion sensors, as well as other sensors located near and surrounding the home. (For a more thorough discussion of basic alarm systems, see Chapter 37.)

**Body armor.** Bullet-resistant clothing worn under or over your own threads. You can even buy bullet-resistant underwear. This kind of protection is becoming so popular that I wouldn't be surprised to see Pierre Cardin create a line of bullet-proof fashions.

If you think you need body armor, you would be wise to consult an expert. The selection must take into account the degree of protection required, the types of activities you'll be engaged in while wearing the armor, your height and build, and the specifications of the armor itself. Often you must make certain trade-offs. After the attempt on his life by Squeaky Fromme, Gerald Ford began wearing a bullet-resistant vest designed to match his two-piece suit. Thus, the armor went unnoticed, but his throat was exposed because of the design of the vest. So he wore a "dicky" under his shirt to protect that area. Naturally, the president did not want his armor to look conspicuous; that would have been quite unnerving.

There are two basic types—soft and rigid. Rigid types are usually made of Fiberglas, ceramics, steel, or titanium. The soft types are usually bullet-resistant nylon, sometimes combined with other materials.

While the highest degree of protection is offered by the rigid armors, some of them cannot withstand multiple hits: Once fractured by bullets, they lose their resistant qualities. Also, they are heavier than the soft type.

The soft armors are lighter and more comfortable, but some types lose their resistant qualities when they get wet. Soft armor will "give" when hit with a bullet, causing the fabric to "bubble in" toward the wearer, or become stretched or deformed. As a result, the bullet may actually hit the body of the wearer, even though the armor will prevent the body from being punctured by the projectile or fragments. The resulting "bullet trauma" is a drawback of soft armor, since it may involve some injury.

**Voice detectors.** In the event of a kidnap or extortion attempt, it is helpful to know whether the caller is telling the truth and whether the voice of the hostage is, indeed, the voice of the hostage. There are several voice detectors on the market, portable enough to fit into an attaché case, that supposedly can detect the level of stress in a voice and determine whether the speaker is telling the truth. Such devices have another use: You can turn them on your employees to see if they have been stealing, accepting bribes, or lying about their past. They have become quite popular.

Another type of voice detector is a voiceprint analyzer. The machine supposedly uses a combination of vocal characteristics to produce a "voiceprint"—a pattern unique to the individual; the vocal equivalent of a fingerprint. One can compare the voiceprint of a caller with a voiceprint on file to see whether the two match.

**Safe rooms.** The safe room is a room that is designed to serve as a refuge in case of an emergency. It should be equipped with food, water, medical supplies, lethal and nonlethal weapons, and communication equipment. And it should be secure and very difficult to break into. No one talks about safe rooms. Many foreign headquarters of American corporations have them in the office complex, and many executives equip a room in the house for this purpose. But the fewer the people who know about the room, the better.

**Dogs.** Dogs are very tough. If properly trained, they will be a very effective form of protection. But they are a big responsibility, and you've got to keep them somewhat mean if you want them to be attack-ready.

**Bug alerts.** Is there a bugging device in the room? On someone's person? Alerts, which range upward from palm size, may be built into desk sets, humidors, or notebooks. Large-scale sweeping devices are also used.

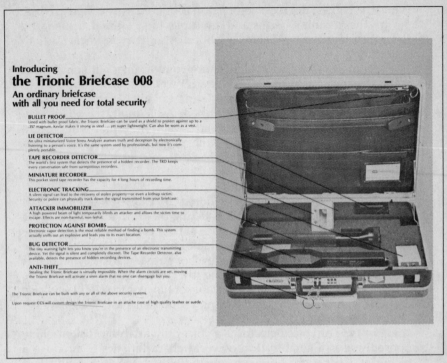

Fig. 69. The incredible "Trionic" briefcase
A traveling security kit modeled after a custom design built
by CCS Communication Control for a special client.

**Tap alerts** let you know if your phone is being tapped. Most of these devices are pretty sophisticated, bulky, and costly, but there are a few built into phones, desk units, and even several excellent portable units that are set into attaché cases.

**Bomb detectors.** Almost all bombs have a trigger device that is hooked to a timer. So a popular type of bomb detector amplifies ticking sounds a thousand times. According to Communication Control Systems (CCS), 90 percent of all bombs involve such timing devices, and CCS makes a detector that fits into an attaché. Another type, the *vapor trace detector*, sniffs out the vapors of the gases emanating from explosive devices. (In a demonstration, one of these picked up the cologne on my chin.) Another popular approach is metal detection, which can be very sensitive. X-ray systems are also good, but not very portable.

*The letter bomb detector.* I love this one. Open the attaché and set up the slide. Just slide the mail through and the sensors will scan the letter for danger. The device usually works by metal or vapor trace detection.

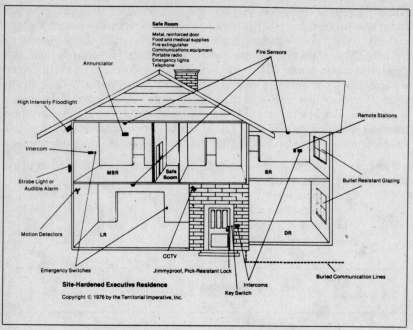

Fig. 70. Executive residence secured against terrorism
The emphasis here is on detection of intrusion.

From Jan Reber and Paul Shaw, *Executive Protection Manual*
(Northbrook, IL: MTI Teleprograms Inc., 1976), p. 125.
Reprinted by permission.

**The security blanket AL 22 (CCS).** This very handy device allows one to immobilize an attacker without doing permanent physical damage. Essentially, it's a flashlight that weighs less than a pound. But it's equipped with what looks like a standard household bulb. But if you look close, you can see that the bulb is really a very oversized version of a flashbulb (photographic type). Even a little olive-pit size flashcube can leave you seeing spots, so imagine what happens when this bulb flashes. "It's as bright," says CCS's Pellosie, "as five suns." It leaves the attacker totally zonked, blind, and disoriented long enough for you to escape. Or, Pellosie points out, you might use the AL 22 as a club. But that would inflict physical harm, no doubt. You can take this device with you when you travel.

**Chemicals.** You can get spray cans, fountain pens, etc. that squirt CS (a type of tear gas), mace, or some other unpleasant liquid into the face of the attacker, making the person so sick that he will be helpless or will forget all about you, or both.

**Kidnap prevention.** We've all seen Mannix, Bond, et alia use concealed radio transmitters to tail criminals to their hideouts or to rescue kidnap victims. Well, now you too can own your own Kidnap Recovery System. The transmitters are small enough to fit into a pack of cigarettes or on a medallion, or they can be sewn into your suit. Wear several, just in case the terrorists find one. The receiver will indicate relative course, distance, and directional path. An optional alert device will sound an alarm at your "home base" when you activate your transmitter, so someone will know you've been snatched during the first few moments it occurs, rather than when you are noticed missing.

For more information about CCS products and other security services they offer, contact:
> Communication Control Systems, Ltd.
> World Headquarters
> 633 Third Avenue
> New York, New York 10017

---

# SUGGESTED READING

---

There has been a great deal written about terrorism and security. But by far the most complete and useful assemblage of information concerning the protection of the executive and the family is the *Executive Protection Manual*, published by MTI Teleprograms, Inc. The authors, Jan Reber and Paul Shaw, are among the nation's experts in executive protection, and they cover every aspect of security, from corporate policymaking and risk management through protective hardware. This book is very well organized and clearly written.
> Contact:
> *The Executive Protection Manual*
> MTI Teleprograms, Inc.
> 3710 Commercial Avenue
> Northbrook, Illinois 60062

# AFTERWORD

## PUTTING IT ALL TOGETHER

The last page seems like the logical place to sum up, even though many of you have arrived here without reading the entire book through. My intention was that you *use* this book as a *tool* rather than labor over it as a textbook. I hope that it has provided some assistance so far.

*Executive Essentials* is about three things: knowledge, experience, and attitude. If I've done my job, you should be more knowledgeable about executive life and methods. You should have a better sense of how, where, and why to get the kind of experience that competitive careers are made of. Finally, you should be inspired to achieve: The difference between the successful and mediocre executive often comes down to the attitude one brings to work, life, and self.

As lengthy as this book is, I've only been able to tell part of the story through it. There are other "executive essentials"—those that are yours alone. I urge you to find them.

# INDEX